Communication
in Everyday Life

Communication in Everyday Life

Personal and Professional Contexts

Sherry Devereaux Ferguson
Jenepher Lennox Terrion

OXFORD
UNIVERSITY PRESS

Oxford University Press is a department of the University of Oxford. It furthers the University's objective of excellence in research, scholarship, and education by publishing worldwide. Oxford is a registered trade mark of Oxford University Press in the UK and in certain other countries.

Published in Canada by
Oxford University Press
8 Sampson Mews, Suite 204,
Don Mills, Ontario M3C 0H5 Canada

www.oupcanada.com

Library and Archives Canada Cataloguing in Publication

Ferguson, Sherry Devereaux, author
Communication in everyday life : personal and professional contexts / Sherry Devereaux Ferguson, Jenepher Lennox Terrion.

Includes bibliographical references and index.

ISBN 978-0-19-544928-0 (pbk.)

1. Interpersonal communication—Textbooks.
I. Lennox, Jenepher A., 1963–, author II. Title.

HM1166.F47 2014 302.2 C2013-908209-3

Cover image: Michael Wheatley/Getty Images
Chapter opening images: Chapter 1: © Frank and Helena/cultura/Corbis; Chapter 2: © Benis Arapovic/Thinkstock; Chapter 3: © skynesher/iStockphoto; Chapter 4: Tibor Bognar/Getty Images; Chapter 5: Anna Bryukhanova/Thinkstock; Chapter 6: william87/Thinkstock; Chapter 7: Bernhard Lang/Getty Images; Chapter 8: © Dave and Les Jacobs/Blend Images/Corbis; Chapter 9: © DonSmith/Alamy; Chapter 10: © track5/iStockphoto

Printed and bound in the United States of America

1 2 3 4 — 17 16 15 14

BRIEF CONTENTS

CONTENTS

CHAPTER 2 | Perceiving Self in Relation to Others 35

CHAPTER 3 | Perception of Others 67

FROM THE PUBLISHER

Communication in Everyday Life: Personal and Professional Contexts is designed to improve readers' communication skills in both their personal and professional lives. To that end, this new and exciting introduction to interpersonal communication includes the following key features:

Attention-grabbing narratives and a compelling writing style. Relatable and engaging narratives and dialogues bring key concepts to life and encourage readers to think critically about their own communication skills. Throughout, clear writing and accessible language guide readers through the occasionally complex world of interpersonal communication.

Functional Conflicts

Functional conflicts occur when people explore their differences and express their opinions in a respectful and productive way.[36] The result is increased trust and the establishment of authentic relationships. To see how the conflict between Maureen and Imran could have been more functional, consider the following dialogue.

Maureen: Hi Imran. Good to see you.
Imran: Hi Maureen. Nice to see you too. How's it going? Long time no news, partner.
Maureen: Yeah, sorry about that.
Imran: I guess they work you hard at UNB. I emailed and texted you a number of times, but you never got back to me. Anyway . . . .
Maureen: Honestly, Imran, things have been hectic. And when I thought of calling, it was too late for you in St John's or too early for me. You know me. I am not a big texter. I kept thinking it would be nicer to talk to you. I am sorry, but it wasn't like I didn't think about you.
Imran: It's okay, I get it. New classes, new profs, roommates. Yeah, roommates. We'll talk about that another time. St John's is way different from Deer Lake.
Maureen: Sounds like we have some things to talk about—but after dinner. I hear mom calling. Maybe when you get back to St John's, we can talk on weekends. Hey, what about Skyping?

In this alternative scenario, Maureen and Imran collaborate to create a supportive communication climate. They respond to each other in an empathic way, taking the perspective of the other person. They acknowledge each other's feelings, and their communication becomes descriptive rather than accusatory. In the end, their friendship moves in the direction of a win–win outcome. In short, the conflict is functional.

As the above example indicates, whether a conflict is functional or dysfunctional depends to a great extent on how both parties respond to the situation. See the "From Theory to Practice" box titled "Making Your Case in the Workplace" for an example of a workplace conflict that could end up as a functional or dysfunctional conflict, depending on the coping style and strategies of the middle manager.

from theory TO PRACTICE

Making Your Case in the Workplace

Imagine yourself in the following situation. You are a middle manager in a leading company that manufactures automobile parts. You have just come into work on a Monday morning after a relaxing weekend. You are in high spirits and looking forward to another week at work. Your secretary has arranged a manageable schedule, and everything seems to be under control. However, you are in for a rude shock. Upon checking your email, you find that upper management has reduced your department's budget; and they have assigned new and unrealistic goals to your team. You want to protest the cuts and the unachievable production goals, but you learn that the financial outlook statement you requested last week is not yet available. Without those figures, you will be unable to argue your case at the afternoon meeting of managers. What kinds of actions can you take to avoid a dysfunctional conflict with your boss? Should you voice your opinion or maintain a loyal silence? Which coping style could work best in this situation (competing, accommodating, avoiding, compromising, or collaborating)? What are the likely results of employing the different coping styles?

DEVELOPING A CIVIL WORKPLACE

The term *civility* implies a respectful awareness of others. In practice, civility means thinking about the impact of your words and actions before you employ them. It means being tolerant of differences and showing consideration for the needs of other people. Sometimes it means restraining yourself from being too blunt—looking for less hurtful words. In other words, civility implies courteous behaviour,

Listening from Your Own Perspective

When listening from your own perspective, you lessen the chances of understanding the other person. Below is the kind of conversation you might overhear in the workplace. Note how neither listener focusses on what the other person says.

Matthew: I met with the marketing team yesterday to get ideas on how to promote our new line of cosmetics. They suggested we should focus on fashion magazines and television.
Aisha: Sure, sounds good. You know, Matt, I was thinking about our upcoming move. Do you think there will be parking at the new location? If not, I don't know how I will be able to afford paying for space.
Matthew: I've got so much to do with this campaign that I haven't thought about the move. I'm concerned we may be missing out if we don't use social media with this campaign.
Aisha: Hey, do you want to grab a coffee? I don't know if I can stay awake without some heavy caffeine. I watched the whole third season of The Walking Dead on Netflix last night.

Although this conversation may sound pretty typical, you can see that Matthew and Aisha are taking turns talking about their individual interests and concerns. Each appears to be waiting for the other person to stop speaking in order to pick up where he or she left off. In other words, as listeners, they are responding from their own perspectives.

Management guru Stephen Covey describes this kind of response as listening through an autobiographical filter, which is not very satisfying for the speaker.[59] When listening from your own point of view, rather than trying to understand what the other person is trying to say, you end up taking the focus of the conversation away from the speaker and putting it on yourself.

"There are people who, inst listening to what is being s them, are already listening to what they are going to say themselves."
ALBERT GUINON

Taking Away from the Other Person's Perspective

As discussed in Chapter 3, most of us look to others for **validation**. That is, we look to others to confirm our sense of worth and value as human beings. Listening is one of the ways by which we can validate others and they can validate us. Failure to listen and respond appropriately to the words of another person has the opposite effect, diminishing the importance of the other person's perspective.

VALIDATION
Confirmation of our sense of worth and value.

Let us examine a typical conversation that might occur in a Canadian organization. Brigitte chats with her co-worker Tomas about one of her work projects. This conversation will illustrate four inappropriate listening responses that can take away from the value of the other person. We will also examine options for more appropriate responses. The conversation begins with Brigitte expressing a concern.

Brigitte: I'm having so much trouble with this project. The deadline is unrealistic, no one is supplying information on time, and the guidelines for data analysis are totally unclear. I feel out of control.

Special features geared towards student learning and engagement. In addition to such learning tools as chapter outlines, a marginal glossary, review questions, and suggested activities, each chapter includes the following boxes to capture readers' interest and involve them with content.

- **"For Starters" boxes** kick-off each chapter with engaging introductory narratives to draw students into the chapter themes.

2 Communication in Everyday Life

forSTARTERS

Intervention

The door opened and a young, frightened boy motioned the two policemen into the house. In the background, the police could hear a loud, angry voice.

"You made the call?" the younger policeman asked.

"Yes." The small voice seemed to fit with the size of the slender boy, and it was hard to hear him over the sound of a blaring television set.

"You've got a problem here?"

The boy nodded but didn't speak. He huddled deeper into the grey and red hoodie he was wearing, as if hoping the jacket could make him disappear.

"Where is your mom? Is she in the other room?" the older policeman asked. "Mind if I turn off the TV?"

"You can turn it off. She's with my dad."

A scream from a woman interrupted the conversation, but it was hard to know if the scream came from the next room or an adjacent apartment. Music and voices from the other half of the duplex invaded the thin plaster walls of the room.

"All right, son, stay here. We'll check it out." The two policemen stepped quickly toward the room from which they thought the scream had come.

Before they could reach the entrance to the room, however, a tall, rough-looking man appeared in the frame of the door, blocking a view of the bedroom. He had a cloth wrapped around his left hand and a half-drunk beer in his right hand. He was wearing tan work pants and a dirty undershirt. A pair of concrete-encrusted workboots lay close to the couch. "What?" The man stared first at the policemen, then at the boy. "What's this about, Jacob?" he asked. "You call the police?" He took a long gulp of the beer.

The boy tried another disappearing act with his hoodie. He didn't answer.

"We need to see your wife, sir," the older policeman indicated. He turned back to his partner. "Joey, do you want to see what's happening in the other room?"

© Radharc Images/Alamy

"Sure thing, Tony," Joey said, moving toward the oversized figure, who had yet to move aside. "What's your name?"

"Ray. Ray Stilton. Hey, stop looking at me like I've got the scabies! We're just having an argument—that's all. Everything is cool." The man tried harder to fill the door frame, which was not too difficult, given his imposing figure.

"Like I said, we need to see your wife." The man did not show any sign of moving, and the policeman's patience was clearly tested.

"Why?" the man demanded. "I told you, everything is okay."

"We know what you told us, sir. But we still need to see your wife to be sure she's okay."

"My wife? To be sure she's okay?" he asked. For a brief moment, the man looked startled, then recovered. He seemed to have had a change of heart. "Irina! They're asking to see you. You'll see. She's fine."

INTRODUCTION

In this first chapter, you will become acquainted with some historical and recent communication models and gain insights into what we can learn from these models. Models serve several different purposes. First, they provide a vocabulary—jargon that allows us to talk about a topic of interest. Just as social workers, police officers, doctors, and other professionals require a job-specific vocabulary that enables them to communicate effectively with their colleagues, so too do you need a common vocabulary in order to discuss communication concepts. Second, models help to explain processes—in this

4 | Understanding, Navigating, and Managing Our Identities 105

from theory **TO PRACTICE**

The Bem Sex-Role Inventory: How Masculine or Feminine Are You?

Rate yourself on a scale from one to seven on the following items, with one representing *never or almost never true* and seven representing *always or almost always true.*

1. Self-reliant ___	21. Reliable ___	41. Warm ___
2. Yielding ___	22. Analytical ___	42. Solemn ___
3. Helpful ___	23. Sympathetic ___	43. Willing to take a stand ___
4. Defends own beliefs ___	24. Jealous ___	44. Tender ___
5. Cheerful ___	25. Has leadership abilities ___	45. Friendly ___
6. Moody ___	26. Sensitive to needs of others ___	46. Aggressive ___
7. Independent ___	27. Truthful ___	47. Gullible ___
8. Shy ___	28. Willing to take risks ___	48. Inefficient ___
9. Conscientious ___	29. Understanding ___	49. Acts as a leader ___
10. Athletic ___	30. Secretive ___	50. Childlike ___
11. Affectionate ___	31. Makes decisions easily ___	51. Adaptable ___
12. Theatrical ___	32. Compassionate ___	52. Individualistic ___
13. Assertive ___	33. Sincere ___	53. Does not use harsh language ___
14. Flatterable ___	34. Self-sufficient ___	54. Unsystematic ___
15. Happy ___	35. Eager to soothe hurt feelings ___	55. Competitive ___
16. Strong personality ___	36. Conceited ___	56. Loves children ___
17. Loyal ___	37. Dominant ___	57. Tactful ___
18. Unpredictable ___	38. Soft-spoken ___	58. Ambitious ___
19. Forceful ___	39. Likable ___	59. Gentle ___
20. Feminine ___	40. Masculine ___	60. Conventional ___

Add your ratings for items 1, 4, 7, 10, 13, 16, 19, 22, 25, 28, 31, 34, 37, 40, 43, 46, 49, 52, 55, and 58. Divide this total by 20. This figure represents your score on the masculinity dimension. Then add your ratings for items 2, 5, 8, 11, 14, 17, 20, 23, 26, 29, 32, 35, 38, 41, 44, 47, 50, 53, 56, and 59. Divide the total by 20. This figure represents your score on the femininity dimension. Consult the following chart to identify your sex type as masculine, feminine, androgynous, or undifferentiated.

	MASCULINITY GREATER THAN 4.9	MASCULINITY LESS THAN 4.9
FEMININITY GREATER THAN 4.9	Androgynous	Female sex typed
FEMININITY LESS THAN 4.9	Male sex typed	Undifferentiated

SOURCE: Based on S. Bem, "On the Utility of Alternative Procedures for Assessing Psychological Androgyny, *Journal of Consulting and Clinical Psychology* 45 (1977): 196–205.

must pick and choose between identities. In some situations, however, people with multiple racial or ethnic identities have an advantage over those with only one identity. For example, some argue that having multiple racial identities can buffer a person

- **"From Theory to Practice" boxes** offer brief, practical activities and encourage critical thought.

professionalCONTEXTS

Listening in Hostage Negotiations

If we believe what we see on television and in movies, hostage negotiators are tough cops, not afraid to leave their guns behind when they go alone to talk to a bad guy holed up with a group of innocent hostages. A close look at real-life hostage negotiators reveals a different and more subtle picture. Rather than relying on a cold, tough exterior to extract concessions from hostage takers, they try to connect with the perpetrators on a human level. Hostage negotiation involves situations with high levels of anxiety, emotion, apprehension, and uncertainty for the hostage taker, his or her victims, and the negotiators. In most cases, a failure on the part of the perpetrator to deal with emotional distresses has led to the crisis. As a result, a psychological counselling approach is necessary to resolve the perpetrator's emotional issues.[89]

Most people in crises—including hostage takers—have a desire to be heard and understood.[90] Therefore, negotiators in hostage situations must be experts in communication, with the ability to hear clearly and to listen effectively. They must be particularly skilled at empathic listening, as one of their goals is to understand the perpetrator's perspective and to help him or her to resolve a problem. In order to accomplish this goal, the negotiator uses strategies such as paraphrasing opinions and feelings expressed by the hostage taker. Through empathic listening, negotiators seek to resolve the crisis in a way that results in "successful containment and arrest rather than escalation and subsequent loss of life."[91]

While police officers are not necessarily trained psychologists, their work in hostage negotiation draws heavily upon the theory and practice of counselling and psychotherapy. Using this body of knowledge, police training in hostage negotiation usually employs role plays. In these role plays, a hostage negotiator is given a scenario and asked to practise his or her new skills in areas that include empathic listening. A typical scenario might involve a man who has abducted his estranged wife and child. He is holding the hostages in an abandoned farmhouse. In a successful scenario, the police officer begins with active listening and then proceeds to show empathy, establish rapport, influence the hostage taker to see things differently, and finally achieve behavioural change. Ideally, the perpetrator will follow the suggestions of the negotiator (in this case, releasing the wife and child and surrendering to police).

Hostage negotiation is difficult and volatile, with the potential for many different and often negative outcomes. However, experts in police tactics agree on one point: using a strategy that includes empathic listening increases the likelihood of a successful negotiation.

Paraphrasing the Speaker's Message

While we are listening closely and using nonverbal cues to demonstrate our interest, we are also gathering information that we can use to confirm our understanding of the speaker's message. For example, if your friend says, "I'll meet you at the coffee shop around the corner after work," you might respond by rephrasing what your co-worker said: "Okay, see you at Second Cup at 5:30." In this way, you confirm your interpretation of the plan. If your friend responds with "No, I meant Tim Hortons," then both of you become aware that the words *coffee shop* carry more than one possible meaning. Paraphrasing, in this case, has helped to clear up what could have been a miscommunication.

Paraphrasing in empathic listening, where we listen from the perspective of the speaker, allows us to reflect back our understanding of what the speaker has said. In this way, we demonstrate our interest at the same time that we enable the speaker to think about what he or she has said.[92] Effective paraphrasing by a listener does more than help the speaker to think about what he or she has said. It also helps the speaker to feel valued, listened to, and understood.[93]

Paraphrasing is not the same as repeating the speaker's exact words. Imagine that your friend says, "I felt so stupid when a client asked me a question about the last quarter profits and I didn't have the answer!" You respond, "You felt stupid that you didn't have the answer to his question?" This response sounds contrived and phony. Effective paraphrasing requires you to put the speaker's words into your own words and, in this

- **"Professional Contexts" boxes** feature examples drawn from a wide range of disciplines, including nursing, policing, business, and social work.

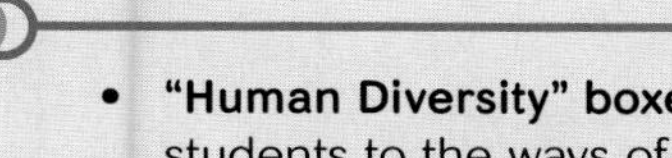

- **"Human Diversity" boxes** introduce students to the ways of life and world views of different cultures and social groups.

humanDIVERSITY

Navigating Anti-violence Work in a Culturally Sensitive Way

A study in Atlantic Canada examined the forms of violence experienced by immigrant women of diverse ethno-cultural backgrounds. In-depth interviews with immigrant women and their service providers took place in five Atlantic Canadian cities: Moncton, Sydney, St John's, Halifax, and Charlottetown. The researchers sought to identify not only the perspectives of the women, but also the views of the service providers about their efforts to help and work with immigrant women who had experienced violence—either in Canada or in their countries of origin. The study identified different kinds of violence, including domestic violence (emotional and/or physical abuse); racism and discrimination in the workplace; and institutional abuse, including targeting of minorities by authorities.

The conclusions were not definitive. Many of the immigrant women said they had received helpful assistance and protection from service providers, churches, friends and family, sponsors, and volunteers after the violence occurred. Other participants complained that immigrant women in Atlantic Canada have less access to services and supports than do women in other provinces. Some service providers identified cultural barriers such as the reluctance of the immigrant women to talk about abuse and violence, their tendencies to deny that the abuse had occurred, and behaviours that suggested a felt sense of shame. A number of the women said that they feared being ignored or singled out by their ethnic communities if their stories became public.

In terms of policy recommendations, the immigrant women and their service providers said the different levels of government, law enforcement agencies, and non-government organizations should work together to create and support culturally sensitive ways of communicating with immigrant women who had experienced violence.[12]

Scarce and Non-distributable Resources and Power Struggles

The term *scarce and non-distributable resource* refers to something that only one person can use or possess at the same time. For example, only one team can win a soccer match, a game of rugby, or a hockey game. Two friends sharing an apartment may want the same bedroom, but only one can have it. If both insist on getting the room, a conflict will develop between them.

In the workplace, conflict develops when people in different departments perceive themselves to be in competition for scarce and non-distributable resources. While the overriding objective of all departments may be to make money for the organization, the individual departments may see themselves as being in competition for space, funding, recognition, or other resources. People in organizations sometimes see others as threats to their own career progress (e.g., "If you get this promotion, I will not get it"). This mentality establishes a "win–lose" dynamic, and people approach the conflict similar to how they might approach a fight. Like wrestlers, they try to maneuver into a superior position, relative to the other party.[13]

Within families and organizations, struggles for power often relate to competition for scarce and non-distributable resources such as time or money. Upset with her husband for going out too often in the evenings, a wife may demand that he give up his poker night with the guys. Or a husband may become upset that his wife is spending too much money on clothes. Sometimes couples struggle over competing goals, such as we discussed earlier. One wants to take a vacation in Hawaii; the other wants to save money to go to Cuba. Within the workplace, employees may resist supervisor demands to work overtime or give up their weekends. People struggle for better positions, greater influence, higher wages, and more desirable work hours.

A contemporary, popular culture focus. Academic research and studies are blended with well-known and relatable references and examples drawn from film, television, and celebrity culture.

iStockphoto

Many changes in language occur in concert with cultural change. In their work at the University of Toronto, Sali Tagliamonte and Derek Denis study the ways that language, culture, and society interact. They say that we can track changes in any one of these three areas by looking at the others.[38]

Tagliamonte argues that upper-class females drove the shift from medieval to modern English (e.g., *ye* to *you*) and that this feminine influence on language continues today. The change agents in this generation, however, tend to be middle-class teenage girls, who are by and large the greatest disseminators of new slang and language forms.[39] When people (especially young people) repeatedly use a word in a way that is different from its more standard use (e.g., the word *bad* to mean "good" or *sickening* to mean "so good that it makes me sick"), then it is possible that the new meaning of the word will become widely accepted. In this way, language evolves. To see the latest updates to the *Oxford Dictionaries Online*, go to http://oxforddictionaries.com/words/whats-new. See the "From Theory to Practice" box for a humorous look at how slang evolves.

In one study, Tagliamonte and Denis tried to find out whether texting by teenagers leads to a breakdown of the English language, as many worried observers claim.[41] According to "language purists," practices such as texting and tweeting lead teens to break grammar rules and to develop their own language—practices seen as destructive by those who want to protect language from evolving.[42] As expected, the researchers confirmed that teenagers are using home computers and cellphones in unprecedented numbers to communicate with their friends. They are also creating new ways of speaking (e.g., slang and abbreviations) that are more informal than our traditional spoken and written language. Despite these most obvious signs of change, however, the communication of teenagers remains firmly rooted in formal linguistic traditions. For example, one teenager texted a friend about a planned rock concert: "Aaaaaaaaagh the show tonight shall rock some serious jam."[43] The sentence contains a subject, a verb, and a direct object—presented in an order that reflects standard rules of grammar. Thus, it seems that adolescents tend to observe the basic rules of grammar at the same time that they bend the rules in new and creative ways.

...TO PRACTICE
...anguage
...de of *Zoey 101* in which Michael ...ord *drippin* as a synonym for ... By the time Michael's friends ...rd, no one remembers that he ... decides to invent a second ... episode ends with Michael ... about how difficult it is to ...ging language.
...ur own language has evolved ...rs. Have you or your friends ...r expressions? Which ones ... not stick? Do the changes in ...nstrate your own development ...?

Universal Pictures/The Kobal Collection

He gives himself away because Germans use their thumb, index, and middle fingers to indicate the number three. This soldier's use of the wrong emblem leads to a barroom gunfight.

Complementing, Repeating, and Accenting Verbal Messages (Illustrators)

When our body movements act in unison with what we say verbally, we call them illustrators.[14] Illustrators may be conscious or unconscious, but they do not stand on their own. They differ from emblems because they accompany—rather than replace—words. For example, you might smile warmly while saying "I love you," point while saying "look over there," form a square with your hands while describing a box, or shake your fist while shouting angrily at a neighbour whose cat has been digging in your garden. These examples all show how we complete, repeat, or accent our verbal messages with nonverbal actions.

"I speak two languages, Body and English."
MAE WEST

While the average person uses illustrators to go along with speech, actors have to be experts in this area. They m... ies to add drama and emphasis to their ... three Emmy awards for his role as Cos... *Seinfeld*, mastered the art of using illustrators. His ... (e.g., flinging open a door to slide into a room), an... to his ability to convert ordinary situations into hi...

Regulating Interaction (Regulato...

In managing a conversation, we rely on what we ... designed to control the flow of conversation. Regu... our turns to speak. Getting in and out of the flow ... traffic on a busy freeway: we have to show others ou...

In the 1960s and early 1970s, sociologist Harve... identify the specific nonverbal signals or regulat... Indicators of willingness to yield to the other pers... intonation (rising or falling voice pitch), drawing o... ing body orientation or position, and looking at th... our turn, on the other hand, we may use turn-requ... breath, raising a finger, leaning forward, finishing t... saying "mmm hmm" or "okay" to signal "I would lik... conversation regulators include the following: pati... to encourage the other speaker to continue, raising ... to answer or ask a question, or holding up a hand t... ing. (See the "From Theory to Practice" box for an ex...

As you can see in the above examples, regulator... nod to encourage another speaker to continue, th...

TURN TAKING The process of deciding who will speak at any given time during a conversation.

overall well-being.[11] Examples include child development,[12] adolescent health,[13] family functioning,[14] high school retention,[15] healthy aging,[16] happiness,[17] and even neighbourhood mortality rates.[18] Simply put, people with more social capital are better off in all of these important areas than those with less social capital. Refer to the "Professional Contexts" box titled "Recovering from Addiction with the Help of Others" for an example of the link between social capital and recovery from addiction to alcohol or other drugs.

REASONS FOR FORMING RELATIONSHIPS

Clearly a number of important benefits come from our relationships with others in family, social, and organizational networks. Let us take a look now at two theories that explain *why* we form relationships with others. The first focusses on our basic interpersonal needs, while the second views interpersonal interaction as a more complex process of negotiation and exchange.

Needs Theory

In 1958, William Schutz introduced a theory of interpersonal relations called **fundamental interpersonal relations orientation (FIRO)**.[19] According to this theory, we are motivated to meet three basic interpersonal needs: inclusion, control, and affection/openness. Schutz suggested that we communicate with others to meet these needs, which exist in all of us to varying degrees.

FUNDAMENTAL INTERPERSONAL RELATIONS ORIENTATION (FIRO) Theory that holds that we form interpersonal relationships in order to meet our need for inclusion, control, and affection.

Need for Inclusion

The **need for inclusion** refers to our fundamental human desire to be connected to other people—to be included in their activities and to feel as if we belong. Generally speaking, if our inclusion needs are met, we feel accepted and valued. If our inclusion needs are not met, we feel lonely and unwanted. These needs play a large role in our organizational and social lives.

NEED FOR INCLUSION The need to be connected to other people.

When our need for inclusion is overly strong, it can lead to negative outcomes. The phenomenon of "groupthink," discussed in greater depth in Chapter 10, happens when people in organizations want so badly to fit into a group that they will go along with any group decision, whether or not they support the decision. They fear being disliked or labelled as *difficult* if they go against majority opinion or threaten the morale of the group. In the worst-case scenarios, the consequences can be deadly; but at best, the feeling of a need to conform at any cost is almost always counterproductive.

The need to be liked and to belong dominates many movie and television plots.[20] In the 2004 film *Mean Girls*, for example, much of the plot revolves around the strong need of the girls to belong to the various cliques or

© AF archive/Alamy

Extensive coverage of communication technologies and social media. Highlighting the influence of digital technologies on interpersonal communication, the discussion explores such current and relevant topics as cellphone usage, online impression management, and cyberbullying.

Managing Impressions in Online Environments

Impression management in online environments has become a ripe area of research.[102] Surveys show that most homes in Canada have computers, and 82 per cent of children are online by the seventh grade.[103] Young people have come of age in an environment full of personal computers (laptops, desktops, and tablets), smartphones, video-game consoles, and other Internet-enabled electronic devices. Most of these devices are socially-oriented—that is, used for social purposes.[104] Most commonly, they are used to facilitate social interaction through online media.

What are the opportunities and challenges for impression management in online environments? According to **social presence theory**, the absence of nonverbal cues in online environments makes it more difficult for users to create the impressions on which relationships are built.[105]

The **social information processing** perspective, on the other hand, says that people can impart impressions of themselves even without the nonverbal cues that characterize face-to-face interactions.[106] They use words, punctuation, and emoticons in emails and instant messages, for example, to convey personality. On social gaming sites and in virtual environments like Second Life, they use avatars and practices such as "gifting" (where social gamers give virtual gifts to other players) to build and transmit impressions.

A related concept, **hyperpersonal theory** goes even further, suggesting that online environments offer *greater* opportunities than face-to-face interactions for the construction of positive impressions of another person. Increased control over what we share, the tendency to exaggerate similarities with another person, the possibility of communicating at convenient times, and the tendency for people to exhibit expected qualities and behaviours all work in favour of positive impression building.[107] Although online relationships develop more slowly than face-to-face relationships, they can develop to the same point as face-to-face relationships when given enough time.[108]

Impression management in online environments can take place on various platforms, including email, computer conferencing, instant messaging, Facebook, Twitter, and dating sites, among others. The communication can be verbal (e.g., emails and comments on Facebook and Twitter) or nonverbal (e.g., photos posted on Myspace or graphic symbols). Electronic platforms, which allow users to overcome constraints of time and space, result in new dynamics in interpersonal relationships. The following discussion looks, in more depth, at how computer-mediated communication (in general) and Facebook and Twitter (more specifically) function as platforms for impression management.

SOCIAL PRESENCE THEORY Theory that explores the effects of sensing another's presence in a social interaction.

SOCIAL INFORMATION PROCESSING THEORY Theory that investigates how we process various types of information in collaborative settings such as social media.

HYPERPERSONAL THEORY Theory that suggests that we use limited online cues to construct idealized images of another person.

Computer-Mediated Communication as a Platform for Impression Management

Computer-mediated communication (CMC) refers to the process of using a computer to communicate messages through channels such as email, instant messaging, or computer conferencing.[109] CMC can involve **synchronous communication** (same time/different place) or **asynchronous communication** (different time/different place). With synchronous communication, the sender and receiver are online at the same time, communicating in real time. With asynchronous communication, someone can send a message while the other is sleeping or involved in another activity. In that situation, the receiver gets the message at a different and often much later time.

COMPUTER-MEDIATED COMMUNICATION (CMC) The process of using a computer to communicate messages.

SYNCHRONOUS COMMUNICATION Communicators exchange messages in real time.

ASYNCHRONOUS COMMUNICATION Communicators exchange messages with a time delay between messages.

TABLE 4.3 Nonverbal strategies for online instructors.

NONVERBAL IMPRESSION-MANAGEMENT STRATEGIES	CORRESPONDING IMPRESSION JUDGMENTS
1. The instructor uses paralinguistic cues such as emoticons thoughtfully to enhance or enrich a written message.	1. The instructor wants to encourage students to be involved and interested in their learning.
2. The instructor gives students plenty of time to complete assignments and shows flexibility with due dates.	2. The instructor is aware of and willing to accommodate student needs.
3. The instructor sends messages regularly to engage students.	3. The instructor is serious about being socially present online.
4. The instructor sends longer messages prudently to stimulate discussion.	4. The instructor is motivated to make the online classroom engaging.
5. The instructor sends error-free messages.	5. The instructor is competent and careful when communicating details.
6. The instructor responds to students promptly.	6. The instructor is approachable and responsive to student needs.
7. The instructor creates and posts a thorough syllabus.	7. The instructor is knowledgeable and passionate about the course.
8. The instructor solicits timely feedback from students.	8. The instructor is committed to teaching and helping students learn.

SOURCE: Column 1 adapted from Y. Liu and D. Ginther, "Managing Impression Formation in Computer-Mediated Communication," *Educause Quarterly* 50, 1 (2001): 50–54.

For example, you can appear more physically attractive by posting your best pictures. You can display information and links to significant accomplishments that make you appear knowledgeable and expert in certain areas. You can also make comments that are in line with the opinions of your imagined audience. Through emoticons and the "like" button, you can display attitudes. When you construct an image of yourself as physically attractive, knowledgeable, and holding acceptable opinions, you are using the impression-management strategy of *self-promotion*.

When you interact on Facebook, you often target your communication to certain groups (e.g., your friends) and ignore others (e.g., potential employers). But concentrating on making yourself sound appealing to one group at the expense of other groups can have negative consequences. Consider the following case. Naseem has applied for a low-paying, entry-level position with a large company. Julio, the human resources manager in charge of filling the position, does not want to hire someone who is overqualified; past experience tells him that such a person will leave the position after a short time. Since the company must invest a lot of money in training new employees, they want employees to stay for a reasonable length of time.

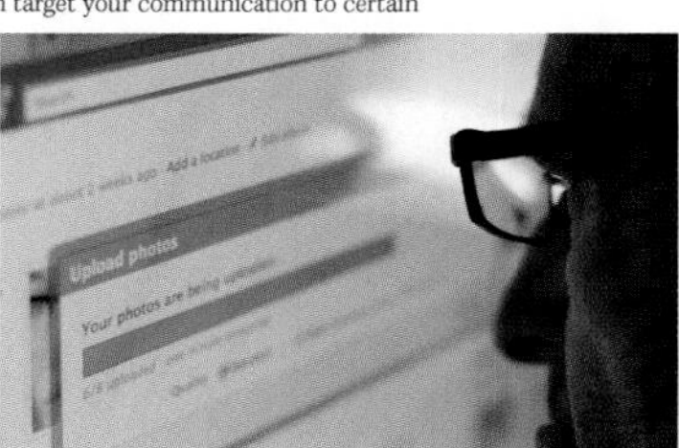

© Chris Batson/Alamy

SUPPLEMENTS

Communication in Everyday Life: Personal and Professional Contexts is supported by an outstanding array of teaching and learning tools for both instructors and students.

For Instructors

- A comprehensive **instructor's manual** includes detailed lecture outlines, questions to encourage class discussion and debate, a wealth of suggested assignments, and links to websites and online videos.
- An extensive **test bank** provides instructors with hundreds of questions in multiple-choice, short-answer, and true/false formats.
- Hundreds of editable **PowerPoint slides** summarize key points from each chapter and incorporate visuals drawn from the text.

For Students

- A **student study guide** features detailed chapter summaries, self-grading quizzes, suggested topics for oral presentations and writing projects, and more.

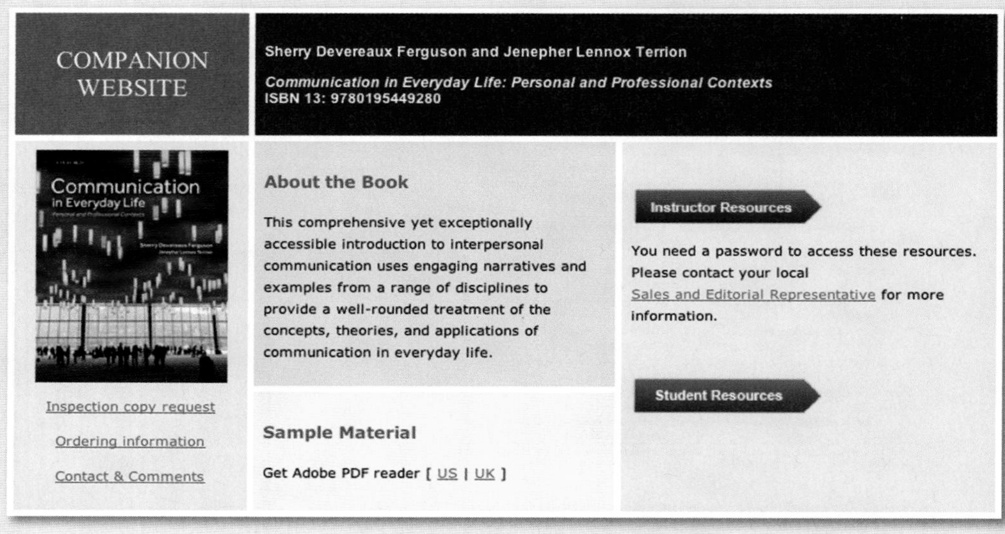

www.oupcanada.com/Ferguson

ACKNOWLEDGEMENTS

We would like to thank the following manuscript reviewers, as well as those who chose to remain anonymous, for their insightful comments and suggestions during the development of *Communication in Everyday Life: Personal and Professional Contexts*:

Diane Demers, Concordia University
Laura Doan, Thompson Rivers University
Dawn Fleming, Saskatchewan Institute of Applied Science and Technology
Victoria O'Connor, Algonquin College
Barbara Rice, Conestoga College
Joanne Spence, Humber College

FROM THE AUTHORS

In 2010, Oxford University Press confirmed their decision to publish this book; and Jenepher and I began our journey to address gaps we had uncovered during more than a half century of collective experience teaching introductory courses in interpersonal and organizational communication.

I first taught the interpersonal and organizational communication course at the University of Windsor in the early 1970s and later co-authored or edited (with Stewart Ferguson) two of the first books in organizational communication. Jenepher's entry into teaching began at the State University of New York (SUNY) at Buffalo in the late 1980s, where she taught interpersonal communication. As a professor at the University of Ottawa, her work continued to include the teaching of courses in interpersonal and organizational communication, for which she has won many awards. Her focus in research and teaching has always been on maximizing the student experience. I am proud to say that Jenepher was one of my earliest students; and while I cannot claim credit for her accomplishments, I am pleased to have her as a colleague and co-author on this book. In short, the two of us bring a large store of experience and commitment to researching and teaching introductory courses in interpersonal and organizational communication.

While the theories presented in this book focus predominantly on the interpersonal, their applications include an equal emphasis on organizational and professional contexts. From its beginnings, organizational communication included a significant interpersonal component because, after all, communication in organizations involves interactions between people who use a variety of media to express themselves. Those media may include air waves (in the case of face-to-face communication), postal services, cellular telephones or land lines, computers, video links, or other. We interact in dyads (groups of two), small groups (three or more), and large groups.

In addition, we carry our private lives, our self-concepts, and our identities into organizations. Our personalities determine our preferences in managerial and leadership styles, and emotional intelligence (EQ) counts as much or more than experience and general intelligence (IQ) when it comes to succeeding in organizations. Our identities also influence how we behave in organizations and how others react to us. In an increasingly multicultural and global world, identity management becomes a critical element in navigating business and corporate environments. So to separate what happens in our personal and work lives makes little sense. That is the premise on which we designed this book, which includes both personal and professional contexts—in other words, communication in our everyday lives.

In a greater sense, it is now extremely difficult to separate communication into discrete fields of study such as media, organizational, interpersonal, and health communication. Courses in media include a focus on how people use media for social gratification, how perception of risks influences behaviours, and how social media change the way we interact with each other in interpersonal contexts. Courses in organizational communication talk about how people interact in small groups, exercise leadership, and respond to cultural influences. Courses in interpersonal communication describe the behaviours of people in virtual space (e.g., Second Life and multi-player games), explore how people manage their online identities, and examine the psychology of perception. Courses in health communication talk about doctor–patient interactions and how health organizations use video links to connect with, diagnose, and prescribe treatment for clients in remote geographic areas. In other words, a wide variety of courses in the social and health sciences now bring together insights from what used to be separate fields of inquiry.

Despite the fact that health, policing, social work, and other professional programs include interpersonal communication courses in their curricula, none of the other introductory textbooks in our field have focussed so strongly on meeting their needs. We have also included an important and necessary emphasis on diversity in our examples, theories, and text boxes; and we have tried to recognize the importance of the Aboriginal heritage in Canada.

We wanted to write a book that was highly readable and student friendly—that contained interesting and current examples of how we communicate with family, friends, romantic partners, work colleagues, and supervisors. In line with this idea, we wrote a number of original narratives and stories to illustrate points. We wanted the students to enjoy the experience of reading this book.

In terms of research, we wanted to include the classical studies that have defined the field, along with major developing areas of research. However, we did not want to include a myriad of relatively isolated studies that have not yet achieved a high level of visibility.

We also wanted students to understand how the concepts in this book apply to their everyday lives. So we have featured a large number of text boxes that ask students to put theories into practice. We have also concluded each chapter with tips for communicating more effectively. We wanted students to be able to see the practical implications of what they are learning—how they can improve their family, social, and work relationships by applying the principles they acquire in this book.

We have made some original contributions in areas such as defining the differences between self-concept and identity—terms that appear in many different and confusing guises in the literature. In the same way, we tried to look at the relationship between personal and collective identities—relationships that are ill-defined in the literature. We devoted an entire chapter to identity management, another novel feature of this book.

We hope that you will enjoy reading this book as much as we enjoyed researching and writing it!

Acknowledgements

All books are a journey. As they progress, so do our lives progress. We are never in the same place at the end as at the beginning of any project. When I began my journey with this book, I was grieving the loss of my husband of 37 years. I am now grieving the loss of a daughter who was with me for 38 years. So acknowledging both the professional and the personal is important to me as this journey draws to a close.

Jenepher and I would like to thank Rukhsana Ahmed and Peruvemba Jaya, associate professors in the Department of Communication at the University of Ottawa, for contributing some interesting examples, theoretical insights, and text boxes in areas such as diversity, health, and impression management.

We would like to acknowledge the representatives at Oxford University Press in Toronto, who showed an early enthusiasm for the project. Stephen Kotowych was the acquisitions editor at the time we proposed this book. We thank both Stephen and managing editor Phyllis Wilson for their interest in—and support for—the project. In addition, we thank Janice Evans, senior editor, for her conscientious efforts with getting this book ready for publication. We have never worked with a more competent or dedicated editor. She is special!

Finally, but not least important, we thank Mark Thompson, developmental editor at OUP, for his dedication and professionalism. Mark never failed to respond to a question, to offer expert advice, or to suggest positive directions for change. This book would be a different and inferior product without his input. On a personal level, I would also like to thank Mark for holding my hand in virtual space at times when I was not sure that I could finish what I had begun. His encouragement and flexibility made all the difference.

I would also like to acknowledge the people in my life who have held a candle for me in my darkest moments. My daughter Cameron and her children (Solan and Harper), my son Eric and his children (Erica, Emilie, William, and Morgan), and my daughter Ali's little girls (Ella and Sasha) continue to be light bearers for me. I love all of them very much, and they help to remind me of the continuity of life—that we are placeholders for the next generation. I particularly want to acknowledge Cameron at this time, because she has shown great strength in this past year. As much as her grief has threatened to overwhelm her at times, she has been a constant support for me; and I am very proud of the woman that she has become. I also want to recognize, with affection, Bruno Lepage, who joined our family many years ago. I thank Eric for coming to help me when he was himself exhausted and not well after a trip abroad.

I would also like to acknowledge my sisters Désiree, Claire, and Barbara, who occupy special places in my heart and life. Ali would be happy to know that her husband, Patrick Hendriks, and I have worked closely together since her death to support the emotional needs of their children. The sharing has been important to me, and I thank him for continuing to include me in the lives of his girls.

I thank my neighbour Jocelyn Burgess for her always cheerful and generous company—especially the Sunday night dinners and evenings at the National Arts Centre. I am grateful to my childhood friend Bobbie Giltner for coming to Canada in 2012 to offer prayers and emotional support to my family. Her presence was comforting to my daughter and to me. I have also appreciated the emotional support offered by psychologist Marie-Sylvie Roy, who has helped me to accept that nothing is ever lost, only changed. Last summer's journey to the sacred valleys and mountains of Peru was wonderful and healing; for that, I owe a debt of gratitude to Pete Bernard, Algonquin medicine man and shaman. I thank renowned medium and author Janet Mayer for the constancy of her friendship. What began as a professional relationship became a personal connection.

And last, but certainly not least, I want to acknowledge the support and valued friendship of esteemed scientist and researcher Dr Henry Lai (*Seattle Magazine*'s Person of the Year in 2011 and recently retired professor from the University of Washington). Despite his own heavy research agenda, he shared medical research and advice with me on a daily basis during the period of my daughter's illness. I have never known a more ethical or caring person, and I will never cease to be grateful to him.

Sherry Devereaux Ferguson
September 2013

I would like to acknowledge my friend and colleague Dr Lynne A. Texter, professor at La Salle University in Philadelphia. As office and house mates throughout graduate school at the State University of New York in Buffalo, Lynne and I spent hours talking about teaching, learning, and education. It was in Buffalo that I began my teaching career, putting into practice the theories about communication and teaching that Lynne and I explored together. I would also like to thank my students, thousands of them over the past two and a half decades, for their willingness to let me test teaching techniques, try out innovative forms of evaluation, and introduce all kinds of multimedia and technology in the classroom. Their feedback and enthusiasm has made my teaching and research so much more meaningful.

My teaching and research assistants over the years have also provided much support and guidance—as well as a lot of fun and youthful energy. I am especially indebted to Victoria Aceti, Geneviève Brisson, Jessica Daoust, Samantha DeLenardo, Dominique Leonard, Vidya Nair, and Jerie Shaw for their collaboration. I must also thank Dr Sherry Ferguson, my co-author, for her feedback on every word I wrote in this book, her commitment to excellence in writing, and her sound leadership on this writing journey.

My parents, Richard and Katharine Lennox, encouraged me to love learning, to be unafraid of change and adventure, and to pursue whatever directions I wanted to. Their belief in me has contributed to everything I have done. I would like to acknowledge the love and support of my children, Jack, Richard, and Katie. So many of the examples I generated in this book came from observing them and their friends and reflecting on the kinds of challenges that young people face in their relationships with family, peers, and members of their community. Finally, I must acknowledge the partnership I have enjoyed with my husband, best friend, and soul mate, Kevin Terrion, for 25 years. We have learned and grown together in so many ways, and it is to him that I turn every day for guidance, affirmation, and love.

Jenepher Lennox Terrion
September 2013

ABOUT THE AUTHORS

Dr Sherry Devereaux Ferguson (Ph.D., Indiana University; MA, University of Houston; BA, Louisiana State University) is a senior professor and former department chair and director of graduate studies for the Department of Communication at the University of Ottawa. She has acted on the editorial boards of numerous journals and yearbooks, including the *Journal of Communication*, the *Communication Yearbook*, *Communication Studies*, the *International Journal of Strategic Communication*, and *Communication, Culture, and Critique*. She chaired the Public Relations Division of the International Communication Association (ICA) and held the position of executive board member-at-large for the Americas. She also chaired the Internationalization Committee for that organization. While acting as chair of the PR division, she established the Global Task Force, a research initiative involving scholars from many countries. She is an honorary board member for the *Systems Theory and Complexity* book series (Aracne Publishing, Rome), in collaboration with the World Complexity Science Academy (WCSA).

Publications include three books on organizational communication, two on public opinion and strategic planning in communication, two on public speaking, one on civic discourse and cultural politics in Canada, and one on interpersonal communication. Publishers include Oxford University Press (New York and Toronto), Sage, Greenwood, Transaction, and others. One of her books has recently been translated into Chinese. Ferguson has published 30 articles in refereed journals and made 45 conference presentations.

Clients in an extensive consulting career have included, in Canada, the Department of Foreign Affairs, the Department of Justice, Transport Canada, Health Canada, the Canadian Space Agency, the National Research Council, the Office of the Auditor General, the Canadian International Development Agency, the Canadian Institute of Management, Petro-Canada, and others. She served on two major federal advisory boards, which oversaw the writing of a vision statement and the defining of curriculum needs for government communicators. She trained more than a thousand government communication officers in public opinion analysis and strategic planning techniques, initially at the request of the assistant secretary of communications to Cabinet. She also did professional speech writing for a former prime minister, government ministers, and top-level bureaucrats.

Dr Jenepher Lennox Terrion is an associate professor in the Department of Communication at the University of Ottawa. She received her Ph.D. in communication from Concordia University.

Dr Lennox Terrion is the winner of many teaching awards, including the University of Ottawa's Award for Excellence in Education, Distinguished Teaching Award, and Capital Educators' Award. She is passionate about teaching and has demonstrated creativity in the design and delivery of both undergraduate and graduate communication courses over the past two decades.

Dr Lennox Terrion is interested in the experiences of vulnerable populations and much of her work connects research with community organizations serving those in need. Her research focusses on evaluating the impacts of a range of programs, including student support services, addiction recovery programs, family support programs, mentoring programs, training programs, and leadership development programs. She is particularly interested in the role of support services in the academic success and engagement of vulnerable populations, including at-risk students, recovering addicts, and students suffering from mental illness. She is also interested in the role of interpersonal relations and social capital in the learning process, in student engagement, and in addiction recovery, and she is generally interested in interpersonal and organizational communication.

Dr Lennox Terrion has also published widely on a range of multidisciplinary topics in international peer-reviewed journals. Her works address such topics as peer mentoring (with articles in the following journals: *Mentoring and Tutoring*, *International Journal of Evidence Based Coaching and Mentoring*, *Journal of College Student Retention*, and *Studies in Higher Education*); addiction and smoking cessation (with articles published in the *Journal of Social and Personal Relationships*, the *Journal of Child and Adolescent Substance Abuse*, and the *Journal of Smoking Cessation*); family support (with publications in *Youth and Society* and the *European Journal of Social Work*); seniors and social capital (with articles in *Social Theory and Health* and *Gestion*); and leadership development (with articles in the *J ournal of Management Development*, *MountainRise*, and *Human Relations*).

Dr Lennox Terrion was recently named a University of Ottawa chair of university teaching. In this role, she is conducting a multiyear study of excellence in the large class. Her research seeks to assess the degree to which highly rated professors of large classes demonstrate teacher immediacy—the verbal and nonverbal communication used by professors to build connections with students—and to catalogue how they do it. Her research will produce guidelines for teaching large classes focussed specifically on building teacher immediacy and, ultimately, positive classroom relationships.

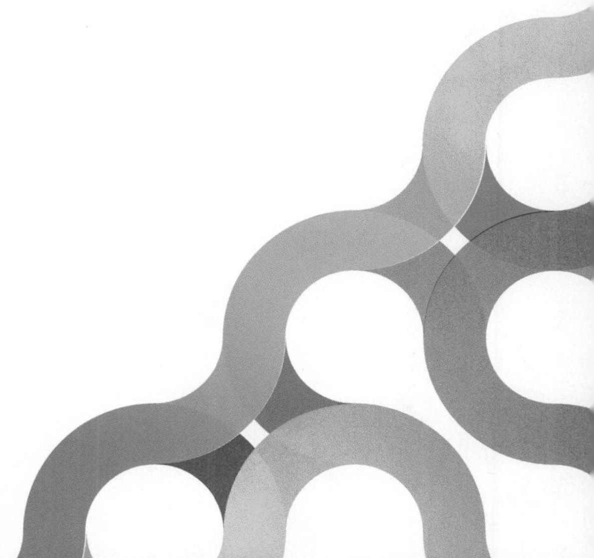

In memory of my beloved daughter
Alexandra Maureen Ferguson Hendriks

And in recognition of her most loved little girls
Ella and Sasha Hendriks
For whom she chose this quote

"If ever there is a tomorrow when we're not together . . . there is something you must always remember. You are braver than you believe, stronger than you seem, and smarter than you think. But the most important thing is, even if we're apart . . . I'll always be with you."
A.A. Milne

—Sherry Devereaux Ferguson

CHAPTER 1

The Communication Process: Learning from Models

CHAPTER OUTLINE

learning OBJECTIVES

- To become acquainted with the most popular communication models
- To become familiar with communication terminology
- To identify what we can learn from the communication models
- To understand how to apply the principles of communication to your everyday lives
- To understand the reasons for communication breakdowns
- To learn about how to communicate effectively

forSTARTERS

Intervention

The door opened and a young, frightened boy motioned the two policemen into the house. In the background, the police could hear a loud, angry voice.

"You made the call?" the younger policeman asked.

"Yes." The small voice seemed to fit with the size of the slender boy, and it was hard to hear him over the sound of a blaring television set.

"You've got a problem here?"

The boy nodded but didn't speak. He huddled deeper into the grey and red hoodie he was wearing, as if hoping the jacket could make him disappear.

"Where is your mom? Is she in the other room?" the older policeman asked. "Mind if I turn off the TV?"

"You can turn it off. She's with my dad."

A scream from a woman interrupted the conversation, but it was hard to know if the scream came from the next room or an adjacent apartment. Music and voices from the other half of the duplex invaded the thin plaster walls of the room.

"All right, son, stay here. We'll check it out." The two policemen stepped quickly toward the room from which they thought the scream had come.

Before they could reach the entrance to the room, however, a tall, rough-looking man appeared in the frame of the door, blocking a view of the bedroom. He had a cloth wrapped around his left hand and a half-drunk beer in his right hand. He was wearing tan work pants and a dirty undershirt. A pair of concrete-encrusted workboots lay close to the couch. "What?" The man stared first at the policemen, then at the boy. "What's this about, Jacob?" he asked. "You call the police?" He took a long gulp of the beer.

The boy tried another disappearing act with his hoodie. He didn't answer.

"We need to see your wife, sir." the older policeman indicated. He turned back to his partner. "Joey, do you want to see what's happening in the other room?"

© Radharc Images/Alamy

"Sure thing, Tony," Joey said, moving toward the oversized figure, who had yet to move aside. "What's your name?"

"Ray. Ray Stilton. Hey, stop looking at me like I've got the scabies! We're just having an argument—that's all. Everything is cool." The man tried harder to fill the door frame, which was not too difficult, given his imposing figure.

"Like I said, we need to see your wife." The man did not show any sign of moving, and the policeman's patience was clearly tested.

"Why?" the man demanded. "I told you, everything is okay."

"We know what you told us, sir. But we still need to see your wife to be sure she's okay."

"My wife? To be sure she's okay?" he asked. For a brief moment, the man looked startled, then recovered. He seemed to have had a change of heart. "Irina! They're asking to see you. You'll see. She's fine."

INTRODUCTION

In this first chapter, you will become acquainted with some historical and recent communication models and gain insights into what we can learn from these models. Models serve several different purposes. First, they provide a vocabulary—jargon that allows us to talk about a topic of interest. Just as social workers, police officers, doctors, and other professionals require a job-specific vocabulary that enables them to communicate effectively with their colleagues, so too do you need a common vocabulary in order to discuss communication concepts. Second, models help to explain processes—in this

"What do you do for a living, Mr Stilton?"

"I'm in construction. Get up at 5:00 in the morning, work by 6:00. See my hands." Putting down the beer, Ray thrust his hands toward the policeman. "I come from a place where people work hard. Get their hands dirty. Not like yours—all clean and manicured. Doesn't mean I have to be treated like this."

In that moment of anger, the man spoke with a strong British accent—one that Tony recognized as common to East End Londoners. He thought about a boy he had known in his youth who had the same accent. The boy had been prone to settling his disputes in a physical way, and Tony wondered if Ray had come from the same street culture as his childhood friend.

A small, frail-looking woman appeared hesitantly at the door. She fit just under her husband's outstretched arm, which was braced against the door frame. "It's all right," she said. "Everything's all right. Ray's just had a few too many beers. Jacob overreacts."

Joey looked in the direction of the boy, who was playing with his tablet computer. Jacob didn't look up when his mother spoke, he just shifted in his seat.

"Come into the room, Ms Stilton. We need to ask you a few questions."

Irina looked uncertainly in the direction of her husband.

With a grunt and a dismissive wave of his arm, the man moved aside and responded, "Might as well. They can't do anything."

"I told you, everything's okay," the woman insisted as she edged her way hesitantly into the room. "We don't need any help here." She looked at her husband, who rubbed his hand nervously. Then she started to cry. "Please, just leave us alone."

"Something wrong with that hand?" Tony asked, glancing at his partner.

"Nah, just a scrape." Ray's face turned red.

"Are you sure?" Tony approached the man and took his hand. Beneath the bandage, the knuckles of the hand were red and swollen. "How did you get this? Been hitting something?" The attention of the policeman pivoted to the woman, who pulled a shawl protectively around her shoulders, hiding her body from scrutiny. He looked back at the man. "Better put the drink down. We need to talk."

"Look, you can see my wife is all right. Our son is all right. I am all right. The call was a mistake. We're a hard-working, respectable family. We pay our bills. We go to church on Sundays. Hell, we pay your salaries. We just want to be left alone. If we have problems, we can solve them without your help." Ray turned to his wife and placed a hand on her shoulder. She winced, drawing back sharply from his touch.

Ignoring his wife's reaction, Ray added with a certain amount of pride: "Irina, she has a good job at the telephone company—a desk job. We're not those street bums asking for some kind of a handout." More a plea than a request, he added, "Now, can you leave us alone?"

A knock at the door interrupted their conversation, and Joey opened the door to a middle-aged woman in a long coat. Removing a scarf from around her neck as she entered the room, she looked as uneasy as Jacob had looked a few minutes earlier. At the same time, she was obviously relieved to see the uniformed officers.

"I'm glad you're here," she said. "We've been dealing with this situation for a while. I'm a case worker with social services. Jacob called earlier, but I wasn't home. I got worried and decided to come around." She extended her hand. "Nancy Corrigan."

"We've got the situation under control, Ms Corrigan. Looks like the woman is okay."

"The woman?" the social worker responded in unconcealed disbelief. "Of course, she's okay. It's her husband we need to be worried about. She tried to shoot him a couple of months ago!"

The two policemen looked at each other, then back at Ray and Irina Stilton. For the first time since the policemen arrived, Jacob showed interest in the happenings. He dropped his tablet on the sofa and ran to his dad.

case, how and why we communicate, as well as the potential impact of our communication. Third, models visually depict relationships among the parts of any picture. And finally, models help us to identify reasons for problems that we may encounter.

This chapter will examine models developed by Aristotle, Harold Lasswell, Claude E. Shannon and Warren Weaver, Wilbur Schramm, Frank Dance, Dean Barnlund, and Sherry Ferguson. It will also briefly describe the simultaneous access model, which first appeared in the work of Stewart Ferguson and Sherry Ferguson in 1988. As we will discuss, these models basically fall into four categories: linear, interactive, transactional, and critical.

Each of the models discussed in this chapter adds something new to our understanding of communication. To show you how, we will revisit the scenario developed in the "For Starters" box with each model in mind. This exercise will also suggest how you can apply the different communication models to understand the role of communication in everyday life.

COMMUNICATION MODELS

Aristotelian Model of Communication

Dating back to fourth century BCE, the Aristotelian model depicts the most basic of communication functions. The model comes from the classical period, when every Greek scholar studied rhetoric—the art of speaking. According to the Aristotelian model, all communication proceeds in a linear fashion, and all communication has the ultimate aim of persuading. That is, communication involves a *communicator* using a *speech* to *persuade* an *audience*. The audience might be one person or many people.[1]

In order to persuade, the communicator must understand the demographics of his or her audience. In other words, the communicator needs to know about the parties in the communication situation—their age, gender, social status, and other relevant characteristics.

In the act of persuading, the communicator relies on three kinds of appeals: appeals based on source credibility, appeals based on logic and reasoning, and appeals based on emotion.

Source Credibility Appeals

By *source credibility*, we mean the personal attractiveness of a communicator to the audience. Aristotle referred to this kind of appeal as *ethical appeal*. Generally speaking, when we talk about **source credibility appeals**, we are referring to the **trustworthiness**, **competency**, **status**, **dynamism**, and **sociability** of the communicator. (Some Asian cultures, however, prefer a less dynamic and more formal presence in their communicators.)

SOURCE CREDIBILITY APPEALS Appeals based on the personal attractiveness of a communicator to the audience.

TRUSTWORTHINESS One's character or integrity.

COMPETENCY One's expertise in a given area.

STATUS One's standing in relationship to others.

DYNAMISM One's boldness, energy, and assertiveness.

SOCIABILITY One's likeability.

Most agree that trustworthiness, or character, ranks above all other qualities when we judge someone. In addition, we tend to trust communicators who are "one of us"—who share our background, our experiences, and our likely fate.[2]

Competency, or expertise, is also essential in a communicator.[3] We are more likely to change our opinions when a communicator has expertise or knowledge of the topic under discussion.[4] A related concept is status—how others see us in relation to others. If we perceive the communicator to have high status and the respect of others, we are more likely to see that person as competent and credible. We get our impressions of status from the reputation, appearance, and occupation of the communicator.

Uschools University Images/Getty Images

In a Western context, we also assign credibility to communicators who are dynamic, or bold, energetic, and assertive. When communicators use powerful (as opposed to powerless) language, they appear confident and strong. In informal communication, however, we deliberately strip our language of some of its power in respect for social norms of interaction. We use *polite forms* such as "Forgive me, sir, but I wonder if I might be able to get a copy of that paper." We also dilute language through the use of *hedges* such as "*I think* that I would like to spend tomorrow at the beach" or "*I guess* that you can use the car."[5]

Finally, we judge communicators on the basis of sociability, or likeability. Studies of student–teacher interactions have found that students like friendly instructors who know their students' names, recount interesting stories, use a conversational manner of speech, have an expressive voice and a dramatic manner, use humor that is spontaneous and relevant to the course content, encourage students to talk, address the issues raised by students, and show openness and a willingness to disclose personal information.[6] When instructors are warm, expressive, involved, and articulate, students also perceive them to be more competent.[7]

Logical Appeals

Communicators also use **logical appeals** in trying to persuade others. In making these sorts of appeals, communicators may use reasoning from example, reasoning from generalization, causal (cause–effect) reasoning, reasoning from sign, or analogical reasoning in an effort to convince the other party to share their views.

LOGICAL APPEALS Appeals based on logic and reasoning.

With reasoning from example, we support our arguments with a number of specific examples. Reasoning from generalization involves moving from the general to the specific. With cause–effect reasoning, we observe effects and look for the causes. We see a student who is failing, and we ask, "What caused this effect?" When reasoning from sign, we see a visible sign of a condition, and we try to figure out what the sign means. Does someone with a cough, high fever, and headache have the flu? If a child has bruises and fractures, has someone abused the child? Finally, when we use analogical reasoning, we

© fotostorm/iStockphoto

conclude that what is true for one situation must also be true for another situation. For example, we may assume that if someone is good at downhill skiing, she or he will also be good at the similar activity of snowboarding.

Emotional Appeals

EMOTIONAL APPEALS Appeals based on the expected emotional responses of an audience.

Communicators must appeal not only to the logical thought processes of their audiences, but also to their emotions. For that reason, communicators often use **emotional appeals**—appeals to the compassion, anger, fear, pride, empathy, guilt, humility, and respect of their audiences.

When we react emotionally to an event or a person, we experience physiological changes. Minute changes in our nervous system and blood chemistry affect our breathing, digestive processes, heartbeat, and muscle control. But what causes an emotional response in one person may create no reaction in another. High steel workers, for example, are able to walk across small beams, hundreds of feet above the ground, without experiencing the sort of transformed physical state or fear that most of us would find debilitating. The same person, however, might sweat uncontrollably if confronted with the need to address an audience of 20 students.[8] Many Canadians, having learned to control their emotions in public settings, see emotional arousal as an unnatural and undesirable state of being—a sign of weakness.[9]

Analysis of a Scenario Using the Aristotelian Framework

Aristotle made a major contribution in terms of helping us to understand how communicators use ethical (source credibility), logical, and emotional appeals to persuade audiences. He also focussed on the importance of knowing the makeup of our audiences. If we use the Aristotelian framework to analyze the scenario depicted in the "For Starters" box, we will be focussing mainly on the linear act of persuasion—that is, individual efforts to persuade another person to adopt a certain point of view.

In the "For Starters" scenario, Ray and Irina hoped to persuade the policemen to go away and to leave them alone with their son. They used source credibility, logical, and emotional appeals in their efforts to convince the policemen to leave. Ray used source credibility appeals when he told the officers that he and his wife work hard, pay their bills, attend church regularly, and contribute to the salaries of the officers. Ray used reasoning from sign when he asked the policeman to look at his wife and son—to see that they had no signs of physical injury. Irina used an emotional appeal (crying) after her appeals to reasoning (stating that everything was "all right," that her husband had simply "had a few too many beers," and that her son "overreacts") failed. Evidence of Ray's emotional involvement occurred when his face turned red from a mix of embarrassment and anger.

The policemen wanted to persuade Ray and Irina to co-operate so they could investigate what appeared to be a dangerous situation. Their efforts at persuasion were assertive in nature, displaying characteristics of dynamic communication. For example, they demanded access to Irina and asked to examine Ray's hand. They also requested information about Ray's occupation. They tempered these demands, however, with polite, socially appropriate language (e.g., referring to Ray as "sir") in order to ease the situation. Like Ray, they reasoned from sign. Ray's size, gender, and manner convinced them that he was capable of abusing his wife. Since Ray was drinking a beer when they arrived, they probably believed that he had acted in an alcoholic rage. They concluded that the bandaged hand was a sign of abusive behaviour on Ray's part. In their eyes, Ray had low source credibility, with questionable trustworthiness and low social status.

In reality, the police officers had little knowledge of the audience to whom they were speaking. Until Nancy Corrigan arrived, they did not have access to background knowledge about Ray and Irina. As a result, they completely misinterpreted the situation; and in the end, none of the communicators effected any real changes in the others. Using the Aristotelian model, we would view the communication as being one-way rather than interactive.

Lasswell's Effects Model

In 1948, Harold Lasswell published a "transmission" model of communication. Like the Aristotelian model, this model focussed on a one-way linear process of communication. The Aristotelian elements of *who* (a communicator), *what* (a message), and *to whom* (an audience, or receiver) resurfaced in this model. However, Lasswell added two components to the earlier model: **channel** and **effects** (Figure 1.1).

CHANNEL The medium used to transmit a message.

EFFECTS The intended or unintended impact(s) of a message.

The emphasis on channel reflected the role that radio had played in communicating to the masses in World War II. The focus on effects reflected the role that propaganda had played in Adolf Hitler's rise to power in Germany. Hitler was not the only one, however, to use propaganda in World War II. As the war progressed, the Allied forces dropped many thousands of flyers and broadcast their own radio shows aimed at demoralizing the enemy and boosting the morale of the Allied forces.

Despite its historical associations with war rhetoric, we can apply Lasswell's model to any communication situation. Let us take the scenario developed in the "For Starters" box. Ray, Irina, Jacob, Tony, Joey, and Nancy took turns acting in the position of communicator (*who*). They used speech to create messages (*what*). The receivers of the message (*to whom*) represented the audience. The *channel* for the messages was air waves, because the communication took place in an interpersonal setting. When Ray placed his hand on his wife's shoulder, however, he was using the channel of touch. Finally, multiple *effects* occurred in the scenario. For example, Ray became angry and his wife became emotional when the police officers refused to leave. The officers became frustrated when the Stilton family refused to co-operate with their requests for information. Jacob reacted with relief to the arrival of Nancy Corrigan, and Nancy was surprised by the officers' concern for Irina. The officers, in turn, were confused by Nancy's clarification of the situation.

In interpersonal and group communication, effects often take the form of emotional reactions. At other times, effects may take the form of physical results: a pay raise that follows a negotiation or a request for a resignation following an inappropriate email. Since Ray Stilton does not intend to press charges against his wife, the effects of Jacob's call are unlikely to produce notable changes in the situation.

FIGURE 1.1 Lasswell's effects model.

Shannon–Weaver Mathematical Model

A third model, developed in the late 1940s by Bell engineer Claude E. Shannon and mathematician Warren Weaver, began life as a one-way transmission model (Figure 1.2) but moved in a later version to an interactive model (Figure 1.3). Many scholars have applied the original model to interpersonal communication as follows. Communication begins when the **information source** gets an idea that he wants to convey to another party. When he encodes or puts this idea into the form of a communication product such as words, a letter, or a broadcast, he becomes a **transmitter**. The communication product is a **signal**. When the second party receives the signal, she has to decode it or figure out what it means. In the decoding process, she acts as a **receiver**. Once she has decoded or reconstructed the idea in her mind, the signal has reached its **destination**.

INFORMATION SOURCE Where the message is conceived.

TRANSMITTER Mechanism for encoding the message.

SIGNAL The message.

RECEIVER Mechanism for decoding the message.

DESTINATION Where the message ends up.

In the original description of this model, only the *source* and the *destination* were human. The *transmitter* was a telephone box that converted information into waves, which travelled over cables to a receiving device. The device at the other end decoded the waves for human consumption. Thus, the original model was an engineering model, applicable to the telephone industry but not to purely human processes. However, through interpretation and adaptation, the Shannon–Weaver model became one of the most popular interpersonal communication models of the twentieth century. Most people would classify it, in its revised version, as an interactive model—not yet advanced to the transactional stage, but a big step in that direction.

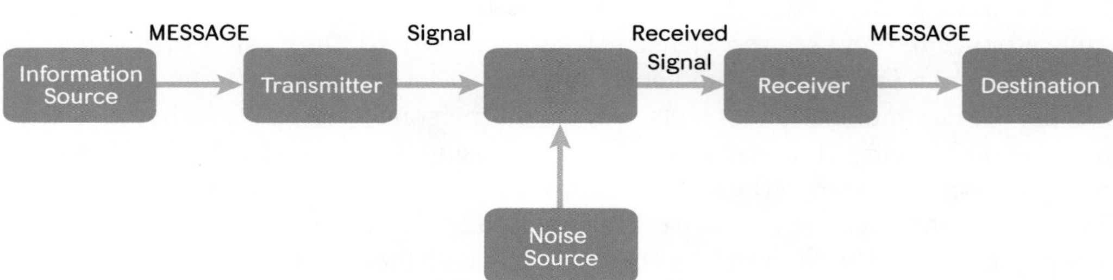

FIGURE 1.2 **Original Shannon–Weaver mathematical model.**

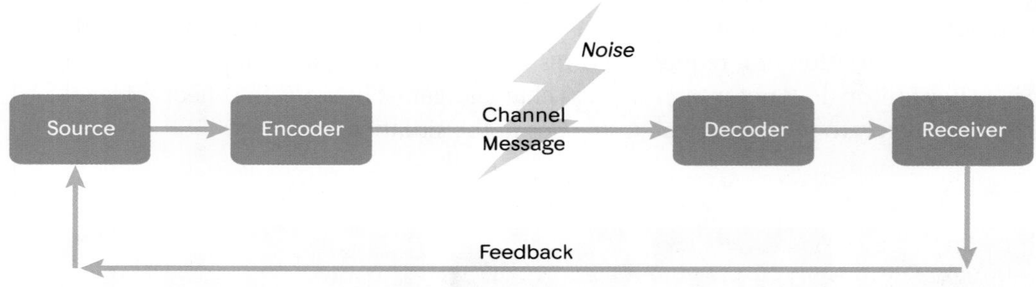

FIGURE 1.3 **Revised Shannon–Weaver model.**

SOURCE: Based on http://www.uri.edu/personal/carson/kulveted/wlsmodel.html.

Note that Shannon and Weaver contributed two additional concepts to the understanding of communication: **noise** and **feedback**. They coined the term *noise* to refer to any interference that occurs in the process of transmitting or receiving signals. In their original description, the term *noise* referred to disruptions caused by bad weather, broken cables, or other problems in the sending and decoding of information via telephone lines. They used the term *feedback* to refer to the response to a message or activity.

NOISE Interference that occurs in the transmitting or receiving of signals.

FEEDBACK Response to a message or activity.

Communication scholars extended the concept of *noise* to include factors that interfere with interpersonal communication situations. Noise can arise in the environment, the channel, the source, or the receiver. Passing traffic on a street outside the room, a ringing cellphone, or coughing can all disrupt the communication process. A malfunctioning microphone can interrupt the ability of a speaker to convey information. A source may be tired, confused, or unsure of how to communicate her ideas. A receiver may lose composure or overreact to an email if he feels insecure or fearful. Sources and receivers may also be biased or prejudiced toward a person or a topic. They may also be distracted by some event in their personal lives. Cultural misunderstandings can short-circuit the transmission process. Expectations related to social norms in dress or codes of behaviour can create communication problems.

As the above examples suggest, noise can be external or internal. **External noise** in a lecture context, for example, could be a loud radio, people talking or laughing in the hallway, a loud air conditioner, vocabulary that you do not understand, or someone texting to you while you are trying to listen to the lecture. **Internal noise** can arise in the form of **physiological noise** or **psychological noise**. An example of physiological noise could be a bad headache or the feeling of hunger that keeps you from concentrating. Psychological noise could be concerns about getting a parking ticket or feelings of sadness about a broken relationship.

EXTERNAL NOISE Interference from an environmental source.

INTERNAL NOISE Interference from an internal source.

PHYSIOLOGICAL NOISE Interference from a biological condition or function.

PSYCHOLOGICAL NOISE Interference from a mental state.

The addition of a *feedback* loop to the later model changed the process from linear to circular—a major contribution to the development of communication theory. With the addition of feedback, the process becomes interactive. The listener is no longer a passive receiver of information, and the roles of source and receiver become interchangeable. The relationship between the source and the receiver acquires importance.

Analyzing the scenario involving Ray and Irina Stilton, we can see both *noise* and *feedback* at play. External noises in the environment include a blaring TV, loud voices and music in the adjacent apartment, a woman's scream, and a knock on the door. Psychological noise differs from person to person, and we can only speculate about the possibilities in this scenario. However, Jacob was probably unwilling to engage in unnecessary conversation with the officers because he was worried about the consequences of his call. Ray's anger and frustration, along with his fears that his wife might be arrested and his son put into foster care, probably influenced his ability to communicate effectively. Alcohol could have

© CEFutcher/iStockphoto

lessened his ability to think clearly and to put his thoughts into words. A fear of going to jail might have influenced Irina's ability to communicate honestly in the circumstances. Tony had preconceived ideas about people from the East End of London, which may have influenced his assessment of—and communication with—Ray. When Ray pointed to the manicured hands of the policemen, he also displayed a cultural bias. This bias would have interfered with the possibility of the two men communicating effectively with each other.

The element of *feedback* was present in all of the interpersonal communications in this scenario. Verbal feedback featured most prominently in the communications involving Ray, Irina, the police, and the social worker. Ray communicated not only through language, but also through body language (e.g., blocking the door with his body). Jacob was the least communicative in terms of verbal feedback. Nonetheless, he reacted nonverbally on a number of occasions—both through his body language and through his efforts to disconnect from his environment. Even his failure to communicate was an act of communication! We can communicate through silence as well as through words. In this scenario, the existence of feedback meant that the parties were involved in interactive communication. The interactive nature of the communication involved in this scenario is further highlighted by the fact that each person took turns acting as *sources* and *encoders*, as well as *decoders* and *receivers*.

Schramm Model

In 1954, Wilbur Schramm developed a human communication model that placed increased emphasis on the *encoding* and *decoding* of messages—that is, how we create, interpret, and assign meaning to words and actions (Figure 1.4). As in the original Shannon–Weaver model, Schramm used the terms *source* and *destination*, but he saw the process as circular: "It is misleading to think of the communications process as starting somewhere and ending somewhere. It is really endless."[10] Schramm's model falls solidly into the interactive tradition. To the previously developed models, Schramm added the idea of **field of experience**—the next major contribution to the development of communication theory.

FIELD OF EXPERIENCE The totality of all we are at the moment of communication.

Schramm said that we can communicate with each other to the extent that we have overlapping fields of experience. So twins raised in the same family will be able to communicate with each other very well because they will have large overlaps in their fields

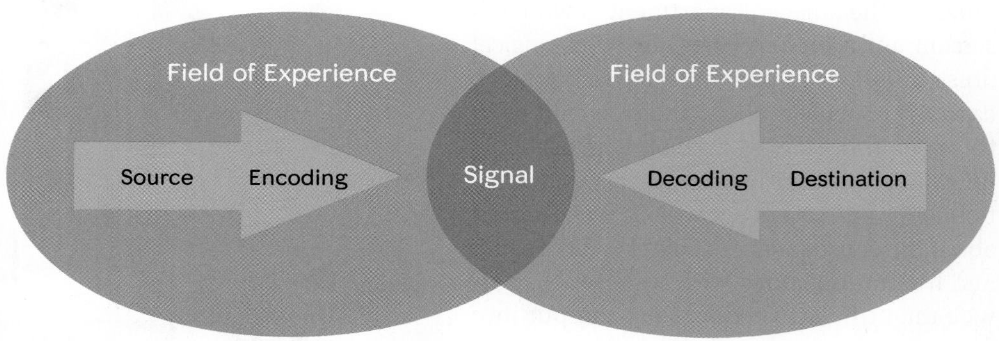

FIGURE 1.4 **Schramm model of communication.**

of experience. Twins raised in different families, on the other hand, will not be able to communicate with each other as well because they will have smaller overlaps. When two people from different countries or **cultures** attempt to communicate with each other, they will have much more difficulty because their fields of experience will be vastly different, with little overlapping relative to people who inhabit the same country or culture.

CULTURE The shared ideas, traditions, norms, symbols, and values that define a community.

In focussing on fields of experience, Schramm introduced the idea that our backgrounds have a large impact on our ability to communicate with others. Background variables can include gender, sexual orientation, age, race, ethnicity, birthplace, socio-economic status, educational level, and many other variables. So even within the same family or culture, differences will exist in our experiences and how we interpret them. A member of Hells Angels, who makes a living by participating in criminal activity, will have different experiences from a social activist who works as a volunteer at a soup kitchen. Likewise, the volunteer at the soup kitchen will probably have different experiences from a person who runs a small business or works as a financial analyst on Bay Street. Thus, according to Schramm, each of us has a unique set of life experiences. To the extent that our experiences are similar to—or different from—other people's experiences, we will find it easy or hard to communicate with those people. All members of the human race will have some overlap in experiences; however, we will have much greater overlap in experiences with some people than with others.

Returning to the episode with Ray and Irina Stilton, we can see that Ray probably had a notably different field of experience from the policemen. He grew up in a different country and in a different culture, and he worked in a blue-collar job that did not require a college education. Jacob's age set him apart from his parents, the social worker, and the policemen. Despite his age, however, he had been through some difficult experiences—probably different from the childhood experiences of the social worker and the policemen. Even though they were both women, Irina probably had different life experiences from the social worker. In their daily routine of dealing with offenders and defusing potentially violent situations, the policemen would have had experiences that coloured how they viewed the conflict between Ray and Irina. They likely assumed that Ray was the abuser and Irina the victim because they knew, from their experiences, that offenders in domestic abuse situations are almost always men.

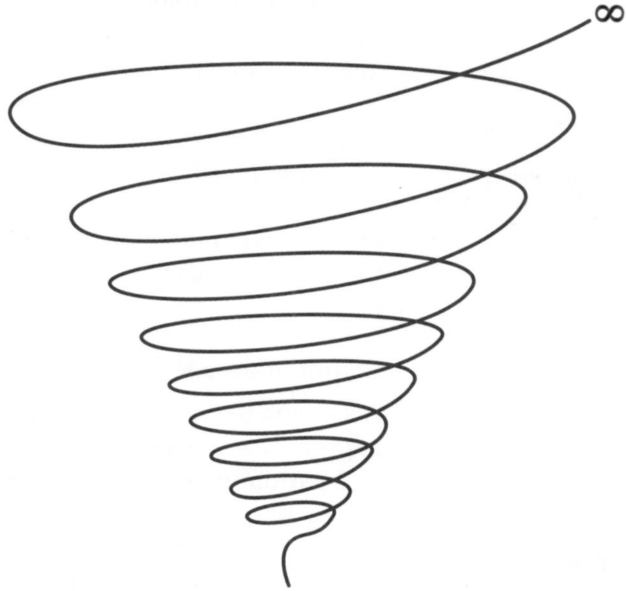

FIGURE 1.5 **Dance model of communication.**

SOURCE: Dance, Frank E.X. "Toward a Theory of Human Communication", pp. 288–309, in F.E.X. Dance, ed., *Human Communication Theory: Original Essays*. NY, Holt, Rinehart and Winston, Inc. (1967). Helical Model, p. 296.

Dance Model

In 1967, Frank Dance contributed the helical model of communication (Figure 1.5). Like Schramm, Dance sees communication as a never-ending story, with no fixed beginning or ending. However, unlike Schramm, he does not visualize the process as circular. Rather, he sees the process as helical in shape and dynamic, ongoing, unrepeatable, additive, and cumulative in its effects. According to Dance, the inward-turning nature of the helix suggests the likelihood that "learning, growth, and discovery" are always taking place.[11] We continue to widen and deepen our perspective and our knowledge base as we go through life. Although progressive over time, the helix continues to loop back in a reflexive way, allowing past events and circumstances to inform the present and the future. Thus, all experiences contribute to the unfolding of the present moment; and even as we move forward, we continue to revisit the past.

These visitations to the past can be positive or negative in their implications. If we have had many positive experiences, we may be able to draw on past information that is helpful—for example, information that enables us to communicate effectively. On the other hand, if we have experienced a great deal of rejection and failure in the past, revisiting those moments may be both difficult and unproductive. In such cases, the consequences for communication may be negative.

The Dance model allows us to apply a few additional principles to the scenario involving Ray and Irina Stilton. We can assume, for example, that Ray's and Irina's prior histories had an important influence on how they interacted with the police officers and with each other in the presence of the officers. Some of these interactions were doubtless negative. We learn, for example, that Irina had tried to shoot Ray on an earlier occasion. We also learn that the social worker had been involved with Jacob's care in the past. Moreover, we can assume that the communication between Ray and Irina will not end when the policemen leave their home. Hopefully, the couple will learn from this experience; however, they will not be able to erase the experience. No matter what happens in their relationship, the experience will always be a part of their past, with the ability to influence future interactions. Nor will they ever experience exactly the same event again.

Barnlund's Transactional Model

In 1970, Dean Barnlund developed the transactional model of communication (Figure 1.6) to respond to perceived weaknesses in the interactive models of communication.[12] **Transactional theory** sees communication as a process in which communicators act simultaneously as senders and receivers. This perspective accepts that not all communication is intentional. It also recognizes that both the history and the quality of the relationship make a difference, because communication takes place in a web of interdependencies. Finally, it sees communication as a dynamic and fluid process, shaped by changes in the communicators and in the environment in which they operate. Thus, the theory recognizes the importance of *context*, which is essential because we do not communicate in a vacuum.

TRANSACTIONAL THEORY Theory that sees communication as a dynamic process, involving continuous changes in communicators and environments.

Simultaneous Nature of Communication and Interchangeability of Roles

According to the transactional model, we never stop communicating. Even when we are listening, we are communicating through our facial expressions, body language, and **paralanguage** (e.g., tone of voice, rate of speech, vocal sounds). For that reason, transactional theory does not separate the roles of sender and receiver. It sees communication as a simultaneous and mutual transmission of information between parties.

PARALANGUAGE Elements of speech that are not recognized as language.

To understand the difference between interactive and transactional models, consider the following example. You send an email or a letter to an acquaintance. She might answer you in ten minutes, ten hours, ten days, or never. The time frame probably depends upon your relationship, the urgency of the communication, and the time available for response. The potential for feedback exists, but the interaction does not involve

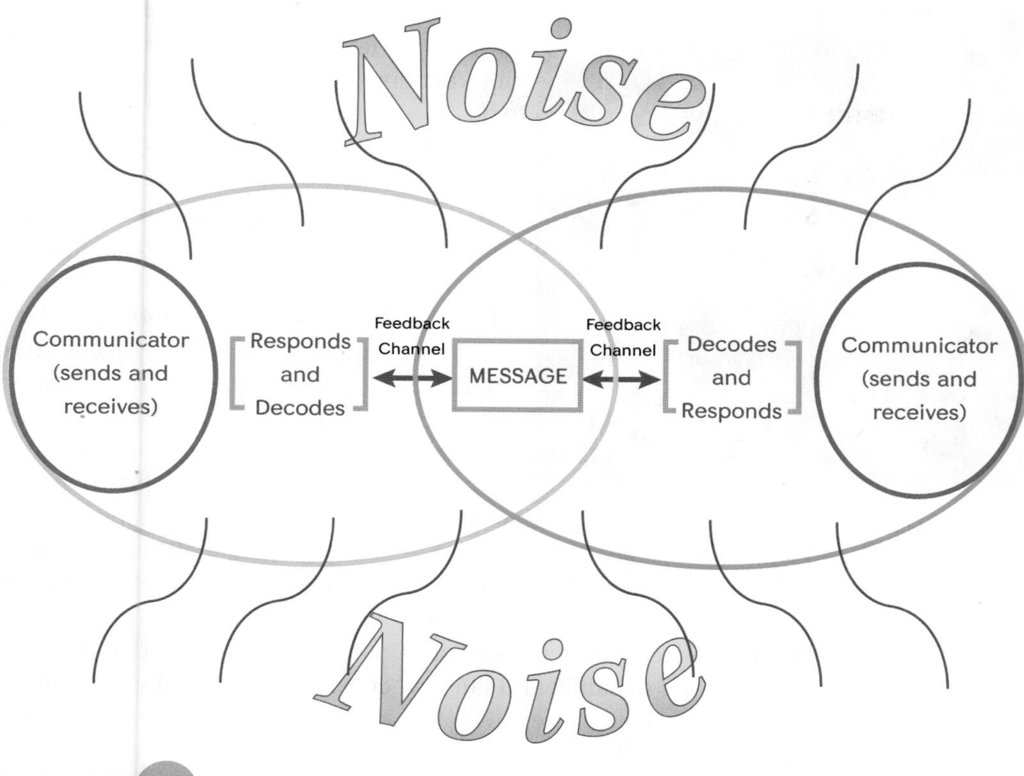

FIGURE 1.6 **Transactional model.**

SOURCE: http://catherinelauraleeds.blogspot.ca/2011/03/communication-theory.html.

simultaneous communication. You and your acquaintance alternate the roles of sender and receiver; thus, the communication is interactive. However, once the two of you meet in person, talk on the phone, or chat on instant messenger, you are engaging in simultaneous communication. Even when not speaking or typing, you and your acquaintance are listening or reacting; thus, the communication is transactional.

Unintentional Communication

We communicate in order to meet our most basic needs for survival, safety, companionship, and love. We also communicate in order to meet higher-level needs for recognition and achievement. However, not all of our communication is intentional or conscious. This observation applies particularly to nonverbal communication. The increased emphasis on the role of the listener as simultaneous sender of messages and the focus on unintentional aspects of communication elevate the role of nonverbal communication in the transactional model.

Importance of Relationships and Interdependencies

The relationship of the communicators becomes very important in the transactional model, because they are interdependent. The source needs a receiver, and the receiver needs a source. Past experiences, attitudes, beliefs, and values influence how they

© Jay Mallin/zumapress.com/Alamy

behave in the moment. How communicators feel about themselves will also influence their interactions with others.

Dynamic and Fluid Nature of Communication

Communicators are constantly in transition, changing with each communication experience. So too is their environment constantly changing. The outside culture influences how we view a situation, and the physical setting influences our interactions. When views in society change, our communication on topics of importance also shifts focus. Once research scientists established a clear link between tobacco smoke and cancer, the dialogue changed. In a similar way, people no longer accept spanking of children, and they see spousal abuse as criminal; neither attitude prevailed even 30 years ago. More recently, the December 2012 shootings in Newtown, Connecticut, created a new climate for protest and debate over gun laws in the United States.

All of these examples illustrate an important principle of the transactional model. That is, communication is a dynamic and fluid process, characterized by continuous change. As society changes, dialogues change. And as actors move from one setting to another, their conversation shifts to reflect their new environment. We do not communicate in a church in the same way that we communicate in a pub or a bar. Locker-room talk is not the same as parlour talk. As the chapter on nonverbal communication (Chapter 7) will indicate, some settings also encourage more positive exchanges than do others.

Analysis Using Transactional Framework

In the scenario described at the beginning of this chapter, we can see how the Stiltons, the policemen, and the social worker simultaneously act as senders and receivers of communication. Even when they are not speaking, they are listening or reacting.

Unintentional, nonverbal communication also plays an important role in this scenario. Jacob communicates his fears and discomfort through his eyes, facial expressions, and attempts to hide in his hoody. He also reveals his lack of ease with the situation through his silence. Finally, he shows his relief toward the end when he runs to his father. Ray unintentionally communicates the stereotypical image of an abusive male through his dress, injured hand, rough language, and drinking.

Relationships and interdependencies also influence communication among all players. Ray and Irina come to the event with a history of interactions. This history doubtless includes many earlier confrontations of the same nature. Their fates are also intertwined. Whatever happens to Irina will influence Ray and Jacob, and vice versa. If Irina goes to jail, she will lose her job and the family will likely face financial difficulties. Irina's future also depends heavily on the loyalty of her husband. The fact that Ray tries to protect his wife indicates his recognition of this interdependence. His efforts to hide his abuse are probably part of a long-term pattern of defensive communication, established early in their marriage.

Self-concept also plays a role in the situation. Cost–benefit theory tells us that if Ray is willing to tolerate the abuse, he must be getting some benefit from the arrangement. When Ray mentions that Irina has a good desk job, we get a clue as to one possible reason for Ray's staying in the marriage: he may identify indirectly with his wife's position, which raises him to a higher social status. Also, since Jacob runs to Ray at the end, we get the sense that Ray has a caring relationship with his son. He may realize that if Irina goes to jail, he could lose Jacob.

Finally, as suggested in our discussion of the Dance model, none of the people in this scenario will be the same in future interactions. Ray has suffered not only spousal abuse, but also the embarrassment of having other people learn about his situation. This embarrassment may lead him to try harder to hide his abuse from other family members, friends, and co-workers. The policemen have acquired new information that might affect their future interactions not only with Ray Stilton, but also with other men who fit his profile. Jacob has learned that he has access to outside help.

Ferguson's Critical Communication Model (CCM)

The critical communication model (CCM), developed by Sherry Ferguson in 2006, adds a further component to the communication process.[13] Like Lasswell's model, this model places a focus on effects; however, it also deals with the ethical and power dimensions of communication (Figure 1.7). Any communication act can have short-term or long-term effects on the receivers of the communication. Consider the example of the telephone prank by Australian disc jockeys Mel Greig and Michael Christian. Pretending to be Queen Elizabeth and Prince Charles, Greig and Christian called the King Edward VII's Hospital in London to ask for an update on Prince Charles's wife, Kate Middleton. Kate had been admitted to the hospital with acute morning sickness. A nurse named Jacintha Saldanha answered the telephone. Unaware that she was being pranked, she gave information on Kate's condition. Three days after taking the hoax call, Saldanha committed suicide. In the aftermath of the tragedy, the radio station cancelled the show, pulled the DJs from the air, and banned prank calls.

In the case of Ray and Irina Stilton, the long-term consequences of their interaction with the police officers could be significant. The social worker could decide to remove Jacob from his home and place him in foster care. If Ray chooses to be more forthcoming, Irina could be charged with domestic abuse. The officers, for their part, might realize that Ray's appearance and uncultured language have led them to the wrong conclusion. In the short-term, they might change their way of communicating with Ray. In the long-term, they might deal differently with others who resemble Ray. The impact of learning that the abuser is not a man, but a woman, could also influence how Tony and Joey approach family conflicts in the future. All of these consequences have ethical dimensions.

OUTCOMES OF COMMUNICATION ACTS

- Short term
- Long term

COSTS OF ACHIEVING OUTCOMES

- To individual
- To groups
- To society

BASES FOR JUDGING COSTS

- Motives of communicator (intent)
- Means employed (legitimacy of strategies & power bases)
- Ethical quality of the outcomes

FIGURE 1.7 Ferguson's critical communication model.

SOURCE: Adapted from S.D. Ferguson, *Public Speaking in Canada: Building Competency in Stages* (Toronto: Oxford University Press, 2006), 12.

In terms of the distribution of power in relationships, not everyone exercises equal power in this scenario. Irina, despite her frail appearance, exercises more power than Ray in the relationship. The social worker holds power in that she can take the child out of his family setting and place him in foster care. The policemen have power that comes from their position as law enforcement officials. Chapter 9 discusses these dimensions of power in more depth.

WHAT WE LEARN FROM COMMUNICATION MODELS

In the preceding discussion, we looked at communication models that help us to understand how and why people communicate, the impact of their communication, and the role of ethics and power in communication. What have we learned from these models?

Communication Can Be Intentional or Unintentional

We are always communicating—with our hands, our eyes, our postures, our words, even our silence.

Rachel stood looking at the train. Deep in thought, she did not notice the people around her until a voice and light touch on her arm startled her into awareness of her surroundings.

A woman approached her. "Excuse me."

Surprised by the unexpected greeting, Rachel emerged from thoughts of the upcoming holiday season to look at the woman. She didn't recognize her. "Do I know you?"

"No, dear, but you need to pay more attention. Do you see the man to your left?"

Rachel looked in the direction the woman had indicated, just in time to see a man disappearing into the crowd of subway traffic.

"He was ready to rob you."

"To rob me?" Suddenly defensive, Rachel grabbed her handbag, which had been hanging loosely on the side of her body. She quickly unzipped the handbag to check for her wallet.

"It's okay. He saw me watching him. He's gone now."

"How did you know he was going to rob me?"

"I worked for the police department for 30 years. I see the signs. His posture, eye movements, efforts to edge closer to you. I also noticed your behaviour. You weren't paying any attention. He was ready to make his move, but he didn't."

In the above scenario, we can see that both the prospective thief and Rachel were communicating even while they intended not to communicate. However, not everyone in the crowd would have read the signs. The background and experience of the retired police officer allowed her to interpret the signs.

Not all cases of unintentional communication turn out so well. Consider the case of two deaf men in Burlington, North Carolina, who were using sign language to communicate with each other when a knife-wielding man appeared on the scene. Using a kitchen knife, Robert Jarell Neal stabbed Terrance Ervin Daniels, one of the deaf men, several times. At trial, Neal said that he believed the men were "flashing gang signs."[14]

Communication Has a Relational, as well as a Content, Dimension

Our knowledge of the other person contributes to our ability to interpret the meaning of a message and to respond appropriately.

"Hey, Antoine, what's up?" Jean was surprised to see his friend coming out of the student pub. He knew that Antoine had a class that afternoon, and it was unlike him to skip a class.

"Not much. I've got to go." Antoine tried to move past Jean, but Jean made a countermove to block him.

"What's happening, dude? You look bummed."

"Yeah, I guess so." He moved backward to stand against the wall and took out his cell phone. Attempting to avoid Jean's gaze, he checked his messages.

"I thought you had class today." Jean closed the distance between them.

"Yeah, what about it? What are you? The hall monitor?" This time Antoine sounded decidedly annoyed.

"I don't know what's going on, Antoine. What's the deal?"

"You don't know, do you? That was my girl you were hitting on."

"Madeleine? Madeleine Lefevbre? She's your girl? I didn't know you were seeing her."

"How would you know? I haven't heard from you for a month. You didn't return my last call."

"Oh, man. I'm sorry. I didn't know about Madeleine, and I didn't get your message. I was sick last week, and I had heavy-duty studying for midterms. If I flunk, I'll lose my scholarship, and my mom just lost her job. It's the end of the line for me if don't ace these exams."

Although Jean and Antoine have been friends for many years, the recent events (Jean's failure to return Antoine's call and his display of interest in Madeleine) have threatened their relationship. Each has read the communication (or lack of communication) in a different way, based on prior interactions. Jean did not think Antoine would be upset when he did not hear from him at a hectic time in the term. He also assumed that Antoine had heard about his mother's layoff. Antoine, on the other hand, assumed that his friend would behave as he had always behaved in the past—calling on a regular basis and making plans to hang out together. When Antoine learned that his friend had hit on the girl he was seeing, he reached the wrong conclusion: he thought Jean's failure to call had come from his interest in going out with Madeleine. Since Jean had never shown special dedication to his studies in the past, Antoine did not imagine that the need to study could be the reason for the lack of communication. Nor did he have any idea that Jean's mother had lost her job or that Antoine was struggling to keep his scholarship.

We can imagine that the two friends will resume their relationship; and in the future, they may be more cautious about reaching hasty conclusions when they do not hear from each other.

Communication Benefits from Shared Fields of Experience

In the below example, James has extreme difficulty communicating with most people because few share his field of experience.

James felt and looked uneasy. He located his place card at the conference table and sat down. When others entered the room, he covered his mouth with his hand, fearful of what he might say if he did not control his speech. He thought about an interaction the previous week at a reception, when he had asked an anorexic-looking woman if she would like some more food. She had stared at him in disbelief before muttering a reply and walking away. Too many episodes of that nature had marked his life and made his social interactions difficult, if not impossible. People did not understand. So placing his hand over his mouth helped him to maintain some control over his communication with others. It helped him to remember to stay quiet.

If James saw someone looking in his direction, however, he removed his hand from his mouth and managed a half smile before looking away. He knew that his emotionless expression was off-putting to people, but he had difficulty with facial displays. Smiling required extreme effort on his part, resulting in situations where people felt he was bored or unhappy. In the same way, James was stoic at funerals and other sad occasions, never able to show emotion, not even when his father died.

A young woman entered the room and sat next to him. She smiled and offered a mint. He took his hand away from his mouth long enough to accept the mint with a quick nod of thanks. Something to do. Something to occupy his thoughts outside of focussing on the panic that was building inside him as he contemplated the upcoming meeting. He did not relax until a man with a broad smile entered the room and offered a cheerful greeting. The man took the last empty spot on the other side of the table. Then he stood. "Sorry, I'm late. We'll get started with some introductions. James, you begin."

James felt as if his heart was going to leap from his chest when he spat out his name and occupation: "James Moscowitz. Cartoonist. Local press." He returned his hand to his mouth, clearly miserable in a setting where interaction was required.

"Thanks, James." Going around the table, the others gave their names and organizational affiliations. Most were from the health care industry—rehabilitation centres, clinics, and nursing homes.

"I want to take a few minutes this morning to introduce our speaker, James Moscowitz. James is here today to talk, from a personal perspective, about how to deal with the special challenges posed by people with Asperger's syndrome. James has had Asperger's his entire life. He copes well with his condition, but he tells me that even well-meaning health care workers don't always know how to communicate with people like him. So he's here to help us out."

James' thoughts were already wandering. Concentrating on the speaker was almost as difficult as socializing. With a short attention span, James often had difficulty focussing in such situations; his lack of attention sometimes appeared rude and inconsiderate to those around him. James slipped his hand into his coat pocket to remove a stress ball, which he squeezed tightly under the table while the speaker continued to talk. Then he noticed that everyone was looking expectantly at him. He wondered how long his thoughts had been drifting.

"James, if you could share some thoughts with us at this time, we would appreciate it."

James stood and moved to the front of the group. At last, he could relax. He could talk for an hour before a group, lecturing on a topic of interest. But he could not engage in a three-minute conversation without experiencing the most intense psychological discomfort.

People with Asperger's syndrome are almost invariably highly intelligent people, but they have extreme difficulty communicating in social environments. Socially awkward and unable to empathize with others, they often make inappropriate comments that offend others. They also experience high levels of stress and anxiety. People who are unfamiliar with this neurological disorder often misinterpret their communication, and misunderstandings result from the lack of shared fields of experience.

Communication Is Irreversible and Unrepeatable

On 3 December 2012, horrified bystanders watched a man die under the engine of a New York Q train. Some yelled and waved for the train to stop. Many stood motionless, glued in place, on the subway platform. No one rushed to aid the man as he died.

In the aftermath of the tragedy, psychologists tried to explain the inability or unwillingness of witnesses to become involved. They said that crowds react differently from individuals in such circumstances. In a crowd, people are more likely to expect someone else to act. On their own, people realize that if they do not act, nothing will happen. Some people are simply frozen in place when a traumatic event occurs, unable to move from fear or horror. Whatever the reason for their inaction, many of those present on the day that Ki-Suk Han died will forever replay that afternoon in their minds. And many will question how they could have let a man die without doing anything to help him. No one assumed responsibility or took control of the situation. No one called for help in lifting the man from the subway tracks.

Given the chance to repeat the event, many of those present would behave differently. But we cannot reverse our actions or take back our words. No one will understand better than witnesses to the death of 58-year-old Han that communication—whether in words or in actions—is irreversible and unrepeatable.

"You can change your world by changing your words."
JOEL OSTEEN

Sending and Receiving Occurs Simultaneously, with both Verbal and Nonverbal Elements

We never abandon the role of sender, even when we are not actively communicating. Consider the following scenario that involves a nurse, his patient, and the patient's daughter.

An older man of Chinese descent looked anxious when a home care nurse entered the room. He turned his head to look at his daughter, who was standing to the side of his bed. Seeing her expression, he cast his gaze downward, staring at the bed covers.

"Mr Zhang." The nurse leaned closer to get his attention. "Mr Zhang, we need to move you to the hospital."

The man didn't speak. Nor did he raise his gaze. It was as if he hoped that one of the Chinese figures on the colourful quilt might come to life and save him from a future he did not want to face.

"Mr Zhang, did you hear me?"

Still no response. The nurse shifted his gaze to the daughter, as if asking for help.

Hesitantly, the young woman moved closer to her father. "Father, you will be better off in the hospital for now. Not for a long time, just until you get better."

"Mr Zhang, it's hard for your daughter to manage right now. She's not strong enough to help you to the washroom. You need help."

The man looked up at the nurse. "I can manage . . . with my walker."

"You're here alone during the day, father. It's not safe. I have to go to work. We can't afford full-time help. I'll come every day to see you until you get better. Lan will come also."

The man looked down again at his covers. Then he raised his eyes. "I'll do what you want, daughter. It's not my choice." A single tear rolled down his cheek. He knew that, when he left for the hospital, he would not see his home again.

Clearly, the communication among the nurse, the older Chinese man, and the man's daughter did not have breaks. Whether speaking or listening, the characters in this scenario were communicating emotions and intentions through nonverbal language. The communication was simultaneous, with each party acting as sender-receiver throughout the episode.

Communication Is a Dynamic, Ongoing Process

On 17 January 2013, a biologically male transgendered candidate appeared on American Idol. *Like other transgendered individuals, she had doubtless engaged in a sometimes painful search for her "real" identity. When Keith Urban asked about the relationships of the woman, she indicated that she would rather not "go there." Even after assuming a new and more comfortable identity, transgendered individuals face other challenges. Most have to find, for example, a new way of relating to friends and family.*

People and their environments are in a constant state of flux. We are never the same from one moment to the next. The changes may be small or large, but they are never insignificant. They become integrated into the person who, according to psychologist Carl Rogers, is always in a state of *becoming*.

When Chastity Bono, child of Sonny Bono and Cher, announced her intention to begin the process of transitioning into a male persona, her mother had a difficult time accepting the decision. Speaking later on the topic, Cher voiced the views of many parents who learn their children have decided to openly express a new gender identity: "It's hard because when she was young, she was just like the cutest girl and I made clothes for her and she was just my little girl."[15]

At the same time, family members are unsure how to communicate with the "new" person. Chaz Bono spoke of this challenge when he said: "We had to really almost relearn how to communicate and how to be around each other. Things had changed. Just me saying the same thing that I would have before with a deeper voice and more of a presence." Even nonverbal mannerisms change, as the transgendered individual learns a new nonverbal communication code. To outsiders, the nonverbal signals sometimes seem exaggerated and unnatural.

While not everyone experiences shifts in identity that are as dramatic as those experienced by transgendered individuals, we all experience change; and the dynamic and ongoing process of communication affects all of us. As we become parents, travel, work at different jobs, participate in relationships, and grow older, our communication styles and patterns evolve. They do not remain fixed or static over time.

Environment Affects Communication

On Thursday, 14 August 2003, just after 4:00 in the afternoon, large parts of Canada (Ontario and Quebec) and the United States (the Northeast and the Midwest) experienced the most far-reaching hydro failure in the history of the two countries. In total, the power outage affected more than 55 million people, including 13 million in New York City, many of whom were attempting to get home at rush hour.

Manmade and natural disasters have the capacity to disrupt our lives and our communication with others. In the aftermath of Hurricane Sandy, many New York residents expressed dismay at the near–communication blackout that occurred in the parts of the state worst hit by the storm, such as the Rockaways—an 18-kilometre strip of land that extends from New York City into the Atlantic Ocean. Nursing homes in this area did not evacuate their residents prior to the storm. During and after the storm, many of these homes did not have access to telephone lines, Internet, or other means of contact with the outside world. Much confusion resulted, with many outsiders unable to reach relatives who resided in the nursing homes.

Consider the case of David Coppedge and his mother Jacqueline Coppedge, who spent days trying to contact David's grandmother.[16] David searched the Internet and called the city's information number, where an operator told him to call the Red Cross. Red Cross personnel suggested, in turn, that he call the city's evacuation shelters. "I basically exhausted every number I could think to call," he said. Told that the phone lines were not working and she would be unable to speak with her mother, Jacqueline Coppedge was no more successful. Finally, a cousin in Atlanta located a patient tracking number, and the Coppedges located their relative at a nursing home in Peekskill, about 60 miles north of New York City. As often happens in natural disasters, the normal lines of communication were disrupted or overloaded during and after Hurricane Sandy.

Noise Affects Communication

Sheryl and Elijah were in the process of taking their oaths from high above the ground. Despite the concerns of their parents and some friends, they had decided to exchange wedding vows in a hot-air balloon. As the balloon bobbled about in the wind, lurching from side to side, Sheryl became increasingly airsick. Rather than focussing on the passages she had memorized for the occasion, she hesitated and stumbled over the words. At the moment that she prepared to say "I do," she heard a faint but distinct sound of air leaving the balloon. Others in the wedding party heard the same whishing sound, and panic took hold of the group. As the balloon plummeted to the ground, the 12 people held fast to each other. All thoughts of wedding bells and cakes evaporated from their heads. After bouncing and rebounding several times on the ground, the balloon came to a stop in a large corn field. Scrambling to his feet and clearly surprised to be alive, the minister extended his hand to the young couple, who were still trying to stand. "I pronounce you a very lucky husband and a very fortunate wife."

This scenario illustrates the effects of noise in a communication environment. As noted in the Shannon–Weaver model, noise can be external, physiological, or psychological in nature. Even before the crash of the balloon, the wind created external noise, which made communication difficult. The combination of air sickness (physiological noise) and fear (psychological noise) inhibited Sheryl's ability to remember her wedding vows. And after hearing the sound of air leaving the balloon (external noise), no one was thinking about the wedding any more.

Channels Matter

It was 1944—the year before World War II ended. Like so many other young women, Barbara had been waiting impatiently for a letter from her husband, a pilot with the Royal Canadian Air Force. Their two children were playing close to her feet when the doorbell rang. She sprang to her feet. When she opened the door, however, she turned pale. A young delivery boy handed her a telegram. With trembling hands, Barbara opened the crinkly parchment paper.

The telegram began, "I am deeply distressed to tell you that . . ." Barbara collapsed at the feet of the boy, who turned pale himself. He picked up the telegram and read the remaining words while Barbara's mother worked to revive her: "I am deeply distressed to inform you that your husband was killed in action." Two streets away, a local clergyman delivered a similar envelope to another young woman; and farther away, in a city factory, a loudspeaker read a list of names of people who should report to the front office. Like Barbara, they knew the reason for the announcement.

Wilbur Dawbarn/Cartoonstock

Jeremy picked up his voice mail messages shortly after arriving home from work. He was glad to hear Jenny's voice with a cheerful greeting, "Hey you, hope you had an awesome day at work!" The words that followed, however, left him in a state of shock. "I know you've been hoping things would work out between us. I did too. But I realized last night that I'm still in love with Ben. I know you're thinking, 'How could I go back to somebody who dumped me?' Yeah, well, it's crazy, but I still love him. Sorry that we couldn't connect where I could tell you face-to-face, but it's probably easier this way. Don't you think?"

Gerald got his layoff notice in a group email.

Wendy learned her husband was divorcing her when she signed for a letter at the post office.

Keira received only a tweet after an argument with her boyfriend, "Bye, KT. See you next lifetime."

As these examples illustrate, channels do make a difference, and some communications require a face-to-face component.

Communication Has a Cultural Component

The palliative care nurse was confused. He did not know what to do in the situation. Entering the room of the dying Filipino woman, he was assaulted by a confusing mix of sounds: music, chanting, and talking. The room was filled with people and flowers, and it seemed more like a party than a vigil for someone who was close to death. While some were praying, others were laughing and telling stories. The woman's husband, originally from Hawaii, explained that the family had gathered to honour the woman's life and to make decisions as they became necessary. The man proceeded to explain the necessity for his presence in the room. He said that his wife was unlikely to ask a question for fear of offending the doctor, and she was unlikely to tell anyone if the pain became unbearable. She would not want to worry her family. Moreover, any response to a direct question would be a "talk story"—a mix of personal experiences, opinions, and an answer to the question.

In other words, if asked about whether she needed additional medication for pain, she might talk first about her experience with getting sick as a child and how difficult it was for her family to visit her in the hospital. She might talk about how her father got a loan to pay for her treatment in a big fancy city hospital and how he worked at two jobs for most of his life to pay off the loans. She might mention that her husband is getting older, and his arthritis makes it difficult for him to drive. She might expand on his problems with arthritis. Finally, she might talk about how her neighbour's daughter had a hard time affording the cost of medications when her son was recovering from surgery. Then she might say that her pain is manageable, she does not want any more medications, and she hopes to return home soon. To understand the "talk story," the nurse needs to listen carefully to the entire account. The answer to the nurse's question is woven into the story, along with the woman's concerns and fears.

In a hospital in western Canada, a doctor prepared to examine a Navajo patient—a man who had recently joined his daughter and her family in Calgary. Since Aboriginal people from the southwestern United States rarely immigrate to Canada, the doctor had little experience with the Navajo culture. Soon after arriving, the man came down with the flu. As the doctor readied to insert an instrument into the man's ear, the man showed visible concern; and when asked to open his mouth for the doctor to examine his throat, he refused. The man's daughter hurriedly explained that, according to Navajo beliefs, the doctor should begin the examination from the feet, not the head. To begin the examination at the top of the body was, in essence, to take the person apart spiritually—the opposite of healing him.

In the emergency room of a Toronto hospital, a Muslim immigrant from Somali expressed strong concern when a male doctor arrived to examine her. A few provinces away, in a Nova Scotia hospice, a Hindu patient's family insisted on moving her bed so that her head faced the east. The patient's husband requested that a light be placed near the head of his dying wife, and her daughter began chanting soft mantras into her mother's ear.

STANDPOINT THEORY Theory that holds that our background and experiences determine our perspective.

We can never divorce cultural elements from any communication act, and similar cultural backgrounds increase our chances of communicating effectively. **Standpoint theory** tells us that our background and experiences determine our perspective, and our perspective influences how we relate to and communicate with others. Our gender, age, socioeconomic status, sexual orientation, race, regional and national affiliations, and other factors influence how we view the world. If we are on a mountain, we can see a valley; but if we are in the valley, we may see only trees and streams. In other words, our position (where we stand) determines what we see and what we do not see. If we have been the victim of a sexual assault or a robbery, we may see danger in places where it is not seen by someone who has not had that experience. People in marginalized communities (whether racial, ethnic, or gender) often see patterns of behaviour in the dominant culture that are invisible to members of the larger culture.

Communication Has a Power Dimension

In October 2011, Principal Justin Vernon asked 170 students at Roger Clapp Innovation School in Dorchester, Massachusetts, to read 10,000 books by the end of the school year. Three-fourths of the students enrolled at the school come from low-income families; one-fifth are special education students. So the challenge was a weighty one, and the students declared that their principal had to do something in return. More specifically, he had to promise to milk a cow while dressed as Lady Gaga!

By the end of the year, the students had fulfilled their part of the challenge. In fact, they had read not 10,000—but 13,000—books. As promised, on the agreed date, "a Lady Gaga–clad figure stepped out of a stretch limousine. It was principal Vernon, wearing a black dress, heels, tiara, and lots of makeup. The students raced to him on the athletic field, happily chanting, 'Milk the cow!' A man of his word, Justin Vernon did just that."[17]

REWARD POWER Power that comes from offering benefits or gifts.

LEGITIMATE POWER Power that comes from holding an office, title, or other legitimate position.

EXPERT OR INFORMATION POWER Power that comes from knowledge or expertise.

COERCIVE POWER Power that comes from making threats or intimidations.

REFERENT POWER Power that comes from personal attractiveness.

According to John French and Bertram Raven, communicators can draw on five different sources of power: **reward power**, **legitimate power**, **expert or information power**, **coercive power**, and **referent power**.[18] In the Lady Gaga example, the principal called upon *reward power* when he promised the students that he would dress as Lady Gaga and milk a cow if they read 10,000 books by the end of the school term. He also exercised *legitimate power*, related to his position as principal.

In the same way that reward power involves the ability to give benefits, it also implies the power to withhold the same benefits. In organizations, this exercise of power might translate into withholding a promotion or a salary increase. In a family context, it could mean the removal of car privileges or taking away an iPod or a computer. With friendships, it could mean turning down a request for a favour or an invitation to participate in some activity. Romantic relationships are rife with instances of partners withholding rewards from the other person—whether it be money, sex, or simply companionship.

Expert or information power manifests in many communication situations. Computer hackers and spies alike recognize the importance of accessing and controlling information. For that reason, many corporations are willing to hire hackers to work on behalf of—instead of against—their organizations. Similarly, governments hire spies to invade and steal the secrets of other countries. Authoritarian regimes control access to all kinds of information, even the products of writers and artists. Dictators know that change stems from new ways of viewing reality, and these new ways of seeing reality come from the most creative people.

Power based on control of information is much more difficult, however, in the age of social media. In earlier times, information trickled down from the higher to the lower echelons of society. Now the information reaches everyone at the same time. Although initially not as dramatic in its impact, the information flow model had already switched from restricted or **trickle-down** to **simultaneous access** by the 1970s, when satellite television came into play. See Figure 1.8 for a visual comparison between the traditional trickle-down model and the simultaneous access model first published by Stewart Ferguson and Sherry Ferguson in 1988. A third **open access model** depicts the open platforms and sharing that take place with social media, with the flow occurring in both directions, both vertically and horizontally.

TRICKLE-DOWN ACCESS Controlled and restricted access to information, flowing mostly downward.

SIMULTANEOUS ACCESS Unrestricted access to information flowing from mass media and reaching everyone at the same time.

OPEN ACCESS Unrestricted and uncontrolled sharing of information on open platforms, accessible to everyone.

Another kind of power is *coercive power*. Consider the case of Lance Armstrong, who denied any involvement with performance-enhancing drugs until January 2013, when he was interviewed by Oprah Winfrey. In the televised interview, he admitted that he was guilty of misleading the general public, his corporate sponsors, the Livestrong Foundation (an organization founded by Armstrong and dedicated to cancer research), and his fans. In addition, he admitted to being a "bully" in how he treated his critics, referring to instances in which he went so far as filing lawsuits against his accusers, thus exercising coercive power and eventually losing *referent power*.

In stark contrast, however, is the case of Spanish athlete Iván Fernández Anaya, who acquired strong referent power when he claimed a second-place finish behind Olympic bronze medalist Abel Mutai of Kenya. The cross-country race took place in Burlada, Navarre, on 2 December 2012. A few metres before the finish line, Mutai slowed, thinking he had already crossed the line. Rather than take advantage of the mistake and claim a hollow victory, Anaya stopped and motioned to Mutai to cross the finish line ahead of him. As a result of his unwillingness to violate his own personal code of ethics by taking advantage of Mutai's confusion, Anaya has gained hundreds of followers on Facebook and Twitter.[19]

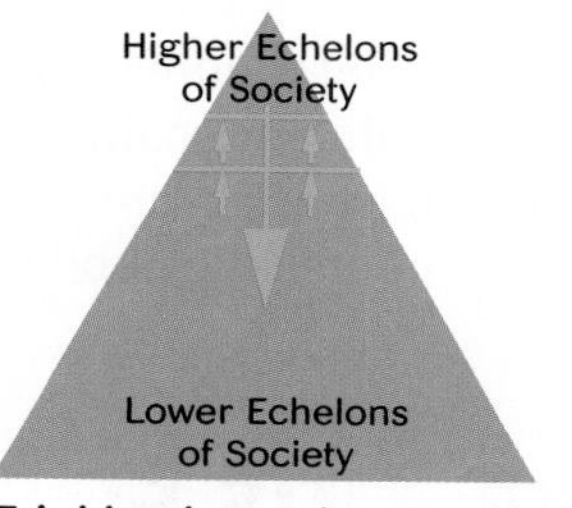

Trickle-down Access Model

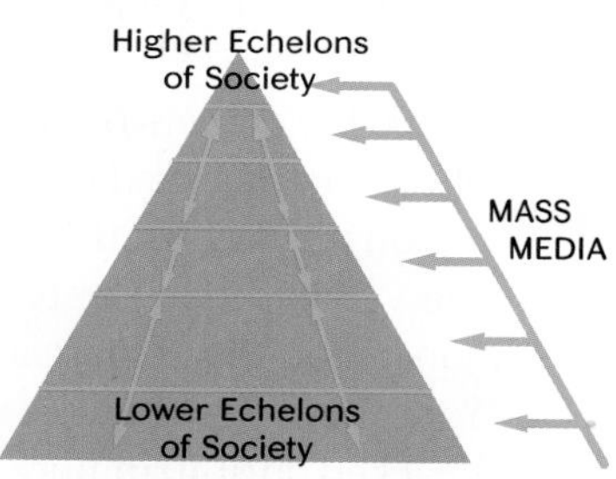

Simultaneous Access Model

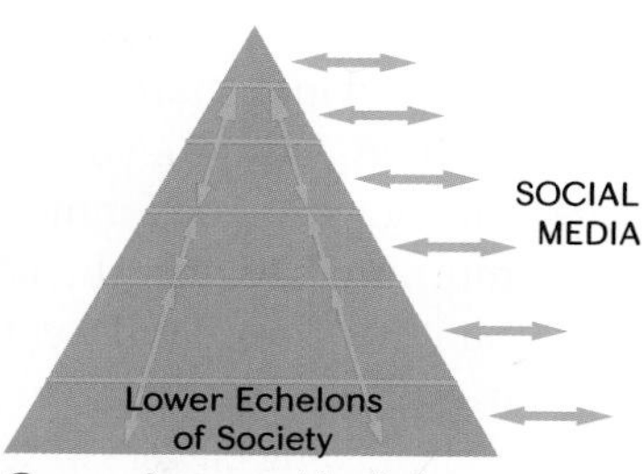

Open Access Model

FIGURE 1.8 Information access models. The arrows indicate transfer of information.

SOURCE: Adapted from "Limited access and simultaneous access models" from S. Ferguson and S.D. Ferguson, *Organizational Communication*, 2nd ed. (New Brunswick, NJ: Transaction Publishers, 1988), 121.

Communication Has a Strong Ethical Dimension

A young accountant named Chad has taken his first job with a large investment firm in downtown Vancouver. After he signs the contract, he and his wife take out a large mortgage to purchase a home. Chad's new position has health benefits, which are particularly important to the care of Chad's young daughter with a rare blood disorder. After joining the firm, Chad reviews the financial records from the past few years. In the process, he realizes that one of the business partners has been doctoring the books. Chad knows that he will lose his job and his daughter's health benefits if he confronts or exposes the partner. At the same time, he worries about the people who have placed their trust in the company, the other business partners (who know nothing of the deception), and his own legal obligations. He sits down to tally the costs and benefits of staying in the firm. After a short delay in which Chad ponders his dilemma, he picks up the telephone and makes a call.

If a doctor or a psychologist discusses a patient's dossier outside of the medical context, the person is engaging in communication of an unethical nature. If an insurance company shares a health profile with an employer or a bank releases personal data on a client, the companies have violated ethical standards of behaviour. When a photographer sold images of partially nude Kate Middleton (Duchess of Cambridge) in 2012, many people accused the photographer of violating ethical standards of journalism. *Not* communicating can also have ethical dimensions, as illustrated by Chad's dilemma.

In the worst-case scenarios, unethical communication poses deadly risks. For example, in October 2012, 10 Canadians fell ill from eating tainted beef imported from the United States. André Picard of the *Globe and Mail* criticized the federal government for failing to issue the *E. coli* warning in a timely fashion. He also accused the government of using the wrong channel to communicate the information: "When you're poisoning people, even unintentionally, a voice message three weeks into the outbreak doesn't cut it, nor do ministerial blandishments, nor do CFIA press releases whining that 'investigations into outbreaks of food-borne illness can be complex.'"[20]

TIPS FOR MANAGING COMMUNICATION BREAKDOWN

In 2004, members of the Federal Aviation Administration (FAA) and the US Department of Defense testified before a national commission that was investigating the communication breakdown that occurred in the 11 September 2001 attacks on the Pentagon and the World Trade Center. As a result of failed communication, the military mistakenly concluded that American Airlines Flight 11 was headed to Washington, DC, not to New York City. Similarly, the military did not learn that United Airlines Flight 93 had been hijacked until 40 minutes after the FAA confirmed the hijacking. Air Force General Ralph Eberhart, commander of the North American Aerospace Defense Command, testified that the military could have "intercepted and shot down all four planes"[21] if they had received information earlier.

Then-acting FAA deputy administrator Monte Belger said: "The most frustrating after-the-fact scenario for me to understand and to explain is the communication link on that morning between the FAA operations center and the NMCC [the Pentagon's National Military Command Center] . . . I know how it's supposed to work, but I have to tell you it's still a little frustrating for me to understand how it actually did work on that day."[22]

Following Belger's orders, a senior official in the FAA opened a "hijacking net" at 9:20 a.m. to bring together all affected federal agencies. Assuming Pentagon personnel were on the net, Belger turned his focus to getting the remaining planes out of the air: "It was my assumption . . . that the NMCC was on that net and hearing everything [in] real time . . . And I can tell you I've lived through dozens of hijackings in my 30-year FAA career, as a very low entry-level inspector up through to the headquarters, and they were always there."[23]

Even stranger, military personnel were at the FAA command centre when the attacks took place: "They were present at all of the events that occurred on 9/11. In my mind, everyone who needed to be notified about the events transpiring was notified, including the military."[24] Belger could only speculate that, since the military has its own "communication web," responsible individuals might have waited to notify headquarters about the hijacking. When questioned, defence officials said they did not know the reason for their absence from the net. Attempts by the military to establish an unsecured link to FAA headquarters failed, leaving the FAA out of an important conference call.[25]

In the end, the communication failure cost the lives of close to 3000 people. Had the military acted sooner, the numbers would likely have been much lower.

Peter Welleman/Cartoonstock

"The single biggest problem with communication is the illusion that it has taken place."
GEORGE BERNARD SHAW

In many cases, we assume that our meaning is understood—that consensus exists in situations of confusion or disagreement. We think that we are clear when we are not. (For an illustrative activity, see the "From Theory to Practice" box.) At other times, as listeners, we assume that we are at fault. We become embarrassed, afraid to look foolish by asking for additional information. Alternatively, we believe that we have been heard when no one was listening. Sometimes the communication failure has few consequences. However, at other times, the consequences are serious, as in the previously mentioned case of the deaf man who was stabbed by an onlooker who mistook his sign language for gang signs. (See the "Professional Contexts" box on medical mishaps for another example of the serious consequences that can result from breakdowns in communication.)

Many crises—personal, organizational, and political—occur because of lack of precision in language. Some linguists claim that misunderstanding of the Japanese word *mokusatsu* contributed to the dropping of the world's first atomic bomb on Hiroshima in August 1945. After issuing the Potsdam Declaration—a dire warning to the Japanese government demanding unconditional surrender—the allied leaders waited for the Japanese response. When Tokyo reporters asked Japanese premier Kantaro Suzuki about his response to the Potsdam Declaration, the premier used the word *mokusatsu*

from theory TO PRACTICE

Communication Breakdowns

Create an abstract drawing that features several interlocking geometric shapes. Next find a partner. Keeping your drawing hidden from your partner's view, describe your drawing using only words; ask your partner to reproduce the drawing from your verbal account. When your partner has finished this task, compare drawings. How similar are the two drawings? What kinds of miscommunication occurred?

*professional*CONTEXTS

All This to Have a Tooth Out?

A nurse called a patient, by name, from the waiting room. She led the patient to an examination room, where she asked about the patient's allergies and other medical conditions. The doctor then entered and identified the patient by her first and last name. The woman confirmed her identity. The doctor then reviewed the planned procedures. With the registered nurse acting as witness, he obtained the patient's written consent for these procedures. At this point, the operating room nurse took over. Using standard hospital procedures, she identified the patient by name and spelled her last name. The patient agreed that "yes," she was that person, and she provided a telephone number for the friend who would provide her with a ride home.

The nurse then led the patient to another room, where the doctor administered a steroid injection. Following this procedure, the patient went to a recovery room. While waiting for discharge, the patient stated, "All this to have a tooth out!"

Embarrassed hospital staff confirmed the woman's true identity and took her to oral surgery to receive the treatment for which she had been booked.[26]

Imagine that you enter a hospital to undergo knee surgery, but you awaken from anesthesia to learn that you are missing a leg, an arm, or a healthy organ. Or imagine that six months after abdominal surgery, you still feel pain in your abdomen. Upon being X-rayed, you learn that the operating team forgot to remove a pair of scissors that ended up in your body. In April 2012, Tasha Gaul and Dale Matlock took their three-year-old son, Jessie, to a hospital in Portland, Oregon, for day surgery to correct his lazy eye. When the surgery ended, the doctor emerged, embarrassed to inform the parents that she had operated on the wrong eye.[27]

Medical mistakes happen—and they can involve wrong sites (i.e., parts of patients' bodies that do not require surgery), wrong procedures, or wrong patients.

Surgeon and author Marty Makary estimates that wrong-site surgeries occur about 40 times each week in the United States.[28] CNN reported that about 2700 operations each year involve the wrong body part or wrong patient.[29] A study of 2.8 million surgeries in Massachusetts over a 20-year period found that about 1 out of every 113,000 operations (excluding surgeries of the spine) were wrong-site surgeries.[30] About 32 wrong-site craniotomies occurred in 2002 in the United States.[31] A wrong-site craniotomy is a procedure in which the surgeon undertakes brain surgery on the wrong side of the patient's head!

A study conducted by the British National Health System (NHS) identified 70 cases of wrong-site surgery and 161 cases of foreign objects being left in patients' bodies in the period from 2011 to 2012. Another 41 people got the wrong implant or prosthesis. In total, the NHS identified 326 "never events"—that is, events that should never happen because they endanger patients' lives.[32]

According to the Joint Commission on Accreditation of Healthcare Organizations (JCAHO) and studies by other groups, the number of wrong-site surgeries may be on the rise. The JCAHO received reports of 20 incidences in 1998 and 60 in 2002.[33] Along with many other research bodies, the JCAHO has identified communication breakdown as the most common root cause of these events.[34] Typically, the problems originate with flawed verbal communication between attending surgeons and other caregivers. The problems typically involve lack of clarity, failure to communicate responsibilities, or confusion about changes in the location of patients. One review of 444 malpractice claims, for example, found that 81 communication breakdowns had occurred in 60 cases that resulted in harm to patients.[35]

to indicate that he did not want to comment. In other words, the premier was trying to say "no comment." To the great misfortune of the world, international news agencies reported that the premier had replied "not worthy of comment." The tone of the statement contributed to the decision of the American government to drop the atomic bomb ten days later on Hiroshima.[36]

Marriage counsellors stress the importance of learning how to communicate more effectively with our partners, and organizations enrol their employees in workshops to assist them in learning how to be better senders and receivers of communication. Problems arise because we frequently assume that communication is easy and that meaning is in words: "I told you so. Why didn't you listen?" Words are only symbols, however, and how we translate those symbols depends upon our life experiences—physical, cultural, interpersonal, and professional. My reality is not necessarily your reality.

As the perception literature demonstrates, we tend to rely on the past to understand the present, to fill in blanks when we don't have a complete picture, and to pick selectively from billions of bits of information with which we are bombarded each day. Our culture and values influence our interpretation of information, and we judge one experience against another. We see what we expect to see and hear what we expect to hear.

Factors that Contribute to Communication Breakdown

The following factors decrease our ability to communicate successfully: speed, personality, linguistic differences, jargon, expectancy, redundant information, fear of pain, and ambiguous or non-specific information. Later chapters will develop these points in more depth.

Speed affects our ability to comprehend. If a communicator speaks too fast and does not repeat information, we may get lost. If we get lost, we often tune out. Nervousness (which can cause us to speak too quickly) and frustration (which can result when we get lost) decrease the probability of successful communication.

Personality affects our ability to comprehend, as well as to communicate. Some of us are more defensive than others in how we respond to communication. When we are sensitive about particular subjects, we may see unintended meaning in someone's words. We may be insulted, for example, by a remark not intended to be taken personally.

Linguistic differences affect our ability to understand. We may not understand the informal expressions or colloquialisms in our second language, or we may interpret words in a literal fashion when they are not meant to be literal.

The use of jargon (e.g., mathematical terms such as *hypotenuse*) can inhibit our ability to understand a concept if we are unfamiliar with the jargon. If we have had similar experiences, training, or backgrounds, however, jargon can help us to communicate more easily. *Hypotenuse*, for example, would be helpful if two mathematicians were communicating with each other.

Expectancy affects comprehension. As noted above, we hear what we expect to hear and see what we expect to see. Perception theory tells us that no two people see the world in the same way. If you ask a friend to recall some shared event, the person may not even remember it, or their recall may be quite different from yours.

Redundant information creates noise in the communication experience. Saying "flat side" is superfluous if all sides are flat. Saying "round cylinder" is redundant. Including too much information can be problematic. Sometimes we get more confused as an explanation continues.

Fear of pain can inhibit communication. When meaning is painful to us, we may switch off or distort. We may not want to know that our partner has been cheating or that our employer is experiencing financial problems. To know is to face the necessity to confront the situation, and confrontation carries risks. In another situation, we may postpone going to a doctor if we fear what we might learn. Or we may simply avoid a topic that recalls some past painful experience. Veterans of war often refuse to discuss their experiences when they return home.

Ambiguous or non-specific information makes communication more difficult. If we are giving instructions on how to put together a kite, for example, references such as "put the small stick on top" or "put glue all around" may be unclear to the listener. On top of what? All around what?

As the above examples suggest, it is generally important to communicate clearly and succinctly. However, some people deliberately speak in vague terms in order to include some audiences and exclude others. For example, communicators in bureaucracies learn the art of communicating vaguely so that their communications cannot be clearly understood or analyzed by outsiders.

How to Avoid Communication Breakdown

We can reduce the chances of a communication breakdown by improving our communication skills. Many factors—such as flexibility, clarity, patience, specificity, common vocabularies, and shared experiences—increase our ability to communicate successfully, and later chapters will address these factors in more depth. The following list presents a brief overview of some relevant tips.

Be flexible in communicating and interpreting communication from others. Meanings are in people, not in words, and flexibility allows us to adapt to meet the different needs of different people.

> "Having not said anything the first time, it was somehow even more difficult to broach the subject the second time around."
> DOUGLAS ADAMS

Be succinct and clear, and listen for unspoken messages. Talking is not the same as communicating, and more words do not necessarily translate into greater understanding.

Wait until someone finishes speaking before responding. If we are patient, we are more likely to receive the message in a clear fashion.

Be specific. The more we speak in specific and concrete (as opposed to general) terms, the greater the likelihood that listeners will understand the true intent of our words.

Use language that is accessible. If we are communicating with a general audience, we should avoid using topic-specific jargon.

Practise communicating with others. The more frequently we interact with others, the higher the likelihood that we will develop a common vocabulary that will allow us to understand and be understood.

Develop a large repertoire of communication skills. These skills will help us to communicate with people from other backgrounds.

Stick to more formal language patterns when working in a second language. These patterns will force us to be more precise in expressing our thoughts.

Be aware of the meaning of nonverbal signals. Usually, nonverbal communication is helpful, since we obtain as much as 93 per cent of our meaning from nonverbal signals—body position, stance, degree of eye contact, facial expressions, grunts or sighs, and other indicators.[37] However, we need to recognize that the meaning attached to nonverbal behaviours varies from culture to culture.

Ask questions and give feedback. We should always ask for clarification of points that we do not understand.

Find alternative ways of explaining a point and use repetition. If the listener cannot identify with our first description, searching for alternative wording can be helpful. Repetition can be effective so long as it is not overdone.

> **"Don't use words too big for the subject. Don't say *infinitely* when you mean *very*; otherwise you'll have no word left when you want to talk about something really infinite."**
>
> **C.S. LEWIS**

Use analogies and comparisons to convey meaning. Examples include "it looks *like a ski slope or roof*," "it looks *like a bridge*," and "it looks *like a drum*." The listener must, however, be familiar with the characteristics of the thing or concept on which the comparison is based.

SUMMARY

This chapter has introduced you to some of the basics of communication, including communication models, what we can learn from the models, reasons for communication breakdowns, and factors that can improve communication. You will learn more about these topics as you progress through the book.

REVIEW QUESTIONS

1. What does the Aristotelian model contribute to our understanding of communication? What are the three kinds of appeals that a communicator can use when attempting to persuade someone?
2. Which elements of communication are common to both the Shannon–Weaver and the transactional models of communication?
3. Are there any similarities between the Schramm model and the Dance model? If so, what are they?
4. What are five characteristics of communication, as identified in the models?
5. According to French and Raven, what are five sources of power?
6. What are five sources of communication breakdown—factors that decrease our ability to communicate effectively?
7. What are five factors that improve our chances of communicating effectively?

SUGGESTED ACTIVITIES

1. Working in a group, create a communication model that uses the terms discussed in this chapter. Try to be as innovative as possible with your model. You can make use of any of the following terms: *sender* or *source*, *message*, *encoding*, *decoding*, *receiver* or *destination*, *channel* or *medium*, *feedback*, *noise*, and *environment* or *context*. Can you think of any elements that are missing from the models in this chapter? Be prepared to display and explain your model to the class.
2. Working in pairs, create skits that make excessive use of some kind of jargon. The jargon can be specific to a profession (e.g., the police, health workers, or social workers); a demographic group such as teenagers; a recreational group such as motorcyclists; or a competitive sport such as figure skating, soccer, or fencing. Then discuss the extent to which the jargon increases or decreases your ability to get meaning from the dialogue.
3. Imagine that you have to explain how to reach your home from your school. Give directions to another student. Then ask the person to repeat the directions. Would the student actually arrive at your home, or would she end up on some dead end street or even dangerous part of the city? Did you feel frustrated trying to explain how to reach your home?
4. Generate three examples of situations that involve unethical communication.
5. Generate three examples of situations that involve unethical use of power in communication.
6. Develop a skit that demonstrates a breakdown in communication stemming from cultural differences.

CHAPTER 2

Perceiving Self in Relation to Others

CHAPTER OUTLINE

learning OBJECTIVES

- To learn about the four faces of self-concept
- To understand the role of internal voice in self-concept
- To learn how external voices influence self-concept
- To understand the challenges of measuring self-concept across cultures

forSTARTERS

Post-Traumatic Stress Disorder and the Self

In October 2009, veterans suffering from post-traumatic stress disorder (PTSD) gathered at a five-day retreat in the eastern United States. The veterans had fought in at least one of three different wars or conflicts—the Vietnam War, the Iraq War, and the War in Afghanistan. Most had fought in Vietnam and/or Iraq. Their stories were gripping, as they spoke of the ways in which war had changed their lives and senses of self. Some referred to themselves as "trained killers," asked after returning home to fit back into society as if nothing had happened. They spoke of being one day in a war zone, charged with taking lives, and the next sitting with family at the dinner table. Before the war, some had gone to elite universities like Yale or held important positions like Wall Street broker.

When they returned, however, they could not go back to what they had been doing before the war. Their priorities had changed, and they saw themselves in a very different way. Unable to cope, some became homeless for long periods of time; others ended up in jail after committing a crime. Almost all had postwar problems with drugs and alcohol. Many found it difficult to accept rules and regulations, since the rules and regulations of war had caused them to commit unspeakable acts of violence. A large number went through more than one divorce after returning from war—divorces that they blamed on their lack of control over anger and depression. Some had contemplated or attempted suicide. One young woman, who had travelled with the first convoys into Baghdad, talked about her thoughts of suicide after being asked to behave in ways that violated her moral code. Such experiences are not unique to this group: "Soldiers who have actively participated in violent combat experience lasting marks, including a higher incidence of suicide, fatal car accidents, poisonings, and drug overdoses, as well as arrests and acts of violence, than comparable groups."[1]

Photo by Suki Dhanda

What is clear is that these men and women had been forever scarred by their wartime experiences, and they carried the burden of knowing they had been forced by rules of war to take the lives of others. Their sense of self had been altered. In their own words, they had come to see themselves as "killers" and "damaged goods." Yet these were the men and women who had been so little able to handle the cost of war that they had collapsed under the emotional burden. Although they perceived themselves in the most negative of terms, in fact they represent society's best hope for a shift in consciousness away from war as a solution to problems.

Consider the following questions as you read this chapter. Have you ever experienced an event in your life that brought your self-concept into question? Did you revise your life script on the basis of this event, or did you discover coping strategies? In what ways, if any, did the event affect your communication with others? To which voices—internal or external—did you pay the most attention?

INTRODUCTION

When we ask the question "Who am I?," many different voices respond to us. Some originate inside us while others come from outside, reflecting the views of close family and friends. Others come from acquaintances at work or in social environments. In trying to figure out who we are, we also look to **reference groups** for guidance. Some of the voices that affect our definitions of self are those of people we know first-hand—a popular friend, a partner, a teacher, or a mentor at work. Others speak to us from media platforms. They may be the voices of politicians or athletes, spiritual leaders or

REFERENCE GROUP A group whose opinions we value and in which we hold or aspire to membership.

celebrities. These individuals may be local, regional, or national figures. Whether close up or far away, other people help us to answer the question "Who am I?"

In this chapter, we will examine the nature of self-concept, the impact of internal and external voices on how we build and maintain self-concept, the challenges of trying to measure self-concept across cultures, and tips for accepting and moving beyond self. We will look also at the impact of self-concept on our functioning in different contexts, including the workplace.

NATURE OF OUR SELF CONCEPT

Self-concept is a relatively stable and organized collection of thoughts and feelings about the self, which lead to attitudes and drive behaviour.[2] For the first six or seven months of life, we have no self-concept—no sense of being different from others.[3] Our sense of self develops only as we interact with others and engage in self-evaluation.[4] As self-concept develops, it separates into at least four different "selves," which are not always the same:[5]

- **self-image**,
- **looking-glass self,**
- **ideal self,** and
- **real self.**

If all of these views of self were the same, we would have no problems. But sometimes, we do not see ourselves (*self-image*) as we think others see us (*looking-glass self*). In the movie series *The Twilight Saga*, for example, Bella sees herself as others see her only after Edward forces her to look in the mirror on their wedding night. Many of us also want to be different (*ideal self*) from how we actually are (*real self*). When our different selves come into conflict with one another, our **self-esteem** and **self-efficacy** suffer.

Self-esteem refers to how we perceive our overall sense of worth or value. *Self-efficacy* refers, on the other hand, to our belief that we can accomplish specific tasks and goals or have an impact.[6] Both are important to how we perform in our everyday lives—in personal as well as professional contexts. If we have high levels of **global self-esteem** and self-efficacy, we will have more confidence to approach personal or work-related tasks. When given highly demanding job tasks or confronted with difficult circumstances, people with high self-esteem function better than people with low self-esteem. They also give up less easily.[7] A significant relationship also exists between self-esteem and job satisfaction.[8]

Although both self-esteem and self-efficacy relate to self-concept, they represent different ideas. Sometimes (although not always) we are high in one and low in the other. We may, for example, have generally high self-esteem but know that we are not good athletes. So long as we do not judge ourselves on the basis of athletics, our weakness as an athlete will not affect our overall self-esteem. If, however, our parents excelled at sports and taught us that we must be also excel at sports in order to be successful in life, then our poor performance in athletics could have a bigger effect on our self-esteem. In this case, our lack of self-efficacy (ability to accomplish the goal of performing well in sports) could have a negative impact on our self-esteem—and by extension, on our self-concept. See the "From Theory to Practice" box for an exercise that will help you to evaluate your self-esteem.

SELF-CONCEPT Relatively constant thoughts and feelings about who we are and how we differ from other people.

SELF-IMAGE Our views of ourselves.

LOOKING-GLASS SELF How we think others see us.

IDEAL SELF The person we would like to be.

REAL SELF The person we actually are.

SELF-ESTEEM Our perception of our overall value.

SELF-EFFICACY Our perceived ability to accomplish something or to make a difference.

GLOBAL SELF-ESTEEM Self-esteem that shows in many aspects of our lives.

from theory TO PRACTICE

How Good Do You Feel about Yourself?

To test your self-esteem, go to the following web page, hosted by the University of Maryland, where you will find the Rosenberg Self-Esteem Scale: http://www.socy.umd.edu/quick-links/rosenberg-self-esteem-scale.

Answering the 10 questions will help you to identify how good you feel about yourself.

To better understand these ideas, take the example of Akashi, a young man who plans to take over his father's business upon graduation from university. Akashi is presently enrolled in the Master of Business Administration (MBA) program at the Edwards School of Business, University of Saskatchewan. Although working toward an MBA, he would prefer to study music, his first love. When he is most honest with himself, Akashi knows that he will never have the same drive as his father to succeed and build the business (*real self*). At the same time, he recognizes that his father sees him as a capable successor to the family business (*looking-glass self*). So Akashi continues to try to fulfill his father's ambitions for him, even as he daydreams about becoming the next Hiroaki Yura, a famous violinist of Japanese heritage (*ideal self*). Although Akashi has done well in school, he sees himself as a failure (*self-image*) compared to his father, who had established a profitable business by the time he was 27 years of age. Sometimes he worries that friends of his father may also see him as a failure (*looking-glass self*). As a result of the conflicts among his various "selves," Akashi often suffers from low self-esteem and worries that he will be unsuccessful in running the family business.

In the discussion that follows, we will explore each of the four faces of self-concept—self-image, looking-glass self, ideal self, and real self—in more depth.

SELF-IMAGE: THE ROLE OF INTERNAL VOICE

At some point in our lives, most of us have awakened to a voice calling our name. This voice comes from somewhere deep inside of us. We hear it, but we know that it is not real in the sense that others can hear it. So we dismiss its importance. We pay more attention, however, to another internal voice—one that whispers to us that we are intelligent or unintelligent, attractive or unattractive, capable or incapable of achieving our goals. While no one else can hear this voice and it is no more tangible than the one that calls our name in sleep, we allow this voice to influence our thoughts and views of self. These views of self may be realistic or unrealistic, but we hold fast to them despite any evidence to the contrary.[9]

LIFE SCRIPTS Storylines that we create to guide us through life.

Beliefs about self also find their way into our **life scripts**. These scripts have characters, plots, settings, and action. The idea of life scripts or life plans appeared in the early literature on transactional analysis (TA), associated with Canadian-born psychiatrist Eric Berne.[10] While some of our stories about self are positive in their unfolding, others have negative beginnings or endings. In other words, sometimes we create "winning" scripts about ourselves; at other times, we make up "losing" ones. When we have low self-esteem, we write negative scripts, repeatedly putting ourselves in situations where we are likely to fail.[11] This behaviour can translate into making poor choices in partners, sabotaging positive relationships, and setting ourselves up for failure. When we anticipate failure, we will usually experience failure.

Consider the following scenario. A young woman named Ashley feels increasingly drawn to a classmate named Charlie. She does not feel overly confident even though she has seen him looking at her a few times in health sciences class. She decides nonetheless to put aside her reservations and invite him to a Drake concert. As she approaches, a popular girl named Jessie grabs Charlie by the arm. Seeing them laughing and talking, Ashley worries that she cannot compete with someone like Jessie. Having convinced herself that Charlie will probably say *no*, she is reserved when asking him to go to the concert.

Although Ashley is normally a warm and caring person, she projects the opposite image on this occasion. Her distant manner does not sit well with Charlie, and he tells her that he already has plans. Ashley leaves the encounter, thinking, "I knew he wouldn't accept my invitation. I'm not good enough." In this scenario, Ashley's expectations have become what we call a **self-fulfilling prophecy**,[12] which can become a recurrent theme in the life scripts of some people.

SELF-FULFILLING PROPHECY A prediction or belief that leads to its own fulfillment.

The following discussion will look at how we create, validate, and revise our scripts as we progress through life.

Creating Our Life Scripts

Some ideas for our life scripts come from direct experience, others from second-hand experience. By *second-hand experience*, we mean reading or hearing about how someone else handles a situation such as the breakdown of a relationship.

At their most basic level, scripts or narratives help us to know how to think and behave in unfamiliar situations or environments. Because we construct many of our scripts from memories, they are highly personal and subjective. No two people perceive or remember events in the same way. So you might recall what someone was wearing at an awards dinner, and someone else might remember the dinner menu. You might remember the pain of falling off a horse on summer vacation with your family, and your sister might remember her peaceful ride on a woodland trail.

Settings are also important in the development of our internal scripts and narratives. We identify on a psychic level with places—towns, cities, regions, and countries. Following the opening ceremonies of the 2010 Olympics in Vancouver, British Columbia, columnist Ian Brown reflected on his reaction to the portrayals of his nation:

> Maybe the opening ceremony of the XXI Winter Games was different on TV, more and less moving at different spots. But on Friday night in a building whose roof is held up with air, it was a strange and moving play, about the wavering but rooted experience of being a Canadian. It was daring. It made me proud to be from here.[13]

Sometimes the places with which we identify are those where we are born and grow up or live for an extended period. At other times, they are places we visit only briefly but adopt in our hearts.

While many narratives associated with place are positive, some come with darker hues. If we grow up in a ghetto setting scarred by poverty and violence, we may feel that we can never escape those boundaries. In status-conscious societies, people often write scripts in keeping with their family status. They assume they cannot get ahead or change their position in society because it has "always been that way"; and this assumption becomes a self-fulfilling prophecy. This example also illustrates the concept of *self-efficacy*, described earlier—the extent to which we believe we can achieve a goal or make a difference. When operating in status-conscious societies, those without status often believe that they cannot make a difference or achieve the same goals as those with higher status. Refer to the "Human Diversity" box for a description of how perceptions of status can impact performance in group situations.

humanDIVERSITY

Social Comparisons Can Diminish Expressions of Intelligence, Especially among Women

Read Montague and colleagues at the Virginia Tech Carilion Research Institute used functional magnetic resonance imaging (fMRI) to study brain processes set in motion when people interact in small groups (e.g., committee meetings, collective bargaining sessions, or cocktail parties). More specifically, they looked at how perceptions of the social status of ourselves and others can affect our ability to process information. The study recruited individuals from two universities. After administering IQ (intelligence quotient) tests to the recruits, the researchers selected men and women who had scored 126 on the tests to participate in their study. In other words, the final test subjects had matching IQs, 26 points above the average IQ in the population. The researchers did not allow the test subjects to see their initial IQ results until after they had completed a series of problem-solving tasks, undertaken in groups of five.

After the participants completed the tasks, the researchers informed all subjects of how they had ranked in performance, relative to the other four members of their small group. Then they assigned additional problem-solving tasks to all group members. The test results showed that something unusual was happening. Dramatic drops occurred in the problem-solving abilities of some lower-ranked individuals, and the researchers concluded that knowledge of their social standing in the group had influenced their ability to complete tasks.

In the final stage of the study, the researchers investigated the brain activity of the high performers versus that of the low performers. They scanned the brains of two people (one high performer and one low performer) from every group of five. They wanted to find out what was happening when the group members were working on the task. Even though all test subjects had scored similarly on the initial IQ tests, the brain activity of the high and low performers varied significantly.

In terms of task performance, the study revealed significant differences in how the men and women performed after being told of their social ranking. Only 3 of the 13 individuals identified as high performers were women, while 11 of the 14 individuals categorized as low performers were women.[14] In other words, feedback on social status appeared to have a strong influence on women—more so than on men. Lead author Kenneth Kishida commented on the results in the following way: "Our study highlights the unexpected and dramatic consequences even subtle social signals in group settings may have on individual cognitive functioning." He also noted that the study raises an important question: "By placing an emphasis on competition, . . . are we missing a large segment of the talent pool?" Thus he cautioned, "We need to remember that social dynamics affect not just educational and workplace environments, but also national and international policy-making bodies, such as the US Congress and the United Nations."[15]

Certain life circumstances may also contribute to the development of negative storylines with negative consequences. When compared with children without motor impairment, for example, children with coordination or other motor problems experience lower self-esteem on almost every measure of self-worth. These children score lower on self-esteem measures related to physical appearance, social acceptance, academic competence, and athletic abilities.[16]

Validating Our Life Scripts

SOCIAL COMPARISON THEORY Theory that holds that we look to others for a standard of comparison.

A common way to ensure the accuracy of our life scripts is to compare ourselves with similar others. According to **social comparison theory**, we look to others for a standard of comparison.[17] And we are most likely to compare ourselves to someone else when that person is closely related to us (e.g., family) or similar in age, race, gender, and background. That does not mean, however, that we always know these people on an intimate or personal basis. We may know them only through television, the movies, or magazines.

These social comparisons can be good or bad for our egos, as we can look upward or downward. When we engage in upward comparison, we look to those who appear better off than we are. That is, we look to "star others" who excel in an area of importance to us.[18] However, we face risks when we make the comparisons at an inappropriate time. If we aspire to become a popular singer like Adele, for example, we fall short if we have not yet acquired the necessary skills. Unlike upward comparisons, downward comparisons involve looking to those who appear to be worse off.[19] For example, we might be looking downward if we compare ourselves to some of the unsuccessful candidates for *Canadian Idol.*

Digital Vision/Thinkstock

In other words, social comparisons can result in positive or negative outcomes for us. We may be inspired and motivated in situations where we imagine becoming our ideal selves. This is known as an **assimilation effect**—where we feel greater self-esteem, with power to reach higher goals, as a result of the social comparison. If we encounter role models whose talents or achievements seem out of reach, on the other hand, the reverse **contrast effect** can occur. A *contrast effect* can leave us in a state where we feel inadequate and deflated, with lowered self-esteem.[20]

These kinds of contrast effects can occur in health-related circumstances—affecting not only our self-esteem, but also our sense of well-being. For example, cancer patients are inspired by the improvement of others (an assimilation effect) only when they can imagine the same improvement in themselves.[21] If a young woman with breast cancer hears about the remarkable recovery of another breast cancer patient, she may or may not believe their situations are comparable. Perhaps the other person went to a world-renowned clinic for treatment or participated in a trial with experimental drugs that are not yet on the market. If the woman does not see her situation as sufficiently similar to that of the other person, she may feel more—rather than less—hopeless after hearing about the case. That is, the story of the breast cancer survivor might create a contrast effect.

ASSIMILATION EFFECT Heightened self-esteem following a favourable social comparison.

CONTRAST EFFECT Feelings of inadequacy and lowered self-esteem following an unfavourable social comparison.

When faced with unfavourable upward comparisons, we can repair our self-regard or self-esteem most easily when we are able to showcase our abilities in other areas.[22] If we do not perform well in sports, for example, we may be able to repair our damaged self-image through successful academic or workplace activities. Positive feedback in one area can make up for negative feedback in another. Even learning about an opportunity to improve in another area can encourage us to take action to reduce the threat.[23]

Revising Our Life Scripts

Sometimes we work with outdated scripts—narratives that have us thinking and acting in ways that may have been appropriate 10 years earlier but no longer apply. We may carry an outdated picture of ourselves as overweight and clumsy even when we have lost 20 pounds and gained in athletic ability. On dating sites, people often list qualities and activities that characterized them at an earlier point in time. Even though someone might not have hiked for 10 years, for example, that person may feel she or he is being truthful in listing hiking as a hobby. Unfortunately for the developing relationship, these outdated views of self can take the mantle of deception for the person who is looking for a fit (not out-of-shape) hiking partner.

*professional*CONTEXTS

Health, Gender, and Self-Concept

More often than males, females integrate an illness into their views of self—that is, they allow the illness to define some significant aspect of self. When ill, females are more likely than males to "embrace" the sick role—taking medication, restricting activities, and seeking the help of a doctor or other health care professional. Males, on the other hand, tend to reject the sick role. Having been socialized to view admission of pain as an embarrassing weakness, males often pretend they are healthy even when they are sick. This behaviour manifests most clearly in gendered sports, where males suppress and conceal pain. In the same way, girls with a chronic illness are more likely than boys to disclose their condition and to see it as part of their identity. Boys, on the other hand, tend to separate the illness from other parts of their identity and not to share their condition with others.

Some classic studies have traced these gender patterns to early childhood—a time at which girls display more dependent behaviours when ill, seek and obtain more sympathy from parents, take more medication, and miss more school. As they get older, females show more of an interest in—and place a greater value on—matters of health. They read more health-related articles in magazines and newspapers. They engage in more preventative health practices such as taking vitamins and going for checkups. Sociologists attribute many of these behaviours to gender conditioning, where parents and other role models treat boys differently from girls.

We become highly attached to the scripts that we write early in our lives, and we work as hard to maintain negative self-views as to protect positive ones.[24] If we become too attached to—or fail for other reasons to update—our scripts, we continue to experience the same endings. We never lose the option to change or rewrite our storylines, and movement from one phase of our lives to another (e.g., adolescence to young adulthood) provides new opportunities for positive change.[25] Our self-concept also becomes more flexible (i.e., we can change it more easily) during periods of role transition—a new marriage or retirement from the workplace.[26] At times, traumatic or stressful events such as divorce or the loss of a partner initiate the unwanted but required update of roles and life scripts. Changes in health (e.g., strokes, disabilities, and chronic illnesses) also affect how we see ourselves and force us to revise our scripts. Stroke victims, for example, feel less capable, less independent, and less in-control of their lives following strokes. Despite efforts at rehabilitation, many report a reduced and more negative sense of self.[27] This reduced sense of self causes them to write new scripts for their lives, with negative storylines. The "Professional Contexts" box discusses the impact of health and gender on self-concept.

> **"How things look on the outside of us depends on how things are on the inside of us."**
> **CONFUCIUS**

The process of aging also brings necessary changes to our life scripts. With the weakening of bodily functions, we may experience higher levels of dependency, lower levels of social interaction, and financial stresses.[28] These changes in circumstances can have a serious impact on self-esteem and self-efficacy—how we feel about ourselves and whether we believe we can make a difference.

LOOKING-GLASS SELF: THE ROLE OF EXTERNAL VOICES

SIGNIFICANT OTHERS People whose opinions matter to us and influence how we perceive ourselves.

Social psychologists and communication scholars argue that we actively construct our views of self.[29] These views come, at least in part, from how we imagine others see us (Figure 2.1). Charles Cooley introduced the idea of *looking-glass self* in 1902 to refer to the power of **significant others** to influence our self-concept.[30] Although Cooley used *looking-glass self* to refer to the *impact* of how we think others view us, scholars have adapted its use over time to mean the same thing as *reflected appraisal*, which refers to how we think others see us (the imagining process). (See the "Professional Contexts" box for an example of how one marketing campaign is trying to improve

FIGURE 2.1 **The looking-glass self.**

*professional*CONTEXTS

Which Is the *Real* Me?

The makers of Dove soap have launched a new component in their "real beauty" campaign to encourage a more positive self-image in young women. In this experiment, which has gone viral on social media (it received over 114 million views in the first month of its release), a forensic sketch artist draws the faces of volunteers. He produces two sketches of each woman, who stands or sits out of view. He bases the first sketch on how the female volunteer describes herself; he bases the second sketch on how a friend sees the person. Then he allows the volunteer to see the difference in the two sketches. The experiment demonstrates that others (*reflected appraisal*) see our physical qualities in a much more positive light than we see ourselves (*self-image*). Some critics have noted, however, that the campaign places an unwanted focus on the physical self.[31]

the self-image of young women by revealing the gap between their perceptions of self and others' perceptions of them.)

The significant others who contribute to perceptions of self may be family, friends, fellow students, health care providers, business acquaintances, or members of organizations with which we identify. These organizations may be political, cultural, social, educational, sports, or other. We may or may not hold formal membership in them. We may hope, for example, to be a member of the next Canadian Olympic team but never reach this goal. We may want to become a famous singer like Celine Dion or Avril Lavigne, a renowned skier like Alexandre Bilodeau, or an expert journalist like Peter Mansbridge or Lisa Laflamme; but we may never realize these ambitions. Nonetheless, these reference groups and the significant others who populate them serve as role models for us even if we are never able to join their ranks.

The following section looks at findings related to the influence of significant others—family, romantic partners, peers, teachers and coaches, caregivers and health care providers, and workplace colleagues and supervisors—on our self-concept.

Family

The term *family* has acquired additional meanings in the last half century. *Family* can imply connections that are biological or developed by the individual. These connections can involve different- or same-sex individuals, close or distant relatives, an intimate or extended network of friends, or married or common-law partners. Whatever the particulars of the relationship, family influences on self-concept and self-esteem are powerful.[32] If we are born to wealthy or highly successful parents, for example, we may struggle with the questions: How can we live up to the standards set by our parents? What is our unique place in society?

> "I've learned that people will forget what you said, people will forget what you did, but people will never forget how you made them feel."
> MAYA ANGELOU

Popular culture holds many examples of youth faced with this dilemma. Some like the children of Donald Trump (billionaire entrepreneur), Bruce Jenner (Olympic athlete and stepfather to the Kardashians), or the Hilton family (hoteliers) are able to carve out a niche for themselves. We may regard Paris Hilton as a good or bad role model, but the fact remains that she is a successful incorporated business entity now—wealthy in her own right. The same applies to the Kardashians. Not all children of celebrity parents are equally able, however, to define themselves in positive ways, as witnessed by problems with drugs, depression, and worse.[33]

When parents expect a lot of their children, the children internalize these expectations.[34] First-born children typically outstrip second-born children when it comes to achievements—even when the second-born children are more intellectually gifted. This effect occurs because parents transmit different messages to different children.[35] No matter the order of birth, however, children benefit from or suffer the consequences of how their parents communicate with them. Parents with positive self-concept tend to send positive messages to their children, and parents with negative self-concept tend to transmit negative messages. Many battered mothers, for example, display inconsistent, punishing, and unemotional

> "Nobody can make you feel inferior without your consent."
> ELEANOR ROOSEVELT

parenting behaviours.[36] In these situations, the parent with low self-esteem communicates similar messages to her children.[37]

The 2009 film *Precious*, based on the novel *Push* by Sapphire, illustrates the damaging effects of negative expectations and treatment by parents and significant others. Set in Harlem in 1987, the film portrays the experiences of a 16-year-old African American teenager named Claireece Precious Jones. The illiterate teen struggles with uncontrolled weight (due in part to forced overeating) and low self-esteem. Subject to daily physical and psychological abuse by her jealous mother, Mary, Precious also suffers incest (which leads to unwanted pregnancies) at the hands of her father. Her mother labels her as "stupid," "a lying whore," and "an uppity bitch." Mary tells Precious that "don't nobody want you" and "I should have aborted your fat ass." To escape from an unbearable existence, Precious learns to live largely in her head until three individuals—a social worker, a teacher, and a nurse—befriend and encourage her to rise above her circumstances. In the end, their efforts succeed; the shift from negative to positive voices in the external world allows Precious to build a more positive self-concept and higher self-esteem.[38]

> **from theory TO PRACTICE**
>
> **Messages that Make a Difference**
>
> Recall messages that you have heard from significant others such as your parents, other relatives, and teachers. Whether you hear the messages repeatedly or only once or twice, these messages can influence how you think about yourself. Can you recall any *positive* messages that influenced how you see yourself? Perhaps significant others commented on your looks, your athletic ability, or your creativity or musical talent? What about *negative* messages? Did someone comment on your clumsiness or body shape or intelligence? Did any of these messages play over and over again in your head? In what ways did they influence your self-concept?

To consider the role of positive and negative messages in your life, see the questions in the "From Theory to Practice" box on messages that make a difference.

Romantic Partners

Our romantic partners can also have a strong impact on our self-concept—in a positive or negative direction. The natural tendency within partnerships is to see the other in an idealized way. That is, we see our partner as better than the person sees herself or himself.[39] Not surprisingly, both dating and married individuals are happiest in relationships where their partner perceives them in an idealized way, sometimes seeing qualities they do not see in themselves.[40]

Unfortunately, low self-esteem in either partner can darken this rosy picture. Individuals with low self-esteem and high levels of insecurity have a poor track record when it comes to long-term relationships, including marriages.[41] When people with low self-esteem fear rejection, they protect themselves by holding others at a distance. They also display less trust in their partners, which places the relationship at greater risk of failure.[42] In addition, over a dozen studies confirm that people with negative self-image actively look for partners who will give negative feedback. They avoid or pull out of relationships that could have more positive outcomes. The negative behaviours of partners with low self-esteem come from these individuals' feelings that they are not good enough.[43]

> **"Low self-esteem is like driving through life with your hand-break on."**
>
> MAXWELL MALTZ

Consider this scenario. Randy, a university student, is the middle child in a family with professional parents. His older sister, now in her late twenties, has just received a promotion to an executive position in a high-tech firm. His younger brother plays competitive tennis, and the family puts a lot of energy and money into supporting his game. Unlike his successful siblings, Randy always seems to be the one without a clear direction. He is intelligent enough, but an underachiever; and while he enjoys soccer, he does not excel at the sport. He is sociable, however, and girls like him. Nonetheless, Randy is surprised when an attractive girl named Nancy shows interest in him. Nancy is outgoing, with a number of friends who stay in daily contact with her. She does well in school. She is an accomplished piano player. Unlike Randy, who sees his life as one uneventful happening, Nancy seems to succeed at everything she does.

For a while their relationship progresses without serious problems, but after a year Randy's old insecurities emerge. He notices that Nancy spends more time texting her friends than talking with him. He loses his part-time job at a hardware store and, in order to pay the rent, must take a job at a snack bar at the local ice arena. He is embarrassed when his friends come to the rink. As Randy becomes less secure in his relationship with Nancy and unhappier with his job, arguments occur more often and last longer. At first Nancy tries to reassure and bolster his confidence. She tells him that he will get a better job soon and everything will be all right. After a while, however, she grows tired of reassuring him. He always seems angry and frustrated, and she begins to question their relationship. Maybe he is not the person she had believed him to be. Sometimes it even seems that Randy is trying to sabotage their relationship. He tells her to find someone else if she is not happy with him, and one day she hears him talking with an old girlfriend. When she confronts him, he walks away from her, slamming the door behind him.

Whatever the cause of low self-esteem, individuals with low self-esteem report less satisfying and less stable relationships than individuals with high self-esteem. Even when the individual with high self-esteem begins the relationship with an idealized view of the other, he or she may come to see the partner with low self-esteem in a less positive way over time. Eventually, the partner with high self-esteem sees the partner with low self-esteem in the same way that the person views himself or herself.[44] But if the individual with high self-esteem does not give up on his or her partner, the person with low self-esteem may gain in confidence over time and the relationship may survive. To learn more about how to build your self-esteem, see the "From Theory to Practice" box.

from theory TO PRACTICE

Self-Esteem Builder

One way to build your self-esteem is to engage in *positive self-talk*. Positive self-talk involves, first of all, identifying and listing the qualities that you appreciate in yourself. For example, your list could include personality traits, abilities, or skills such as the following: sense of humour, athletic ability, or eye for fashion. After identifying some of your best qualities, stand in front of a mirror and read your list aloud. Begin each statement with the words "I love my . . . . " To have noticeable impact on your self-esteem, repeat this exercise on a regular basis.

Peers

Peers are especially important to the development of self-concept in children and adolescents. During elementary school years, children begin to describe themselves in terms such as *smart* or *stupid*, *popular* or *unpopular*—terms that suggest both self-image (how they see themselves) and looking-glass self (how they think others see them). The opinions of others have a major impact on how children perceive their physical, academic, and social selves.[45] When faced with extreme forms of discrimination such as bullying, children become anxious and depressed, with lowered self-esteem. As in the tragic cases of Amanda Todd of Port Coquitlam and Rehtaeh Parsons of Halifax, this lowered self-esteem can have fatal consequences.

Recognizing the seriousness of the problem, Canadian parents have begun to take actions against school boards. Parents in Kanata and Waterloo, Ontario, for example, have filed lawsuits against local school boards for failing to protect their children against bullies.[46] Groups have rallied to produce documentaries and public service announcements to discourage bullying among school-aged children, and celebrities are speaking out on the problem. Facebook launched a Canadian anti-bullying campaign in November 2012, with the aim of getting 18 million Canadian subscribers to commit to an anti-bullying pledge.[47] A growing number of politicians are taking a public stance in the media, and some courts are sentencing bullies to time in detention or jail. In November 2011, a 13-year-old youth in Durham, Ontario, faced court charges for bullying schoolmate Mitchell Wilson to the point that the 11-year-old tied a plastic bag around his own head and suffocated to death.[48] In October 2012, the police arrested eight teenage girls in London, Ontario, on charges of emotional and physical bullying, as well as **cyberbullying**.[49] On 27 September 2012, the Supreme Court of Canada issued the Bragg decision, which gave underage victims of cyberbullying the right to anonymously seek court disclosure of their bullies.[50]

CYBERBULLYING Malicious communications in the form of text messages, emails, or postings on social and personal websites.

Teachers and Coaches

Teachers and others in authority positions can also have a serious impact on the self-esteem and self-efficacy of the children they teach. In a classic 1968 study, Robert Rosenthal and Lenore Jacobson[51] told teachers in one California classroom that certain students had shown exceptional promise on an IQ test and that the teachers should expect strong academic performance from these students. In fact, the information was false, as the researchers had pulled the names randomly from a classroom list. Rosenthal and Jacobson wanted to know whether teacher expectations could influence academic performance.

At the end of the first school year and again at the end of the second year, the researchers examined records indicating the progress of these students. Although the students received no additional time to complete assignments and no special curriculum or private tutoring, their grades and teacher evaluations improved significantly in both years—not only under the first teacher but also under a different teacher. Rosenthal and Jacobson concluded that unconscious communication from instructors (e.g., nods of approval, smiles, encouraging words, and calling more often on the students for their opinions) had made the difference. In other words, the expectations of others can influence how we see ourselves and how we perform.

Although some question the methods used in these early studies and others say that gender and social skills may have influenced the results, the large majority of studies confirm the importance of teacher expectations in predicting student success.[52] Several attempts at replicating the Rosenthal and Jacobson study produced similar results, and a review of 345 experimental studies[53] and more non-experimental studies[54] offer further evidence to support the conclusions reached by this ground-breaking study. To

from theory TO PRACTICE

Labelling Ourselves

Do you think of yourself as a procrastinator, bad at math, lazy, or disorganized? These and other negative self-labels can influence how you think about yourself. They can also influence the way other people treat you. Researchers Michelle R. Hebl and Eden B. King from Rice University, Houston, Texas, wanted to teach undergraduate students about the powerful effect of the self-fulfilling prophecy—the idea that our beliefs about self will come into being if we believe them strongly enough. They asked volunteers to wear a hat with a sticker, which indicated a personal quality or attribute (e.g., intelligent, attractive, good leader, annoying, lazy). Then the instructor told the students to treat the volunteers as if the labels were accurate.

At the end of the study, the researchers found that the volunteers (those wearing the labels) ended up acting as though the words they were wearing accurately described them. For example, a student with a *good leader* sticker on her hat demonstrated leadership qualities. A student labelled as *lazy* showed little initiative. In analyzing the results, the researchers speculated that this effect may have occurred because the other students treated the volunteers in a way that conformed to their labels.[55] In other words, what we tell others about ourselves (in this case, labels on a hat) influences how they see us. In turn, how they see us influences how we behave.

What do you tell others about yourself? Does this information reflect how you would like to be perceived and treated? If not, which labels best represent how you would like others to see you?

learn more about how labels affect our self-concept, see the "From Theory to Practice" box on self-applied labels.

Indirect communication can be as powerful as direct communication in sending messages to students. When schools provide low-income and minority students with inadequate help and poor facilities, the message is clear: "We care less about you than we care about other students." While some students may resist these messages, others accept them as true and behave in a way that supports the negative judgments.[56] For these students, the message becomes the kind of self-fulfilling prophecy discussed earlier. To learn about a Canadian campaign designed to send positive messages to Aboriginal youth, see the "Human Diversity" box.

> "Someone's opinion of you does not have to become your reality."
>
> LES BROWN

Many examples of the strength of expectations come from the world of coaching. Studies of athletes, for instance, have uncovered a relationship between season of birth and success at athletics—a finding linked to the power of expectations of coaches and others with whom young athletes interact. In a study of National Hockey League (NHL) professionals, researchers found the players were twice as likely to have been born in the first quarter of the year as opposed to the last quarter.[57] In the junior hockey leagues, which feed the NHL, the relationship was even more pronounced, with four times as many players born in the first quarter of the year than in the final quarter.[58] A third study, which examined the birthdates of 837 major-league baseball players, uncovered the same connection.[59]

Why would birthdate influence the success of professional athletes? The answer lies in the expectations of others, which contribute to expectations of self. Because children born in the first quarter of the year are older when they try out for their first

humanDIVERSITY

The I Am Aboriginal Campaign, Building Self-Esteem through Positive Messages

In 2009, the Rainbow District School Board in Sudbury, Ontario, partnered with Urban Aboriginal Youth Leading the Way and the Eshkiniijig Advisory Circle to launch the I Am Aboriginal campaign. The campaign aimed to encourage Aboriginal students to identify with—and develop a sense of pride in—their Aboriginal heritage. The initiative asked Aboriginal elementary and secondary students and their families to complete a survey in which they indicated whether they self-identified as First Nations, Métis, or Inuit. It also asked the students to create and submit videos and posters that explained why the campaign mattered. An outdoor activity at Whitefish Lake First Nation allowed Aboriginal youth to learn and practise traditional survival skills such as building shelters and starting fires, to engage in traditional games, and to learn about preparation of traditional foods.

Asked how they felt about the campaign, students expressed overwhelmingly positive opinions. Dakota Recollet of Lockerby Composite School explained, "I feel it is important to identify with your Aboriginal background so you can be proud of where you come from."[60] Sudbury Secondary School student Jericho Pettifer expressed a similar view: "Young Aboriginal people need to know where they came from and to understand the emotional, physical, and spiritual aspects of their beings."[61]

Jennifer Hansford, contributor to the Aboriginal publication *The Windspeaker*, sees this campaign as the first—but not the last—step in local efforts to support and celebrate diversity. Although targeted primarily at Aboriginal students and their families, the campaign also aimed to engage non-Aboriginal students in learning more about the history, culture, and languages of Aboriginal Canadians.[62]

sports teams, they have an initial advantage over children who are younger, weaker, and less mature in their physical development. As a result, these older children experience greater success at the games, receive more attention from coaches, and get more rewards and recognition from the sports community. They acquire higher self-esteem and self-efficacy than their younger peers. Others expect them to succeed, and they feel empowered to meet the expectations. Their success, over time, becomes a self-fulfilling prophecy—long after the age variable loses importance. (At 8 years of age, a few months can make a difference in performance ability; at 18 years of age, the difference is insignificant.)

Caregivers and Health Care Providers

People who experience serious health or mobility problems often complain that their caregivers treat them as if they have mental, as well as physical, limitations.[63] They say that health care practitioners, caregivers, and family members frequently discuss their cases as if they are absent from the room. Older adults feel particularly vulnerable to this kind of treatment.

As discussed earlier, children and others with motor impairment or a chronic illness often experience relatively low levels of self-esteem. This low self-esteem can aggravate an already sensitive situation. In order to address the problem, health care workers need to assess and try to build self-esteem and a sense of self-efficacy in children and others with physical limitations—to help them to understand that they have multiple abilities outside of the area of impairment and that the impairment should not define them.[64]

In recent years, health care practitioners have become more aware of the importance of addressing these kinds of issues and speaking directly to people with disabilities or illness. If someone behaves as if we do not exist, we feel worthless and incompetent; as a result, an already fragile self-concept can undergo a dramatic turn for the worse. In situations involving illness and disabilities, a poor mental attitude has serious implications for health outcomes.

Workplace Colleagues and Supervisors

As in other contexts, the term *self-fulfilling prophecy* is common in the business literature, where economists talk about the influence of expectations on market performance. However, expectation effects can be found throughout the workplace. For example, managers experience greater success when they hold a strong belief in their own abilities to select, train, and motivate others. In a classic case called "Sweeney's Miracle," a Tulane University professor named James Sweeney, successfully trained an uneducated janitor to run the school's biomedical computer centre and to train others in using the computers. Sweeney's belief in his own teaching abilities outweighed any questions about the abilities of the janitor, who had scored low on IQ tests. The tests had indicated that the janitor might have difficulty even learning to type, let alone run a computer centre.[65]

In another classic case, supervisors at a bank reduced the lending power of some branch managers. Afterwards, these managers became increasingly less effective. First, the demoted managers resorted to making only "safe" loans. When these actions resulted in loss of business to competing banks, the managers reversed their approach and took unnecessary risks in reaching for new loans. This irrational behaviour led to even larger credit losses. The expectations of the supervisors—that the managers' lending would result in financial loss—then became a self-fulfilling prophecy.[66]

As this example illustrates, actions can be more important than words. If a manager gives increased responsibility to an employee, this action communicates belief in the employee's abilities. Being given a job with limited or decreased responsibility, on the other hand, reads as a negative evaluation or a request to resign.

Another management study found an important relationship (correlation of 0.72) between what managers expected of new employees in the first year and the contribution of the employees over the next five years. In the first year, managers voiced their expectations, set standards, encouraged the employees to adopt attitudes that would enable them to achieve their goals, and reinforced successes. These early expectations influenced the later performance of the employees.[67]

Many studies demonstrate that women have less confidence than men in the workplace. The American Sociological Association, for example, found that women feel less sure than men about their work-related expertise.[68] This finding is particularly true in areas such as science and technology.[69] Author and life coach Ann Daly says that women learn very early that they must get everything right to land at the top of their classes. This stress on perfectionism continues to have an impact on their attitudes once they enter the workplace. They assume, for example, that they cannot apply for a promotion or a job unless they meet every requirement listed in the job description. Men, on the other hand, will often apply for a job for which they are not qualified on paper. Their thought process follows: "Well, I don't have the qualifications, but I can learn the job. So what can I lose by applying?" In support of this argument, Daly cites a Hewlett-Packard study that found that men believe they need to meet only 60 per cent of the requirements to apply for a job, while women believe they must meet all requirements before applying.[70]

The UK-based Global Entrepreneurship Monitor (GEM) found that female entrepreneurs display less confidence than their male counterparts in their ability to succeed. The 2010 GEM report showed that fewer women (47.7 per cent) than men (62.1 per cent) believe in their ability to begin and run a business. They perceive fewer opportunities in their environments, anticipate more problems, and fear failure more than their male counterparts. As a result, they are more likely to pass up opportunities and to be dissuaded from attempting a startup.[71] Despite these glum global statistics, once in business, female microbusiness entrepreneurs in Canada have higher success rates than their male counterparts.[72]

Despite some grounds for optimism, these predominantly negative self-assessments follow women into the workplace. For example, a study by the Columbia Business School found that men assessed their performance as 30 per cent higher than records supported. Women tended, on the other hand, to be more modest in assessing their performance and in accepting compliments.[73] In the same way, the overconfidence of men makes it easier for them to justify faking or exaggerating their credentials, giving them an edge when it comes to job applications. But the picture is not all positive. Overconfidence and exaggeration of credentials sometimes mask deep insecurities that can lead individuals (especially men) to engage in high-risk behaviours. Refer to the "Professional Contexts" box on the impostor syndrome for one explanation of this phenomenon.

*professional*CONTEXTS

Less than Perfect: The Impostor Syndrome

Social psychologist Gerri King discusses a phenomenon called *the impostor syndrome*—a psychological condition in which an individual (usually a male) feels like a fake because he believes he does not deserve the success he has achieved. This syndrome often leads powerful men to engage in risky, potentially destructive behaviours such as having sex with multiple anonymous partners—especially call girls—and/or cheating on their intimate partners. Attempting to explain why powerful men in married or dating relationships risk destroying their relationships by turning to sex workers, King says that low self-esteem and life changes are the main contributors to this behaviour. Any change in a person's life—even a positive change—can trigger this behaviour because "with every gain, there is also a loss."[74]

As King explains, when we occupy "normal" roles in society, our self-concept allows us to make mistakes. After all, our friends are "normal." They make mistakes, and they do not expect more from us. Nor do we expect more from ourselves. If we see ourselves as "normal," we can be less than perfect and still feel good about ourselves. The problem arises, however, when a life change (e.g., a promotion) suddenly catapults us from our position as "average" into an elite level of business or society. In those situations, we have to "retrofit" our identity and adopt behaviours that fit the new norm. For example, if we receive a promotion from a low-level position to a high-level, high-profile position, we may have to interact more with the media and high-ranking executives. In that situation, we may have to abandon our tendency to use sarcastic language. We will lose some friends and gain others, but the expectations of the new friends may be different from those of the old. We may have increased privileges, but fewer freedoms. We may feel nervous about whether we can cope and meet expectations, and we may react by engaging in self-destructive behaviour.

We see many examples of men and women who experience a wide range of serious problems when they achieve a higher position in life. Marilyn Monroe never stopped seeing herself as Norma Jean, the unwanted daughter of a mentally ill mother and a father she never knew; her insecurities undoubtedly contributed to her suicide at the age of 36. In a similar way, Elvis Presley (born in a two-room shotgun house in Tupelo, Mississippi, to parents who had struggled through the depression years) was not able to manage an altered self-image in a healthy way; rumour mills claimed that he entertained many of the women who lined up at Las Vegas engagements for the opportunity to experience a moment of intimacy with "the King." More recently, people were shocked to learn that Sandra Bullock's husband, television personality Jesse James, had been having multiple affairs. People asked, "Why would a successful man, who is married to one of the world's most adored women, feel the need to look outside the marriage for sexual fulfillment?" At least part of the answer may be that he felt like an impostor in his role as a celebrity, and his hidden insecurities led him to engage in behaviours that had the potential to (and eventually did) harm his celebrity status.

IDEAL SELF: THE ROLE OF THE MEDIA

In arriving at the ideal self, we look to role models. In today's environment, a large number of these role models come to us via the media. People use the most readily available sources as a standard of comparison.[75] So if the images that come to us on television, in films and fashion magazines, and on the Internet are easily accessible and known to us, we will look to those sources for benchmarks for personal comparisons. When the images depict people in a realistic way (i.e., when the images are not doctored or changed to make the celebrities appear more glamorous), they can make us feel better about ourselves. On the other hand, if the images are unrealistic and idealize the people they portray, our self-concept may suffer from the comparison. If a gap develops between the real self and the ideal self, we may experience **body-image disturbance** and lowered self-esteem and self-efficacy. For some ideas on how to battle against negative body image, refer to the "Professional Contexts" box on thoughts, feelings, and consequences.

BODY-IMAGE DISTURBANCE Reduced levels of satisfaction with our bodies and a downward spiral in how we see our physical selves.

The following sections consider the interaction of children and adolescents with media images, shifts in media depictions of women over time, media influence on body satisfaction, and variations across cultures.

Interaction of Children and Adolescents with Media Images

From a very young age, children engage with mass media images, which allow them to compare themselves to others with whom they may never have personal contact.[76] Cultural icons such as sports stars and pop stars capture the imagination of children, who often copy the fashions worn by these celebrities.[77] The trend continues as girls and boys move into later adolescence, comparing themselves in an upward fashion with these role models. Surveys suggest that children consume about 6.5 hours of media content each day. The greatest reliance on media as a basis for comparison occurs between the fourth and eighth grades, a time when adolescents are developing a strong awareness of their bodies.[78] Teenage girls say that media rank second only to parents and peers as sources of information and influence on their attitudes and behaviour.[79]

© Lya_Cattel/iStockphoto

Shifts in Media Depictions of Women over Time

Given the media consumption patterns of adolescents, we must ask ourselves, "What are these young people getting?" A 1985

professionalCONTEXTS

Thoughts, Feelings, and Consequences

Can holding onto our thoughts make a difference to our self-concept? Psychologists at Ohio State University in the United States and Universidad Autónoma de Madrid in Spain believe it can.[80] In a series of three experiments, Richard Petty and his colleagues asked high school students to write down their thoughts on paper and then to keep or discard the papers.

In the first experiment, the students wrote what they liked or disliked about their bodies. After recording their thoughts, some students checked what they had written for writing or spelling mistakes and kept the papers, while others threw their papers away without doing any corrections. Afterward the students filled out rating scales, indicating how they felt about their bodies.

The findings revealed that the students who had corrected and kept the papers also kept the thoughts. Those who had discarded the papers discarded the thoughts. In other words, if a student retained a paper on which she had written positive things about her body, she transferred those attitudes to the scales on body image. On the other hand, if she threw the paper away, the attitudes did not transfer to the same extent from paper to the scales. Whether positive or negative in nature, thoughts that landed in the trash bin did not receive the same level of importance as thoughts retained in paper form.

A related study found that carrying around a piece of paper on which an individual had written her or his thoughts made it even more likely the person would retain the attitude written on paper. Petty commented on the conclusions: "This suggests you can magnify your thoughts, and make them more important to you, by keeping them with you in your wallet or purse."[81] A third study showed that just imagining you have discarded a thought does not make a difference. You have to perform a physical action—writing and keeping the thought or saving it on a computer—for the thought to be retained. Petty and his colleagues hope that they can apply these findings to help people to get rid of destructive thoughts and feelings such as those of despair after the death of a loved one.

Albert Ellis's widely publicized theory on rational emotive thought conveys similar ideas about the relationship between thoughts and feelings.[82] Ellis says that thoughts are real in the sense that they can help or hurt us. Words, on the other hand, are only words—symbols to which we give meaning. If someone shouts at us from the window of a prison, we attach a different meaning to the action and the words than we do if a supervisor yells at us in the workplace. We also experience different emotions. The action is the same: someone yells at us. The words are the same—abusive in both cases. But our thoughts control our emotional responses to the words. We can feel angry or frustrated or even sad for the prisoner.

Ellis says that thoughts can be *facilitative* (constructive and helpful) or *debilitative* (destructive and unhelpful). He proposes a three-step model for better understanding the process. In this rational emotive model, an *activating event* (e.g., a supervisor yelling at us) leads to a *thought or belief* (e.g., my supervisor does not like me). The thought or belief leads to a *consequence* (e.g., I feel angry). Ellis says that if we can control our thoughts, we can control our emotions. A visual illustration of the process follows:

Activating Event → Thought or Belief → Consequences.

Consider two possible interpretations of a departmental transfer:

Activating Event	**Thought or Belief**	**Consequence**
My manager has transferred me to another department.	My manager thinks I am incompetent.	I feel hurt and disappointed.

Activating Event	**Thought or Belief**	**Consequence**
My manager has transferred me to another department.	My manager thinks I will have greater opportunities in another position.	I feel proud and self-confident.

As you can see from Ellis's rational emotive model and the research conducted by Petty and his colleagues, thoughts play a critical role in our everyday lives. To the extent that we can channel those thoughts in positive directions, we will lead more fulfilling lives. Ellis's work has led to many suggestions for therapies that can improve our stress levels, our relationships with others, and our mental health in general.

study found that 1 out of every 10.8 television commercials included messages about attractiveness;[83] and between 1900 and the mid-1980s, female body sizes depicted in advertisements had decreased by as much as 50 per cent.[84]

An analysis of shifting trends in weight and body size of Miss America contestants and *Playboy* centrefolds between 1959 and 1978 showed that the weight of these women fell significantly below the weight of average women in the same period. At the same time that height increased, bust and hip sizes decreased. In other words, female role models in the media grew steadily taller and thinner over the two decades.[85] A repeat of this study in 1992 found that this downward trend in weight continued through 1988 for Miss America contestants but remained the same for *Playboy* centrefolds. The women participating in the beauty competition weighed 13 to 19 per cent less than expected for their height. The trend was toward taller, leaner, and straighter bodies.[86] Around the same time, magazines targeting females contained 10.5 times as many features on diet and weight loss as magazines targeting men.[87]

This focus on a thin ideal has not changed in the years that followed these studies.[88] The women who populate films, daytime and prime-time television, and music videos in 2013 reflect the continuing obsession of Western societies with thinness. A review of 28 prime-time situation comedies found that 33 per cent of female actors appearing regularly on these shows were below average in weight. A 2002 issue of *Us Weekly* reported questionably healthy weights for film stars such as Halle Berry (5'7", 112 lbs), Cameron Diaz (5'9", 126 lbs), Gwyneth Paltrow (5'9", 120 lbs), and Julia Roberts (5'9", 120 lbs). Today, media sources continues to glamourize such ultra-thin celebrities as Nicole Richie (reality TV star), Victoria Beckham (former member of the Spice Girls), and Mary-Kate Olsen (TV and film star)—even as they question the healthiness of these women's weight.

Too often, media reports about female celebrities place the focus on thinness as an indicator of beauty. Consider the following description of movie star Megan Fox two months after having given birth:

> If we wiped your memories and told you that this woman has just given birth, would you believe us? . . . The *Transformers* actress looked slim and relaxed . . . At this stage, most new mothers would have to be reminded to brush their hair, slap on some lipstick and actually leave the house but Megan is taking it all in her stylish stride . . . As if to illustrate just how good the beauty's figure looks, she wore the most unforgiving of items: the dreaded leggings . . . And unlike most of us, who will be retreating to the elasticated beauties after a Thanksgiving feed . . . Megan wore her leggings with short tops rather than a baggy T-shirt . . . Megan obviously had no qualms about showing off her post-baby body in all its glory.[89]

The article from which this passage is taken is accompanied by 13 photographs of Fox and a caption that describes Fox as "impossibly slender," reinforcing the focus on physical appearance.

The media set equally high standards for middle-aged and older women. They hawk the importance of "looking younger than you are" and "defying aging" through the use of anti-aging creams, hair colours, plastic surgery, and weight loss regimes. They assume that the physical effects of aging are socially undesirable and capable of being reversed. More importantly, they assume that everyone should want to achieve the ideal of a youthful appearance.[90] The increasing application of the term *cougar* (meaning an older woman who tries to attract younger men) to describe women in their thirties—and the use of the term in the first place—confirms the negative connotations of aging. A woman on one forum complained: "I get mad when I hear the ages some people consider a cougar to be. I've seen women who are like 28 and people are calling them a cougar and . . . she still has baby fat."[91]

Media Influence on Body Satisfaction

What is the impact of the media focus on thin and youthful bodies for women and muscular bodies for men? A large number of studies suggest that body-image disturbance or body-image dissatisfaction results when a gap occurs between the real and ideal self.[92] Some estimate that as many as two-thirds of all young women are extremely unhappy with the shape, size, condition, and/or appearance of their bodies.[93] The gap between the real (what we actually are) and the ideal (what we would like to be) affects women of all ages—children, adolescents and young adults, and middle-aged and older adults. Using silhouette drawings and self-report measures, researchers have consistently documented the seriousness of the problem across the female population.[94]

Evidence of the prevalence of this gap between the real and the ideal appeared in one study where only 29 per cent of adolescents chose ideal bodies that matched their actual bodies.[95] Studies with college-aged and older females have generated similar findings.[96] A *Psychology Today* survey found that 15 per cent of female readers and 11 per cent of male readers said they would give up five years of their lives to be their ideal weights; 24 per cent of women and 17 per cent of men said they would give up at least three years.[97] These kinds of results suggest that many believe in the **myth of perfection**—the idea that it is both desirable and possible to achieve perfection.[98]

MYTH OF PERFECTION
The false notion that a state of perfection exists and is attainable.

In North America, almost everyone is or has at one time been on a diet. According to one 2005 survey, 45.6 per cent of high school students said they were trying to lose weight. Breaking down the statistic by gender, two-thirds of high school girls and one-third of high school boys claimed to be taking active measures to decrease their body weight.[99] See the "Professional Contexts" box titled "Dying to Be Thin" for a narrative about a woman named Melissa that reveals some of the more drastic consequences that can result from an obsession with thinness.

Melissa's story is not unique. A recent Health Canada survey (2007–2009) reported that 0.6 per cent of Canadian women between the ages of 6 and 79 suffer from at least one kind of eating disorder, and eating disorders accounted for more than 5200 hospitalizations in Canada between 2009 and 2010. Women made up 90 per cent of the patients.[100]

While a number of factors contribute to the declining sense of self-worth of many young women, the media undoubtedly play a significant role. As discussed earlier, researchers have long warned about the negative impact of the media on the body image of women.[101] Moreover, those most at risk of being negatively influenced by the media include individuals (1) who are already extremely dissatisfied with their bodies, (2) who place a high value on personal appearance, and (3) who suffer from eating disorders.[102] People with low self-esteem are also more likely to be negatively influenced by media images because their self-concept is less stable.[103]

Studies show that unhappiness with our body image also leads us to *underestimate* the weight of role models in the media[104] and to *overestimate* our own body sizes. That is, we think the role models are skinnier than they actually are, and we think we are larger than we are. One study showed that women overestimated their weight by an

*professional*CONTEXTS

Dying to Be Thin

Melissa had been a high school and college athlete with hopes of becoming an Olympic competitor in track. She surrendered that dream, however, soon after graduating from college. She chose instead to marry, begin a family, and venture into the business world. In many regards, Melissa was an over-achiever, what many call a "Type A" personality. She was hard on herself and expected similar output from others. In her first two years of marriage, she continued to live in the world of the athlete. She swam, bicycled, and jogged in the summer; and in the winter, she went cross-country skiing before leaving for work in the mornings.

Before they married, her husband, Brad, had often told Melissa how much he admired her figure and her athleticism. After marrying, he had made negative comments about a friend who was not in shape. Although Brad did not realize the potential effect of his casual statements, they had an impact on Melissa. She concluded that her outward appearance meant a great deal to her husband; and when she became pregnant with their first child, she tried to keep up a modified physical regime. She attended exercise classes for expectant mothers and took long daily walks in the neighbourhood.

Things were going well until she experienced unforeseen complications with her pregnancy. Faced with a life-threatening situation, she had to give up the exercise classes and stay in bed for most of the last month of her pregnancy. Confined to bed, she became immensely depressed and found herself munching on Twinkies, Oreo cookies, and other junk foods—indulging cravings she had controlled in past years. Her appetite seemed bottomless, and she gained 30 pounds in her pregnancy, 15 more than she had intended.

At 5'7" tall, Melissa's 145-pound weight was not excessive for a woman who eventually delivered an 8-pound baby. The average weight gain in pregnancies is 25 to 30 pounds. But Melissa felt defeated and depressed by the loss of control over her body—and by extension, her life. She remembered her high school coach urging her to shed 10 pounds for a major track meet. It had taken a heroic effort to lose those 10 pounds, and she wondered how hard it would be to lose the 25 pounds she had added to her figure during pregnancy.

Brad unwittingly aggravated the situation when he purchased DVDs and magazines for Melissa during her months of confinement to bed. Unfortunately, these products had unforeseen and extremely negative consequences for Melissa's self-image. Rather than reducing her boredom, they fuelled her insecurities. The movies and the magazines overflowed with images of skinny celebrity moms such as Angelina Jolie, Keri Russell, Bethenny Frankel, and Beyoncé. As the days turned into weeks, Melissa fell into a deep state of depression, which became worse after the birth of her son.

In the early days of caring for her new baby, she had no opportunity to do more physical exercise than taking strolls with her son. Brad left early for work each day, and she remained at home. Her freelance work, helping two small businesses with their accounts, consumed any extra moments during the day. The baby's naptime was her only real opportunity to accomplish work tasks.

The pounds gained during pregnancy stuck to her in the year following the birth of her son; and Melissa's

average of 25 per cent after viewing pictures of ideal bodies in fashion magazines. They overestimated body parts such as their hips and their waist by at least 50 per cent.[105]

Unrealistic standards in the media lead to serious health consequences for pregnant women who feel the need to stay thin during pregnancy or to rid themselves of unnecessary weight immediately following childbirth. Merryl Bear, director of Toronto's National Eating Disorder Information Centre, has stated that pregnancies once allowed women to "relax" into their bodies and experience the natural process of growth. But now, she says, "there are more challenges to a pregnant woman's self-perception that are exacerbated by the images and the stories of celebrities who get pregnant, have their babies, and throughout the process . . . just have their pre-pregnancy body with a bump."[106] Dr Blake Woodside, who heads the country's largest eating disorders treatment program at Toronto General Hospital, has also noted that instances of eating disorders in pregnant women (dubbed *pregorexia* in the media) have increased in recent years. He sees widespread "fatphobic" and "fat discriminatory" attitudes as contributing to the problem.[107]

spirits continued to spiral downward, affecting not only her sense of self-esteem but also her relationships with her husband and her child. Brad attributed the first months of depression to a postpartum disorder, a common condition of women in the weeks following the birth of a child. But Melissa's reaction was longer lasting. At one point, she decided to do something about the situation. She might not be able to control the time available for exercise, but she could control her eating. As a serious college athlete, she had developed the ability to make sacrifices and to follow a demanding regime. Now, she decided, she must draw upon that past ability.

Her intention in place, Melissa cut back the number of calories she was consuming to 1200 per day, the lowest number recommended for losing weight at a safe rate. She was ecstatic when she weighed herself six weeks later to learn that she had lost 10 pounds. She was now down to 135 pounds. Determined to lose more, she cut her calories to 900 per day. A month later, she was relieved and happy to learn that she had shed another 10 pounds. She was now at a weight that, at one time, would have been ideal for her height. But she was receiving so many compliments from Brad, her friends, and even her mother that she decided the loss of a few more pounds would not hurt. Again she cut the number of calories she was consuming, this time by going on a vegetarian diet with little protein and mostly leafy vegetables. She cut potatoes, rice, bread, and other carbohydrate-heavy foods completely from her diet. She rejected any offers of dessert, even on special occasions; and she learned how to push the vegetables around on her plate so that it looked as if she had eaten more than appeared.

Once again, Melissa felt good about herself. Her life was under control, and she felt a renewed sense of power. Moreover, she no longer missed the foods she used to eat. In fact, she rarely had any appetite. At the same time, however, she was experiencing a decrease in energy, finding it difficult to take care of her young son, and sometimes feeling weak and faint. Friends and family began to have a worried look when they saw her, especially those who had not seen her for some time. Her mother questioned her diet, and her sister finally voiced the fears of others: was Melissa anorexic? Melissa did not understand their concern because when she looked in the mirror, she saw herself in a different way from how they saw her. She did not see a dangerously underweight individual but rather a young woman who was finally looking the way she was supposed to look—or close to it. In her mind, there was always more work to be done, however, to attain the standards of women like Heidi Klum. She might not be able to have the muscular, toned body of her earlier role models in the world of athletes, but she could compete with the figures in the media if she tried hard enough. This mindset was possible until one morning, when she was alone with her son, she collapsed. Brad found her later that morning when he returned from work after being unable to reach her. At 22 years of age, Melissa was forced to recognize that she had entered the scary world of anorexia. Not only had she endangered the life of her son, left unattended for several hours that morning; but she faced almost certain death if she did not change her perception of herself. At her family's urging, Melissa accepted psychological counselling.

While studies on the influence of media on body image have dealt more often with the plight of women, researchers now worry about the impact of media images on men as well.[108] One-third of young men experience unacceptably high levels of dissatisfaction with the shape, size, condition, and/or appearance of their bodies.[109] However, for the most part, males tend to worry more about degree of muscle bulk and development of the upper body than about thinness.[110] One study showed that male interest in developing muscle bulk appeared as early as middle school.[111]

The current ideal for men is a lean and muscular build, with a well-developed chest and narrow hips and waist. When confronted with media images that project this ideal, men experience the same kind of body disturbance as women do when they view images that embody the ideal of thinness.[112] The result can be eating problems, obsessive exercising, depression, and low self-esteem.[113] The increased use of steroids among men may reflect the felt need of men to fit this stereotype of masculinity.

The celebration of youth and physical attractiveness carries over into the gay community. Although hotly debated, the theory of accelerated aging contends that gay men see themselves as older earlier than their heterosexual peers. According to one source, many in the gay community perceive a man as "old" when he turns 30.[114] This statement recalls the earlier discussion of *cougars*, women in their mid-30s or older who are characterized as being "old." In both cases, the views of significant others, friends, family, and the media have an impact on self-esteem and overall self-concept.

Social media are not helping the situation. Controversy has enveloped a dating website called BeautifulPeople.com, which restricts its membership to individuals deemed attractive by the existing community. At the end of 2009, the website deleted the accounts of about 5000 users, based on weight gain over the holiday season. This website is not alone, however, in its focus on appearance. Other online dating sites such as Darwin Dating include similar criteria in their membership requirements. Judging people on the basis of biology is not that unique in the sense that Mensa was founded many years ago to bring together a community of intellectuals. A person has to score within or above the ninety-eighth percentile on an intelligence test to qualify for membership in Mensa. Rejection from these sorts of exclusive communities sends the most disconfirming of messages because we cannot easily change our physical or intellectual selves. Yet this sort of rejection can have an impact on both self-esteem and self-efficacy.

Other websites are more subtle but equally toxic in their implications for self-concept. A website called Chatroulette, for example, connects users to live video chats with random strangers. The site does not contain options for filtering out "the rude, the nude, and the outright bizarre."[115] Users do not pick or choose the connections. In essence, Chatroulette involves channel surfing with humans, and the disconnections can be as fast as the connections. Either party can click for the next random connection; no explanations or "goodbyes" occur. All of the formalities and courtesies of face-to-face interactions, or even usual web interactions, go by the wayside. Appearance becomes very important because all the users see initially is a webcam image of the other person. A fast click is an obvious rejection of that image.

Cyberbullying has become a common phenomenon, especially among young people. This form of malicious communications has the potential to destroy self-image and feelings of self-worth.[116] As discussed earlier, some cases lead to devastating consequences, including loss of life.

Variations across Cultures

When reaching conclusions about self-concept, we find that variations occur across cultures. A study involving 750 respondents in five European cities, for example, found cross-cultural differences in how people think about health and beauty. When asked to choose the photograph that was closest to their own ideal self-image, respondents in different countries chose different images.[117] Moreover, another study showed that the viewing of idealized female or male bodies had no impact on the self-esteem of Chinese female or male subjects. In fact, male participants in the study showed *higher* self-evaluations after looking at the idealized images of other men.[118]

Even within Western cultures, differences exist between mainstream and minority groups. In North America, African American girls report higher self-esteem than Caucasian and Hispanic girls.[119] Some researchers speculate that the higher levels of self-esteem may come from African American girls' rejection of negative images in the media.[120] A study of ninth and tenth grade students found, for example, that black females do not typically compare themselves to white female models in mainstream media.[121] Other studies have also found that black women tend to disregard media figures as a reference group. The images of black women that appear on television or in the movies are often not ones these women would choose to copy since media tend to depict black women as either sexually permissive or well-meaning but domineering mother figures.[122] For these and other reasons, black women do not seem to internalize the negative images in the media to the same extent as white women. Consequently, they experience less of a gap between their actual and ideal body images.[123] Some say these findings explain the healthier body image, higher self-esteem, and lower incidence of eating disorders in black women.[124]

REAL SELF: CHALLENGES IN DISCOVERING THE INNER SELF

Although psychologists refer to the "real" or "actual" self, we have to wonder whether we can ever completely escape the boundaries of self-perception, looking-glass self, and idealized self. We may know our height and weight, hair colour, gender, liking or disliking of particular foods, level of success at school, how we react to stress, and what attracts others to us. But we will probably never know all parts of our multifaceted personalities.[125] The exception may be members of minority racial and ethnic groups, first-generation citizens, and gay and lesbian individuals, who are forced to come to terms with the fact that the "real me" has many parts.[126]

> "I am afraid to show you who I really am, because if I show you who I really am, you might not like it—and that's all I got."
> SABRINA WARD HARRISON

It is also likely that people with high self-esteem are better able to access and feel comfortable displaying the "real self." They are willing to stand up for—and defend—themselves when necessary. In general, they think well of others and expect the same in return. Studies have found that these individuals feel comfortable in situations that are often uncomfortable for those with lower levels of self-esteem. For example, their performance does not suffer when others observe them closely. They work harder under managers with high standards, and they are at ease with people they consider to be superior in some way. They tend to evaluate their workplace performance in favourable terms. The opposite applies to people with low self-esteem, who are probably also more likely to protect and hide the "real self" from view.[127] For a discussion of how we seek to influence how others see us, see Chapter 4 on identity and impression management.

CHALLENGES IN MEASURING SELF-CONCEPT ACROSS CULTURES

Some say that we need to move away from Caucasian male–dominated ideas about self-concept, which are tied to values such as individual achievement.[128] When we assess self-esteem on the basis of individual accomplishments, Caucasian males have the highest levels of self-esteem out of all the racial groups. But when broader measures are used, African American and Hispanic adolescent males may have the highest levels of self-esteem.[129]

With the exception of African American women, women in general tend to score lower than men on almost all measures of self-esteem. The lowest self-esteem scores come from Asian and Native American women. Asians and Native Americans get higher scores than others, however, on the relational dimension; and women in general score higher than men on the relational dimension.[130] (By *relational dimension*, we refer to measures that concern how we handle relationships. Typically, women tend to be more relationship-oriented in their behaviours, and men tend to be more instrumental or task-oriented.)

Generalizing across genders and cultures can be hazardous when some of the tools used to measure self-esteem have built-in biases. The Japanese, for instance, believe that modesty is a virtue. Therefore, when they respond to explicit questions about self-esteem, they describe their self-concept in modest terms and score middle-of-the-road on measures of self-esteem. If you do not take culture into account, you might think that the Japanese have a lower sense of self than Canadians. In reality, however, researchers have been unable to agree on questions such as "Do the Japanese demonstrate lower self-esteem than Canadians?"[131] The answer is "We don't know."[132]

SELF-ENHANCEMENT The tendency to pay more attention to information that supports a positive view of the self.

SELF-CRITICISM The tendency to pay more attention to information that supports a negative view of the self.

SELF-SERVING BIAS The tendency to credit our successes to internal or personal factors and our failures to external or situational factors.

INDIVIDUALISM Focus on individual needs and goals.

COLLECTIVISM Focus on group needs and goals.

Cultural variations exist in areas such as **self-enhancement** and **self-criticism**. Self-enhancement is common in many Western cultures. For example, over half of American undergraduate students participating in one study said that they would rank in the top 10 per cent on "interpersonal sensitivity."[133] Other studies with American adults show the same tendency to overestimate positive attributes.[134] Such immodest statements would not show up in Japanese studies, where self-criticism tends to be the norm.[135]

North Americans are also more likely to display **self-serving bias**. When we succeed in the workplace, for example, we are likely to credit our success to internal qualities such as intelligence, talents in a particular area, or expertise. When we fail, we are likely to place the blame on external factors such as interference from others, incompetency on the part of co-workers, or lack of support from our supervisor. Sometimes we blame our failures on situational factors like unreasonable deadlines or poor economic conditions. An analysis of 23 studies conducted in Japan, on the other hand, failed to find a single instance of any self-serving patterns. Japanese participants explained their successes in terms of luck or hard work and their failures in terms of lack of ability or lack of talent.[136]

Cultural approaches to self-concept undoubtedly reflect cultural views of the importance of the individual versus the community. Most Western cultures, for example, value **individualism** and independence. The culture of Japan, by contrast, is **collectivist** in nature; thus, Japanese people tend to value others' needs over their own. Consider the following findings, which illustrate this difference. When asked about whether they expected more positive or negative events to befall themselves or their siblings, individuals of Japanese ancestry anticipated more negative future events for themselves and fewer for their brothers and sisters. Americans of European ancestry, on the other hand, expected more positive events for themselves and more negative events for their brothers and sisters.[137] From a collectivist perspective, then, it seems that the practice of putting oneself down and bolstering others does not necessarily reveal anything about self-esteem. Rather, it indicates a stronger interest in the welfare of the collective than in the welfare of the individual. See the "Human Diversity" box on preserving self-esteem through **face work** for another example of such cross-cultural differences.

FACE WORK Politeness strategies aimed at making other people feel better about themselves.

TIPS FOR ACCEPTING AND MOVING BEYOND SELF IN COMMUNICATION

Building upon the previous discussion, the following recommendations suggest how to confirm and reinforce a positive self-image.

Whenever you or someone else questions one part of your identity, think about some of your other identities. If your physical self appears to be threatened, look to your academic, social, or emotional selves for confirmation of your value. Try out alternative ideal identities; evidence suggests that practice helps people to integrate positive aspects of these identities into their real selves.

If you are operating from a negative script, rewrite it. Be sure to delete any outdated information from the script. Your high school self may be quite different from your university self. Acknowledge the potential for growth in yourself and others.

humanDIVERSITY

Preserving Self-Esteem through Face-Work Strategies

A young model, flown to Japan for a cover shoot with the most celebrated rock star in Japan, had a puzzling experience. Repeatedly during the photo shoot, the makeup and hair artists complimented the young woman in the most elaborate terms. At the same time, they apologized repeatedly for her having to do the photo shoot with such an unattractive man. In actual fact, the Japanese singer was not unattractive at all; and his celebrity was well established. The young woman, who was relatively new to modelling at that time, did not understand what was happening. Why would the makeup team put down the young and popular singer, one of their own? Had she known more about Japanese culture, she would have understood. The Japanese believe that self-effacement (putting oneself down) and self-criticism have a positive social value. In a similar way, the Japanese would say "I am there and you are here," whereas Canadians would say "I am here and you are there."

The term for this kind of cultural behaviour is *face work*—politeness strategies that make our interactions more pleasant and our words less harsh or threatening. Face work can take many forms. Some cultures show politeness by complimenting or putting more focus on the other person. Others show politeness through personal rituals that precede business transactions. Whereas many English-speaking people value directness or bluntness in speech, saying exactly what we think, many other cultural groups avoid "baldness" of speech. Instead of saying "she forgot to sign the paper," someone from South America might say "the paper was left unsigned." All face-work strategies aim to help individuals to preserve their dignity and self-esteem. See Chapter 6 for further discussion of cultural differences and face-work strategies.

© Dean Mitchell/iStockphoto

Check to see if your actions suggest low self-esteem. Look, for example, at your choice of partners. Do your partners display high or low self-esteem? If you have been choosing people with low self-esteem or avoiding people with high self-esteem, you have probably been setting yourself up for failure. Get out of the negative relationships and look for more positive situations and partners. Periods of transition in your life offer the best opportunities for change. When you are in a better relationship, be open to accepting and giving positive messages.

Engage in positive self-talk if some aspects of your self-concept appear to be threatened. Many books have been written in recent years on the power of positive thinking—the idea that we attract positive energy to us when we think positively and negative energy when we think negatively. In an interview with a CTV commentator, 2010 Olympic champion Alexandre Bilodeau said that he always engaged in positive self-talk as he waited for the signal to begin his run in the men's mogul event, repeating key encouraging words to himself.

Set realistic goals for yourself. Are you striving for an ideal self that is unrealistic, obsessing about weight loss or physical characteristics that you cannot easily control? Do you give in to the "myth of perfection" promoted by the media? If so, look elsewhere for upward social comparisons. Identify "real" people in your personal, social, educational, and organizational environments to use as role models. Notice that even the most popular, attractive, and interesting people have strengths and weaknesses. If you tend to look downward, on the other hand, for social comparisons, you may be setting your goals too low.

If your ego is too "noisy," aim for balance in self-concept; otherwise, your friends may go elsewhere for company. Many have labelled Generation Y as the "me" generation, a cohort of youth born after 1982 with scripts that focus on egotism. A number of studies have focussed in recent years on "quieting the ego." Whereas the noisier ego tends to tune out people in a manner similar to tuning out background noise, the quieter ego shows greater interest in—and empathy for—others. The quieter ego recognizes the strengths and weaknesses of the self but also acknowledges that the self is "ultimately a construction or story."[138] The noisier ego attempts, by way of contrast, to defend the story of self. Too much concern for the ego can result in a selfish approach to relationships, whereas too quiet an ego can result in our not being ourselves. Most researchers agree that some balance is required to achieve the best state of being in relation to others. If you are unsure how to relate to others in positive ways, look to those who are most respected in your reference groups or seek expert advice from one of the many self-help books that focus on self-esteem books.

Celebrate and learn from differences. Rumi, a thirteenth-century Persian poet and mystic, once said: "Out beyond ideas of wrongdoing and rightdoing, there is a field. I'll meet you there." In order to meet others in a place that is mutually comfortable, we must understand that differences do not threaten our individual or cultural identities. I am not right and you are not wrong; we are just different.

Believe in positive outcomes. Bestselling author and motivational speaker Wayne Dyer stresses the importance of believing in positive outcomes when he says, "When you change the way you look at things, the things you look at change."[139] Like Aboriginal Australians, he believes that we have the power to "dream" our future into existence. In his 2012 book *Wishes Fulfilled: Mastering the Art of Manifesting*, he says that "everything that now exists was once imagined. So if you want something to exist, you must first imagine it."[140] He argues that positives attract positives, and negatives attract negatives; so if you expect positive happenings in your life, they are more likely to happen. This philosophy reflects the advice of many earlier writers and leaders such as Mahatma Gandhi of India, who stressed the active nature of positive thinking when he said, "We must become the change we want to see."

SUMMARY

This chapter has focussed on the importance of developing a positive self-concept, accepting and acting on confirming messages, and encouraging positive self-concept in others. We have looked at how we create, validate, and revise the scripts that guide our lives. Internal voice plays a significant role in how we see and position ourselves in the world. The views of others (external voices) also influence our self-concept and self-efficacy—that is, the extent to which we believe we can accomplish the goals we set for ourselves. Family, romantic partners, peers, teachers and coaches, caregivers and health care providers, and workplace colleagues and supervisors all have a role to play in our personal scripts.

The media also have a strong impact, especially with regard to self-image—and by extension, self-esteem. In our earliest years of life, we learned about ourselves and others primarily through direct experience and face-to-face interactions. Today many of these interactions involve traditional and social media. While these media have much to offer in the way of information and entertainment value, they also carry risks. This chapter has discussed the impact of unrealistic depictions of body image in fashion magazines, advertisements, and TV shows. Tips and recommendations for how to build a more positive self-concept conclude the chapter.

REVIEW QUESTIONS

1. How can internal and external voices influence each other in constructing and maintaining self-concept? Use illustrations to support your arguments.
2. How do the concepts of self-esteem and self-efficacy differ from each other? Has your sense of self-esteem or self-efficacy changed over time? If so, identify events that could have contributed to the changes.
3. Do you agree that women have less confidence when it comes to applying for jobs and promotions? If so, why?
4. What are some challenges of measuring self-concept across cultures? Can you think of any challenges not discussed in the chapter?
5. Of the eight chapter recommendations concerning affirmation and reinforcement of the self through communication, which ones are likely to work best? Why?
6. Do you agree that positives attract positives and negatives attract negatives? Support your arguments with examples from your experience.
7. This chapter discussed media influence on body image. Can you suggest other sources of comment on body image that have the potential to affect our self-concept?

SUGGESTED ACTIVITIES

1. List at least two qualities about yourself under each of the four faces of self-concept: *self-image* (how you see yourself), *looking-glass self* (how you think others see you), *ideal self* (how you would like to be seen), and *real self* (how you actually are). Examples of terms that you might use to describe the four selves are *friendly*, *nervous*, *dependable*, *shy*, *honest*, *motivated*, *outgoing*, and *intelligent*. After you have listed your qualities, discuss the ideas in small groups. Are the descriptions similar or different for your four selves? Do they change, depending on contexts and relationships?

2. Scan fashion magazines to identify examples of what the media depicts as *desirable* female and male bodies. Using the pictures you find, create a collage. Present and discuss your collages in class. Do you think the images are *idealized*? Do you think the standards of beauty, set by the media, are realistic? Do these kinds of images have any impact on your own self-image? How do you feel about them?
3. Describe lead female characters in your three favourite TV shows. Do they conform to the media ideal for "perfect" female bodies? If so, do you feel any pressure to conform after viewing the shows?
4. Identify three male characters in your favourite TV shows. Do they conform to a media ideal of what constitutes the "perfect" male body? Do you think that men feel the same pressure as women to look like the models or actors appearing in advertisements, films, and TV shows?
5. Interview individuals from three different cultures. You can conduct the interview in person, over the telephone, or by email. Ask each person to describe the physical characteristics of an ideal female and male in their respective cultures. Do these descriptions vary from culture to culture?
6. Spend 15 minutes on the website Chatroulette. Be prepared to describe to your classmates what happened. How did you feel about the interactions? Comfortable or uncomfortable? Why?

CHAPTER 3

Perception of Others

CHAPTER OUTLINE

learning OBJECTIVES

- To understand the nature and characteristics of perception
- To understand how perception influences how we see others
- To learn how the characteristics of perception can have an impact on our communication with others
- To gain insights into how to apply what we know about perception to our interactions at home and in social and workplace settings

forSTARTERS

Cultural Diversity and Aboriginal Perceptions of Time[1]

A typical psychiatric assessment relies on mainstream cultural conventions. The client goes to the office of the psychiatrist at a specific time. The psychiatrist asks a series of questions that move from past to present: family history, personal history, and present situation. If the doctor wants to see how well the client can remember material, she might ask the person to list the days of the week or month backwards. Having a set amount of time for the interview, she will try to keep the appointment moving; and the tests will have time limits. At the end of the appointment, the client will receive directions on how to take certain medications or perform other actions to improve future mental health.

Problems can arise when psychiatrists follow these same procedures in interviews with people from many different cultural backgrounds. For example, individuals from certain cultures do not like to commit to time schedules that are not flexible enough to take family needs into account. They may not want to go to the office of the health care worker—an environment they see as cold, unfamiliar, and unsafe. Whether from shyness or embarrassment, they may not want to respond to some questions, in which case they might say, "We can talk about it some other time." In other situations, they may want more time to think about their answers.

By looking at differences in how people perceive time, we can learn a great deal about issues associated with the culture-bound nature of time. Most Westerners, including Canadians, see time as linear, moving on a one-way path from past to present to future. Like many Indigenous peoples, however, Aboriginal Australians interpret time in a different way. They see people as standing in the middle of "time circles."

The time circles surround the individual like hula hoops of different sizes, and he or she positions events into one of the circles. The most important events appear in the time circles that are closest to the individual. Those least important appear in the outer time circles. Conceived in this way, the wedding of a close relative might be near in time, and a scheduled medical appointment might be far in time. This situation could be true even if the medical appointment is happening next week and the wedding next month. So if a person must decide between helping a relative choose flowers for a wedding and attending a doctor's appointment, the person might arrive an hour late for the doctor's appointment or might not go at all.

Like Aboriginal Australians, many Aboriginal Canadians do not believe that time schedules should dictate our daily lives. Rather what is important should determine what we do in any given day. An Aboriginal saying goes as follows: "It is not important *when* things happen, it is important *that* they happen." Consider the following fictitious conversation between an Australian social worker and her Aboriginal client.

Social worker: Can you be available next week for an appointment? Say 10:00 on Thursday?

INTRODUCTION

PERCEPTION The process of sensing, interpreting, and reacting to the physical world.

What is the nature of **perception**? How does perception influence how we see others? How can we apply what we know about perception to our interactions with others? A number of studies have found that perception is learned and backward looking; culture bound and racially biased; selective and self-serving; spontaneous, largely unconscious, and value driven; relative and context bound; mood dependent; and completion seeking. All of these characteristics affect our perception of—and interaction with—others. In this chapter, we will examine each of these characteristics of perception, along with their

Client: I will try.
Social worker: You have another appointment at that time?
Client: I don't know.
Social worker: Perhaps we should set a different time? How about Friday morning?
Client: That might work.
Social worker: What is a good time for you?
Client: I can't say.
Social worker (increasingly frustrated): Could you tell me when you think you will be available next week?
Client: Next Thursday morning.
Social worker: Good. What time?
Client: 10:00 or thereabouts.
Social worker: You said you couldn't be available at 10:00.
Client (also frustrated): How can I know what will be happening next week? My friend might come by my place or I might need to run an errand for my wife.

Obviously the Aboriginal client has placed the meeting with the social worker in one of his outer time circles. Because Aboriginal cultures tend to place family and community above self, an Aboriginal person might cancel even an important medical appointment to attend to the needs of family or friends.

Many Aboriginal people also tend to downplay the importance of planning for the future. For health care professionals, this disregard for the future can be problematic. Aboriginal people may not see the need, for example, to follow therapies that can prevent illness in the future such as a diet to lower cholesterol. Since their cultures focus on the here and now, as opposed to the future, they may not appreciate the importance of correcting behaviours with long-term risk factors (e.g., smoking, drinking, or eating a poor diet).

Health care workers who follow culturally sensitive practices will get a better response from Aboriginal people than those who stick strictly to mainstream practices. Rather than asking Aboriginal clients to place events in the past, present, or future, for example, a psychiatrist might use culturally relevant benchmarks such as hunting season, summer or winter solstice, National Aboriginal Day, or a traditional feast. In the same way, psychiatrists can improve the odds that their Aboriginal clients will stay with a treatment program if they link medication times to culturally meaningful events in the day. For example, a psychiatrist might direct an Aboriginal client to take medication at a time when the client would be checking on an elderly relative—not necessarily at mealtime, since many Aboriginal people have less structured routines than mainstream society.

Testing will not involve stopwatches, since Aboriginal people do not accept the importance of completing a task within a specified time frame. In addition, psychiatrists may allow for periods of silence after questions in order to accommodate preferences in communication. A psychiatrist or other health care worker may also need to focus on the immediate (rather than delayed) benefits of lifestyle changes. They may need to emphasize the link between present behaviours and future health outcomes. Finally, the medical practitioner may need to consult extensively with family and community members, since many will potentially participate in the care of the patient.

As you read this chapter, consider the following questions. How do some of the basic characteristics of perception (e.g., its culture-bound, racially biased, and value-driven nature) affect our interactions with people whose cultural backgrounds differ from our own? Do Canada's education, health, and legal systems recognize the needs of Aboriginal and other culturally diverse groups? To what extent does stereotyping characterize our interactions with people from other cultures? In what ways could some of the strategies discussed in this chapter apply to our interactions with such people?

implications for communication. We will also look at strategies and tools for increasing our awareness and controlling our perception biases.

NATURE AND CHARACTERISTICS OF PERCEPTION

As infants, we learn to organize information received through the senses of sight, touch, smell, sound, and taste. Most of the time, the visual is most important to us. Our eye is

© Andres Rodriguez/Alamy

drawn to whatever we hear, touch, or smell.[2] Experience and research tell us, however, that no one sense operates on its own.[3] For example, the look, touch, and smell of food interact to influence our perception of taste.[4] More surprisingly, research reveals that sound also interacts with taste.[5]

A study conducted at the University of Oxford, England, examined the influence of background noise on how we experience food.[6] As noise levels increase, people describe foods as being less salty and less sweet. A greater sense of taste returns when the noise levels decline. Perhaps this association between loud noise and poor taste explains why travellers on planes and trains often complain about the tastelessness of the foods they eat while travelling. Some bars and restaurants have discovered that people drink more and faster when the music is louder and faster. Fast music also encourages people to eat quickly, contributing to faster turnover in tables. Slow music, on the other hand, encourages diners to linger and to eat in a more leisurely way. Ocean soundtracks can enhance people's appreciation of seafood, and the heavy metal music of Axl Rose can make people taste a cabernet sauvignon as heavier and more robust. Top chefs and food companies around the world are paying attention to these and other findings about how our sense of taste relates to our other senses.

In the following sections, we will consider in greater depth how what we see, feel, smell, hear, and taste influence how we experience the world around us. More specifically, we will look at how the characteristics of perception—the tendency of perception to be learned and backward looking; culture bound and racially biased; selective and self-serving; spontaneous, largely unconscious, and value driven; relative and context bound; mood dependent; and completion seeking—influence our interpersonal interactions.

Perception Is Learned and Backward Looking

This section explores the learned and backward-looking nature of perception, as well as implications of these characteristics for interpersonal communication.

Perception Is Learned

All of the senses have a learned dimension.[7] Consider the learning that occurs with the sense of sight. In a well-known experiment, which occurred in the early part of the twentieth century, a researcher named George Stratton constructed some special goggles that not only distorted his vision but also inverted everything that he saw (i.e., turned the world upside down). He wore the goggles day and night for an extended period of time. By the end of the orientation period, he had adapted to his altered vision so well that he was able to fly an airplane and ride a motorcycle while wearing the goggles. At the completion of the experiment, Stratton removed the goggles to find that his world without the goggles now appeared to be distorted. He had to retrain his brain to organize the incoming visual information in a way that put the world right again.[8] Our visual systems are programmed to recognize learned patterns.[9]

Just as we learn sight by experience, we also learn touch by experience. To illustrate the point, ask another person to close her eyes. After she closes her eyes, touch her arm *lightly* with varying combinations of fingers (e.g., three fingers from one hand and two fingers from the second hand) placed *simultaneously* on the skin. Ask her to tell you how many fingers you have placed on her arm. Repeat the experiment several times. (In order for the experiment to work, all fingers must touch the skin at the same time.) On the first couple of tries, she will probably not be able to tell the difference between one, four, five, or more fingers on the skin. That is, you can place one finger on her arm, and she might think you are touching her with four or five fingers. Or you can put seven fingers on her skin and she might think you are touching her with one or two fingers. After several tries, however, she will learn to discriminate. Similarly, a person who has learned Braille can discriminate between various combinations of six raised dots, representing the letters of the alphabet, placed about an eighth of an inch apart.

"Nothing is in the understanding, which was not first perceived by some of the senses."
JOHN LOCKE

How we perceive taste, sound, and smell is also learned. Professional wine tasters, for example, develop an advanced sense of taste that allows them to judge the quality of wines. In judging the wines, they learn to be aware of all the taste zones of their tongue (Figure 3.1). Regarding sound, we learn to identify different voices as belonging to different people, to tell the difference between the sound of a loon and the sound of a robin, and to recognize when a baby's cry means he is hungry as opposed to tired. Further, with practice we can learn to tell the difference between sounds that are at first indistinguishable.[10] Finally, we learn to react in certain ways to the smell of different foods, perfumes, or even body odours. We also learn to associate smells with certain people, places, or things.

Culture has a large influence on whether our reactions to what we see, feel, taste, hear, and smell are positive or negative, as much of our learning comes from our cultural experiences. Some Middle Easterners regard the eyes of sheep, for example, as a delicacy; and quite a few Scots like tripe (the lining of a cow's stomach). Many natives of Louisiana consider alligator to be a delicacy, and people in Thailand and China enjoy insects coated with chocolate. Unappealing, you say? Well, it is all in the mouth (eye and nose) of the beholder.

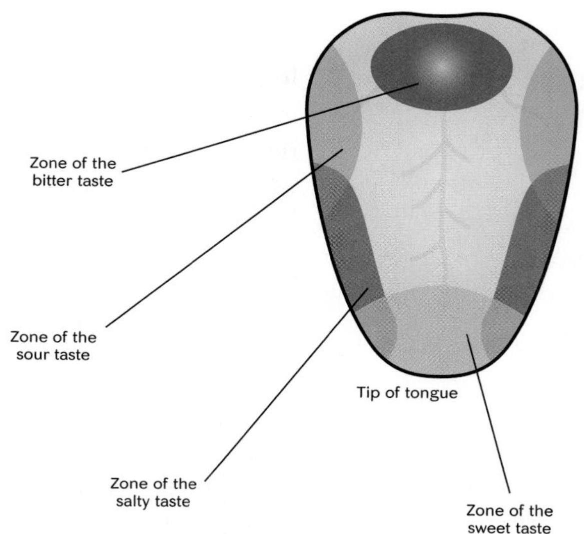

FIGURE 3.1 **Taste zones of the tongue.**

SOURCE: https://www.healthtap.com/#topics/causes-for-loss-of-taste.

Perception Is Backward Looking

The learned nature of perception means that it is backward looking in its interpretation of the present. We constantly anticipate the past. That is, we see what we expect to see.[11] In a classic experiment, Jerome Bruner and Leo Postman found that participants in their study failed to notice obvious irregularities in a deck of playing cards.[12] When presented with a deck that included a red queen of spades or a

black king of hearts, for example, they saw the expected colours. They saw the red queen of spades as black and the black king of hearts as red.

Horror films such as *The Others* (2001) are able to succeed in building plot lines based on deception because audiences have learned perceptual sets about horror films. That is, people tend to respond to horror films in predictable ways, based on past encounters with these sorts of films. In *The Others*, a single mother and her two children grow increasingly fearful that they are living in a haunted house with servants whom they suspect to be the living dead. We follow the movie, convinced that we know the familiar plot line. We ignore many signs such as the failure of the children to respond to sunlight (despite having a life-threatening allergy to this light), the ability of the mother to communicate with her dead husband, the characters' old-fashioned dress, and their outdated way of speaking. Our expectations lead us to suspect the wrong child of being the ghost. In short, we ignore many signs that could lead to a different conclusion about what is going on. In the end, however, we realize that our perceptions have led us to the wrong assumptions. We have been duped. Yes, the house is haunted; but no, the haunted are not the ones we believe them to be. If you watch the film a second time, you see many signs that you did not see on the first viewing. You approach the film from a different perceptual set—a framework that includes what you learned the first time you watched the film.

"The eye sees only what the mind is prepared to comprehend."
HENRI BERGSON

In 1915, cartoonist W.E. Hill conceived a well-known optical illusion that demonstrates this same principle. Tongue in cheek, Hill titled the drawing *My Wife and My Mother-in-Law*. Prior expectations lead the viewer to see either a young woman or an old hag. Numerous studies of eyewitness accounts also demonstrate how past learning influences our interpretation of present events.[13]

Implications for Communication

In social interactions as in other situations, our expectations are grounded in past experience. Even when we want to learn something new or to see someone in a new light, we use old frameworks to interpret and file the information. In *The Act of Creation*, Arthur Koestler argues that innovations often come from people in dream states or outside of a particular field of study because they are not bound by existing ways of thinking.[14] The more we know about a subject, the more expertise we acquire, the more difficult it becomes to think "outside of the box."

As audience reactions to *The Others* and other similarly deceptive films demonstrate, we pick out what we regard as significant detail in any event and interpret the information in the light of what we already know, believe, and expect to see. Letting our expectations influence our perception of others can be problematic, however, when we rely on **stereotypes**.[15] We will develop this topic in more detail in the section on the completion-seeking nature of perception.

STEREOTYPES
Popularly held beliefs about a type of person or group of persons that do not take individual differences into account.

Perception Is Culture Bound and Racially Biased

The idea of a cultural and racial bias in perception has close connections with the learned and backward-looking nature of perception. A classic 1929 study of Trobriand

Islanders found, for example, that the islanders saw children as resembling their fathers, even when the children looked much more like their mothers. The Trobriand society had influenced the islanders to see their children in this way.[16] Like most people, the islanders looked for (and found) cues that fit with what they had been conditioned to expect.[17] This section discusses the culture-bound and racially biased nature of perception, as well as implications of these characteristics for communication. To learn more about a Harvard University study into the unconscious cultural and racial biases of people, see the "Human Diversity" box.

Perception Is Culture Bound

As illustrated in the "For Starters" box at the beginning of this chapter, Aboriginal people often experience time in a way that is different from how most members of mainstream cultures experience time.[18] Because they do not see time as linear, they see the past as closely woven into the present. Daily conversations, for example, might give equal attention and importance to recent and long-past events. An Aboriginal person might speak of the death of a family member or respected elder that happened many years ago as if the event occurred the previous day or week. He or she might also become extremely agitated when referencing this crucial life event. Consider the following example of a conversation between a police officer and an Aboriginal man who has placed a complaint against a neighbour.

Police officer: What is the nature of your complaint, Samuel?
Samuel: Willy took my best hunting rifle off the back of my truck. He won't give it back.
Police officer: Willy?
Samuel (pointing to the house next door): Yes, my neighbour. He can't be trusted.

humanDIVERSITY

Hidden Biases

Since the early 1980s, Mahzarin Banaji and Anthony Greenwald have been studying how unconscious biases influence the decisions we make in our everyday lives. These two psychologists currently help to run Harvard University's ongoing Project Implicit, a collection of studies that examine unconscious thoughts and feelings. In their book *Blindspot: Hidden Biases of Good People*, Banaji and Greenwald argue that hidden biases influence many of our everyday decisions and choices. These biases have an impact on our hiring and promotion policies, our interactions with colleagues in the workplace, and our perceptions of people accused of having committed crimes.

The biases surface in often subtle ways. For example, a doctor might pay more attention to the complaint of a man than to the complaint of a woman. He or she might show more attentiveness to the questions of a highly educated patient than to the questions of a patient with limited education. A sales clerk might go first to someone whose dress, mannerisms, or colour of skin suggests a dominant group. It is not so much that we are likely to harm someone from another group, Banaji says, as that we are likely to try harder to help someone with whom we identify.

The Harvard studies have revealed some unexpected results. For example, over 40 per cent of African American respondents show a pro-white bias. Workplace biases lean in favour of tall over short people, extroverts over introverts, slim people over heavy people, and men over women. When asked whether the election of Barack Obama was surprising, Banaji replied, "Yes, but don't forget he was running against a woman and an elderly man who's short."[19]

To see how you rate on a four-category test for racial bias, log into Harvard's Project Implicit (https://implicit.harvard.edu/implicit) and prepare yourself for some potentially surprising results.

Police officer: No? Why is that?
Samuel: He ran off with my Sheila.
Police officer: Sheila? Is that Sheila Sitter? Willy's wife?
Samuel: Yes, you know her?
Police officer: We've met. But Sheila is 50 years old. They've been married for at least thirty years. Are you saying that you don't trust your cousin today because of something he did more than thirty years ago?
Samuel: Darned right. Haven't hunted or fished with him in 33 years. Now what about my rifle?

In the above case, Samuel refers to an event that occurred 33 years earlier, when Sheila was 17 years old. Yet the event is still unsettling to him, and it has forever coloured his view of Willy. Samuel perceives the event as timeless, stitched into today's fabric even though it happened many years earlier. Because of the close connection between the past and the present, events in some Aboriginal cultures have no end point.

BREADTH OF PERCEPTUAL FIELD The amount of information we take into our visual or other perceptual systems.

Studies have found that East Asians differ from Westerners in areas such as the size or **breadth of their perceptual fields**.[20] To understand this concept, think about what you see when you look through a set of binoculars. You focus on a very narrow field, perhaps a bird building a nest in a tree. If you remove the binoculars, however, your field of vision expands to include much more information—the tree in which the bird is building its nest, the surrounding forest and fields, and the backdrop of the sky. Extending this idea to include cultural norms, an East Asian entering a banquet hall during a party might notice the arrangement of tables, the buffet area in the back, the dance floor in the front, waiters moving about the room, and people engaged in conversation—that is, the room as a whole. A Westerner, on the other hand, might quickly focus on the set-up of band equipment at the front of the room, several band members tuning their instruments, and the size of the dance floor—a much tighter view.

OPTICAL COMMUNITIES A social group that shares a similar view of the world.

Different historical periods also create "**optical communities**"—groups of people who see the world differently from those in other historical periods.[21] If you look at paintings from different historical periods, you can see how perceptions of the human body changed over time. In some periods such as the Classical period of ancient Greece, artists focussed on the anatomy of the body, often creating lifelike representations of full-figured women and muscular men. In other periods, artists depicted the human body in less detail or rejected realism completely in favour of the psychological. The distorted faces in van Gogh's paintings illustrate the focus on the psychological. Scientists are also influenced by the time periods in which they work. The most popular theories of the day affect how they interpret the results of their work.[22]

Perception Is Racially Biased

OWN-RACE BIAS The idea that accuracy increases when we identify specific members of our own race.

Own-race bias refers to the idea that we are more accurate when asked to identify specific members of our own race than when asked to identify specific members of another race. In fact, we are more than 1.4 times more likely to make correct same-race than other-race identifications. Similarly, we are 1.56 times more likely to make a false identification with someone from another race. Because of own-race bias, eyewitness accounts are considerably less reliable when we must identify suspects from a race other than our own.[23]

Innocence projects in Canada, the United Kingdom, Australia, New Zealand, Ireland, the Netherlands, and the United States have confirmed the problems that come from own-race and other forms of bias. These projects provide assistance to individuals who claim to have been wrongly convicted of a serious offence. According to American statistics, three out of four wrongful convictions stem from eyewitness accounts. In 2011, the American Innocence Project found that 77 per cent of their first 225 investigations revealed a dependence on eyewitness accounts. Many of the convictions involved members of minority races.[24]

> "We don't see things as they are. We see them as we are."
>
> ANAÏS NIN

Despite the problems associated with both line-up and photo identifications, jurors place a lot of credibility in eyewitness accounts.[25] Jurors also tend to rely on the confidence of the eyewitnesses, but a highly confident eyewitness is as likely to be wrong as a less confident eyewitness.[26] The value placed on eyewitness accounts poses a particular threat to Western court systems since we rely so heavily on visual content.

Implications for Communication

Despite the difficulties, we can overcome own-race bias. In a series of four experiments, researchers asked subjects to think about a time when they had treated someone from another race unfairly. Afterwards the subjects responded to a series of faces of individuals from that racial group, as well as faces of people from their own race. They did not have time to think about their choices. Encouragingly, the responses showed that the participants had discarded their negative stereotypes of people from the other race.[27]

In a second study, participants made a conscious effort to avoid stereotyping when they interacted with members of an **out-group**. Afterwards their responses showed less stereotyping. As in the previous case, the participants did not have time to plan their responses. Thus, with the right intentions and efforts, we may be able to discard our stereotypes and to see strangers as individuals—not just as members of a larger group to which they may belong.[28] To understand more about how misperceptions of new immigrants affect their Canadian experience, go to the "Human Diversity" box.

OUT-GROUP A group of which one is not a member.

humanDIVERSITY

(Mis)Perceptions of New Immigrants

Each year, Canada welcomes over two hundred thousand new immigrants from many different countries. These immigrants come from diverse cultural backgrounds, not always recognized or understood by those charged with overseeing and protecting their welfare. Consequently, misperceptions on the part of educational, health care, and social workers sometimes create obstacles to the successful integration of these new immigrants into Canadian society.

Children of new immigrants often have difficulty integrating into the schools they attend and adjusting to life in Canada. Many face language barriers, and most struggle to adjust to new and unfamiliar cultural norms and practices. Many refugee children also carry memories of traumas they and their families experienced in their home countries. Sometimes social workers fail to take culture and background into account when they work with immigrant youth. They may associate frowning or angry children with bad mothering. Sometimes they even recommend removal of the children from their homes. When the mothers realize they are perceived as incompetent, they feel alienated and resentful. In their minds, they had struggled—often in extreme circumstances—to provide a better life for their children. Now they are victims of a system that does not recognize their values or sacrifices.[29]

Perception Is Selective and Self-Serving

SELECTIVE PERCEPTION The process by which we see and retain certain kinds of information while ignoring or discarding other kinds of information.

In order to get by in our everyday lives without becoming overwhelmed, we must rely on **selective perception.**[30] Many stimuli compete for our attention on an ongoing basis.[31] For example, when we are standing on a street corner waiting for a bus, visuals competing for our attention might include bumper-to-bumper traffic, colourful displays in store windows, advertisements taped to light posts, and the clothing of people walking past on the street. Sounds could include honking from cars, the conversations of passersby, or the whir of drilling at a construction site. We might smell roasting nuts at a concession stand, odours coming from a flooded sewer, or cinnamon and vanilla from a nearby candle shop. Because we are bombarded by approximately two million bits of information a second, we must disregard a great deal of what we receive. The challenge is to retain the significant since we are only able to process 134 bits of information a second.[32]

The experience of a man who regained his sight after thirty years of blindness illustrates that knowing *what to retain* and *what to discard* is far more important than grasping every detail of our environments:

> When I could see again, objects literally hurled themselves at me. One of the things a normal person knows from long habit is what not to look at. Things that don't matter, or that confuse, are simply shut out of their seeing minds. I had forgotten this, and tried to see everything at once; consequently I saw almost nothing.[33]

LOAD-INDUCED BLINDNESS Inability to see as a result of information overload in the visual field.

As the preceding example illustrates, **load-induced blindness** can occur when we receive more visual information than we can process.[34]

In retaining what is significant, we tend to filter out information that does not serve our needs. If we have just purchased a new car, we might disregard commercials that promote alternative choices. We are more likely to notice and remember the commercials that reinforce our decision. The following discussion considers both the selective and **self-serving** nature of perception.

SELF-SERVING A focus on what serves our own purposes and makes us look best.

Perception Is Selective

Judges and lawyers know that two people may see the same robbery from virtually the same angle and distance and yet disagree on almost every detail of the event, including the height, weight, eye colour, hair colour, and dress of the robbery suspect. The selective nature of perception leads us to focus on some details and to ignore others. In the 2001 sniping murders that took place around Washington, DC, numerous eyewitnesses described the presence of a white truck or van at the locations of the sniping incidents. For weeks police searched for a white van before arresting the suspects in a completely different kind of automobile—a blue Chevrolet sedan. No eyewitnesses had reported seeing such a vehicle at the crime scenes.

Factors such as gender and occupation come into play when we talk about selective perception.[35] Studies of eyewitness accounts have found, for example, that men and women note and remember different aspects of a crime scene, depending on what catches their interest.[36] Women tend to remember more "female-oriented" details such as clothing or hair style. They are also better at recognizing facial features. Men, on the other hand, tend to remember more "male-oriented" details such as the kind of gun someone is carrying or spatial information such as the direction in which a person ran. In the same way, our occupations can influence what we see and retain. An athlete might notice the degree of muscularity in a robbery suspect. A fashion designer might notice the suspect's dress. A plastic surgeon might make mental notes about the person's bone structure.

Our past experiences and current needs also make a difference. A structural engineer, visual artist, and carpenter will probably focus on different features when they look at a house. The structural engineer is likely to note the integrity of the building. The artist will judge the aesthetic appeal of the house—whether it is original and interesting in design. The carpenter will notice whether the house needs serious repairs or repainting. Our needs also influence the details to which we pay attention. A potential home buyer may pay attention to the amount of traffic on the street, the nearness to a school, the availability of parking, and the amount of yard space—as well as features of the house itself. We often use expressions such as "I saw it with my own eyes," "Seeing is believing," or "A picture is worth a thousand words." In truth, each of us sees a different picture.[37] For another example illustrating the selective nature of perception, try the exercise suggested in the "From Theory to Practice" box.

Perception Is Self-Serving

When we talk about the selective nature of perception, we speak of "filters" through which we pass information about our world. In this process of filtering, much gets left in the strainer. For example, focussing on the sex of someone leads us to pay less attention to characteristics such as the person's weight, size of nose, shape of earlobes, and skin colour. We pay attention instead to the amount and type of facial hair, the presence or absence of breasts, and the shape of the person's hips. In this situation, we filter out a lot of information about the individual's body because it does not serve our needs or purposes.[38]

We pay attention to and recall information that makes us look better, and we judge ourselves more generously than we judge others. For example, if a co-worker arrives late at work on a few occasions, we might decide the person is irresponsible or has a poor work ethic (personality traits). If we arrive late at work on the same number of occasions, on the other hand, we might attribute our lateness to heavy traffic, fatigue from working hard the previous day, or an alarm clock that frequently malfunctions. In other words, we look for *external* factors (those that originate outside ourselves) to explain our late arrival at work, but we look for *internal* factors (those that originate within the individual) to explain the late arrival of a colleague.

from theory TO PRACTICE

Do You See What I See?

Count the number of *f*'s in the following statement:

> *Full flavourful cuisine is made of everything that we value in fantastic foods—fine herbs, lots of fresh ingredients, and a touch of genius!*

Compare your answer with the answers of your classmates. What is the correct answer?

This exercise illustrates that even when we make a serious effort, we do not see everything in our environment. In this case, many people fail to count the *f*'s in short words such as *of*. Can you think of any logical reason that they might make this omission?

> "It is one of the commonest of mistakes to consider that the limit of our power of perception is also the limit of all there is to perceive."
> C.W. LEADBEATER

In Chapter 2, we referred to this tendency to credit our successes to internal or personal factors and our failures to external or situational factors as *self-serving bias*. The reverse applies when we judge other people. When judging others, we are more likely to place blame on factors related to personality (internal) and less likely to accept the situation (external) as the reason for the person's failures.

Implications for Communication

The events leading to the My Lai massacre of Vietnamese citizens by American troops in 1968 illustrates the communication risks in selectively perceiving and filtering information:

> A war correspondent was present when a hamlet was burned down by the United States Army's First Air Cavalry Division. Inquiry showed that the order from division headquarters to the brigade was "On no occasion must hamlets be burned down." The brigade radioed the battalion: "Do not burn down any hamlets unless you are absolutely convinced that the Vietcong are in them." The battalion radioed the infantry company at the scene: "If you think there are any Vietcong in the hamlet, burn it down." The company commander radioed his troops: "Burn down that hamlet."[39]

In this situation, the information became more and more distorted each time the message was received, interpreted, and retransmitted. In the end, the selective filtering of those who heard the messages resulted in the deaths of several hundred civilians.

Selective perception carries many risks because we are quicker to perceive, remember, and respond to the negative than the positive.[40] So we might focus on what is wrong with someone else before we see what is right about the person. We are also quicker to perceive and more likely to recall the unusual and the sensational. In an experiment conducted at the University of Windsor, student participants invariably noted the most sensational and unexpected aspects of a film about "Cajun" Mardi Gras. They remembered details such as the wringing of a chicken's neck, masked riders on horseback, and a young man dressed in female clothing. (See the "Human Diversity" box titled "Perceptions of the Unfamiliar" for a description of this experiment.) A study of eyewitness accounts revealed a similar focus on the sensational. Eyewitnesses had better recall when suspects were holding unusual or unexpected objects such as raw chicken, celery, or a weapon.[41]

Perception Is Spontaneous, Largely Unconscious, and Value Driven

This section explores how perception is a spontaneous, largely unconscious, and value-driven process. Perception happens spontaneously, before we are even fully aware that it is happening. Because it occurs without conscious thought, what we perceive depends to a great extent on our existing values.

Perception Is Spontaneous and Largely Unconscious

We often think of perception as having four distinct phases. In the first phase, we pick out cues that might be important such as the designer dress a person is wearing. In the second phase, we use the cues to decide on personal characteristics (e.g., high economic status). Based on this opinion, we then make connections in the third phase to other qualities that might fit with the personal characteristics (e.g., conservative political views). Finally, in the fourth phase, we put everything together in order to know how to respond to the other person. Our response may be mental (thoughts) or behavioural (actions).[42]

While these phases of perception may sound logical and linear, they often occur in a largely spontaneous and unconscious fashion, taking only seconds of time. We perceive race and gender, for example, within 100 to 150 milliseconds of meeting another person;[43] indeed, "even a split-second glimpse of a person's face tells us his identity, sex, mood, age, race, and direction of attention."[44] Our values also play into these perceptions, as the following discussion will illustrate.

Perception Is Value Driven

We are quicker to perceive information that fits with our existing cultural, religious, and social values than information that goes against these values.[45] After testing participants to identify their values, researchers in one experiment flashed words representing the values on a screen for a millisecond. Then they gradually increased the display times for the words until everyone could recognize them. The findings revealed that the most religious people saw the word *religion* almost immediately. Less religious people saw the word only after it had displayed for a longer period of time. In other words, we most quickly perceive the things that matter most to us—the things we value.[46] We are also most likely to perceive what we already believe to be the truth and to block information that does not fit with our existing belief structures.

Implications for Communication

When we meet other people, our first impressions—largely unconscious, spontaneous, and value driven—become the foundation for later interactions[47] and for representations of the person to others.[48] We use readily accessible cues to arrive at these impressions, which form in the first few minutes of interaction.[49] When we perceive similarities in dress between ourselves and the other person, for example, our first impression is more likely to be positive.[50]

We are also more likely to arrive at a favourable opinion of another person when positive information about the person comes from a third party, not from the person herself.[51] This idea illustrates **warranting theory**, which says that we are more likely to believe information about someone if that person cannot manipulate the information.[52]

Impression formation theory also concerns itself with how we represent ourselves to others. In fear of making a bad first impression, sometimes we make comments such as "I know I might seem bored, but I'm really not" or "I might appear prejudiced, but it's not so." In fact, we hurt ourselves when we make such disclaimers because they tell other people that we might be bored or prejudiced. As a result, people are more likely to expect us to display the trait we have disowned.[53]

In the same way, we put ourselves at risk when we make bad comments about another person. People react positively to those who express liking for other people and negatively to those who make derogatory comments about others. Rather than

WARRANTING THEORY Theory that says we are more likely to believe information that someone cannot manipulate.

IMPRESSION FORMATION THEORY Theory related to how we put together different pieces of information to form an impression of a person.

humanDIVERSITY

Perceiving the Unfamiliar[54]

The 1975 documentary film *The Good Times Are Killing Me* depicts an annual Mardi Gras celebration quite unlike the world-famous carnival of New Orleans, Louisiana. This "Cajun" Mardi Gras takes place many miles from New Orleans in rural locations like Church Point, Basile, and Mamou, Louisiana. The celebrants are Acadians, originally from Nova Scotia. In this traditional celebration, masked men in clown outfits, pointed hats, and colourful pyjamas ride on horseback through the countryside, begging for chickens, sausages, rice, vegetables, and other donations. Dressed in black capes and cowboy hats, their *capitaines* carry white flags. Accompanied by a band of musicians, a lone celebrant sings the haunting Mardi Gras song.

The rules of conduct follow:

> The authority of *le capitaine* is absolute. He leads the procession and distributes any liquor that is consumed. No member of the colourful band of beggars may enter private property without his permission. He approaches each farmhouse with raised white flag to ask permission from the homeowners for *les Mardi Gras* to enter. If he receives an invitation, he drops or waves the flag to signal the others. They are expected to sing and dance and beg with great energy at homes that are donating to the gumbo. Before departing, the masked beggars and their *capitaines* chase down live chickens to take back to the villages, where the women prepare chicken and sausage gumbos for the evening celebration. The dancing and festivities continue at the local dance hall until midnight, the beginning of the Lenten season.

Apart from the costumes and the drinking, the festivities involve few elements that would be familiar to people from other cultures. There are no parade floats, grand balls, or thrown beads that outsiders might recognize from the better-known Mardi Gras of New Orleans.

The unfamiliar details and context of *The Good Times Are Killing Me* made it very suitable for a classroom-based perception experiment conducted with first-year students at the University of Windsor. The experiment resembled the telephone game, where people pass whispered messages from one to another and the last person reveals what she or he has heard. To conduct the classroom experiment, the researcher asked two students to volunteer to leave the room for the showing of the film on the Cajun Mardi Gras. Following the viewing by the larger group, the researcher recruited a third student from the group who had seen the film. She asked this student to relay her understanding of the film to one of the two volunteers (Volunteer #1) who had not seen the film. Then the researcher asked the first volunteer (Volunteer #1) to offer her understanding of the film to the other student who had not seen the film (Volunteer #2). In the final step of the exercise, this student (Volunteer #2)—the third person in the chain—described the film to the larger group. All three descriptions were presented aloud to the class so that peers could note which elements were retained, dropped, added, or distorted as the three students relayed their understanding of the film.

What was retained? First, the recounting of the events demonstrated the *sharpening* effect in perception—how receivers of communication tend to retain in sharp detail the most outrageous and sensational details, such as the wringing of a chicken's neck. Participants also tended to remember the colourful beggars and caped men riding on horseback through the countryside. Some remembered the highly sensory images of boiled crawfish and corn cobs being poured from vats onto picnic tables. Typically participants remembered that the "Cajuns" like to drink, party, go horseback riding, and chase chickens.

forming a bad impression of the person who is being put down, we form a bad impression of the person who is making the negative comment. The term ***TAR effect*** refers to this transfer of negative feeling to the person who expresses dislike.[55]

TAR EFFECT A tendency to dislike the person who criticizes someone else rather than disliking the person who is criticized.

To learn more about how pickpockets take advantage of the unconscious and largely spontaneous nature of perception, see the "Professional Contexts" box. Pickpockets achieve their ends in part by controlling the focus of our attention, over which we have little conscious control.

Perception Is Relative and Context Bound

As discussed in earlier chapters, our gender, sexual orientation, age, regional and national affiliations, and other demographic factors have an impact on how we perceive and relate

What was dropped? Overall, the accounts tended to be simplistic and underdeveloped (the *levelling* effect in perception), with much lost from the original film. As the information passed from one student to the next, the transmission time grew shorter; each account contained fewer details than the last. A classic article by G.A. Miller argues that people can usually recall no more than seven points, "plus or minus two"; some say the number may be closer to five than seven. Supporting this principle, the communicators tended to omit major contextual details such as the costumes and the music. Yet context is very important to our sensing of the world, as well as to our communication of our perceptions to others. When questioned about the omissions, one participant said, "I heard the music in my head all of the time that I was recounting the story. I just didn't think to mention it."

What was added? Communicators often embellished the story, adding details not present in the film. Sometimes they made up a conversation where the women on farms begged the costumed men to sing a song for them; or they said that the men were on their way to a masquerade ball. The added details made the communicator appear better informed and the story more interesting. The new information often added "spice" to the story. One participant said, for example, that the women were frightened when the masked men arrived; another said that the masked men were drinking heavily. At other times, the fictitious additions seemed to be attempts to make sense of what participants had seen and heard—to find some logical and reasonable explanation for the events that they had witnessed (*assimilation* to their cultural expectations).

What was distorted? Communicators changed the story to fit their understanding of the world. When some aspect of the film did not make sense to them, they invented explanations or changed the story line (another example of *assimilation*). One said, for example, that *les capitaines* were modern-day pirates who rode in bands through the countryside, forcing people to give chickens to them. The documentary was sometimes relabelled as a music video featuring John Fogerty, who appeared in the film.

Overall, the descriptions generated by the students give great insight into how we try to make sense of culturally alien information. Participants in the experiment—even those who had viewed the film—found it difficult to describe the seemingly bizarre events. They did not understand why masked men would be riding through the countryside, begging for chickens. They found the wringing of a chicken's neck to be unsettling. Unfamiliar with the French Acadian dialect, they did not understand the Mardi Gras song or the context and meaning of the celebration. In short, they had no existing perceptual frames within which to position the information. The students who had not viewed the film (but had heard the descriptions of others) were even more confused. When our past experience fails us, we fill in the missing pieces or add content to make a more complete puzzle. At the same time, we drop or distort information that confuses us or does not fit our perceptual frameworks.

When we encounter unfamiliar information in our everyday lives, the need to understand our world leads us to eliminate details from our perceptual fields (*levelling*), to exaggerate striking features (*sharpening*), and to fit what we perceive into pre-existing ideas and cultural expectations (*assimilation*). These processes occur when we come into contact with people from other cultures. We may not understand why these people behave as they do, why they hold the values that they hold, or why they misinterpret our behaviours and attitudes. Eliminating, adding to, or distorting what we perceive in these situations helps us to make sense of our world. At the same time, these reactions to diversity can stand in the way of effective communication between individuals from different cultures. By understanding how and why information can become distorted in cross-cultural interactions, we can take steps to avoid miscommunication.

to others. Standpoint theory tells us that we can never escape our place in the economic, social, and political order of things.[56] (See Chapter 1 for a discussion of this theory.) In other words, we live in a relative world, in which our perceptions depend on who we are, where we are, and how we got to this point. In the following discussion, we will consider the relative and context-bound nature of perception.

> **"What you see and hear depends a good deal on where you are standing; it also depends on what sort of person you are."**
>
> **C.S. LEWIS**

Perception Is Relative

Asked to describe the suspect in a robbery, a six-foot individual might say that a 5'8" suspect is short. Someone who is 5'3" tall, on the other hand, might see the suspect as

*professional*CONTEXTS

"Pick a Pocket or Two": Stealing Your Attention[57]

Considered to be the "pickpocket of pickpockets," young and charming sleight-of-hand artist Apollo Robbins plies his trade in clubs and shows in cities such as Las Vegas. He works quickly and effortlessly, removing all manner of objects from the clothing and bodies of unsuspecting audience members. He then returns the items in entertaining ways to his shocked victims.

One of the best-known stories about Robbins's extraordinary abilities relates to an incident that occurred in 2001. At one show venue, Robbins began a conversation with several agents from the secret service detail in charge of protecting former US president Jimmy Carter. Before the end of the conversation, Robbins was in possession of almost everything in the men's pockets—badges, watches, keys to the Carter motorcade, and even Carter's trip itinerary. The agents were embarrassed and annoyed when Robbins revealed what he had done. At other shows, Robbins has moved cigarettes from one man's breast pocket to another's side pocket, replaced a cell phone with a piece of fried chicken, and transferred a woman's engagement ring to a key chain in her husband's pants pocket.

Robbins uses strategies of diversion to move closer to his victims without alerting them to his techniques. For example, he approaches them and begins performing impressive coin tricks to get their attention. While they are focussed on the coin, Robbins breaks eye contact and steps into their personal space with a semi-circular and barely noticeable motion. Were he to move head-on into their space, he would make them uncomfortable and anxious. Instead he ends up standing next to the person, with easy access to rings, watches, wallets, and other items of value or interest. But Robbins says that physical positioning is only a tool: "It's all about the choreography of people's attention. Attention is like water. It flows. It's liquid. You create channels to divert it."

Robbins describes how focussing someone's attention in one area allows him to operate unnoticed in another area outside the person's attention frame. Leaning close to a person's face, for example, will take that person's attention away from her lower body, giving Robbins the opportunity to remove a cell phone from her side pocket. Alternatively, if he wants to shift attention from a person's front coat pocket, he might ask the person to check his back pants pocket to see if anything is missing. While the person is checking his back pocket, Robbins is removing a wallet from the person's front pocket.

Robbins's interest in factors of attention has led him to participate in several projects that explore the functioning of the mind. The US Department of Defense asked to consult with him on military applications of pickpocketing, manipulation of attention, and con games. As one Special Operations Command official explained, knowing how it actually works is important.

Neuroscientists have also demonstrated interest in Robbins's area of expertise. One idea in which they have expressed interest, for example, relates to Robbins's assertion that objects that move in an arc (semi-circular motion) will draw and hold our attention more than those that move in a straight line. In an experiment with a coin, Robbins demonstrated that when he pulled his hand away in an arc-like motion, the attention of the audience followed the hand motion, abandoning the focus on the coin. However, when he pulled his hand away in a straight line, the attention of the viewer was more likely to stay with or return to the coin. The results of this experiment appeared in *Frontiers of Human Neuroscience*.

Robbins's collaborators in this experiment included neuroscientists Stephen Macknik and Susana Martinez-Conde, whom Robbins met at a conference for the Association for the Scientific Study of Consciousness. At that conference, Robbins talked about what he had learned about the management of attention; and subsequently he began working with Macknik and Martinez-Conde, who co-chaired the conference. The three collaborated on a book called *Sleights of Mind*, which deals with how we perceive, process, understand, and respond to information.

A popular lecturer now, Robbins frequently speaks at professional conferences. He presented at a conference in Baltimore for example, that featured Nobel Prize–winner Daniel Kahneman. According to observers, the two men talked at length about the concept of "inattentional blindness," where we focus so strongly on one task that we fail to pay attention to—or even see—anything else.

tall. Serious consequences sometimes result from these perceptual discrepancies. Kirk Bloodsworth spent eight years in jail (two on death row) before being found innocent of the rape and murder of a nine-year-old girl. His wrongful conviction stemmed in part from an inaccurate description of the guilty party. The authorities were looking for a 6'5" man—a suspect described as extremely tall. In the end, the confessed murderer proved to be only 5'7" tall.[58]

In the movie *Annie Hall* (1977), the viewer sees Alvin Singer (played by Woody Allen) talking to his psychiatrist on one side of a split screen. The psychiatrist asks about Alvin's relationship with Annie Hall, "How often do you sleep together?" Alvin replies, "Hardly ever, maybe three times a week." On the other side of the split screen, Annie (played by Diane Keaton) speaks with her counsellor. Asked the same question, Annie responds, "Constantly, I'd say three times a week."[59]

How we view our physical world is also relative, influenced by people and circumstances. For example, when accompanied by friends, we will judge a hill to be less steep than if we face the climb alone. In other words, the presence of social support influences visual perception.[60]

Perception Is Context Bound

Context also makes a difference in how we perceive others. If someone is smoking a cigarette in front of an office building, we assume the person is smoking tobacco. If someone is holding a cigarette in an alleyway, surrounded by homeless people, we assume the person could be smoking an illicit drug. The 2004 documentary *Fahrenheit 9/11*, directed by Michael Moore, shows former US president George W. Bush stating, in a serious tone, that all nations must "do everything they can" to fight terrorism. As soon as Bush finishes his statement, the camera opens up to show the former president on a golf course, preparing to swing a golf club. Bush says to the interviewer, "Now watch this drive!"[61] Contextually, his previous comments have just lost their impact.

Implications for Communication

Consider the following conversation between a supervisor and her employee to see an example of how the relative and context-bound nature of perception can influence our interactions with others:

Alexia: What do you think about the new sick-leave policy?
Mark: It's okay.
Alexia: Okay? I'm excited to get the extra days.
Mark: Yeah, I am too. But the policy at my last job offered more days.
Alexia: True, but your last company went under. You have to take economic times into account.

Relative to the number of sick days in Mark's last job, the new sick-leave policy does not look so good. But when you expand the picture to include the larger context—difficult economic times and firms going into bankruptcy—the picture changes. Sometimes, however, we fail to perceive the bigger picture or we judge words or actions against some standard that makes them appear worse than they would appear in some other context. For example, while you might appreciate a friend telling you about a new weight-loss program when you are shopping at a health-foods store, you might be offended if the same friend tells you about the diet just after you have filled your plate at an all-you-can-eat buffet.

Perception Is Mood Dependent

Our moods influence how we respond to our external circumstances. For example, we experience pain more strongly when we feel sad or depressed.[62] We are more likely to be persuaded by a sales clerk when we feel happy.[63] We perform better at work and perceive our leaders as more charismatic when we are in a positive mood.[64]

> **"The appearance of things changes according to the emotions, and thus we see magic and beauty in them, while the magic and beauty are really in ourselves."**
>
> **KAHLIL GIBRAN**

Implications for Communication

Somewhat ironically, we may be able to communicate most effectively when we are in a mildly negative mood. For one thing, we are more likely to process information *accurately* (rather than distorting it) when we are in such a mood. We are also more likely to remember information and to make fewer errors in recalling it.[65] Our persuasive abilities will be better.[66] Because we are more skeptical when we are in a negative mood, we are also more likely to detect deception on the part of others.[67] Finally, we are more likely to place less importance on first impressions.[68] Since first impressions are often wrong, this by-product of negative mood could have benefits in terms of interpersonal and work relationships. Thus, negative mood does not always have a negative outcome. Nervousness and frustration, on the other hand, can interfere with the processes of perceiving accurately and communicating effectively.

MOOD CONTAGION The idea that we can "catch" the mood of someone else much like we catch a cold.

We "catch" the moods of other people much as we might catch a cold.[69] Some apply the term **mood contagion** to this phenomenon.[70] We feel good when our leaders are in a positive mood and bad when our leaders are in a negative mood.[71] When listening to someone read aloud in an upbeat voice (as opposed to a sad voice), our facial features and postures suggest that we experience a correspondingly positive mood.[72]

Advance knowledge of a partner's mood can influence our mood.[73] If we learn that our partner had a bad day at work, we may "catch" that person's mood before she or he ever arrives home.[74] These feelings influence our later interactions with the person.[75] In close relationships, we sometimes make a conscious effort to match our partner's mood.[76] This sort of mood matching occurs, however, only when we want to get along with the other person and to have a good interaction.[77]

Perception Is Completion Seeking

We fill in missing information when there are gaps in our perceptions.[78] The completion-seeking nature of perception manifests itself in the practice of stereotyping. When we stereotype, we attempt to fill in the blanks about another person. That is, we make guesses about the person's beliefs and opinions, based on the most obvious characteristics of the person such as hair and skin colour, manner of dress or speech, or ethnicity. We often do this sort of stereotyping in order to know how to interact with someone we do not know well.

bst2012/Thinkstock

Imagine that you are a nurse, new on the job. You are assigned to the geriatrics ward at the local hospital, where many older people struggle with a range of illnesses. Your colleagues mention that one of the patients with whom you will be working is Turkish. You do not know anything about the person other than a brief medical history. When you meet her, she is wearing a hospital gown; so you cannot get information from her dress. You know almost nothing about Turkish culture, but you remember a Turkish family who lived in your neighbourhood when you were growing up. You also recall a few news stories you have heard about people from Turkey. Based on this limited information, you call upon stereotypes of Turks; and you apply perceived characteristics of the larger group to the individual in order to know how to behave with the patient—what to say and do (or avoid saying and doing).

Your motives for stereotyping may be honourable, but your understanding of this older Turkish woman may have no basis in fact. You may not know, for example, that her family hid and sheltered a Jewish family during World War II and that her politics are very liberal. You may not know that she is an award-winning artist or that her son works as a film producer in Hollywood. You may not know that, until stricken with advanced heart disease in her sixties, she ran marathons in support of breast cancer research. In short, you may know almost nothing about her; but you may assume that she is a new Canadian, with the traditional values, religion, and politics of her home country. Members of visible minority groups sometimes complain that, no matter how many generations their families may have been in Canada, many people still assume (on the basis of their skin colour and name) that they are newly arrived from another country. To better understand how stereotyping works, refer to the "From Theory to Practice" box titled "Can You Be Sure?"

Stereotypes often have ties to nationality, race, ethnicity, gender, and sexual orientation. When shown photos of the faces of unknown sprinters (black and white), novice Canadian coaches said that the black athletes had succeeded because they were born with the gift of speed. They said that the white athletes had succeeded because of a supportive environment (e.g., interest on the part of their parents, money, or access to good coaches or facilities). In other words, despite the fact that these coaches had a sophisticated knowledge of players, they still engaged in stereotyping on the basis of race.[79] Try the exercise in the "From Theory to Practice" box titled "Stereotyping Our World" to identify some of the markers on which you rely in judging people.

As you can see, we tend to rely on visual cues (e.g., skin tone, facial features, and observable behaviours) when we apply stereotypes to individuals. While characteristics such as gender, race, ethnicity, and age are often fairly easy to identify

from theory TO PRACTICE

Can You Be Sure?

If a nurse were to walk in the room right now, how would the person look? Would the nurse be a man or a woman? If an off-duty police officer were to enter the room, how would the officer relate to your class members? If an Aboriginal leader were to come into the room, how would he or she be dressed? How would you describe a victim of domestic abuse? Have you had any personal experiences with people who fit into these broad categories but do not match the pictures that came first to your mind? How confident are you in your assumptions?

To better understand the process of stereotyping, complete the following sentences:

Women are ____________________.
Men are ____________________.
Teenagers are ____________________.
Artists are ____________________.
Italians are ____________________.
Older people are ____________________.
Homeless people are ____________________.
Newfoundlanders are ____________________.

Now describe exceptions to the stereotypes you have formed. Be specific in describing individuals who do not conform to these stereotypes.

from theory TO PRACTICE

Stereotyping Our World

Try to guess how the people shown in the four photographs would feel about the topics listed below. Assign a number from one to seven for each person in each category, with the number *one* indicating an *extremely unfavourable* attitude toward the topic, and the number *seven* indicating an *extremely favourable* attitude toward the topic. Avoid using the number *four*.

Photo 1

Alexa-Mitiner/Thinkstock

Photo 2

DragonImages/Thinkstock

Photo 3

Big Cheese Photo/Thinkstock

Photo 4

Mike Watson Images/Thinkstock

Hockey							
Photo 1	1	2	3	4	5	6	7
Photo 2	1	2	3	4	5	6	7
Photo 3	1	2	3	4	5	6	7
Photo 4	1	2	3	4	5	6	7

Seal Hunt							
Photo 1	1	2	3	4	5	6	7
Photo 2	1	2	3	4	5	6	7
Photo 3	1	2	3	4	5	6	7
Photo 4	1	2	3	4	5	6	7

Sororities and Fraternities							
Photo 1	1	2	3	4	5	6	7
Photo 2	1	2	3	4	5	6	7
Photo 3	1	2	3	4	5	6	7
Photo 4	1	2	3	4	5	6	7

Reality TV Shows							
Photo 1	1	2	3	4	5	6	7
Photo 2	1	2	3	4	5	6	7
Photo 3	1	2	3	4	5	6	7
Photo 4	1	2	3	4	5	6	7

Heavy Metal Music							
Photo 1	1	2	3	4	5	6	7
Photo 2	1	2	3	4	5	6	7
Photo 3	1	2	3	4	5	6	7
Photo 4	1	2	3	4	5	6	7

Legalization of Marijuana							
Photo 1	1	2	3	4	5	6	7
Photo 2	1	2	3	4	5	6	7
Photo 3	1	2	3	4	5	6	7
Photo 4	1	2	3	4	5	6	7

Increased Tuition Fees							
Photo 1	1	2	3	4	5	6	7
Photo 2	1	2	3	4	5	6	7
Photo 3	1	2	3	4	5	6	7
Photo 4	1	2	3	4	5	6	7

What did you use as the basis for your judgments? The person's gender? Clothing? Hairstyle? Age? Race? Share your perceptions with your classmates. Did most people make the same judgments? You can also try this same exercise with your classmates early in the term (before you get to know them). Have a volunteer go to the front of the class and then guess how you think the volunteer would feel about the above topics. Try the exercise with several volunteers and different topics (ones that would not be too personal).

based on appearances, other characteristics such as sexual orientation are less visible. Nonetheless, people tend to make assumptions about a person's sexual orientation—and subsequently apply stereotypes to that person—based on observable facial features, hairstyle, manner of dress, and gestures.[80] Gay men, in particular, are often victims of stereotyping that relies on these kinds of indicators.

We stereotype not only on the basis of visual cues, but also on vocal qualities, including the extent to which a voice sounds "feminine" or "masculine."[81] In one study of gender stereotyping, participants saw those with more masculine voice qualities (whether male or female) as more capable than those with female voice qualities. The participants connected female voices with babyish qualities and female resumes with warmth of personality.[82] This stereotyping occurred regardless of the quality or content of the resumes.[83] Other studies have found that men in general get more respect than do women. This respect can carry over to hiring decisions that discriminate against women.[84]
To see how the Canadian job market reflects gender stereotyping, see Figure 3.2.

Less acknowledged stereotypes pertain to the single or marital status of individuals. For example, people believe that single individuals are more likely than those in a relationship to have sexually transmitted diseases (STDs). Given the choice, they say they would choose a partner who has been in a relationship over a single individual. People also see males as more likely than females to carry STDs.[85]

Other less apparent stereotypes relate to people with mental or chronic illnesses. Although different illnesses affect us in different ways, people often assign group characteristics to all people with such illnesses. They sometimes see those with mental

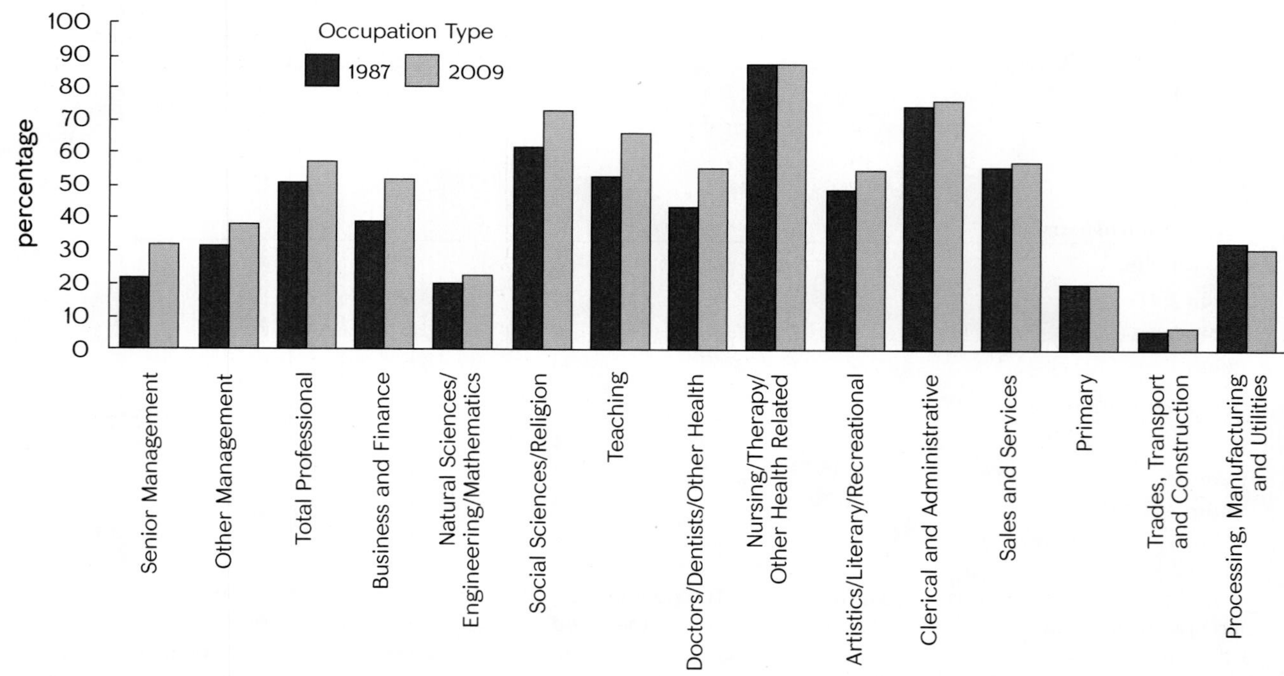

FIGURE 3.2 **Women employed as a percentage of all occupations, 1987 and 2009.**

SOURCE: Statistics Canada, "Chart 7," www.statcan.gc.ca/pub/89-503-x/2010001/article/11387/c-g/c-g007-eng.htm. Reproduced and distributed on an "as is" basis with the permission of Statistics Canada.

illness as incompetent and dangerous, personally responsible for their problems.[86] They also see people with chronic illnesses as all alike and dependent on others.[87] Even caregivers for the mentally ill tend to rely on these stereotypes.[88]

Perhaps the most widely held stereotypes are age-related. In Western societies, many see older people as less healthy, attractive, active, and interesting than younger people. As a result, their interests are often considered to be less important than the interests of younger people. In May 2012, Kathy Bates tweeted that NBC had cancelled the TV series *Harry's Law*. This popular legal drama, which featured Bates, catered to the older demographic. Despite having one of the highest Nielsen ratings (fluctuating between 7.5 and 9 million viewers in the second season), the producers cancelled the show. Featuring older actors, the series had failed to attract younger viewers. In fact, the show had a rating of only 0.8 in the 18 to 49 demographic—too low in the eyes of the network.[89] See the discussion of the communication predicament of aging (CPA) model on page 94 to learn more about how to improve our communication with older people. The "From Theory to Practice" box titled "Questioning Your Stereotypes" also encourages you to think more about the stereotypes on which you rely.

from theory TO PRACTICE

Questioning Your Stereotypes

Think back to a time when you treated someone from another race, ethnicity, gender, or other group in a way different from how you would like to be treated. Why do you think you acted in this way? Do you think the views of others influenced your behaviour? Did your behaviour influence how other people around you treated the person? Did you have a chance to get to know this person better at a later time? If so, in what ways (if any) did these later interactions change your initial impression of the person?

Self-categorization theory tells us that we see ourselves both as individuals and as members of groups. Whether we see others as individuals or members of a group depends on context and our relationship with them.[90] We do not usually apply stereotypes to people we know well. So if, for example, we develop a relationship with a gay man prior to learning about his sexual orientation, we are less likely to ground the relationship in stereotypes.[91] In the same way, we see friends from other racial or ethnic groups as having individual personalities and traits; but we see strangers as behaving like members of the groups to which they belong. So we might like and trust a friend who holds membership in a group that we generally distrust or fear.

SELF-CATEGORIZATION THEORY The idea that we see ourselves as both individuals and group members, whereas we see others as either individuals or group members based on other factors.

Many studies confirm that poor outcomes in much intergroup and interracial communication trace back to negative stereotypes.[92] If we hold a stereotype of women as overly emotional, we might not be willing to promote women to higher-level positions in an organization. Or if we have a stereotype of some racial group as lazy, we might be unwilling to hire a member of that group for a job. Even positive stereotypes can be problematic because they can lead us to expect too much from a person or group. If an employer assumes that every Asian worker should be able to complete complex mathematical tasks, the expectation might place an unfair burden on Asian employees who do not have strong math skills.

In addition, reliance on stereotypes reduces our curiosity—our felt need to find out more about someone. If we assume that we know the attitudes and actions of others, we may not bother to take the time to get to know them:[93] Stereotypes affect how we seek, attend to, interpret, and recall information.[94]

In the most extreme cases, stereotyping can be deadly. One American study showed that people are more likely to shoot first and ask questions later when the target has physical traits associated with the black race. Both black people and non-black people responded to split-second "shoot/don't shoot" situations in a way that stereotyped those with more classic black features and skin tone.[95] We are not without our share of similar stereotypes in Canada.

Implications for Communication

Almost everyone relies to some extent on stereotypes. Stereotypes originate because we feel more comfortable and secure when we believe we can predict how someone will respond to our words and actions. On the surface, stereotyping reduces some of the unknowns in an unfamiliar situation. Students draw upon their stereotypes of professors in deciding how to talk to them about a problem. Patients relate to their doctors in a certain way, based on stereotypical expectations of how patients should behave in a medical setting. But sometimes we get surprises. We may have constructed an image of a carpenter, for example, in our minds; but if we learn that the person building our new patio is an Oxford graduate or a mother of five, we face the need to find a new category for that person. In such situations, we have to work harder. When our stereotypes fail us, we have to engage in more complex reasoning processes.[96]

> **"When you meet someone better than yourself, turn your thoughts to becoming his equal. When you meet someone not as good as you are, look within and examine yourself."**
> **CONFUCIUS**

PERSPECTIVE TAKING Looking at a situation from the other person's point of view.

COUNTER-STEREOTYPING Effort to eliminate stereotypes by focussing on similarities.

Practices such as **perspective taking** and **counter-stereotyping** help us to see beyond our stereotypes and to model more sensitive communication behaviours. By *perspective taking*, we mean looking at a situation from another person's point of view. One study asked participants to write about a fictitious African American man and an elderly man. After writing about the two men, the participants judged the African American man as less aggressive and the elderly man as less dependent than they had before completing the written task.[97] Perspective taking does not require that we *agree* with the other person. It requires only that we try to understand that person's point of view. For an exercise in perspective taking, see the "From Theory to Practice" box titled "Taking the Other's Point of View."

IN-GROUP A group of which one is a member.

Counter-stereotyping involves a conscious effort to eliminate stereotypes. *The Cosby Show*, an American sitcom that was popular in the 1980s and early 1990s, represents one such effort by the American media to question and dispute stereotypes related to African American individuals. This show depicted the Huxtables, an upper-middle-class African American family, whose problems were common to others of their socio-economic status. The producers of the show tried to downplay the differences and focus on the similarities in African American and white American cultures.

xflickrx/Flickr at www.flickr.com/photos/environment/2167097486/

Positive intergroup contact can also reduce prejudice and eliminate biases.[98] Our friends and other **in-group** members influence how we see others.[99] Groups tend to share and reinforce stereotypes of out-group members. That is, they cling to shared stereotypes but surrender unshared ones.[100] Even so, some group members give up their ideas more readily than others.

Findings related to active versus passive perceivers help to explain why some people are more resistant than others to changing their opinions. **Active perceivers** choose the amount and type of information they receive about a person, whereas **passive perceivers** rely on others to select the information. Given the task of hiring someone to fill a job opening, for example, an active perceiver might go online (perhaps to Facebook or Twitter) to seek additional information on candidates for the job. A passive perceiver, on the other hand, would probably wait for the job interview. Ironically, passive perceivers tend to be more confident in their judgments of other people; and this confidence makes them more resistant to changing their views of people.[101] To promote more effective communication behaviours, we should aim to be active perceivers. The more information we have, the greater our chances of judging people and situations in an accurate, not stereotypical, way.

from theory TO PRACTICE

Taking the Other's Point of View

Find a partner and role-play the following fictitious situation. Imagine that you work in a retail store that allows only one employee to be on vacation at any given time. You have just found out that one of your co-workers has applied for vacation time in early July, and you are angry because you usually take your vacation in early July. Taking your co-worker's point of view, however, you realize that she has a good reason for requesting the time off. Act out the scenario, filling in the specific details of the situation as you interact with your partner.

ACTIVE PERCEIVERS
Individuals who choose the amount and type of information they receive.

PASSIVE RECEIVERS
Individuals who rely on others to select information for them.

For a review of many of the characteristics of perception, see the "Professional Contexts" box on perception errors in performance appraisals.

STRATEGIES, TOOLS, AND TIPS FOR GAINING AWARENESS AND CONTROLLING PERCEPTION BIASES

Through conscious efforts, strategies, and education, we can manage our perception of others and learn to communicate in more productive ways.[102] In this discussion, we will review what we have learned so far about perceptual errors. We will look at ways to minimize the errors, and we will examine strategies and tools for improving our communication.

Adopting Strategies to Control for Bias and Improve Communication

Remember that your first impressions are more often wrong than right. Snap judgments do not allow time for the other person to reveal his or her personality and character. Overvaluing first impressions encourages us to dismiss someone as unworthy of our attention or friendship before we have given the person a chance.

> "Too often we colour our perception with other people's pencils."
> TIM WINTER

Be aware that you perceive and remember negative and sensational information more quickly and easily than positive information. A focus on the negative and/or sensational can lead to disregarding more positive and less sensational information.

Remember that you will have more difficulty identifying differences in people from other racial groups. If you are offering an eyewitness account to police or jurors, you need to

*professional*CONTEXTS

Perception Errors in Performance Appraisals

In the career of an employee, periodic reviews of performance have a significant impact on job retention, promotions, bonuses, and salary increases. Although this process is meant to be objective, subjective impressions influence these appraisals; and errors in perception can interfere with a fair evaluation. These errors include judging a person in relation to her peers or the appraiser instead of using objective criteria, judging on the basis of only one quality, placing inappropriate emphasis on the rank or status of the person, focussing too heavily on one period in time, or placing undue emphasis on the order of the questions.[103]

Contrast errors occur when we compare employees to their peers rather than judge them on independent criteria. This error relates to the *relative* nature of perception—how we see people and objects in relationship to each other.

A second error involves judging an employee on points of similarity with—or difference from—the appraiser. If the employee is similar to the appraiser, she is more likely to receive a positive appraisal than if she is different from the appraiser. In other words, our perceptions are often *culturally bound and racially biased*, favouring people of the same gender, ethnic background, nationality, sexual orientation, and other demographic characteristics.

A third error involves basing the appraisal on one perceived quality of the person, either good or bad. For example, if the appraiser sees an employee as "agreeable," he might give an overall good appraisal based on that one trait (*halo effect*). Someone perceived as "less agreeable" might receive an overall poor evaluation based on that one quality (*horn effect*). This error relates to the *completion-seeking* nature of perception, our desire to extend what we know into areas less known to us.

A fourth commonly observed error involves status. Those in higher-level positions tend to receive more favourable appraisals than those lower in the hierarchy. This error relates to the *value-driven* nature of perception.

A fifth error occurs when the appraiser fails to look at the entire period of time the review is meant to reflect and instead pays too much attention to one more restricted time period. This narrow focus may place too much emphasis on either very recent or long-past behaviour. This error relates to the *selective* nature of perception.

A sixth error occurs when the appraiser places undue emphasis on the order in which questions appear. For example, errors can occur when earlier appraisals unfairly influence the current one. These ideas relate to the *primacy effect*: what comes first has a greater impact than what occurs in the middle or later. At other times, appraisers give similar ratings on different points if they follow closely after each other on the evaluation form, demonstrating the *recency effect*: what comes last has greater impact. These sorts of errors often relate to the *backward-looking* nature of perception.

recognize the limitations of your ability to make these distinctions. Otherwise you may contribute to the false conviction of an innocent person.

Be aware that not everyone else has the same goals, needs, and values. People with different interests and backgrounds tend to order their priorities in different ways.

Recall that level of confidence in your judgments about people is no measure of correctness. The most confident people are often wrong.

Recognize that you see the world through a filter that is different from that of everyone else in the world, including your closest friends, parents, and co-workers. Arguing over who is right and who is wrong is counter-productive. Instead try to find common ground for understanding and moving the relationship forward.

Recognize that people from other cultures have different filters through which they see the world. They also have different communication patterns. The student who looks down at his feet when an instructor asks whether he plagiarized a paper may be showing respect for the person in authority rather than displaying guilt about his paper.

Be sure you are not judging others against an unrealistic standard, perhaps a standard that you cannot meet yourself. It is easy to miss good qualities if your only gaze is critical. Be aware that you may be blaming the failures of others on weaknesses in character and motivation but blaming your own failures on outside forces beyond your control.

Realize that your mood influences how you see and react to other people, as well as how they react to you. Overreacting on a bad day can endanger your relationships in the workplace, at home, and in social settings. Avoid "catching" the mood of someone else when they are in a bad mood.

Set an example for others in your group by treating people in the way you would like to be treated.[104] Your example influences others, either positively or negatively. Moreover, putting down other people only makes you look bad. According to the TAR effect, the negative impression transfers from that person to you.

Assume the perspective of the other person. Attempt to see the world through her eyes in order to understand why she behaves in a particular way. If a group member does not show up for one or two meetings, get more facts before judging the person. Remember that it is not always obvious when someone is facing a serious personal challenge such as a life-threatening illness, the loss of a loved one, or the end of a valued relationship.

Make a conscious effort not to stereotype other people. Not all men want high-powered careers; some enjoy being full-time stay-at-home dads. Not all Baptists are politically conservative, and not all hockey players are jocks. Although media reports might suggest otherwise, not all famous musicians have drug problems. Try to view others as individuals instead of seeing them as members of a larger group.

Using Perception Checking to Minimize Error

Perception checking can help us reduce errors in communication. Most commonly, perception checking entails three steps.[105] First, we describe the behaviour we have noticed in the other person. Second, we give two possible interpretations of the behaviour. Third, we ask for clarification. The following examples illustrate the process of perception checking.

PERCEPTION CHECKING A process for confirming what we think we have seen, heard, or experienced.

> *Example #1. You haven't said much since getting home from work today* (behaviour). *I was wondering whether something happened at work to upset you* (interpretation 1) *or whether I have done something to upset you* (interpretation 2). *What is going on* (request for clarification)*?*
>
> *Example #2. You haven't called lately* (behaviour). *Has your schedule prevented you from calling* (interpretation 1)*, or do you want us to see less of each other* (interpretation 2)*? Is there something I should know* (request for clarification)*?*

It is also possible to shorten the process by leaving out one of the steps.

> *Example #3. You've been very quiet this afternoon* (behaviour). *Is anything bothering you* (request for clarification)*?*
>
> *Example #4. You haven't called lately* (behaviour). *Is it because you are really busy* (interpretation 1)*, or do you want us to see less of each other* (interpretation 2)*?*

Because perception checking involves a highly explicit form of communication, **low-context cultures** such as those of Canada and the United States are most comfortable with the practice. By *low-context culture*, we mean a culture that relies heavily on words to transmit meaning. Statements need to be explicit, not leaving room for more than one

LOW-CONTEXT CULTURES Cultures that rely heavily on words rather than context.

interpretation. Low-context cultures also tend to be individualistic, valuing independence and accomplishing tasks without assistance from others. Their communication relies heavily on logic and linear thinking—going from point A to point B in a direct fashion.

HIGH-CONTEXT CULTURES Cultures that place great importance on context and rely to a lesser degree on words.

High-context cultures, on the other hand, place less importance on words and more importance on context. Context includes nonverbal elements such as facial expressions, tone of voice, gestures, and posture. Context also includes cultural and other background information (e.g., social standing and occupation). People in high-context cultures rely more heavily than people in low-context cultures on unspoken elements in communication. Examples of countries with high-context cultures include Japan, Saudi Arabia, and Mexico, which are collectivist in their orientation. That is, they place great importance on the group, as opposed to the individual, and on long-term relationships and loyalties. These countries are less logical and more intuitive in their reasoning. Like Americans and Canadians, members of high-context cultures want to get from point A to point B; but they get there by a much more roundabout way. For example, Saudis tend to talk a bit about the personal, then a bit about business. Then they loop back again to the personal before returning to the matter of business. Eventually, they reach point B—but in a much more indirect fashion.[106]

People in high-context cultures often consider perception checking to be overly controlling and inappropriate communication. North Americans and the British, on the other hand, place a high value on explanations and clarification of meanings. So perception checking works well for them.

Using the Communication Predicament of Aging (CPA) Model to Improve Interactions with Older People

COMMUNICATION PREDICAMENT OF AGING (CPA) MODEL A model that predicts the relationship among aging cues, stereotyping, and communication behaviour.

The **communication predicament of aging (CPA) model** helps us to understand how to communicate with older people in a sensitive and productive way.[107] The logic of the model follows. When encountering an elderly person, a younger person recognizes old-age cues. These cues could be grey hair, a cane, wrinkles, or a hearing aid. The cues have the potential to trigger negative expectations associated with ageism, including the conclusion that the older person cannot understand, hear, or see clearly. The negative expectations lead the younger person to modify her speech to reflect this negative stereotype and compensate for the perceived lack of competence of the elderly person.

Communication behaviours that reflect "elderspeak" might include simplified, patronizing, or condescending speech. A staff member in a retirement home, for example, might refer to a resident as *dear* or *sweetie* or use baby talk to communicate with the older person. This kind of communication reinforces the negative stereotype already present in the caregiver's mind. More importantly, however, this kind of patronizing speech can lead an elderly person to integrate the negative stereotype into his own identity.

As a result of this self-stereotyping, the older person might begin to behave in a more childlike and dependent fashion. Or fearful of looking childish, she might avoid social interaction altogether. Finally, the elderly person might experience low self-esteem and, ultimately, changes in behaviour (including declining physical health) that reinforce the old-age cues observed by younger people. The CPA modelgives communication a central role that reveals itself at every stage of the model (Figure 3.3).

So how do we change the behavioural patterns in the CPA model to encourage more positive outcomes? Along with a number of other researchers, Martine Lagacé and

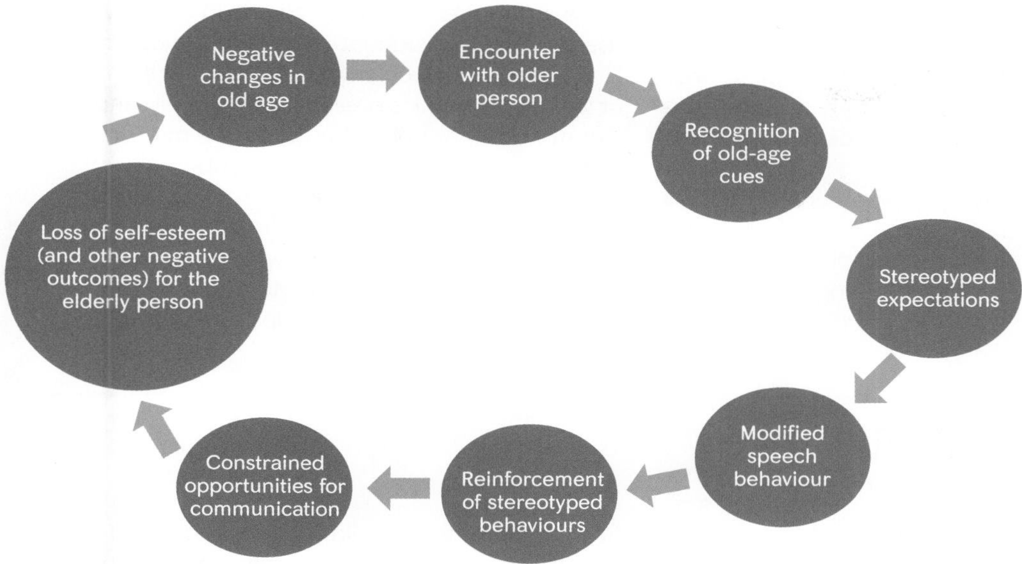

FIGURE 3.3 **The communication predicament of aging (CPA) model.**

SOURCE: J. Lennox Terrion and M. Lagacé, "Communication as Precursor and Consequence of Subjective Social Capital in Older People: A New Perspective on the Communication Predicament Model," *Social Theory and Health* 6 (2008): 239–49.

Jenepher Lennox Terrion of the University of Ottawa propose that communication training in listening and conversation skills provides valuable tools to seniors and their caregivers. Sensitivity training can also enhance the health outcomes and overall well-being of seniors. This result will come from improved relationships, more positive attitudes, more realistic perceptions, and better understanding. By openly discussing and dismantling the negative stereotypes, seniors and their caregivers can construct a new model for communicating more respectfully and productively.[108]

SUMMARY

In this chapter, we have examined how perception is learned and backward looking; culture bound and racially biased; selective and self-serving; spontaneous, largely unconscious, and value driven; relative and context bound; mood dependent; and completion seeking. All of these characteristics of perception influence and interact with each other in the communication situation.

Communication can fail when we block information with which we disagree, ignore or discard information that appears to be of little interest or value, or lack the background to process the information. We undermine our communication with another person when we apply characteristics that do not apply, rely too heavily on first impressions, judge the person by standards that are culturally defined and racially biased, believe that our past experience should be the guiding force for future interactions, and focus on negative and sensational elements while ignoring positive and less sensational elements.

We lose the opportunity for rewarding interactions with other people when we place others into compartments that do not allow for individual differences. Stereotypes play on the most easily recognized characteristics of a group—age, gender, skin colour, manner of dress, and other obvious markers. In stereotyping, we use a minimal amount of information to construct profiles of people who belong to groups other than our own, or we rely on profiles passed to us by family and friends. Our motives may not be bad ones. We may simply want to know how to interact with members of unfamiliar groups. But these most obvious characteristics probably tell us little about the character, personality, or belief system of a single person. So when we rely too heavily on stereotypes, we impair our ability to communicate or develop meaningful relationships with individuals.

REVIEW QUESTIONS

1. How have the characteristics of perception described in this chapter influenced your communication with friends, co-workers, or family? Give specific examples related to each characteristic (*learned* and *backward looking*; *culture bound* and *racially biased*; *selective and self-serving*; *spontaneous, largely unconscious*, and *value driven*; *relative* and *context bound*; *mood dependent*, and *completion seeking*).
2. Think about some dominant stereotypes in our culture (e.g., stereotypes of used car salesmen, morticians, professors, hockey players, scientists, accountants, artists, engineers). How do these stereotypes reduce our ability to send and receive positive messages?
3. Have you ever tried a type of food that is popular in another country but uncommon in Canada? Did you have difficulty understanding the popularity of the food? How did your perceptions differ from those of people who grew up in a country or culture in which the food is popular?
4. Have you ever shared perceptions of some event from your past—for example, a school trip, a scary encounter, or a family gathering—with a friend or family member who also experienced that event? Were you surprised to learn that each of you has different memories of the event? Did you argue over who was right or wrong or which details were correct? How does what you have learned about selective perception help to explain this phenomenon?
5. Have you ever worked with someone from another culture who dressed or behaved differently from you? How did you react to the unfamiliar behaviours? Did any misunderstandings arise between the two of you as a result of cultural differences? Explain.

SUGGESTED ACTIVITIES

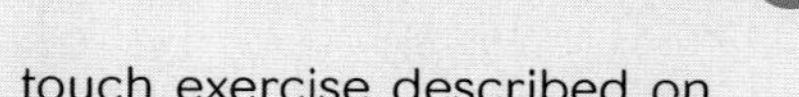

1. Participate in the touch exercise described on p. 71 and discuss the significance of the results.
2. Close your eyes for a moment. Think about what you can recall of your immediate surroundings. Shielding as much of your gaze as you can, glance down at the piece of paper in front of you and make a few notes about what you can remember about your physical environment. Then look up and compare your notes with those of other members of the class. Note the differences in observations.
3. Think of an experience that you have had with individuals who are traditionally seen as members of a marginalized group (e.g., people with disabilities or homeless people). Describe this experience to the class and comment on how your interaction leads you to see the people as individuals rather than as members of a group.

4. In a short written paragraph, describe your most frightening experience. Then read the description in private to another class member. That person will then whisper details of the story to a third person, the third person will whisper details to a fourth, and so on. Once everyone has heard the story, the last person will recount it to the class. Afterwards read the original description to the entire group. Then discuss what happened, considering questions such as the following: What was added? What was dropped? What was changed or distorted? How do these additions, drops, and changes relate to what you have learned about perception?
5. Ask a friend to enter the class long enough to make an announcement. Following the person's departure from the classroom, ask your classmates to provide and share descriptions of the person. Then have the person re-enter the room so that others can check their perceptions against reality. Why do you think the differences in perception occurred? How does this experience cause problems in courtrooms and other settings?

子供連
子供連

CHAPTER 4

Understanding, Navigating, and Managing Our Identities

CHAPTER OUTLINE

learning OBJECTIVES

- To understand the relationship between self-concept and identity
- To learn about how we navigate multiple identities with collective dimensions
- To understand the importance of having our identities validated by others
- To learn about managing personal identities in different contexts
- To become acquainted with impression-management strategies
- To understand how people manage impressions in online environments

forSTARTERS

The Catfish: Who Are You?

Several controversies have erupted in the past few years over people taking false identities online. One of the most widely discussed of these deceptions involved star football linebacker Manti Te'o. Over a period of many months, while he was playing for Notre Dame, Te'o fell in love with a "woman" he believed to be Lennay Kekua. In fact, his online "girlfriend" was Ronaiah Tuiasosopo, a troubled 22-year-old man who used a photo of a woman named Diane O'Meara to lure Te'o into the relationship. O'Meara knew nothing about the deception; nor did Te'o. When Tuiasosopo found it increasingly difficult to sustain the act, he "killed off" his fake alias, only to bring her back to life again three months later.

Shortly before Christmas, Te'o received a call that informed him of the hoax. Embarrassed, confused, and humiliated, Te'o spoke with his coaches at Notre Dame soon after he returned from the holidays; and the university launched an investigation to uncover the facts of the case. In the days that followed, Te'o had to deal with a barrage of press coverage, which questioned his credibility and authenticity. Internet users made fun of Te'o, posting pictures of the college football star with his arm around an imaginary girlfriend. They attached the term *Te'oing* to the phenomenon. People found it difficult to believe that anyone could have been fooled for so long. Some accused him of using the deception as a means of securing support for the Heisman Trophy, for which he was nominated at the time. They felt the hoax, revealed only after the award ceremony (at which Te'o was named runner-up), was a ploy for voter sympathy. Fans felt duped.

In fact, this phenomenon (now known as *catfishing*) has grown increasingly common; and Te'o is not the first or the

© Richard Levine/Alamy

most serious case of Internet deception. In 2005, 46-year-old Thomas Montgomery and 45-year-old Mary Shieler became entangled in an online romance with strong ironic dimensions and deadly consequences. Montgomery pretended to be an earlier version of himself—a six-foot, muscular 18-year-old Marine with broad shoulders and bright red hair. His Internet moniker was "MarineSniper," an exaggeration of his former role in the military. Using the moniker "Talhotblond," Mary took the identity of her 18-year-old daughter, Jessi.

For an extended period of time, neither knew of the other's true identity. Eventually, however, Montgomery's wife learned that her husband was engaged in an obsessive online relationship with an "18-year-old high school senior" from West Virginia; and she sent a letter with family photos to her husband's romantic interest. At that point,

INTRODUCTION

In Chapter 2, we focussed on self-concept. In talking about self-concept, we ask the question "Who am I?" Many different voices can respond to this question. Some of those voices come from inside of us, whereas others come from outside—friends, family, or others. When we talk about **identity**, on the other hand, we answer the question asked by others: "Who are *you*?" *Self-concept* refers to how we think of ourselves, whereas *identity* refers to the characteristics that allow others to recognize us.[3] (Note that both concepts differ from *reflected appraisal*, which refers to how we *think* others see us.)

IDENTITY The characteristics that allow others to recognize us.

So what are the characteristics or markers that enable other people to recognize us? Just as the DNA of one person is never the same as the DNA of another, the characteristics that make up our identities are also unique. These identity markers can be physical (e.g., appearance and athletic abilities), social (e.g., competence in relationships), academic the situation got more complicated. Still hiding her true identity, Mary berated Montgomery for his deception and launched an online romance with Brian Barrett. Barrett was a 22-year-old student at Buffalo State College, who worked part-time as a machinist at the same company as Montgomery. Unaware of Mary's true identity, Barrett became involved in Internet exchanges with "Talhotblond." But when he decided to add a personal dimension and make an impromptu visit to "Talhotblond" in 2006, Montgomery found out about Barrett's plans, became enraged, and murdered him. In a 2009 documentary titled *Talhotblond*, filmmakers exposed the extraordinary circumstances that led to the death of Brian Barrett.

The following year (2007), a young girl named Megan Meier hanged herself after learning that her Myspace boyfriend named *Josh Evans* was, in fact, the daughter of a 47-year-old neighbour named Lori Drew. Lori Drew created the fictitious Josh, and her daughter used the profile to deceive Megan into believing that Josh liked her. Eventually, however, the mythical Josh posted insults on Megan's Facebook page and proclaimed that he hated her. Unaware that Josh was not a real person, some of Megan's peers followed suit and posted vicious messages on her Myspace page. Like Manti Te'o, Megan became the brunt of a cruel online assault; but in this case, it ended in even greater tragedy.

As mentioned earlier, the term *catfishing* is now used to describe the practices of people who pretend to be someone else online in order to lure another person into a fraudulent relationship. *Catfishing* involves posting someone else's photographs or other misleading information on social media websites with the intent of getting another person to fall in love with the alias. The term *catfish* (used to signify the person doing the online luring) came from a film by the same name, which received rave reviews at the 2010 Sundance Film Festival. In the documentary, filmmakers Henry Joost and Ariel Schulman recorded the development of an online romance between Ariel's brother Nev and a constructed identity named Megan. Suspecting that something was fishy, the two filmmakers sought to document the fraudulent behaviour. On a spin-off television show (*Catfish: The TV Show*), Nev Schulman gives advice to those who have been catfished.

In the aftermath of the Manti Te'o story, many people have come forward in Internet postings to describe their own experiences with catfish. Ronnie Williams, for example, wrote: "This is so sad, this has happened to me a couple of times in the past when I first started dealing with Internet dating. I got my heart broken just like this, so trust me, this is a creepy, deceptive low life way of . . . playing with someone's emotions."[1]

Not all people who assume false identities online have malicious intent, however. Nev Schulman, for example, discusses the case of "Amanda," who was really Aaron, a gay man who had not come to terms with his real identity. At other times, people are looking for a more exciting life, and they do not want to hurt the other person. But Schulman warns that we can become so immersed in our alternative identities that we fail to live our real lives.[2]

This discussion should lead you to think about the following kinds of questions, which are addressed in this chapter: Which of your identities are most important to you? Intellectual? Physical? Emotional? Social? Do you think that others see you as you see yourself? Do you ever experiment online with your identity? Does your "ideal self" emerge in these experimentations? What kinds of impression-management strategies do you use to influence how others see you?

(e.g., intellectual capabilities), or emotional (e.g., how we feel).[4] Physical markers can include characteristics such as body type, skin colour, muscle tone, and physical coordination. Social markers relate to factors such as personality (whether we are shy or outgoing) and social skills (how well we get along with other people). Academic markers include characteristics related to our performance in school and our ability to engage in reasoning and analysis. Emotional markers can include the extent to which we show impulse control (e.g., manage anger), demonstrate maturity in our interactions with other people, or cope with negative events in our lives.

Our identity may contain elements that are not part of our self-concept, and our self-concept may contain components that are not part of our identity. Newborn babies lack a self-concept, but they have an identity that includes their names and recognizable

© mammamaart/iStockphoto

physical characteristics. Once we develop a self-concept, our less visible or hidden qualities may be absent from our identities. While others may see us as students or part-time employees at fast food restaurants, we may see ourselves as aspiring dancers or singers. Alternatively, others may see us as successful members of the Canadian ski team, but we may view ourselves as failed athletes because we did not make the last Olympic team. We are often shocked to learn the identity of people who commit acts of terrorism such as the 2012 shooting at the Eaton Centre in Toronto or the 2013 Boston marathon bombings. Traumatized family members and friends of the offenders typically proclaim that that the people they knew could not have committed these acts. Clearly, the perpetrators saw themselves in a different way from how others viewed them. Their self-concept had many hidden parts, not seen by others.[5] In the same way, there may be a gap between how we *think* someone sees us and how they *actually* see us.

We also have multiple identities; and in different situations, we place importance on some more than on others.[6] Consider the example of Dilavar, a 20-year-old Turkish Canadian youth. Dilavar is comfortable in his interactions with his family, eating *dolma* and talking excitedly in Turkish about vacation plans to travel to Istanbul. However, when he is at school with his friends or working in a part-time job at Tim Hortons, he is equally at ease talking about hockey or nominations for the Juno Awards. According to psychologist and philosopher William James, our self-presentations often respond to what others expect of us.[7] And at the same time that we are managing our identities, we are interacting with others who are managing their identities. Hence self-presentation becomes a process of selecting the appropriate identity for any given situation or circumstance.

In this chapter, we will look at how we navigate and manage multiple identities in face-to-face—as well as online—environments. We will also look at tips for more effectively managing our identities.

NAVIGATING MULTIPLE IDENTITIES WITH COLLECTIVE DIMENSIONS

As individuals, we are both authors of and principal characters in our "self-as-story";[8] and much like actors on a stage, we put a good deal of effort into developing our roles. In our life scripts, we play many different roles. That is, we have multiple identities. For example, a young woman may be a university student, daughter, sister, aunt, girlfriend, Newfoundlander, graphic artist, figure skater, good conversationalist, and human rights activist—all at the same time. Similarly, a young man may be a student,

> **"As much as being Indian is my identity, that is not all I am. I am not just an 'Indian'; I am a woman, a business student, an artist, a writer, an adventurer, and a sensitive yet bold person who cannot be summarized in one word."**
>
> AARTI SHAW[9]

brother, son, uncle, boyfriend, hockey player, amateur sports writer, musician, and member of the Liberal Party. To explore your various identities, refer to the "From Theory to Practice" box.

Our multiple identities have a collective dimension. That is, we share parts of our identity with larger groups. The collective or shared aspects of our identities contribute to a sense of "we-ness." We see evidence of these kinds of identifications in the enthusiastic cheering of players at college or university sports games or in the tears of Canadian athletes marching with their flag at the Olympics. Regional identifications surface when Canadians gather for a lobster festival in eastern Canada or attend a rodeo in Calgary. The LGBTQ community, the African Canadian community, and many ethnic groups sponsor days of pride to encourage **collective identities**. For an example of how communities can develop a collective

from theory TO PRACTICE

What Are the Different Aspects of Your Identity?

To understand the different aspects of your identity, go to the following link, respond to the questionnaire, and score yourself: www.wellesley.edu/Psychology/Cheek/aiq_iv.html. Did you learn anything new about yourself as a result of answering this questionnaire?

COLLECTIVE IDENTITY The characteristics of our personal identity that we share with members of a larger group.

human DIVERSITY

The Saints (and Others) Go Marching Home

When we think of New Orleans, we think of Bourbon Street, jazz musicians such as Louis Armstrong, and Mardi Gras. In February of each year, hundreds of thousands of celebrants from around the globe gather to drink, party, watch the parades, and participate in the festivities. Students often find sleeping space on the floors of dormitories and homes of friends. To accommodate the crowds, owners of restaurants and bars strip their establishments of chairs and tables. Outside on Canal Street and in the French Quarters, partygoers shove, mingle, and shout for beads to be tossed in their direction. Music is everywhere, and the excitement is infectious.

On 7 February 2010, the city began its celebrations earlier than planned. On that date, the New Orleans Saints met the Indianapolis Colts on neutral ground in Miami, Florida, to play in the widely publicized Super Bowl XLIV; and the unexpected happened. The Saints defeated the heavily favoured Colts by a score of 31–17. Fans went wild, celebrating in pubs and homes across the continent. Post-game analysis revealed that this super bowl was the most watched sports event in TV history, generating almost as much interest in Canada as in the US.

Louisiana had suffered two debilitating hurricanes in recent history; New Orleans had endured the horrors of Hurricane Katrina; and Saints fans had been waiting more than forty years for this celebration. Ironically, the father of Colts quarterback Peyton Manning had quarterbacked the Saints' team in its losing years—years when the Saints were dubbed the "Ain'ts" by cynical outsiders. Now it would be a bittersweet victory to see the Saints win against the team quarterbacked by his talented and celebrated son. These and other human interest stories set the scene for the emotional conclusion that has been widely seen as a comeback not only for the Saints, but also for New Orleans and Louisiana. The "Who Dat Nation" (the name many fans apply to themselves as a group) went wild. Schools declared a holiday. Eight thousand fans waited at the Louis Armstrong airport for returning team members, and Mardi Gras celebrations began in earnest with floats populated by the Saints players. On crowded streets and in public places, "Who dat, who dat, who dat say dey gonna beat dem Saints" became a mantra.

In the days and weeks following the Saints' victory, Louisiana residents repeatedly spoke of the Saints' rise from years of defeat to national prominence as a symbol of a revitalized Louisiana. The stadium where the Saints played their home games, which had been a site of suffering and despair in the aftermath of Hurricane Katrina, became a reminder of the city's resilience. Political, religious, and cultural leaders pronounced that the city was on its way to recovery. People who had fled the city in the aftermath of Katrina spoke of returning to rebuild their lives. Former and current residents who had lost homes, jobs, family members, and community affiliations basked in the reflected glory of a "close other." The Saints had become more than a sports team to the people of Louisiana; they had come to represent the spirit and collective identity of the community. Thus, the Saints' victory took on a greater significance—it became a new winning script for the people of New Orleans and the larger state community.

© Taylor Hinton/iStockphoto

identity in the wake of natural or manmade disasters, see the "Human Diversity" box on the 2010 Super Bowl victory of the New Orleans Saints.

Sometimes our collective identifications are so strong that we are willing to sacrifice our lives for group causes. For Japanese suicide bombers in World War II, national affiliation trumped commitment to personal well-being. In more recent years, we have seen religious affiliations drive some individuals to engage in similar acts, as with the 2001 destruction of the World Trade Center towers in New York City. In this case, as in many others, religion topped both personal preservation and national affiliation as a source of inspiration.

The following discussion identifies some important collective identifications, including gender, ethnic, religious, cultural, regional, and national affiliations.[10]

Navigating Gender Identities

GENDER IDENTITY Characteristics we share with others of a particular gender.

ANDROGYNOUS A mix of both feminine and masculine traits.

UNDIFFERENTIATED Low scores on both feminine and masculine traits.

The Bem Sex-Role Inventory, developed by researcher Sandra Bem in the early 1970s, allows users to classify themselves according to traditionally recognized sex (or, more accurately, gender) roles. (See the "From Theory to Practice" box.) The inventory includes the following categories: masculine, feminine, **androgynous**, and **undifferentiated**.[11] We land in one category or another, depending on how we rate ourselves on 60 physical, social, academic, and emotional characteristics. According to Bem, high scores on either masculinity or femininity suggest that we are displaying behaviours that could result in gender-typing by others. In other words, our friends and colleagues rely on gender displays to know how to interact with us. When their responses place us in a masculine or feminine trait category, they can influence us to exhibit these behaviours more strongly in the future. Sensitivity to this possibility can help us to move outside the gender categories into a more desirable androgynous zone. In recent years, however, critics have labelled Bem's inventory as culturally insensitive, outdated in its dependence on 1970s values and flawed in its methodology.[12]

Navigating Ethnic and Racial Identities

ETHNIC IDENTITY Characteristics we share with others with a common ancestry.

Ethnic identity refers to the extent to which we identify with—or connect to—others who share our ancestry.[13] Some characteristics of ethnic identity include a distinct sense of belonging to a particular ethnic group; a commitment to this group's core values and beliefs; and a support for traditional values, which we often hold in common with many other ethnic groups.[14] Ethnic groups often (but not always) have race in common. Names used to designate some of the ethnic groups in Canada include *Hispanic*, *Latino*, *African Canadian*, *Asian Canadian*, *Chinese*, *Filipino*, *First Nations*, *Aboriginal*, *Mexican Canadian*, *Caucasian*, and *Italian Canadian*. For many new Canadians, ethnic identity plays a critical role in home, social, and work lives. (See the "Human Diversity" box for a brief look at ethnic identity in second-generation Canadians.)

RACIAL IDENTITY Characteristics we share with others with respect to racial heritage.

A related concept is **racial identity**. We can identify our *racial identity* by considering our sense of connection or shared heritage with a racial group.[15] Individuals with multiple racial identities face a particular challenge in social interactions, because they

from theory TO PRACTICE

The Bem Sex-Role Inventory: How Masculine or Feminine Are You?

Rate yourself on a scale from one to seven on the following items, with one representing *never or almost never true* and seven representing *always or almost always true.*

1. Self-reliant ___
2. Yielding ___
3. Helpful ___
4. Defends own beliefs ___
5. Cheerful ___
6. Moody ___
7. Independent ___
8. Shy ___
9. Conscientious ___
10. Athletic ___
11. Affectionate ___
12. Theatrical ___
13. Assertive ___
14. Flatterable ___
15. Happy ___
16. Strong personality ___
17. Loyal ___
18. Unpredictable ___
19. Forceful ___
20. Feminine ___
21. Reliable ___
22. Analytical ___
23. Sympathetic ___
24. Jealous ___
25. Has leadership abilities ___
26. Sensitive to needs of others ___
27. Truthful ___
28. Willing to take risks ___
29. Understanding ___
30. Secretive ___
31. Makes decisions easily ___
32. Compassionate ___
33. Sincere ___
34. Self-sufficient ___
35. Eager to soothe hurt feelings ___
36. Conceited ___
37. Dominant ___
38. Soft-spoken ___
39. Likable ___
40. Masculine ___
41. Warm ___
42. Solemn ___
43. Willing to take a stand ___
44. Tender ___
45. Friendly ___
46. Aggressive ___
47. Gullible ___
48. Inefficient ___
49. Acts as a leader___
50. Childlike ___
51. Adaptable ___
52. Individualistic ___
53. Does not use harsh language ___
54. Unsystematic ___
55. Competitive ___
56. Loves children ___
57. Tactful ___
58. Ambitious ___
59. Gentle ___
60. Conventional ___

Add your ratings for items 1, 4, 7, 10, 13, 16, 19, 22, 25, 28, 31, 34, 37, 40, 43, 46, 49, 52, 55, and 58. Divide this total by 20. This figure represents your score on the masculinity dimension. Then add your ratings for items 2, 5, 8, 11, 14, 17, 20, 23, 26, 29, 32, 35, 38, 41, 44, 47, 50, 53, 56, and 59. Divide the total by 20. This figure represents your score on the femininity dimension. Consult the following chart to identify your sex type as masculine, feminine, androgynous, or undifferentiated.

	MASCULINITY GREATER THAN 4.9	MASCULINITY LESS THAN 4.9
FEMININITY GREATER THAN 4.9	Androgynous	Female sex typed
FEMININITY LESS THAN 4.9	Male sex typed	Undifferentiated

SOURCE: Based on S. Bem, "On the Utility of Alternative Procedures for Assessing Psychological Androgyny," *Journal of Consulting and Clinical Psychology* 45 (1977): 196–205.

must pick and choose between identities. In some situations, however, people with multiple racial or ethnic identities have an advantage over those with only one identity. For example, some argue that having multiple racial identities can buffer a person from cultural stereotypes that negatively influence self-concept. In addition, research suggests that multiracial people often make conscious efforts to adapt their racial identities to circumstances and contexts.[16] In the 2008 and 2012 US presidential campaigns, for example, President Barack Obama sometimes focussed on his white grandparents or mother in promoting his candidacy; at other times, he focussed on his African heritage. His choices depended upon the audience, the circumstances, and the occasion.

> **"I confused gender identity with sexual orientation. Your gender identity is about who you are, how you feel, the sex that you feel yourself to be. Sexual orientation is who you're attracted to."**
>
> CHAZ BONO

Navigating Religious Identities

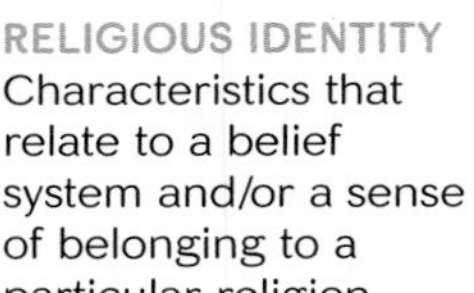

RELIGIOUS IDENTITY Characteristics that relate to a belief system and/or a sense of belonging to a particular religion.

Religious identity plays an important role in the lives of some Canadians. Our *religious identity* involves a sense of belonging to a certain faith or religion.[18] Sometimes we maintain religious identities as a way of preserving ethnic and other group identities. The maintenance of religious identities is especially important to many immigrants, especially those who are minorities within Canada.[19] Religion helps immigrants to maintain ties with their home countries and cultures, to achieve solidarity, and to come together with others with similar beliefs and values.

Take the fictitious example of two young women, Radhika and Nasreen. Radhika migrates with her family from Mumbai, India; and Nasreen and her family migrate from Teheran, Iran. Both families live in Mississauga, Ontario, where the two girls form a close friendship in grade school. Growing up, the girls are always conscious of the religious practices and rituals common to their respective faiths.

Nasreen's family practises Islam. She participates in the annual Ramadan fast and observes other important occasions such as Eid al-Adha. In the traditions of Islam, she prays five times each day, often with her parents at the local mosque. Along with her brother, Hanif, Nasreen attends Quran classes for youth. Her parents are active in the local Iranian Canadian Association. Despite her Canadian connections, Nasreen feels very close to her extended family in Iran, and she stays in touch with them through occasional phone calls and social media sites like Facebook. Her Iranian relatives were surprised but pleased when Nasreen continued to follow Islamic practices even after her family relocated in Canada.

*human*DIVERSITY

Ethnic Identity in Second-Generation Canadians

To what extent do second-generation ethnic youth identify with the roots and ethnic origins of their parents and grandparents? We might expect these links to weaken over time and for the youth to see themselves as more Canadian than Turkish, Pakistani, Somali, Brazilian, Swedish, or any other nationality. In one study that aimed to discover the answer to this question, researchers interviewed second-generation Finnish Canadian youth in Ottawa. The resulting data showed that the youth participated only infrequently in Finnish community events, and not all were fluent in the Finnish language. Nonetheless, they spoke of emotional ties to Finland and visits to Finnish grandparents and other relatives. They said that some cultural items in their homes held special meaning for them. The researchers concluded that the youth identified with their Finnish ethnicity on a symbolic level but also identified strongly with being Canadian.[17]

Radhika and her parents adhere to the Hindu faith, and they never tire of talking about religious events in their home country of India. These conversations revolve around visits to the temple, social gatherings, and activities associated with important religious holidays. Radhika and her sister, Seema, hear countless accounts of the annual Ganesha festival in Mumbai. Her parents are active members of the local Indian Temple Association. Radhika learns classical Indian dance, and Seema learns to play the flute in the classical Indian music tradition. Sometimes Radhika and her sister feel frustrated, however, that they must spend so much time on religious and other practices related to their Indian heritage.

The parents of both Radhika and Nasreen believe that their religious affiliations serve as vital links to their home countries and ethnic heritage.

Navigating Linguistic and Cultural Identities

Language can be a major mediator in preserving or threatening cultural identities. Because of its ties to oral histories and cultural knowledge, language affects how we perceive the world and our relationship to the world.[20] In North America, **linguistic** and **cultural identities** play a particularly important role in the lives of Aboriginal people. In February 2010, the band council of the Mohawk reserve at Kahnawake, located 15 minutes from downtown Montreal, issued eviction notices to 25 individuals deemed to be non-Native. The council stated that the evictions, issued on the basis of racial heritage, were meant to preserve the identity of the Mohawk community. The council's actions generated a fierce debate, both within and outside the Mohawk community. Central to the debate are questions of how band membership should be determined—through bloodlines or through cultural participation—and how First Nations people can best preserve their cultural identities in the face of the growing threat of **assimilation**.[21]

LINGUISTIC IDENTITY Characteristics we share with others who speak a common language.

CULTURAL IDENTITY Characteristics we share with others from the same or similar cultural backgrounds.

ASSIMILATION The process of being absorbed into a larger group.

Many people believe that minority groups cannot survive as distinct cultural entities without preservation of their languages. In the United States, a project is underway to preserve the oral and cultural histories of the Assiniboine tribe of the northern plains of Montana. This tribe presently has only 50 living members fluent in the group's native tongue.[22] In Canada, the federal government has established the Aboriginal Languages Initiative with a similar objective: "to support the preservation and revitalization of Aboriginal languages for the benefit of Aboriginal peoples and other Canadians."[23]

In a similar way, the province of Quebec has long worried about loss of French cultural identity in an overwhelmingly English Canada. For that reason, politicians introduced and approved the controversial *Charter of the French Language* (also called Bill 101) in 1977, which defined Quebec as a unilingual province. This law requires all merchants to display French most prominently on signs, a concern to businesses operating in ethnic or predominantly English parts of Quebec. Additional actions by Quebec governments in recent years have continued to provoke a heated debate over questions of language and identity.

When we want to preserve and maintain our linguistic and cultural identities, we can engage in a number of different strategies. We can support language programs such as the ones discussed above. We can also participate in cultural events.[24] Canada hosts many cultural festivals, including the Caribana festival in Toronto, the South Asian and Lebanese festivals in Ottawa, the Caribbean Days Festival in North Vancouver, the Festival du Voyageur in Winnipeg, the Carnaval de Québec in Quebec City, and the Calgary Stampede. These festivals act to promote and preserve cultural identities.[25] In addition, ethnic media create and produce cultural content, which various ethno-cultural and ethnic groups consume.[26] Omni TV (which broadcasts in Alberta, British Columbia, and Ontario) targets various ethnic and linguistic groups such as Somali, South Asian, Polish, Italian, Chinese, Russian, and Ukrainian with its programming.

> **"Anybody who works in the English language in Ireland knows that there's the dead ghost of Gaelic in the language we use and listen to and that those things will reflect our Irish identity."**
>
> JOHN MCGAHERN

Navigating Regional and National Identities

REGIONAL IDENTITY
Characteristics we share with others from a particular region of a country.

NATIONAL IDENTITY
Characteristics we share with others from a particular country.

We can identify our **regional** and **national identities** by considering the regions or countries to which we feel connected.[27] For Canadians, geography has a major influence on identity. Events experienced as significant in Ottawa, for example, may generate few ripples in cities as far away as Halifax, Calgary, Vancouver, or even Montreal or Toronto. Western Canadians often express a feeling of alienation from central and eastern Canada. Crossing the country on the Trans-Canada Highway, we can recognize the origins of this psychic distance. Sparse populations in Manitoba and Saskatchewan and steep mountains separating British Columbia from the rest of Canada contribute to the feeling of separateness from the highly populated provinces of Ontario and Quebec. In a similar way, the Aboriginal peoples of the northern territories often express a feeling of alienation from those who live in the southern provinces, and people in Labrador and Newfoundland see themselves as unique populations within Canada.

The nearness of Canada to the United States has an impact on how Canadians perceive their identities. After all, 90 per cent of Canadians live within 160 kilometres of the Canada–US border, and we have close historical and economic ties to Americans. As a result, we also share many values. A major international study by Dutch psychologist Geert Hofstede confirms, for example, that Canadians cluster with Americans on four major dimensions of culture:[28]

- *power distance*—the extent to which hierarchical power and structure set people psychologically apart from one another (i.e., those in power should look, act, and feel more powerful than those with less power);
- *uncertainty avoidance*—the extent to which people accept and need rules,

regulations, and clear delineation of responsibilities (i.e., they see unfamiliar, uncertain, and ambiguous situations as threatening and anxiety-producing);

- *individualism–collectivism*—the extent to which people value and reward individuals versus groups; and
- *masculinity–femininity*—the extent to which people value assertiveness, independence, and achievement (stereotypically masculine values) versus nurturance and sympathy (stereotypically female values).

In his study, Hofstede administered psychological inventories to more than 116,000 IBM employees based in 40 countries around the world. The following examples illustrate the nature of his findings.

Employees in Scandinavian countries scored high on the femininity dimension. Scandinavian management stresses consensus-based, intuitive decision-making and reliance on informal personal contacts. In contrast, employees in the United States scored high on the masculine dimension. Americans value fact-based management and fast decisions that depend on clear establishment of responsibilities. An American consultant going into a Scandinavian organization would probably not feel comfortable with the intuitive decision-making style of his Scandinavian client. (In later studies, Hofstede labelled the *masculinity–femininity* dimension as *achievement–nurturance*. Using the revised terminology, Sweden would have ranked high on the nurturance dimension and the United States high on the achievement dimension.)

Hofstede found that people in France are most comfortable with large power distances. They like centralized power and clear status differences. So when IBM asked the direct supervisors of employees to initiate all proposals for salary increases, the French branch modified the policy. It required the *superior's superior's* superior, three levels above, to initiate the salary proposals.

Germans scored high on the need for uncertainty avoidance. That is, they expressed a desire for formal rules, specialization, and assignment of tasks to experts. In this context, it should not be surprising that Max Weber, the author of bureaucratic theory, was a German. Bureaucracy makes order possible even in conditions of change. Power exists in the role, not in the person; and rules protect the lower-ranking employees from abuse by those who outrank them.

The United States offers the best example of a country rating high on the individualism scale, followed closely by Australia and Great Britain. Canada is also more individualistic than collectivistic in its orientation. Canadians value and protect individual rights over the rights of groups. The *Canadian Charter of Rights and Freedoms* incorporates this focus on the individual, as does the American *Bill of Rights*. Strong historical and cultural links exist between individualism and capitalism. In collectivist societies such as Japan and many African nations, on the other hand, loyalty is to the clan, the organization, or society. In return, the organization or group assumes responsibility for protecting its members. The Japanese regard "hire and fire" policies as poor ones, and traditionally they have offered lifetime employment to many members of their organizations.

Canada and the United States both scored slightly below average on cultural value placed on power distance, well below average on uncertainty avoidance, very high on individualism, and well above average on the achievement dimension. Other countries with values similar to those of Canada and the United States included Ireland, New Zealand, and Great Britain.

In the years following his study, Hofstede added three more dimensions:

- *short-term versus long-term orientation*—a focus on the present and past (traditional values, social obligations, and saving face) versus future rewards (perseverance and thrift);
- *indulgence versus restraint*—enjoyment of the pleasures of life (partying, leisure time, sex, spending, and consumption) versus holding back or controlling the extent to which one indulges in the pleasures of life;
- *monumentalism versus self-effacement*—emphasis on pride and rigidity versus humility and flexibility.

Hofstede drew these last three categories from the results of studies conducted by Michael Bond and Michael Minkov. Bond surveyed students in 23 countries, and Minkov analyzed responses from people in 81 countries.[29] Considered together, Hofstede's seven dimensions help us identify and understand the distinct characteristics that contribute to national identities.

"Canadians often define themselves by what they are not—and what they are not is American."
SHERRY DEVEREAUX FERGUSON

Despite the fact that Canadians agree that we are more like Americans than like other nationalities (55 per cent believe our values are similar),[30] we also argue for differences. We see ourselves as more compassionate, peace-loving, and egalitarian than Americans.[31] In "Fire and Ice" surveys of Americans and Canadians, conducted by the Environics Research Group (Toronto) between 1992 and 2000, other differences also surfaced:[32]

The United States	**Canada**
Religious	Secular
Risk-taking	Risk-averse
Money is everything	Money is suspect
Winner takes all	Income redistribution
Highest standard of living	Best quality of life
Will win the lottery	Have won the lottery
Aspiration	Accommodation
Traditional authority	Question traditional authority
Moralism relativism	Pluralism
Conservative social values	Liberal social values
Outer-directed (conformity)	Inner-directed (autonomy)
Violence is normal	Violence only on skates
Civil-war rebellions	Legal separation
Death penalty	No death penalty since 1976
Neo-conservatism	Sustainable social welfare state
Direct democracy	Parliamentary democracy
Gated communities and SUVs	Multicultural cities and minivans
Unilateralism, pre-emptive strikes/wars	UN, International Criminal Court, Kyoto Protocol, peacekeeping
Jazz, baseball, movies, Internet, and Man on the Moon	Medicare, hockey, and Cirque du Soleil

A number of other surveys also record differences in Canadian and American values. A 2002 Communication Canada survey identified family (79 per cent), respect (66 per cent), peace (65 per cent), freedom (64 per cent), and helping others (63 per cent) as the values most often chosen by Canadians. More than half of surveyed Canadians also selected safety and security (57 per cent), fairness (56 per cent), co-operation (54 per cent), appreciation of heritage and history (54 per cent), openness and tolerance (54 per cent), democracy (51 per cent), sharing (51 per cent), and caring (51 per cent).When asked to identify their top values, Americans listed patriotism, achievement, competitiveness, caring, dominance, egalitarianism, responsibility, culture, materialism, and morality. Canadians agree that American values include patriotism, achievement, competitiveness, dominance, and materialism; however, they question the extent to which Americans incorporate the other values into their daily lives.[33]

> **"Patriotism is, fundamentally, a conviction that a particular country is the best in the world because you were born in it."**
> GEORGE BERNARD SHAW

from theory TO PRACTICE

Who Am I?

Think of your own background and try to describe yourself in terms of gender, ethnic, racial, religious, linguistic, cultural, regional, and national identities. Was it difficult for you to separate all these different parts? If so, why?

EXPERIMENTING WITH OUR IDENTITIES

While we often think of identities as relatively unchangeable, some parts of our identity are highly flexible. For example, we can improve our athletic abilities by undergoing physical training. We can immerse ourselves in another culture and eventually assume an identity associated with that culture. We can even change relatively static physical characteristics through surgery. In other words, we may present ourselves at different times to different people in different ways. Only we know our "real self."

Most of us experiment with our identities at some point. Sometimes we experiment in a casual way. We may colour our hair or change our style of dressing (physical identity), assume a new name on Twitter (social identity), enter a new field of studies (intellectual identity), or practise being less emotional in professional environments (emotional identity). We may even pretend to be someone else. Some studies have found that approximately 50 per cent of all Internet users have, on some occasion, pretended to be someone else.[34] At other times, our experimentations may be rooted deeply in a desire to locate and exhibit the "real" self. The lives of many gay, lesbian, and transgendered individuals reveal such searches for self-identity and self-expression.

We are most likely to use the Internet to experiment with our identities in our adolescent years,[35] and preadolescents and younger adolescents experiment more often than older adolescents. Lonely adolescents experiment with their identities more than others in their age group.[36] The most extreme cases of experimentation with identities involve young males who, in a desperate search for a new identity, become mass murderers. See the "Professional Contexts" box on rampage killings.

In the age of social media, many people construct alternative identities through self-presentations on blogs, personal websites, Second Life, Facebook, Myspace, Twitter, YouTube,

*professional*CONTEXTS

Rampage Killings: The Quest for a New Identity?

On the morning of 14 December 2012, Adam Lanza shot his mother, Nancy Lanza, before proceeding to Sandy Hook Elementary School, where he shot and killed 20 first graders as well as their principal and several of their teachers with an assault-style weapon. These actions left the community reeling and the larger nation wondering "What went wrong?"

The work of researcher Katherine Newman offers some answers to this question. In 2004, along with two co-authors, Newman published a book called *Rampage: The Social Roots of School Shootings.*[37] This book documents a landmark study conducted by Newman and four doctoral students at Harvard University. Newman began her research in the year following the 1999 shootings at Columbine High School in Littleton, Colorado. The research team looked at 18 rampage shootings that had occurred in small-town American high schools in the years following 1970.

Based on close to two hundred interviews, Newman and her team arrived at some novel conclusions. They discovered that the high school shooters were not loners, as many people had believed. Instead the boys were at the outer margins of society. They aspired to membership in the groups populated by their more popular peers; but they were socially inept, awkward in how they interacted with other people. In Newman's words, they were "failed joiners."

Residing and going to school in small towns did not make their daily lives easier, because small towns foster a climate that supports conformity and group norms—the most difficult environment for someone who feels different. Although the stability of small towns makes these locations ideal for family life, they can be like a "death sentence to those at the margins."[38] Newman says that in small towns, marginalized youth face a situation with few options.

Why do young rampage killers choose school populations? Newman notes that the shooters are typically strong students, but they feel out of place in school cultures that value athletic over academic performance.[39] Their peers see them as "unattractive," "weak," and "unmanly" losers. Facing rebuff, they look for unconventional ways to change the way that others see them; and once an outcast starts dropping hints that he might kill someone, others pay attention. Typically, the shooting is the "last act in a long drama: a search for acceptance and recognition"—undertaken only after all other strategies fail.[40]

Take the case of Michael Carneal, a bright 13-year-old boy whose 1997 shooting spree at Heath High School in Paducah, Kentucky, resulted in three deaths and one paralysis. Carneal was a good student but a poor athlete, and his peers often teased and bullied him. Prior to the shooting spree, Carneal had tried more harmless means of getting attention. He had played the jokester—acting silly, playing tricks on people, and stealing small items. But not until he started talking about killing people did he get the attention of the school goths, the group he desperately wanted to join. When questioned afterwards about his motives, Carneal said that he thought the goths would become his friends after the shooting—that they would invite him to their homes and come to see him at his home. He would be part of the "cool" crowd. He never thought about the consequences of his actions or the pain he would cause others. According to Newman, "all he was after was another identity." Like others who commit similar acts, Carneal was trying to cast himself in the lead role in a movie that ends in gunfire and infamy.[41]

Schools provide an appropriate setting for such staged events, because they reside at the hub of small towns. Attacks on schools draw the undivided attention of the entire community. And, according to Newman, the underlying cause for these attacks is almost always the same: "a fragile or damaged identity, an experience or fear of rejection, and a perceived failure to fit into a family, a school, or a larger community."[42]

and other social media sites. Online dating sites in particular afford people the opportunity to craft and experiment with profiles that highlight or glorify their lives and personalities.[43]

As in many other areas of communication, differences emerge between men and women in terms of the ways in which they play with their identities. For example, women lie more often about their weight and men lie more about their height. Women are more honest in disclosing their status as single, divorced, or separated.[44] Although both men and women post misleading photographs, women are more likely than men to post outdated, retouched, or otherwise deceptive photographs. They are also more likely to post photographs taken by a professional. At the same time, women worry about posting a photograph so far removed from reality that their online correspondent will not accept them when they meet in person. They aim to achieve a balance between enhancing their physical appearance and presenting a recognizable view of self.[45]

Given that people experiment online with their identities, what is the impact of this experimentation? Do these public presentations, constructed online, alter or shape offline identities? In fact, online experimentation with identities can lead us to manifest our online personality characteristics in offline interactions. That is, we may begin to internalize the characteristics and behaviours we present online, influencing how we present ourselves in real-world encounters.[46]

> **"Perhaps it's impossible to wear an identity without becoming what you pretend to be."**
> **ORSON SCOTT CARD**

In the sense that experimentation involves manipulation, all experimentation with identities requires a certain amount of deception. However, the motives for the deception vary from situation to situation. On a whim, someone with brown hair and brown eyes may decide to build an online avatar with blonde hair and blue eyes. The person may have no ulterior motives. The sole motive is novelty or experimentation. In another case, a young boy with a slight build may decide to construct an avatar with large biceps and a broad chest. In this case, the avatar reflects the boy's ideal physical self. In a third instance, a woman may pretend to be single when she is in a committed relationship. This pretense may reflect her desire to find another relationship, to cheat on her partner, or just to enjoy another person's company without having to explain the details of her personal life.

Alternatively, people may misrepresent themselves without realizing that they are being deceptive. For example, the posting of an outdated photograph may reflect a person's inattention to the ways in which she or he has changed over time. When people interact online, they often present features of some earlier or **historical self**. For example, if a middle-aged woman enjoyed outdoor sports such as cross-country skiing and bicycling as a youth, she may still see herself as "loving the outdoors and leading an active lifestyle" even if she has not bicycled or put on a pair of skis for 10 or 20 years. She may genuinely believe what she puts into her profile. Similarly, a young man may list himself as an activist on social issues if he signs online petitions on a regular basis. The social justice community, on the other hand, may see him as no more than a passive supporter of causes. Furthermore, when youth participate in deceptive presentations of selves, they rarely see the strategies as unethical. Rather they are likely to see their inaccurate self-representations as presentations of who they would most like to be—their ideal selves.

HISTORICAL SELF An outdated self, someone we used to be.

Problems can arise nonetheless when someone wants to make the transition between the "ideal" or "historical" self and the "real" or "present" self. This kind of dilemma occurs, for example, when online chat leads to a face-to-face meeting. If a photograph posted online bears little resemblance to the person who appears at the coffee shop, the online correspondent may resent the deception or question the credibility of other claims made by the person.

Some cases of deception (online and offline) relate to efforts to conceal conditions that carry negative stigmas. Examples of such conditions include "history of mental illness, rape, molestation, epilepsy, domestic violence, previous incarceration, HIV/AIDS, and substance abuse."[47] Eating disorders also carry stigmas. We often hide these sorts of conditions—and the **concealable stigmatized identities** associated with them—out of fear that others might see us in a less positive light if they know about the condition.[48] In our view, the condition carries a potential mark of failure or shame.[49]

CONCEALABLE STIGMATIZED IDENTITY An identity that carries a stigma and that can be hidden from others.

Stigmas can have an impact on both the affected individual and close others, who fear being shunned or avoided if people learn about the stigmatized condition. The impact varies from country to country and from group to group. Hispanics, Asian Americans, and Native Americans report greater effects from stigmatized social identities than do European Americans; and African Americans report smaller effects.[50]

VALIDATING OUR IDENTITIES

We look to others to validate or confirm our identities.[51] When others within our social context are not willing to validate certain parts of our identities, we sometimes choose to abandon those parts. On the morning of 26 January 2013, prominent Ontarian politician Harinder Takhar delivered a speech to delegates at the Ontario Liberal leadership convention. Speaking of his immigrant roots in India, Takhar said that he had been forced to cut his hair and give up wearing a turban in order to secure a job in Ontario. In other words, he had been forced to give up part of his identity—a decision that meant "losing a part of himself forever."[52]

Sometimes the losses that we suffer, in terms of identities, do not come from choices we make ourselves—but from circumstances. Sometimes our identities are stolen from us. To learn more about the growing problem of identity theft, refer to the "Professional Contexts" box titled "Stolen Identities."

Psychologist Milton Rokeach describes what can happen in other circumstances—when people question or fail to validate *some part of our* identity. In a classic work, he discusses the case of the "Three Christs of Ypsilanti."[53] In this study, Rokeach placed three mental patients, all of whom believed they were Jesus Christ, in a facility together. He forced them into daily physical and social contact. Eventually two gave up their identities when confronted with an assault to core beliefs about their identity. (Milton Rokeach labels these core beliefs about self as "Type A" beliefs.) The result was sweeping changes to their entire belief system—changes in self-perception, identification with authority figures, beliefs that came from those authority figures, and trivial matters of taste.

SELF-VERIFICATION THEORY Theory that says that we want others to see us as we see ourselves.

Self-verification theory says that we want others to see us as we see ourselves.[54] So how do we respond to feedback that is incompatible with how we see ourselves and how we want others to see us? An experiment with female undergraduate psychology students at the University of Texas at Austin found that participants made intensive

*professional*CONTEXTS

Stolen Identities

What happens when someone steals our identity? In many regards, identity theft is the most extreme example of a threat to identity; and understandably victims of this sort of theft feel angry and helpless. Some even apply the term *rape* to their feelings of violation. They face the possibility of losing their credit ratings, which affect their ability to make major purchases such as a home or automobile. They can lose their life savings. They can even lose their reputations. Sometimes the perpetrators of identity theft commit crimes in their victims' names. After a major drug dealer stole the identity of a high-tech executive in the United States, the executive had to carry explanatory documents from law enforcement whenever he travelled out of the country. Otherwise he faced interrogation by customs personnel upon re-entry. On one occasion, armed law enforcement officers entered his home in the middle of the night to arrest him. They had not read the complete entry on the FBI's database, and they thought he was the criminal. A CALPIRG survey found that victims have to invest an average of 175 hours over two years to restore their financial status. Some cases take more than four years to reach resolution, and the invisible scars remain for much longer periods of time.[55]

efforts to change views that did not correspond to how they wanted others to see them.[56] In other words, they sought feedback that would verify or validate the views they held of themselves. As you will see later in this chapter, we can choose among a number of different strategies when we feel the need to improve negative impressions.[57] And most of us—some more than others—engage in ongoing **self-monitoring** to ensure we are creating the desired public impression.

SELF-MONITORING The extent to which we regulate our behaviours in order to look good to others.

HIGH SELF-MONITORS People who are very aware of the opinions of others.

LOW SELF-MONITORS People who do not worry about the opinions of others.

High self-monitors pay great attention to the opinions of others, and they alter their behaviours to fit different kinds of situations. They also have different public and private faces, and they try to be the person you want them to be. If someone is a high self-monitor, he will probably engage in a variety of activities designed to challenge incompatible feedback.[58] High self-monitors make good managers because they can influence people to follow their lead.[59]

Unlike high self-monitors, **low self-monitors** do not pay much attention to how others perceive them. Nor do they make an effort to manage these perceptions. They behave in much the same way across different contexts (e.g., family, work, recreational), and they tend to rely on their own values to guide their behaviour. Low self-monitors expect you to "take them as they are." They make good researchers and project members. The behaviours of low self-monitors are much easier to predict than those of high self-monitors, who are good at assuming different roles.[60]

> **"That ain't me, that ain't my face. It wasn't even me when I was trying to be that face. I wasn't even really me then; I was just being the way I looked, the way people wanted."**
>
> KEN KESEY, *One Flew over the Cuckoo's Nest*

MANAGING OUR IDENTITIES

The term impression management refers to the way we use presentation styles to create impressions of ourselves in the eyes of family, friends, workplace associates, romantic partners, and others. Simply put, impression management is the art of self-presentation.[61] The following discussion focusses on how we manage our multiple and collective identities in face-to-face and online environments. We will look at various contexts and strategies.

IMPRESSION MANAGEMENT The way we create impressions of ourselves in the eyes of others.

Why do we feel the need to manage impressions? Scholars in psychology and sociology agree that expectations of others, setting or context, and the value placed on opinions of others drive our desire to present ourselves in a given way.[62] We behave differently with different people in different situations. The levels of formality and rules of interaction vary from setting to setting.[63]

For many years, concepts related to self-presentation and impression management appeared in the popular literature under the label of "how to win friends and influence people," after the title of a highly influential 1936 book by Dale Carnegie.[64] Because some acts of self-presentation involve conscious effort, people tended to see early impression-management strategies as manipulative. Self-presentation and impression management

Wavebreak Media/Thinkstock

became an area of academic interest only after Erving Goffman entered the discourse in the mid-1950s.[65] Using theatre settings as a metaphor for understanding social interactions, Goffman said that some interactions take place "onstage" and others occur "offstage." In other words, some interactions are public and others are private; and we take concrete steps to construct, protect, and maintain our public identities.

We no longer see self-presentation as a manipulative act that happens only in special circumstances such as job interviews or first dates. Instead we see impression management as an everyday occurrence that characterizes all social interactions. Self-presentation communicates who we are to others,[66]and we perform most impression-management strategies without thinking about them. In other cases, we make not only conscious but also unconscious efforts to create a specific impression. For an example of a conscious effort, see the "Professional Contexts" box on image makeovers.

*professional*CONTEXTS

A Makeover for Your Image

Thirty-five years old, Stella is a successful investment banker. She is attractive and intelligent, a good conversationalist. She wants to find someone with whom she can settle down, but she has had a lot of bad luck in relationships. She has been thinking about reactivating her membership on an online dating site; however, her last experience with meeting people through this site was not a good one. She worries that, once again, she might attract someone who is not truly interested in pursuing a serious relationship. How can she present herself in a way that attracts the kind of person she would like to meet? Browsing the Internet, she locates the name of a firm that specializes in personal-image construction in online environments.

Aden has a different problem. He is a 50-year-old former manager of a large industrial supply company in Saskatchewan. He joined the firm more than twenty years ago, shortly after graduating with a marketing degree from Dalhousie University. He rose quickly in the firm; however, economic problems spurred the company to lay off a large number of employees, including Aden and several other high-salaried managers. Demoralized, Aden worries that his image is outdated and that his age will work against him in a job market saturated by young people. Unsure of how to proceed, he looks online for ideas; and one day he comes across an advertisement for a firm that offers assistance with executive-image management.

Manon just graduated from a publishing program at Simon Fraser University in British Columbia. She is excited to learn that a position has just opened at a commercial publishing house in Toronto—her dream job. When she goes to the publisher's website, however, she sees pictures of men and women who dress quite differently from her. With the computer images still in mind, Manon surveys her closet. Instead of solid-coloured suits and conservative shirts, she sees brightly coloured and patterned fabrics—the leftovers of her earlier studies at a design school in Montreal. She looks at herself in the mirror and sees a more recently formed schoolgirl look—long straight hair falling around her shoulders and a minimum of makeup. What to do? She pulls out old notes from one of her design classes and runs across the name of an image-consulting firm.

What do the three have in common? All ended up going to image consultants. Stella sought the help of a firm that specializes in personal-image construction. Aden sought the help of a firm that specializes in executive-image management. Manon located the name of a company that focusses on professional-image management.

Image consulting is the business of helping people to create and perfect their self-presentation strategies. As noted with the above examples, image consulting takes different forms. Some firms specialize in personal-image management. Personal-image consultants might suggest how to adapt or change your hair style, clothing, personal grooming, manners, or other behaviours in order to draw positive instead of negative notice in various social settings. Professional-image management firms aim to achieve similar goals in business, government, and political contexts. Professional-image consultants might work with employees in areas such as business etiquette and grooming, which can have an impact on customer relations and sales. Other firms restrict their clientele to executives. Many also offer advice on how to build a personal, professional, or corporate image online.

To learn more about image consulting, you can go to the website of the Canadian chapter of the Association of Image Consultants International (AICI): www.aicicanada.com.

In the following sections, we will discuss the different contexts in which people manage impressions and common impression-management strategies.

Managing Impressions in Different Contexts

Impression management can occur within the contexts of family, friendships, romantic relationships, or professional relationships. We learn to behave in certain ways (i.e., to create impressions) in order to maintain or promote these relationships. (See Chapter 8 for additional coverage of family, friendship, professional, and romantic relationship contexts.)

Managing Impressions in Family Contexts

The movie *Monster-in-Law* offers an amusing example of how a prospective daughter-in-law and future mother-in-law seek to manage impressions in a family context. While the daughter-in-law (played by Jennifer Lopez) tries to create a favourable impression with her future mother-in-law (played by Jane Fonda), the mother-in-law behaves in the opposite way. She aims to create a negative and unfavourable impression as she distances herself from her son's fiancée. The movie illustrates both negative and positive approaches to impression-management in a family context. It also illustrates the complexities of managing impressions in family contexts.

As in other cases, impression management in family contexts involves controlling the information that we share with others.[67] Achieving this kind of control in situations involving family is tricky when others question or interfere with our efforts at impression management.[68] For example, family members often accompany youth and older adults on medical visits.[69] In these situations, family members may answer questions on behalf of the patients and take the role of advocates in the medical decision-making process.[70] Sometimes these efforts at advocacy contradict the views of the patient. They may also make the patient feel unimportant, without influence or power. At other times, the advocates may share more information with the medical providers than the patient wants to share. In these cases, the family members violate the impression-management goals of the patient.[71]

Consider the case of an adult daughter who acts as an advocate for her father. The older man suffers from serious heart disease. During a medical visit, the doctor asks the father whether he has stopped smoking. The father hesitantly responds that he has given up smoking. The daughter knows differently, however, and she tells the doctor that her father has not quit smoking. This disclosure embarrasses and upsets the father; his daughter has portrayed him as a liar. The daughter, on the other hand, is upset because her father hid the truth about his smoking. The doctor is caught in the middle—unwillingly entangled in a family conflict.[72]

Managing Impressions in Friendship Contexts

We want others to like us; so we may be cautious about what we say when we interact with new friends. We want to create a good impression. As we become more familiar and comfortable with our new friends, however, we probably think less often about managing impressions with these individuals. We become more relaxed, informal, and natural.

Bonds of friendship can create safe spaces for mastering certain impression-management skills. Friendships allow children, for example, to experiment with positive—as well as negative—impression-management strategies. When they experiment with negative strategies (such as insulting others), they experience negative consequences (e.g., being insulted in return), but without the more serious outcomes that can occur outside the context of friendship (e.g., being charged with verbal assault). Friendships provide a setting for testing activities that may be improper elsewhere.[73]

Some cautions are nonetheless in order. Social relationships, social standing, and socio-demographic backgrounds also play a role in impression management.[74] An old saying tells us that we are "known by the company we keep." In fact, others do form impressions of us based on the social and other circles in which we move. If we socialize with the wealthy and elite, others may see us as valuing money and social status. If we surround ourselves with people who are concerned about the environment and social justice, others may see us as having the same values. The education levels, income, personalities, and relative positions of our friends and acquaintances influence the perceptions that others hold of us. As a result, we may have difficulty forging identities that are independent of the people who surround us.[75] Yet we can still achieve our impression-management goals by understanding how others' perceptions of our friends impact their perceptions of us. Through this understanding, we can make these judgments work in our favour.[76]

BENEFICIAL IMPRESSION MANAGEMENT Efforts to create positive impressions of close others.

Sometimes we use **beneficial impression-management** strategies to benefit close others. That is, we try to create a positive image of the close other in the eyes of another person. If we believe a friend, for example, has a romantic interest in a casual acquaintance named Maya, we might try to paint our friend in the most positive light when speaking with Maya. If Maya likes people who are talkative and outgoing, we might describe our friend as talkative and outgoing. If we think Maya likes someone who is quiet and reflective, we might highlight these qualities in our friend. In another instance, if our niece or nephew secures a job interview with someone we know, we might try to create a positive impression of that person when speaking with the potential employer.[77]

Managing Impressions in Romantic Contexts

Let us look at an example of impression management in a romantic context. Raj (a 19-year-old male) and Devika (an 18-year-old female) meet at Second Cup for their first date. After ordering coffee for himself, Raj turns to Devika to ask what she wants. An impressed Devika orders coffee too. They sit across from one another at an unoccupied table, and the conversation flows easily between them. Each tries to maintain the positive first impressions that led to their date—that is, until Devika's cellphone rings. To Raj's annoyance, Devika answers the phone and engages in conversation with the caller. Clearly, Devika has not lived up to Raj's initial impression of a considerate young woman—an impression that made him eager to pursue the relationship. (A 2012 study revealed that simply having a cellphone on a table during a social interaction lowers the perceived quality of the interaction.[78])

Romantic desires can lead both men and women to adopt strategic self-presentation strategies; however, the strategies most often used differ for the two sexes. Romantic motives often lead men to increase their spending on "conspicuous purchases" such as a new watch, a new cellphone, or a new car. Men also tend to focus on their ambitions and financial successes in communicating with desirable partners.[79] Women, on the other hand, are more likely to talk about charitable activities such as volunteering at a homeless shelter, offering to help build housing for poor families, or volunteering at a hospital for sick children.[80] They also focus on their faithfulness in relationships when they desire a long-term romance. To demonstrate this commitment, they might distance themselves from other females who have a reputation for being unfaithful.[81]

> **"When you break up, your whole identity is shattered. It's like death."**
> **DENNIS QUAID**

Women acquire impression-management skills in areas such as relationships early in life, and they tend to present themselves as more willing to adapt and less assertive than men in their romantic relationships. If they believe their partner values a particular quality such as modesty, for instance, women are likely to display behaviours consistent with that quality.[82] In line with their image as nurturing individuals, women are also more likely than men to engage in protective behaviours such as apologizing and **hedging** to minimize negative impressions.[83] Examples of hedging include comments such as "You could have done *a bit* better on that task," "She was *somewhat* unhappy about the results," and "You were *a little* off in your calculations." Words such as *a bit*, *somewhat*, and *a little* soften the edge of statements. Men would be more likely to say "You could have done better on that task," "She was unhappy about the results," and "You were off in your calculations." (See Chapter 6 for additional discussion of gender differences in language use.)

HEDGING Using words that show uncertainty or reduce the negative impact of what we are saying.

Managing Impressions in Professional Contexts

Managing impressions in the workplace involves a delicate dance between being ethical and being effective. Andrew DuBrin, who has conducted in-depth research into the topic of impression management in the workplace, says that many people see impression management in professional settings as "inherently manipulative, deceitful, and unethical."[84] Unfortunately, we reinforce this perception when we lie on our resumés—an action that can derail the careers of both entry-level and top-level executives.[85] Embellishing or including false information on resumés can backfire if the employer discovers the misrepresentation. The job candidate will lose the opportunity for the position, and she or he may also lose credibility with other potential employers if they hear about the deception.

> **"I began wearing hats as a young lawyer because it helped me to establish my professional identity. Before that, whenever I was at a meeting, someone would ask me to get coffee."**
> **BELLA ABZUG**

Even if a person secures a job after making false claims, the benefits may be short-lived. A case in point is that of former Radio Shack CEO David Edmondson, who resigned in 2006 after the company learned he had lied about his education. Edmondson misstated his academic record on his resumé, claiming that he had earned two bachelor's degrees (in psychology and theology) when in fact he had no degrees.[86] In a similar case, Yahoo board members fired the company's recently hired CEO, Scott Thompson, shortly after discovering that he had misrepresented his educational background on his resumé.[87] As these cases illustrate, the discovery that an employee has lied about his or her credentials almost always results in immediate dismissal.[88]

Despite the risks, an AOL Jobs survey found that one out of every four people reported that they had lied on a resumé or in an interview to get a job.[89] So what do people most commonly lie about in job applications? Forbes.com put together the following list:[90]

- important dates such as year of graduation,
- academic degrees,
- past salaries,

- claims of having made a huge profit or gain for a previous employer,
- job titles,
- technical abilities,
- language fluencies,
- addresses, and
- grade point averages.

Common Impression-Management Strategies

Both men and women use the following five strategies in managing impressions: self-promotion, ingratiation, intimidation, exemplification, and supplication.[91] However, men are more likely to use strategies traditionally considered to be appropriate to men—for example, assertive or dominant strategies such as intimidation. Women, on the other hand, are more likely to rely on strategies traditionally expected of women—for example, passive and cooperative strategies such as supplication. The impression-management tactics used by men tend to lead to better performance evaluations and better salaries than those used by women.[92] In the following discussion, we will examine each of these strategies.

Self-Promotion

People who use the strategy of self-promotion communicate their strengths in an effort to make a positive impression on others. Also known as self-enhancement, this strategy involves placing an emphasis on the competencies, abilities, or accomplishments of the communicator. An individual might want, for example, to be seen as independent, outgoing, and open-minded. In that situation, she might talk proudly about her study abroad in order to create an image of herself as a competent world traveller who appreciates other countries and cultures.

Extreme cases of self-promotion involve narcissism, an obsession with having others see us as highly attractive. Self-enhancement strategies used by narcissists are characterized by positivity (i.e., thinking about oneself in a highly positive way), egocentrism (i.e., thinking about oneself without taking the perspective of others), and a sense of uniqueness or specialness.[93] We can find many examples of narcissistic individuals in popular media. Pro-sports trainer Ryan Bowers, for example, repeatedly described himself as romantic, charming, and personally "blessed" by God when he appeared in season eight of *The Bachelorette*. Notably, his efforts at self-promotion were unsuccessful; he not only failed to win the bachelorette, he also captured the title of one of the most disliked bachelors to have ever appeared on the show. Other memorable examples come from the films *American Psycho* (2000) and *Wall Street* (1987). In *American Psycho*, the main character (played by Christian Bale) is an egocentric, self-obsessed, narcissistic investment banker who spirals into a psychopathic serial killer.

Wall Street features a self-obsessed, power-hungry corporate executive (portrayed by Michael Douglas) who has almost no regard or empathy for others.

Ingratiation

People who use the strategy of ingratiation worry about being liked by others. In order to increase their likeability, they may compliment others, use flattery, or behave in ways designed to get favourable responses from others. In the movie *The Devil Wears Prada* (2006), we see Andrea Sachs (played by Anne Hathaway) desperately trying to make a favourable impression on her boss, Miranda Priestly (played by Meryl Streep). An aspiring journalist, Andrea has recently graduated from Northwestern University; Miranda is the cutthroat editor-in-chief of *Runway* fashion magazine. In an attempt to impress her boss, Andrea completely changes her style of dress, adjusts her priorities, and goes to extreme lengths to run personal errands for Miranda.

Intimidation

People who use the strategy of intimidation try to achieve their goals by provoking fear in others. They do not care about being liked; they want to establish control. They may come across, for example, as highly assertive or even aggressive.[94] Although this impression-management strategy can create distance between people and make the strategist less well-liked,[95] it can be helpful in responding to **bullying**.[96] Projecting assertiveness in response to peer aggression can make a potential victim of bullying feel less frightened and vulnerable and more brave and self-confident.[97] To learn more about how to respond to bullying, see the "From Theory to Practice" box titled "Managing Impressions to Prevent Bullying."

BULLYING A form of aggressive behaviour that includes punching, name calling, or spreading rumors.

Exemplification

People who use the strategy of exemplification focus on moral worthiness. That is, they attempt to earn respect by showing sincerity and devotion and taking responsibility for their actions. If an employee stays late in the office and checks her emails on weekends, for example, she demonstrates her dedication and commitment to work. People who want to build and maintain positive images can benefit from this impression-management strategy. However, studies show that "exemplifiers" can run the risk of being perceived as hypocrites by those they are trying to impress. To avoid such risks, they must live up to their claims and demonstrate good moral qualities.[98]

from theory TO PRACTICE

Managing Impressions to Prevent Bullying

To learn more about how to respond assertively to peer aggression, visit the Eyes on Bullying website (sponsored by the Education Development Center). There you will find the chart "Bullying Actions and Victim Responses" (www.eyesonbullying.org/pdfs/responses.pdf). This chart will help you to understand the differences between submissive, assertive, and aggressive behaviours and to learn more about how to communicate self-confidence and a sense of control to a bully. Try putting some of these ideas into practice at the next opportunity.

Supplication

People who use the strategy of supplication attempt to get sympathy and attention by talking about their limitations or lack of knowledge.[99] They present themselves as vulnerable and weak in order to receive help from others. By playing dumb or appearing incompetent, they discourage others from asking for their help or assigning responsibilities to them.[100] Sometimes the strategy results in offers of assistance or extra attention from others. However, these kinds of actions (especially playing dumb) can also have negative side effects. Some may conclude that the helplessness or confusion indicates poor mental health. The person using the strategy may begin, after a time, to feel alienation, unhappiness, and low self-esteem.[101]

Communication Behaviours Associated with Impression-Management Strategies

Certain kinds of communication behaviours typically accompany the five impression-management strategies discussed above. Table 4.1 lists some of these behaviours, as they relate to workplace contexts. Bear in mind that this table is descriptive, not prescriptive. That is, we do not recommend that you use these strategies; we describe them so you can recognize them.

TABLE 4.1 Communication behaviours associated with impression-management strategies in the workplace.

IMPRESSION-MANAGEMENT STRATEGY	COMMUNICATION BEHAVIOUR
Self-Promotion	The self-promoter • talks proudly about his or her experience or education, • makes others aware of his or her talents or qualifications, • makes others aware that he or she is valuable to the organization, and/or • makes others aware of his or her accomplishments.
Ingratiation	The ingratiator • compliments colleagues to seem likable, • takes an interest in the personal lives of colleagues to demonstrate friendliness, • praises colleagues for their accomplishments in order to come across as a nice person, and/or • does personal favours for colleagues to increase likeability.
Intimidation	The intimidator • threatens or frightens coworkers with the aim of getting work done, • makes others aware of his or her power to make things difficult if necessary, • deals forcefully with colleagues when they hamper his or her ability to complete work, • reacts strongly or aggressively when coworkers interfere with his or her business activities, and/or • uses implicit or explicit threats to get colleagues to behave as he or she deems appropriate.
Exemplification	The exemplifier • stays late at work in order to be seen as hard working, • tries to appear busy, even when things are slow, • arrives at work early to look dedicated, and/or • goes to the office at night or on weekends to show dedication.
Supplication	The supplicator • pretends not to understand in order to get people to help him or her, • acts like he or she needs assistance so that others will offer help or sympathy, and/or • pretends to know less than he or she knows in order to avoid an unpleasant assignment.

SOURCE: Adapted from K.M. Kacmar, K.J. Harris, and B.G. Nagy, "Further Validation of the Bolino and Turnley Impression Management Scale," *Journal of Applied Behavioral Management* 9 (2007): 16–32, pp. 29–30.

Managing Impressions in Online Environments

Impression management in online environments has become a ripe area of research.[102] Surveys show that most homes in Canada have computers, and 82 per cent of children are online by the seventh grade.[103] Young people have come of age in an environment full of personal computers (laptops, desktops, and tablets), smartphones, video-game consoles, and other Internet-enabled electronic devices. Most of these devices are socially-oriented—that is, used for social purposes.[104] Most commonly, they are used to facilitate social interaction through online media.

What are the opportunities and challenges for impression management in online environments? According to **social presence theory**, the absence of nonverbal cues in online environments makes it more difficult for users to create the impressions on which relationships are built.[105]

SOCIAL PRESENCE THEORY Theory that explores the effects of sensing another's presence in a social interaction.

The **social information processing** perspective, on the other hand, says that people can impart impressions of themselves even without the nonverbal cues that characterize face-to-face interactions.[106] They use words, punctuation, and emoticons in emails and instant messages, for example, to convey personality. On social gaming sites and in virtual environments like Second Life, they use avatars and practices such as "gifting" (where social gamers give virtual gifts to other players) to build and transmit impressions.

SOCIAL INFORMATION PROCESSING THEORY Theory that investigates how we process various types of information in collaborative settings such as social media.

A related concept, **hyperpersonal theory** goes even further, suggesting that online environments offer *greater* opportunities than face-to-face interactions for the construction of positive impressions of another person. Increased control over what we share, the tendency to exaggerate similarities with another person, the possibility of communicating at convenient times, and the tendency for people to exhibit expected qualities and behaviours all work in favour of positive impression building.[107] Although online relationships develop more slowly than face-to-face relationships, they can develop to the same point as face-to-face relationships when given enough time.[108]

HYPERPERSONAL THEORY Theory that suggests that we use limited online cues to construct idealized images of another person.

Impression management in online environments can take place on various platforms, including email, computer conferencing, instant messaging, Facebook, Twitter, and dating sites, among others. The communication can be verbal (e.g., emails and comments on Facebook and Twitter) or nonverbal (e.g., photos posted on Myspace or graphic symbols). Electronic platforms, which allow users to overcome constraints of time and space, result in new dynamics in interpersonal relationships. The following discussion looks, in more depth, at how computer-mediated communication (in general) and Facebook and Twitter (more specifically) function as platforms for impression management.

COMPUTER-MEDIATED COMMUNICATION (CMC) The process of using a computer to communicate messages.

Computer-Mediated Communication as a Platform for Impression Management

Computer-mediated communication (CMC) refers to the process of using a computer to communicate messages through channels such as email, instant messaging, or computer conferencing.[109] CMC can involve **synchronous communication** (same time/different place) or **asynchronous communication** (different time/different place). With synchronous communication, the sender and receiver are online at the same time, communicating in real time. With asynchronous communication, someone can send a message while the other is sleeping or involved in another activity. In that situation, the receiver gets the message at a different and often much later time.

SYNCHRONOUS COMMUNICATION Communicators exchange messages in real time.

ASYNCHRONOUS COMMUNICATION Communicators exchange messages with a time delay between messages.

EMOTICONS Graphic representations of facial expressions that convey mood.

CMC allows for many choices in impression management. For example, communicators can use carefully chosen words and phrases not only to transmit information, but also to set the tone of the interaction and convey mood. Communicators can also use nonverbal elements such as **emoticons** to convey mood.[110] Some emoticons are simple; others are more complex. (Visit the website http://pc.net/emoticons for a list of commonly used text-based emoticons). Emoticons such as smiley or sad faces can produce a positive or a negative response in the other person.[111] For examples of how verbal and nonverbal strategies can enhance communication in online environments (specifically, in online learning environments), see tables 4.2 and 4.3.

The basic principles of impression management in CMC apply across all computer-based social environments, from blogs to message boards to social media sites. To give you a better understanding of how impression management happens in such environments, the following section explores Facebook as a platform for impression management.

What We Can Learn about CMC from Facebook

Facebook allows people to strategically promote interpersonal relationships by selectively sharing certain aspects of their lives—for example, hometown, birthday, relationships status, and preferred activities. Facebook also allows for image management.

TABLE 4.2 Verbal strategies for online instructors.

VERBAL IMPRESSION-MANAGEMENT STRATEGIES	CORRESPONDING IMPRESSION JUDGMENTS
1. The instructor greets the students when communicating online.	1. The instructor cares about the students.
2. The instructor uses a variety of online applications (e.g., bulletin boards, private email, online student forums) and activities (e.g., small group and large group discussions).	2. The instructor wants to create a classroom that involves dynamic and collaborative exchanges with students.
3. The instructor uses strongly worded messages (e.g., "Important notice!") to emphasize the importance of the communications.	3. The instructor is a competent communicator.
4. The instructor uses "we" when talking with the students.	4. The instructor cares about the students.
5. The instructor looks for multiple ways of explaining concepts when responding to students' questions.	5. The instructor is an effective communicator.
6. The instructor carefully crafts written messages and avoids verbal hedges (e.g., "In my opinion . . ."), qualifiers (e.g., ". . . isn't it?'"), and fillers (e.g., "Uhm . . .").	6. The instructor is credible.
7. The instructor uses appropriate language and actively participates in discussion of ideas.	7. The instructor wants to foster a dynamic and collaborative learning environment.
8. The instructor tries to avoid overly harsh language in responding to inappropriate private emails or postings on a public forum or bulletin board.	8. The instructor wants to foster a safe and friendly environment.

SOURCE: Column 1 adapted from Y. Liu and D. Ginther, "Managing Impression Formation in Computer-Mediated Communication," *Educause Quarterly* 50, 1 (2001): 50–54.

TABLE 4.3 Nonverbal strategies for online instructors.

NONVERBAL IMPRESSION-MANAGEMENT STRATEGIES	CORRESPONDING IMPRESSION JUDGMENTS
1. The instructor uses paralinguistic cues such as emoticons thoughtfully to enhance or enrich a written message.	1. The instructor wants to encourage students to be involved and interested in their learning.
2. The instructor gives students plenty of time to complete assignments and shows flexibility with due dates.	2. The instructor is aware of and willing to accommodate student needs.
3. The instructor sends messages regularly to engage students.	3. The instructor is serious about being socially present online.
4. The instructor sends longer messages prudently to stimulate discussion.	4. The instructor is motivated to make the online classroom engaging.
5. The instructor sends error-free messages.	5. The instructor is competent and careful when communicating details.
6. The instructor responds to students promptly.	6. The instructor is approachable and responsive to student needs.
7. The instructor creates and posts a thorough syllabus.	7. The instructor is knowledgeable and passionate about the course.
8. The instructor solicits timely feedback from students.	8. The instructor is committed to teaching and helping students learn.

SOURCE: Column 1 adapted from Y. Liu and D. Ginther, "Managing Impression Formation in Computer-Mediated Communication," *Educause Quarterly* 50, 1 (2001): 50–54.

For example, you can appear more physically attractive by posting your best pictures. You can display information and links to significant accomplishments that make you appear knowledgeable and expert in certain areas. You can also make comments that are in line with the opinions of your imagined audience. Through emoticons and the "like" button, you can display attitudes. When you construct an image of yourself as physically attractive, knowledgeable, and holding acceptable opinions, you are using the impression-management strategy of *self-promotion.*

When you interact on Facebook, you often target your communication to certain groups (e.g., your friends) and ignore others (e.g., potential employers). But concentrating on making yourself sound appealing to one group at the expense of other groups can have negative consequences. Consider the following case. Naseem has applied for a low-paying, entry-level position with a large company. Julio, the human resources manager in charge of filling the position, does not want to hire someone who is overqualified; past experience tells him that such a person will leave the position after a short time. Since the company must invest a lot of money in training new employees, they want employees to stay for a reasonable length of time.

© Chris Batson/Alamy

As part of his job, Julio must check the credentials of all prospective employees. He performs a standard online search and finds Naseem's Facebook page. Because Naseem is typically careful to avoid posting embarrassing or offensive content on her Facebook page, she has made much of her account publicly available, and Julio is able to consult her profile and timeline. To his annoyance, he finds that Naseem has misrepresented her accomplishments. In fact, she has held several higher-profile (and higher-paying) positions that she did not include on her resumé. From what he can see online, Naseem's former employer laid off a number of employees when he ran into financial difficulties. Naseem was a casualty of those layoffs.

When Julio reads the comments on Naseem's Facebook page, he realizes that she has had difficulties securing a comparable position; so she has lowered her expectations. In one comment, she even mentions her application to Julio's company; and she expresses concerns about being able to make ends meet with such a low-paying job. As a result of this misrepresentation, Naseem loses the opportunity to be hired in Julio's company even after she is short-listed for the open position. In other words, her effort to create a favourable impression with her friends (e.g., by explaining her need to apply for less prestigious positions) has led to an unfavourable impression with a prospective employer.

Other kinds of sharing on Facebook pages can also affect hiring decisions—for example, listing activities and interests such as going to clubs and bars, heavy partying, drinking, doing illegal drugs, or revealing religious and political views. As more employers turn to Facebook pages to screen potential employees, our online lives will have an increasingly significant impact on our professional lives. Even people who generally restrict public access to their Facebook pages are not exempt from this sort of scrutiny. Many employers now insist that applicants provide them with unrestricted access to these pages. With no current regulations that state otherwise, employers are legally able to use online profiles and postings of job applicants in arriving at hiring decisions.[112]

As people post increasingly large amounts of personal information online, they also face risks that relate to more than just potential job opportunities. Internet predators use Facebook and other social media profiles to identify likely victims. Aggravating the situation, the most vulnerable young women (those with a history of childhood abuse) are most likely to self-present in provocative ways online, thus attracting predators.[113] (Refer to the discussion of clothing and personal artifacts in Chapter 7 for a description of this research.) Individuals who use Facebook and other social media sites must be aware of such risks in order to take steps to protect themselves from potential predators.

In considering how and to what ends we can use Facebook as a platform for impression management, the question arises: What does it mean to be a "friend" on social media sites such as Facebook?[114] Some studies suggest that being labelled as an online "friend" does not necessarily imply that the same relationship exists offline. It is technologically easy to establish online relationships; and they require little emotional, financial, or physical investment. In addition, social norms make us reluctant to refuse friend requests, even from people we do not know very well. So online networks may become much larger than offline networks, but they may be much more superficial in nature.[115]

For these kinds of reasons, we cannot assume that popularity on social media sites such as Facebook necessarily translates into popularity offline. Studies in this area are inconclusive. Tong and colleagues found that an overabundance of friends on Facebook did not increase positive evaluations by others.[116] Kleck and colleagues, on the other hand, found a link between the number of Facebook friends and positive social judgments by observers. Facebook users with a large number of online friends were perceived to be more popular, confident, pleasant, and sexy than those with fewer online friends.[117] Other researchers have looked at the frequency of Facebook use instead of number of online friends, and the results seem to indicate that frequent users have a greater ability to create and maintain connections with others.[118]

TIPS FOR NAVIGATING AND MANAGING IDENTITIES

Navigating and managing our identities requires us to understand ourselves, others, and the social conventions of the environments in which we interact with other people. The following tips will help you to navigate and manage identities in a variety of contexts.

Recognize that not everyone is like you, and not everyone values the things that you value. Be respectful of the differences among people with regard to age, gender, sexual orientation, culture, ethnicity, race, and socio-economic backgrounds.

Pay attention to your goals and contexts when using the different impression-management strategies. For example, during a medical visit, you can create a favourable impression with your doctor by adopting a respectful manner when asking questions about your health.

Do not include false information on your resumé. Be honest, avoid embellishment, and own your strengths and accomplishments in order to receive long-term rewards. Remember that many potential employers will perform an Internet search to determine if you are telling the truth.

If you are travelling to another country for an extended period of time, take the time to learn about the culture. Doing so will help you find a culturally appropriate identity that will increase your chances of fitting into the local culture.

Be sensitive to rules of etiquette in online environments. For instance, post appropriate materials and use suitable emoticons that take the context and recipient into account. Avoid deception or misrepresentation of the truth when communicating and presenting online.

Develop good communication skills. These skills will help you control the impression you make on others. For example, you can get a potential employer to see you as a good candidate for a job by presenting yourself—through verbal and nonverbal communication—as a good candidate.

SUMMARY

In this chapter, we have looked at the labels that others put on us, as well as how we seek to present ourselves. We discussed how, in our everyday social interactions, we choose among multiple identities and manage these identities in multiple contexts (family, friendship, romantic relationships, and professional relationships). Some of these identities have collective dimensions. Through communication strategies, we seek to present ourselves in the ways we want others to see us. Thus, our conscious and unconscious efforts at managing our impressions become integral to our everyday lives. While online environments open new possibilities for experimentation and impression management, online interactions also come with new responsibilities and risks.

REVIEW QUESTIONS

1. What is the definition of *identity*? What are the different kinds of identity, and how do they differ from one another?
2. How can our online interactions influence how we present ourselves in offline environments? How can this crossover influence others' impressions of us? Use illustrations to support your arguments.
3. What does the term *impression management* mean? How can impression management be used in a friendship context? What is its relevance in a workplace context?
4. How have you managed impressions in family, friendship, romantic, and professional (including academic) contexts? How successful were you in your attempts to present yourself in a certain way?
5. Do you agree that men and women use different impression-management strategies in organizational settings? If so, why?
6. Of the impression-management strategies discussed in this chapter, which one(s) could work best for corporate reputation management? Why?
7. In addition to the verbal and nonverbal impression-management strategies for online instructors discussed in this chapter, what other impression-management strategies could an online instructor adopt in order to facilitate student–teacher interactions?
8. What are the main challenges of using social media tools for managing impressions in a professional context? Can you think of any challenge(s) not discussed in this chapter?

SUGGESTED ACTIVITIES

1. Our collective identities include gender, ethnic, racial, religious, linguistic, cultural, regional, and national dimensions. Create a list, ordering these dimensions according to their importance in your life. Be prepared to share your responses with other members of your group. How are they similar? How do your priorities differ from the priorities of your classmates?
2. List some characters in popular movies and TV shows who think about themselves in extremely

positive and narcissistic ways. Put together a collage of these characters.

3. Review the impression-management strategies discussed in this chapter and create skits that allow you to act out the different strategies (self-promotion, ingratiation, intimidation, exemplification, and supplication).
4. Reflecting on your personal experience and what you have learned in this chapter, create a list of *dos* and *don'ts* for online communication exchanges. After creating the list, share it with others in your class. Discuss your ideas.
5. Based on the ideas discussed in this chapter, identify the most common impression-management strategies used by people in popular online dating forums. To complete this task, you will need to undertake some Internet research.

CHAPTER 5

Listening

CHAPTER OUTLINE

learning OBJECTIVES

- To learn about the difference between hearing and listening
- To understand the listening process
- To understand the importance of effective listening in personal, academic, business, and professional contexts
- To recognize barriers to effective listening
- To improve your own listening behaviours

forSTARTERS

A Sickening Situation: Bosses Who Don't Listen

Did you know that bad bosses can make you sick? In fact, they can. A Swedish study found that people who worked for bad bosses had a 39 per cent greater chance of having a heart attack than those with good bosses.[1] Whether employed in a paid position or as a volunteer, you have probably experienced your share of both good and bad supervisors. And you have probably found that the communication patterns of your boss made a difference to your work experience and how you felt about your job.

After extensive research, Stanford University professor Robert Sutton concluded that your direct supervisor—rather than the company's CEO or senior managers—has the biggest impact on your stress level at work, as well as your job satisfaction. Sutton says that it is easy to recognize bad bosses because they suffer from what he calls "power poisoning." That is, they focus on their own needs rather than those of their staff. They are hypercritical of others, and they do not offer praise even when people have earned it. Perhaps most importantly, they do not listen.

According to Sutton, bad listeners tend to follow certain patterns. First, they do most of the talking and steer the conversation in the direction they want it to go. They look away and appear disinterested (eyes glazing over, stifled yawns) when it is your turn to speak. They interrupt your story to tell one of their own; and, in myriad small ways, they make you feel boring and unimportant. In a social setting, you can look for another conversation partner. At work, however, you cannot escape a poor listener when he or she is your boss. To make matters worse, the listening skills of your boss may influence the quality of your work (whether you perform to the best of your abilities) and

"I haven't read your proposal yet, but I already have some great ideas on how to improve it!"

INTRODUCTION

Even before birth, we begin to develop the first of our communication abilities. By about five months, the hearing organs form; and around six months, the developing fetus responds to sound.[3] By about eight months, the fetus can distinguish between different sounds in his or her own language and between different voices.[4] At birth, babies can recognize the sound of their mothers' voices, and they respond to the music to which they were exposed while in the uterus.[5] These findings demonstrate that babies are busy listening to the outside world while they (and their parents) await their arrival.

Although most of us are born with the ability to hear and the capacity to listen, listening is a challenging but critical communication skill that is rarely taught in a formal way.[6] This lack of training has some serious consequences. When tested immediately after a 10-minute presentation, for example, the average listener hears, comprehends, and remembers only about 50 per cent of the information. After 48 hours, the amount retained has gone down to 25 per cent.[7] In classroom situations, 10 per cent is a common retention rate.[8]

In this chapter, we will look at the nature and importance of listening, barriers to effective listening, and the impact of ineffective listening. We will also suggest tips for putting effective listening skills into practice in a variety of contexts.

the quality of your work environment (whether you look forward to going to work).

Poor listeners also tend to disregard the feedback and advice offered by others. Imagine the following workplace scenario. You are tasked with researching the purchase of some new computer software. After you report the findings of your investigation and make a recommendation, your boss makes a decision that seems to completely disregard your input. Given this response, you will probably feel that your boss does not value your contribution and that you have wasted your time.

To learn more about how bosses respond to input from their employees, Kelly See (of New York University) and her colleagues surveyed hundreds of professionals across a range of organizations and industries.[2] See wanted answers to the following two questions: To what extent do people in power act on advice from their staff? What is the impact of these behaviours on employees? To find the answers, See asked close co-workers of managers about the extent to which the managers acted on the advice of their employees. She also gathered data in controlled laboratory experiments, where people (managers and non-managers) received advice from others.

A consistent pattern of results emerged. The greater the power of the managers, the more they tended to be overconfident in their decision-making and the more they tended *not* to act on advice from others. This discounting of good advice often resulted in poor decisions and sometimes costly mistakes. In addition, the ignored employees felt undervalued. See and her colleagues believe that the unwillingness to take advice from others—even experts who are paid to offer advice—may stem from a perception that asking for help shows weakness.

This research led See and her colleagues to offer some recommendations for improving the organizational effectiveness of managers. First, they recommended that managers should surround themselves with people who are going to disagree with them and who are willing—and confident enough—to challenge them. In other words, bosses need subordinates who will point out when they are wrong. Second, managers should seek as many opinions as possible from a variety of sources. Finally, bosses need to *listen* to those opinions. In conclusion, good decision-making and a satisfied workforce result when managers surround themselves with smart people and listen closely to what those people have to say.

This discussion should lead you to think about the following kinds of questions, which this chapter addresses: How do the listening behaviours of the bosses in these studies mirror the poor listening habits of many of us? Why is it so difficult to listen effectively to other people? What can we do to improve our listening skills? Why is it important for us to develop effective listening skills in order to perform our jobs in a competent way?

THE NATURE OF LISTENING

Of all the communication activities in which we participate on a daily basis—speaking, listening, reading, and writing—we spend the most time by far on listening. In the 1970s (before the Internet, the iPod, and the cellphone), Larry Barker and his colleagues wondered whether the advent of television had had an impact on the amount of time that college students engaged in various communication activities.[9] Their findings were similar to those of earlier studies.[10] That is, the researchers found that college students spent most of their time (53 per cent) listening, 17 per cent of their time reading, 16 per cent of their time speaking, and 14 per cent of their time writing (Figure 5.1). More recent studies suggest that, despite the growing number of electronic communication devices, young people today spend about the same amount of time listening as they did in the past (Figure 5.2).[11] More specifically, college students spend almost 56 per cent of an average day listening, followed by reading (17 per cent), speaking (16 per cent), and writing (11 per cent), with much of this time involving the use of electronic communication tools.

> **"A good listener is not only popular everywhere, but after a while he gets to know something."**
> **WILSON MIZNER**

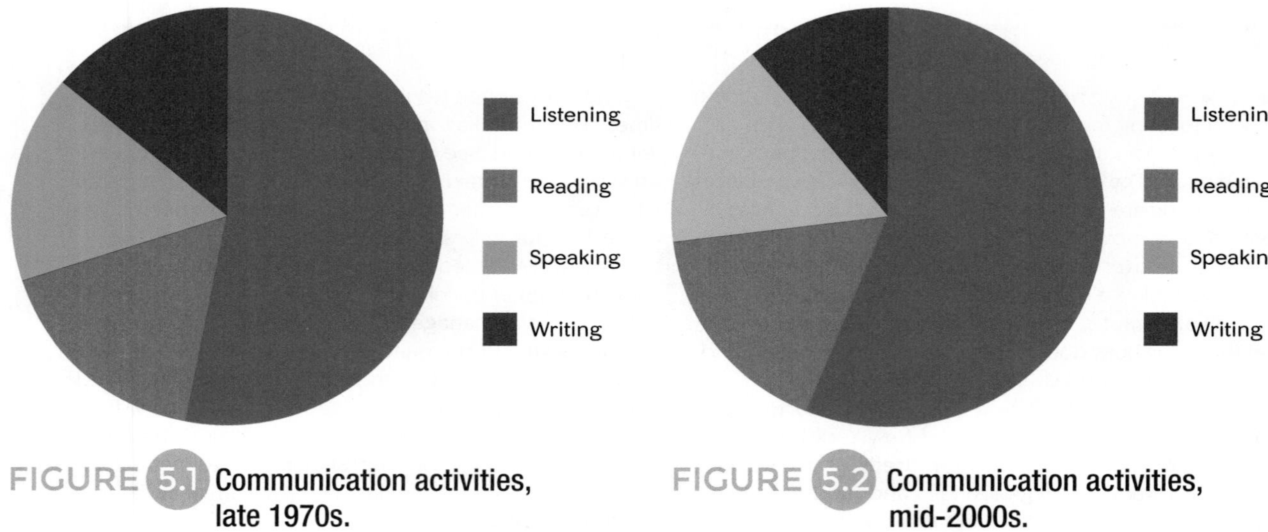

FIGURE 5.1 Communication activities, late 1970s.

SOURCE: L. Barker, K. Gladney, R. Edwards, F. Holley, and C. Gaines, "An Investigation of Proportional Time Spent in Various Communication Activities by College Students," *Journal of Applied Communication Research* 8, no. 2 (1980): 101–10.

FIGURE 5.2 Communication activities, mid-2000s.

SOURCE: R. Emanuel, J. Adams, K. Baker, E. K. Daufin, C. Ellington, E. Fitts, and D. Okeowo. "How College Students Spend Their Time Communicating," *International Journal of Listening* 22, no. 1 (2008): 13–28.

Given how much time we spend listening to others, it is important to understand this process. Let us begin by differentiating between hearing and listening.

Hearing and Listening: Not the Same

HEARING A physical process that occurs when the eardrum absorbs sound vibrations and sends the sensations to the brain.

LISTENING A mental process that involves interpreting messages that others have transmitted.

The physical process of **hearing** occurs when the eardrum absorbs sound vibrations and sends the sensations to the brain. To this purely physical process, **listening** adds the critical dimension of making sense of the sounds we hear. In relation to interpersonal communication, listening can be defined as a "process that involves the interpretation of messages that others have intentionally transmitted."[12] We listen in order to understand and respond appropriately to verbal or and other audible messages. Of all the sounds that you hear as you sit in your classroom, for example, you will choose to pay attention to some and to ignore the others. Sometimes you hear the professor's voice but fail to process what she or he is saying. Then suddenly you hear the words "This will be on the exam!" At that point, you become fully alert.

The Listening Process

Four distinct phases characterize the listening process: selecting, understanding, remembering, and responding (Figure 5.3). Although movement from one phase to the next often happens so quickly that we do not notice the change we will examine each one in turn.

Selecting

SELECTING The process of focussing on certain stimuli and ignoring others.

Sounds, sights, and smells constantly bombard us; and if we paid attention to all of them, we would be completely overwhelmed and incapable of doing anything. To avoid this condition of overload, we select certain stimuli and ignore others. **Selecting**, the first phase of listening, refers to the process of paying attention to some sounds and ignoring others. We are more likely, for example, to pay attention to sounds that are extreme

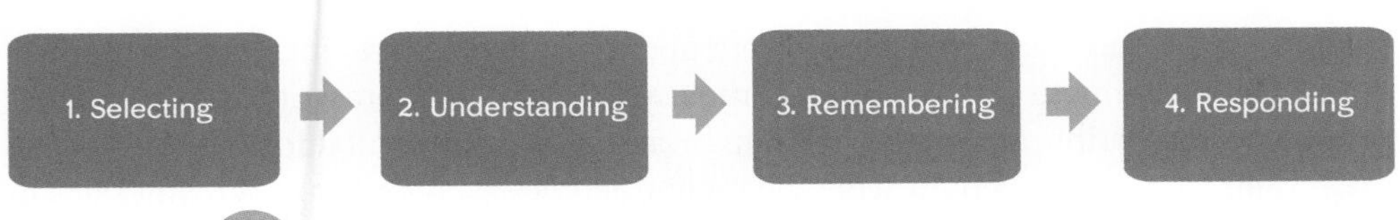

FIGURE 5.3 The listening process.

in nature—very loud or very soft. We also attend to those that are important to our personal needs and interests. Despite the many sounds competing for our attention at a busy airport, for example, we will probably hear the boarding call for our flight. The term **cocktail party effect** refers to this ability to pay attention to what matters to us in any given situation.[13] The term comes from the idea that, even in a crowded "cocktail party" environment, we are able to focus on one out of many conversations and sounds. Despite the high level of noise in the setting, we will hear our name if someone mentions us. Refer back to Chapter 3 for a more detailed discussion of the factors that determine which stimuli draw our attention.

COCKTAIL PARTY EFFECT A phenomenon where we hear one voice out of a medley of conversations and background noises.

Understanding

Once we have selected a sound that merits our attention, we figure out what it means. At the stage of **understanding**, we decode sounds into a meaningful pattern.[14] When assigning meaning to what someone is saying, we rely on more than just our knowledge of what the words mean. Imagine that you are visiting a foreign country where you do not speak the language. If a young woman wearing an apron and carrying a menu approaches your table in a restaurant, smiles while saying something, and holds a jug of water over your glass, you will probably understand her words as either a friendly greeting or a question about whether you would like some water. Depending on her tone of voice and facial expression, you will attach meaning to her words and respond with facial expressions and gestures that you deem to be appropriate. You are able to attach meaning to the interaction because of prior knowledge of restaurants and pre-existing expectations about how people behave in these settings.[15]

UNDERSTANDING The process of assigning meaning to the stimuli we have selected.

At least three influences operate at the understanding stage. First, **context** (e.g., the setting) exerts an influence.[16] In the preceding example, the restaurant setting helps you to make sense of what is being said.

CONTEXT Circumstances surrounding a situation.

Second, prior knowledge and expectations about the meaning of the stimuli influence your understanding.[17] When you hear words that are familiar, you draw on your pre-existing knowledge of what those words mean. When you do not have the knowledge required to fully understand the sounds (e.g., when travelling and interacting in a foreign country), you are forced to make an **inference**.[18]

INFERENCE An educated guess when we do not have all the necessary information.

Finally, **cognitive complexity** influences the understanding process.[19] Consider the following example. An executive with a large pharmaceutical firm, Eric learns that his company's European sales have not reached the desired levels. They are considerably below projections; and as a result, the company has a large surplus of drugs with a limited shelf life. At first Eric assumes that the problem could be their main competitor, who launched an aggressive marketing campaign for a new drug. Eric fears that the marketing campaign could have pulled interest away from his company's product.

COGNITIVE COMPLEXITY The capacity to use a number of viewpoints to make sense of complex information.

Then he pauses and thinks more deeply about the problem. He considers the possible impact of other factors such as the poor economic conditions in Europe, missed shipping dates, confusion over some orders, and the decision not to increase the marketing budget to compete with the other company. Eric talks to representatives in production, sales, marketing, and distribution in order to get additional information. And he takes their views into account when he recommends a strategy for improving sales in the next quarter. One of the company's top directors, however, has a different response to the problem. Based solely on the current sales figures, he recommends immediate cuts in production. While Eric's response demonstrates a high level of cognitive complexity—a willingness to take many different factors into account—the director's response reflects a much lower level of cognitive complexity.

People who are cognitively complex are able to listen more attentively, to understand more accurately, and to remember more of what is said.[20] In addition, they are able to process messages more deeply.[21] They rely on factors such as context to help in interpreting and evaluating messages.[22] For these kinds of reasons, cognitively complex listeners are able to respond more appropriately and effectively than those who are less cognitively complex.

Fortunately, most of us increase our levels of cognitive complexity and related communication skills over time. So teenagers tend to be more cognitively complex than children, and young adults tend to be more cognitively complex than teenagers.[23]

Activities that challenge us to see things from a different perspective, to question our existing ideas, and to look at ourselves critically expand our cognitive complexity.[24] Other helpful strategies include meeting people from outside our usual network, trying to understand the moods and feelings of others, modelling our communication techniques after those of people whose communication skills we admire, and processing information from the viewpoint of the other person.[25] One of the characteristics of cognitively complex individuals is flexibility—a willingness to try new things and to incorporate new patterns of thinking into existing frameworks.

REMEMBERING The process of recalling information.

Remembering

Once we have selected and made sense of information, we need to be able to recall it. **Remembering** refers to the process of recalling information. You may have noticed that, during a long lecture, you have difficulty staying focussed on the professor. As a result, you probably do not remember much of what the professor said. Some studies have investigated how certain behaviours make it more or less likely that you will remember the information you encounter.

In one study, Jackie Andrade asked 40 participants to listen to a boring telephone message that contained the names of people and places. Half of the participants were asked to doodle while listening, and the other half were asked to listen without engaging in any other activity. Those who doodled were able to recall 7.5 names and places (on average), while those who did not doodle could recall only 5.8 names and places (on average). Andrade found that doodling helped participants to daydream less and to stay more focussed on the message.[26] Try the experiment suggested in the "From Theory to Practice" box to see if doodling can help you to retain information from your class lectures.

What we have learned about laptop use in classrooms is less encouraging. A large number of studies indicate that laptops have a strong negative impact on several measures of learning, including understanding and remembering course content.[27] These results do not mean that laptops themselves are the problem; rather it is what students choose to do with their laptops during class time that affects their ability to recall course content. An increasingly large number are using their laptops for activities other than note taking (e.g., emailing, instant messaging and texting, checking Facebook, twittering, and watching videos).[28] Indeed, one study found that the more time students spend browsing the Internet during class, the lower their final grades.[29]

from theory TO PRACTICE

A Doodle a Day Might Give You an "A"

Try doodling during the first half of the next class lecture you attend. At the midpoint of the lecture, stop to think about what you remember of the lecture to that point. Then listen attentively without doodling in the second half of the lecture. At the end of class, take another moment to think about what you remember. Do you think you remember more or less than when you were doodling? Was it easier or harder to concentrate when you stopped doodling? What other techniques might help you to recall information when listening?

Responding

In the final phase of the listening process (**responding**), we provide feedback to show the speaker that we have understood his or her message. Responding can vary from a simple facial expression (e.g., a nod or smile) to a verbal response (e.g., "I know what you mean"). Sometimes our responses indicate that, in fact, we are not listening at all. In the French film *Le Fabuleux Destin d'Amélie Poulain* (2001), Amélie responds in the following way to her father's query about how she is doing: "I had two heart attacks, an abortion, did crack . . . while I was pregnant. Other than that, I'm fine." When her father responds "That's nice," it is clear to Amélie (and to the audience) that he was not listening.

RESPONDING The process of providing feedback to show that understanding has occurred.

The most appropriate and effective responses depend on the context and the relationship between the communicators. Imagine you are late for a job interview, and you cannot find the office. The most appropriate response to your question "Where is the hiring manager's office?" would be a quick verbal direction and perhaps a pointing arm. In this interaction, you are not looking for a lengthy and intimate conversation, but a quick and accurate instruction for finding the office. When speaking to a friend about an upsetting event, on the other hand, you are looking for a more supportive and detailed response.

THE IMPORTANCE OF LISTENING

Why does good listening matter? Good listening matters because, in personal contexts, it helps us to develop satisfying friendships[30] and intimate romantic relationships.[31] When we need support, we look for good listeners who make us feel valued. Positive, supportive, and appropriate responses contribute to the development of intimacy in relationships.[32] (See the "Human Diversity" box titled "PostSecret: Looking for a Listener" to see how one blogger invented a creative way to help people to find listeners for their most intimate secrets.)

Imagine two students, Kristen and Ryan, talking over coffee after a first-year criminology class. Kristen tells Ryan that she is taking the course a second time because she failed it the previous year. Ryan's response to this disclosure could set the tone for their entire relationship. If he laughs and comments that she must be pretty dumb to fail such an easy course, it is unlikely that the couple will move in the direction of intimacy. If,

humanDIVERSITY

PostSecret: Looking for a Listener

You may have heard of PostSecret, the online blog where people share their most intimate secrets. They send these secrets on postcards to blogger Frank Warren, who posts the secrets every Sunday. Perhaps you have even submitted a secret yourself. The popularity of Warren's "community mail art project"—the most visited advertisement-free blog in the world[33]—seems to indicate that many people are looking for a listener who is nonjudgmental, quiet, and discrete.

The PostSecret project began in 2004 when Warren was working on a national suicide hotline, offering support to callers in need of sympathetic listeners. His experience with the loneliness and despair of callers resonated with his growing awareness of people's need to share deeply personal and often untold secrets. Warren gave out 3,000 postcards to strangers around Washington, DC; he asked each person to write a secret on the postcard—a secret they had never shared with anyone—and return the card to him by mail. Since that time he has received over 500,000 postcards from writers around the world. His website, PostSecret.com, gives a voice to people with a deep need to be heard but not judged. As Warren says, "The secrets I receive reflect the full spectrum of complicated issues that many of us struggle with every day: intimacy, trust, meaning, humor, and desire."[34] Following are a few examples of messages written on postcards posted on Warren's site:

"I'd elope tomorrow if you asked me."

"A month ago I decided not to kill myself. But it wasn't until today that I decided to start living!"

"When you travel, mom and I are free."

"I want to join an online dating website but I am terrified of meeting someone I know."

*"*Fifty Shades of Grey *makes me sad."*

In addition to hosting the website, Warren has published several books that share many of the most moving, interesting, startling, and provocative of the postcards he has received over the years.

With permission from Frank Warren

on the other hand, he makes a supportive comment like "What a bummer—for you to have to sit through the same lectures again this year," the response might pave the way for more personal exchanges in the future. Such exchanges will occur, however, only if Kristen perceives that Ryan's response is honest, understanding, and accepting.

In educational contexts, good listening is essential to learning. To get the most out of a classroom lecture, students must actively engage in the listening process: they must selectively focus on the instructor's words, make an effort to understand what is being said, remember the most important information for future use, and respond to the lecture by developing their own ideas about this information. Unfortunately, many students in Canada struggle with this process, at least in part because mainstream Western culture does not emphasize the connection between listening and learning. In contrast, as you will see in the "Human Diversity" box titled "Listening and Aboriginal Storytelling," Aboriginal cultures tend to place a strong focus on this connection.

Good listening is also crucial in professional contexts. Experts tell us that poor listening skills carry a significant price tag in the business world.[35] Poor listening will cost a corporation with 100,000 employees $3 million each year if each of its employees makes a $30 mistake (e.g., taking a wrong number or placing a wrong order). Think of how many times you have decided to go to another business after receiving poor service from your first choice.

humanDIVERSITY

Listening and Aboriginal Storytelling

Central to the oral traditions of Aboriginal communities in North America, storytelling involves the transmission of narratives by word of mouth from generation to generation. This practice functions to inform and educate young people by passing along history, traditions, lessons, values, literature, and knowledge. The learning process is highly inclusive, co-operative, and enjoyable.

Storytelling requires the presence of listeners with refined abilities to hear, comprehend, and retain the words of the speaker. For this reason, Aboriginal youth are encouraged from a young age to be attentive and respectful listeners. Deeply embedded in Aboriginal cultures is the recognition that for stories to be remembered—and thus for the culture to remain alive and vibrant—the act of listening needs to figure prominently into social and communication practices.

The Aboriginal Human Resource Council of Canada offers recommendations on working with Aboriginal colleagues, all of which centre on the concept of listening. These recommendations include giving full attention to the speaker and to what she or he is saying, maintaining eye contact, not interrupting the speaker, providing nonverbal cues to show you are paying attention, and listening from the heart rather than just with the head. This advice embodies the basic elements of effective listening.[36]

Given that the oral tradition of storytelling has always been (and continues to be) at the core of Aboriginal society, we can learn much about genuine and successful listening from Inuit, Métis, and First Nations peoples in this country.

Listening affects productivity in the workplace. Salespeople who *speak less* and *listen more* make more sales than those who *speak more* and *listen less*. When salespeople listen well, they can identify the needs of their potential customers and respond effectively to those needs by offering the right products or services.[37] Moreover, when customers perceive that a salesperson is really listening, they have greater trust in the salesperson and they want to continue the relationship in the future. In other words, when salespeople listen to their customers, the customers plan to come back.[38]

Active and supportive listening also promotes understanding and builds trust between patients and health care providers. When doctors allow patients to talk about their problems without interrupting and try to understand their patients' perceptions, they improve the quality of the medical encounter and build good relations. Patients in one study rated their physicians as excellent when they saw these professionals as respectful, accessible, willing to explain symptoms, and interested in listening to them.[39] Another study found similar results, with patients reporting that good listening skills and willingness to spend adequate time with them were important to their interactions with health care providers.[40] Many doctors, however, are poor listeners. One of the most common complaints of patients in medical encounters is that their physicians do not listen to them.[41] Some patients report that doctors interrupt them within 18 to 30 seconds of the start of a conversation.[42] Physicians face not only poor ratings but also financial repercussions when they do not establish good relations with their patients. Studies show that dissatisfied patients are more likely to file malpractice suits.[43]

Restaurant servers also benefit from good listening behaviours. Their reward comes in the form of increased tips. In a study designed to test the influence of nonverbal communication on tipping, servers either squatted near the customer or stood while taking orders in a restaurant. When servers squatted beside their tables, the patrons left more generous tips. The enhanced sense of nearness and eye contact made the servers seem friendlier and, as a result, encouraged the customers to leave a better tip.[44] These same kinds of behaviours also suggest good listening.

As indicated in the "For Starters" box at the beginning of this chapter, good listening skills are very important in managers. Good listeners meet our needs and make us feel respected. They are rare; but when we find them, the experience is immensely satisfying. In *The Lost Art of Listening*, Michael Nichols calls good listening—which he defines as a willingness to listen with a minimum of defensiveness, criticism, or impatience—the "gift of understanding."[45] When offered by managers, this "gift" can have a positive impact on the job satisfaction and productivity of employees. When Judy Brownell asked employees to rate both the listening skills of their managers and their job satisfaction, 92 per cent of those who rated their managers as good listeners said they were satisfied with their jobs.[46] Brownell also found that training makes a difference. For example, 58 per cent of the managers rated as good listeners by their employees had received training in listening, whereas 89 per cent of managers rated as poor listeners had received no training.[47] Through training, managers gain an awareness of the need to listen well, learn techniques for becoming better listeners, and discover how to model good listening behaviours to their employees.[48]

Unfortunately managers often fail to recognize their inability to listen effectively. Virtually all managers in Brownell's research project perceived their listening skills as *good* or *very good*, but many of their employees evaluated them as *infrequently* demonstrating effective listening. Despite the generally bad showing of managers, women fared better than men in this study, with 58 per cent falling into the good listener group.[49] In explaining these results, Brownell suggests that women are more likely than men to use nonverbal cues to indicate they are listening. These behaviours include nodding, making eye contact, smiling, and saying "uh huh"—mannerisms that people see as indicators of good listening. Speakers react positively to these nonverbal responses.[50]

To find out if you are a good listener, complete the quiz in the "From Theory to Practice" box.

BARRIERS TO EFFECTIVE LISTENING

If listening is so important, why does the average person have such poor listening skills? As discussed earlier, a big difference exists between hearing and listening. Hearing what someone has said does not mean that you have processed the information. So many different stimuli compete for our attention that it is no wonder we are often asked, "Are you listening to me?" In fact, we may be taking in the *sounds*, but we may not be taking in the *message*.

> **"Two monologues do not make a dialogue."**
> **JEFF DALY**

In contrast to hearing, listening requires us to focus physically and mentally, to select the information to which we want to attend, to understand the information, to remember it, and to respond appropriately. Unfortunately, a number of factors can negatively influence our abilities to achieve these goals, including information overload, the difference between the rates at which we speak and listen, listening from our own perspective, and taking away from the perspective of the other person.

Information Overload and Multi-Tasking

According to Torkel Klingberg, we are in a constant state of information overload. As a result, we must engage in serious multi-tasking to keep up.[51] A professor of cognitive neuroscience at the Stockholm Brain Institute in Sweden, Klingberg states that people report

from theory TO PRACTICE

How Well Do You Listen?

Use the following rating scale to answer each of the ten questions below:

1 = always false, 2 = usually false, 3 = sometimes false, 4 = usually true, and 5 = always true.

As you answer the questions, think about how you typically respond to a friend or family member who is telling you about a problem.

1. I try to offer advice when I listen to others. ___
2. I check new information against what I already know when I listen to others. ___
3. I have an idea of what others will say when I listen to them. ___
4. I am sensitive to others' feelings when I listen to them. ___
5. I think about what I am going to say next when I listen to others. ___
6. I try to put myself in the other's shoes when I am listening. ___
7. I can't wait for others to finish talking so I can take my turn. ___
8. I try to reflect back what the other person is saying to confirm my understanding. ___
9. I focus on determining whether others understand what I said when they are talking. ___
10. I ask others to elaborate when I am not sure what they mean. ___

To score: Reverse your responses for the *odd numbered questions* (if you wrote 1, make it a 5; if you wrote 2, make it a 4; if you wrote 3, leave it as is; if you wrote 4, make it a 2; if you wrote 5, make it a 1). Add all the numbers next to each statement. The higher the score, the better your listening behaviours.

As you can see, good listening involves practising the kinds of behaviours we have discussed in this chapter.

SOURCE: Based on W. Gudykunst, *Bridging Differences*, 2nd ed. (Thousand Oaks, CA: Sage, 1994).

being interrupted or distracted every three minutes while at work. Using a computer analogy, he says that we have an average of eight windows open at the same time—all of which are dedicated to responding to the various stimuli that demand our attention.

Today's students face all kinds of distractions, many of which come from having constant access to digital technologies. Most students are extensively wired and connected to friends, the media, and the Internet through cellphones, MP3 players, and laptops. Since large lecture halls typically allow unmonitored wireless Internet access, students engage in the ultimate in multi-tasking as they check their email, text their friends, visit Facebook, and surf the web, while at the same time listening to the lecture and taking notes.

While it may seem efficient (and more interesting) to engage in all these activities at the same time, the human brain is not as good at multi-tasking as we like to think. Researchers at Carnegie Mellon University asked students to compare two rotating objects while listening to a recording of someone reading sentences aloud. This task engaged two different parts of the brain—one dedicated to processing visual information and the other dedicated to processing audio information. Results showed that each of these parts of the brain was significantly less active when students performed the two tasks at the same time, compared to when they performed each task separately. (Activation dropped by 29 per cent in the area of the brain that processes visual information and 53 per cent in the area that processes audio information.) Thus, while we may think we are good at juggling many activities at the same time—for example, texting a friend while checking Facebook or listening to a podcast while reading a book—we are

professionalCONTEXTS

Improving Your Brain Function with Music

We all know that when we hear a certain song, we cannot help but tap our toes, nod our heads, or even get up and dance. We react this way because music activates parts of the brain that control the function of movement. However, music also triggers activity that is related to mental functions such as attention, information processing, and memory.[52]

You may have seen the film *Awakenings* (1990), in which an innovative physician (played by Robin Williams) discovers that certain songs (as well as other familiar stimuli) can break through his patients' catatonic states. The idea for *Awakenings* came from neurologist Oliver Sacks's work in the 1960s. More recently, in the twenty-first century, researchers have found that patients suffering from Parkinson's and Alzheimer's diseases can benefit from music therapy. The therapeutic work with Alzheimer's patients demonstrates, in particular, the impact of music on memory. For example, the patients can remember song lyrics that are sung better than those that are spoken.[53]

Music also helps stroke patients. When they focus their attention on the beat of a specific type of music, these patients report an easier time performing other tasks.[54] Singing helps them to retrieve and form words (even when not singing), and they find it easier to walk while listening to music: "It's almost as if they're using past memories of how to move with music."[55] One study of 60 stroke patients found that focussed attention and verbal memory improved much more in a group that listened to music than in groups that used other learning strategies. In addition, participants in the music group experienced less depression and confusion.[56]

Music therapy—the power of listening to rhythm and sound—offers a glimmer of hope to those afflicted by strokes and Alzheimer's and Parkinson's diseases. Go to www.cbc.ca/news/canada/story/2012/12/28/music-as-therapy.html to view a CBC News clip that profiles the music therapy work of neurologist Frank Russo of Ryerson University and Constance Tomaino (a pioneer in the field). Also turn on some quiet music or hum a tune the next time you have difficulty concentrating or remembering what you have read.

doing all of these tasks less effectively than if we focussed on one activity at a time. When asked to engage in two complex tasks at once, we devote less brainpower to each task.[57]

Despite these findings, however, some researchers have uncovered a more positive connection between music and task performance. For example, researchers are now exploring the role that music can play in helping Alzheimer's patients improve their memory. See the "Professional Contexts" box above to learn more about this research.

Difference between Thought Rate and Speech Rate

SPEECH–THOUGHT DIFFERENTIAL The difference between the rate at which a speaker conveys a spoken message and the speed at which a listener processes the information.

Another barrier to effective listening is the **speech–thought differential**—the difference between a speaker's rate of speech and a listener's rate of thought. A typical speaker says about 125 words per minute, but the brain can process thoughts at a rate of 400 to 500 words per minute.[58] This means that when you are listening to someone speak, your brain is capable of processing much more information than the speaker is conveying.

Put another way, you have lots of "free time" to think about other things when people speak to you. While it can be tempting to think about last night's date, your afternoon plans, or your boss's habit of scratching his ear while talking, problems arise when you allow your thoughts to wander too far from what a speaker is saying. First, lack of attentiveness conveys a lack of respect for the speaker. People can tell when you are not fully listening, and they will feel hurt and offended by your lack of interest in what they have to say. Second, if you daydream while others speak, you may miss important information. Have you ever shown up late, at the wrong place, or on the wrong day for a meeting or date? It is possible that someone told you the right time, place, or day, but you were not listening.

Listening from Your Own Perspective

When listening from your own perspective, you lessen the chances of understanding the other person. Below is the kind of conversation you might overhear in the workplace. Note how neither listener focusses on what the other person says.

Matthew: I met with the marketing team yesterday to get ideas on how to promote our new line of cosmetics. They suggested we should focus on fashion magazines and television.

Aisha: Sure, sounds good. You know, Matt, I was thinking about our upcoming move. Do you think there will be parking at the new location? If not, I don't know how I will be able to afford paying for space.

Matthew: I've got so much to do with this campaign that I haven't thought about the move. I'm concerned we may be missing out if we don't use social media with this campaign.

Aisha: Hey, do you want to grab a coffee? I don't know if I can stay awake without some heavy caffeine. I watched the whole third season of The Walking Dead on Netflix last night.

Although this conversation may sound pretty typical, you can see that Matthew and Aisha are taking turns talking about their individual interests and concerns. Each appears to be waiting for the other person to stop speaking in order to pick up where he or she left off. In other words, as listeners, they are responding from their own perspectives.

Management guru Stephen Covey describes this kind of response as listening through an autobiographical filter, which is not very satisfying for the speaker.[59] When listening from your own point of view, rather than trying to understand what the other person is trying to say, you end up taking the focus of the conversation away from the speaker and putting it on yourself.

> **"There are people who, instead of listening to what is being said to them, are already listening to what they are going to say themselves."**
> **ALBERT GUINON**

Taking Away from the Other Person's Perspective

As discussed in Chapter 3, most of us look to others for **validation**. That is, we look to others to confirm our sense of worth and value as human beings. Listening is one of the ways by which we can validate others and they can validate us. Failure to listen and respond appropriately to the words of another person has the opposite effect, diminishing the importance of the other person's perspective.

VALIDATION
Confirmation of our sense of worth and value.

Let us examine a typical conversation that might occur in a Canadian organization. Brigitte chats with her co-worker Tomas about one of her work projects. This conversation will illustrate four inappropriate listening responses that can take away from the value of the other person. We will also examine options for more appropriate responses. The conversation begins with Brigitte expressing a concern.

Brigitte: I'm having so much trouble with this project. The deadline is unrealistic, no one is supplying information on time, and the guidelines for data analysis are totally unclear. I feel out of control.

First Inappropriate Response: Evaluating (Agreeing or Disagreeing with the Speaker)

> *Tomas: I know what you mean. I had a similar problem last year, and it took forever for my team members to get their acts together. We got in trouble because we couldn't meet deadlines either, and you know what Ben did . . . .*

In this response, Tomas uses the phrase "I know what you mean" as a springboard to talk about *his* past experience. Sometimes, in a casual conversation, we tell stories about funny movies we have seen or times we had to pull an all-nighter to finish an assignment. In these conversations, springboarding back and forth is okay. We can take turns telling our stories without worrying that we are harming the other person's sense of self-worth. However, when someone has a problem, a frustration, or exciting news, we should not jump in right away and say, "Oh, that reminds me of the time . . . ."

You might think that you are showing empathy for the other person—letting that person know she or he is not alone in the situation—when you respond "That happened to me too." It is true that people like to know that others have had similar experiences. However, your interruption acts as a barrier to good listening if it takes the focus of the conversation away from the speaker before she has a chance to tell her story.

Similarly, you should avoid making statements such as "I agree" or "I disagree." As psychotherapist Carl Rogers points out, responding with either agreement or disagreement implies a judgment.[60] Because evaluation comes from our personal frames of reference, the comment is ultimately about our views, not about those of the other person.

Second Inappropriate Response: Shifting the Focus (Asking Questions from Your Perspective)

> *Tomas: Did you ever get reimbursed for expenses on your last marketing project? It's been almost two months since I submitted my receipts for my last trip to British Columbia, and I still haven't got paid.*

In this example, Tomas redirects the conversation away from Brigitte's problems with her current project. He does so by using Brigitte's reference to *her project* to shift the focus of the conversation to one of *his projects*—a topic in which he is more interested. Clearly, Tomas wants to talk about not getting paid for his last trip, but Brigitte probably has no interest in going in that direction. As a result, she has to wait for her next turn to pick up where she left off: voicing concerns about her current project.

> **"The opposite of talking isn't listening. The opposite of talking is waiting."**
> FRAN LEBOWITZ

Not all questions reflect poor listening. You can ask a question, for example, to encourage the speaker to share more information ("Where did that happen?"), to show interest ("So what did you do then?"), or to enable the speaker to further develop his or her ideas ("How did you feel about that?"). These kinds of questions encourage the speaker to finish her turn and to expand her ideas. If you are not careful, however, you can move the subject away from what the speaker wanted to discuss and focus attention on your ideas and interests.

Third Inappropriate Response: Advising (Trying to Provide a Solution to the Problem)

Tomas: You should try to get Nan to take over that project. She handled it last year, and she knows the contacts. You could take her project. That's what I'd do.

When you have a problem you want to talk about, what do you want from the other person? A solution? Emotional support? Understanding? An ear while you work things out? When given these four options, few people respond that they are looking for a solution from the listener. The vast majority select emotional support, understanding, or an ear while they work things out. Extensive research has confirmed that people rarely want advice when they are trying to work through a personal problem.

People want to believe they are capable of solving their own problems and making their own decisions. They appreciate a listener who provides the attention and focus they need while they explore—and perhaps resolve—their own problems. Solutions offered by others might not be the right fit.[61] Instead of offering messages that say "Let me solve this problem for you" or "Here's what you should do," good listeners keep the focus on encouraging the listener to explore multiple perspectives. When we encourage the speaker to consider multiple perspectives, we also encourage the development of cognitive complexity in the person. (Recall from our earlier discussion that cognitive complexity helps us to arrive at well-considered conclusions.)

> **"When we honestly ask ourselves which person in our lives means the most to us, we often find that it is those who, instead of giving advice, solutions, or cures, have chosen rather to share our pain and touch our wounds with a warm and tender hand."**
>
> **HENRI NOUWEN**

The above is not to say that we never want advice or a proposed solution to our problems. Sometimes we need specific information or advice to solve a problem—for example, help with choosing a new tablet computer. At other times, we need an expert like an accountant, a lawyer, or a physician to show us our options and guide us in making a decision. Most of the time, however, we are looking for a non-judgmental listener—someone who will listen without making suggestions.

Fourth Inappropriate Response: Interpreting (Trying to Figure People Out)

Tomas: I guess you're really questioning your decision to join this organization, eh? I always wondered if you were really cut out for it.

Given the above response, we can imagine that Brigitte might be surprised by Tomas's interpretation of her comment. He has shifted the conversation from Brigitte's feelings about one project to her feelings about the organization as a whole. Brigitte never said that she wanted to leave the organization (or even the project), but Tomas assumes he knows what she is thinking and feeling. Sometimes the attempt to interpret redirects the conversation to areas of greater interest to the listening partner, which devalues the speaker. Perhaps Tomas would like to share his own insecurities about his position, but Brigitte clearly did not intend to go in that direction.

© Squaredpixels/iStockphoto

Summary

The exchange between Tomas and Brigitte illustrates four common pitfalls in listening: evaluating, shifting the focus, advising, and interpreting. Like most of us, Tomas and Brigitte should heed the advice: "Seek first to understand, and then to be understood."[62] The following behaviours will help us to avoid these four pitfalls: responding with silence or saying "mmm hmm," summarizing and showing interest in what the speaker has said, and asking questions that encourage the speaker to reflect on the problem from different points of view. We will develop these ideas in more depth as we proceed through the chapter.

GETTING THE MOST OUT OF LISTENING

As we have seen in this chapter, listening is not easy in most situations. But you can make the task easier by adopting some simple behaviours that promote effective listening. The following discussions outline some of these behaviours and show you how they can help you get the most out of listening—both to learn and to sustain and improve your relationships with other people. Before you continue, take a moment to turn to the activity in the "From Theory to Practice" box.

> *from theory* **TO PRACTICE**
>
> **Modeling a Good Listener**
>
> Think of people you know whom you consider to be good listeners. List the behaviours (both verbal and nonverbal) that you think make these people effective listeners. Once you have finished this chapter, add to this list any additional behaviours you have overlooked. How can you use these behaviours in your own life to get the most out of listening?

Listening to Learn

When listening to learn, we engage in **deliberative listening**. Deliberative listening involves hearing, understanding, evaluating, and storing information for later recall. It also involves analyzing and drawing conclusions from the information. With deliberative listening, we seek to assess the quality, relevance, and usefulness of the information we receive.[63] We approach the task from a critical rather than empathic perspective. In an environment where information moves quickly and spreads easily, we must be able to differentiate between fact and opinion, truth and exaggeration. We develop deliberative listening skills in classroom contexts, and we apply them in business contexts.

DELIBERATIVE LISTENING Listening to learn, often from a critical perspective.

Let us look at some of the key actions we can undertake to improve our ability to engage in deliberative listening.

Sitting near the Front

Sitting close to the front of a lecture or conference hall can help you to listen more effectively. First, your close proximity to the speaker means that you will face fewer distractions. You will be less likely to check Facebook or otherwise let your attention drift. In addition, you will be able to hear more easily and have fewer distractions from people coming and going from the room or engaging in unrelated activities.

> "It's only through listening that you learn, and I never want to stop learning."
> DREW BARRYMORE

Second, a front-row seat tells the speaker that you are interested and engaged. In classroom settings, professors respond differently to students whom they perceive as serious. And when others have positive expectations of you, you are more likely to meet those expectations. See Chapter 2 for a review of this cyclical relationship, known as the self-fulfilling prophecy.

Third, sitting near the front puts you in contact with other serious listeners. In classroom contexts, these listeners can become good study friends, lab partners, or work-group buddies. Furthermore, surrounding yourself with others who are working hard to pay attention, answering questions, and taking good notes can improve your own performance: observing their good work habits might rub off on you!

Eliminating Distractions

As discussed earlier in this chapter, most people overestimate their capacity to multi-task. While it can be tempting to surf the Internet, text with friends, and surf the web while attempting to listen to a lecture, extensive research shows that grades suffer when students multi-task in this way. When students browse the Internet instead of listening or taking notes, their final marks are lower.[64] So you need to eliminate distracting stimuli in order to listen to learn. The "Professional Contexts" box reminds us of the risks in multi-tasking.

*professional*CONTEXTS

Risky Behaviours and Double Jeopardy

Most people are aware that using a cellphone while driving creates distractions that can lead to accidents. In fact, an Alberta study found that drivers who use cellphones while they are driving have a four to six time higher collision rate. Nationally the statistics are not much better. As a result, most provinces have enacted some kind of legislation to ban cellphone use in the absence of a hands-free device while driving. Internationally, at least forty countries have placed similar restrictions on cellphone use.[65]

These laws may not, however, get at the real problem. While it may seem like the accidents result from drivers looking away from the road or taking their hands away from the wheel—to text, dial a number, or hold their cellphone—the real distraction in cellphone use is *listening*. Recall our earlier discussion of a study from Carnegie Mellon University that found that people experience problems with processing visual content (rotating figures) and audio content (someone reading sentences aloud) at the same time. Researchers at the same university have identified similar problems in studies of cellphone practices. Their research involved measuring participants' brain activity as they engaged in two unrelated tasks. More specifically, the participants listened to spoken messages, which they rated as true or false, while driving in a simulated situation.

Using MRI pictures of the brain, the researchers found that activity in the part of the brain associated with driving decreased by 37 per cent in participants charged with the two tasks.[66] As a result, those drivers made more errors than those who performed only one task (i.e., driving). The errors included missing exits, weaving in and out of lanes, and even hitting guard rails. The researchers concluded that the brain can handle only so much information at once and, for that reason, a hands-free phone device may not prevent traffic accidents. Thus, while it may be legal to use a cellphone with a hands-free device, this "safety feature" can lull drivers into thinking they are paying attention when, in reality, they are not fully focussed on driving.

You might wonder why talking to a passenger does not seem to carry the same risks. The answer is simple. Both drivers and passengers can adapt their conversation to the driving conditions. When searching for a street sign or taking an exit, for example, they can more easily pause the conversation to take environmental demands into account.

Paying Attention

As we saw earlier in this chapter, the speech–thought differential (the gap between how quickly a speaker conveys a message and how quickly the listener can process the information) is also important.[67] For every word spoken in a lecture, listeners have the time to think of four or five other words. Good listeners work at using all of this "extra time" to think about the ideas being discussed, to anticipate where the speaker will go next, to compare new ideas to what they have learned before, and to think critically about the information. Bad listeners use the time to daydream: to think about their next appointment or to evaluate the clothing, hairstyle, or accent of the speaker. Clearly, when it comes time to make use of the information in a work project or classroom exam, the individual who focussed on the lecture rather than on the speaker's shoes will be better prepared.

Taking Good Notes

Taking good notes helps to ensure academic and career success because you use these notes to study, to review instructions, and to tailor your assignments to the expectations of the professor or job supervisor. Good note-taking requires listening effectively *during* meetings, but it also involves preparing *before* you arrive at the session. Doing the required readings and reviewing proposals and slide presentations ahead of time can give you an idea of the agenda—not only what will be discussed, but also what will be emphasized. These kinds of practices lead to higher academic success and prepare you for the workforce.[68]

Once you arrive in the meeting room (and have taken your seat near the front to maximize your listening ability), prepare to write down the important information. You will not be able to note every word because the speaker will likely speak faster than you can write or type. Instead, listen for key ideas. The following kind of statement alerts you to key ideas: "One of the most critical elements in this process is . . . ." In making notes, you will want to identify these key ideas by underscoring or highlighting the points.

"Wisdom is the reward you get for a lifetime of listening when you'd have preferred to talk."
DOUG LARSON

© David Hills/iStockphoto

In addition to noting key ideas, record how the various ideas and topics fit together. Use headings and subheadings to identify major sections and number these sections to assist you in recreating the structure of the talk at a later time. Structure your notes to reflect the structure of the lecture. To identify this structure, listen to cues from the speaker. A speaker might say, for example, "There are three phases to this process. Let's look at each one in turn." Other indicators of structure could include the following: "First, we will talk about . . ." or "Next we will cover . . ." or "In conclusion . . . ." Transitional words such as *so*, *however*, and *therefore* also point to the structure of a lecture and help a listener to anticipate the next points. Reviewing ahead of time also helps you to anticipate the possible structure of a lecture. If you have an idea where the lecture is going, you will be better able to recognize the sequence of ideas when they appear.

If you have time, explain ideas in your own words. **Paraphrasing** what another person has said forces you to process that person's ideas in your own mind. By actively thinking about and rephrasing what the speaker is saying, you will gain a better understanding of her or his meaning. You will also remember the ideas more easily, because you have created links in your personal computer (your brain).

PARAPHRASING Using our own words to help us understand and/or reflect back our understanding of what another person has said.

It is good practice to leave blank space in your notes so that you can add details after the class has ended. You can, for instance, add illustrations or examples under the headings and subheadings that you have created. Many students use a note-taking approach called the "Cornell System." This system requires that you divide each note page into two columns. The left column occupies about one-third of the total width of the page. During class, you record your notes in the right column. After class, you use the left column to record additional ideas, definitions, and themes from the lecture and related readings.

Reviewing Your Notes

It may seem time consuming to review notes after class, but research shows that the amount of information retained after listening to a lecture drops dramatically by the next day if you do not review what you have learned. As mentioned earlier in the chapter, the retention rate for a 10-minute presentation is only 50 per cent. After 48 hours, the rate falls to 25 per cent or even lower in class situations.[69] Thirty days later (just in time for a mid-term test), you retain only 2 to 3 per cent of what you knew when you left the class.[70]

You can, however, dramatically increase retention of lecture material if you review your notes for 10 minutes the day after the lecture, 5 minutes a week later, and 2 to 4 minutes after 30 days. This schedule should enable you to keep your level of retention close to what it was on the day of the lecture. [71]

*professional*CONTEXTS

Speed Listening to Increase Productivity

Both students and working professionals have always had to manage a large amount of reading in order to manage their class loads and work tasks. In past years, some took courses in speed reading in order to learn techniques that could reduce the amount of time spent reading. But now they face a new challenge. In addition to relying on written text for essential information, they must listen to podcasts, TED talks, and audiobooks. What if you could listen to—and understand—an hour of material in 30 minutes or less? Imagine how much more you could do with the extra time.

Suppose your work project or class assignment requires listening to 60 minutes of audio content. Audio files play at a default speed that is digestible by most people. However, you can increase the speed on media players to 1.5 times, 2 times, or even 3 times faster than the default speed. In other words, you can listen to 60 minutes of information in roughly 40, 30, or 20 minutes. ou can set the speed for faster playback of audio files on media players such as Windows Media Player and QuickTime. (Search on the Internet for instructions for your particular device.[72])

Most people feel comfortable playing spoken text at 1.4 times the normal speed. Begin at this rate and gradually increase your speed until you can no longer comprehend the information. Perhaps you think that, when sped up, the speaker will sound like Alvin and the Chipmunks with high-pitched and squeaky tones. In fact, most players automatically adjust the pitch so that the tone is not squeaky even though the speech rate is faster.

Remember, when you listen to a faster-paced podcast or other audio file, you will need to focus and concentrate more closely than during normal listening. Wearing earphones seems to enhance the ability of people to absorb content while speed listening, probably because the earphones block outside sounds that interfere with comprehension. You will not be able to text a friend, check Facebook, or watch a clip on YouTube while you listen; however, you will have more time for all of these activities once you finish listening to the audio recordings!

Why is it effective to spend such a small amount of time in review? The act of reviewing moves the lecture material into your long-term memory. Once in the long-term memory, the material will be more accessible at exam time or when you next need it. When you engage in review, you tell your brain that the information is important to remember. Without this review, most of the information will stay only briefly in your short-term working memory.

While it may seem that you do not have enough time to bother with reviewing—after all, you have to prepare for all your other work projects and lectures—the time you invest in ongoing reviews saves time later. Instead of having to re-learn all of the material you have forgotten, you can simply review it.

Becoming Aware of Confirmation Bias

CONFIRMATION BIAS The tendency to attend to information that confirms our beliefs and to ignore information that contradicts our beliefs.

As explained in Chapter 3, we tend to seek out and attend to information that confirms what we already believe and to ignore or discount information that contradicts these beliefs. We refer to this tendency as a **confirmation bias**. When we choose to listen only to what we already believe, we put ourselves at risk of doing poorly in school and in our careers. We live in an information age, characterized by many new ideas that challenge existing frameworks of thought. Even if we do not agree with all of these ideas and concepts, we need to understand them. When we are aware of our confirmation biases, we seek to understand ideas before accepting or rejecting them. We also try to see where new ideas might fit into what we already know. Our thoughts may be something like "I don't agree with that idea, but I can see where it fits with the rest of the speaker's logic."

Practising Active Listening

Learning is an active process. To do well in learning environments, you must do more than show up.[73] If you sit passively in a lecture and wait for the speaker to entertain you, you will get little out of the experience. Rather, you must make a conscious effort to find something of interest in the lecture. Think about how the information affects you and what you might be able to do with it. In a classroom lecture, you should also think about how the information relates to the assigned readings and how it links to previous lectures in this or other classes.

An idea for increasing the efficiency of your learning experience outside the classroom is to engage in speed listening. The "Professional Contexts" box on speed listening suggests a way to develop and incorporate this communication skill into your learning experience.

Listening to Sustain or Improve Relationships

EMPATHIC LISTENING Listening from the perspective of the other person.

Listening to sustain or improve relationships involves **empathic listening**: that is, limiting your own talking, using both verbal and nonverbal cues to indicate you are listening, and paraphrasing the speaker's message. Empathic listening requires you to hear what the other person is saying—both at the content level (what the words say) and at the emotional level (how the speaker feels about the information). You listen with your ears, your eyes, and your heart: "You listen for feeling, for meaning. You listen for behaviour. You use your right brain as well as your left. You sense, you intuit, you feel." [74] You try to understand not only the message, but also the person.[75] You try to

professionalCONTEXTS

Carl Rogers: On the Impact of Empathic Listening

The renowned psychologist Carl Rogers wrote about the importance of empathic listening in the therapeutic relationship. His words resonate today not only for counsellors and therapists, but also for everyone wanting to connect more meaningfully with others:

> I find, both in therapeutic interviews and in the intensive group experiences which have meant a great deal to me, that hearing has consequences. When I truly hear a person and the meanings that are important to him at that moment, hearing not simply his words, but him, and when I let him know that I have heard his own private personal meanings, many things happen. There is first of all a grateful look. He feels released. He wants to tell me more about his world. He surges forth in a new sense of freedom. He becomes more open to the process of change . . . . I have often noticed that the more deeply I hear the meanings of this person, the more there is that happens. Almost always, when a person realizes he has been deeply heard, his eyes moisten. I think in some real sense he is weeping for joy. It is as though he were saying, "Thank God, somebody heard me. Someone knows what it's like to be me." In such moments I have had the fantasy of a prisoner in a dungeon, tapping out day after day a Morse code message, "Does anybody hear me? Is anybody there?" And finally one day he hears some faint tappings which spell out "Yes." By that one simple response he is released from his loneliness; he has become a human being again. There are many, many people living in private dungeons today, people who give no evidence of it whatsoever on the outside, where you have to listen very sharply to hear the faint messages from the dungeon.[76]

imagine, as they tell their stories, what others have experienced in the past; what they may be experiencing in the present; and how they feel about these experiences. See the "Professional Contexts" box above for an inspirational comment on the role of listening in interpersonal relationships.

Limiting Your Own Talking

As the Greek philosopher Epictetus once said, "We have two ears and one mouth so that we can listen twice as much as we speak." Many of us have a hard time limiting our talking, but the first rule of good listening is to talk less. This task may be difficult because most of us are uncomfortable with silence, and we feel obliged to fill the empty spaces. For many Westerners, periods of silence and conversational lapses can be awkward, especially if they last longer than three seconds and if it appears that the speakers are not sure how to fill the lapse.[77]

We tend to see people who hesitate in conversations as socially awkward or lacking in social skills. For this reason, it may be important to communicate that your silence is intentional—that you are leaving space for others to continue their thoughts.[78] You can convey this intention by nodding encouragingly, saying "mmm hmm," maintaining eye contact, and appearing comfortable with the conversational lapse.

Using Nonverbal and Verbal Cues to Show Attention

Approximately 93 per cent of the emotional content of our communications comes through our body language.[79] For that reason, it makes sense to use these same channels to indicate to others that we are listening.

Making eye contact is a particularly subtle, yet effective, sign of attention. We all know what it is like to speak with someone at a party and to have that person continually looking past us at each new person who comes in the door. When this kind of

© twohumans/iStockphoto

inattention happens, we feel uninteresting, unimportant, and ignored. Looking away from someone who is talking is a form of social exclusion.[80] Therefore, while it might be tempting to check out a new arrival in the room, to look at your watch, or to check your cellphone, these behaviours have negative consequences. When we look into the eyes of a speaker, that person responds much more positively than when we look away while she or he is speaking.[81] Eye contact with a speaker says that we are interested in the conversation—and by extension, the person.

CULTURE BOUND Restricted by cultural influences.

Like all verbal and nonverbal communication, behaviours related to eye contact are **culture bound** (meaning that culture influences how we make and interpret eye contact). Along with many others, Marsha Mason and her colleagues at the University of Aberdeen in Scotland concluded that most Westerners respond positively to eye contact, but that too much eye contact can give the impression of an overly dominant personality.[82] While most Canadians and Americans perceive direct eye contact as a sign of respect and interest, members of some minority cultures in North America (e.g., Canadian First Nations and Asian cultures) view such behaviour as overly dominant and disrespectful.[83] People in Muslim cultures may see direct eye contact between men and women as unacceptably flirtatious behaviour.[84] In general, many Asian cultures place a higher value than North Americans on the nonverbal and emotional aspects of listening.[85] Chapter 7, on nonverbal communication, will explore these ideas in more depth.

Aaron Bacall/Cartoonstock

"You're a very good listener. You hear my feelings."

Other nonverbal signals that tell people we are listening include nodding the head to show support, leaning toward the speaker to show that we are engaged in the interaction and not trying to get away, and mimicking the facial expressions of the speaker to show that we identify with her or his emotional experience.[86]

Empathic listening also has verbal aspects. Empathic listeners use words that explicitly acknowledge that they understand and empathize with the other person's experience (e.g., "That must have been awful!" or "I can see how you would have been upset").[87] With empathic listening, we avoid words that imply judgment or criticism because our aim is to understand the other person and to sustain or improve the relationship. Mutual respect, support, and trust characterize the process. Empathic listeners also use many of the nonverbal cues discussed under the previous point to show they are listening.

Empathic listening plays an important role in policing and many of the helping professions such as counselling, nursing, and social work. See the "Professional Contexts" box to find out more about how hostage negotiators use this communication skill.

professionalCONTEXTS

Listening in Hostage Negotiations

If we believe what we see on television and in movies, hostage negotiators are tough cops, not afraid to leave their guns behind when they go alone to talk to a bad guy holed up with a group of innocent hostages. A close look at real-life hostage negotiators reveals a different and more subtle picture. Rather than relying on a cold, tough exterior to extract concessions from hostage takers, they try to connect with the perpetrators on a human level. Hostage negotiation involves situations with high levels of anxiety, emotion, apprehension, and uncertainty for the hostage taker, his or her victims, and the negotiators. In most cases, a failure on the part of the perpetrator to deal with emotional distresses has led to the crisis. As a result, a psychological counselling approach is necessary to resolve the perpetrator's emotional issues.[88]

Most people in crises—including hostage takers—have a desire to be heard and understood.[89] Therefore, negotiators in hostage situations must be experts in communication, with the ability to hear clearly and to listen effectively. They must be particularly skilled at empathic listening, as one of their goals is to understand the perpetrator's perspective and to help him or her to resolve a problem. In order to accomplish this goal, the negotiator uses strategies such as paraphrasing opinions and feelings expressed by the hostage taker. Through empathic listening, negotiators seek to resolve the crisis in a way that results in "successful containment and arrest rather than escalation and subsequent loss of life."[90]

While police officers are not necessarily trained psychologists, their work in hostage negotiation draws heavily upon the theory and practice of counselling and psychotherapy. Using this body of knowledge, police training in hostage negotiation usually employs role plays. In these role plays, a hostage negotiator is given a scenario and asked to practise his or her new skills in areas that include empathic listening. A typical scenario might involve a man who has abducted his estranged wife and child. He is holding the hostages in an abandoned farmhouse. In a successful scenario, the police officer begins with active listening and then proceeds to show empathy, establish rapport, influence the hostage taker to see things differently, and finally achieve behavioural change. Ideally, the perpetrator will follow the suggestions of the negotiator (in this case, releasing the wife and child and surrendering to police).

Hostage negotiation is difficult and volatile, with the potential for many different and often negative outcomes. However, experts in police tactics agree on one point: using a strategy that includes empathic listening increases the likelihood of a successful negotiation.

Paraphrasing the Speaker's Message

While we are listening closely and using nonverbal cues to demonstrate our interest, we are also gathering information that we can use to confirm our understanding of the speaker's message. For example, if your friend says, "I'll meet you at the coffee shop around the corner after work," you might respond by rephrasing what your co-worker said: "Okay, see you at Second Cup at 5:30." In this way, you confirm your interpretation of the plan. If your friend responds with "No, I meant Tim Hortons," then both of you become aware that the words *coffee shop* carry more than one possible meaning. Paraphrasing, in this case, has helped to clear up what could have been a miscommunication.

Paraphrasing in empathic listening, where we listen from the perspective of the speaker, allows us to reflect back our understanding of what the speaker has said. In this way, we demonstrate our interest at the same time that we enable the speaker to think about what he or she has said.[91] Effective paraphrasing by a listener does more than help the speaker to think about what he or she has said. It also helps the speaker to feel valued, listened to, and understood.[92]

Paraphrasing is not the same as repeating the speaker's exact words. Imagine that your friend says, "I felt so stupid when a client asked me a question about the last quarter profits and I didn't have the answer!" You respond, "You felt stupid that you didn't have the answer to his question?" This response sounds contrived and phony. Effective paraphrasing requires you to put the speaker's words into your own words and, in this way, check your understanding. In the above case, it might have been better to say, "I guess you're worried you might have looked bad when you weren't sure how to respond to his question?" Alternatively, you could say, "I guess it was embarrassing when you weren't able to provide the figures?" These paraphrases build on the speaker's original words but demonstrate deeper processing of the message on the part of the listener.

PARAPHRASING CONTENT Summarizing the main verbal message.

PARAPHRASING EMOTIONS Summarizing how the speaker feels about what he or she is telling you.

You have two options in paraphrasing: **paraphrasing content** or **paraphrasing emotions**. Paraphrasing the content of the message requires summarizing the main verbal message. In this way, you can clarify unclear references or words that may carry multiple meanings (e.g., the building's *main entrance*). To begin a paraphrase of content, you can use a "lead-in" such as "It sounds like you're saying . . ." and then rephrase what you think you heard. (See Table 5.1 for more lead-ins.)

In addition to paraphrasing the content of the message, you can look for cues to indicate how the speaker feels about what he or she is telling you, and you can paraphrase at the emotional level. For example, you can paraphrase what you think a person is feeling by using expressions such as "You're kidding!" or "Seriously!" or "No way!" You can also paraphrase feelings by making statements that begin with lead-ins such as "You must feel . . ." (see Table 5.1). In these ways, you show empathy with the speaker. Cues to the emotions of speakers may appear in their facial expressions, tone of voice, or body language.

Sometimes you may worry that you have not identified the right emotion in your paraphrase, or you may wonder how the other person will respond. For example, imagine that Jamal, upset about losing a contractor, expresses his worry to his co-worker Maeve.

Jamal: Damn. I knew I should have called that contractor back sooner. I'm not sure what's going to happen now that he's dropped out.
Maeve: You're worried about getting a bad evaluation?
Jamal: No. I'm upset about losing my vacation. I've got to find another contractor. My boss won't care if I find someone else to do the work.

In this case, Maeve mislabelled Jamal's emotion as "worried." In fact, his emotion is more akin to frustration and annoyance. Speakers will usually respond positively to an honest attempt at paraphrasing—one that does not stray too far from the "right" label. Misinterpretations can even allow speakers to think about and relabel their emotions. To avoid offending people by incorrectly paraphrasing their emotion, you can offer your interpretation tentatively.[93] For example, you can end your paraphrase with a question like "Is that what you're feeling?"[94]

See the "Professional Contexts" box for an example of how a good listener might use paraphrasing and other techniques of effective listening to respond to a worried friend.

TABLE 5.1 Lead-ins for paraphrasing.

PARAPHRASING CONTENT	PARAPHRASING FEELINGS
• It sounds like you're saying	• You must feel . . . .
• If I understand correctly, you're saying	• It sounds like you're feeling . . . .
• Let me make sure I get what you're saying	• You must have been so [*name of emotion*] when [*rephrase what happened*].

*professional*CONTEXTS

A Conversation with Danika and Mike

The following conversation between two friends, Danika and Mike, begins with Danika's anxious statement about a downturn in company sales. Note how Mike responds, using good listening techniques and effective paraphrasing of both content and feelings.

Danika: I'm worried about whether we'll meet sales quotas this year. The figures don't look promising.

Mike (requesting more information): What do you think is the problem?

Danika: I'm not sure. I think it might be one or two people who are having more problems than usual. I guess I need to look more closely at individual sales figures.

Mike (paraphrasing content and asking for confirmation of interpretation): You think the lower sales of one or two people could be creating your problems?

Danika: Maybe. But it's possible that they can't do much better right now, given the economic problems in some of their territories. I don't have enough information at the moment, but I'm worried the situation could worsen before I figure it out.

Mike (paraphrasing feelings): You sound pretty concerned.

Danika: Yes, I am. I'm losing a lot of sleep. This company's been good to me, and I don't want to be responsible for its failure.

Mike (paraphrasing content and feelings): I know your job means a lot to you. It's easy to feel stressed when things are not going as well as you would like.

Danika: Totally.

Mike: So what do you think you should do now?

In this example, Mike works hard to understand both the content and the emotion conveyed in Danika's words. He asks a question to be sure he understands the content, uses effective paraphrasing, and helps Danika to focus on coming up with a solution to the problem—but only after she has had a chance to "vent" about her anxiety. While Mike has not had a chance to talk about his own interests or worries, he has given Danika the gift of good listening; and at some point in the future, Danika will probably return the favour.

TIPS FOR EFFECTIVE LISTENING

With practice, you can improve your listening skills. The following tips will help to guide you on your journey to become a more effective listener.

Make an effort to enhance your cognitive complexity. You can do this by interacting with people from outside your usual network, working to understand the moods and feelings of others, modelling your communication after people whose communication skills you admire, and processing incoming information from the viewpoints of other people.

Avoid checking your email or social media accounts during challenging listening situations. Limit texting, tweeting, and surfing the web when attending a lecture or participating in some other activity that requires you to listen. If you are having trouble focussing, try doodling, note taking, or playing soothing music. Although it can be difficult to pay attention, good listening pays off in a variety of ways.

Use silence to communicate. Understand the value of silence in building nurturing relationships. Giving people the time and space to talk is a gift that provides many returns in the quality of our relationships.

Use words that explicitly acknowledge that you understand and empathize with the speaker's experience. For example, if someone tells you about a time when she or he was afraid or upset, you might say "That experience must have been frightening!" or "I can see how you would have been upset." These statements show understanding; they validate what the other person has experienced.

Use nonverbal cues and vocal sounds to show you are listening. Nodding your head, making eye contact, leaning toward the speaker, and saying "mmm hmm" all indicate that you are listening. As you will learn in Chapter 7, people trust nonverbal information more than they trust words. Just saying "I am listening" may not convince people if your body language does not support this message.

Summarize and paraphrase what the speaker has said. Doing so will force you to think about and make sense of the information, and it will communicate to the speaker that you have been listening. Paraphrasing will also help you to clarify the meaning of vague language and avoid miscommunication.

Ask questions. Asking questions is another behaviour that shows you have been paying attention to what the speaker has said. It can also help the speaker work through a difficult issue by encouraging her or him to reflect on the problem from different points of view.

Actively think about what the speaker is saying. When listening to complex information such as a lecture or a professional presentation, try to anticipate where the speaker is going next, compare any new ideas to older insights, and think critically about the information (but not about the speaker). These activities will help you to pay attention, to process the information more effectively, and to remember it when needed.

SUMMARY

We have seen in this chapter that *hearing* is not the same as *listening*. Too often, we think we are listening to others when, in fact, we are just hearing the sounds they are making. In looking at the listening process, we learned that the four phases—selecting, understanding, remembering, and responding—are not easy. However, working hard to become a good listener has many benefits. We also saw that numerous barriers can stand in the way of effective listening. Those barriers include distractions (which contribute to information overload), the difference between our rate of thought and others' rate of speech, the tendency to listen from our own perspectives, and the tendency to take away from the other person's perspective. We learned about listening effectively in business meetings and classrooms in order to perform better as students and to further our careers. Finally, we learned how to display good listening behaviours such as talking less, using nonverbal and verbal cues to show we are listening, practising empathic listening, and using paraphrasing to reflect back what we think we have heard. We also looked at some tips for effective listening.

Although good listening takes work, it is "one of the ways, one of the best ways, we can be good to each other."[95] Good listeners put themselves and their interests aside temporarily in order to look at the world through other people's eyes and to focus on other people's ideas, worries, experiences, and feelings.

REVIEW QUESTIONS

1. How is hearing related to listening? How is hearing different from listening? Give examples.
2. How would you define effective versus ineffective listening? What specific communication behaviours

are associated with each kind of listening? Why is it important to develop effective listening skills?

3. Think about all of the professionals with whom you have come into contact—doctors, nurses, professors, guidance counsellors. What is the importance of effective listening to their ability to perform their jobs?
4. Which of the barriers to effective listening discussed in this chapter—information overload, the difference between thought rate and speech rate, listening from your own perspective, or taking away from the other person's perspective—causes you the most difficulty as a listener? Why? How can you address this challenge?
5. Why is taking away from the other person's perspective (through evaluating, shifting the focus and probing, advising, or interpreting) a bad listening habit? Can you think of any situations where taking away from another person's perspective could be appropriate and/or justified?
6. What are the benefits of empathic listening? Have you ever used empathic listening when talking with family or friends? What was the impact of your empathic listening on the other person?
7. What are the benefits of paraphrasing? How is paraphrasing content different from paraphrasing emotions?
8. Think about the different bosses you have had. In which ways do their behaviours resemble those of the bad bosses described in this chapter? What could they do differently to improve their listening skills?

SUGGESTED ACTIVITIES

1. Imagine a family member or friend came to you after having lost his or her job. Using the principles of empathic listening, write a script for a conversation with that person.
2. Watch an interview from a news broadcast or a talk show and observe the listening skills of each speaker. Pay special attention to any ineffective behaviours. How do the listeners show respect for the speakers? How do they use nonverbal cues to encourage the speakers? Do you notice any empathic listening behaviours? Any attempts to paraphrase? Critique each listener. Identify the best listeners and justify your choices.
3. Write a few paragraphs describing how the knowledge acquired in this chapter has helped you to better understand your interactions with other people. What kinds of listening and feedback behaviours have made your interpersonal experiences more pleasant? What kinds of behaviours have made your experiences more difficult or unpleasant? Think of friends who have demonstrated supportive or unsupportive listening behaviours.
4. Ask one of your classmates to tell you about a problem or concern she or he is currently facing at school or at work. Pay attention to how you behave in this encounter and evaluate your own listening behaviours. Have you made any inappropriate responses that could take away from the other person's perspective? Has this encounter made you aware of any habits you need to work on to become a better listener?

CHAPTER 6

Communicating Verbally

CHAPTER OUTLINE

learning OBJECTIVES

- To be able to describe the characteristics of language
- To be able to identify the rules that influence words and meanings
- To understand the role of context and culture in creating meaning through words
- To recognize the evolving nature of language
- To understand how we socially construct our world through language
- To recognize barriers that prevent understanding the verbal communication of others
- To improve our own verbal communication skills

forSTARTERS

Barriers to Communication

When we hear on the news that an airplane has crashed, we ask ourselves "Why?" and "How did this happen?" While mechanical errors, bad weather, fuel contamination, and other issues may contribute to these occurrences, the number one reason for plane crashes is pilot error.[1] What types of errors do pilots most commonly make? According to Malcolm Gladwell, in his book *Outliers*, the answer is lack of teamwork and communication errors.[2]

The miscommunication leading to crashes happens in two places: in the cockpit of the plane and between pilots and air traffic controllers (ATCs) on the ground. A major reason for this miscommunication relates to the cultural value of respect for authority. In many cultures, subordinates hesitate to challenge those with a higher rank even when they know something is amiss. A show of respect becomes more important than correcting mistakes. The Power Distance Index (PDI) provides one way to measure how much a particular culture values and respects authority.[3] For example, Americans have a low PDI score, which means they do not value authority as much as Colombians, who score high on the PDI. As we will see in the following examples, attitudes toward authority sometimes play a significant role in cockpit decisions by pilots and co-pilots.

Consider the following example. On paper, fuel exhaustion and subsequent engine failure accounted for the crash of Avianca Flight 052 in January 1990. More specifically, bad weather and poor visibility forced the Colombian plane to abort landing and to continue circling while dangerously low on fuel. But when investigators looked more closely at the events leading to the crash, they realized this crash could have been avoided if the flight team had communicated more effectively.

The captain of the plane was Laureano Caviedes; his first officer was Mauricio Klotz. In the following transcript, notice the length of the silences and the tone of Klotz's remarks as the pilots abort their first landing attempt at John F. Kennedy International Airport in New York City:[4]

Terry Ashe/Time & Life Pictures/Getty Images

Caviedes: The runway, where is it? I don't see it. I don't see it.

They take up the landing gear. The captain tells Klotz to ask for another traffic pattern. Ten seconds pass.

Caviedes [seemingly to himself]: We don't have fuel . . . .

Seventeen seconds pass as the pilots give technical instructions to each other.

Caviedes: I don't know what happened with the runway. I didn't see it.
Klotz: I didn't see it.

An ATC comes in and tells them to make a left turn.

Caviedes: Tell them we are in an emergency!
Klotz [to the ATC]: That's right to one-eight-zero on the heading and, ah, we'll try once again. We're running out of fuel.

INTRODUCTION

INTERDEPENDENT Reliant on other people for safety, survival, and support.

When we say that humans are social animals, we mean that (as a species) we rely on other people to meet our most basic survival needs—water, food, protection from the elements, and safety. Of course, our relationships with others serve many more purposes than meeting these basic needs. We also turn to other humans for comfort, companionship, laughter, knowledge, and creativity. In other words, we are **interdependent**. As we

To say that one is "running out of fuel" when landing a plane is not out of the ordinary; planes should be low on fuel by the time they approach landing. So the lack of urgency in Klotz's message caused the ATC to interpret Klotz's words as a passing comment.[5] Indeed, Klotz was engaging in "mitigated speech," which downplays the importance of what is being said.[6] This kind of speech is less common in North America than in other areas of the world; but even in North America, subordinates often hesitate to be overly blunt in their communication with superiors. In a typical flight situation, captains do not speak in mitigated language. They give orders. First officers, on the other hand, tend to "hint" when communicating with their superiors.

As the plane continued to circle, the ATC suggested a new landing plan. The final respectful exchange between Klotz and the ATC illustrates the perceived power distance between the Colombian co-pilot Klotz and the American ATC. Klotz's unquestioning acceptance of an unworkable plan has deadly consequences for those on Avianca Flight 052.

Klotz: Climb out and maintain three thousand and, ah, we're running out of fuel, sir.
ATC: And Avianca zero-five-two heavy, ah, I'm gonna bring you about fifteen miles northeast and then turn you back onto the approach. Is that okay with you and your fuel?
Klotz: I guess so. Thank you very much.

Psychologist Robert Helmreich wrote the following analysis of the accident: "The high power distance of Colombians could have created frustration on the part of the first officer because the captain failed to show the kind of clear (if not autocratic) decision making expected in high power distance cultures."[7] The pilot did not take control of the communications at any point. Additionally, the low power distance of the American ATC caused him to underestimate or disregard Klotz's passive warnings, as he expected a more explicit and clear message.[8]

With a $300 million machine and the lives of human beings at risk, flight teams cannot afford to adopt indirect or overly respectful communication styles.

Let us take a look at a second example of miscommunication involving a pilot and his co-pilot. In this second case, the first officer tries three times (using subtle hints) to tell his captain about a dangerous accumulation of ice on the plane's wings. Again the respectful nature of the communication has disastrous consequences.

Hint #1: First Officer: Look how the ice is just hanging on . . . ah, back, back there, see that?
Hint #2: First Officer: See all those icicles on the back there and everything?
Hint #3: First Officer: Boy, this is a, this is a losing battle here on trying to de-ice those things, it [gives] you a false feeling of security, that's all that does.

This Air Florida plane later plunged into the Potomac River outside of Washington, DC.

Human error explains a large number of airplane crashes, and better communication could prevent many of these tragedies. To reduce the possibility of miscommunication, every major airline now has a program called crew resource management training. This program instructs junior crew members on how to communicate directly and clearly with their superior officers.[9] When they establish clear communication pathways and seek input from their junior officers, the senior officers establish a supportive environment for sharing information.

This case study should lead you to think about the following kinds of questions, which this chapter addresses: What is the impact of culture on language? How does culture influence our interpretation of words and our ability to communicate effectively with others? What sorts of barriers interfere with our ability to understand language? What is the relationship between language and power?

have seen throughout this book, our capacity to connect with other people depends on our ability to communicate with them.

In this chapter, we will look at the characteristics of language, the social functions of language, and the difficulties we encounter when we confront language barriers. Finally, we will explore some tips for more effective **verbal communication**.

VERBAL COMMUNICATION
Communication that involves spoken, written, or signed language.

THE CHARACTERISTICS OF LANGUAGE

As you read this page of written text, your brain attempts to make sense of the black lines that make up the words. When you listen to someone speak, your brain interprets the sounds the speaker is making in order to understand what she or he is saying. Because you are human, you are able not only to identify words, but also to understand the ideas expressed by the words. In turn, you are able to use words to communicate ideas to others. While we take this ability to communicate through words for granted, the process is complex and challenging. To gain a deeper understanding of what happens, let us look at the characteristics of language in general. Those characteristics include its symbolic, rule-bound, culture-bound, dynamic, and social nature.

Language Is Symbolic

SYMBOL Something that stands for or suggests something else.

Words are **symbols** that stand for things. Consider the famous René Magritte painting of a pipe with the words "Ceci n'est pas une pipe" (this is not a pipe) beneath the picture. Just as the *picture* of the pipe is not itself a pipe, the word *pipe* is not a pipe. Both the picture and the word have symbolic functions. As symbols, they represent the object that a person picks up, fills with tobacco, and lights.

Triangle of Meaning

TRIANGLE OF MEANING A model that explains the relationship among words, things, and their meanings.

REFERENT The object or idea to which a symbol refers.

THOUGHT The mental image that we associate with a symbol and its referent.

ONOMATOPOEIA Words that sound like what they describe.

Charles Ogden and I.A. Richards developed a model called the **triangle of meaning** (Figure 6.1) to explain the relationship between a word (the symbol), the thing it describes (the **referent**), and the idea or **thought** associated with the word and the thing (the meaning).[10] As Figure 6.1 demonstrates, there is a strong connection (solid line) between symbols (e.g., words) and the thoughts or mental images they stimulate. There is also a strong connection (solid line) between these thoughts and the actual objects or things. For example, the word pear (a symbol) conjures the image of a yellow edible fruit (thought). In most cases, this mental image bears a resemblance to (solid line) the actual object or referent (the pear). There is not an equally strong connection, however, between referents and the symbols that represent them—hence the dashed line.

In language, the link between a word (symbol) and the thing it describes (referent) is almost always arbitrary. That is, we cannot explain logically why a dog is called *a dog*, a table is called *a table*, the city of Edmonton is called *Edmonton*, or the need for food is called *hunger*. A few exceptions exist, however—words that sound like what they describe. Examples include *buzz*, *hiss*, and *purr*. The term used to describe words that sound like their referents is ***onomatopoeia***.

As we go through life, we create words—or, more often, we learn the words others have created—to describe the things we encounter. The size of the vocabulary we develop to discuss these things depends on our need to be more or less precise. For example, snowboarders acquire a large and specific vocabulary to discuss types of snow. According to an article on the snowboarding website YoBeat, snowboarders have at least 39 different words to describe different types of snow. Following are a few examples:[11]

champagne powder: Freshly fallen snow that is light and fluffy.

sludge: Sticky snow that slows the rider.

concrete: Deep and heavy snow that creates a wall when ridden.

boiler plate: Snow that has become ice.

untouched: : Freshly fallen snow that no one else has ridden

tracked out: Freshly fallen snow that has been ridden

Someone unfamiliar with snowboarding might refer to all types of snow as *snow*.

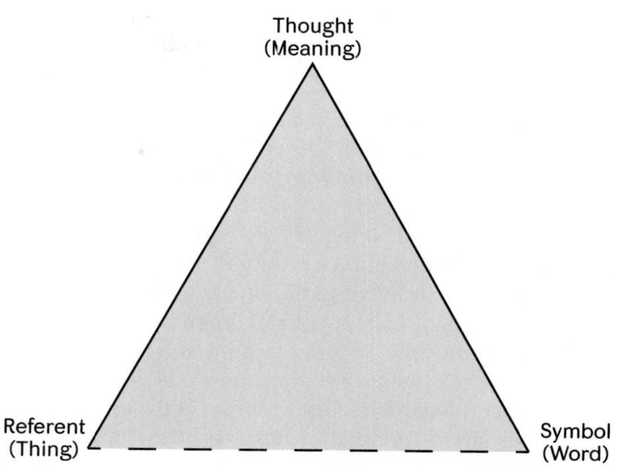

FIGURE 6.1 **Ogden and Richards's triangle of meaning.**

Given how differently each of us experiences the world around us, any given symbol or referent can stimulate a variety of thoughts. For example, consider the words *hockey game*. What comes to mind? Perhaps you think of an exciting, fast-paced team sport that you love to watch and play. Alternatively, a boring evening spent watching *Hockey Night in Canada* could come to mind. Perhaps the phrase *hockey game* conjures visions of violence and irritatingly overpaid professional athletes. Maybe you think nostalgically of your parents driving you to early morning practices at cold rinks when you were a kid. Or perhaps you think about how hockey seems to reflect national pride for many Canadians. The range of possible interpretations associated with symbols and referents demonstrates an important principle of human communication: meanings are in people, not in words or things. That is, humans give meaning to the symbols and things around them, and many interpretations are possible. See the "Human Diversity" box for an example of how certain words can have quite different meanings for different people, depending on the context.

Let's consider another example, this time with the help of a diagram. In Figure 6.2, we see the symbol *sport utility vehicle (SUV)*. The referent for this symbol is an SUV (or at least a picture of it). The referent and its symbol can trigger a variety of thoughts, ranging from *gas guzzler* to *safe vehicle* to *freedom and independence*. Our personal experience with a referent or a symbol influences our thoughts on the topic. One study found, for example, that perceptions of SUVs depended largely on whether a person drove an SUV (drivers reported more positive perceptions of SUVs than did non-drivers).[12] This finding supports the principle that meanings reside in people, not in words or things.

> **"The word experience is like a shrapnel shell, and bursts into a thousand meanings."**
> GEORGE SANTAYANA

Denotative versus Connotative Meaning

DENOTATIVE MEANING The literal or dictionary meaning of a word.

CONNOTATIVE MEANING Meaning that takes context and relationships into account.

The meaning we attach to words (as symbols) can be **denotative** or **connotative** in nature. *Denotation* refers to the literal or dictionary meaning of a word. It relates to content—that is, information about the topic being discussed (e.g., assignment due date, time for dinner, or the results of a medical test). At the simplest level, denotation refers directly to the observable world around us. For example, the statement "your

humanDIVERSITY

Gender Differences in Saying Those Three Little Words

When we talk about turning points in relationships (see Chapter 8), we cannot ignore the impact of three little words—*I love you*—on a romantic relationship. For most people in a committed relationship, these words imply loyalty and exclusivity. But outside of the context of a committed relationship, do these words mean something different to different people? In fact, according to a 2011 study, men and women differ in important ways in their responses to a partner's first confessions of love; and their reactions depend (at least in part) on factors related to sexual activity.[13]

The study found that men tend to respond more positively to first confessions of love—and think they are more genuine—if these confessions are offered before sex. When men hear the words *I love you* before sex, they also interpret the words as an invitation to physical intimacy, which could account for their positive responses. This finding emerged as especially true for those interested in short-term sexual relationships as opposed to long-term committed relationships. The study also found that women, on the other hand, tend to feel more positive about first confessions of love when they come *after* sex. When their partners offer such confessions after sex, women perceive the confession to imply a desire to pursue a serious relationship. Unlike men, women believe that confessions of love before sex reflect *less* trustworthiness and sincerity on the part of their partners. On reason for this difference may be that women fear that their partners' motivations for professing love could come from a desire to have sex rather than a desire for commitment.[14]

In brief, this research demonstrates that the words *I love you* have different meanings to different people, depending on the context and who is doing the confessing.[15]

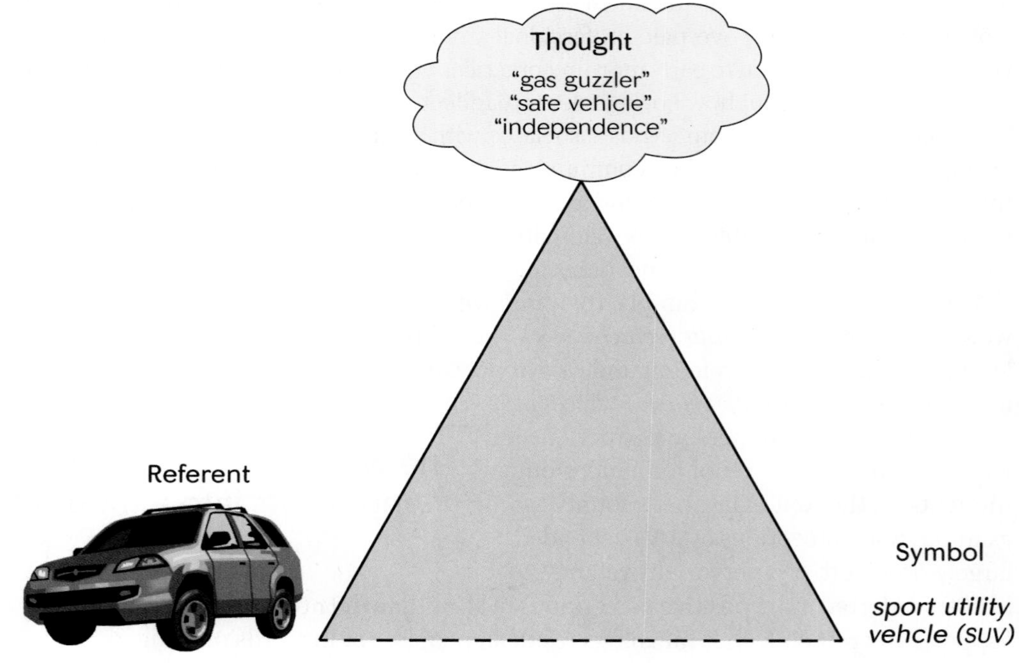

FIGURE 6.2 **An example of Ogden and Richards's triangle of meaning.**

assignment is late" makes direct reference to an object (*your assignment*), time (*late*), and the relationship between the terms (*is*). The meaning of this sentence comes from understanding the definition of the terms and their references in the objective world.

The connotative meaning of words arises from the relationship of communicators (e.g., their feelings toward each other, their history together, the nature of the relationship, and power dynamics within the relationship). Imagine that a woman named Sandy says to her teenage son Robert, "Your assignment is late." Assume that Sandy has always taken an excessive amount of responsibility for Robert's school performance. She helps him more than necessary with homework. She keeps track of his assignments and tests. She bails him out of tight spots to ensure he does not fail. In this situation, the comment "your assignment is late" may send the message that Sandy doubts her son's ability to manage his own work. This relational message may undermine Robert's motivation to take ownership for his own life.[16]

Unlike denotative meaning, connotative meaning takes the complex cues within and around a message into account. These cues enable us to arrive at a meaning that is deeper and richer than the literal meaning of a word. If Sandy's and Robert's relationship had been different and Sandy had stated "your assignment is late" in a calm and nonjudgmental way, her son might have interpreted the message differently. He might have felt empowered to take control of his own life.[17] In the latter case, the connotative meaning of the message could have been the following: "Your assignment is late. However, I am confident you will handle it. What are your plans for solving this problem?"

Language Is Rule Bound

Although language is symbolic and meanings are in people, we have developed conventions to help us to understand each other. For example, if someone were to say to you "perfect are every fresh occasion for flowers," you would not understand what that person said. While you can recognize the individual words, their organization within the sentence does not follow any conventional rule of English grammar. Let us take a look now at some of the rules for making and arriving at meaning through language. Those rules can be phonological, syntactic, semantic, or pragmatic in nature.

Phonological Rules

All languages have **phonological rules**. These rules govern which sounds appear in a language, where they appear, and how they combine to form words. If we look at the Hawaiian language, for example, we might be surprised to see the following three phonological rules:[18]

PHONOLOGICAL RULES Rules governing the sounds that appear in a language.

- Words in Hawaiian must not end in a consonant.
- Words in Hawaiian must not have two consonants in a row.
- Words in Hawaiian must begin with a consonant.

Because all words in the Hawaiian language end with a vowel (e.g., *hau'oli*, meaning "happy"; *mahalo*, meaning "thank you"; and *wailele*, meaning "waterfall"), people think the language "sways like a palm tree in a gentle wind and slips off the tongue like a love song."[19] How and where the sounds appear in a language makes a difference to the overall character of the language.

The English language has different phonological rules from the Hawaiian. One rule requires the presence of a vowel in every syllable.[20] For that reason, the word *zjrtnc* would be an unlikely candidate for a new word in English. The Czech language, on the other hand, does not require vowels in every syllable; so words such as *zmrzl* (meaning "frozen solid") appear in that language. Although the word *babrod* does not exist in

English, it would meet phonological requirements to become an English word because it contains appropriate combinations of vowels and consonants.

Phonological rules also help us to know how to pronounce a word. For example, the word *table* is pronounced "*tay*-bl" according to the phonological rule for pronouncing this word in English. If you are speaking French, on the other hand, a different phonological rule applies; and you pronounce the word "tah-*ble*". Although these words look alike, we pronounce them differently, depending upon which language we are speaking. When learning a new language, we must master the phonological rules of that language in order to understand, as well as speak, the language.

Syntactic Rules

SYNTACTIC RULES
Rules governing the arrangement of words and punctuation in a sentence.

Syntactic rules govern the structure of sentences, limiting the arrangement of words and punctuation. For example, a young child looking for his mother might confuse the order of words and call out "Where you are?" rather than "Where are you?" The child has not yet learned the syntactic rules governing where you place the words in a sentence.

The title of the popular grammar book *Eats, Shoots and Leaves* plays on how punctuation influences the meaning that we give to words. If we include a comma between *Eats* and *Shoots* (as in the title of the book), we understand that someone (perhaps a cowboy) comes into a restaurant, eats a meal, shoots up the place, and then leaves. If we omit the comma—as in *Eats Shoots and Leaves*—the phrase could refer to the diet of pandas.[21] To ensure that the readers get the joke, the cover of the book pictures two pandas, one of whom is holding a gun. The second panda stands on a stepladder, painting over the comma between *Eats* and *Shoots*. These images inform the reader of two possible interpretations of the title.

Semantic Rules

SEMANTIC RULES
Rules that relate to the agreed-upon meanings of words.

Noam Chomsky, a professor of linguistics, famously used the example "Colourless green ideas sleep furiously" to illustrate how a sentence can be grammatically correct (it follows syntactic rules) but make no sense whatsoever (it breaks **semantic rules**).[22] In other words, following syntactic rules does not guarantee clarity of thought if we do not observe semantic rules.

Every language has its own set of semantic rules, but these rules evolve over time and within cultures. Adults sometimes struggle to keep up with the meanings of new words appearing in the vocabulary of their teenage children.[23] For example, although most adults would not recognize *YOLO* as an English word, teenagers understand that it means "you only live once" (so do what you want to do). Teenagers use slang to demonstrate to themselves and to each other that they are part of an in-group. Through their choices of language, they exclude others such as parents.[24] (We will develop this point in more depth later in the chapter.)

> "Language is a process of free creation; its laws and principles are fixed, but the manner in which the principles of generation are used is free and infinitely varied."
>
> NOAM CHOMSKY

Pragmatic Rules

PRAGMATIC RULES
Rules that take context into account when arriving at meaning.

Given the range of possible meanings for any set of words, we rely on **pragmatic rules** to tell us the likely meaning of the words. In arriving at the meaning, we take social conventions and context into account.[25] If a friend greets you with the question "How are you?,"

you might respond "Fine, you?" or "Pretty good, and yourself?" Social conventions in Canada require a brief, positive response to a personal greeting of this variety. Someone from another country who is unfamiliar with this social convention, on the other hand, might be confused by the initial question and not know how to respond. In addition, the question might have a different meaning in a different context. If a medical doctor asks "How are you?", he or she is looking for a detailed description of your health.

"The word 'good' has many meanings. For example, if a man were to shoot his grandmother at a range of five hundred yards, I should call him a good shot, but not necessarily a good man."
GILBERT K. CHESTERTON

All language relies on context to establish its meaning. Imagine you are at work and your boss says, somewhat sternly and without smiling, "I'd like to see you." You will probably feel nervous. You might wonder what you have done wrong. If an attractive person at a party says the same words while smiling and looking into your eyes, you will probably understand "I'd like to see you" as an invitation to a date—a quite different interpretation of the same words.

So how do we differentiate between the communication from our boss and the communication from our conversation partner at a party? In all likelihood, we rely on contextual cues such as the body language of the speaker, our relationship to the speaker, the time and place of the exchange, and the events that preceded and followed the comment. Keeping in mind the five *W's* of journalism, we can ask *who* (is involved), *what* (the message is about), *when* (the interaction is occurring), *where* (the conversation is taking place), and *why* (the discussion is taking place). When we answer these questions, we take contextual cues into account. These cues help us to assign meaning to the communication.

Language Is Culture Bound

Chapter 3 included a discussion of the impact of culture on perception. This chapter considers the ways in which language and culture interact. Recall from Chapter 1 that we can define *culture* as the shared ideas, traditions, norms, symbols, and values that define a community.[26] The community may include a few people (e.g., cyclists or poets) or the residents of a province or a whole country. Cultural differences can create barriers to communication between members of different cultures. See the "Human Diversity" box titled "What Did Y'all Say?" for examples of cultural differences in how we label our world.

When we travel or meet people from other countries, we become aware of these differences. For example, what do you call a sweetened, carbonated beverage? Do you say *pop*? *Soda*? *Coke*? *Soft drink*? Your location, regional or national affiliation, and age will determine your choice of words.[27] Younger Canadians generally use *pop* to refer to carbonated beverages, while older Canadians and Americans use the term *soft drink*. Americans are more likely than Canadians to use the term *soda*, and people in the southern United States (and some other states) refer to all carbonated beverages as *coke*. (To see a map that tracks the use of these terms in North America, take a look at this website: www.popvssoda.com.)

Many words that exist in other languages do not translate into English as a single word. For example, the Hopi word *Koyaanisqatsi* means "life out of balance"; English contains no one word that conveys this exact meaning. In researching his 2006 book *The Meaning of Tingo and Other Extraordinary Words from Around the World*,[28] Adam Jacot de Boinod studied 280 dictionaries and 140 websites. In the process, he identified an extensive list of words with no equal in English. Following are a few examples:

humanDIVERSITY

What Did Y'all Say?

British people commonly use words that are a mystery to Canadians. These words, generally used in informal discussions, have entirely different meanings (or no meaning at all) to most Canadians. Imagine that you heard the word *gob*, dropped in conversation. Like most Canadians, you'd probably think of a droplet of something, or maybe the band. But to a Brit, the word *gob* is simply slang for "mouth."

Imagine you are at a pub in England and you want something to put in your gob. You could ask for *bangers and mash* (sausage and mashed potatoes). Or you might request a *chip butty* (a French fry sandwich). For dessert, you might order a *spotted dick* (a cake-like pudding).

Looking around the pub, you find yourself staring at a very fine-looking man. To be a true Brit, you could say something like "That bloke is quite fit" in lieu of "That guy is hot." And if the pub is located in London, you could say, "I fancy that Cockney; he is so tick, man."

Okay, so now you've left the pub and you're walking down the street. Suddenly, a man begins to yell at you, "Find a bobby! They're copping it up. There's claret all over the place!" At this moment, you might be tempted to give the man a dirty look and walk the other way. But if you know that *bobby* means "policeman," *copping it up* means "getting in trouble," and *claret* is another word for *blood*, you might actually try to help. The distraught man is just trying to say, "Find a policeman! They're getting in trouble. There's blood all over the place!" If you want to calm the man, you can say, "Hold it down an ickle, mate."

Your next stop is a local sports venue, which carries supplies for football (i.e., soccer), rugby, and cricket. As you enter, the shopkeeper tells you that *kits* and *trackies* are for sale; and after wandering around the shop, you realize that he must have been referring to uniforms and sweatshirts. But why didn't he just say so! You overhear a nearby conversation that refers to one side being "skinned on the pitch" during the last match. You flinch but then realize that the speaker is simply saying that one team was badly beaten during the last game.[29]

tingo (Rapa Nui): To borrow objects from a friend's home one-by-one until there is nothing left.
iktsuarpok (Inuit): To keep going outside to check if anyone is coming while you are waiting.
tartle (Scottish): The experience of hesitating when you are introducing someone whose name you can't remember.
drachenfutter (German for "dragon fodder"): A gift a husband bestows on his wife when he has stayed out late or otherwise engaged in inappropriate behaviour.
gumusservi (Turkish): The light of the moon as it shines upon the water.
vybafnout (Czech): To jump out and say "boo."

English also contains words that have no equals in other languages. Until recently, the word *cancer*—so familiar in the Western world—did not exist in most of the roughly 2000 languages of African countries. Sadly, diseases like breast cancer and cervical cancer have now become common causes of death in a part of the world that did not formerly need a word to describe them.[30] As we will discuss later in the chapter, we cannot address a problem until we can name it.

When we talk about the relationship between culture and language, we must discuss the widely acknowledged but controversial ideas developed by linguist Edward Sapir and his student Benjamin Whorf.[31] These researchers proposed that language shapes culture, and culture shapes language. This argument makes sense to most people. We create our language to reflect our culture; and these words, in turn, influence how we see the world. Sapir and Whorf called this part of their theory **linguistic determinism**. (Refer to the "Human Diversity" box titled "Keeping Culture Alive through Language" to learn about how keeping a culture's language alive can help to preserve that culture's world view.)

LINGUISTIC DETERMINISM The idea that language determines our thinking.

humanDIVERSITY

Keeping Culture Alive through Language

Language is a gateway to culture. When you learn a new language, you gain increased access to the culture surrounding that language. For example, you might understand more jokes and popular references, or you might appreciate a certain holiday because you are familiar with its historical significance. By way of contrast, when people stop speaking a language, they lose parts of their culture—a warning that Canadians need to take seriously. Our 2006 census showed that almost all of the 60-plus Aboriginal languages in Canada fall into the endangered category.[32] Undoubtedly, residential schools played a massive role in the decline of Aboriginal languages and cultures in Canada. As a former residential school student said, "They knew without language and culture, they would be breaking our spirits and we wouldn't know really where we came from."[33] Whatever the reasons, the fact remains: Aboriginal languages in Canada are at risk.

Recognizing the need to preserve these languages, a number of programs now aim to revitalize Aboriginal languages and transmit them to younger generations. Most have the mutual goal of protecting Aboriginal culture from disappearing altogether. In British Columbia, for example, the First Peoples' Heritage, Language, and Culture Council offers a "preschool language nest" program. This program helps parents and their young children to practice everyday words, concepts, and traditional practices on a daily basis.[34] Language and culture immersion camps provide additional avenues for Aboriginal children, youth, and elders to strengthen their languages and promote the transmission of traditional knowledge.[35] Another example is the Yawenda project, launched in 2007. This federally funded project seeks to revitalize the Huron-Wendat language on the Wendake reserve in northern Quebec City.[36]

Keeping a language alive keeps a culture alive by preserving that culture's world view—its unique way of looking at the world. Through efforts such as those outlined above, we honour and show respect for the heritage of Aboriginal peoples. Since this heritage represents part of Canada's heritage, the loss of these languages would be a loss for all of us, Aboriginal or not.

Sapir and Whorf's more extreme position, called **linguistic relativity**, is the aspect of their theory to which a number of scholars object. Linguistic relativity proposes that people who speak different languages perceive and think about the world quite differently from each other. In other words, they have different human experiences. This position implies that we must have a word for any concept that we want to understand or think about. Those who object to this position argue that our experience tells us this is not the case. For example, we may not have a word in English for laughing so hard that one side of the abdomen hurts (*katahara itai* in Japanese), but we can still understand this experience. Thus, while we may need to label a concept in order to *discuss* it with other people, we do not necessarily need to label it in order to *think about* or *understand* it.

LINGUISTIC RELATIVITY The idea that people who speak different languages perceive and think about the world differently.

Language Is Dynamic

The coining of words such as *website*, *download*, *unfriend*, and *OMG*, demonstrates that language evolves to meet needs.[37] In the same way, our slang and other expressions change over time. Children growing up in Winnipeg in the late 1960s, for example, sang "Halloween Apples" (emphasis on *ween* and *ples*) when they went door to door on Halloween night. At each house, they repeated the song, growing louder and louder until someone opened the door. Most of these children thought their tradition was universal until they met children from other regions who said "trick or treat." It is unclear whether the singing of "Halloween Apples" was regionally bound—used only by children in Manitoba—or whether this tradition originated elsewhere in earlier times. In any case, the cry of "Halloweeeeen App-ulz" is rarely heard today.

© ersoy emin/Alamy

Many changes in language occur in concert with cultural change. In their work at the University of Toronto, Sali Tagliamonte and Derek Denis study the ways that language, culture, and society interact. They say that we can track changes in any one of these three areas by looking at the others.[38]

Tagliamonte argues that upper-class females drove the shift from medieval to modern English (e.g., *ye* to *you*) and that this feminine influence on language continues today. The change agents in this generation, however, tend to be middle-class teenage girls, who are by and large the greatest disseminators of new slang and language forms.[39] When people (especially young people) repeatedly use a word in a way that is different from its more standard use (e.g., the word *bad* to mean "good" or *sickening* to mean "so good that it makes me sick"), then it is possible that the new meaning of the word will become widely accepted. In this way, language evolves. To see the latest updates to the *Oxford Dictionaries Online*, go to http://oxforddictionaries.com/words/what-s-new. See the "From Theory to Practice" box for a humorous look at how slang evolves.

> ## *from theory* TO PRACTICE
> ### The Evolution of Language
> You may recall an episode of *Zoey 101* in which Michael introduces the slang word *drippin* as a synonym for *awesome* or *great*.[40] By the time Michael's friends catch onto his new word, no one remembers that he invented it. So Michael decides to invent a second new word, *flump*. The episode ends with Michael expressing frustration about how difficult it is to receive credit for changing language.
>
> Think about how your own language has evolved over the past few years. Have you or your friends invented any words or expressions? Which ones lasted? Which ones did not stick? Do the changes in your use of slang demonstrate your own development as a person? If so, how?

In one study, Tagliamonte and Denis tried to find out whether texting by teenagers leads to a breakdown of the English language, as many worried observers claim.[41] According to "language purists," practices such as texting and tweeting lead teens to break grammar rules and to develop their own language—practices seen as destructive by those who want to protect language from evolving.[42] As expected, the researchers confirmed that teenagers are using home computers and cellphones in unprecedented numbers to communicate with their friends. They are also creating new ways of speaking (e.g., slang and abbreviations) that are more informal than our traditional spoken and written language. Despite these most obvious signs of change, however, the communication of teenagers remains firmly rooted in formal linguistic traditions. For example, one teenager texted a friend about a planned rock concert: "Aaaaaaaaagh the show tonight shall rock some serious jam."[43] The sentence contains a subject, a verb, and a direct object—presented in an order that reflects standard rules of grammar. Thus, it seems that adolescents tend to observe the basic rules of grammar at the same time that they bend the rules in new and creative ways.

Adolescents also lead all other demographic groups in changing the ways that words are pronounced, and they have invented new rules of inflection.[44] One example of evolution in the speech patterns of youth is **up talking**, in which the voice rises into a question at the end of a sentence. Examples include "I like popcorn?" and "We went to the mall today?" Today, up talking is quite common among North American youth, but it is a relatively new

UP TALKING A speech pattern in which the voice rises in pitch at the end of a statement.

development in the history of the English language. The rise of this speech pattern is linked to the spread of **Valleyspeak**, a style of speaking that originated in the San Fernando Valley area of Los Angeles, California, and spread throughout North America via popular media beginning in the 1970s. Valleyspeak also introduced the use of *like* as a filler word, as in "I'm, *like*, not into him." Teenage girls drove (and continue to drive) the popularization of Valleyspeak. You can recognize this way of talking in Alicia Silverstone's character in the 1995 movie *Clueless* and in the voices of characters in the reality TV show *The Hills*.

VALLEYSPEAK A variety of English characterized by up talking and excessive use of the word *like*.

Many of the words and expressions introduced in Valleyspeak have entered our everyday language. Examples of words common to Valleyspeak include *like* (placed anywhere in the sentence), *whatever* (placed anywhere in sentence), *Helloooo*... (with rising voice), *awesome*, *classic*, *cool*, *bad* (for something good), and *rad*. Examples of expressions from Valleyspeak include "I'm like so totally not into him," "She was like freaking me out," "I'm sure!," and "Let's just veg."

A more recent example of shifting speech patterns involves **vocal fry**.[45] *Vocal fry* is characterized by a low, staccato vibration during speech. A slow fluttering of the vocal cords allows the production of this sound. Often used at the end of a sentence, it is most noticeable when a speaker's pitch drops. You might recognize the use of vocal fry by the Kardashian sisters or Reese Witherspoon (especially in in the 2001 movie *Legally Blonde*); you might also recognize it from the songs of Britney Spears and Ke$ha. You can find what it sounds like at http://news.sciencemag.org/social-sciences/2011/12/vocal-fry-creeping-u.s.-speech.

VOCAL FRY A low vocal register that often sounds creaky or rattling.

While some changes in language use and speech patterns spread across countries or even continents, others are restricted to smaller regions. Tagliamonte and her colleagues have examined how (and with what speed) the language in Toronto changes from generation to generation.[46] One change has involved the use of **quotatives**, words used in quoting what other people have said. Many Torontonians use a form of the verb *to say* more frequently than any other quotative (e.g., "She *said*, 'You've got to be kidding). The quotative *be like* is also gaining in popularity, especially among younger people in Toronto. This more recently developed quotative appears to have its roots in Valleyspeak: "She *was like*, 'Get out of here!'" or "*I'm like*, 'This can't be happening.'" According to the researchers, people over 40 years of age use *say* when quoting the words of another person, while people under 30 use the phrase *be like*. Members of the in-between group (30- to 40-year-olds) alternate between *say* and *be like*.[47]

QUOTATIVES Words used to introduce quotes in conversation.

Viewed in the light of the above discussion, the evolutionary changes in language do not suggest the death of formal grammar as we know it. Rather the changes reflect a dynamic and ongoing process that occurs in all speech communities, including the one in which teenagers live.[48]

SOCIAL FUNCTIONS OF LANGUAGE

While the work of Sapir and Whorf may have fallen out of favour because of controversial claims, their ideas nonetheless made an important contribution to our understanding of how we use communication to create social reality. As philosopher Martin Heidegger said, words and language are not "wrappings" for things we use in speaking and writing.[49] Instead our words and language create the things that we wrap. In other words, instead

"Man acts as though he were the shaper and master of language, while in fact language remains the master of man."
MARTIN HEIDEGGER

of just describing the social world, words help us to create and populate our world with people, things, and ideas.

In the following section, we will explore the ways by which language allows us to socially construct our world, to name our world, and to bring us together or separate us.

Language Allows Us to Construct and Name Our World

In *The Social Construction of Reality*, Peter Berger and Thomas Luckmann argue that thoughts, on their own, have no meaning until we put them into words and make them real through communication. [50] Until we have attached a label to an object, idea, activity, or person, we cannot talk about it. Nor can we address associated issues. For example, many physical and psychological problems such as obsessive-compulsive disorder (OCD), attention-deficit/hyperactivity disorder (ADHD), and narcolepsy went unnamed and unaddressed for centuries. Women who suffered from postpartum depression after giving birth received no special care until someone labelled the health issue. Post-traumatic stress disorder (PTSD) received no attention until mental health researchers defined and named the condition in the years following the Vietnam War. While veterans of earlier wars doubtless suffered from symptoms that characterize PTSD (e.g., high levels of anxiety, disturbing flashbacks, difficulty relating to others and accepting authority), few connected the personal difficulties (e.g., alcohol abuse, failed marriages, homelessness, and difficulty holding jobs) to their war experiences.

In the late 1980s, Japanese lawyers attached labels to two serious consequences of growing job demands on employees. One was *karoshi*, meaning "death from overwork"; the other was *karojisatsu*, meaning "suicide induced by overwork and work-related depression." Once named, however, the risks associated with overworking received official recognition as a workplace injury, eligible for compensation.[51] Equivalents for the words *karoshi* and *karojisatsu* do not exist outside the Japanese language. However, since the negative experience of overwork characterizes many countries in the Western world, we can be sure that eventually the Japanese terms will find companions in the English language.

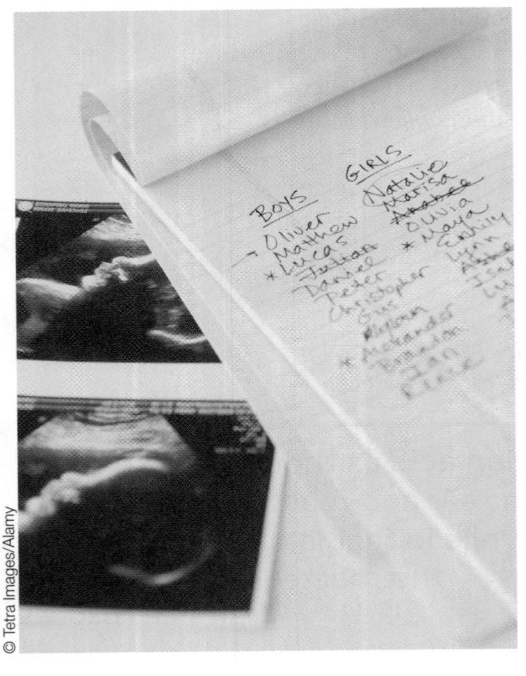

© Tetra Images/Alamy

Names influence how we see ourselves and how others view us. For this reason, parents often put great effort into choosing a name for their child. In one episode of the television show *How I Met Your Mother*, Lily and Marshall discuss possible names for their yet-to-be conceived child.[52] When Marshall suggests *Rob*, Lily immediately says "no," thinking of an obnoxious child named Rob in the kindergarten class she teaches. Next, Marshall suggests *Ryan*, prompting Lily to think of a student who stabbed her with a pencil. When Marshall suggests *Johnny*, Lily thinks of a boy who swallowed the class's pet goldfish. In response to Marshall's suggestion of the name *Jeremy*, Lily recalls a student devilishly flinging red paint around the classroom. Clearly, names have powerful associations, although these associations differ from person to person.

In a real-life example, *Washington Post* columnist Carolyn Hax responded in April 2013 to a correspondent's concern about naming a child after an ex—a choice promoted by her current partner. The woman did not want to transfer unpleasant associations to her child.[53]

As the above examples indicate, people assign personal characteristics to names. Research by Albert Mehrabian gives an academic foundation to our intuitive feelings that people form impressions of us based on our names.[54] At different points in time and in different cultures, names may suggest masculinity or femininity, athleticism, intelligence, or creativity. As Linda Rosenkrantz and Pamela Satran discuss in *Beyond Jennifer & Jason, Madison & Montana*, our given names carry stereotypes and vary (across time and from person to person) in perceived attractiveness.[55]

Names can speak volumes—not only about the hopes and dreams that parents have for their baby, but also about the future identity of the child.[56] Ima Hogg, daughter of a former governor of Texas, had to deal with constant jokes about her name. In actual fact, her family did not intend to inflict a cruel punishment on her. Ima's name had appeared in a civil war poem written by her uncle. Nonetheless, Ima felt the necessity to downplay the effects of the name by signing illegibly; and her stationery never contained her full name—only "I. Hogg" or "Miss Hogg." How do you feel about your given name? Go to the "From Theory to Practice" box to pursue this question in more depth.

from theory TO PRACTICE

What Does Your Name Say About You?

As we have seen in this section, your name is not just a label. It influences how you see yourself and how others see you. How do you feel about your name? What do you think it says about you? Do you wish it were more common? Less common? Go online and search for more information about your name—what it means, when it was first used, and its level of popularity now or in the past. (You might want to begin at www.babycenter.ca or www.ssa.gov/oact/babynames.) Do you feel differently about your name after doing this research?

> **"We don't know when our name came into being or how some distant ancestor acquired it. We don't understand our name at all, we don't know its history and yet we bear it with exalted fidelity, we merge with it, we like it, we are ridiculously proud of it as if we had thought it up ourselves in a moment of brilliant inspiration."**
>
> **MILAN KUNDERA**

Language Brings Us Together or Separates Us

Language can bring us together or separate us. The term ***convergence*** refers to language practices that unite us. For example, we may use the same vocabulary or have the same accent as others in our network or community. We may adapt our speech patterns to show affiliation. We may even create private words or develop **restricted codes** to confirm that we are insiders. In one episode of the television show *The Office*, Michael offers Josh and Jim drinks.[57] Josh replies, "A shot of midori, perhaps!" Josh and Jim both laugh, but Michael (and many viewers!) do not understand the joke. Jim starts to explain the humour but ends up saying that Michael just had to be there in order to understand the joke. This example shows how language (in this case, an inside joke) identifies in-group versus out-group members.

CONVERGENCE Uniting or bringing together, as in speech that emphasizes similarities.

RESTRICTED CODE Language and gestures with special meanings that only the members of a certain group understand.

In contrast to convergence, ***divergence*** refers to language practices that emphasize the differences between one group and another. As discussed earlier, using slang that parents do not understand has long been a way for teenagers to distance themselves and create their own community. Like teenage anglophones, teenage francophones have created their own phonetically based language on Facebook, which many adults do not understand. For example, in communicating with each other, eastern Quebec teens spell the word *quelqu'un* (someone) as *kelkun*. They shorten *j'espère* (I hope) to *jesper* and *je veux* (I want) to *jveu*. Instead of *vraiment* (really), they write *vrm*. Decoding this sort of language can be challenging to francophones from other regions and age groups, especially those who expect the language to follow the established rules.

DIVERGENCE Separating, as in speech that emphasizes differences.

*from theory*TO PRACTICE

Do You Know Your Foreign Slang?

While you may be familiar with the slang used by you and your friends here in Canada, you might want to test your understanding of slang terms in Australia and Britain. Visit these websites to test your knowledge: http://alldownunder.com/games/quiz/slang.htm and www.squidoo.com/british-slang-quiz.

Many Canadian teens now use the term *bro* in preference to *dude*, long popular as a reference to a male individual. The substitution probably occurred as a way to stay ahead of adults' use of the term. Once parents (the out-group) start using the language of teens, teens (the in-group) abandon the old slang expressions and develop new language codes. As we discussed earlier in the chapter, changing speech patterns (reflected in practices such as *up talking* and *vocal fry*) also illustrate language codes that bring youth together.

Online slang dictionaries include up-to-date examples of current street lingo common to the youth culture. Note the following examples from www.urbandictionary.com:

dorkus malorkus: (Fake) Latin for *dork*. From the Simpsons when Bart says to Lisa: "You are . . . as we say in Latin . . . a *dorkus malorkus*."

friending spree: Randomly adding anyone you come across on a social network, including complete strangers.

armchair activist: A so-called activist, who thinks he is helping a good cause by making a topic famous via blogs or social media.

See the "From Theory to Practice" box for an exercise that will introduce you to some slang terms that are popular outside of North America.

CONVERSATION STYLE The way we present and express ourselves when conversing with others.

POWERFUL LANGUAGE Language that conveys authority.

CREDIBILITY The extent to which you are believable to others.

POWERLESS LANGUAGE Language that does not convey authority.

REPORT TALK Talk that focusses on content rather than relationships.

INSTRUMENTAL Aimed at achieving a specific goal or purpose.

ONE-UP, ONE-DOWN SITUATIONS Two-person interactions in which one person clearly holds more power than the other.

Language Conveys Credibility to the User

Have you seen the viral videos on the Internet called "Sh*t Girls Say"—a YouTube series that showcases expressions used by girls and women? Toronto comedians Graydon Sheppard and Kyle Humphrey, the creators of the series, argue that these expressions do not appear in the language of men. While no research exists to support these claims, many researchers have found ample support for the proposition that men and women have different **conversation styles**, including the words they choose to use.[58] Researchers have also found gender differences related to pattern of inflection and tone of voice. Through our conversation style, we convey messages—intended or unintended—about who holds power in the exchange.

In Western cultures, we see people who use **powerful language** as more **credible** than those who use **powerless language**.[59] University students perceive professors who use powerful language, for example, as more dynamic than those who use powerless language.[60] Powerful language is generally direct, not weakened by qualifiers such as *somewhat*, *maybe*, or *perhaps*. Powerful language does not beat around the bush.

According to linguist Deborah Tannen, men tend to use more powerful language than do women. They have a more direct style of communicating, and they are more likely than women to engage in **report talk**. Men use language to give or receive information and to achieve results. In other words, their communication goals are **instrumental**. Men prefer to be in control, and they strive to avoid **one-up, one-down situations** in which they are not always in power.[61] (See the "Professional Contexts" box for an example of the dominant–submissive relationship that characterized nurse–physician relations for many years.)

Women display more interest in **rapport** than in report talk. Whereas men are more likely to talk about the content of their work at the end of the day, women are more likely to talk about the interactions that occurred. Women use conversation to establish relationships, share feelings, and build intimacy.Typically, women try to avoid sounding bossy or aggressive,[62] and they aim for balance in their interactions with others.[63]

In an effort to avoid one-up, one-down situations, women give orders and feedback in a more indirect way than do men. They might say, for example, "It would be good if you could submit your report by tomorrow." When a female professor asks her research assistants if they would "mind" undertaking a task, she is suggesting that the assistants have a choice. In all likelihood, however, the professor expects the work to be done; she is not really offering a choice. In another instance, a female professor might say, "You need to work a little harder"; in the same situation, a male professor might say, "You need to work harder."

As mentioned earlier, women also use less powerful language, characterized by uncertainty, expressions of self-doubt, and hesitations. **Tag questions** such as "It's hot in here, isn't it?" imply that the speaker is uncertain and seeks approval from the listener. **Disclaimers** such as "This may be a bad idea, but . . ." or "This is just my opinion, but . . ." or "I'm not an expert in this area, but . . ." announce that the speaker is unsure about her viewpoint. Self-doubt also finds expression in an excess of words such as "I think" and "I'm not too sure about this." **Question statements** such as "You do want to go?" (in which the speaker's voice rises rather than falls at the end of the sentence) likewise imply doubt and uncertainty. **Hesitations** (*well*, *um*) and **hedges** (*I guess*, *sort of*, *somewhat*) are fillers that we associate with a lack of certainty and lack of confidence.[64] Many people, especially in Western contexts, perceive excessive use of these kinds of expressions as showing weakness.[65]

Yet some disagree with this assessment. Critics say that many communication habits that might appear to indicate uncertainty and weakness are in fact signs of collaboration

RAPPORT A positive relationship characterized by mutual liking and effective communication.

TAG QUESTIONS Phrases that, when tagged onto the end of sentences, change statements into questions (e.g., "don't you think?").

DISCLAIMERS Phrases that devalue statements by drawing attention to potential faults.

QUESTION STATEMENTS Statements spoken as questions, expressing doubt through rising intonation.

HESITATIONS Words such as *um* or *well* that act as fillers and convey uncertainty.

HEDGES Phrases or words such as *sort of* and *somewhat* that protect against the risk of making a direct statement.

*professional*CONTEXTS

Nurse–Physician Communication: A Helping Hand

For many years, medical doctors treated nurses as assistants whose sole purpose was to offer them support. The physician (historically a male) acted in a dominant role; the nurse (historically a female) took the submissive role—the role of helper. This unbalanced power equation contributed significantly to the low retention rates among nurses.[66] On the positive side, the model is changing.[67] And so we ask ourselves: How much of this change relates to the communication and language styles adopted by nurses and physicians? The traditional "doctor–nurse game" required the nurse to "communicate her recommendations [to the physician] without appearing to be making a recommendation."[68] However, nurses today are much more actively involved in decisions on the care of their patients.[69] Their language styles have also shifted from deferential to more authoritative.

These changing communication styles have an impact on the effectiveness of health care services. When health care providers use clarity, humour, appropriate introductions, immediacy, listening, and empathy in their communications, patients express higher levels of satisfaction with the system.[70] Indeed, the same communication strategies have positive effects when applied by physicians to their interpersonal relationships with nurses.[71] Skillful communication deconstructs the negative power relations between nurses and physicians, ultimately increasing job satisfaction for both and improving the health care experience for patients.

and what some label as lack of assertiveness is really interpersonal sensitivity.[72] By using tag questions, for example, women are able to request input from others in a polite way. This kind of language encourages the building and maintenance of relationships. Consider the following example. A head nurse asks the other nurses for their input on an important decision. Even though you could categorize the nurse's request for input as weak or indecisive,[73] studies show that health care organizations get better results with participatory decision-making.[74]

> "We tend to look through language and not realize how much power language has."
> DEBORAH TANNEN

DEFERENTIAL LANGUAGE Language characterized by courteous respectfulness and submissiveness.

Another term for what we have thus far referred to as *powerless language* is ***deferential language***. The term *deferential* contains two ideas: submissiveness and respect. The element of submissiveness carries undercurrents of powerlessness, as discussed above. However, the second element (respect) also carries weight. Deferential language enables a speaker to project humility, warmth, and likeability. See the "Human Diversity" box for examples of how people around the world use deferential language as a politeness strategy.

In summary, how we speak influences how other people perceive us, and we establish credibility through our verbal communication skills.[75] Within the Western context and most of the English-speaking world, especially in business, we strengthen these communication skills when we employ powerful language. Before moving to the next section, see the "Professional Contexts" box on victim impact statements (VIS) for an additional illustration of the empowering qualities of language.

BARRIERS TO EFFECTIVE VERBAL COMMUNICATION

To this point in the chapter, we have talked about words and their meanings; and we have emphasized the role of verbal communication in creating understanding and enhancing our credibility. Now let us look at some of the barriers to communication that take away from our understanding, ability to establish and maintain relationships, and credibility.

BALD LANGUAGE Blunt or direct language.

humanDIVERSITY

Deferential Language as Face Work

Unlike English-speaking people who place a high value on directness, many cultures in the world equate baldness of speech with rudeness. Most Japanese people, for example, dislike **bald language**. When the Japanese say *maybe*, they usually mean *no*; but *maybe* allows the speaker and the listener to save face. In fact, in many regions of the world, use of indirect or deferential language functions as a politeness strategy—a form of *face work* (see the "Human Diversity" box on page 61, in Chapter 2).

When English speakers want to be polite or courteous, they tend to use direct terms such as *please* and *thank you*. As noted earlier however, people in many non–English-speaking regions express courtesy more subtly. When someone from Japan or Korea offers a gift, she or he might say: "Sorry, accept this gift, sorry."[76] In such cases, the gift giver apologizes because the receiver (by accepting the gift) will feel obligated to return the generosity at a later time. People from India often use deferential support noises to show polite regard for a person who is speaking. Urdu speakers, for example, use a term equivalent to *very nice* to show support for the other person. If you said, "My name is Josée," an Urdu speaker might respond, "Very nice."[77] Clearly, the Western interpretation of deferential language as a sign of weakness or powerlessness is not a universally agreed upon conclusion.

professionalCONTEXTS

Giving Victims of Crime a Voice

Imagine that you or someone you love has been the victim of a crime. While you may gain satisfaction from seeing the perpetrator arrested and imprisoned, you may feel that justice has not been served until you have had a chance to express your pain, loss, and trauma in words. While victims suffer the most from crimes, they often feel that the criminal justice system pays more attention to the rights of the perpetrator.[78] The victim impact statement (VIS) offers one of the most effective means for victims to be heard by the criminal justice system. This statement describes how the crime has affected the life of the victim and her or his family and friends. It details the short- and long-term psychological, physical, and financial effects of the crime on the victim and on the victim's close others. Victims of crime prepare these statements in advance of the sentencing date, at which time they present them on paper, videotape, or orally in a court room.

In a survey conducted by Mothers against Drunk Driving (MADD), victims who had the chance to submit a VIS reported that this experience increased their satisfaction with the entire criminal justice system. After being given the opportunity to present a *written* VIS, 66 per cent expressed satisfaction with the criminal justice system; 62 per cent expressed satisfaction after being given the opportunity to present an *oral* VIS.[79]

Bafflegab

When you use words (especially **jargon**) that other people do not understand, you may be erecting the barrier called **bafflegab**. If the other person does not know your language code, misinterpretation will occur. Lawyer Milton A. Smith coined the word *bafflegab*. Jokingly, he defined it as "multiloquence characterized by consummate interfusion of circumlocution or periphrasis, inscrutability, and other familiar manifestations of abstruse expatiation commonly utilized for promulgations implementing Procrustean determinations by governmental bodies." In other words, Smith used incomprehensible language to define the term that means *the use of language that is incomprehensible*. If you are a *Doctor Who* fan, you may recall the fourth doctor saying in one episode, "Bafflegab, my dear. I've never heard such bafflegab in all my lives." He made this comment after Queen Xanxia used big words and jargon to explain how she planned to gain eternal life.[80]

JARGON Words or expressions that have meaning for members of a specific profession or other group but that have little or no meaning to outsiders.

BAFFLEGAB The use of unnecessarily long or complicated words that other people do not understand.

Organizations cannot afford to use bafflegab to communicate with clients and customers. Government and business employees must speak a different and more accessible language when communicating with general audiences. For example, bureaucrats should avoid using terms such as *stakeholders*, *target groups*, and *portfolios* outside of their work environments. Business people need to avoid terms such as *impact*, *punt*, *vertical*, and *over the wall*. This sort of language has little to no meaning to outsiders.[81] People may have no idea what you are saying.

Despite the above warning, not all jargon is bafflegab; and jargon can be very useful in communicating within work cultures (e.g., legal or medical settings). Like shorthand, such language makes it easier and faster to communicate with those who know the restricted language codes. The use of jargon within an organization also enables employees to talk about sensitive information without fear that outsiders will understand and spread this information.

Shared language codes—made up of jargon, slang, jokes, rituals, and nicknames—also foster a sense of community among those inside the group.[82] For example, you may have been part of a sorority or fraternity that developed special language and secret rituals. Or you may have been part of a club that used a nickname for someone or something that only the group understood—for example, calling rabbits *hoppers*. These restricted codes allow members to bond while excluding others who do not understand the verbal and nonverbal codes.

Some groups change their language codes from time to time to prevent out-group members from penetrating their ranks. For example, after Craigslist put restrictions on advertisements for "erotic services," providers and users of these services developed new language codes to discuss "adult services" among themselves.[83] A dollar symbol in place of the letter *s* (as in $exy $indy) or the word *generous* used in connection with someone looking for a date indicates that a professional escort is offering sexual services for a price.[84] Similarly, men who frequent sex-trade workers use language codes that change over time; these codes both speak to in-group membership and make it more difficult for outsiders (especially police officers) to infiltrate or bring charges against the group.[85]

Equivocality

EQUIVOCALITY
Possibility for words and actions to have multiple interpretations.

The term ***equivocality*** refers to the many possible meanings in any word, act, or situation. Almost everything we say or do has more than one possible interpretation. Equivocality creates difficulties because it can lead us to misinterpret a message or a situation. For example, if you say to your friend "I'll meet you outside after class," your friend may wait outside the building in which your class is held. However, you may mean "I'll meet you in the hall outside the classroom." As noted in Chapter 5, we can avoid this kind of miscommunication by paraphrasing and confirming what we think the other person meant. As a listener, we could ask the follow-up question, "You mean outside on the front steps?" In this situation, context has created the difficulty in interpretation.

Other issues related to equivocality include the use of abstract and relative language. By abstract language, we mean words that lack concreteness. For example, we can imagine a range of meanings for the word *barbaric*. *Barbaric* can imply a lack of manners or, alternatively, behaviours that include extreme levels of violence, as in the following description: "The Huns ate raw meat, drank fermented mare's milk, and murdered captives by allowing their children to club them to death." After reading this description, we know exactly what the writer was trying to convey when he said the Huns were *barbaric*. In the same way, relative language (involving comparisons) is problematic. Words such as a *few*, *many*, *several*, and *not a lot* create a range of meanings in people.

STRATEGIC AMBIGUITY
Use of unclear and vague language to accomplish goals.

While equivocality often poses a barrier to effective communication, it also serves important purposes in communication.[86] Within bureaucracies and some large corporations, for example, the multiple possibilities for interpretation allow for **strategic ambiguity** or vagueness.[87] The idea of strategic or purposeful ambiguity has particular relevance for organizations. When managers become too specific in describing proposals for changes, they eliminate the possibility for "wiggle room." Wiggle room enables employees to buy into policies or programs that they might accept but not want to support publicly. Thus, strategic ambiguity allows groups to get along as if they share meanings when, in fact, they may have different interpretations of words and actions. Mission statements such as "this university will be responsive to the communities that it serves" allow for many interpretations and thus flexibility in implementation.

Politicians and government agents are well known for their lack of directness in language. Consider the following statement: "It is important to recognize that a diversity of views may exist on this policy." In fact, the government organization may be facing strong opposition to the policy; but the statement carefully avoids either telling or bending the truth.[88]

In highly structured organizations such as government, subordinates also tend to word requests in a way that leaves room for the superior to reject the request. In this way, both the subordinate and the superior can save face. When higher-level executives behave in ways that pose a risk to policies or plans, subordinates rely on ambiguous wording to express their concerns. For example, instead of saying "the deputy prime minister blocked our plans at the last minute," the bureaucrat might say "last-minute adjustments prevented our moving ahead with our plans" or "unavoidable delays mean that we will need to move the date forward."[89] In this way, the government representative is able to address the issue without stating anything concrete or framing anyone in a bad light.

Bureaucrats also avoid words with negative connotations. You will never find government communicators using the term *problems*. Instead they speak of *challenges*. For these kinds of reasons, some critics accuse bureaucrats of using the "language of non-responsibility."[90]

Within government bureaucracies, strategic ambiguity also eases the shifting of loyalties, when necessary, from one group or individual to another. When new political parties assume leadership in Canada, for example, the bureaucrats must support the party in power, no matter their political allegiances or personal loyalties. The nurturing of formal cordiality and politeness in relations helps to reduce tensions. In the same way and for similar reasons, heads of state often use ambiguous language when they speak in forums such as the United Nations (UN). They use **metaphors**, especially **archetypal metaphors,** to reach people from different backgrounds and perspectives. Archetypal metaphors are figures of speech that refer to things we all recognize, regardless of our background—light and darkness, birth and death, weather and the seasons, heat and cold, and other natural forces.[91] Examples include "the winter of our despair," "the winds of change," "fanning the flames of anger," and "the birth of a new order." Archetypal metaphors are broad, nonspecific, and abstract in nature. Thus, they are useful in international contexts. In forums such as the UN, members come from many different countries; and they hold many different—and often conflicting—views on issues. When speakers become too specific, they alienate those with contrary views. When they use ambiguous language, on the other hand, they reach larger numbers of people.

METAPHOR A figure of speech that reveals something about one thing by implicitly comparing it to something else.

ARCHETYPAL METAPHOR A metaphor that refers to basic elements of the earth and human experience.

Euphemisms and Doublespeak

Speakers commonly use **euphemisms** to avoid offending or upsetting listeners, but sometimes the euphemisms confuse rather than clarify. For example, if you hear that your favourite television show has been "pulled indefinitely," is "off the schedule," or is "on a permanent hiatus," you might not realize that the program has actually been cancelled. Because television networks do not want to broadcast bad news about shows that have not made the cut, executives use euphemisms to soften the blow.[92]

EUPHEMISM An expression meant to be less offensive or disturbing than the word or phrase it replaces.

Let us look at some additional common examples of terms that "soften" language:

- *mature* in place of *old* or *elderly*,
- *pre-owned* (or *pre-loved*!) in place of *used*,
- *held back* in place of *failed* (e.g., *he was held back a grade level*),
- *crossed over* or *kicked the bucket* in place of *died*,
- *correctional facility* in place of *prison*,

- *sanitary landfill* in place of *garbage dump*, and
- *adult entertainment* in place of *pornography*.

In certain contexts, these terms may be appropriate; but speakers should use euphemisms only when they know that their listeners will understand what they mean.

DOUBLESPEAK
Language that deliberately disguises the true meaning of a potentially unpleasant idea.

A particularly troublesome kind of euphemism is **doublespeak**. The term *doublespeak* describes language that aims to disguise the true meaning of a potentially unpleasant or unpopular idea, often for strategic reasons. William Lutz considers doublespeak to be the most deceptive, irresponsible, and dangerous form of euphemism. In times of war, governments often use doublespeak to deceive publics with respect to the human cost of the war.[93] Examples of military doublespeak include the following:

- *elimination of unreliable elements*, meaning imprisonment, execution, or exile of people deemed to be the enemy;
- *non-operative personnel*, referring to dead soldiers;
- *enhanced interrogation*, referring to the use of torture tactics to extract information from prisoners of war;
- *collateral damage*, referring to innocent people who were unintentionally injured or killed in an attack;
- *servicing the targets*, referring to killing enemy soldiers;
- *softening up*, referring to dropping bombs in anticipation of an invasion; and
- *terminate with extreme prejudice*, meaning *kill* (often in a violent manner).

These examples illustrate what Lutz calls "the language of non-responsibility," a language that (as previously mentioned) also characterizes some bureaucratic language and many advertising campaigns.[94] See the "Professional Contexts" box on consumerism and language for an example of an early campaign that encouraged women to take up smoking.

*professional*CONTEXTS

Consumerism and Language

Today we are familiar with advertisers' never-ending efforts to convince us to buy goods we do not need. Perhaps you bought the newest iPhone, for example, when you already owned a perfectly functioning smartphone. In the early 1900s, however, the question of how to encourage consumers to buy unneeded products was new.[95]

Corporate executives arrived at the answer when the tobacco industry hired Edward Bernays (considered to be the father of public relations) to figure out how to bring women into the tobacco market. A cultural taboo had existed for many years against women smoking in public. In researching the problem, Bernays spoke with a psychoanalyst, who told him that cigarettes symbolize male power. Picking up on that theme, Bernays marked his campaign with the slogan "Torches of Freedom"; and he convinced a group of upper-class women to light up during the Easter Sunday Parade of 1929 in New York City. Bernays's efforts effectively connected the symbol of women smoking in public to the idea of challenging male power. Females smoking cigarettes became socially acceptable and ultimately changed the cultural and consumer landscape in North America.

Happily, we are seeing a cultural shift away from smoking in North America today.[96] Recognizing the power of language, government health agencies have pushed for heavy restrictions on the language and images tobacco companies use in promoting their products. In addition, Canadian and American legislation requires these companies to place warnings about the health hazards of smoking on the packaging of tobacco products.

Language Misuse

LANGUAGE MISUSE Use of words in the wrong context, improper grammar, or incorrect pronunciation.

MALAPROPISM Switching of an intended word with another word of similar sound or spelling that has a different meaning.

Language misuse can create a barrier to effective communication in at least two ways. First, a listener may completely misunderstand the message. Misunderstandings often occur when a speaker uses the wrong word (e.g., **malapropism**). Saying "I need to fill my *subscription*" (rather than *prescription*) at the drug store can cause confusion. In some cases, a wrong word can even sound nonsensical. For example, in an episode of *Friends*, Joey introduces the malapropism *moo point*, which he defines as something that doesn't matter, like a cow's opinion). He meant to say *moot point* (an unimportant or debatable point).[97] Joey's friends are visibly confused by his mistake.

Language misuse also stands in the way of communication when it discredits the speaker. If you heard a colleague at work—a native speaker of English—say something like "Me and Jack was real worried about the report," the credibility of your colleague would probably go down in your eyes. As a result, you might pay less attention to what your colleague was saying or even ignore future attempts to communicate with you. Consider the following common errors that can detract from a speaker's credibility:

- use of *irregardless* (a nonstandard combination of *irrespective* and *regardless*);
- *could of, should of,* or *would of* (instead of *could have, should have,* or *would have*);
- *between you and I* (instead of *between you and me*); and
- *if I was you, I would . . .* (instead of *if I were you, I would . . .*).

While these latter mistakes might not cause the same misunderstandings as malapropisms, they can lower the credibility of the speaker and her or his message.

Static Evaluation

STATIC EVALUATION Use of language that does not take change into account.

We have seen in this chapter that language is dynamic: it evolves to accommodate changes in culture, values, technology, and usage. Sometimes, however, the way a person uses language does not change when it should. **Static evaluation** suggests that the speaker has not evolved with changes in the world. An older adult might recall, for example, a time when ten cents bought a chocolate bar at a corner store. If that person walked into a store today expecting to exchange a dime for a chocolate bar, she or he would be committing static evaluation. Similarly, the way we talk about people, ideas, and objects can reflect our failure to recognize change. If a father calls his daughter *baby* or *little girl* when she is in her twenties, he sends the message that he does not see her as an adult. Ignoring change in others works as a communication barrier because it "freezes" the person in time and fails to acknowledge growth and development. In other words, it sends

from theory TO PRACTICE

Am I *Dating* or *Seeing* Him?

Most people used to agree on the meaning of the word *dating*. Dating implied an early and non-exclusive stage in a relationship. *Going steady*, on the other hand, implied an exclusive relationship. Not everyone agrees on such terms today. For example, one person responded on a Yahoo forum: "Dating is different from seeing someone. Seeing someone is when you are in an open relationship and you guys are getting to know each other. Dating is when you're in a relationship . . . . If you ask someone if they're dating anybody it usually means [asking] if they are involved with someone."[98] A member of the Plenty of Fish dating website gave the opposite interpretation: "From what I've gathered in my experiences, dating someone means squat. You can date many people at the same time, it's your 'choosing period.' Seeing somebody means you're taken."[99] How do you use the terms *dating* and *seeing*? Is dating the same as seeing someone to you? What other words to you use to refer to someone with whom you have a romantic relationship? Do you think your parents or grandparents would agree with your definitions of these terms?

an inaccurate—and often confusing—message. See the "From Theory to Practice" box on *dating* versus *seeing* for an example of how the language used to describe romantic relationships changes over time.

Politically Incorrect Language

When speakers use politically incorrect language, they both offend others and discredit themselves. As a result, listeners may dismiss or reject whatever they are trying to communicate. The following discussion addresses some common examples of politically incorrect language and offers advice on how to avoid such language.

Use inclusive, gender-neutral language. Some women find terms such as *policeman, fisherman, chairman, fireman,* and *mailman* to be offensive since they imply that only men can hold these jobs or positions. Terms such as *police officer, fisher, chairperson* (or *chair*), *fire fighter*, and *letter carrier* have broader applications. Rather than saying *mankind*, say *human beings* or *humanity*. Substitute *human resources* for *manpower*. In addition, avoid using gendered terms such as *girlfriend, boyfriend, husband,* and *wife* in formal or unfamiliar situations; instead, use *friend, partner, significant other,* or simply the name of the person.

When referring to people with disabilities, avoid the term *handicapped*, which has negative associations for many people. Also avoid referring to people with disabilities as *the disabled* or *the blind*. Instead, say *people with disabilities, differently abled people*, or *people who are blind*. Like all of us, people with disabilities prefer to see themselves as people first, with strengths and weaknesses. Also avoid terms like *wheelchair-bound, people suffering from HIV*, or *cancer victims*. People with disabilities or illnesses usually see themselves as coping with their challenges, not handicapped by or suffering from them. Many overcome remarkable obstacles in their quest to lead independent lives; they are fighters, not victims. People who are deaf have their own language, and many consider their communication system to be equal or superior to those of us who communicate with oral language.

In referring to members of visible minority groups, be careful to avoid outdated terms such as *Oriental*. Reference to a specific national origin (e.g., *Chinese, Nigerian, Colombian*) is usually preferable to broader categories (e.g., *Asian, African, South American*). On the other hand, many families of Asian, African, and other non-North American origins have been in Canada for generations; and not all want to be labelled by the countries of their long-dead ancestors.

Over time and among different groups, variations occur in what minority groups consider desirable or even acceptable. At the present time, the term *Aboriginal* is most widely accepted when referring to the Inuit, First Nations, and Métis populations of Canada. However, some Aboriginal groups still prefer the term *Indian* or *Native*. In a similar way, Americans of African descent have shifted their preferred names over time from *Afro-American* to *African American* to *black* to *people of colour*. In Canada, some citizens of African descent refer to themselves as *African Canadian*, but most prefer *black Canadian*. Some Canadians and Americans of Latin American descent ask to be called *Latino*; others prefer *Hispanic* or *Hispano*.

As demonstrated in the 2003–2007 television series *Queer Eye*, members of the LGBTTIQQ (lesbian, gay, bisexual, transgender, transsexual, intersex, queer, or questioning) community have added positive content to words such as *queer*, which used to be politically incorrect. In 2005, *The Passionate Eye* aired a documentary on "fag hags," in which a woman discussed how two negative words (*fag* and *hag*) have acquired positive meanings for women with strong ties to gay men.[100] Other expressions, developed outside the gay community, continue to be seen as offensive. YouTube commercials by stars such as Hilary Duff counsel teenagers that it's "not okay" to say "That's so gay."[101] In brief, beware! Language is always evolving, and not everyone agrees on the appropriate terminology in any given time period.[102]

In general, avoid unnecessary descriptors such as *lady* lawyer or *gay* activist or *black* student. When you add such descriptors, you show bias toward a certain group. Widespread media coverage of Luka Magnotta, accused of murdering Concordia student Jun Lin, illustrates this point. The early coverage identified Magnotta as a "gay porn star." This labelling offended some members of the gay community, who said that the coverage would never have read "heterosexual porn star."

TIPS FOR EFFECTIVE VERBAL COMMUNICATION

As we have seen in this chapter, the word choices we make—our verbal communication—have an important impact on the relationships we build with others and on their perceptions of us. In short, effective communication requires us to be mindful of how others will perceive, understand, and respond to our words. To conclude this chapter, let us look at some tips for effective verbal communication.

Speak with confidence, especially when you need to demonstrate leadership. The odd "umm" or "I think" can indicate humility, which others may perceive positively. If you litter your language with statements implying self-doubt, however, others will question your credibility as a communicator.[103] Try to choose words that convey strength rather than weakness. Say "I'd like to ask a question" rather than "Umm, is it ok if I ask a question?" Or say "This is a really well-written report" rather than "I think this is a good report, don't you?" In Western cultures, we also convey confidence through dynamism and energy in our voice and body.

CONVERSATIONAL SELF-FOCUS Focus on oneself to the exclusion of others in a conversation.

Don't talk too much. If you dominate the conversation, most people will not enjoy talking with you. In fact, researchers have applied the term ***conversational self-focus*** to those who spend too much time talking about themselves.[104] *Self-focus* means that you show little interest in the other person and instead keep turning the conversation back to yourself. As discussed in Chapter 5, you should make the effort to ask about and show interest in others.

Read the crowd and adapt to the situation. Jokes that seemed funny in the locker room might not seem so funny at a business luncheon. Adapt your word choices, examples, slang, and efforts at humour to the people with whom you are communicating and to the setting in which you are communicating. Pay attention to cues from others in order to identify appropriate behaviour for the interaction. In other words, take context into account.[105]

Guide the listener. When presented with too much information, we cannot easily follow a message. To help listeners understand and remember what you say, use techniques such as the following.[106] Identify the points you plan to make by number (e.g., "I'll answer your question in two parts"). Accompany your words with hand gestures and use pauses for emphasis. Summarize and repeat what you have said from time to time.

Be positive. Emphasize what people *can* do or *can* have rather than what they *cannot* do or *cannot* have. Focus on what *can* work rather than what *cannot* work or what *will* happen rather than what *will not* happen. If you take this approach, people will perceive you and your message more positively.[107] Try "You're welcome to wait here" rather than "You can't come in yet." Consider saying "You can make a copy yourself" rather than "We will not be handing out copies." Substitute "We can meet tomorrow" for "We cannot meet today." The positive emphasis of these statements shows concern for the needs and interests of the other person. Comments such as "That makes no sense" diminish the other person and invite conflict. Saying "If I understand you correctly . . ." shows respect for the other person and allows you to explain your point of view. Sometimes we have to convey negative or upsetting information; but when given the choice, we should frame our messages in more positive terms. People are more likely to agree with positive rather than negative messages.[108]

OTHER-ORIENTATION
Thinking about the other person's interests, needs, knowledge, and situation when you speak.

Demonstrate ***other-orientation*** *in your talk*. Other-orientation (or "you attitude")[109] refers to the extent to which you care about the welfare of others.[110] Other-orientation strategies include seeking common ground; trying to identify areas of mutual interest; and varying your vocal pitch, volume, and rate of speech to match those of your conversation partner.

Use clear, correct, non-threatening language. Avoid confusing or misleading the listener by using unclear language (e.g., bafflegab, equivocality, or euphemisms intended to deceive). Also avoid using the wrong word or otherwise misusing language, which can also create confusion. In addition, use language that does not threaten the ego of the other person. People respond defensively when you threaten their egos and defensiveness creates a negative communication climate for relationships.

Try to keep up with the changes in language. Telling a group of students to "hook up and form a threesome" in order to do group work in the classroom may seem harmless to a professor who takes the meaning of these words to be "get into a group of three." To the students, however, this language sounds dated and inappropriate. When we use words that are out of date, we display static evaluation, one of the barriers to effective communication.

Avoid politically incorrect language. Be respectful of groups that have experienced discrimination in the past and pay attention to language choices that exclude people. Use gender neutral language (e.g., *nurse* rather than *male nurse*). Avoid unnecessary descriptors (*lawyer* instead of *black lawyer*). Avoid labels that were acceptable in the past but that have changed (e.g., *Eskimo*). Avoid language that implies a judgment or negative bias against a group (e.g., "That's so gay"). Pay close attention to how others refer to themselves and, if unsure, ask about their preferences.

Translate abstract words like brave, generous, and peaceful into concrete terms. If you say that someone went into a burning home to save a child, your listeners will probably agree that the person is brave. If you say that someone gave a significant amount of money to charity, most people would understand why you call the person *generous*. But abstract words create debate. What is the difference, for example, between *peace keeping* and *war*? Many people would argue over those definitions because they cannot see, taste, smell, touch, or hear the meaning of the words. Abstract words carry different meanings for different people.

SUMMARY

We have seen in this chapter that language is a human creation. While the words that we use to describe our world are arbitrary, they are absolutely essential to our ability to communicate. We have also seen that we cannot make up rules for language as we go; but we do have room for creativity in terms of word choice, meanings given to the words, and slang that we use to communicate. We have looked at the characteristics of language and discovered that language is symbolic, rule bound, culture bound, and dynamic. We also talked about the social functions of language that allow us to construct and name our world and to bring us together or separate us. We reviewed barriers that keep us from understanding one another, and we concluded with tips on being a more empathic, powerful, other-oriented, and credible speaker.

As we noted in earlier chapters, we cannot *not* communicate. In other words, we cannot avoid communicating. We send messages even when we do not intend to send them—through our silence, our failure to respond (neutrality), and other means. Others are always reading these signals. While we may take verbal communication for granted, most of us know it is easy to say the wrong thing. Unfortunately, we may not realize our mistakes until we see the reaction of the other person. Because communication is irreversible (we cannot undo or take back what we have said), we have to become effective at formulating messages that will have the desired impact on our credibility, relationships, and work life.

REVIEW QUESTIONS

1. What are the four types of language rules discussed in this chapter? Why do we need to follow these rules? What are the implications of breaking them?
2. What is a *symbol*? How does a symbol relate to its referent? How do thoughts relate to both symbols and referents?
3. Do you think that people can understand or experience a concept even if they have no word for that concept? Why or why not?
4. In what ways are young people (particularly young women) leading the evolution of language?
5. What are the connections among power, gender, and credibility? What types of behaviours might take away from your credibility?

What are some of the ways to build your credibility with others?

6. Discuss the following two principles: "We cannot not communicate" and "Communication is irreversible." Can you think of a time when you or someone you know has experienced negative consequences from ignoring these principles?

SUGGESTED ACTIVITIES

1. Think about the flag of your home country. What are some of the symbols (or words) that come to mind when you think about this object? Do you think that classmates from other countries would share these same meanings? Why or why not? Think about how your discussion reflects the communication principle that meanings are in people and not in words.
2. Consider one of your male friends and one of your female friends. Think critically about differences in the ways that these friends communicate. Do they differ in their word choices? In their conversation style? Explain your responses.
3. Visit the website http://whaddayaapp.com to check out an app (available for iPhone and Android smartphones) involving a humorous Newfoundland translator and soundboard. Make a note of some of the expressions used by people from Newfoundland and Labrador. Think about how these words reflect the cultural reality of these Canadians.
4. Make up a new word and start using it in conversations with your friends or family. Pay attention to how others respond, noting whether or not they seem to understand your new word based on the context in which you have used it. See if anyone else starts using your new word.
5. Form a group with three or four of your classmates. As a group, identify words or expressions that were unfamiliar or amusing to your friends when you used them. What do your experiences say about you or your culture? Share your findings with your class.
6. Find a partner and discuss what you have learned in this chapter. Listen to each other as you communicate and identify any barriers to effective communication.

CHAPTER 7

Communicating Nonverbally

CHAPTER OUTLINE

learning OBJECTIVES

- To understand the difference between verbal and nonverbal communication
- To appreciate the importance of studying nonverbal communication
- To understand the primary and secondary functions of nonverbal communication in our lives
- To be able to identify the channels through which we communicate nonverbally
- To understand the impact of space and time on nonverbal communication
- To understand how culture influences nonverbal communication
- To improve our own nonverbal communication skills

forSTARTERS

Liar, Liar, Pants on Fire!

© ImageZoo/Alamy

We all tell lies. People who claim they do not lie are probably lying! Most of the time, however, we tell "little white lies." For example, we might say to a friend something like "That dress looks amazing on you!" In reality, the dress might not be a great fit; but we want to avoid hurting our friend's feelings. Or we might decline an invitation at work by saying "I would love to be part of that committee, but I've taken on too many new assignments lately." In reality, the thought of being on the committee may have drawn a deep internal groan.

At other times, we lie without uttering a single word. Take the game of poker. Expert poker players have mastered the "poker face," allowing them to disguise their hand and betting strategy. These players also have a strong ability to "read" other players. Nonverbal cues and the timing of bets help them to determine whether or not opponents are bluffing. In the television show *Lie to Me*, the main character Cal Lightman (played by Tim Roth) has "reading" people down to a science. Lightman analyzes nonverbal cues such as facial expressions, hand gestures, and posture to detect deception. Needless to say, his skills are in high demand with law enforcement, military agencies, and politicians. The show follows Lightman as he tries to determine if and why a criminal suspect, for example, is lying.

The research of Paul Ekman of the University of California served as the basis for *Lie to Me*. In the mid-1960s, Ekman began to focus on the link between the face and emotion. He was especially interested in how "micro expressions" can help us to detect deception.[1] According to Ekman, these small, rapidly occurring facial cues reveal if a person is attempting to conceal something. These cues can include raised eyebrows, a slight downturn in the lips, touching the forehead, and changes in pupil size, to name a few. Typically, they appear for only a microsecond, but onlookers are able to identify their fleeting presence. Ekman designed the Facial Action Coding System (FACS) to identify which facial muscles work together to create various micro expressions.[2]

INTRODUCTION

NONVERBAL COMMUNICATION Communication that does not involve language.

In Chapter 6, we focussed on verbal communication—communication that involves spoken, written, or signed language. In this chapter, we will learn about **nonverbal communication**—communication that does not involve language. When we speak of *nonverbal communication*, we are talking about the way we utter words—tone of voice, pitch, accents, and use of pauses. We are also talking about facial expressions, body language, and gestures. In addition, the study of nonverbal communication includes the impact of physical appearance and clothing on how others see us, the possessions that help to define us, and how we use space and time to communicate. All of these descriptors communicate who we are and what matters to us.

In the sections that follow, we will look at how we differentiate between verbal and nonverbal communication, the functions and channels of nonverbal communication, and the impact of space and time on nonverbal communication. Finally, we will explore some tips for more effective nonverbal communication.

More recently, Ekman has designed online training tools to put his research into practice. These tools include hour-long modules that train individuals to identify concealed emotions and deception. Groups such as law enforcement, national security, therapists, health professionals, salespersons, human resource groups, and negotiators have participated in this kind of training.[3] Border control and airport personnel regularly use nonverbal indicators to decide whom to question or detain.[4]

In addition to studying facial expressions as indicators of lying, researchers look at body language. If you (like some 28 million other television viewers)[5] watched American pro-cyclist Lance Armstrong's admission of guilt in his interview with Oprah Winfrey in January 2013, you probably studied Armstrong closely as he spoke, wondering what you would see and hear. Until this televised statement, Armstrong had repeatedly denied using performance-enhancing drugs; and many of us had believed this acclaimed seven-time Tour de France winner, cancer survivor, and activist. But what did we actually observe when Winfrey interviewed Armstrong? Carol Kinsey Goman, author of *The Truth about Lies in the Workplace*, says that Armstrong minimized the seriousness of his actions when he shrugged his shoulders as if to say "no big deal." In addition, signals such as the tightening of muscles around his mouth, licking his lips, covering his mouth with his hand, and rubbing his upper lip showed stress and the withholding of information. When Armstrong denied pressuring other players to use performance-enhancing drugs, he rubbed his hands (a nonverbal indicator of lying).[6] While the casual observer would not have noticed these nonverbal indicators of lying, experts would have been quick to note their significance.

Other common indicators of lying include greater lag time in responding to questions, reduced eye contact, increased shifts in posture, unfilled pauses, slower and more careful speech, and higher pitch to the voice.[7] Lying requires thought and effort, leaving little time for concern with issues such as body language, facial expressions, or voice control. The slower and more careful speech and unfilled pauses come from efforts to maintain consistency in stories. Practised liars learn to mask and control many of these cues; however, facial expressions are easier to control than body language. As a consequence, leaks often come from the hands and the feet; and the more complex the lie, the more the liar will leak cues. As with all other areas of communication, however, differences surface across cultures.

As you read this chapter, consider the following kinds of questions. How does nonverbal communication influence our perceptions of others? What is the influence of culture on nonverbal behaviours? In what ways might overconfidence in our ability to interpret nonverbal behaviours compromise our relationships at home, in social settings, and at work? What are some of the channels through which we transmit nonverbal information?

DIFFERENTIATING BETWEEN VERBAL AND NONVERBAL COMMUNICATION

What is the difference between verbal and nonverbal communication? As suggested above, the difference depends on whether or not *language* is involved. Spoken and written communication fall clearly into the category of language. However, we can also identify other verbal codes that we might mistake as nonverbal. Examples include semaphore, Morse code, and sign languages. In each case, a one-to-one correspondence exists between symbols and the letters or words they represent. For this reason, these communication systems fall into the category of verbal—*not* nonverbal—communication.

Semaphore involves someone holding a pair of flags to spell a message, letter by letter. As with other language systems, a direct connection exists between each symbol (in this case, the arrangement of flags) and a specific letter of the alphabet. Refer to the

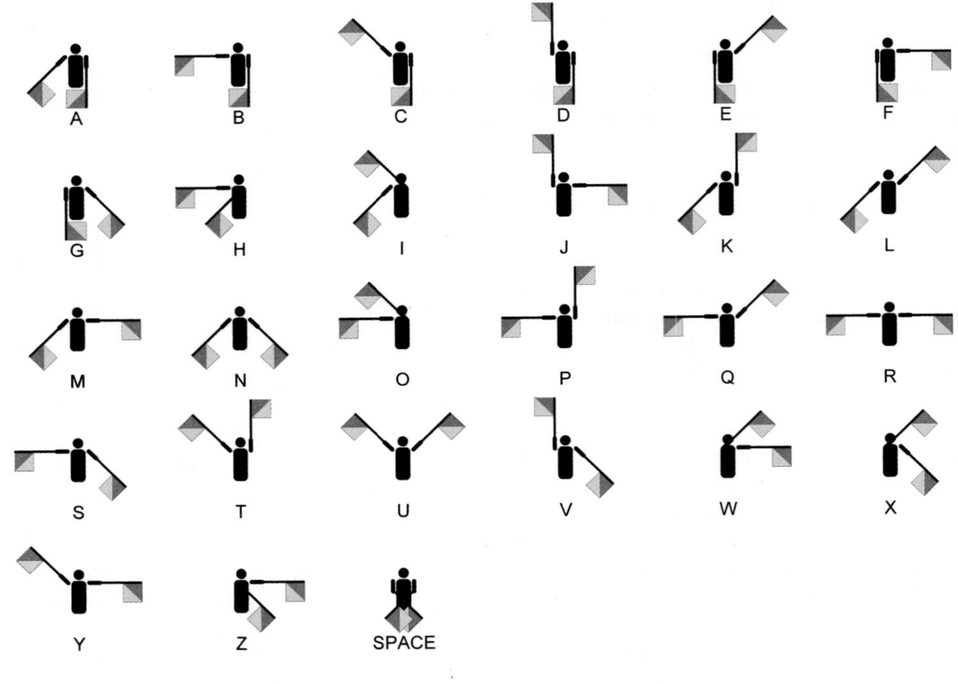

FIGURE 7.1 **Semaphore.**

chart in Figure 7.1 to see how you can use this system to spell your name. Of course, if you spell out your name (or any other message) using semaphore, the receiver of the message must also be able to decipher the code!

Like semaphore, Morse code connects letters of the alphabet to specific symbols. In this case, the symbols are combinations of short and long signals (commonly called *dots* and *dashes*). The symbol for the letter *a*, for example, is a short signal (a dot) followed by a long signal (a dash). Users employ instruments such as mirrors or flashlights to convey these symbols visually (i.e., through long and short flashes of light). They can also tap objects (e.g., telegraph keys, stones, sticks) to convey these symbols through sound vibrations. Historically, early radio and telegraph operators made the most frequent use of Morse code. Although little used today, Morse code continues to intrigue people and to draw together communities of enthusiasts. For an interesting observation relating to the move away from Morse code, see the "Human Diversity" box.

The deaf community uses a third type of language code, sign language. In signing, people rely on a combination of hand gestures, facial expressions, and body postures to communicate. Different communities around the globe use different sign languages, but the most widely known and used of these languages is American Sign Language (ASL). In French-speaking Canada, people with hearing impairments often employ Quebec Sign Language. The Canadian Association of the Deaf notes that we should always capitalize the terms *American Sign Language* and *Quebec Sign Language* since these communication systems are as much languages as English, German, or Russian.[9] American Sign Language has become more familiar to television viewers thanks to *Switched at Birth*, "the first mainstream television series to have multiple deaf and hard-of-hearing series regulars and scenes shot entirely in ASL."[10]

Conceptual Lag

While a visiting lecturer at the University of Sierra Leone in the 1960s, Stewart Ferguson had an opportunity to witness the transition from telegraph to telephone in action. When travelling into a remote region of the country, Ferguson witnessed an event that illustrated what he later called *conceptual lag*—the idea that it takes time to integrate any new idea into our way of thinking and behaving.

What happened on this occasion was that the local telegraph operator, while in Ferguson's presence, received a telephone call from someone a distance away. Instead of carrying on a normal voice conversation, however, the man began to use the telephone to communicate his message in Morse code! The conversation sounded something like the following: "Dot, dash, dot, dot, dash, dot, dash, dot, dot, dot, dot. . . ." At the end of the conversation, the sender inquired, "Have you received me?" The receiver replied, "Yes, over." This tendency for people to look backward in dealing with the present became one of Marshall McLuhan's most popular media theories, which he dubbed the *rear view mirror syndrome*.[8]

PRIMARY FUNCTIONS OF NONVERBAL COMMUNICATION

Now that we have seen what nonverbal communication *is* and *is not*, let us look at the functions that it serves. These functions include replacing or substituting for verbal messages (**emblems**), complementing or adding to verbal communication (**illustrators**), regulating interaction (**regulators**), relieving tension or satisfying bodily needs (**adaptors**), and conveying emotion (**affect displays**).[11] Although Paul Ekman and Wallace Friesen originally conceived of these categories as primarily relating to gestures, later researchers have applied the functions to body movements in general (facial expression, vocal cues, gestures, posture, and other body language).

EMBLEMS Body movements that stand on their own as a replacement for words.

ILLUSTRATORS Body movements that accent or work in unison with what is said verbally.

REGULATORS Body movements that control the flow of conversation.

ADAPTORS Body movements that relieve tension or satisfy self or bodily needs.

AFFECT DISPLAYS Body movements that tell others about our emotional state.

Replacing or Substituting for Verbal Messages (Emblems)

In his pioneering work on the measurement and meanings of nonverbal communication, Paul Ekman identified some body movements that stand on their own as a replacement for words. These nonverbal cues, which Ekman called *emblems*, convey a clear and obvious message to all members of the same culture or community.[12] For example, nodding the head replaces the word *yes* in many cultures, while shaking the head from side to side says *no*. Using these head movements in this way can can have unexpected results for visitors to Bulgaria, however, because Bulgarians shake their heads from side to side to say *yes* and nod to say *no*. Similarly, if you use the "thumbs up" gesture to signify approval of something (e.g., a movie), you should be aware that many Middle Easterners read this gesture as a crude insult.[13]

> "I can't just tell the guys I want the ball, I have to do it with my body language."
> LAMARCUS ALDRIDGE

Learning the emblems of other countries can be critically important if you want to blend into the local culture on visits. Not knowing these emblems may even have serious consequences. You may recall the scene in Quentin Tarantino's World War II movie *Inglourious Basterds* (2009) where a Jewish American soldier (pretending to be a Nazi officer) holds up three fingers to order three glasses of scotch in a bar in Nazi-occupied France.

Universal Pictures/The Kobal Collection

He gives himself away because Germans use their thumb, index, and middle fingers to indicate the number three. This soldier's use of the wrong emblem leads to a barroom gunfight.

Complementing, Repeating, and Accenting Verbal Messages (Illustrators)

When our body movements act in unison with what we say verbally, we call them illustrators.[14] Illustrators may be conscious or unconscious, but they do not stand on their own. They differ from emblems because they accompany—rather than replace—words. For example, you might smile warmly while saying "I love you," point while saying "look over there," form a square with your hands while describing a box, or shake your fist while shouting angrily at a neighbour whose cat has been digging in your garden. These examples all show how we complete, repeat, or accent our verbal messages with nonverbal actions.

"I speak two languages, Body and English."
MAE WEST

While the average person uses illustrators to go along with speech, actors have to be experts in this area. They must use their faces, hands, and bodies to add drama and emphasis to their words. Michael Richards, who won three Emmy awards for his role as Cosmo Kramer on the television show *Seinfeld*, mastered the art of using illustrators. His facial expressions, physical humour (e.g., flinging open a door to slide into a room), and wild gesturing added enormously to his ability to convert ordinary situations into hilarious stories.

Regulating Interaction (Regulators)

In managing a conversation, we rely on what we call regulators—body movements designed to control the flow of conversation. Regulators tell us when to start and stop our turns to speak. Getting in and out of the flow of conversation is a lot like entering traffic on a busy freeway: we have to show others our intentions through obvious signals.

In the 1960s and early 1970s, sociologist Harvey Sacks and his colleagues began to identify the specific nonverbal signals or regulators that characterize **turn taking**.[15] Indicators of willingness to yield to the other person include the following: changes in intonation (rising or falling voice pitch), drawing out the last syllable of a word, changing body orientation or position, and looking at the listener.[16] When we want to begin our turn, on the other hand, we may use turn-requesting cues such as sharply taking a breath, raising a finger, leaning forward, finishing the other person's sentence, or rapidly saying "mmm hmm" or "okay" to signal "I would like to speak!"[17] Additional examples of conversation regulators include the following: patiently nodding or making eye contact to encourage the other speaker to continue, raising a hand in class to indicate the desire to answer or ask a question, or holding up a hand to keep someone else from interrupting. (See the "From Theory to Practice" box for an exercise related to these observations.)

TURN TAKING The process of deciding who will speak at any given time during a conversation.

As you can see in the above examples, regulators can also substitute for words. If we nod to encourage another speaker to continue, the nod acts as a regulator; however, it also substitutes for saying "please continue." If we raise our hand to indicate we would like a turn at speaking, the raised hand substitutes for saying "I would like to speak." In that sense, there can be overlap between gestures that replace words (emblems) and those that regulate conversation (regulators).

> **from theory TO PRACTICE**
>
> **It's My Turn!**
>
> As we discussed, a number of cues can alert us to when speakers want to begin or end their conversational turns. Watch one of your favorite television shows and carefully observe the characters as they speak. Do they make use of the cues we have discussed here? How natural does their conversation appear? Do more believable actors use more natural turn-taking cues?

Relieving Tension and Satisfying Bodily Needs (Adaptors)

Adaptors (sometimes called *manipulators*) are body movements that relieve tension and satisfy self or bodily needs.[18] They involve manipulation of the physical self. We may be unconscious of these movements, which often fall into the category of habits. When we scratch our head, push our hair out of our eyes, play with a pen, stroke our arms, change our position, or adjust our glasses, these signals convey information. Others may perceive these nonverbal messages as displaying some kind of anxiety or distress. Sometimes they will be correct in their interpretations; at other times, however, we may be scratching a bug bite, moving in our chair because we are uncomfortable, or stroking our arm because it is hurting. Some adaptors, such as smoothing our clothes, can also be signs of romantic interest. Like many other nonverbal signs, adaptors can have more than one interpretation; so knowing the person can be important in coming to the most accurate interpretation of the adaptor. If you look at the "Professional Contexts" box on doctor–patient interactions, you will see the important role that reading adaptors once played in medical contexts.

> **professional CONTEXTS**
>
> **Doctor–Patient Interactions: Listening to the Nonverbal**
>
> In recent decades, a shift has occurred from an emphasis on the nonverbal to the verbal in doctor–patient interactions.[19] Many families in Canada no longer have a family doctor; they go to clinics, where they see different doctors each time. Unacquainted with these walk-in patients, the doctors rely heavily on short structured interviews and computerized data banks to acquire the information needed to diagnose and prescribe treatments.
>
> While the verbal dimension of communication suffers in these brief structured encounters, the nonverbal almost totally disappears. Yet the nonverbal has traditionally played a critical role in doctor–patient interactions. The old country doctor of the early to mid-twentieth century visited his patients at home. He had an intimate acquaintance with all members of a family. In small communities, doctors sat around wood stoves with their patients and exchanged stories when they were not treating patients. The doctors knew not only the medical but also the personal histories of the patients. And they listened—not only to words, but also to bodies—when their patients came to them with problems.
>
> Patients reveal many health problems through body movements (e.g., rubbing a sore neck, favouring one arm when the other is injured, involuntarily shaking due to a neurological disorder). They also convey their concerns about their health through tone of voice, body language, and other nonverbal cues. But deciphering the nonverbal requires familiarity with the person. As a result of the reduced emphasis on face-to-face communication and lessened opportunity to read the whole patient (characteristics of modern doctor–patient interactions), outcomes can suffer.[20] In other words, patients are more likely to be misdiagnosed or given the wrong treatment when doctors disregard nonverbal information.

Conveying Emotion (Affect Display)

Although we use words to tell others how we are feeling, we convey most of the emotional content of our messages through nonverbal means.[21] For example, we convey happiness with smiles or laughter, sadness with tears, and boredom with a slouched body posture. The term *affect display* refers to the nonverbal messages that convey information about our emotional state.

> **"When the eyes say one thing, and the tongue another, a practised man relies on the language of the first."**
> **RALPH WALDO EMERSON**

In a classic series of studies, Albert Mehrabian concluded that we convey 93 per cent of the emotional content of a message through nonverbal channels and just 7 per cent of the emotional content through spoken words.[22] In a follow-up study by different researchers, participants watched videotapes of a performer reading friendly, neutral, or hostile messages in a friendly, neutral, or hostile nonverbal style.[23] When the performer mixed verbal and nonverbal signals—e.g., when she read a friendly message in a hostile manner—participants believed the tone of voice more than the words.

Our body posture, movements, and gestures also play a key role in conveying emotion. Viewed independently, facial expressions can be difficult to read.[24] However, we gain more accuracy when we look at facial expressions in conjunction with body language. One study asked participants to identify emotions such as pleasure, victory, or pain in a series of photographs. The first group looked only at facial expressions. The second looked only at body language. The third group looked at facial expressions *and* body language. Participants who were most accurate relied either on facial expressions *and* body language or on body language alone. Thus it seems that while the face does provide some limited information about feelings, body positions and hand gestures convey more valuable information.[25]

Like the face and the body, touch transmits much information about our emotions to others. A study by American psychologist Matthew Hertenstein asked volunteers to communicate eight different emotions to a blindfolded stranger. Using only touch, the volunteers achieved as high as 78 per cent accuracy in communicating anger, fear, disgust, love, gratitude, sympathy, happiness, and sadness. When the researchers repeated the studies in countries including Spain, Pakistan, and Turkey, they received even higher rates of accuracy.[26]

SECONDARY FUNCTIONS OF NONVERBAL COMMUNICATION

In addition to the primary functions discussed above, nonverbal communication also fulfills secondary functions of a social nature. We rely heavily on nonverbal communication in arriving at first impressions, and we depend on consistency between verbal and nonverbal messages to maintain these impressions. We also use nonverbal techniques to connect with others. Finally, we use nonverbal communication to build and maintain our relationships.

Making First Impressions and Violating Expectations

Imagine meeting a co-worker for the first time—perhaps your new boss, a member of your work team, or the person moving into the cubicle next to yours. Immediately you take in the clothes, hair, facial features, and body language of the newcomer; and you quickly form several judgments. It takes you less than a minute to form these first impressions and to decide whether you like or dislike the person.[27] (See the "Professional Contexts" box titled "It's the Way She Walks" to find out how criminals quickly choose their targets based on these sorts of first impressions.)

We use readily accessible cues to arrive at these first impressions, which often have a lasting impact even though they form quickly.[28] We see physically attractive people as more likeable,[29] confident, and comfortable in social situations than people who are less physically attractive.[30] We respond favourably to people who come across as agreeable, outgoing, open, conscientious, and emotionally stable. In judging another person, we place more importance on the perceived **agreeableness** of the person than any other personality characteristic; and we judge agreeableness largely on the basis of nonverbal mannerisms.[31] Despite the confidence that we may feel in using nonverbal indicators to judge the agreeableness of another person, however, we make more mistakes in judging this quality than any other.[32] Worse, when we assume we are right, we may not pay attention to information that contradicts what we believe to be true.[33] Most of the time, no connection exists between our level of confidence in our judgments and our actual level of accuracy.[34]

AGREEABLENESS The perceived warmth and friendliness of a person.

*professional*CONTEXTS

It's the Way She Walks

In the early 1980s, Betty Grayson and Morris Stein conducted an experiment that acquired the status of a classic in the field of nonverbal communication.[35] The researchers asked convicts serving time for rape, murder, and robbery to view videos of pedestrians (filmed without their knowledge) on a busy New York City street. Then they asked the offenders to identify the pedestrians they would choose as victims. To the surprise of the researchers, the convicts had a high level of agreement as to whom they would choose to victimize. They also made their choices within a matter of seven seconds.

The results puzzled the researchers because age, gender, race, and size did not appear to be deciding factors. Even though small and frail, a woman might not be selected as an easy victim. A large man, on the other hand, might be chosen. Nor were the offenders themselves able to explain their choices. They did not know why they believed that some people looked like easy targets and others less so.

To find the answers to the puzzle, the researchers analyzed the videos to identify differences in the selected victims versus non-victims. By studying the movement and body language of the pedestrians, Grayson and Stein arrived at the following conclusions.

People selected as easy targets had a noticeably awkward or unusual walk. They dragged, shuffled, or lifted their feet in an unnatural way. Their strides were either abnormally short or long. They walked either much slower (suggesting lack of a clear purpose) or much faster (suggesting nervousness or fear) than those around them. The non-victims had a much smoother and more natural walk, stepping in a heel-to-toe fashion at an average pace.

People selected as easy targets also had less coordinated and more erratic body movements. Sometimes they jerked or lurched from side to side. Their arms were loose and disjointed, swinging out of harmony with the rest of their body movements. Non-victims moved in a smooth, balanced, and centred way, with confidence and strength.

Finally, people selected as easy targets often had a slumped posture and downward gaze. These behaviours can be signs of someone who is weak or submissive—less likely to put up a fight. Alternatively, these behaviours can indicate someone who is distracted, unaware of his or her surroundings and thus easier prey. Non-victims, on the other hand, tended to stand up straight and look directly ahead.

Once aware of the indicators that mark us as victims, we can work to change these behaviours. If we learn how to move more confidently, we can reduce our risk of becoming victims of assault or other crimes. Taking self-defence classes is also a good way to learn strategies for preventing and protecting ourselves in the event of attacks.[36]

Mike Baldwin/Cartoonstock

"Thank God we're cute. You only get one chance to make a good first impression."

Even though we are often wrong in our first impressions, we rely on these impressions to guide our interactions with people we do not know very well. We take scraps of information such as a firm handshake, a wink, or a wrinkled brow as indicators of a confident, flirtatious, or disagreeable personality; in turn, we treat people as though they possess these personalities. Being able to make these sorts of quick judgments is important, as we feel at risk when we do not know what to expect from another person. In the absence of contradictory information, we may continue to rely on these early judgments in later encounters with the individual—long after we have forgotten *why* we believe that someone is intelligent, compassionate, or honest.

The difficulty arises when we over-value first impressions and rely strictly on outer appearances, group memberships, and the most obvious personality characteristics in deciding how to interact with a person.[37] First impressions almost never tell the full story. Someone may be generous in nature but have little money or few goods to contribute to a charitable function. Someone may dress in a flamboyant fashion but hold highly conservative values. When faced with serious life events and illness, people often show less agreeableness than they would normally display. Nonetheless, we expect people to be consistent in both their verbal and their nonverbal behaviours. So if their behaviour does not match their words or their appearance contradicts their words, we may not trust them.[38]

Cultural factors also play a role in first impressions. Let us imagine that your new co-worker (of whom we spoke earlier) has just arrived from another country. Others in your workplace will have expectations of this individual, since first impressions come with expectations. In a diverse workplace, these expectations often find their origins in stereotypes. For example, we may expect older people to be more conservative, younger people to be more rebellious, and gay people to be more artistic. Based on past experiences and cultural stereotypes, co-workers may initially perceive a newcomer from Korea to be serious, highly motivated, and conscientious. They may perceive a newcomer from Brazil, on the other hand, to be more relaxed and sociable but less task-oriented. Based on these first impressions, co-workers will decide what to expect from the newcomer.

Our expectations also come from contexts. For example, we do not expect supervisors in professional settings to swear or curse. We do not necessarily have the same expectations on a construction site. When something unexpected happens, it violates our expectations; as a result, we must react. Based on this idea, **expectancy violation theory** tells us that our first impressions can change direction (either positively or negatively) if a person violates our expectations.[39] In the workplace, we might expect that a new employee with lots of relevant experience will do well in his new position, but our expectation will change quickly if this person fails to deliver several reports on time. Similarly, we might expect a new employee with no relevant work experience to struggle at first, but our expectation will shift if this person successfully leads several projects in her first weeks at the job. Although first impressions usually rely most heavily on nonverbal cues, expectancy violation relies equally on verbal and nonverbal factors.[40]

EXPECTANCY VIOLATION THEORY Theory that explains how violation of expectations can alter first impressions.

Take a look at the "Professional Contexts" box titled "Thanks for Applying—but No Thanks" for an example of the impact of nonverbal communication in the hiring interview. The hiring interview is often the first—and sometimes the only—opportunity for a job candidate to make a personal sales pitch to the organization. Thus, first impressions matter a great deal.

professionalCONTEXTS

Thanks for Applying—but No Thanks

Have you ever landed a coveted job interview, felt as if you had nailed it, and later received the dreaded rejection letter? Maybe it wasn't what you said but what you *didn't* say that made the difference. Did you know that your body language influences a big part of the hiring process? Body posture, hand gestures, eye contact, grooming gestures, and facial expressions all contribute to the impression that you give to a prospective employer.[41]

According to experts, ideal nonverbal behaviours in an interview setting follow the rule of moderation. That is, avoid extremes such as staring at the interviewer without taking appropriate breaks, allowing your eyes to dart nervously around the room, or leaning aggressively toward the interviewer. (A slight lean toward the interviewer, on the other hand, suggests liking and interest in the person.)

To most of us, a limp handshake suggests a weak, uncertain, and unsociable personality. Too strong a grip indicates a potentially over-strong and dominant personality. As with other nonverbal behaviours, moderation remains the key to a positive impression. A medium-strong handshake allows us to connect in a socially acceptable way with a stranger.[42]

Fiddling with your hair, jewellery, or other objects suggests lack of confidence and nervousness. Putting your hands in your pockets, behind your back, or across your chest suggests that you are hiding something or you are defensive. Leaning away from the interviewer suggests boredom. On the other hand, sitting up straight with a confident posture conveys intelligence and composure.[43] Experts suggest filming a mock interview with a friend and playing it back to correct whatever negative nonverbal habits you might demonstrate.

Career coach Debra Benton offers some additional advice to follow when interviewing via online video conferencing services such as Skype. She warns against visibly poor hygiene, wearing orange (because it may make you look like a convict), allowing pets and children to enter the viewing frame, and appearing jittery. This advice is particularly valuable in today's job market, as more than 60 per cent of companies report using video interviews prior to inviting a candidate to appear for an in-person meeting.[44]

Making Connections through Immediacy

Albert Mehrabian, one of the most prominent researchers of nonverbal communication, conducted a series of experiments in the 1960s and 1970s on how we respond to the nonverbal behaviours of others. He was particularly interested in ideas related to **immediacy**. At first sight, the immediacy principle appears to state the obvious—that we are attracted to people and things we like, evaluate positively, and prefer. At the same time, we avoid those we dislike, evaluate negatively, or do not prefer.[45] Identification of this principle led, however, to a flurry of research and interest in the communication behaviours that make a communicator more or less likeable or approachable.

IMMEDIACY A sense of likeability and approachability established through communication behaviours that draw people closer together.

So what are immediacy behaviours? In short, they are communication behaviours that increase our feelings of closeness to and liking for another person.[46] Imagine a person turns his or her body toward you, leans in your direction, makes eye contact, nods warmly at you, and exhibits a pleasant facial expression while speaking or listening to you. All of these signals decrease both the physical and the psychological distance between you and the other person, and they have the potential to create mutual feelings of liking.[47]

In interpersonal encounters, we are most likely to be drawn to people who exhibit immediacy behaviours. These behaviours can also help to build connections in more formal contexts. In public speaking, for example, audiences judge speakers who use more immediacy cues—speaking in a warm and pleasant voice, smiling, making eye contact, leaning toward the audience, and so on—as more competent, composed, credible, and persuasive.[48] Similarly, salespersons experience more success when they exhibit immediacy cues. One study found that sales improved when pharmaceutical representatives demonstrated more nonverbal immediacy.[49]

Nonverbal immediacy also influences the likeability of political candidates. In one experiment, participants watched excerpts from a 1992 debate between American presidential candidates Bill Clinton and George Bush.[50] The researchers found that when the debaters showed nonverbal expressiveness and immediacy, these behaviours were contagious. That is, observers imitated the charismatic nonverbal behaviours and, as a result, felt more positively toward the candidates. In a 2008 documentary film, former political adviser Richard Greene identified the importance of immediacy behaviours in sweeping Barack Obama to the presidency.[51] Greene pointed out both verbal and nonverbal elements in these immediacy behaviours. In terms of the verbal, he talked about the way in which Obama shared his feelings and emotions with his audience. In terms of the nonverbal, he talked about Obama's eye contact, empathetic listening style, and warmth and sense of humanity. For more insight into the impact of nonverbal communication on people's perceptions of leadership ability, take a look at the "Professional Contexts" box.

IMMEDIACY BEHAVIOURS Verbal and nonverbal behaviours that suggest a teacher's willingness to approach and to be approached by students.

Few concepts have received as much attention in the instructional communication literature as **teacher immediacy**.[53] Educators establish this sort of immediacy by engaging in verbal and nonverbal behaviours that reveal their willingness to approach and to be approached by students.[54] Examples of nonverbal immediacy behaviours include smiling; using expressive vocal tones; leaning toward students; facing students; moving closer to students; decreasing physical barriers (e.g., moving out from behind a podium); and using relaxed body movements, gestures, and positions.[55] Verbal immediacy behaviours include addressing students by name, asking questions for class discussion, and calling on students to answer questions.

As a college or university student, you will have noticed that some educators seem able to reach across the rows of desks to build a connection with most or all of their students. These instructors tend to use immediacy behaviours to reduce the distance between themselves and their students. Others have a more detached teaching style, perhaps because they believe they do not need to build rapport with the class in order to deliver information. These two approaches reflect different attitudes toward the teacher–student

*professional*CONTEXTS

Nonverbal Communication in Leadership

In a 2011 book called *The Silent Language of Leaders: How Body Language Can Help—or Hurt—How You Lead*, Carol Kinsey Goman says that mastering body language should be higher on the agenda of leaders.[52] The most effective leaders convey not simply power and status, but also warmth. Think about a time when your supervisor gave you an encouraging smile and a nod when you floated a new idea in a company meeting. Did you feel more confident afterwards? Warm gestures can help to build trusting relationships between workers and managers, ultimately improving the work environment and the quality of an employee's work.

Goman says that greater use of visual communication technologies requires leaders to be increasingly aware of their nonverbal messages. While the new technologies help to build connections, they also have the potential to contribute to feelings of self-consciousness, apprehensiveness, and even alienation. It is important, therefore, to achieve a balance between using technology to facilitate work (especially across distances) and building immediacy through more face-to-face and personal channels.

relationship, and they potentially have different outcomes for the students.

© David Hills/iStockphoto

Teacher immediacy helps to motivate students to learn—in large part because students are more apt to pay attention when they like their instructor. To benefit the most from the learning experience, students need to be motivated, interested, and engaged.[56] Teacher immediacy affects both the amount of knowledge students gain and the amount they recall later.[57] Immediacy also enhances the development of logical and reasoning processes in students.[58]

In addition to having a positive effect on learning, teacher immediacy also plays a critical role in other positive outcomes for both students and educators. For students, these outcomes include improved attendance and participation,[59] as well as more frequent and meaningful out-of-class communication with instructors.[60] Teachers, for their part, receive benefits in the form of more positive student evaluations in areas such as the overall quality of instruction and the perceived value of the course.[61]

Teachers can more easily achieve high levels of both nonverbal and verbal immediacy in classrooms with fewer students (e.g., under 30). The reduced distance between students and teachers in such settings enables students to see the facial expressions, body gestures, smiles, and eyes of the instructor. As well, smaller class sizes make it easier for teachers to learn students' names, interact one-on-one with students, and take questions from students who might not participate in a larger class setting.

Instructors in large classes can also achieve immediacy, especially if they rely less on the traditional lecture[62] and employ technologies in creative ways.[63] Instead of simply delivering a one-sided monologue, instructors can encourage students to ask questions and participate in the discussion. The simple act of smiling—even if viewed from a great distance—can make an instructor seem approachable. In terms of technologies, using a cordless microphone allows an instructor to walk around the classroom and get closer to students. These kinds of teacher behaviours can make a large class feel much smaller.[64]

Building and Maintaining Relationships

We pay close attention to the subtle cues of our friends, family members, and other relational partners. We watch attentively for signs of increased or decreased interest, closeness, or intimacy (e.g. a smile, meaningful silence, or a forward lean). Nonverbal communication has acquired the label of the "relationship language" because of its importance in initiating, maintaining, and dissolving close relationships.[65] Nonverbal communication tells the people involved in a relationship—as well as observers—a lot about the state of their union.

Nonverbal behaviours can be particularly significant in romantic relationships. As we will discuss in more detail in Chapter 8, the first stage in developing a romantic relationship (the initiation stage)[66] usually involves the sending and receiving of subtle unspoken cues or "nonverbal flirting."[67] We use these nonverbal cues to signal our romantic interest in another person.[68] These cues include eye contact, touch, leaning toward the person of interest, **self-grooming**, and smiling. Examples of self-grooming are running your

SELF-GROOMING
Cleaning and tidying behaviours, which often characterize courtship behaviours.

fingers through your hair, twirling a stand of your hair, adjusting your tie, smoothing your clothing, or fixing your makeup.

Although most people see men as initiators in the courtship process, some studies have shown that women regulate the process.[69] Women use subtle cues (e.g., standing close to or making eye contact with their target) to encourage movement from one stage of intimacy to the next. While researchers have studied the role of nonverbal communication in initiating romantic relationships for more than half a century, they have tended to focus on the heterosexual relationships of young adults. More recent work, however, has expanded the focus to include children, adolescents, gay and lesbian individuals, and older adults.

Flirting also occurs at the maintenance stage of romantic relationships. Flirtatious and playful behaviours help couples to deal with tension, express difficult messages, provide mutual pleasure, and solve problems.[70] Established couples also signal intimacy and closeness through nonverbal behaviours—for example, by standing or sitting close together, facing or leaning toward each other, smiling, exchanging meaningful facial expressions, making eye contact, and touching.[71] Long-term satisfaction in a relationship depends on each partner learning to read the other's nonverbal messages effectively.

Touch plays an increasingly important role in the positive progression of romantic relationships. Touch moves from being private and exploratory in the early stages of a relationship to increasingly familiar and public as the relationship intensifies. The amount of touching usually peaks early in a romantic relationship and then decreases as the partners become more comfortable with each other. Where a couple fails to achieve a comfortable middle ground, the relationship may suffer or even fall apart.[72]

> **"There's a language in her eye, her cheek, her lip; Nay, her foot speaks. Her wanton spirits look out at every joint and motive of her body."**
> **WILLIAM SHAKESPEARE**

Nonverbal communication also plays a role in the ending of romantic relationships. Telltale signs of an ending relationship include withdrawal behaviours such as reduced eye contact and decreased talk time. Couples in the process of terminating relationships also increase the physical distance that separates them from each other. Less smiling and touching often accompany these behaviours.

While the end of a relationship may appear inevitable once a couple starts to separate, a change in communication behaviours—increased eye contact and touch, more verbal communication, and more physical closeness—can change this dynamic and rebuild the relationship. Stephen Covey, author of *The Seven Habits of Highly Effective People*, suggests that to rebuild a relationship, the partners need to behave as people in love behave. He recounts the story of a man who said he was worried because he was no longer in love with his wife. Covey replied that the man had to "love her." The man repeated, "I told you, the feeling isn't there." Covey then explained: "My friend, *love* is a verb. *Love*—the feeling—is a fruit of *love*, the verb. So love her. Serve her. Sacrifice. Listen to her. Empathize. Appreciate. Affirm her."[73] In other words, Covey was advising the man to *act* as though he loved his wife in order to once again *feel* love for his wife.

NONVERBAL COMMUNICATION CHANNELS OR MEDIA

Throughout this chapter, we have looked at the importance of nonverbal communication in our interactions with one another. At this point, let us take a closer look at the many channels that carry our nonverbal messages. We will examine facial expressions; eye contact and gaze; vocal cues; silence; body movement, posture, stance, and gestures; touch; clothing and personal artifacts; and colour as conveyers of nonverbal information.

from theory TO PRACTICE

Guess the Emotion

How good are you at interpreting emotion through facial expressions? To find out, go to the following link: http://greatergood.berkeley.edu/ei_quiz.

Facial Expressions, Eye Contact, and Gaze

The face, with its 43 muscles, is capable of conveying thousands of expressions. All of these expressions help us to communicate with one another. While some facial expressions have different meanings in different cultures, at least a few mean the same thing in all cultures. Paul Ekman and Wallace Friesen identified six facial expressions that appear across cultures: anger, disgust, fear, happiness, sadness, and surprise.[74] Test your own skills at interpreting facial expressions by going to the "From Theory to Practice" box titled "Guess the Emotion."

"The eyes are the window to the soul."
SIXTEENTH-CENTURY PROVERB

Eye contact serves many purposes. We use our eyes to show interest in what someone else is saying,[75] to convey understanding or confusion, to express emotion, to signal sexual interest,[76] and sometimes to demonstrate respect.[77] As we have seen, eye contact also plays a role in regulating conversation by indicating that we would like to speak or that we would like the other person to speak.[78] In face-to-face communication within North America, we view those who make eye contact as confident and outgoing.[79] We see public speakers who maintain direct eye contact as more credible and charismatic than speakers who do not maintain direct gaze.[80]

Avoiding eye contact, on the other hand, can be a way to reduce hostility when we face an aggressive verbal attack. We also avoid eye contact to create distance when we feel uncomfortable—for example, when someone looks at us for too long or stands too close to us.[81] In such instances, our eyes serve as a barricade to protect us.

How people interpret directness of eye contact can vary, however, across cultures. While most North Americans and Europeans see direct eye contact as a sign of confidence and interest in the other person, members of some Latin American, Asian, and African cultures see direct eye contact as disrespectful. Indeed, members of some cultures show respect for a higher-status individual by lowering their eyes or avoiding direct eye contact.[82] People in some Muslim cultures perceive direct eye contact between men and women as an expression of inappropriate sexual interest.

Research has found that depressed people tend to avoid eye contact with others.[83] This behaviour can make the condition worse, as it isolates the depressed person from others who might be able to offer support. Happy people, on the other hand, tend to seek eye contact; and, as a result, they are more likely to make connections with other people.

Vocal Cues and Silence

PARALANGUAGE Speech elements that we do not categorize as language.

INTONATION The way the voice rises and falls as we speak.

TONE The vocal quality that conveys emotion.

PITCH The degree of highness or lowness with which we speak.

The term ***paralanguage*** refers to elements of speech that we do not recognize as language, including **intonation**, **tone**, **pitch**, speech rate, volume, and hesitations. Each of these elements impacts the communication process in its own way.

Intonation gives the voice its melodic nature and adds dynamism to a speaker's words. For English speakers, falling intonation at the end of a sentence indicates certainty (a statement); rising intonation indicates uncertainty (a question). In Chapter 6, we discussed a "question statement," where the voice rises into a question even though the speaker is making a statement (e.g., "This is John calling?"). This intonation raises doubt about the speaker's words and, in some cases, lowers his or her credibility.

Tone can indicate emotions such as sadness, happiness, joy, or irritation. A speaker's tone is very important because others tend to pay more attention to tone than to words. A confident tone encourages others to accept or agree with what the speaker is saying. An uncertain or unenthusiastic tone, on the other hand, tells listeners that what is being said is not important.

Pitch can impact a speaker's credibility. Research shows that listeners perceive speakers with lower-pitched voices as more credible.[84] One study found, for example, that voters perceived male candidates with lower-pitched voices to be more honest and trustworthy than those with higher-pitched voices. They also perceived candidates with lower voices to be more attractive and more dominant.[85] Because women tend to have higher-pitched voices than men, they sometimes seek voice coaching to improve their chances in the workplace.

Speech rate varies from person to person and across cultures. Westerners typically speak at a rate of about 125 words per minute. Slower speech rates may cause listeners to see the speaker as lacking intelligence or credibility. On the other hand, listeners perceive people who pack more words into their speech—195 words per minute in one study—as more credible.[86]

Hesitations—or disfluencies—are pauses or filler sounds such as *umm* or *ahh* in otherwise fluent speech. As mentioned in Chapter 6, use of hesitations can lead to reduced credibility in a speaker because listeners associate these speech patterns with a lack of certainty and confidence.[87] Disfluencies become a problem if they draw attention to themselves.[88]

> **First they came for the Jews and I did not speak out because I was not a Jew. Then they came for the Communists and I did not speak out because I was not a Communist. Then they came for the trade unionists and I did not speak out because I was not a trade unionist. Then they came for me and there was no one left to speak out for me.**
>
> MARTIN NIEMÖLLER

Silence serves many different functions. Silence comforts when words cannot express how we feel. Simply sitting and holding the hand of someone who is grieving can communicate more meaningfully than offering a five-minute speech of condolence. Silence creates a space for listening without judging. Silence punishes when we feel anger or upset with a partner, friend, or family member. Silence adds drama, weight, and impact when we speak in public situations. Most politicians know the power of pausing after making a statement of importance. Comedians use silence to give audiences a chance to process and react to a joke. We employ silence to show defiance. Sometimes our silence conveys our fear, reluctance, or unwillingness to take a stand on an issue. In Germany during World War II, most citizens were afraid to say anything against the Nazi party; in the end, their silence allowed the societal wrongs of those in power.

In talk-oriented cultures, silence demands a response. Canadians and Americans, for example, are often extremely uncomfortable with silence. We feel the need to fill silence with words. For that reason, therapists use silence to force a response from clients who have difficulty expressing their feelings. Investigators use silence to pressure suspects to talk and reveal information. Interviewers use silence to see how job candidates will handle the lapse in verbal communication. Salespersons sometimes use silence to encourage potential customers to reveal what they might be willing to spend on a product.

> "Silence is an integral element of communication; in its absence, words rich in content cannot exist."
> POPE BENEDICT XVI

Although some people are more comfortable than others with silence, few want to live in a world of total silence. To punish and control unruly inmates, prison officials sometimes put them into isolation cells, where they have no communication with other prisoners. Some traditional societies such as the Balinese have used shunning as a means of punishing individuals (and their families) who have committed an offence against the community. For example, Made Rai, an 80-year-old Indonesian man, still feels the effects of a shunning that began many years ago. No villager will look at or speak to Rai or other family members when they leave the family compound. They cannot attend services at the local Hindu temple, and Rai's grandchildren cannot attend the local school. The family will not be able to bury its members in the village cemetery. The Indonesian version of shunning, *kasepekang*, has been likened to "a social and spiritual death sentence."[89]

> "Silence is so freaking loud."
> SARAH DESSEN

Body Movement, Posture, Stance, and Gestures

If you asked people on the street for a definition of nonverbal communication, they are most likely to say *body language*—a term that entered the popular culture in the 1960s as a result of work by Ray Birdwhistell.[90] Birdwhistell coined the term ***kinesics*** in 1952 to refer to communication through body movements, posture, stance, and hand gestures. After filming and analyzing people interacting in social situations, Birdwhistell and his colleagues concluded that no more than 30 to 35 per cent of our communication depends on words—a finding similar to (but not the same as) that of Mehrabian. The remainder depends on nonverbal communication, in which body language plays a large role.

KINESICS Communication through body movements, posture, stance, and hand gestures.

According to the research of Birdwhistell and others, we are less aware of the information we transmit nonverbally than what we transmit verbally. This lack of awareness means that we "leak" information through nonverbal channels, and this **nonverbal leakage** reveals our true inner states. For this reason, the police often pay a lot of attention to the nonverbal behaviour of suspects. Examples of often unconscious body movements include posture changes, repetitive toe or finger tapping, and muscle twitches. Researchers Paul Ekman and Wallace Friesen have suggested that the feet and legs may be the best sources of leakage because we are usually unaware of their activity while we are busy managing facial expressions. The hands are easier to conceal and control, but sometimes they also send unintended information.[91] Take a look at the "Professional Contexts" box for examples of nonverbal leakage that can hamper the career success of women.

NONVERBAL LEAKAGE The nonverbal behaviours that unintentionally reveal true inner states.

> "What you do speaks so loud that I cannot hear what you say."
> RALPH WALDO EMERSON

professionalCONTEXTS

Common Body-Language Mistakes of Women

Raquel Laneri disagrees with teaching young women to speak in soft tones, to sit straight with their legs crossed, and to place their hands on their laps.[92] While others may perceive these nonverbal behaviours as attempts to be polite, respectful, and modest, supervisors and colleagues may see them as weaknesses in a workplace setting. Table 7.1 lists the most common body-language mistakes women make in professional contexts, as well as the messages these nonverbal cues may send.[93]

TABLE 7.1 Common body-language mistakes women make and their perceived messages.

BODY LANGUAGE	PERCEIVED MESSAGE
Tilting head	A sign of listening that some see as an act of submission or even flirting
Folding hands in lap	A sign of weakness and passivity
Hiding hands under a conference table or desk	A sign of untrustworthiness
Crossing legs	A sign of resistance
Excessive smiling	A sign that the person is not serious
Folding arms in front of chest	A sign of insecurity or defensiveness
Playing with or tugging at hair, jewellery, or clothes	A sign of anxiety or flirting

SOURCE: Adapted from R. Laneri, "Body Language Decoded," *Forbes*, 23 June 2009, www.forbes.com/2009/06/23/body-language-first-impression-forbes-woman-leadership-communication_print.html.

When speaking in public, we should try our best to avoid unintentional body movement and remain *centred*. Being centred implies standing tall, with shoulders up and square, and staying—emotionally and physically—in a calm and stable state. As Richard Greene points out in his 2008 documentary, Barack Obama has mastered the art of appearing centred. Greene also discusses the importance of downward gestures that "plant ideas" rather than upward gestures that release ideas to the atmosphere. Gesturing within the power zone (between the shoulders), Greene says, enables speakers to convey "strength and authority."[94]

In addition to affecting how other people perceive us, our body movements and posture also influence how we feel about ourselves. For example, adopting a "power pose" (a physical stance that conveys competence and power) for as little as two minutes leads to changes in testosterone and cortisol levels. These physiological changes make people feel more confident and optimistic; and as a result, they begin to act in a more powerful and assertive way.[95]

from theoryTO PRACTICE

Nonverbal Expressions of Power and Dominance

Harvard University professor Amy Cuddy delivered a TED talk on nonverbal expressions of power and dominance, which is available at www.ted.com/talks/amy_cuddy_your_body_language_shapes_who_you_are.html. Cuddy says that we can change other people's perceptions of our credibility—and even our own body chemistry—simply by changing body positions. After watching the talk, try to apply Cuddy's research findings. Do you have a job interview, a presentation, or a sales pitch coming up? If so, practise your power pose for two minutes before this event and see what happens!

Touch

Touch is, in many regards, our first language. While still in the womb, babies receive vibrations from their mothers' heartbeats, and the amniotic fluid magnifies the experience.[96] Mothers use touch to communicate affection, to warn children of hazards in the environment, and to offer comfort. Tiffany Field, director of the Touch Research Institute at the University of Miami, identified a wide range of benefits linked to massage therapies in babies and young children. These benefits include improved growth in premature babies, more sociable behaviour in children, improved sleep patterns, and better moods.[97] Other studies indicate that even the lightest touch (sitting next to a child on the couch, brushing past them as we move through a room, or giving a quick pat on the head) result in positive benefits.

> **"We need four hugs a day to stay sane, eight hugs a day to stay healthy, and twelve hugs a day to really grow on."**
> **SUE PENDELL**

The messages conveyed through touch also play a vital role in our overall well-being in adulthood. Touch conveys comfort and affection, and these emotional messages help to relieve stress—a contributing factor to many health problems such as high blood pressure, heart disease, and a weakened immune system.[98] Studies have shown that even self-touching—rubbing our necks, arms, or hands; brushing our hair back from our forehead; massaging our temples—can have positive health benefits.[99] See the "Professional Contexts" box for a discussion of how new touch-sensitive technologies can help us transmit messages of comfort and support across great distances.

A classic 1976 experiment demonstrated the importance of even fleeting touch with a stranger. Two conditions applied in the experiment. In returning library cards to students, clerks at a university library either briefly touched the hand of the person or

*professional*CONTEXTS

Need a Hug?

Scientists at several different institutions have designed vests and other devices that add a physical dimension to the online experience. A Media Lab team at the Massachusetts Institute of Technology, for example, created a vest called "Like-a-Hug" that inflates whenever a friend presses the "like" button on your Facebook account. The inflated vest gives a squeeze, which you can return by pulling the fabric more tightly around your body. If also vested, your friend will receive a hug in response. One of the developers of Like-a-Hug, Melissa Chow, says that the virtual hug offers the important sensation of touch that we often lack in our day-to-day lives.[100]

In Japan, designers Dzmitry Tsetserukou and Alena Neviarouskaya advanced the work of the MIT team when they designed a vest that offers "hugs, shivers, tickles, butterflies in the stomach, and thumping heartbeats." The more complicated iFeel_IM (I feel, therefore I am) employs a backpack harness with two fabric hands, a butterfly over the stomach, and a googly eyed heart over the chest. When activated by words with an emotional component, small motors tighten the vest into a hug or create other physical sensations. The software attached to the vest scans the social media for words that would cause an emotional response in face-to-face communication.[101]

Research by Temple Grandin in the 1960s laid the groundwork for these more recent projects. When Grandin visited a relative's cattle ranch in her youth, she noticed that agitated cattle seemed to relax when placed in "squeeze boxes" that applied pressure to large parts of their bodies. Like many other autistic and hyper-sensitive individuals, Grandin could not normally tolerate hugs or other close contact with people; so she decided to transfer her observations of cattle behaviour in the squeeze boxes to her own situation. She designed and constructed a human-sized "hug box," which provided the touch sensation she was unable to get from human contact. She found the pressurized "hug box" calmed her nerves and reduced the frequency of her anxiety attacks.[102]

According to developers working in the area of touch-substitution technologies, the growing and heavy trend toward replacing face-to-face communication with online interaction may prevent us from giving and receiving vital messages of comfort and support through touch. While devices such as Like-a-Hug and iFeel_IM may not be the ultimate answer for most of us, they may be a step in the direction of the future.

returned the card without touching the student's hand. Follow-up interviews revealed that students who had been touched gave higher evaluations to both the clerk and the library. The results applied even when the students did not notice the touch.

Research has also shown that waitresses get bigger tips if they touch their customers. People buy more if someone greets and touches them as they enter the store. Strangers are more apt to help others who make physical contact at the time they make their requests. We give higher evaluations to doctors, teachers, and managers who are not afraid to connect through touch with patients, students, and employees.[103]

We also gain much information about others by touching them. We learn whether people are open or closed to contact, whether they are tense or relaxed, and whether they are warm or cold (both physically and emotionally). That knowledge can help us to interact more sensitively with others.[104]

The exact meaning of a touch can vary, based on a number of factors. We react differently to touch in the workplace than in dance clubs or doctors' offices.[105] Thus, context matters, with most forms of touch being off bounds in office environments. Other factors include the intensity and duration of the touch, as well as its location. The identity and gender of the person who touches us—and our relationship to that person—also matter. Finally, as is the case with most other communication behaviours, cultural norms and expectations affect how we interpret touch.

Along with Brits and Americans, Canadians live in a largely touch-phobic but touch-hungry society. We fear touch at the same time that we crave it. Some say that the only truly acceptable touch zones for casual acquaintances in North America are the back, the shoulder, the arm, and the hand.[106] We restrict contact with other parts of the body to close family members and intimate partners. The only real exceptions come in moments of deep grief, fear, or extreme joy, when our desire for comfort or emotional sharing is strong enough to overcome our reservations about being touched. Most people list hugs, pats, and other more intimate touch behaviours as appropriate in those circumstances.[107]

The tendency to restrict touch to family and intimate partners is far less common in most other countries in the world. According to Sue Johnson, author of *Hold Me Tight: Seven Conversations for a Lifetime of Love*, Americans "hold, hug, pat, stroke, fondle, and caress each other" much less often than do people in other countries.[108] The French, Italians, and Africans, on the other hand, see touch as a natural and vital way of interacting with others. Most southern European women walk arm-in-arm; and many Arab, Indian, and African men hold hands as they walk.[109] In 1987, the cameras captured then Canadian prime minister Brian Mulroney walking uneasily and self-consciously, hand-in-hand, with Zimbabwean leader Robert Mugabe. To avoid further hand-holding at one point, Mulroney clasped his hands behind his back; undeterred, Mugabe reached behind Mulroney's back to grab his hand.[110]

© Alex RF/Alamy

Canadian psychologist Sidney Jourard visited coffee shops in countries around the world in an informal effort to discover how many times people touch each other when interacting in those settings. The numbers (based on an hourly average) varied markedly from country to country: London, England, 0; Gainesville, Florida, 2; Paris, France, 110; and San Juan, Puerto Rico, more than 180. People tend to touch more in warm than in cold climates, perhaps because of more accessible skin and the positive effects of sunlight on mood. In addition, less religious people touch more than more religious people, possibly because of religious taboos against inappropriate contact.[111]

Conservative Mid-range Provocative

Photo source: J.G. Noll, C.E. Shenk, J.E. Barnes, and F.W. Putnam, "Childhood Abuse, Avatar Choices, and Other Risk Factors Associated with Internet-Initiated Victimization of Adolescent Girls," *Pediatrics* 123, (2009).

Clothing and Personal Artifacts

Clothing and personal artifacts play an important role overall in how we perceive a person's social identity, attitudes, mood, and values.[112] A necklace with a Star of David suggests, for example, the religious identity of the person. The garb of a Roman Catholic priest suggests both the order to which he belongs and his position within the hierarchy. Youth cultures and motorcycle gangs have their own modes of dress, intended to identify members' affiliations.

In short, our manner of dress conveys messages, intended or unintended, to others. A 2009 study by Jennie Noll and her colleagues looked for connections between how adolescent girls presented themselves on the Internet and a childhood history of abuse. The researchers also looked for connections between these self-presentations and victimization by Internet predators.[113] They asked participants in their study (girls aged 14 to 17 years) to fill out personal surveys and to create 3-D **avatars** for their online interactions. The adolescents designed and dressed the avatars from a range of body types and clothing. Afterwards, the researchers categorized these avatars as conservative, mid-range, or provocative. (See the photo above.) In their analysis, the researchers found that the girls with a history of abuse were more likely to create provocative avatars that conveyed messages about sexuality. Furthermore, girls who created provocative avatars were more likely to receive online sexual advances with the potential to lead to offline encounters, thus opening the door for sexual victimization. (Complete the activity in the "From Theory to Practice" box to see what you might communicate about yourself through an avatar.)

> **"Clothes and manners do not make the man; but when he is made, they greatly improve his appearance."**
> HENRY WARD BEECHER

AVATAR An online visual representation of an individual.

Researchers at the University of Calgary published a study in February 2013 on how dress affects our perceptions of physicians.[114] In their study, they asked visiting family members in intensive care units (ICUs) whether the dress of the ICU doctor was important to them. The participants stated that they did not believe dress made a difference. However, a second set of responses proved the opposite. Following the initial questioning, the researchers showed participants photos in which models posed as doctors and asked them to pick out the photos of their preferred

from theory TO PRACTICE

Creating an Avatar

Join the virtual reality community Second Life and create an avatar for yourself. Discuss your choices of body type and clothing with other members of your class. Does your avatar resemble you? Do you feel a personal connection with it? Would you feel uncomfortable if another avatar made an inappropriate comment about the appearance of your avatar? What do you think your avatar reveals about who you really are?

physicians. More than half of the participants chose pictures of models wearing white coats, and nearly one-quarter chose models wearing surgical scrubs. Less often chosen were models in business attire and casual clothing. Participants judged the models in lab coats and surgical scrubs to be competent, honest, caring, and knowledgeable—judgments that were largely unconscious and based on dress. (See the "Human Diversity" box titled "Muslim Women and Workplace Discrimination" for a related discussion on how clothing can affect hiring practices in the workplace.)

Stanley Milgram's classic experiment on obedience also identified the role of dress in conveying status and authority.[115] In the aftermath of the atrocities of World War II, Milgram set out to determine how far people would go when someone in authority told them to obey orders. In this experiment, a man in a technician's coat (a symbol of authority) told participating volunteers to administer increasingly strong electric shocks to "learners" whenever the learners made a mistake. The volunteers thought that the purpose of the experiment was to discover the effects of physical punishment on learning, and they did not realize that the learners were allies of the researchers, trained in advance to act as though they were being shocked. Close to two-thirds of the volunteers followed orders until the end, administering shocks even when the learner screamed out in pain and begged for the experiment to end. Eventually the "learners" grew silent (suggesting death). Like the more recent study by the University of Calgary researchers, Milgram's study demonstrated how people attach credibility to certain modes of dress.

Objects also communicate. To see how, let us take a look at the room of Carol Ann, a 19-year-old university student who lives with her parents. Her room is brightly lit. She always keeps her door closed. She keeps her clothes folded neatly in her closet. A box of incense and several candles are lying on her bureau. Two copper statues of dolphins are on display beside her bed. A pink teddy bear sits on her bed. A laptop rests on her desk. A number of school books are lying on a table near the window.

What do you think Carol Ann is saying about herself through her personal objects? Her use of bright lighting may signify a spontaneous and happy personality. Since she keeps her door closed, we can conclude that she probably values her privacy. The neatly folded clothes suggest that she likes organization in her life. The incense and candles give the impression that she might appreciate quiet moments of alone time. The dolphin statues could indicate her love of dolphins or be a reminder of special time spent

humanDIVERSITY

Muslim Women and Workplace Discrimination

When we finally get an interview after sending out what seems like hundreds of applications, we want to look our best. We dress to convey to our potential employer that we are confident, professional, and the right person for the job. In a professional environment, a very short skirt or a low-cut blouse can send the wrong message and compromise a woman's chances of being hired. But what about religious attire like the hijab, a headscarf worn by Muslim women?

In a study conducted in the United States, some candidates applying for jobs at stores or restaurants wore a hijab; others did not.[116] The researchers found evidence of formal discrimination against the hijab-wearing candidates, who received significantly fewer job callbacks than the other women. They were also less likely to be asked to complete an application.

Workplace discrimination affects everyone. The employee experiences lower self-esteem and a lessened sense of well-being, including increased stress, anxiety, and depression.[117] Negative work environments contribute to low organizational commitment, poor job performance, and high turnover rates.[118] In this lose–lose situation, the organization as a whole suffers.

professionalCONTEXTS

The Message of the Pearls

On 4 February 2013, Canadian geneticist Turi King took the speaker's podium at the University of Leicester, England. In a much-anticipated and internationally televised event, King stood ready to announce the results of DNA testing on a skeleton unearthed at the Grey Friars excavation in Leicester. Many believed the skeleton to be the long-lost remains of Richard III; however, the university had refused to release the findings prior to this occasion. They had sworn all participants, including King, to secrecy.[119] King had devised, however, her own secret code with her father for this occasion. She had told him that if she wore a specific strand of pearls for the announcement, he would know the DNA was a confirmed match. That Monday, King wore the pearls. "That was my little signal to him . . . . I wanted him to know."[120]

on the ocean. Carol Ann's attachment to her pink teddy bear could symbolize a close relationship with the person who gave it to her. The laptop and school books probably suggest her status as a student. In short, based on the display of her personal belongings, we can conclude that Carol Ann is probably a private, studious, and happy young adult who values comfort and relationships.

As this example reveals, our personal artifacts—the things we keep and display to others—communicate who we are. Much of the time, we are not conscious of the extent to which our personal belongings convey information about us. However, sometimes people use objects in a deliberate way to convey a nonverbal message. In the example cited in the "Professional Contexts" box titled "The Message of the Pearls," you can see how one young woman used jewellery to convey a special message to her father.

Colour

In 1971, Swiss scientist Max Lüscher conducted one of the earliest studies into colour preferences. His research resulted in the well-known but controversial Lüscher colour test, which claims to be able to reveal deep psychological truths about individuals who take the test. As an example, Lüscher assigned personality characteristics to people based on how they ranked eight different colours: blue, green, red, yellow, violet, brown, black, and grey.[121]

Ignoring the personality dimension of colours, a 1973 study by Charles Osgood focussed on cross-cultural differences in perceptions of colour. Osgood asked people from 23 different cultures how they felt about different colours. What meanings did they attach to the colours? What were their emotional responses to the colours? Osgood found that most cultures felt similarly about the colours. For example, most people (regardless of cultural origins) saw red as a strong and active colour and black as a strong but passive colour. They saw yellow, white, and grey as weak colours. They felt good about white, blue, and green; and they felt bad about grey and black. Overall, they preferred brighter colours.[122]

© Adafir/Alamy

Culture influences the meanings that people attach to colours. For example, *white* is the colour of mourning in China and Japan, whereas *purple* signifies mourning in Thailand. In Egypt, *yellow* and *orange* indicate mourning; in some parts of Africa, *red* is the colour of mourning. *Black* is the colour of mourning and death in the United States, Canada, Britain, and most European nations. When a Japanese company marketed black scooters in India, Indian mothers would not allow their sons to purchase the scooters because they also associated the colour *black* with death.[123]

A 1991 study used the Lüscher colour test to compare how people in China, South Korea, Japan, and the United States felt about colours.[124] The researchers asked participants to indicate the colours they associated with 13 words such as *expensive*, *happy*, *love*, and *dependable*. As in Osgood's study, the responses attached to some colours showed consistency across cultures; however, the meanings attached to other colours varied from country to country. Table 7.2 shows some examples of what the researchers found.

In today's global economy, businesses are increasingly concerned with how people in other countries will perceive their products. Using a colour with negative associations can be a costly mistake. A Canadian airline had to revert to its original colour scheme after discovering that its South Asian clientele associated the new colours with bad luck.[125] In other cases, businesses are ignoring traditional colour preferences within their own countries in an effort to appeal to a global market. Thai Airways, for example, adopted purple for its brand colour, despite the negative associations of purple in Thailand. In much of the rest of the world, purple evokes connections with royalty, wealth, and luxury.[126]

Cultural colour associations are also changing in other areas. Despite the historical associations of white with mourning, for example, most Chinese brides now choose white gowns with red jackets. The traditional colour for a wedding dress in China is red, the colour of good luck and happiness. As design expert Cassandra Gill has noted, companies are in many regards in a "colour no-man's land"—a business landscape with few stable rules regarding colour association. Globalization is bringing common understandings of colour to many parts of the world; yet at the same time, we will probably never see agreement across all cultures and people.[127]

TABLE 7.2 Colour associations in China, South Korea, Japan, and the United States.

	ASSOCIATIONS IN			
COLOUR	China	South Korea	Japan	United States
Grey	inexpensive, low quality	—	inexpensive, low quality	expensive, high quality
Brown	inexpensive	—	inexpensive	inexpensive
Purple	expensive, love	expensive, love	expensive	inexpensive, love
Black	expensive, powerful	expensive, powerful	expensive, powerful	expensive, powerful
Red	love, adventure	love, adventure	love, adventure	love, adventure
Blue	high quality	high quality, sincerity, trustworthiness	high quality, sincerity, trustworthiness, dependability	high quality, sincerity, trustworthiness, dependability
Green	pure, sincerity, trustworthiness, dependability	pure	pure	—
Yellow	happiness, progress	happiness	happiness	—

SOURCE: Adapted from L. Jacobs, C. Keown, R. Worthley, and K. Ghymn, "Cross-cultural Colour Comparisons: Global Marketers Beware!," *International Marketing Review* 8, no. 3 (1991): 21–30.

Although its meaning might not always be set in stone, colour remains a silent but powerful communication tool with close links to culture, religion, social traditions, and politics. It influences our wardrobes, our home decorations, and our product choices.

HOW SPACE, TIME, AND PHYSICAL SETTINGS COMMUNICATE

Concepts of space and time fundamentally shape how we perceive our world. Not surprisingly, then, our notions about personal space, **territoriality**, **chronemics**, and spatial arrangements play important nonverbal roles in how we communicate with others. The following sections will discuss the many ways in which these concepts convey information, influence how we interpret information, and establish contexts in which communication can occur.

TERRITORIALITY Our desire and efforts to mark our territory and defend it against invasion.

CHRONEMICS The study of how people perceive, structure, value, and react to time.

PROXEMICS The study of how people perceive and use space.

Personal Space

The term ***proxemics*** refers to how people perceive and use personal space and distance. Edward T. Hall, anthropologist and pioneer in the field of intercultural communication, says that an invisible bubble surrounds each of us. This bubble moves with us wherever we go, and it expands or contracts to enable us to interact comfortably with others at four different distances: intimate, personal, social, and public (Figure 7.2). Our culture, the circumstances surrounding the interaction, and the nature of the social relationships determine the distance at which we choose to interact with others. Typically we are aware of the existence of this bubble only when someone violates its boundaries.[128]

For many cultures, especially in the West, the intimate zone extends from our bodies to a maximum of 0.5 metres. Within this zone, we make physical contact and exchange close personal communication. The personal zone, which we reserve for interactions with close friends and family members, extends from 0.5 metres to 1.5 metres. We use social distance, which goes from 1.5 metres to 3.5 metres, to interact with more casual acquaintances. The zone used for public discourse and speaking extends from 3.5 metres to 7.5 metres. The appropriateness of gestures, postures, and vocal qualities differs from zone to zone.[129] In addition, the exact boundary of each zone differs from person to person, depending not only on cultural influences but also on personality and personal preferences.

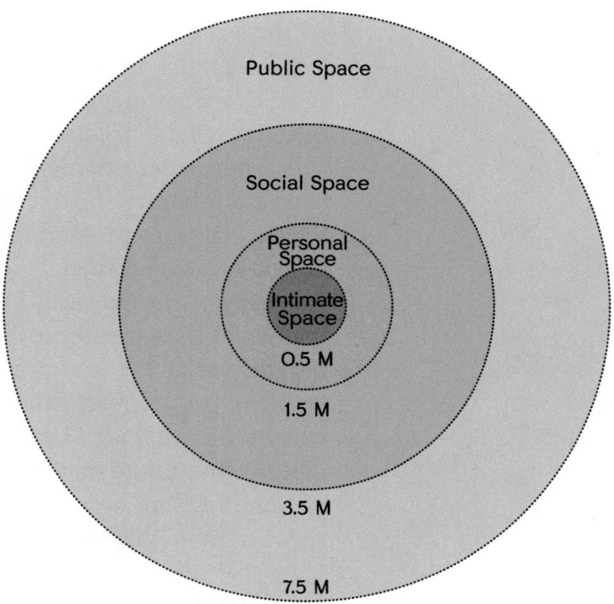

FIGURE 7.2 **Zones of space used in interpersonal transactions.**

SOURCE: Based on http://en.wikipedia.org/wiki/File:Personal_Space.svg.

Territoriality

The term *territoriality* originally referred to the way by which animals mark and defend their territory against trespassing by others of their species. Dogs and cats establish claims to territory, for example, by urinating on trees and vegetation. Some animals will defend their territories to the death.

Although most of us do not go to such extreme lengths to identify and protect our personal territory, we all engage in territorial behaviours. In an open-concept office, for example, an employee might become extremely agitated if a co-worker places her belongings—even temporarily—on a desk that he considers to be his territory. In response to such an act, the employee might silently move the co-worker's belongings to a different spot to communicate his disapproval. Homeowners often build fences or plant hedges to establish personal territory. If someone violates these territorial markers, the homeowner might send a nonverbal message to deter future violations—for example, by making a fence taller or planting shrubs with painfully sharp leaves.

Chronemics

Chronemics refers to the study of how people perceive, structure, value, and react to time.[130] Based on his work in this area, Edward T. Hall identified two types of cultures, which view time in drastically different ways: **monochronic cultures** and **polychronic cultures**.[131]

MONOCHRONIC CULTURES Cultures that view time as rigidly linear and rely heavily on clocks and schedules to regulate events.

POLYCHRONIC CULTURES Cultures that view time as elastic and believe events will happen when they are meant to happen.

Western societies typically take a monochronic approach to time. In Western societies, we buy, spend, manage, save, dedicate, waste, pass, arrange, make, and account for time. We divide our years into months and weeks and our days into hours, minutes, and seconds. We live by the clock, with deadlines, timelines, and rigid schedules. We arrive at our places of employment at a given time, take scheduled breaks, and end the work day at a pre-set time. We have agendas and calendars to inform us of meeting times and appointments, and we are impatient when kept waiting. In monochronic time systems such as ours, people engage in only one activity at a time. Once they complete one activity or task, they move to the next in a sequential way. In monochronic systems, time is money—a valuable commodity to be preserved and respected. We can find monochronic systems in countries such as Canada, the United States, Switzerland, Germany, and the United Kingdom.

This obsession with measuring time does not characterize all cultures. Some regard time as a much more elastic concept. They believe that we are where we are supposed to be at any given moment, and things happen when they are supposed to happen. To question a person's lateness or failure to show up for an appointment is to question the role of fate in determining our lives. Polychronic societies see the emphasis on time and clocks as arbitrary and out of phase with the cycles of nature and the seasons. They value relationships over tasks; and as in the case of Aboriginal Australians, they place family obligations over artificially set schedules (see the "For Starters" box in Chapter 3). Plans are easily made and easily broken in polychronic time systems, where many things can happen at the same time. So someone might schedule several different tasks or meetings for the same time period. People who live in a more elastic time culture know that they can postpone or cancel some tasks to accommodate others, and no one will be surprised or offended by the delays. When people speak of *tomorrow* in a polychronic culture, they might mean *the day after today* or they might mean *next week*. We can find polychronic time systems in countries such as Brazil, Saudi Arabia, Egypt, Mexico, and those of sub-Saharan Africa.

Buildings and Spatial Arrangements

Buildings, their layouts, and furnishings tell employees and others a great deal about organizations and their values. A building from the 1970s in Germany, for example, employed a staircase design to encourage employees to work hard to rise through the ranks. At the base, the twelve-tiered structure housed the lowest-echelon workers. The building visibly narrowed in stair-step fashion at each additional floor until, at the highest level, the top administrators occupied only a fraction of the floor space used at the lowest levels. The building stood as a strong symbol of the very limited number of employees who would reach the highest levels of the organization.

This building also typified the tendency of management to set aside the top floors for the president of the company, the chairman of the board, and other top-line executives.[132] In modern offices, these upper levels are often accessible only by private elevators, to which top executives hold keys. Locating senior executives in secure offices on the top floors implies a tight control over the day-to-day activities of the organization. The residence of senior executives on the ground floor, on the other hand, implies surrendering responsibility for the routine functioning of the organization.[133]

The arrangement of offices on any given floor also communicates the office hierarchy. Corner offices with windows usually house senior executives and heads of departments. The most powerful executives have the offices with the greatest square footage and the most windows. Secretaries and receptionists often control access and act as gatekeepers to these executives and department heads.[134]

The furnishings and décor of office buildings also send messages to employees and visitors. Law firms use dark woods, muted colours, deep reds, leathers, and antiques to attract wealthy clients. Studies have shown these kinds of rich tones and hues have better drawing power than glass, chrome, and other more modern design elements. Rare, expensive office decorations (e.g., valuable works of art) can point to the fact that little (if any) power is available to newcomers.[135] Such decorations also communicate the financial standing of the organization to current and potential clients.

As suggested with the earlier example, the layout of an office or building can communicate a great deal about the status of employees within the organization. The following points summarize major findings with respect to the interaction between physical setting and status.

First, the higher your position in the organization, the greater and better space you will enjoy.[136] CEOs and other executives command larger offices located at corners, situated farther from the centre of activities, and often on top floors of buildings. They also have higher-quality furnishings. In most buildings, secretaries, clerks, and others with low statuses occupy the least desirable spaces (e.g., noisy areas that lack dividing walls, doors, and windows).[137]

Second, the higher your position in the organization, the less likely you are to require or use the space. The executive who spends his day in board meetings, lunches with clients, and takes tours of the plant gets the oversized office with scenic views, bookcases, and comfortable seating. The secretary, who is responsible for doing the paper work and being available to answer the telephone and greet visitors, gets the small office with no windows. In most organizations, an upside-down relationship exists between the amount of space occupied by an individual and the time spent in the office.

Third, the higher your position in the organization, the more likely your space will be guarded by secretaries, doors, and rules governing access.[138] These barriers discourage employees and others from entering higher-level employees' spaces without first calling to make an appointment or at least knocking on the door. Little prevents the spaces of lower-level employees from being invaded by others.

Fourth, the higher your position in the organization, the more flexibility you will have to alter the setting.[139] Lower-level employees operating in public and highly visible positions

© mediaphotos/iStockphoto

are expected to treat their physical space as unchangeable and inflexible. Higher-status employees are often allowed or even encouraged to put up artwork, choose furnishings, and adjust the layouts of their spaces.

Fifth, power weakens with distance from the source of power. Those located closest to sources of power gain status from the nearness, as in the case of a secretary or an assistant. Aides or colleagues located on another part of the floor or in another building do not benefit in the same way from the closeness to power.[140]

In addition to organizing spaces to communicate the relative status of employees, some organizations try to create workspaces that are warm and inviting. These organizations recognize that most employees are more productive when they feel comfortable in the physical spaces in which they work. One way to make employees feel at ease is to use **soft architecture** and allow employees to personalize their workspaces—to paint walls in colours of their choice, to hang pictures, to reposition furniture, and to place personal artifacts as they wish. In contrast to soft architecture, **hard architecture** establishes a much colder atmosphere, as it discourages efforts at personalization. We can see examples of hard architecture in buildings with concrete walls and stairways, graffiti-resistant paint, and metal hand railings. We can also see evidence of hard architecture in the granite floors of shopping malls, seats bolted to the floors in college and university classrooms, the steel cages that house prisoners, and the metal fences around school yards.[141] In hard office buildings, employees cannot move their desks or other furnishings, they cannot control the temperatures of their personal workspaces, and rules discourage them from displaying personal items.

SOFT ARCHITECTURE Buildings and other structures that allow personalization of spaces.

HARD ARCHITECTURE Buildings and other structures designed to stand strong and to resist human imprint.

Finally, physical settings have the power to bring people together or to push them apart. Humphrey Osmond identified these tendencies as the **sociopetal** and **sociofugal** functions of settings.[142] Sociopetal layouts include chairs set facing one another or set in a circle, oval, or horseshoe pattern. Such layouts encourage people to maintain eye contact and to talk to each other. Sociofugal layouts, on the other hand, tend to make eye contact and conversation more difficult. We can see these sorts of layouts in the straight lines of bolted-down seats in auditoriums, airports, railway stations, and many college classrooms.

SOCIOPETAL SETTING A physical setting that brings people together.

SOCIOFUGAL SETTING A physical setting that pushes people apart.

QUESTIONING THE WORK OF PIONEERS IN THE FIELD OF NONVERBAL COMMUNICATION

A number of critics have questioned the work of Paul Ekman and Albert Mehrabian, the acknowledged pioneers and groundbreakers in the field of nonverbal communication.

The results of some studies have called Ekman's findings on lie detection into question. A 2010 study tried to determine, for example, whether viewers of *Lie to Me* had more sophisticated abilities than non-viewers to identify liars. (Recall from the "For Starters" box at the beginning of this chapter that Ekman's research served as the basis for this show, and Ekman acts as the show's science consultant.) The results of this study indicated that viewers, despite their "training," were no better able than non-viewers to pinpoint liars. They were, however, more suspicious.[143] On the basis of studies such as this one, some critics urge that law enforcement and security personnel should rely less heavily on nonverbal cues when interviewing and questioning suspects.[144]

Others say that part of the difficulty in relying on nonverbal behaviour comes from its culturally specific nature.[145] For example, not every culture responds to the loss of a loved one in the same way.[146] The research of anthropologist Margaret Mead showed that the Balinese people celebrate rather than mourn the death of a loved one, as they see death as passage into the next life.[147] Consequently, you cannot rely on their facial expressions to determine their loss. Similarly, African Americans in New Orleans traditionally honoured the lives of deceased family members with lively street parades. On the way to the cemetery, the musicians played mournful and spiritual songs; however, on the return, the music and mood became more joyful. A "second line" of onlookers joined in, dancing and twirling umbrellas to spirited tunes such as "When the Saints Go Marching In." An onlooker unfamiliar with this custom would never have known by the facial expressions and body language of the mourners that they had just buried a loved one.

Critics also question the claims of Albert Mehrabian that more than 90 per cent of our communication occurs through nonverbal as opposed to verbal channels. In defence of his work, however, Mehrabian says that the popular media have extended his findings beyond appropriate limits. Authors of popular books and expert commentators in televised courtroom trials apply his findings to almost every communication event. Mehrabian himself says that his findings apply only to situations where communicators are talking about their feelings or attitudes.[148] In other words, when we try to understand the emotional message of another person (what they are feeling), we will rely more heavily on *how* they express their feelings than *what* they say.

TIPS FOR IMPROVING NONVERBAL COMMUNICATION SKILLS

As we have seen in this chapter, effective nonverbal communication involves attentiveness and awareness of context and cultural norms. The following offers some practical tips that will help you to improve your nonverbal communication skills at work, at school, and in your personal encounters.

Use nonverbal channels of communication to communicate emotional information and offer support. If your partner arrives home stressed or sad, give her a sympathetic smile, offer him a massage, or simply hold her hand. Give a reassuring hug to a family member who is upset or frustrated.

Remember that certain facial expressions, gestures, and other nonverbal cues mean different things in different cultures. If you are travelling to a foreign country, do some research on what common gestures and expressions mean in that country; such preparation can save you from making an awkward, embarrassing, or confusing mistake.

Use immediacy behaviours to increase your likeability. When you are listening to someone speak, nod your head, smile, lean toward the other person, and make eye contact. Interacting with others in this way will encourage them to like, trust, and value you.

Adopt a "power pose" before your next job interview or presentation. Stand tall and strong, put your hands on your hips, take up space, and hold your head high. The physiological changes that come with the power posture will help you to feel more confident and, in turn, you will *look* more confident.

Ensure your nonverbal messages match your verbal messages. If your words say one thing and your nonverbal cues demonstrate something else, others may question your sincerity.

Use nonverbal cues to demonstrate that you are listening and to regulate conversations. As we saw in Chapter 5, nonverbal cues that tell the speaker he or she is important. Remember to take turns when conversing with others and use nonverbal cues to let others know when you want to speak and when it is their turn to speak.

Avoid nonverbal leakage as much as possible. Try to see yourself as others might see you and watch to be sure you are not displaying signs of nervousness or discomfort. Examples include jiggling your foot, playing with your hair, or tapping your pen. Once you have identified your leakage behaviours, make a conscious effort to avoid them.

Use touch in a manner appropriate to the context. Remember that not everyone is comfortable with being touched, and touching others is not socially acceptable in all settings. Be particularly careful to avoid overly familiar or aggressive physical contact in professional environments, as co-workers may feel offended or even assaulted by this sort of contact.

Wear clothing that reflects the image you want to present to others. If you are going to a job interview, wear neat, relatively conservative business clothes. If you are going to a friend's birthday party, wear something casual that suggests to others that you are friendly and approachable. Remember that other people form their first impressions of you based on the clothes you wear and other aspects of your personal appearance. Making a good first impression is important, as it will improve your future interactions with a person.

SUMMARY

In this chapter, we have explored the differences between verbal and nonverbal communication. We learned that confusion sometimes exists with respect to language codes in which unspoken symbols represent letters or words on a one-to-one basis (e.g., semaphore, Morse code, American Sign Language, and Quebec Sign Language). We saw that nonverbal communication fulfills some primary functions such as replacing or substituting for verbal messages, complementing or adding to verbal communication, regulating interaction, relieving tension and satisfying bodily needs, and conveying emotion. We also saw that nonverbal communication fulfills social functions of a secondary nature—making first impressions, violating expectations, getting people to like us, making connections, and building and maintaining relationships.

Next we examined the many channels that convey nonverbal messages: facial expressions; eye contact and gaze; vocal cues; silence; body movement, posture, stance, and gestures; touch; clothing and personal artifacts; and colour. We looked at how concepts of space and time—personal space, territoriality, chronemics, and spatial arrangements—convey information, influence how we interpret information, and establish context for communication. Finally, we critically examined the work of early pioneers working in the realm of nonverbal communication, and we concluded with some tips for improving nonverbal communication skills in professional and everyday contexts.

REVIEW QUESTIONS

1. What are the primary and secondary functions of nonverbal communication? How have you used nonverbal communication in your own interactions with others?
2. What are the benefits and challenges of attaining immediacy in different contexts? Refer to specific contexts (e.g., public speaking, working in an office, teaching).
3. What is the role of nonverbal communication in helping to build and maintain relationships? Why is nonverbal communication particularly important in romantic relationships?
4. In Western cultures, eye contact is a sign of confidence and interest in others. Can you think of some cultural contexts where direct or sustained eye contact is *not* appropriate? What other cross-cultural differences in nonverbal communication might arise?
5. What is paralanguage? What are some common examples?
6. What are some situations in which nonverbal communication might play a role in displaying power in the workplace? How could these situations affect the organizational climate?
7. Which of the tips for improving nonverbal communication discussed in this chapter do you think might help you the most in improving your communication skills? Can you think of other helpful pointers not discussed in the chapter?

SUGGESTED ACTIVITIES

1. The next time you are in a public place, look carefully at the people around you. Who looks approachable and who does not? What types of body language are these people using? Do you think you look approachable?
2. Create and video record a mock job interview with a friend or classmate. Watch the recording and analyze what you did well or badly in the interview in terms of nonverbal behaviours.
3. Grab a group of friends or classmates and play charades. (You can find specific rules online.) Did you find it difficult to understand what the actor was conveying? What kinds of nonverbal channels did players use to convey messages? Which channels were most effective in getting the ideas across?
4. Get into a group and write down several emotions. Taking turns, select an emotion from your list and express it to the group. Use only facial expressions—no words or gestures. Once the group guesses the emotion, move to the next person. Which emotions were easier or harder to convey?
5. Watch a Charlie Chaplin movie clip on YouTube and jot down your ideas regarding what is happening in the clip. Be prepared to share your responses with the whole class. Discuss any difficulties you encountered in trying to interpret the messages in the silent film.
6. Display some nonverbal expressions for happiness, such as smiling and laughing. Now display some nonverbal expressions for anger, such as frowning and pouting. Was one message more difficult to demonstrate than the other?

CHAPTER 8

Building and Maintaining Relationships

CHAPTER OUTLINE

learning OBJECTIVES

- To learn about the importance of healthy relationships
- To recognize the needs that influence our relationships
- To differentiate between relationships of circumstance and relationships of choice
- To understand the contexts in which people develop relationships
- To recognize the predictable stages through which romantic relationships move
- To learn about self-disclosure and its role in building trust and intimacy
- To learn how to improve your own relationships with family, friends, work colleagues, and romantic partners

forSTARTERS

Emotional Contagion

Andrea worked for Trans-Texas Airways, based in Houston, Texas, in the mid-1960s.[1] Unlike its larger competitors—Braniff, Delta, and American—Trans-Texas was a small boutique airline. When flying with Trans-Texas, customers often had to go out of their way and switch flights several times before arriving at their final destination. Worse, the wait times and layovers were often inconvenient. When customers called to book flights, however, they were rarely familiar with the schedules of the other airlines and they did not know their options. Unlike today's travellers who usually find their own routings on the Internet, customers in the 1960s relied heavily on the recommendations of airline personnel.

Because Andrea was concerned about the well-being of her customers, she did not feel comfortable booking them on unnecessarily expensive or unreasonable routings. If she felt that the routing was too difficult or costly for an older person or a family, she directed them to the other airlines rather than offering options on Trans-Texas. At other times, she suggested ways to combine travel on Trans-Texas with travel on the other airlines. She always tried to find the best routing for customers, whether that happened to be on Trans-Texas or a competitor.

This behaviour did not reflect company policy. Like most companies, Trans-Texas expected reservation clerks to book as many flights as possible on their airline. However, Andrea believed—and Daniel Goleman, author of *Working with Emotional Intelligence*, agrees—that empathic responses secure more business for companies in the long run. These responses secure more business because they put the needs of the customer above the bottom line, and people return to businesses that care about them: "Top sales people . . . apply a different approach: empathic concern, where you sense and care about the person's needs. Rather than persuade someone to buy the wrong thing, these sales stars make sure they match the customer's needs to what they offer—and may even send them elsewhere if need be. This builds a lasting relationship of trust—and a customer who returns again and again."[2]

© Steve Debenport/iStockphoto

In his studies of emotional intelligence, Goleman identified four major components: empathy (as described above), self-awareness, motivation, and social skills. He says that these four qualities play a major role in personal and professional success. He further argues that EQ (emotional quotient) is more important than IQ (intelligence quotient), in life in general and in the workplace in particular.

A favourite example of the benefits of emotional intelligence comes from an early study with four-year-old preschool children. In this study, Walter Mischel of Stanford University placed a single marshmallow before each child. Then he told the children that they could eat their marshmallows immediately, or they could wait for him to return

INTRODUCTION

Humans are social animals, connected with others in a complex web of relationships that are built and sustained through communication. In prehistoric times as now, these interpersonal relationships helped to ensure the survival of our species. We have always relied on others to assist in meeting our most basic needs such as food, safety, companionship, and reproduction.

In this chapter, we will look at different kinds of relationships, contexts within which relationships develop, reasons for forming relationships, the importance of setting boundaries in relationships, and the stages through which our most personal from an errand. If they waited, they would get a second marshmallow. In other words, the children had the opportunity for a second marshmallow if they were able to show enough self-control to delay eating the first one.

Fourteen years later, Mischel returned to the children, who had just graduated from high school. To his surprise, he learned that the children who had resisted the temptation of gobbling the first marshmallow in his absence had dramatically different outcomes from those who showed less impulse control. They had scored more than 200 points higher on their college entrance exams (SATs), they were more popular with their peers, and they were better able to function in situations where they did not get immediate rewards. Goleman relates the results of the marshmallow study to his ideas of emotional intelligence. He says that the impulse control, demonstrated by one-third of the children, related more to EQ or social intelligence than to IQ.

Out of the four characteristics of emotional intelligence (empathy, self-awareness, motivation, and social skills), Goleman puts a particular emphasis on empathy. By *empathy*, we mean the ability to feel with another person, as Andrea did in her interactions with customers of Trans-Texas Airways. Andrea was able to look at each booking request from the perspective of the other person. Empathy does not require us to believe as another person believes or even to accept another's point of view as our own. But it does imply that we have to be open to other ways of seeing reality. Goleman believes that emotional intelligence relates to love and spirituality—the best parts of the human spirit.

In line with this idea, Goleman coined the term *emotional contagion*. He says that we can "catch" the emotions of other people much like we catch a cold. So if we sense that our boss is feeling frustrated and angry, we may begin to feel frustrated and angry. If a colleague at work is feeling insecure and troubled, we may contract the same emotions. On the other hand, if our boss is feeling happy and positive, we may "catch" those feelings. Goleman also says that optimism is a predictor of success in the workplace and in life in general. When we are around positive and optimistic people, we feel more positive and confident. Many people who practise meditation recommend "zipping" oneself up after a session. Like Goleman, they believe that the emotional energy of others can have a physical impact and that meditation opens us to those potentially negative energies.

If you look around on the Internet, you will find that EQ has gained an important place in the organizational world. Employers are using scores on EQ tests to profile, interview, hire, and evaluate employees. They are sending lower-level employees for EQ training in customer relations and customer service. They are sending managers for leadership training, and executives are signing up for private coaching in EQ. Goleman says that we may not be able to improve our IQ, but all of us can improve our emotional intelligence. By googling "emotional intelligence," "social intelligence," or "EQ," you can find much more about recently published books and activities related to EQ.

This discussion should lead you to think about the following kinds of questions, which are addressed in this chapter: Have you experienced emotional contagion in your personal or professional relationships? In other words, have the good or bad moods of your friends or colleagues rubbed off on you? How can you protect yourself from the impact of negative people and benefit from the influence of optimistic and positive people? How does Goleman's theory relate to the development of healthy relationships in workplace settings? Are managers and employees with high EQ more likely to meet the needs of workers in terms of inclusion, control, and affection/openness? Why?

relationships move. We will also cover tips for building and maintaining healthy relationships with friends, family, romantic partners, and co-workers.

THE VALUE OF RELATIONSHIPS

Social capital theory explains that our social relationships and networks have value that can translate into important personal and business outcomes. Pierre Bourdieu defined social capital as a resource, based on connections between and among people, that can be converted into economic and other benefits.[3] Bourdieu says that we can bank or accumulate social capital in the same way that we accumulate money. Our opportunities to generate social capital depend on both the size of our social networks (the number of connections) and the quality (good or bad) of our relationships. Large networks consisting of many good relationships can advance the social, economic, and other interests of an individual. In the following discussion, we will look at three different kinds of social capital—**bonding**, **bridging**, and **linking**.[4]

SOCIAL CAPITAL A resource based on interpersonal connections that can be converted into economic and other benefits.

BONDING SOCIAL CAPITAL Benefits that result from close relationships with parents, children, and other family members.

BRIDGING SOCIAL CAPITAL Benefits that result from connections with friends and close associates.

LINKING SOCIAL CAPITAL Benefits that result from relationships with people in positions of power who are outside of our usual network.

Bonding social capital refers to the benefits that come from close relationships such as those between parents and children or other close kin.[5] Critical to a sense of well-being, social capital of the bonding variety fulfills our immediate needs for attachment, love, emotional support, and solidarity. When children experience rejection or hostility in these early relationships, however, they develop a pattern of insecure attachment.[6] As we will see later in this chapter, whether we develop secure or insecure attachments with parents or other primary caregivers has important implications for other relationships in our lives, as well as our health and overall well-being.

Bridging social capital refers to the benefits that come from connections with work colleagues, friends, classmates, and neighbours who are outside the immediate network of family and kin but who are similar to us in some way.[7] Similarities may include educational or occupational training and experiences; demographic variables like age, ethnicity, or sexual orientation; and corresponding beliefs, attitudes, and values. We accumulate bridging social capital when we join an employer-sponsored curling team, plan a camping trip with a neighbour, invite a friend to a party, or help a peer solve a problem. These close contacts can provide new ideas, perspectives, and information, as well as offer emotional support. When college and university students have a strong social network of peers, they are less likely to drop out and more likely to do well in school.[8]

Linking social capital resides in the relationships we have with people in positions of influence who are outside our usual networks.[9] These people might include business leaders or entrepreneurs with whom we interact on a casual and infrequent basis, church ministers, or community leaders. They can offer access to specialized information and resources such as jobs, spiritual guidance, and educational programs. As sociologist Mark Granovetter says, even "weak" ties (connections characterized by infrequent contact and low levels of intimacy) hold benefits. These connections expose us to large numbers of people and opportunities that we cannot access through our more intimate networks. "Weak" ties can help us, for example, in getting a job or promoting an idea or a product.[10]

"Communication—the human connection—is the key to personal and career success."
PAUL J. MEYER

A common way in which many of us build linking social capital is by participating on social media sites such as LinkedIn, Twitter, and Facebook. Many of the connections to which we are exposed through these sites are second- or third-level connections. LinkedIn, in particular, offers the opportunity for professional networking that can lead to jobs. Members can endorse the skills and competencies of other members, thus bringing these members to the attention of potential employers and business acquaintances. The site also allows for statements of reference. Anyone who participates in a person's network has access to that person's references and other information.

As this discussion suggests, who you know can have a positive impact on getting a job or helping you to meet other work-related goals. In addition, some studies have found that the number and quality of our connections also predict many aspects of our overall well-being.[11] Examples include child development,[12] adolescent health,[13] family functioning,[14] high school retention,[15] healthy aging,[16] happiness,[17] and even neighbourhood mortality rates.[18] Simply put, people with more social capital are better off in all of these important areas than those with less social capital. Refer to the "Professional Contexts" box titled "Recovering from Addiction with the Help of Others" for an example of the link between social capital and recovery from addiction to alcohol or other drugs.

REASONS FOR FORMING RELATIONSHIPS

Clearly a number of important benefits come from our relationships with others in family, social, and organizational networks. Let us take a look now at two theories that explain *why* we form relationships with others. The first focusses on our basic interpersonal needs, while the second views interpersonal interaction as a more complex process of negotiation and exchange.

Needs Theory

In 1958, William Schutz introduced a theory of interpersonal relations called **fundamental interpersonal relations orientation (FIRO)**.[19] According to this theory, we are motivated to meet three basic interpersonal needs: inclusion, control, and affection/openness. Schutz suggested that we communicate with others to meet these needs, which exist in all of us to varying degrees.

FUNDAMENTAL INTERPERSONAL RELATIONS ORIENTATION (FIRO) Theory that holds that we form interpersonal relationships in order to meet our need for inclusion, control, and affection.

Need for Inclusion

The **need for inclusion** refers to our fundamental human desire to be connected to other people—to be included in their activities and to feel as if we belong. Generally speaking, if our inclusion needs are met, we feel accepted and valued. If our inclusion needs are not met, we feel lonely and unwanted. These needs play a large role in our organizational and social lives.

NEED FOR INCLUSION The need to be connected to other people.

When our need for inclusion is overly strong, it can lead to negative outcomes. The phenomenon of "groupthink," discussed in greater depth in Chapter 10, happens when people in organizations want so badly to fit into a group that they will go along with any group decision, whether or not they support the decision. They fear being disliked or labelled as *difficult* if they go against majority opinion or threaten the morale of the group. In the worst-case scenarios, the consequences can be deadly; but at best, the feeling of a need to conform at any cost is almost always counterproductive.

© AF archive/Alamy

The need to be liked and to belong dominates many movie and television plots.[20] In the 2004 film *Mean Girls*, for example, much of the plot revolves around the strong need of the girls to belong to the various cliques or

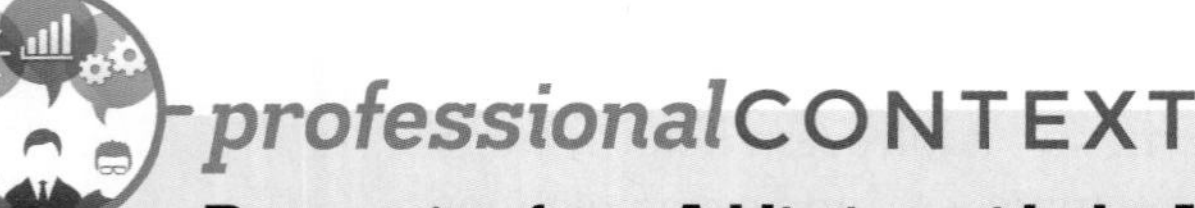

professionalCONTEXTS

Recovering from Addiction with the Help of Others

According to the Canadian Centre on Substance Abuse, the leading cause of poor performance in the workplace is substance abuse. Alcohol and other drugs impair a worker's ability to stay awake and alert on the job, reason and make sound decisions, control emotions, and operate equipment that requires motor skills and coordination. Even if an employee abuses a substance outside the workplace, the effects can persist into the next day or longer. The employee may be hung over or experience withdrawal symptoms. In addition to poor performance, long-term dependencies on alcohol and other drugs can also lead to conflicts with co-workers and supervisors, absences related to physical and stress-related illnesses, chronic fatigue, and mental and emotional issues resulting in depression and even suicide. The cost in financial terms is also great. Organizations have to pay higher insurance premiums to insurance providers and salaries to replacement workers. They also suffer financial losses resulting from lowered productivity. A recent study in Alberta estimated the cost to employers at $67 million.[21]

While many factors play a role in a person's recovery from addiction to alcohol and other drugs, experts have identified one that is particularly important when considering the treatment process for addiction. That factor is recovery capital. Closely linked to social capital theory, the term *recovery capital* refers to the quality and quantity of resources available to someone who is trying to recover from addiction.[22] External resources can include a safe place to live, a good job, healthy relationships, and financial security. Internal resources can include personal beliefs and values, self-esteem, self-efficacy, hope, education, and social skills.[23]

Key to long-term recovery are healthy relationships—the bonds with peers, family, teachers, co-workers and supervisors, counsellors, and therapists that support recovery efforts.[24] Friendship networks are especially important for adolescents and young adults, who view their peers as a primary support. To maintain sobriety, people in recovery often try to build new relationships that align with their goals of recovery. This realignment may mean making new friends and connecting with people who will help in recovery rather than those who might encourage relapse.[25] In the workplace, many employers offer programs to assist employees with substance abuse problems. They know the financial cost of not offering this assistance.

Let us look at two examples of recovery capital. The first involves a laboratory technologist named Lee, who became addicted to sleeping pills while working at a local hospital. Lee had become extremely depressed when his brother died in a car accident. The roads were slippery the night that his brother left his place to drive home, and Lee felt guilty that he had not pressed his brother to sleep over. In the weeks following the death of his brother, Lee had trouble sleeping, and he had periodic panic attacks. He would awaken in the middle of the night, drenched in a cold sweat. The next day, he felt exhausted. On late night

social groupings at North Shore High School. While not every girl wants to be part of the most exclusive clique (the Plastics), they all want to belong to a group. This movie illustrates that belonging to some kind of social group—even if it is just a couple of friends—is important to social success (sometimes even to survival) in high school.

Schutz points out that, in fact, some people need more interpersonal interaction (as opposed to alone time) than others. Most of us, however, feel most comfortable when we achieve a balance between being with others and being alone. The **ideal social person** can enjoy being with others but can also find satisfaction in being alone. Less balanced individuals, on the other hand, tend to be either **oversocial** or **undersocial**.

IDEAL SOCIAL PERSON An individual who meets her inclusion needs in a balanced way.

OVERSOCIAL The tendency to work extra hard to seek interaction and attention from others.

UNDERSOCIAL The tendency to avoid interaction with others.

Imagine a young couple, Ivana and Marco, who experience tension because one has a greater need than the other for socializing. Ivana wants to be with others—Marco and their mutual friends—most evenings after work, while Marco wants to go home and enjoy some quiet downtime listening to music. Resolving the tension between them could begin with Ivana's and Marco's acknowledgement that she is more of a "socializer," while he is more of a "loner." They also need to recognize, however, that neither is wrong for having different needs. With that recognition, they can work to find a way to satisfy their different inclusion needs and reduce the tension in their relationship.

shifts, the problem was especially serious. It often took him three or four hours to get to sleep when he returned home, and his sleep was not sound.

After a few weeks of sleeplessness and exhaustion, Lee asked a doctor at the hospital for a prescription for sleeping pills. The doctor obliged, and the pills allowed Lee to get better rest; as a result, he felt much better and more alert in his daily activities. When he requested a refill, the doctor obliged. The third time that Lee asked, however, the doctor expressed concern. She suggested that Lee could become addicted if he continued to take the sleeping pills. But when he stopped taking the medications, once again Lee had problems sleeping. Feeling that he was not susceptible to addiction (he had never had any problems of that nature), he decided to take a month's supply of pills from one of the storage cabinets at the hospital. He didn't imagine that anyone would notice or care if a few pills were missing.

This pattern persisted over a period of months, and Lee found that he had to take an increasing number of pills to get the same effect. He also began to combine the medication with a couple of beers at night. At first, he managed all right at work. However, after a time, he found that he was becoming groggy on the job; he took off work more often; and he had trouble concentrating on the tissue and fluid samples that he had to prepare for analysis. As a result, he feared that some of his analyses might be incorrect—problems that could have an impact on the health of patients. He also feared that someone would notice the quantity of pills that were missing when it came time to place another order.

Finally, Lee decided to go to the hospital administrator and disclose his problem. To his surprise and relief, the administrator was supportive. He offered grief counselling, time off with pay to participate in a rehabilitation program, and the name of a local support group. Lee also gained enough courage to discuss the situation with his friends and family, who pledged their assistance. With access to these external supports, Lee regained his self-confidence and came to believe that he could overcome his addictions (internal supports). In memory of his brother, he decided to become a big brother to a boy who did not have a male role model. This decision helped Lee to overcome his sense of guilt and subsequently his problem with addiction (internal support).

The second example involves a college student named Madison. Madison has successfully recovered from addiction, but she risks relapsing due to the pressures of her academic program, easy access to alcohol and drugs, and the frequency with which her friends use alcohol and drugs. Positive feedback from a professor and regular meetings with an on-campus counsellor (external resources) could potentially have a strong and positive impact on her level of confidence in her academic abilities and coping skills (internal resources). As a result, she might feel more hope for the future (internal resource), which may help her to stay sober.[26]

In a similar way, some of us enjoy working in jobs that allow us to be on our own. We like offices with closed doors or jobs that allow us to work at home, tasks that do not require group work, and time for introspection. Others of us have a greater need to be part of a busy work environment, moving about the office and interacting with others. We like open-concept offices, noisier environments, and team projects. In short, different people have different degrees of need for inclusion.

Need for Control

In addition to varying levels of need to connect with others and be included in their activities, we all have some **need for control**. We want to exercise influence over our relationships, decisions, and activities. In an organizational setting, we might want to make a decision about the timing of a company announcement, when to implement a new policy, or the choice of a consulting firm to carry out a project.

NEED FOR CONTROL The need to influence our relationships, decisions, and activities and to let others influence us.

The extent to which we try to "get our way" over others with different opinions will give a clue as to our need for control. Some people, who prefer to take charge most of the time, are uncomfortable following the lead of others. Others are uncomfortable when placed in leadership positions. Most of us, however, fall somewhere in between: at times wanting to be the leader and at other times choosing to be the follower.

RELATIONSHIP BOUNDARIES The limits to which we are willing to go to establish or maintain a relationship.

Whether we are happiest in the role of leader or follower, all of us need to know how to set **relationship boundaries** in our personal and work lives. For example, we must decide how many concessions we will make before we say "enough is enough." When we speak of "setting boundaries," we are talking about establishing a line that we will not cross in order to maintain the relationship. That line may relate to how someone else treats us (e.g., touching us inappropriately, cheating on us, or putting us down in front of other people). At other times, the line may relate to an action that we are not willing to take against someone else (e.g., engaging in an illegal or immoral act, rejecting our family, or harming another individual). Boundaries are about respecting and protecting ourselves *and* expecting and demanding a certain level of respect from others. If we say "yes" in order to please someone when we really mean "no," for example, we have allowed someone to cross a personal boundary. If we allow someone to speak to us in a disrespectful or abusive way, we have accepted the lack of boundaries in the relationship.

Much of our knowledge about setting and observing boundaries comes from our experiences as children. In healthy environments, we learn when to say "yes" and when to say "no"; and we learn socially acceptable patterns of communicating and behaving. In abusive or unhealthy environments, on the other hand, we may not learn how to set or respect boundaries. Studies support the idea that many rapists and violent offenders have parents who set fewer ground rules and looser boundaries than do the parents of other kinds of offenders.[27]

Anyone who followed the 2013 trial of confessed murderer Jodi Arias will be familiar with the term *boundaries*. In that trial, defence witness and domestic violence expert Alyce Laviolette discussed times that she felt Arias had "set boundaries"—that is, taken a position or stood up for herself. An overwhelming majority of the public disagreed with Laviolette's assessment; however, the example serves nonetheless to illustrate the currency of the term *boundaries*.

Boundaries—whether physical, emotional, or other—are important not only in our personal lives, but also in our work lives. Teachers and professors face the need to define and respect boundaries with their students. When managers or employees fail to respect the boundaries of their employees or co-workers, organizational climate suffers; and in turn, this climate negatively affects job satisfaction, retention levels, and productivity.

Individuals working in the helping professions—doctors, nurses, psychologists, counsellors, and therapists, among others—face a particular need to establish boundaries with their patients and clients. Becoming too emotionally involved carries high risks—to the professional and to the client. In the Jodi Arias trial, the prosecutor (Juan Martinez) accused both Alyce Laviolette and psychologist Richard Samuels of crossing that ethical line—becoming emotionally invested in Arias. He pointed to examples such as their giving her books, apologizing to her, and disregarding evidence that did not support their conclusions.

Sometimes workers in the helping professions develop a fondness for an individual patient or client that leads them to favour that person over others in similar circumstances. They may also come to identify too strongly with the person's perspective or problems. In some cases, they may even put their patient's or client's needs above their own. This sort of overinvestment in another person can lead to burnout—a state of extreme physical and mental exhaustion, which can disrupt a person's personal and work life. In other situations, patients develop an inappropriate dependency or "crush" on their caregivers. Some patients attempt, for example, to establish a personal connection with nurses or other hospital staff.

To protect both patients and their caregivers, practical and ethical guidelines caution against gift giving, physical contact, and the development of personal friendships that blur professional boundaries. Those in the helping professions can be at great risk if they do not follow these guidelines. Setting limits on interactions, establishing and sticking to roles, and recognizing when boundaries are breached—all are critical and necessary steps to be followed by those in the helping professions. All of these steps also allow us to meet our need for control in our personal and work lives.

> **"I'm on the patch right now. Where it releases small dosages of approval until I no longer crave it, and then I'm gonna rip it off."**
> **ELLEN DEGENERES**

Need for Affection

In his early work, Schutz referred to the third basic interpersonal need as the **need for affection**. This need reflects our desire to give and receive love and support from others. Outward displays of caring and recognition tell us that we are important to other people: a thank-you card from a supervisor for a successful marketing campaign, a phone call from a co-worker who knows that we are not feeling well, or a box of chocolates from a romantic partner. All recognize our value as human beings—not just as cogs in an organization or caregivers in the home. In developing a behavioural scale to measure need for affection, Schutz later added the idea of openness. He says that when our need for affection is met (that is, we feel liked), we are more open with other people.

Despite the almost universal need to be liked, Schutz describes the **ideal personal type** as someone who can handle not being liked in certain situations. For example, a work supervisor may have to fire someone who is well liked by the other employees; a teacher may have to assign some low grades; a parent may have to force a child to go to school despite the child's wishes. Each of these situations will probably result in some dislike for the person who makes the unpopular decision.

When someone's need for affection is not met, he or she may develop **underpersonal** or **overpersonal** characteristics. Holding the belief they are not liked or valued, underpersonal people often protect themselves by withdrawing from others or establishing superficial relationships. In other words, they become less open. In an organizational setting, the underpersonal employee may choose to avoid social events such as receptions or company picnics. He may develop friendships but limit interactions to casual conversation about the weather, an upcoming hockey game, or the relocation of a local coffee shop.

Those who are overpersonal, on the other hand, strive to establish close relationships with everyone they meet, regardless of whether or not the others show interest in developing this kind of relationship. The overpersonal employee might share details of her sex life or marital problems with co-workers. She might put her supervisor and co-workers on email lists for jokes and cartoons or send notices about upcoming social events to them. See the "Professional Contexts" box on oversharing in the workplace for an example of the risks in being overpersonal.

Closely associated with the need for affection is the need for **intimacy**. As we will see later in this chapter, intimacy is critical to building and maintaining healthy interpersonal relationships; however, choosing the

NEED FOR AFFECTION The need to feel liked by others.

IDEAL PERSONAL TYPE An individual who wants to be liked but feels comfortable in situations that may result in dislike.

UNDERPERSONAL Characteristic of an individual who feels undervalued and seeks to avoid close relationships.

OVERPERSONAL Characteristic of an individual who seeks to establish close relationships with everyone, regardless of whether others show interest.

INTIMACY The state of having a close, authentic connection with another person.

> **"Communication is a continual balancing act, juggling the conflicting needs for intimacy and independence. To survive in the world, we have to act in concert with others, but to survive as ourselves . . . we have to act alone."**
> **DEBORAH TANNEN**

professionalCONTEXTS

Oversharing in the Workplace

A 2012 *New York Times* article by Peggy Klaus discussed the current trend toward oversharing in the workplace. To illustrate the problem, she cited four examples taken from the experiences of different managers and executives. In the first instance, several employees asked their manager, "How many times can I be absent before you fire me?" In the second case, an employee at a health care organization told her boss that she was looking for a new job; and she expected her job search would take six to eight months. In the third case, a senior manager asked an employee how he was doing. The employee responded, "Well, I haven't had sex for five years, so I guess I'm not doing so good." In the fourth and final example, after congratulating a new grandmother, the chief executive officer (CEO) of a small company received a lengthy and medically explicit account of the birth of the employee's granddaughter.

Why are people engaging in this new "obsessive sharing disorder" (OSD)? Many studies show that people in some cultures (warm climates in particular) tend to be more open than those in other cultures. According to Klaus, Facebook and other social media sites are driving the current trend. Used to oversharing in social media, people have stopped taking context into account. As a result, offices are becoming chat rooms, where people share highly personal information (e.g., drinking patterns, sex lives, and other previously taboo topics) with colleagues, supervisors, and clients.

A second possible motivation for oversharing in the workplace, according to Klaus, could be the "desperate" need for connection. As employees spend increasingly long hours in the workplace, it becomes a second home; and colleagues and bosses become a family.

In concluding her discussion, Klaus emphasizes that the act of sharing offers some important benefits. Sharing allows us to build trust and establish relationships that make our lives more agreeable and our workplace more productive. However, we should think carefully about what we share and when and where we share the information.[28]

right person, the right time, and the right place is important. Refer to the "Professional Contexts" box titled "Killing for Love" for an example of how the search for intimacy can sometimes lead to unhealthy and risky relationships.

SOCIAL EXCHANGE THEORY Theory that explains how people weigh the perceived costs and rewards of relationships in deciding to maintain or end them.

Social Exchange Theory

In contrast to needs theory, which focusses on how we fulfill essential social needs through our relationships, **social exchange theory** uses an economic model to explain

professionalCONTEXTS

Killing for Love

In the 2003 film *Monster*, which is based on true events, actress Charlize Theron plays Aileen Wuornos, a prostitute who becomes a serial killer. Born into an abusive family, raped as a child by a family friend, and shunned by her peers, Aileen turned to prostitution at the age of 13. The film begins with Aileen's voice-over, where she describes herself as a dreamer who truly believed that one day she would be a movie star—beautiful and rich, like Marilyn Monroe. As a child, she created a world in her mind where she felt safe from the horrors of her reality. In her quest for acceptance and love, Aileen began to perform sexual favours for men. As she recounts, "Even if they couldn't take me all the way like Marilyn, they would somehow believe in me just enough, they would see me for what I could be."[29]

Aileen's story demonstrates the negative impact of unhealthy and abusive relationships on a child's understanding of love and social acceptance. While Aileen searches to fulfill two basic human needs (affection and inclusion), she has never had the opportunity to develop high-quality relationships; therefore, she accepts whoever offers something vaguely resembling the fulfillment of these needs. In addition, Aileen has trouble making friends and getting legal employment due to her lack of communication skills. Only when Aileen meets and begins a romantic relationship with a young woman named Selby does she learn what it means to love and be loved in return.

© digitalskillet/iStockphoto

how people weigh the perceived costs and rewards associated with their relationships. This assessment helps them to decide whether to stay in or leave the relationships.[30] The theory predicts that people will leave relationships when they think that the effort or cost of maintaining the relationship outweighs the advantages.

Imagine a dating couple, Morgan and Jamie, who are enjoying the early stages of their relationship. Morgan, a police officer, works a lot of shifts that begin at various times throughout the day and night; Jamie has a day job in sales. Both Morgan and Jamie have to weigh the benefits (e.g., companionship, fun times, quality of sex life, and not being alone) against the costs of this relationship (e.g., pressures to be available, investment of time and money, and lack of opportunity to date other people). Jamie may decide that the challenges of dating someone who is often unavailable because of shiftwork—along with the worry associated with dating someone who works in a potentially dangerous job—are not worth the benefits offered by the relationship. In this case, a breakup may be likely.

According to Samuel Bacharach and Edward Lawler, we are dependent on a person or organization to the extent that we can or cannot replace that relationship with another equally attractive option.[31] If an employee believes that jobs are scarce, she is likely to very feel dependent on her employer. If that same employee receives several job offers from other organizations, on the other hand, she will not feel as dependent on the employer. A company can refuse a pay raise to its employees; but if the employees have options, they will probably look elsewhere at the first opportunity. The same reasoning applies to more intimate relationships. If Jamie has other attractive options, she may be more apt to leave the relationship with Morgan.

TYPES OF RELATIONSHIPS

We are connected to other people in a variety of contexts, including families, neighbourhoods, workplaces, schools, sports teams, and clubs. Some of these links happen by chance, others by choice. Let us take a look at the difference between these two types of relationships.

Relationships of Circumstance

Relationships of circumstance arise from situations or circumstances in which we find ourselves. For example, we may not have chosen the associations we have with our work colleagues, classmates, or next-door neighbours; rather we got to know these people because of the circumstances that brought us together. We may like these people well enough, and perhaps we would have chosen them as friends anyway; but the situation led to the relationship. Our connections with parents and other relatives are likewise decided by circumstances beyond our control.We may be glad to have them in our lives, but we did not actually choose them.

RELATIONSHIPS OF CIRCUMSTANCE
Relationships that develop because of situations or circumstances in which we find ourselves.

> "You don't choose your family. They are God's gift to you, as you are to them."
> DESMOND TUTU

As a result of the long hours, at-times stressful conditions, and need to cooperate to get work done, conflict often arises in relationships of circumstance in the workplace. After all, we seldom choose these people as colleagues; and we may not have much in common with them. To get along, we may need to disregard small irritants. We may also need to become more accepting of diversity. The "Human Diversity" box titled "The Human Library" provides an interesting example of how we can learn about—and get along better with—different people.

Relationships of Choice

RELATIONSHIPS OF CHOICE Relationships we actively seek out and choose to develop.

Relationships of choice stand in contrast to relationships of circumstance in that we actively seek out and *choose* to develop these relationships. Many relationships of circumstance, at some point, become relationships of choice. If we become friends with a co-worker, for example, and undertake after-hour activities together—going to the theatre, joining a soccer team, or practising for a marathon—this relationship has evolved from one of circumstance to one of choice. We can even argue that all relationships of choice begin as relationships of circumstance. After all, how would we have met the people with whom we choose to form relationships if circumstances had not brought us together in the first place?

The Human Library

While many people rely primarily on the Internet to conduct research, most have borrowed a book from the library at some point. Less likely, however, is the borrowing of an actual person; and yet the "human library" involves just that kind of loan. Essentially, the human library is a resource whereby we borrow a "human book"—someone we might otherwise never meet—for a designated period of time. The "human book" and the person doing the borrowing typically meet at a formally organized activity and then engage in meaningful conversation.

Although relatively new to parts of North America, the human library has been a regular practice in Europe for over ten years. The idea first appeared with a "Stop the Violence" campaign undertaken by five young adults in Copenhagen, Denmark. The organizers conceived the library as a festival event, meant to raise awareness and mobilize youth against violence.[32]

The guiding principle of the human library is to promote dialogue and build relationships. Volunteers in the human library aim to reduce prejudice and encourage understanding among people of diverse cultural, occupational, and other backgrounds. The range of human books is vast: from former gang members to male nannies to post-operative transsexual individuals to Muslim extremists.

Organizations such as the Canadian Broadcasting Corporation (CBC) have joined the movement, seeing it as a way to build and encourage positive community relations. In 2011, the city of Toronto, Ontario, hosted the human library at four different branches of its public library system. At this event, citizens met with Toronto police officers and the new chief customer service officer for the Toronto Transit Commission (TTC). As one police foundations student reported, "You can't build relationships through a cop-car window. You've got to be on the ground, you've got to talk to people—just like this—face to face."[33]

A growing number of other major organizations have recognized the benefits of this new public relations approach. And given the positive public response, the trend is likely to increase in the years to come.

RELATIONSHIP CONTEXTS

Whether by circumstance or choice, we are part of relationships in a number of different settings or contexts. Four major contexts in which we find ourselves involve our families, friends, workplace colleagues, and romantic partners. Let us take a closer look at each of these important bonds.

Family

Our earliest interactions with our family members—in particular with our mother, father, or other primary caregivers—help us to learn about our environment. They also lay the groundwork for future relationships with others. In the context of family, we develop **internal working models** of relationships—mental pictures of the nature of relationships and what we can expect from them.[34]

INTERNAL WORKING MODEL A mental picture that helps us understand some aspect of our world.

Working models help us to make sense of our world, and they influence both our perceptions and our behaviours. Our childhood experiences with other people—in particular our primary caregivers—serve as a model for how we perceive and enact relationships throughout our lives.[35] A child who has formed a secure attachment to a caregiver will probably see other people as available, responsive, and helpful.[36] He will also likely see himself as a lovable and valuable person. In turn, he is likely to be confident about forming relationships with other people. Thus, when our early relationships are secure and satisfying, they help to ensure high-quality relationships later in life.[37] If, on the other hand, we do not get the chance to form secure relationships as children, we may not be able to form high-quality relationships as adults. See the "Human Diversity" box for an example of the impact of negative childhood experiences on the development of internal working models in Aboriginal children enrolled in residential schools.

"The mother-child relationship . . . requires the most intense love on the mother's side, yet this very love must help the child grow away from the mother, and to become fully independent."

ERICH FROMM

Our early interactions with our primary caregivers also influence our interpersonal communication skills. Children who are securely attached to their mothers communicate more effectively. They are also more responsive, more outgoing, more empathic, and less aggressive than less securely attached children.[38] In one study, children who were securely attached to their mothers at age three showed better language skills at age four and a half than children who were not so securely attached. They were also better able to talk about their emotions.[39]

A second study identified similar connections among maternal attachment, communication, and the quality of subsequent friendships.[40] This study examined how mothers talked about mental states (emotions, desires, and thoughts) with their 24-month-old children during play. The findings revealed that a secure infant–mother attachment promotes the later abilities of a child to engage in positive interactions with friends. To measure the quality of your friendships, follow the link given in the "From Theory to Practice" box on the next page.

"Feelings of worth can flourish only in an atmosphere where individual differences are appreciated, mistakes are tolerated, communication is open, and rules are flexible—the kind of atmosphere that is found in a nurturing family."

VIRGINIA SATIR

humanDIVERSITY

The Impact of Residential Schools on Aboriginal Survivors in Canada

Most Canadians see our country as multicultural and inclusive; however, our history is not without a dark and disturbing past. For more than a century, the Canadian government (in partnership with multiple Christian institutions) used the residential school system to promote the forced assimilation of more than 150,000 First Nations, Inuit, and Métis children.[41] The system had been in place since the 1870s.

Based on the perceived need to "civilize the Indian population,"[42] the government established schools across the country to house and educate all Aboriginal children under the age of 16. Amendments to the Indian Act made attendance mandatory.[43] Threatened with fines and imprisonment, Aboriginal parents were forced to watch as their children were taken away to be "Christianized" under the harsh conditions of residential schools.

To enforce the disconnection of Aboriginal children from their history and culture, residential school staff used varying degrees of abuse. For example, they forbade the children from using their native languages; and common punishments ranged from beatings to the shaving of heads.[44] Although hard to believe, the last federally run residential school, the Gordon Residential School in Saskatchewan, did not close its doors until 1996.

Without question, the impact of such traumatic practices affected how several generations of Aboriginal children learned to approach and develop human relationships. Good relationships with family members and other children at a young age predict good relationships in adulthood.[45] Yet the children who attended residential schools had little contact with their families, and tight control over recreational and social activities allowed little opportunity to interact with their peers. Many survivors have reported that their experiences in residential schools made it difficult to relate to others because they had become less trusting and loving. Fearful of being touched and lacking the communication skills to deal with conflict, they were prone to outbursts of anger and displays of violence later in life.[46]

Many residential school survivors continued to suffer long after they reached adulthood. The harsh discipline of residential staff and the lack of contact with loving parental figures left survivors without the emotional breadth or skills to form secure relationships with their own children. Thus, a cyclical pattern of unhealthy relationships was set in place.[47]

In the intervening years, Aboriginal leaders have fought hard for public acknowledgement of the mistreatment of children in residential schools. In 2007, the federal government developed a $1.9 billion compensation package for former residential school students, and Prime Minister Stephen Harper issued an official apology on behalf of the government on 11 June 2008.[48] Though much work remains, Aboriginal-managed organizations such as the Aboriginal Healing Foundation continue to be instrumental in the recovery of residential school survivors.[49]

Friends

FRIENDSHIPS Relationships involving people with shared activities and interests, ranging from the personal to the intimate.

While family relationships represent our most important social connections in the earliest years of life, **friendships** also play a central role in social and emotional development.[50] In the following discussion, we will look at friendships that reflect different stages of our lives: childhood, adolescence, early adulthood, middle adulthood, and later adulthood.

from theoryTO PRACTICE

Think about the Quality of Your Friendships

Responses to the McGill Friendship Questionnaire, developed by Frances Aboud and Morton Mendelson, offer insights into how children develop friendships and classify others.[51] Take a tour of Aboud's lab at this website: www.psych.ualberta.ca/GCPWS/Aboud/Aboud_tour.html. Once you have toured the lab, you can measure the quality of your relationships with friends by completing the online McGill Friendship Questionnaire.

Friendships in Childhood

The single best childhood predictor of our ability to fit into society as an adult is not school grades or classroom behaviour, but rather how well we get along with other children.[52] Children gain many benefits from time spent with peers, including companionship, intimacy, and self-validation.[53] Peer friendships also help in the development of social competence and confidence.[54]

When children enter the school system, they behave in ways that invite either positive or negative responses from their peers. A child who expects rejection sometimes tries to bypass this negative outcome by being disruptive or aggressive with other children. By taking the role of aggressor, the child avoids the possibility of being rejected on the basis of other personal characteristics.[55] According to William Bukowski and his associates at Concordia University[56] and Evelien Gooren and her associates at VU University Amsterdam,[57] these kinds of negative behavioural cycles begin most often in elementary school; however, the effects can persist into adulthood.

Kai Chiang/Thinkstock

Different communication skills emerge at different stages of childhood. For example, toddlers learn to listen and to acknowledge others; they also learn turn-taking skills. By preschool age, children become adept at keeping the conversation going and using appropriate attention-getting cues. Between the ages of 6 and 12, the skill sets become more complex. Children in this age range develop the ability to recognize relevant content in interactions and to respond appropriately. In other words, they begin to learn how to process more advanced information, and they develop **empathy**. A good repertoire of skills learned in childhood should lead to high-quality relationships in later years. See the "From Theory to Practice" box titled "Are Your Electronic Devices Getting in the Way?" for a discussion of the role that personal electronics can play in inhibiting the building of close friendship bonds in childhood, early adolescence, and beyond.

EMPATHY An active and mindful effort to understand the experience of another person and share that person's feelings.

Friendships in Adolescence

An increasing independence from parents and a growing movement toward peers for confirmation, intimacy, and companionship mark the entry to adolescence.[58] In fact, in middle adolescence, young people turn more often to peers than to parents for expressions of support and intimacy.[59]

Adolescent friendships require specific skill sets that build on—but are different from—those acquired in childhood.[60] As adolescents move into a more "talk-focussed" and less "play-focussed" stage of life, they become skilled at initiating and sustaining conversations. As well, because the activities—or play—of adolescents move away from more supervised settings, adolescents show more initiative in opening conversations and making plans with friends.[61] To manage well, they learn empathic listening skills and **self-disclosure** skills.[62] Adolescents who are able to self-disclose—or share personal information about the self—are better able to build intimacy in their friendships.[63] Intimate friendships allow youth to explore and develop their identities in safe spaces.[64] Through self-reflection and conversation with friends, adolescents find the answers to questions such as "Who am I?" and "What is my place in the world?" Finally, the growing dependence on friends for social support creates a need to learn how to manage conflicts.

SELF-DISCLOSURE Sharing of personal information about oneself in conversations.

"Friendship . . . is not something you learn in school. But if you haven't learned the meaning of friendship, you really haven't learned anything."
MUHAMMAD ALI

Just as rejection during childhood years has many negative consequences, the impact of rejection from adolescent friendships can be significant. Rejection in

from theory TO PRACTICE

Are Your Electronic Devices Getting in the Way?

Stanford University researchers found that the more time tweenage girls (girls aged 8 to 12) spent watching videos and multi-tasking with digital devices, the poorer their perceived social well-being. Girls who multi-tasked the most (1) saw themselves as less socially successful and less normal, (2) slept less, and (3) reported having more friends of whom their parents disapproved than did girls who spent less time multi-tasking. On the positive side, the more these girls engaged in face-to-face communication, the better they felt about their levels of social success and other important outcomes. Increased levels of face-to-face communication helped them to develop greater feelings of normalcy, more healthy sleep patterns, and fewer friendships to which parents objected.[65]

Think about your own multi-tasking with electronic devices. Do you spend too much time online, checking your email, or texting friends? Do you engage in these activities when you are with friends and family members? Does your multi-tasking limit your ability to develop healthy social relationships? If you are concerned, you might put down your electronic devices and talk—face to face—with someone. To learn more about the multi-tasking study conducted at Stanford University, visit the following site: www.youtube.com/watch?feature=player_embedded&v=XHxrspmjbwl.

adolescence predicts later maladjustment, including behavioural problems such as dropping out of school and engaging in delinquent and criminal activities.[66] These sorts of behavioural problems lead, in turn, to even poorer peer relationships, greater rejection, and a damaged sense of self. One study found, for example, that university students identified peer rejection during adolescence as their most traumatic life event.[67]

Friendships in Early Adulthood

Friendships also play a central role in the lives of young adults, especially those who are not in a serious romantic relationship. Young adult friendship can be a source of support, advice, and companionship. Because young adults tend to leave their family home to take on new roles (e.g., at a new school or a new job), they encounter many opportunities to establish new friendships.

While adolescence offers time for exploring the self and discovering one's identity through social interactions, the primary social task for young adults is the development of intimate relationships.[68] As a result, when young adults move out of the activity-based interactions of childhood and adolescence, they turn to talk and the exchange of personal information as a way to build intimacy.[69] Shared time and self-disclosure become pathways to intimacy—findings that apply equally to women and men.[70] While young men prefer to build intimacy through shared activities (e.g., recreation and sports), young women rely more on the sharing of personal information to establish closeness and trust.[71] To consider the role and impact of friends in your life, refer to the "From Theory to Practice box titled "Friendship Inventory Exercise."

from theory TO PRACTICE

Friendship Inventory Exercise

Divide a piece of paper into two columns. In one column, write the names of all the friends who have played an important role in your life. (It may take several weeks to compile your list, as some names will come to you later than others.) Go all the way back to childhood. Then evaluate the current shape of the relationships that have mattered to you: *excellent*, needs little work; *good*, could use a bit more care; *poor*, needs lots of work; *strained* or *hardly existent*; or *no longer existent*. Record your assessment in the second column. What do you think about your list? How many of your early friendships remain intact? Are you happy with the state of your friendships? If not, do one thing to improve the quality of each of these friendships.

Friendships in Middle Adulthood

Friendships often take a back seat during our middle adult years. Between the ages of 35 and 55, we tend to focus on work, marriage (or domestic partnerships), and/or raising children.[72] Following marriage, both women and men report a decline in cross-gender friends.[73] Given how much time spouses spend with each other—along with time spent on parenthood and/or work—the time available for visiting with old friends and making new ones may be limited. Also once people marry, they generally turn more often to their spouses and less frequently to their friends to meet their social needs.[74] Nevertheless, many parents find that they develop new friendships through their children—with other parents they meet at playgrounds, playgroups, sports games, recitals, and their children's schools.

Friendships in Later Adulthood

It might seem that our friendship networks would reduce in size as we age—the result of transitions into seniors' residences, health concerns and limitations, and loss of friends due to death. In fact, changes in the size of friendship circles depend on the characteristics of the older adults and the contexts in which they live.[75]

Consider the cases of Arthur (an elderly man) and Ruth (an elderly woman). Arthur moves from an apartment, where he lives alone, to a seniors' residence. The new living arrangement allows him to develop friendships with other residents, and he begins to participate in shared activities such as fitness class, choir, and a book club. In contrast, Ruth has a history of being active in volunteer work, her church, and activities such as bingo and bridge club. But when she falls ill and remains at home for many months, her network shrinks to a few contacts who visit from time to time. These cases show that one person may experience a growth in the number of friendships in older adulthood while the other experiences a decline.

Older Canadians gain many benefits from having a network of friends. Those benefits include better health and social outcomes and the maintenance of independence in later life.[76] Community support enables older citizens to lead more productive, independent, and fulfilling lives;[77] and those who engage in positive social interactions enjoy a longer life.[78]

Work Colleagues

In adulthood, a large number (if not the majority) of our daily interactions and relationships involve colleagues in the workplace. Some of these relationships emerge from circumstance—simply being in the same organization as the other people. Others arise from choice—friendships and romantic relationships that we choose to develop and foster.

Relationships of Circumstance in the Workplace

We do not choose our co-workers in the way that we choose our friends or romantic partners. Instead the circumstances of our shared workplace bring us together. Nonetheless, we spend a great deal of time with these people; and in some cases, our lives may depend on how well the relationship is functioning. Police work, for example, occurs primarily within the context of teams. Police officers rely heavily on their partners and back-up units in dangerous situations, and they need to trust that the support will be there when they need it. Firefighters also depend heavily on their relationships with co-workers for safety and security.

Even in less dangerous lines of work, failed working relationships can pose a serious threat to the emotional and physical well-being of workers. See the "Professional Contexts" box for a discussion of the relationship challenges facing nurses who work in correctional services.

Relationships of Choice in the Workplace

We also have an opportunity within most workplaces to develop relationships of choice. These relationships can take the form of friendships or romances. Most of the time, friendships with co-workers have positive benefits. They can increase the flow and openness of information moving through job-related communication networks. They also

*professional*CONTEXTS

When Nurses Go to Jail

When nursing students imagine the kind of setting where they will work, they may visualize a hospital, a clinic, or a doctor's office. They may imagine working in public health, as a researcher, or in a mobile health care practice. A correctional facility or jail may not be the first workplace that comes to mind. And yet, for thousands of nurses across Canada, working in a provincial correctional system is their reality. In this situation, they face many challenges as they juggle security concerns with providing health care for inmates.[79]

A number of key issues differentiate nursing in correctional settings from nursing in other sectors (e.g., doctors' offices, hospitals, and nursing homes). To work in a correctional facility, nurses need to have not only strong nursing skills but also the ability to interact professionally with a challenging clientele. Compared to nurses in other sectors, correctional nurses encounter more conflict in the workplace and endure higher levels of emotional abuse. These negative encounters lead to increased levels of stress, job dissatisfaction, and feelings of depersonalization.[80]

Despite what we might expect, not all of these negative encounters occur between nurses and inmates. In one study, 43 per cent of correctional nurses reported being the subject of bullying by correctional officers and nursing colleagues.[81] This kind of intragroup conflict was a significant predictor of job dissatisfaction, burnout, and intent to leave.

When nurses work in correctional facilities, they confront many complex relational challenges. They must be equipped to deal with a wide range of people in different roles: correctional officers, lawyers, inmates, social workers, physicians, and other nurses. Flexibility, listening skills, assertiveness, and proficiency in conflict management are all essential to success in this important but challenging role.

lead to higher levels of engagement and better job performance when they provide employees with support and resources (e.g., information and professional contacts). Romantic relationships that begin in the workplace, on the other hand, can be more problematic.

Working and Social Friendships

In the workplace, friendships often develop between colleagues who spend a lot of time in close contact (e.g., behind a counter in a coffee shop, on an assembly line, or in a police car). Committee work creates additional opportunities for building organizational friendships. Receptions, charity drives, and other organized social events also allow work colleagues to interact on a personal level and explore shared interests. When organizations create common meeting areas such as kitchens or lounges, establish office sports teams, and promote social events outside of work, they create a culture that fosters friendships.[82]

According to William Rawlins, two types of friendship can develop in the workplace. Restricted to the workplace, **working friendships** involve a limited amount of emotional investment. Nonetheless, they fulfill an important social need at work, and we maintain them for as long as their benefits exceed their costs.[83] **Social friendships**, on the other hand, transcend the boundaries of the workplace. Social friends get together outside of work, and both parties develop a strong commitment to the relationship. These friendships enrich both work and private life.

WORKING FRIENDSHIPS
Friendships that are restricted to the workplace and limited in emotional investment.

SOCIAL FRIENDSHIPS
Friendships that go beyond the boundaries of the workplace.

Both working friendships and social friendships can make work more interesting and more satisfying. However, the cultivation of both kinds of friendship takes effort and time and, on occasion, can result in conflicts between getting work done and maintaining the friendship. Consider what could happen if a work friend becomes your supervisor after a promotion. The promotion would likely change the dynamic of your relationship. Asked to perform a task that you do not want to do, you could develop feelings of resentment toward your work friend. On the other hand, if your friend consistently avoids giving you undesirable assignments, she could face accusations of favoritism. Or if the work suffers, she might have to defend her decisions to higher-level supervisors.

In the 2008 book *Remember Me?*, by Sophie Kinsella, 28-year-old Lexi Smart wakes up in a hospital to find that four years of her life have disappeared from her memory. She no longer has out-of-control hair, crooked teeth, and a sparse wardrobe from Giant Tiger. She has a tanned and fit body, perfect teeth, and a clothes closet that is the size of a bedroom. She is wealthy and attractive. Nor does she have a lowly job with friends who love and admire her. Instead she has a hot and wealthy husband, a new set of friends, and a position as supervisor of women with whom she previously went pubbing. She learns that no one likes her any more—that she became a tyrant after gaining the position of supervisor and her friends abandoned her. Now she is brunt of jokes in the workplace, as she tries desperately to regain her memory and her old life. The promotion to supervisor had resulted in many unwanted changes in her personality, values, and friendships. Like most relationships, these kinds of changing dynamics can be challenging to negotiate and manage.

Romantic Relationships in the Office

Many workplaces provide an ideal setting for romance to grow between workers. Emotional attachments can develop easily in situations involving close proximity (physical closeness), stressful or challenging work, and long work hours. As illustrated in the television series *The Office*, an office romance between co-workers can move from flirtation to dating to marriage. In this show, co-workers Pam and Jim experience a relatively seamless and easy transition from one stage to the next. In real life, however, workplace romances can be more complicated.

Office romances have benefits as well as drawbacks. The benefits include the ease of connecting, the emotional support of someone who understands the demands of the work, and the enjoyment of frequent encounters with the object of one's affection. The dangers include potentially negative impacts on someone's career. An unpleasant breakup between colleagues can make coming to work difficult or awkward for the former couple. To be perceived positively, workplace romances should not involve bosses and subordinates. Moreover, the motivation for the romantic relationship should appear to be genuine affection, not money or power (e.g., desire to move up in the organization).[84]

Co-workers can also experience discomfort when a couple breaks up or fights in a workplace setting. One episode on the television hospital drama *Grey's Anatomy* showed how bad it can be for co-workers when a couple argues at the workplace. When doctors Cristina and Owen (who are married to each other) have an ugly confrontation within hearing distance of their colleagues, the other doctors become upset. These colleagues have difficulty interacting with the couple for some time afterwards.

The period following the end of an office romance holds particular risks, including the possibility for allegations of **sexual harassment**. Whether founded or unfounded, these allegations can have a negative impact on the disputing parties, other workers, and the organization as a whole. The Canada Labour Code requires companies to develop sexual harassment policies. The companies, for their part, consider that it is in their interest to manage this behaviour—not only for legal reasons, but also because sexual harassment has a negative impact on employees and productivity.[85]

SEXUAL HARASSMENT
Unwanted sexual attention or the inappropriate promise of rewards for sexual favours.

Romantic Partners

In adulthood, our most significant relationships involve romantic connections with other people. In the 2005 film version of *Pride and Prejudice*, Mr Darcy (Matthew Macfadyen) expresses his feelings for Elizabeth (Keira Knightley) in a way that is typical of romantic passion: "You have bewitched me, body and soul, and I love . . . I love . . . I love you. I never wish to be parted from you from this day on." Most people who have experienced romantic love can identify with Mr Darcy's desire to be with the object of his affection at all times.

Not long ago, most people met their future spouses while still in high school or shortly after graduation. After dating for several years, they married and often began families. The situation is quite different now. The majority of high school graduates postpone the task of finding a mate until after they have completed their post-secondary education or training for a profession. Others delay this task in order to travel or focus on work. Between 1972 and 2008, the average age at first marriage in Canada increased from 22.5 to 29.1 years for women and from 24.9 to 31.1 years for men.[86] When young adults finally turn their efforts to forming a romantic relationship, many report great difficulty in finding potential partners.[87] It should be no surprise then that people are turning in growing numbers to creative sources in their quest for a soul mate.

With the development of computer technologies and the Internet, new ways to find a romantic partner and engage in courting behaviours have emerged. The trend of seeking romantic partners online is clearly growing, with an estimated 30 to 40 million North Americans using online dating services.[88] In 2008, the dating website Plenty of Fish enjoyed 18 million hits per month in Canada and 58 million worldwide.[89] Dating websites function by providing, usually for a fee, a platform on which individuals seeking a romantic partner can create and share a profile of their qualities and characteristics. These sites allow users to open themselves to being contacted by others, search for and assess potential partners, and initiate interaction through email.[90]

The phenomenon of online dating has become a popular social practice for several reasons. First, most people have access to affordable Internet services and a computer or other Internet-enabled devices. Second, individuals can quickly and easily register with dating sites from the comfort of their own homes. Third, the increasing sophistication of the software used to match people helps users identify compatible partners.

Chris Taylor/Cartoonstock

...honestly I just feel like we don't communicate like we used to!

The main concerns for online daters seem to be how to balance the desire to meet a mate with privacy concerns (How much do I want to reveal about myself?), misrepresentation concerns (Are others being honest with me?), and personal security concerns (What if someone is dangerous?). To respond to these concerns, online daters use a variety of uncertainty-reduction strategies including doing online searches for information about their potential partner, examining public records, and asking direct questions of the other person.[91]

While online communication with strangers may sound risky, online daters are conscious of the risks—including physical dangers, the possibility of deception, and embarrassment. They are nonetheless confident about their abilities to manage the risks.[92] Given these findings, it is likely that the future will see a growing number of couples crediting their successes at finding satisfying relationships to an online dating website.

As we consider the beneficial role of technology in helping us find potential partners and form romantic relationships, we should observe some final words of caution. While technology may give us new ways to interact with people, it can also interfere with our ability to connect in a meaningful way. This observation applies to relationships in general, but it is particularly significant in relation to romantic partnerships. See the "From Theory to Practice" box titled "Expecting More and Getting Less" for a discussion of this problem.

In the following section, we will continue our examination of romantic relationships by taking a closer look at the stages through which these relationships typically progress. We will also look at the communication patterns that characterize each stage.

from theory TO PRACTICE

Expecting More and Getting Less

Sherry Turkle, a researcher at the Massachusetts Institute of Technology (MIT), has studied the impact of texting and electronic communication on human relationships. In her 2012 book *Alone Together: Why We Expect More from Technology and Less from Each Other*, she argues that we limit our ability to connect with each other when we give so much of our attention to our electronic devices.[93] Even when we spend time with each other—at breakfast, during meetings, at the playground, during funerals—we seem unable to let go of our electronics. She suggests that texting can come between us and our ability to talk to each other. Although it sounds simple, she recommends reducing our use of electronics and being mindful of the need to connect with others in simple, face-to-face communication.

To learn more about these and related ideas, listen to Turkle's TED talk at www.ted.com/talks/sherry_turkle_alone_together.html. While you are listening, ask yourself if you think our electronic communications cause us to "edit" ourselves too much, as Turkle suggests. Does this editing get in the way of our ability to establish real intimacy with people?

STAGES OF ROMANTIC RELATIONSHIPS

Shared talk and increased levels of intimacy characterize friendships as well as romantic relationships. So what is it that makes a romantic relationship so special? As Sternberg's **triangular theory of love** suggests, characterizing features of romantic relationships include passion (sexual attraction), commitment (a desire to stay together and to maintain the relationship over the long term), and intimacy (feelings of closeness and attachment).[94] This definition applies to same-gender as well as mixed-gender relationships.

The extent to which each of these qualities appears in the relationship often changes over time. For example, in the early stages of a romance, passion may dominate the relationship; whereas commitment and intimacy may grow in importance over time. Nonetheless, all three dimensions are typically present when a relationship lasts.

Mark Knapp developed a model that describes the predictable stages through which most romantic relationships (and some friendships) progress.[95] Two phases (**coming together** and **coming apart**) constitute the model. Each phase has five stages (see pages 242–4). Using Knapp's model, we can identify the stage of a relationship by the kind of talk in which the two partners engage. Communication moves the relationship from stage to stage, and **turning points** in behaviour and conversation signal the direction of the change. Common turning points in a relationship include the first date, an argument, meeting the other person's family or close friends, moving in with each other, or getting married. Refer to the "From Theory to Practice" box on *Notes for a Film about Donna and Gail* for an example of how people move through the different stages of relationships.

TRIANGULAR THEORY OF LOVE Theory proposing that passion, commitment, and intimacy characterize romantic relationships.

COMING-TOGETHER PHASE Five stages through which couples move as they build intimacy.

COMING-APART PHASE Five stages that contribute to a movement away from intimacy.

TURNING POINTS Events or interactions that signal changes in the relationship.

from theory TO PRACTICE

Notes for a Film about Donna and Gail

Produced by the National Film Board of Canada (NFB) in 1966, the award-winning *Notes for a Film about Donna and Gail* depicts the story of two young women whose lives intersect when they take jobs in a Montreal factory. Although the women meet in a workplace setting, their personal lives soon begin to merge; and the two take on a shared identity for a period of time. In this film, a narrator of questionable ethics takes the viewer on a trip through the various stages of a relationship from initiating to terminating.

Described in the *Canadian Film Encyclopedia* as the "first English Canadian film to feature lesbian characters and to reflect a strong European influence,"[96] *Notes for a Film about Donna and Gail* is considered the seminal work of director Don Owen. Given the time period, however, Owen only hints at the lesbian content of the relationship. For more on this film, go to the NFB website at http://onf-nfb.gc.ca/en/our-collection/?idfilm=10774.

Coming Together

Knapp suggests that the coming-together phase can be a fast ride from first meeting someone to achieving intimacy, or it can be a long slow evolution. During this phase, couples typically move through five stages: initiating, experimenting, intensifying, integrating, and bonding. Knapp notes, however, the possibility for exceptions. He says that some people skip some stages, move back and forth between stages, or move from a more advanced stage to an earlier one.

Initiating

During the initiating stage, two people who have noticed each other begin to communicate about themselves. The intent is to create a good impression and to gather information about the other person. Nonverbal communication plays a role by conveying information through physical appearance—dress, hairstyle, jewellery, and so on. Body language also sends information about levels of confidence, personality, and attraction to the other person. At this stage, talk tends to be superficial and predictable, touching on topics such as the weather or current events in the news. If the exchange of information during the initiating stage goes well, the two communicators may choose to move to the next stage.

Experimenting

While small talk characterizes the initiating stage, the experimenting stage involves a move into more personal areas of conversation. That is, the two people attempt to find common ground through sharing information about their interests, hobbies, school, or work ("I just started a new job" or "I plan to study nursing"). To move beyond the experimenting phase, the two individuals must show a mutual interest in pursuing a more in-depth relationship. If not, the relationship will either remain at the experimenting stage (with the two continuing to enjoy an acquaintanceship) or dissolve over time.

Intensifying

At the intensifying stage, the two people will explore more intimate topics of conversation, increase their physical contact, and show verbal and nonverbal signs of affection. In a romantic relationship, they may begin to ask for commitment or declare plans to be exclusive in some way. Self-disclosure becomes more risky as the two share confidences that may not be known to others ("I lost my last job because I couldn't get along with my boss" or "I'm hoping to get into nursing, but my chemistry marks were really bad in high school"). Given the risks that each person is taking with disclosing highly personal information, further development of the relationship may depend on the other's reaction to the disclosure.[97]

Integrating

During the integrating stage, the relationship takes on an existence that both couples and observers can easily recognize. The lives of the couple merge in a recognizable way. They become a social unit, with shared friends, activities, rituals, interests, and property. They receive invitations and attend events as a couple. They plan holidays together. Sometimes they dress alike or adopt dress codes that reflect the personal style of the other. They use terms such as *ours* rather than *yours* or *mine*. Self-disclosure has become deep and intimate by this stage. The words "You complete me," from the 1996 movie *Jerry McGuire* (starring Tom Cruise and Renée Zellweger), illustrate how partners feel about each other in this relationship stage. These words also reflect the kind of communication that occurs at this stage, as partners are often able to complete each other's thoughts and may even finish each other's sentences.

> **"The more connections you and your lover make, not just between your bodies, but between your minds, your hearts, and your souls, the more you will strengthen the fabric of your relationship, and the more real moments you will experience together."**
> **BARBARA DE ANGELIS**

The development of restricted codes (private or "insider" language) also signals the emergence of the integrating stage. For example, the couple might agree that the comment "I forgot to let the dog out" will signal the desire of one partner to leave a party. One study on the use of insider language by couples found that silly names, made-up terms, and covert requests for sex were indicators of a positive relationship.[98] Similarly, another study found that (especially in the early stages of marriage) restricted codes—or private talk—contributed to marital satisfaction.[99]

Bonding

While signs of intimacy and a deep personal connection tell us when two people have reached the integrating stage, a more public stance indicates the bonding stage. At this stage, the couple communicate the status of their relationship in a more formal way. Getting engaged, getting married, or moving in with each other—all signal that the couple has reached the bonding stage. However, the true test of having reached this stage is the extent to which both partners trust that the other will accept his or her "real self." At this stage, couples often talk about their personal commitment to be present for each other through difficult times ("We'll get through this together").

Coming Apart

The romantic ideal, presented on television and in novels and movies, shows couples remaining happily ever after at the bonding stage. In reality, however, many couples experience at least some movement into the coming-apart phase at one or more points in their relationship. Occasional questioning of the relationship does not mean that a couple will never enjoy the satisfaction of the bonding stage again, but it probably indicates that the pair will have to do some work to return to the earlier and more positive stage. However, if the partners do not work to improve their relationship, they may progress through all five stages of the coming-apart phase. These five stages are differentiating, circumscribing, stagnating, avoiding, and terminating.

Differentiating

Along with a decrease in physical contact and interaction, the first sign of a couple's movement away from bonding may be a shift from the words *us* and *ours* to *me* and *mine*.

Differentiating involves shifting the focus away from the shared identity and toward individual identities. Differentiating is not necessarily bad, in that it allows each member of the couple to bring new ideas and new information to the relationship—thus keeping the relationship alive and vibrant ("Tell me about what you did at your art class" or "I'm so proud of you for going back to school!"). However, differentiating can be destructive if it pulls the partners too far away from each other and encourages the establishment of separate lives and identities ("I want to take a holiday on my own" or "Why don't you go to the meeting on your own? I've never enjoyed that crowd").

Circumscribing

At the circumscribing stage, a marked decline occurs in the quantity and quality of communication between the partners. Talk may revolve around safe and impersonal topics ("Did you feed the cat? She hasn't seemed hungry lately"). The couple withdraws from sharing or discussing problems. Commitment to the relationship declines. You go through the motions, but you no longer care. At this stage, the relationship may still seem stable to outsiders; and the couple may be able to repair any damage if both partners work at rebuilding intimacy.

Stagnating

If the relationship continues to decline, it may move into the stagnating stage. Like a stagnant pool of muddy water, the relationship does not grow or change; and nothing happens to renew or revitalize it. The little talk that occurs at this stage is likely routine and superficial. As in the circumscribing stage, the couple may avoid areas that have led to conflict in the past ("Let's not talk about that" or "I wish you wouldn't bring that up"). Most important, boredom characterizes this stage, as the couple faces the same daily routines with the same people, same activities, and same conversations. At this point, the couple will have to try much harder to save the relationship.[100]

Avoiding

At the avoiding stage, the lack of commitment becomes even more obvious as couples limit both their talk *and* their physical contact. The relationship has gone even further downhill. They may ignore the other person and not respond to questions or even avoid being in the same room. An emotional gulf separates them. They may be superficially polite or openly hostile, but they no longer depend on the other person for confirmation of self-worth. Because of reduced physical contact and limited interest in talking, the partners have little chance to work on the relationship ("I've got to go to the office to pick up some papers. Don't wait up for me"). It is exceedingly difficult at this stage to rebuild or repair the relationship. When faced with the necessity to be in the same location, they may simply "tune them out" or ignore their presence.

Terminating

The relationship comes to an end in the terminating stage. At this point, conversations tend to revolve around practical matters (e.g., the division of goods and property or informing others about the breakup). Terminating may be done informally (e.g., simply saying goodbye) or formally (signing legal documents). While most people see this stage as a difficult time in their lives, they can experience it negatively or positively. The nature of the experience depends on the kind of communication that takes place.[101] Hurtful and angry words lead to more negative outcomes, while efforts at reaching a mutual understanding and expressing sincere regret about the ending make positive outcomes more likely. In a best case scenario, the couple returns to the level of friendship—an important outcome in situations involving children.

Predicting Relationship Failure by Analyzing Communication Patterns

John Gottman began studying marriage in the early 1970s in his "love lab" at the University of Washington. With the help of his team, Gottman has studied over 3000 couples to try to understand the dynamics and communication patterns of healthy and unhealthy relationships.[102] He invites married couples to come to his lab, where he asks them to discuss a contentious issue in their relationship. Using technologies such as video equipment and heart-rate monitors, the researchers record participants' physiological and other responses to the conversation. After analyzing the data, they track the relationship status of the couples over a number of years. Do they stay together? Are they happy? Do they divorce? Based on the results of these studies, the researchers are able to predict with 94 per cent accuracy which couples will stay married and which will divorce.

What types of factors predict the success or failure of a relationship? People often think that arguing is a predictor of relationship failure. The findings of Gottman's study suggest otherwise. Constructive arguments, where the couple focus on the problem and avoid attacking each other, represent a normal and healthy response to conflict. However, conflict can be damaging when the "four horsemen of the apocalypse" make their presence known. According to Gottman, these four destructive forces are criticism, contempt, defensiveness, and stonewalling.[103]

Criticism occurs when one partner attacks the personality or character of the other person, rather than focussing on the specific behaviour that is bothersome. It is healthy to discuss frustrations and irritants in a relationship; it is unhealthy to make personal attacks on a partner. For example, saying "I felt embarrassed to see that the living room was still untidy when the guests arrived. How did this happen?" focusses on your own feelings and on finding a solution to the problem. Saying "I can't believe you didn't clean up the living room. You're so thoughtless" is an attack on the other person. The first illustrates a healthy approach to conflict. The second leads to destructive consequences.

The expression of *contempt*, which usually follows criticism, is a step further down the path of relationship decline. Contempt involves using insults and other signs of disrespect to attack the self-worth of the partner. Examples of contempt include put downs, name calling and insults (e.g., "you idiot"), eye rolling, and even sneering or lip curling. The most destructive of the horsemen, contemptuous messages convey disgust.

© Chris Rout/Alamy

When one partner criticizes and expresses contempt for the other, the partner who is criticized is likely to respond with *defensiveness*. Defensiveness occurs when one partner sees himself or herself as the victim and, in response, tries to create defences to a perceived attack. Examples include denying responsibility ("I didn't have anything to do with it"), making excuses ("It wasn't my fault that I didn't call! My cellphone was dead"), and meeting one complaint with another ("That's not true. You're the one who . . .").

Like the avoiding stage in Knapp's model, *stonewalling* implies withdrawing and disengaging from the conflict instead of discussing the problem. Stonewalling involves turning away from the relationship by tuning out the other person, ignoring the person's words and body language, showing little reaction, or physically leaving the discussion. Sometimes it can be healthy to walk away from a conflict in order to "cool off." However, too frequent reliance on avoidance can be a destructive habit.

All couples engage in each of these types of behaviour at some point in their relationship. However, relationships that show the chronic presence of the four horsemen have a high likelihood of failure. Unless the two parties to the conflict change their communication patterns, the relationship will likely dissolve. It is important to note that the four horsemen do not appear only during conflict. These destructive patterns can typify the everyday talk of couples and, in that way, erode a relationship quietly but steadily. The good news, however, is that when couples choose to work on their relationship—often through counselling or coaching—they can change these negative communication patterns and replace them with healthy ones.

If the four horsemen prevail and the relationship fails, we will carry with us the leftover impacts of the relationship. That is, we will be different people as a result of our interaction with our now ex-partner. In some cases, our ex-partner will continue to play a role in our lives. This role may be supportive, as when ex-partners remain friends or continue to co-parent their children; or it may interfere with the building of new relationships. Refer to the "Human Diversity" box titled "When an Ex Gets in the Way" to learn more about the potentially negative impact of relationships with ex-partners.

humanDIVERSITY

When an Ex Gets in the Way

Have you ever felt jealous of your partner's warm feelings for his or her ex? Perhaps you have wondered about the impact of those warm feelings on your relationship. New research from the University of Toronto suggests that, in fact, you may have cause to worry.[104]

In the Toronto study, couples reported on their current relationships three times over a six-month period. They discussed the quality of their current relationships, their emotional attachment to ex-partners, and the perceived quality of relationship alternatives. The results showed that participants in a declining relationship (one that appeared to be going downhill) reported increased longing for a previous partner. This increased longing did not necessarily mean that they wanted to leave their current relationship. Instead they probably saw the ex as a fallback—an alternative if the current relationship failed.

When one partner in a committed relationship acts on a yearning to reconnect with an old flame—by making contact through social media or other means—there is a high likelihood of infidelity. Reaching out and rekindling a former relationship can lead to an "accidental affair." By *accidental affairs*, Nancy Kalish refers to situations where people do not set out to have an affair but become swept up in the nostalgia and romance of their newly rediscovered lost love.[105]

Tracking down old lovers leads to more positive results with single people.[106] In a study of 1,000 lost-and-found romances, Kalish found that nearly three-quarters of the reunited couples were still together ten years later. The divorce rate for those who married was 1.5 per cent or lower. This percentage is surprisingly low, given that the overall divorce rate is above 40 per cent in both Canada and the United States.[107]

BUILDING TRUST AND INTIMACY THROUGH SELF-DISCLOSURE

As we have seen throughout this chapter, intimacy—or the state of having a close, authentic connection with another person—lies at the foundation of meaningful interpersonal relationships. And being authentic or honest about ourselves requires trust. But how do we build the kind of trust that leads to intimacy? Most communication scholars believe that we can establish trusting—and ultimately intimate—relationships when we self-disclose or share personal information about ourselves.[108] Two important models of self-disclosure explain how this process works: social penetration theory and the Johari window. Let us take a look at each one in turn.

Social Penetration Theory

Irwin Altman and Dalmas Taylor developed the **social penetration theory**[109] to describe how sharing information about ourselves builds closeness in relationships. Long before the Disney character Shrek explained to Donkey that ogres are like onions because they have layers, Altman and Taylor compared people to onions. They explained that people (like onions) have layers, which they peel away as they get to know each other more intimately. Through this voluntary shedding of layers, they reveal more information about their inner selves. Altman and Taylor suggested that the layers have both breadth and depth.

SOCIAL PENETRATION THEORY Theory that suggests the importance of self-disclosure in moving from less intimate to more intimate relationships.

Breadth refers to the number of conversational topics that allow you to reveal aspects of yourself (e.g., hobbies, career ambitions, health, sports played, and other interests). As a relationship progresses, you explore more and more topics with the other person. In other words, you develop greater breadth in your relationship as you move into new areas of conversation.

Depth refers to the amount of information available on any of these topics. The information can be superficial—for example, the fact that you play hockey. Or it can be more intimate: you are thinking of quitting the varsity hockey team in order to focus on your studies. The outer skin represents superficial information that is easy to uncover or observe (e.g., gender, home town, or occupation). Moving toward the inner layers, people start sharing increasingly personal information about themselves (e.g., personal fears and secrets).

JOHARI WINDOW A self-awareness model that helps us to identify and understand the open, hidden, shared, and unknown parts of the self.

Johari Window

A second model, which explains how we develop intimacy through self-disclosure, is the **Johari window**. This model was named after a combination of the first names of the researchers who developed it: Joseph Luft and Harrington Ingham.[110] The Johari window is divided into four panes or quadrants, each representing a different dimension of the self (Figure 8.1).

The *open quadrant* contains information that we and others know about ourselves. The information may be known because it is obvious (e.g., gender) or because we have chosen to share it (e.g., sexual orientation).

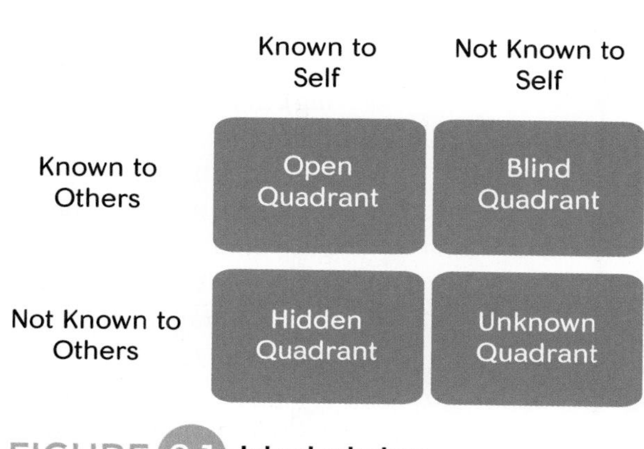

FIGURE 8.1 Johari window.

The *hidden quadrant* contains information that we know but have not chosen to share with others. People often put irrational fears or concealable stigmas (e.g., a history of mental illness, a criminal record, or an eating disorder such as bulimia) into the hidden quadrant.

The *blind quadrant* holds information that others may know about us but we do not know. Our parents may know that we are adopted, for example, but they may not have shared that information with us. Sometimes people see positive qualities in us that we do not see in ourselves, or we may not recognize our impact on others. In an episode of the television show *Gossip Girl*, Dan makes a statement to Serena that clearly illustrates his awareness of her blind quadrant: "You're totally unaware of the effects you have on me. You're also completely unaware that you laugh like a four year old."

Finally, the *unknown quadrant* contains information about us that is not known on a conscious level to ourselves or others. Examples of this sort of information include undeveloped artistic or other abilities or forgotten memories of our childhood. While these memories may be tucked away somewhere in our unconscious, they may never resurface.

According to the Johari model, we can increase our intimacy with others by increasing the size of our open quadrant (i.e., by sharing more information about ourselves). Doing so requires moving information about ourselves from the hidden quadrant to the open quadrant. We can use the model of the Johari window to gain insight into the level of intimacy we have with others. A window representing our relationship with our romantic partner or closest friend will probably have a large open quadrant; a window representing our relationship with a casual acquaintance, on the other hand, would probably have a much smaller open quadrant.

The Internal Drive to Self-Disclose

In Chapter 5, we talked about PostSecret, the website that publishes postcards mailed from people around the world. These postcards contain the senders' most intimate secrets. We may wonder what would motivate people to write a secret on a postcard and mail it to a stranger, to be shared on the Internet. Obviously, the senders of the postcards want their voices to be heard. The anonymity and the lack of a feedback component ensure that the senders will not be judged. But beyond those explanations, we can ask, "What else might explain the thousands of postcards, with intimate self-disclosures, that Frank Warren receives each year?"

We may find at least part of the answer in a study by Harvard researchers Diana Tamir and Jason Mitchell. The study used neuroimaging to scan the brains of people while they either talked about their own beliefs and opinions (e.g., whether they liked snowboarding) or speculated about those of other people (e.g., whether Barack Obama likes snowboarding). Reward centres in the brain lit up much more when people talked about themselves than when they talked about other people.[111] That is, the parts of the brain that register pleasure showed much more activity when people discussed their own views.

When offered money to talk about themselves or other people, participants willingly gave up between 17 per cent and 25 per cent of their potential earnings for the opportunity to reveal personal information. Simply thinking about oneself was sufficient to light up brain regions associated with reward, but the effects were even stronger when participants believed their thoughts would be communicated to someone else. In other words, sharing thoughts about oneself seems to be much more rewarding than just reflecting on them; and self-disclosure has many benefits beyond building intimacy and trust in relationships.

Adding support to this conclusion, James Pennebaker has shown that writing about traumatic, stressful, or emotional events boosts our emotional and physical health.[112] In a study of what they called "expressive writing," Pennebaker and his colleague Sandra Beall asked a group of college students to write for 15 minutes on four consecutive days about traumatic or upsetting experiences in their lives.[113] A second group of students wrote about superficial topics (such as their dorm room or their shoes). Participants who wrote about their deepest thoughts and feelings reported significant benefits in their physical health four months later. They also made fewer visits to the campus health centre than those students who wrote about superficial topics. The researchers concluded that the act of thinking about, writing down, and letting go of personal, private, and troubling thoughts can be therapeutic.

The findings of Pennebaker and Beall, as well as those of Mitchell and Tamir, may well explain why we enjoy sharing our secrets. They may also explain why almost half of everyday speech relays information about our private experiences or personal relationships.[114] Further, they may offer insight into the growing movement to disclose intimate information about ourselves on Facebook, Twitter, and other websites.

The Dangers of Self-Disclosure

Some say that we live in a period of time when our desire to disclose intimate details about our lives also leads us to expect similar disclosures by others. That is, we expect reciprocity. If we are going to share our most intimate secrets with others, we expect them to do the same with us—an expectation that leads to what some call *voyeurism*. The term *voyeurism* refers to spying on the intimate lives of others. In today's society, voyeurism often translates into an obsession with following the lives of celebrities and public figures in the media.[115] Photographers can earn huge sums of money for obtaining pictures of celebrities and their families. These actions sometimes result in tragedy, as happened in January 2013 when a Los Angeles photographer died while trying to get a photograph of Justin Bieber. More often, the celebrity is at risk, as happened with Princess Diana in 1997 when photographers engaged her driver in a deadly car chase in a Paris tunnel.

Individuals who disclose personal information about themselves online also face many dangers. Through their postings, other people can quickly and easily learn much about their lives; and it is difficult to control who sees the information once it is online. The danger may be physical (e.g., someone may use our posts and check-ins on social media sites to find us and harm us), or it may be financial (e.g., someone may use our information to make fraudulent transactions that compromise our finances). These sorts of threats often have consequences that are easy to spot. At other times, the danger may be less obvious but equally harmful—for example, psychological or emotional damage caused by cyberbullying. When we self-disclose, we open ourselves to risks—the reason that trusting and knowing the other party becomes so important. See the "From Theory to Practice" box titled "Sharing Our Private Thoughts in Public Ways" to learn more about the relationship between blogging and self-disclosure.

Workers in the helping professions must be especially careful not to allow or encourage disclosures that could have an impact on their ability to treat their patients or clients. In brief, while self-disclosure may contribute positively to the building and maintenance of certain kinds of relationships, it may not be desirable in every situation.

from theory TO PRACTICE

Sharing Our Private Thoughts in Public Ways

Web and video blogs have become hugely popular over the past decade or so. As an online place where anyone can record and share personal thoughts, observations, and analyses, the blog is at once very private and very public.[116] When only the writer and her or his closest friends can access the online journal, the blog can be a safe place to disclose personal information and reflect on daily experiences. However, the writer faces certain risks when she or he self-discloses in an unsecured blog.[117] Anonymous readers may ridicule or reject the writer—a threat to the writer's sense of self and identity. Bloggers may also receive nothing in return when they share intimate details of their lives. One-sided disclosure differs markedly from the in-person self-disclosure that can build trust and intimacy in a relationship. In face-to-face interaction—or even when exchanges occur in writing—people build relationships through mutual sharing. And when one person self-discloses in a two-sided interaction, the other is likely to respond in kind.

Blogs also present challenges in terms of impression management.[118] As discussed in Chapter 4, we engage in impression management whenever we interact with others. We are highly conscious of the fact that we are "on stage," and we behave in certain ways to influence how others perceive us. When we share our innermost thoughts and socially embarrassing moments in online environments, however, we have a weaker ability to engage in damage control or impression management.[119]

While many of us will join the millions of bloggers and share our innermost thoughts online, we should remember that the Internet is a "small, small world."[120] It is relatively easy for readers—intended or not—to access the personal thoughts we post online. For that reason, some people prefer to record their most private thoughts in a diary that they can lock away from the eyes of others. If you are a blogger, you might want to visit the following web page to learn some tips on safe and appropriate blogging: http://ilookbothways.com/learn-safety/blogging.

TIPS FOR BUILDING AND MAINTAINING RELATIONSHIPS

As we have seen in this chapter, healthy interpersonal relationships contribute to many different and important aspects of our health and well-being. In short, people who enjoy positive relationships with others tend to be healthier, happier, and even wealthier.[121] To conclude this chapter, then, let us look at some tips for building and maintaining satisfying relationships.

Catherine Yeulet/Thinkstock

Show interest in others, ask questions, and avoid talking too much about yourself. Charles Derber describes the "conversational narcissist" as someone who keeps turning the focus of the conversation back to himself or herself.[122] This person competes for attention rather than cooperating to build a good conversation. You have probably chatted with a conversational narcissist, and you know the negative impact of this behaviour on interactions and relationships.

Be realistic about the people who populate your home, social, and work life. If you expect the people in your life to be perfect and they cannot live up to your expectations, you may become bitter and judgmental. On the other hand, some research shows that having high expectations for the quality of your relationships can lead to happier relationships. Therefore, when someone disappoints you, focus on dealing with the issue that caused the disappointment rather than blaming the person for not being perfect. [123]

Instead of dwelling on the irritating habits of a co-worker, roommate, or family member, try to note the good qualities of that person. Although this suggestion sounds cliché, experts in marital communication have found that the longest and happiest marriages involve couples with positive attitudes toward each other and the relationship.[124]

Work at seeing the other person's perspective rather than explaining others' behaviour from your own point of view. Healthy relationships are built on empathy—an active and mindful effort to understand the experience of the other.[125]

Recognize that you and your work colleagues, friends, family members, or partner will have differences of opinion; but you do not need to address all of these differences. If you want an enduring relationship, "pick your battles" and "agree to disagree." Some topics, which may never be resolved, are better ignored.[126]

Use your words and nonverbal communication to make what John Gottman calls "repair attempts" when you feel a conflict developing.[127] Examples of repair attempts include using humor, acknowledging the importance and needs of the other person ("I know how much this means to you"), showing that you are on common ground ("Okay, we have a problem; how can we fix it?"), backing down ("I see what you are saying; maybe you are right"), or choosing your battles ("Let's agree to disagree").

Self-disclose to build intimacy. Research shows that when you self-disclose appropriately, the other person will probably reciprocate by sharing information of an equally personal nature. This kind of response is called the "norm of reciprocity."[128] These sharing behaviours build trust that, in turn, leads to more self-disclosure and ultimately more intimacy. Trust and intimacy are essential to healthy relationships.

Set boundaries. The boundaries you set with a romantic partner may not be as rigid as those you set with a co-worker or a client, but they are important nonetheless. Boundaries communicate to others that you respect yourself and expect them to respect you as well.

Don't let electronic devices replace or interfere with face-to-face interaction. If you want to build a close relationship with someone, make an effort to interact with that person face to face. When you are spending time with friends, family, work colleagues, or a romantic partner, overcome the impulse to browse the Internet or check your texts or email.

SUMMARY

In this chapter, we saw that healthy relationships have positive consequences for our lives. They help us to meet our needs for inclusion, control, and affection. We also looked at the different types of relationships into which we may enter—relationships of circumstance (those created by the situations in which we find ourselves) and relationships of choice (those we have deliberately created). We then took a close look at the characteristics of some of the most important types of relationships, including those with family, friends, and romantic partners.

We saw that romantic relationships follow a predictable pattern of development, and we discussed how an awareness of the stages of coming together and coming apart can help us to build and maintain healthy relationships. We also saw how self-disclosure builds intimacy and trust, which are both essential to satisfying relationships. Finally, we learned some specific techniques for building and maintaining better relationships. While a good relationship requires serious effort on the part of both parties, this chapter has shown that we are capable of establishing this kind of connection through our communication and that the benefits make the effort worthwhile.

REVIEW QUESTIONS

1. What is social capital? What does social capital theory tell us about the importance of interpersonal relationships?
2. What is social exchange theory? How might this theory explain why we choose to maintain some relationships but not others?
3. Why do people feel the need for inclusion? What is meant by the terms *oversocial* and *undersocial*? What are some drawbacks to being either oversocial or undersocial?
4. How are relationships of choice different from relationships of circumstance? Are there any similarities between these two kinds of relationships?
5. What are the stages of coming together and coming apart in romantic relationships? How can knowing the patterns through which these relationships typically grow and deteriorate help us build healthy relationships?
6. What is self-disclosure? How can self-disclosure help to build intimacy and trust in friendships?
7. Which of the tips for building and maintaining relationships offered in this chapter are likely to work best? Why? Can you think of other principles for building and maintaining relationships not discussed in the chapter?

SUGGESTED ACTIVITIES

1. Form a group with three of your classmates. Review the stages of relational development discussed in this chapter. Then consider the following question. If you meet someone online, do you think the relationship will follow the same predictable pattern as happens with someone you meet in person? Why or why not? Explain and elaborate on this point. After discussing your ideas within your group, share your findings with the class.
2. Consider a friendship you have with a male and one that you have with a female. Think critically about how you use self-disclosure to become closer with these friends. Are you more open in your disclosure with one than the other? What affects the kind of disclosure? Does gender make a difference? Does personality make a difference? Is one person a better listener than the other? Does either reciprocate by self-disclosing to you? Explain your responses.
3. Form a group with several of your classmates. List the differences and commonalities between the social penetration model and the Johari window. Use each model to explore a relationship with one of your closest friends.

CHAPTER 9

Managing Conflict and Practising Civility

CHAPTER OUTLINE

learning OBJECTIVES

- To become acquainted with the sources and characteristics of conflict
- To understand the difference between overt and covert conflict
- To understand the role of power in conflict
- To become acquainted with coping styles used by different people
- To learn about the difference between functional and dysfunctional conflict
- To understand the importance of practising civility in the workplace
- To learn how to deal with conflict in constructive ways

forSTARTERS

Alternative Forms of Justice in Canada

Phillip lived on a First Nations reserve in Saskatchewan. At 19 years of age, he stole a truck from a local gas station for an afternoon joy ride with two friends. Along with his friends, he then purchased a 12-pack of beer. By the time a police officer spotted the truck a few hours later, Phillip and his friends had finished the beer. Afraid of being caught and charged, they sped away, ignoring the police siren. In his haste to escape, Phillip (the driver) lost control of the vehicle and ran into a tree, causing serious damage to the truck. In court the next day, he faced criminal charges of theft, dangerous driving, operating a motor vehicle while impaired, and failing to stop for a police officer. As an adult offender, he would almost certainly receive a jail sentence under the Canadian justice system in most provinces. In Saskatchewan, however, the courts sometimes offer an alternative—the sentencing circle—to Aboriginal offenders.

This alternative developed as a way to respond to the justice needs of Aboriginal communities.[1] Although most Canadians agree that our justice system does not always work as well as it could, we disagree on how to fix the system. At one extreme, we see greater punishment of offenders as the answer. The term *retributive justice* refers to the idea of making offenders pay by sentencing them to time in jail. At the other extreme, we see options such as restorative justice. The term *restorative justice* refers to an approach that sees community service, therapy, and restitution (or compensation) to victims as more productive than putting offenders behind bars.

Restorative justice has a long history in many Aboriginal cultures, as well as in some faith communities such as the Mennonites. Aboriginal peoples have long used healing circles (the basis for the more recently developed sentencing circles) as a means of restoring harmony within their communities. In the early 1990s, the territory of Yukon and the province of Saskatchewan began experimenting with sentencing circles as an alternative to criminal trials. In the United States, activists such as Little Rock Reed encountered much resistance when they tried to incorporate healing circles into the prison system in that country.[2]

CP Photo/Winnipeg Free Press—Ken Gigliotti

In order to illustrate what typically happens at sentencing circles—a unique group process—we can look at the fictitious case of Phillip. Phillip must first agree to receive his sentence in the sentencing circle rather than in the courtroom, as the process is voluntary. His victims must also agree. In accepting this forum for sentencing, Phillip realizes that he will face the owner of the stolen car (the uncle of a friend and owner of the local gas station), the victim's family, his own family, the police officer who charged him, and representatives of the community in which he lives (e.g., respected elders). No lawyer will be present to speak for him.

Ideally, circle members consider all the facts in the case, discuss the situation, and decide upon a plan of action for the offender. In other words, they proceed through a typical problem-solving sequence—defining and analyzing the problem, identifying possible solutions, and arriving at the best solution. The unique aspects of this group process, however, relate to (1) the fact that criminal actions call the circle into being; (2) the composition of the group, with offender and

INTRODUCTION

CONFLICT
Disagreement between two or more parties who see themselves as having opposing goals or values.

Disagreements and disputes between and among people are natural and inevitable, and our most frequent **conflicts** occur with the people who matter most to us. Often the conflicts are minor and short term; however, they can be serious and long term, even threatening the existence of a relationship. In addition to reduced productivity, workplace conflict results in lower employee morale, higher levels of absenteeism, and interpersonal and organizational confrontations.[4] Managers spend at least 25 per cent of their time in the workplace resolving conflicts.[5]

victims in the same room; and (3) the voluntary nature of the group.

Once the group members have arrived at a sentencing plan, they present their plan to a court judge. Judges almost always accept the recommendations of the sentencing circles, which most often include repaying the victim in some way, performing services for the community, and accepting counselling or treatment. In Phillip's case, the members of the circle might recommend that Phillip work weekends at the gas station until he has repaid the owner for all damages to his truck. If circle members suspect that Phillip has a drinking problem, they might also propose that he participate in substance abuse and safe driving programs.

Sentencing circles and other restorative justice initiatives aim to reintegrate the offender into the community. Supporters say that social control and community support work better than jail in rehabilitating offenders. If Phillip does not follow through with the terms of the sentence, he will be letting down his victim, his victim's family, his family, and the community at large. He will also face the possibility of imprisonment.

Sentencing circles have faced their critics—both in the legal system and in some Aboriginal communities. Many Aboriginal critics disapprove of the modifications to their peoples' traditional peacekeeping practices. The legal community, on the other hand, complains that procedures are inconsistent from one sentencing circle to the next, appeal processes are unclear, and victims and other community representatives do not always receive proper representation. Most importantly, they complain that, too often, no one has verified the facts of the case prior to the sentencing. In the absence of tested facts, it is difficult (if not impossible) to decide on appropriate sentences. Debates over facts, they say, should occur at an earlier stage—not at the sentencing circle. Despite these criticisms, however, many Canadians continue to support the use of sentencing circles; and sentencing circles continue to occur in some provinces and territories.

Other groups have also faced critics when trying to implement alternative justice systems. For example, many people protested when the Islamic Institute of Civil Justice (IICJ) announced in 2003 that it planned to offer legally binding arbitration based on sharia law in Canada. The group argued that this sort of arbitration fit with the guidelines presented in Ontario's 1991 Arbitration Act, which allowed faith-based arbitration on family issues such as divorce, custody, and family inheritance. Several Jewish, Christian, and other religious groups had been offering arbitration services under the act for more than a decade, without objection from the general public.

The response from many women's groups was almost immediate. Protests over establishing sharia-based arbitration panels came from the National Association of Women and the Law, the Canadian Council of Muslim Women, and the National Organization of Immigrant and Visible Minority Women of Canada. They expressed the fear that women would feel pressured to participate in a system that does not accord them the same rights as men. Critics of the IICJ's proposal also expressed concern about the political implications of allowing religious beliefs to influence the legal system.

In an attempt to resolve tensions, officials asked former attorney general of Ontario Marion Boyd to investigate the potential impact of sharia-based arbitration in the province. In her official report, released in December 2004, Boyd ruled that Ontario Muslims should have the same privileges as Christians and Jews to seek faith-based arbitration for certain kinds of disputes. Responding to widespread concerns about women's rights, she also stated that all legal actions must conform to the *Canadian Charter of Rights and Freedoms*. In September 2005, however, then premier of Ontario Dalton McGuinty announced that Ontario would reject the use of sharia law.[3]

As you read this chapter, consider the following questions: Does culture have an impact on perceptions of conflict? How much weight should we give to the role of culture in conflict resolution? How do sentencing circles give "voice" to Aboriginal people? How does access to sharia justice give voice to members of the Muslim faith? How do these forms of justice attempt to redress power inequities in society? What are some of the pitfalls or dilemmas in implementing alternative justice systems in Canada?

Dudley Weeks, a professor in political science, conducts workshops in mediation and conflict resolution with people from around the world. One of the workshop exercises asks the participants to list words that describe how they view conflict. The most commonly mentioned words include *fight, anger, pain, war, impasse, destruction, fear, mistake, avoid, lose, control, hate, loss, bad,* and *wrongdoing*.[6] In fact, people in conflict feel a wide range of emotions—mostly negative. Depending on the circumstances, they may feel out of

> **"Conflict is an important part of the totality of human communicative behaviour."**
>
> **FRED JANDT**

control, fearful, angry, confused or disoriented, uncertain, distrustful, powerless and vulnerable, or defensive.

In this chapter, we will examine various aspects of conflict: sources and types, stages, the role of power, coping styles, outcomes, the kind of language and behaviours that characterize civil workplaces, and the benefits of using the awareness wheel.

SOURCES OF CONFLICT

Conflict occurs as a result of many different factors. Let us take a look at some of the primary factors causing interpersonal conflicts. These factors include differences in beliefs, attitudes, and values; personality differences; incompatible and conflicting goals or roles; interdependencies; insufficient or different information; poor communication; scarce and non-distributable resources and power struggles; and stressful situations.

Differences in Beliefs, Attitudes, and Values

Differences in beliefs, attitudes, and values give rise to conflict and influence the way we view and manage conflict. These differences may involve gender, race, ethnicity, religion, language, age, education, sexual orientation, political orientation, socio-economic status, or other factors.

Mississippi Masala is a romantic film released in 1991. Set mainly in the rural areas of Mississippi, the film examines an intercultural and interracial conflict involving an Indian American family and an African American family. The film documents how a romance, which develops between the daughter of the Indian American family and the son of the African American family, leads to friction and conflict between the families. A sensitive portrayal of the conflict allows us to see how the families deal with—and ultimately resolve—their differences as they come to terms with the couple's love for each other.

In multicultural societies such as those found across Canada, diverse workplaces give rise to conflicts growing out differing beliefs, attitudes, and values.[7] New Canadians and internationally trained professionals presently account for the majority of growth in our country's labour pool. To address this trend, consulting firms such as the Civility Group Inc. have established centres that offer training in intercultural competencies. Business schools also aim to prepare students for working in a multicultural environment.[8] Employers who want to establish more inclusive hiring policies and more respectful and diverse workplaces seek help from these centres, colleges, and universities.[9]

Personality Differences

Differences in personality can account for conflict between individuals. For example, one member of a project team may want everyone to participate and agree on decisions, while another may want to proceed in a less democratic way in order to meet deadlines. In this case, the different personality styles (relationship-oriented versus task-oriented) can cause tension within the team.

Consider the case of two colleagues, Kevin and Ethan, who disagree over whether to set deadlines for different stages of a project. Kevin does not want to commit to multiple deadlines; rather he prefers a more flexible approach, with only a final deadline. Ethan, who is more comfortable in structured situations, feels uncomfortable with Kevin's approach. Whichever approach these colleagues decide to take, they will likely face conflict; and this conflict may interfere with their productivity.

In order to better position individuals in organizations, many organizations pay for potential employees to take personality tests such as the Myers–Briggs Type Indicator (MBTI). These tests help the organization to identify the basic personality styles of the job candidates and to place the candidates accordingly. As in the case of Kevin and Ethan, one employee may work best in a highly structured environment while another may work best with lack of structure. At other times, an organization may need someone who is detail-oriented in one position but someone who can see the big picture in another position. Appropriate placements lower the chances of conflicts that result from personalities colliding or competing with each other.

Incompatible and Conflicting Goals or Roles

Incompatible and conflicting goals can also cause disagreements between individuals or groups. For instance, a couple may be saving money for two different reasons. One partner may want to take a trip to Mexico, while the other may want to make bigger payments on their mortgage. The couple may struggle over which goal should achieve priority. In the workplace, co-workers may face conflict if their individual duties are incompatible. In a hospital, for example, conflicts may arise if a staff member needs to consult with a patient in order to complete extensive paperwork, but a nurse needs to finish prepping the patient for tests. Conflicts can also arise when managers convey different priorities to employees. For instance, the head teller of a bank may say that quick customer service should be a priority, but the bank's community relations director may insist that employees slow down and spend time getting to know customers.

Being assigned responsibilities that lie outside our regular job roles can also give rise to disagreements. In some cases, the colleague normally responsible for a task may resent our intrusion into her or his territory. In other cases, we may think that another person should complete the work—that it is not our responsibility to take up the slack.

Interdependencies

Many interdependencies exist in organizations. For example, one group may depend on a second to complete a particular stage of a project. If the second group does not complete its work on time, then the first cannot meet its target date. Similarly, if a manager assigns the same deadline to two different groups for completing their contributions to a staged project, one group will not be able to meet its deadline. At other times, employees depend on the delivery of materials or the reliability of equipment to complete their work. If the employees responsible for ordering or maintaining the equipment do not carry out their tasks in a timely way, conflicts can arise with groups that depend on the materials and equipment.

In a similar way, we may become engaged in conflict if we believe that someone else is making us look bad. If we think that someone on whom we depend is not making a full effort, we may grow resentful—out of fear that the results will reflect badly on us. Such perceptions account for almost all small-group conflicts, especially in college and university classrooms where grades depend on dedicated efforts by all group members. The same kinds of conflicts can arise, however, in project work in organizations.

Insufficient or Different Information

Our level of access to information can lead to differences in perception of situations. These perceptual differences, in turn, can result in interpersonal conflict. In the 2012 movie *The Twilight Saga: Breaking Dawn—Part 2*, we see Rosalie (played by Nikki Reed) and Jacob (played by Taylor Lautner) disagreeing over who will get more time with baby Renesmee. In one scene, Jacob watches Rosalie closely while she plays with Renesmee. Jacob's apprehension arises from his concern about the safety of the half-human, half-vampire baby. He perceives the need to protect Renesmee from Rosalie's vampire instincts, whereas Rosalie does not see the situation in the same way.

Consider another example. An employee named Laidi learns that she is being relocated to a much more spacious office on a different floor of the building. Kim, a male co-worker, worries that Laidi has requested the move to get away from him. He had invited her, the previous week, to get together for drinks after work; Laidi had declined the invitation. A female co-worker (Paula) thinks the move is unfair because Laidi has done nothing to deserve the bigger office. Having been in the organization longer than Laidi, Paula thinks she should have priority. Kim reacts by becoming moody and silent whenever he is around Laidi, and Paula complains about Laidi to other staff members. What neither of them knows, however, is that Laidi's boss decided to relocate her so she can be closer to the group with whom she will be interacting on an important but unannounced project. This example shows that people come to different—and often inaccurate—conclusions when they have incomplete or different information; and these sorts of conclusions can result in conflict.

Conflicts in the workplace can also arise from the perception that employment equity legislation favours some groups over others. In Canada, the Employment Equity Act provides protection for four groups in particular: women, visible minorities, persons with disabilities, and Aboriginal peoples. Some candidates and employees believe this legislation results in reverse discrimination—a perception that can lead, especially in situations of insufficient information, to resentments and confrontations.

Royston/Cartoonstock

"Apparently many companies experience problems including: a lack of direction, poor accountability, lack of respect among members, pushing personal agendas, poor communication ..."

Poor Communication

Poor communication can lead to conflict between individuals or groups. Our neglect or inability to express ourselves clearly, state our needs, or listen effectively can cause frustration, annoyance, and anger in relationships.[10] We can see examples of poor communication in unclear conversations, office memos, company policies, performance reviews, and customer feedback. These flawed attempts at communication influence interactions between employees and managers, government agencies and their clients, doctors and patients, and others.[11] The "Human Diversity" box describes some of the communication problems that can arise when government agencies try to help immigrant victims of violence. Doubtless some of these encounters will have produced unnecessary conflicts.

humanDIVERSITY

Navigating Anti-violence Work in a Culturally Sensitive Way

A study in Atlantic Canada examined the forms of violence experienced by immigrant women of diverse ethno-cultural backgrounds. In-depth interviews with immigrant women and their service providers took place in five Atlantic Canadian cities: Moncton, Sydney, St John's, Halifax, and Charlottetown. The researchers sought to identify not only the perspectives of the women, but also the views of the service providers about their efforts to help and work with immigrant women who had experienced violence—either in Canada or in their countries of origin. The study identified different kinds of violence, including domestic violence (emotional and/or physical abuse); racism and discrimination in the workplace; and institutional abuse, including targeting of minorities by authorities.

The conclusions were not definitive. Many of the immigrant women said they had received helpful assistance and protection from service providers, churches, friends and family, sponsors, and volunteers after the violence occurred. Other participants complained that immigrant women in Atlantic Canada have less access to services and supports than do women in other provinces. Some service providers identified cultural barriers such as the reluctance of the immigrant women to talk about abuse and violence, their tendencies to deny that the abuse had occurred, and behaviours that suggested a felt sense of shame. A number of the women said that they feared being ignored or singled out by their ethnic communities if their stories became public.

In terms of policy recommendations, the immigrant women and their service providers said the different levels of government, law enforcement agencies, and non-government organizations should work together to create and support culturally sensitive ways of communicating with immigrant women who had experienced violence.[12]

Scarce and Non-distributable Resources and Power Struggles

The term *scarce and non-distributable resource* refers to something that only one person can use or possess at the same time. For example, only one team can win a soccer match, a game of rugby, or a hockey game. Two friends sharing an apartment may want the same bedroom, but only one can have it. If both insist on getting the room, a conflict will develop between them.

In the workplace, conflict develops when people in different departments perceive themselves to be in competition for scarce and non-distributable resources. While the overriding objective of all departments may be to make money for the organization, the individual departments may see themselves as being in competition for space, funding, recognition, or other resources. People in organizations sometimes see others as threats to their own career progress (e.g., "If you get this promotion, I will not get it"). This mentality establishes a "win–lose" dynamic, and people approach the conflict similar to how they might approach a fight. Like wrestlers, they try to maneuver into a superior position, relative to the other party.[13]

Within families and organizations, struggles for power often relate to competition for scarce and non-distributable resources such as time or money. Upset with her husband for going out too often in the evenings, a wife may demand that he give up his poker night with the guys. Or a husband may become upset that his wife is spending too much money on clothes. Sometimes couples struggle over competing goals, such as we discussed earlier. One wants to take a vacation in Hawaii; the other wants to save money to go to Cuba. Within the workplace, employees may resist supervisor demands to work overtime or give up their weekends. People struggle for better positions, greater influence, higher wages, and more desirable work hours.

Stressful Situations

Stressful situations can cause or aggravate conflicts. In stressful situations, we often respond in ways that we would not normally react. Unrealistic deadlines and heavy workloads cause us to have a lower level of tolerance for the behaviour of others. Acts that might not have bothered us so much under normal circumstances become magnified. When we lack money to cover the rent, fear losing our job, or worry about failing an exam, we bring those stresses into our relationships. The result is often unnecessary conflict with family, friends, and co-workers. We may make unrealistic demands on someone who works under us, or we may speak in an angry way to a family member. Similarly, when we experience personal loss or trauma, our relationships may suffer. Parents of murdered children often separate once the crisis has peaked. One or both cannot handle the grief, and the family falls apart. The relationship of Katniss Everdeen (played by Jennifer Lawrence) and her mother in the 2012 movie *The Hunger Games* deteriorated with the death of her father. Unable to cope with the death, Katniss's mother became catatonic, creating a stressful home environment for a preteen Katniss, who had to become the breadwinner of the family and caregiver for her younger sister. The resulting resentment contributes to conflicts in the relationship between Katniss and her mother.

"An eye for an eye will only make the whole world blind."
MAHATMA GANDHI

When we feel good about our situations, on the other hand, we are much more likely to be empathetic in our responses to others and to experience less conflict in our relationships. See the "Professional Contexts" box for an interesting case from the Israeli justice system.

TYPES OF CONFLICT

Conflict can be overt (open) or covert (hidden).[14] The following discussion will examine characteristics of these two types of conflict.

Overt Conflict

OVERT CONFLICT
Conflict involving open disagreement.

Overt conflict occurs when we openly disagree with another person or group.[15] In this situation, we address the problem or issue in a direct way. According to Albert Hirschman, dissatisfied employees have three options.[16] They can voice their opinions

*professional*CONTEXTS

Give the Judge a Break! I Want Parole

Shai Danziger of Ben-Gurion University of the Negev in Israel analyzed the results of 1112 parole board hearings in Israeli prisons over a ten-month period. Danziger looked for possible connections between the morning, lunch, and afternoon breaks of judges and the decisions the judges made in the parole board hearings. Astonishingly, he discovered that the odds of a successful request start off at about 65 per cent. As the morning progresses, the odds plummet to zero. After the judges return from breaks, the odds return to 65 per cent before beginning another downward turn. Danziger also found that the first three prisoners to appear before the board each day had a better chance of getting parole than the three last applicants—regardless of other factors such as the length of their sentences or the number of times they had been in prison. Eight judges with an average experience of 22 years made these judgments. The verdicts accounted for 40 per cent of all parole requests over the ten-month period.[17]

or concerns, exit the organization, or maintain a loyal silence. When people engage in overt conflict, they tend to use the voice option. Voicing of opinions can take the form of asking about the problem, seeking advice from others, or engaging in debate to try to work things out.

People in open conflict often use **metalanguage** to talk about their concerns. For example, one partner might say to the other, "When you said, 'I'm not angry,' what did you really mean?" or "Does *reaching an agreement* mean the same thing to you as it means to me?" Metalanguage enables people in conflict to voice and talk through their problems.

METALANGUAGE Language that describes or comments on language.

To encourage the voice option in organizations, management can provide suggestion boxes or websites for feedback, conduct regular sessions to listen and respond to employee questions and concerns, and act on credible suggestions. If management does not provide these options, punishes employees who hold unwelcome views, or stifles employee voices, the organization will suffer. When employees feel rejected or ignored, most either leave or air their concerns in social media forums such as Twitter and Facebook, which are open to public scrutiny. If they remain, they may engage in covert conflict (e.g., neglect their duties or secretly spread rumours about the business).

According to social exchange theory (discussed in Chapter 8), three factors influence the strategy a person will choose in an overt conflict. These three factors are the level of satisfaction with the relationship before its decline; the amount of financial, emotional, or other investment in the relationship; and the quality of the best alternative. When people remain loyal, they usually hope or pray that change will occur; but they do not voice their concerns.

Covert Conflict

Unlike those who are engaged in overt conflict, people involved in **covert conflict** do not address issues directly. Sometimes only one of the disputants even realizes that a conflict exists because the other hides his resentment or upset.[18] In the movie franchise *Harry Potter*, we see that Hermione and Ron have romantic feelings toward each other, but they never profess their love openly. Because they do not tell each other about their feelings, tension and jealousy sometimes surface in their friendship. In the 2010 movie *Harry Potter and the Deathly Hallows—Part 1*, for example, Ron abandons the quest to find the Sword of Gryffindor when he thinks Hermione and Harry have become a couple. In this case, the conflict is covert because he does not tell his friends that he is upset with them.

COVERT CONFLICT Hidden conflict, not always known to the other party.

People involved in covert conflict are likely to display passive-aggressive behaviours.[19] By *passive-aggressive behaviours*, we mean indirect acts of aggression. Examples of passive-aggressive behaviours include pretending we do not hear the other person when she or he speaks to us, not answering the phone when the person calls, deliberately submitting a report late, or withholding information. Disputing neighbours might call the police to report a late party or call the pound to pick up a dog that is not on a leash when the real source of the conflict relates to ownership of a parking space. Rather than talking through the conflict, the parties in conflict take actions that have the potential to harm, annoy, or "punish" the other person.

Covert conflict often results in misdirected displays of aggression. Take the fictitious case of Hiro, who has recently started a new job. In his first few weeks in the position, he encounters a number of frustrations. A co-worker fails to tell him about an important meeting. His boss tells him that he will have to work extra hours to help fix a problem in another department. He discovers that he does not have as much authority or influence as he had anticipated. Not wanting to risk losing his job, Hiro does not express his frustration or annoyance at work. Instead he yells at his teenage sons when he returns home—transferring his feelings of aggression from his boss and coworkers to his family.

Sometimes covert conflicts transform into overt conflicts.[20] The following example illustrates this point. Emma and Amarina work, on a commission basis, in customer sales at a small clothing boutique. Soon after beginning their part-time jobs, the two become friends—that is, until Amarina notices that Emma is stealing customers that she has already approached and helped. She grows more resentful as the days pass, but she does not say anything directly to Emma. Instead she complains to another sales clerk and mentions the problem to her manager. (Those involved in covert conflict often try to muster group support for their positions or grievances.) Finally, however, what has been a covert (unspoken) conflict becomes overt. The open conflict begins when Emma takes a particularly large sale away from Amarina, who is already feeling stressed about her finances. The argument, which begins in the front part of the store, escalates until the manager eventually moves both of the girls to the back room and tells them to work out their differences. Amarina begins crying, and Emma realizes that both will lose their jobs if the tension continues. The girls decide to address the issue in a direct way, and they reach agreement on how they will approach and deal with customers in the future. Once the conflict becomes overt, the issues get resolved.

Not all conflicts that move from covert to overt end equally well. Some relationships continue to deteriorate, as can happen in marriages where one partner confronts the other about an affair. Sometimes a partner uses such a confrontation as an excuse to leave the relationship—an action she or he wanted to take in the first place. At least partly for that reason, some spouses choose not to address issues of infidelity. Go to the "From Theory to Practice" box titled "Talking It Over or Acting It Out?" and reflect on some overt or covert conflict you have experienced.

> ### *from theory* TO PRACTICE
> **Talking It Over or Acting It Out?**
>
> Think about a recent conflict that you experienced with a colleague at work. How did you deal with the conflict? Did you openly disagree? Try to work out your differences? Avoid and fail to resolve the issue or totally lose control? Use someone else as a scapegoat? Did you display any hostile, adversarial, or passive-aggressive behaviours in dealing with your work colleague? After identifying your reactions, respond to the following question: Was the conflict addressed in an overt or covert fashion?

STAGES OF CONFLICT

According to Jeffrey Rubin, conflict moves in cycles and continues to resurface until people address the underlying causes.[21] A typical conflict resembles a three-act play. In Act I, conflict escalates and issues multiply. A dispute over coffee breaks in the workplace can give rise to arguments over lunch breaks, pay increases, compensation for overtime, and parking privileges. If one spouse accuses the other of spending too much money on lottery tickets, the accused might in turn criticize the accuser for spending too much on hair care, pets, or clothes. A parent–child disagreement over the use of a car could escalate into a fight over curfew, rights to sleepovers, or choice of friends. In other words, a single issue opens the door for the emergence of multiple issues.

Other shifts also occur in Act I of a conflict. People change from focussing on specific issues and behaviours to focussing on personalities. The rhetoric becomes accusatory:

"You show no consideration for anyone but yourself." Behaviours become generalized: "You're *never* on time." People in conflict also begin to shift from "light" to "heavy" tactics in Act I. They begin by pointing out problems, but they move on to making threats if that strategy does not work. If threats fail to achieve results, the opponents may use other means to force their point of view. For example, they may try to back up their threats with action or embarrass the other person into agreeing with them. They pull more people into the conflict. What begins as a conflict between two co-workers may now involve multiple colleagues and supervisors. A conflict that begins with intimate partners may expand to involve the couple's friends and family members.

All of the above—the accusations, the move from light to heavy tactics, and the number of people involved in the conflict—make it more difficult for parties in conflict to back down. They fear losing face with others, and they believe they have invested too much to change their positions on the issues. In other words, they have become over-committed and locked into a pattern of behaviour that encourages the conflict to continue. In this behavioural set, the parties in conflict begin to view each other as stereotypes. They see and hear only what they want to see and hear, they distort messages, and they become suspicious of the other person's motives and actions. In Act I, conflict escalates to the maximum extent. While some conflicts will end at this point—usually when one party dominates the other and forces an agreement—many will continue unresolved.

In Act II, parties lose hope the other will change. They may not like each other more than they did in Act I; however, they realize that they will not prevail over the other by coercive means. For that reason, Act II marks a transition stage, where people begin grudgingly to accept the necessity for compromise or collaboration. They have simply "run out of steam," lacking either the energy or resources to continue the fight. At this stage, saving face becomes important; neither person wants to be perceived as the loser. Rubin cites the world championship chess match between Bobby Fischer and Boris Spassky. Neither player wanted to be the one to call a draw (tie) even though they both—and everyone watching—could see that a draw was inevitable. At one point, the commentator (Shelby Lymon) observed that the two men were playing "forehead to forehead," but avoiding eye contact. The situation changed when the two "apparently looked up, glanced at each other, smiled, and nodded their heads. The referee eagerly said, 'Do I take it that there is a draw?' And so a draw was reached." By agreeing to the draw at the same moment, both players were able to save face.

In the above example, the shift from stubbornly avoiding the issue to agreeing to the draw signaled the move from Act II to Act III. Act III brings a certain measure of closure. The parties to the conflict move toward settlement. Settlement does not necessarily imply resolution, but it implies a de-escalation of the conflict. In the best-case scenario, the parties begin to talk again. They discard stereotypes and see the other as having strengths, not just weaknesses. They brainstorm and try to identify ways to build momentum. They look for a bigger goal to which they can both commit, and they become more flexible on means to achieve the goal. That flexibility can translate into varying strategies for resolving the issues. For example, if the parties in conflict have been trying to solve all the issues at once, they might change their strategy to take one issue at a time. If taking the issues one at a time is unproductive, they might put multiple issues on the table in order to allow "give and take" on different ones. Alternatively, they might look for solutions to the easiest issues before proceeding to the more difficult ones. As they try new approaches, they listen more carefully to each other and look for mutually agreeable solutions.

ROLE OF POWER IN CONFLICT

Whenever conflict arises, questions of power come into play. According to John French and Bertram Raven, five sources of power are available to those who want to prevail over others. Those sources of power are reward power, coercive power, legitimate power, referent power, and expert or information power (Figure 9.1).[22] You may recall that we introduced these sources of power in Chapter 1, when we discussed the power dimension of communication. In the following discussion, we will take a closer look at each one.

Reward power comes from offering benefits or gifts. An individual in conflict can offer rewards in an attempt to increase his attractiveness to those who will profit from the benefits. To gain the favour of a small group, an individual might offer to have a meeting at his home, provide a meal for everyone, pay for supplies, or do extra work for the group. Reward power increases our ability to influence decisions and encourages others to listen to our opinions.

A second source of power, *coercive power*, comes from threatening or intimidating people. An individual in conflict can exercise coercive power by threatening to punish anyone who does not go along with her ideas. In a small group, a leader could threaten to pull out of the group and leave the remaining members without the necessary numbers to perform a task. Popular television celebrities sometimes threaten to leave a show if they do not receive more money or perks. In March 2012, teen moms Jenelle Evans and Leah Messer threatened to leave the hit MTV show *Teen Mom 2* unless network executives met their salary demands.[23] A month earlier, contestants on *The Biggest Loser* walked off the set after NBC made a surprise announcement. The network had invited former contestants to rejoin the show to compete for a $250,000 prize.[24] One of the stars of *The Real Housewives of New Jersey*, Teresa Giudice, threatened to leave the show unless Bravo offered her more money for the fall 2012 season.[25]

> "The measure of a man is what he does with power."
> PLATO

The effectiveness of coercive power depends on whether the other party can avoid or survive the threat. After reality television personality Victoria Gotti threatened to leave *Celebrity Apprentice* in 2012, Donald Trump ousted her from the show. Trump knew the viewing audience would not turn against him for firing Gotti. Getting rid of Gotti also allowed him to retain model Cheryl Tiegs, a more popular and likeable contestant; as a result, most audience members supported Trump's decision. Even if Gotti had remained on the show, her threat to leave would have damaged her appeal. Coercive power decreases the attractiveness of the person who chooses to use it.

A third source of power, *legitimate power*, comes from holding a position of authority. This power is the rightful power (often limited in scope) that we grant to others in the belief we will gain benefits from the transfer. In many situations, we freely give the right to act on our behalf to leaders whom we trust. Figures of authority such as members of Parliament, classroom teachers, and supervisors in

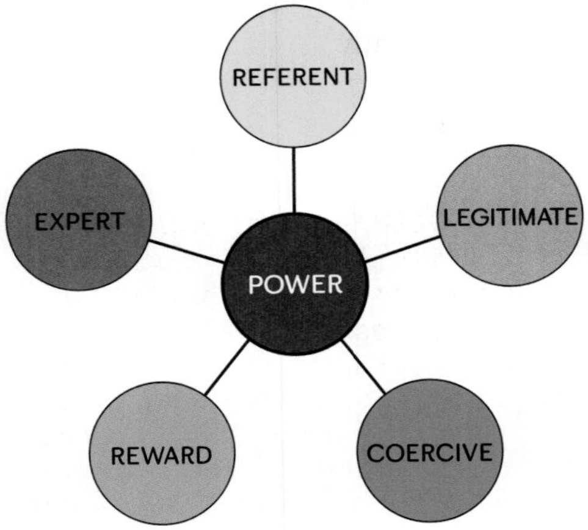

REFERENT
EXPERT
LEGITIMATE
POWER
REWARD
COERCIVE

FIGURE 9.1 Five sources of power.

SOURCE: Based on Babou Srinivasan, "How to Manage Power," accessed at http://leadershipchamps.wordpress.com/2008/04/30/managing-power/ on November 26, 2012.

organizations hold power that derives from their position. We question their power only when we believe they have abused the trust placed in them.

© Travel Pictures/Alamy

Individuals acquire legitimate power when they accept a formal position of authority or status in an organization or some other network or hierarchy. Judges, priests, and prime ministers all hold legitimate power granted to them by an official organization. Executives and other higher-level employees hold power based on their job descriptions. In many traditional societies such as those of the Inuit and First Nations peoples of Canada, elders acquire legitimate power based on age. Being born into some castes in Hindu society gives special status and power to the occupant. For a discussion of how status and power interact in the Indian workplace, see the "Professional Contexts" box.

If someone attempts to exercise power outside the limits of legitimacy, she decreases her attractiveness to others. She also decreases her chances of being granted similar powers in the future. Imagine that a city councillor votes to award a contract to a company in which she holds shares. While the councillor may truly believe that the company is the best candidate for the job, she risks being accused of abusing her legitimate power for personal gain. In a similar way, when members of Parliament promote projects in their ridings, many people will believe they are trying to buy votes in the next election. In both of these examples, people may question whether the politicians have exceeded

*professional*CONTEXTS

Conflict and Power in the Workplace: The Lingering Influence of the Caste System in India

The dynamics of status and power can have an impact on how conflict plays out in the workplace. These dynamics have a particularly strong influence in India, whose caste system dates from ancient times. The caste system began as a loosely based division of labour among the Brahmins (priests and scholars), the Kshatriyas (rulers and warriors), the Vaishyas (food producers and traders), and the Shudras (labourers). In addition, another group of people (viewed as outside the system) performed all tasks considered to be "unclean." Eventually, however, the people in India began to see the different occupational groups in a hierarchical way. That is, they saw them as occupying different places on the social ladder—some higher and some lower. This view led to stereotyping of people in lower castes, along with discrimination in the workplace.

After the departure of the British in 1947, the Indian government passed legislation similar to the employment equity legislation in Canada to prevent discrimination against members of certain caste groups. To protect the interests of groups covered by the legislation, employee associations and unions developed along caste lines.

Despite the efforts of Indian governments and unions to neutralize the effects of the caste system, status-conscious organizations created their own sets of power dynamics. And even today, many employees perceive continuing inequalities in the system. Some complain that managers (intentionally or unintentionally) use their higher social status and positional power to discriminate against employees from lower castes. Whether the accusations are true or false, the perception of discrimination causes misunderstandings and conflicts—a serious problem for organizations.[26]

the limits of their legitimate power. As a result, they may be less likely to vote for these politicians in the future.

A fourth source of power, *referent power*, comes from personal attractiveness. We are attracted to people with beliefs or values similar to our own. These identifications lead us to behave in ways that indicate the connection. For example, we might become a follower on Twitter, share the person's comments on Facebook, or attend a conference where the person is keynote speaker. In Canada, Justin Trudeau has strong referent power for many members of the Liberal Party. They see him as someone who will uphold the values and legacy of his father (former prime minister Pierre Trudeau). In the United States, Republicans Sarah Palin and Paul Ryan have strong referent power for some Americans. Members of the Tea Party believe in highly conservative political values and reduced federal powers, and they see Palin and Ryan as strong advocates for these values.

Many celebrities also hold referent power. For that reason, companies often use celebrities in advertising their products. A "halo" effect can occur, where the attractiveness of the person allows him or her to exercise influence in a wide range of areas. Olympic personalities often promote products such as cereals that have little to do with their areas of expertise. Former Canadian figure skating champion Elizabeth Manley promoted Herbal Magic weight loss products for many years. Referent power increases with attractiveness. So the greater the attraction to—or identification with—someone, the stronger his or her referent power and the more likely the person will have influence that extends to many areas. If teenagers see Justin Bieber, Katy Perry, or Rihanna as highly attractive, for example, they may pay attention to what these singers have to say on a number of unrelated and diverse subjects—clothes, cars, sex, use of drugs, and other topics.

Finally, *expert or information power* comes from access to knowledge or perceptions that we do not have. In other words, people with this sort of power have access to—or the ability to control—information. Secretaries, personal assistants, and housekeepers often have such information power. Following the death of Princess Diana, her butler held information power over the royal family; he had been privy to much confidential information in the years preceding her death. Doctors, lawyers, and other professionals have expert power, generally limited to areas in which they hold advanced knowledge. Dr Oz has expert power, for example, on matters related to health; whereas TLC personality Randy Fenoli has expert power when it comes to wedding dresses (*Say Yes to the Dress*). David Suzuki exercises expert power on a wide range of topics pertaining to nature and wildlife, and Canadian finance ministers exercise this sort of power on topics pertaining to the economy.

An additional source of power is the ability to stimulate debate and generate support for ideas and points of view. In today's environment, access to the media can be

from theory TO PRACTICE

Winning the Lottery

Imagine the following scenario. Every week for the past year, you and your friend have pooled your money to buy a lottery ticket. Last week, while you were out of town visiting your family, your friend bought a lottery ticket and won. You feel that your friend should split his winnings with you. He disagrees. The two of you begin a heated debate over the issue. How would you draw on the five main sources of power—reward power, coercive power, legitimate power, referent power, and expert or information power—to argue your point? Create a strong argument related to each one.

After creating your arguments, find a partner. First, assign the role of the lottery-winning friend to your partner and make your case. Next, switch roles and let your partner make her or his arguments. Once you have finished, consider the following questions. Did you find some sources of power to be more persuasive than others? How did you respond when your partner used coercive power? Did you find the use of referent power to be convincing? Why or why not? Did you find the use of expert or information power to be more persuasive than more emotional arguments? How did you respond to the use of reward power? Did the offer of a reward appear sincere to you?

a major source of power for a group seeking support for a cause such as environmental protection or Aboriginal rights.[27]

Now that you have a better understanding of the major sources of power, take a moment to think about how you might draw on these types of power in a personal argument. Refer to the "From Theory to Practice" box for an exercise that will help you with this task.

COPING STYLES

The Thomas–Kilmann Conflict Mode Instrument (TKI) identifies five coping styles commonly used by individuals in conflict: competing, accommodating, avoiding, compromising, and collaborating. The developers of the instrument refer to these approaches as *coping styles*, and they say that each of us has a dominant coping style or way of handling conflict.[28] Let us consider these styles in the light of win–lose dynamics.

Competing

Competing involves arguing a position and aiming to win at the expense of the other party. Members of organizations compete for many different kinds of resources, including positions, power, pay increases, and recognition. The competing style relies on an assertive approach, with win–lose dynamics: that is, *I win; you lose*. It does not involve co-operation. As a result, some see this style as overly controlling and selfish. Nonetheless, some situations demand a competing or controlling style. In an emergency situation, forcing a decision might save lives. At other times, pressing strongly for an important policy or action may be ethical and necessary.

COMPETING Forcing a resolution by pushing for one's own needs or solution.

Accommodating

Accommodating requires that you yield to the other person's point of view, whether you believe in the position or not. Thus, this coping style is co-operative but passive. It works well when you care more about the person than the issue or the issue does not hold the same importance for you as for the other person. However, when you use the accommodating style on a regular basis, you risk being generous to the point of selflessness. People with an accommodating style often give in to the other point of view just to keep the peace. Again the dynamics are win–lose, but the winner changes: *you win; I lose*.

ACCOMMODATING Resolving a conflict by giving in to what the other party or individual wants.

In the following scenario, we can see an accommodating style (as well as a competitive style) in action. A jewellery chain has decided to open a store in Vancouver. The owners have contracted a marketing firm to promote the opening. At the request of their boss, two members of the marketing firm (Mei and Sean) sit down to plan for the opening.

Sean: Hello, Mei. Let's get started.

Mei: Sure thing. I've been thinking about some ideas for the opening, and I prepared a PowerPoint presentation so you can see what I have in mind.

Sean: Mei, stop for a minute. Why didn't you wait for our meeting? I have ideas too, and we should be making the plans together.

Mei: I was trying to save time; that's all. I. . . .

"Do not think of knocking out another person's brains because he differs in opinion from you. It would be as rational to knock yourself on the head because you differ from yourself ten years ago."

HORACE MANN

Sean: Yeah, well, I think we should begin from scratch. Seems you're trying to get some extra points with management.
Mei: What do you mean?
Sean: Don't pretend you don't know about it! Come on, Mei. The opening of a new managerial post at our home office in Victoria.
Mei: Honestly, I had no idea. Besides I can't move to Victoria. What would happen with Wan? I just wanted to get a head start on planning.
Sean: I hear you, but regardless, I want to make a contribution at the idea stage to this project. Understand?
Mei: Sure, if that's how you feel about it. What did you have in mind?

Sean displays a strong competitive style throughout the interaction, and Mei eventually yields to pressure from Sean. Her yielding demonstrates the accommodating style of dealing with conflict.

Avoiding

AVOIDING Withdrawing from a conflict.

Avoiding means you refuse to deal with the conflict. You might skirt the issue entirely, moving to another topic. If you want to be courteous, you might say that you will talk about the issue at a later date. Or you might withdraw from a potentially threatening environment. In any case, the approach does not have a co-operative or assertive dimension. On the surface, avoiding leads to a situation with *no winners and no losers*: the conflict goes unresolved. The end results are usually *lose–lose*, because unaddressed conflicts tend to have bad endings.

The following encounter between an Arab Canadian man (Emon) and his mother (Haseena) illustrates an avoiding style. Emon immigrated to Canada from Riyadh, Saudi Arabia. His parents did not support his decision to emigrate. As an only son, Emon was expected to remain in Riyadh and to take care of his parents. In this scenario, Emon calls home to wish his parents Eid Mubarak. The conversation unfolds in the following manner.

Emon: Hello. Assalamu alaikum, Amma. How are you? How is Abba?
Haseena: Walikum as salam. (She starts crying.) How do you expect us to be? With my arthritis and your Abba's (father's) heart condition, it is becoming very difficult for us to take care of ourselves. You know how your sisters are all busy with their own families. I don't know what your Abba and I will do for Eid.
Emon: I know it's not easy, Amma. But Nadia and I, we're working hard to save for a trip to Riyadh. And we sent some money to help you get by.
Haseena: So you think we need help now? Your Abba and I have become a burden to you? You know how hard it was for us to raise you and your sisters? You can never understand the pain of not being with your children and grandchildren—especially Maryam and Mahdi, whom we have not seen at all except in the pictures you sent us.
Emon: Amma, can I speak to Abba now?
Haseena: Your Abba does not want to speak to you now, Emon; and I have to prepare supper. Good-bye now.

In this encounter, Emon repeatedly avoids his mother's attempts to engage him in a debate about how he has disappointed her and, in turn, she avoids the possibility that her husband might respond differently (and maybe more positively) if allowed to speak to Emon.

Compromising

Compromising, which requires co-operation, typically involves meeting in the middle or splitting the difference. When time matters, compromising offers a quick solution. As we will see, however, it does not necessarily represent the best solution. When two people compromise, each gets about 50 per cent of what he or she wants. They have to lose part of what they want in order to win anything. In that sense, the outcome is neither win-win, nor lose-lose. Rather it is win-lose for each person.

Imagine that two work colleagues compete for department funding to attend a conference. The organization has a conference fund of $1000, normally awarded to only one individual. This year, however, the awards committee sees that they have two equally deserving candidates; and they decide to split the funding between the two. Each will receive $500. This decision demonstrates a compromising style on the part of committee members, which sometimes makes sense. If the two individuals have sufficient personal income to cover the remaining cost of attending the conference, they will doubtless be satisfied with the compromise.

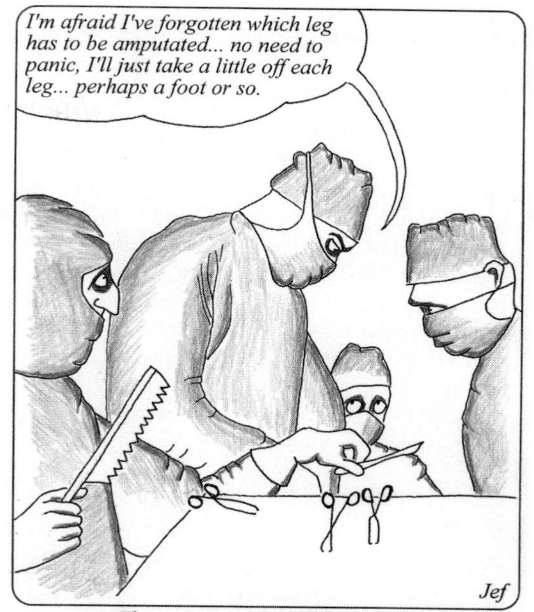

The eminent orthopaedic surgeon proposes a compromise solution.

Jef Clark. By permission of Theo Clark.

Imagine, however, that neither has sufficient personal funds to make up for the missing $500. Consequently, neither can afford to attend the conference. Calling upon a collaborative style, the two approach the committee with a suggestion. One is willing to give up her funds this year if the committee will commit to funding her trip the following year. In this case, collaboration works better than compromise. The following discussion will expand on this idea.

COMPROMISING
Resolving a conflict by meeting in the middle.

Collaborating

Collaborating requires a spirit of co-operation, active listening skills, good communication skills, and an environment of mutual respect. In collaborating, we search for a solution that will satisfy both of our needs to the maximum extent. The classic example, developed by Roger Fisher and William Ury, involves a dispute over an orange.[29] Two people want the orange. If they compromise, they will split the orange in half. However, if they explore their mutual interests in the orange, they may learn that one of them wants to use the orange peel in cake icing. The other wants to make a drink from the orange. With this deeper understanding of the situation, they can share the orange more effectively—with one person getting the peel and the other getting the inner fruit. Had they compromised, neither would have fully met their needs. One would have ended up with a small drink, the other with less peel than required for the icing. By collaborating, however, both can meet their needs in the most effective way. The two individuals are able to satisfy 100 per cent (not just 50 per cent) of their wants. Collaborating involves learning enough about the needs and interests of the other person to arrive at the best possible solution.

COLLABORATING
Resolving conflict in a way that allows both sides to satisfy their wants.

> "Peace is not the absence of conflict but the presence of creative alternatives for responding to conflict."
>
> DOROTHY THOMPSON

from theory TO PRACTICE

What Kind of Animal Are You?

In 1983, Norman Sawchuck introduced the idea of using animals to represent the five coping styles identified earlier.[30] These representations (along with variations) now appear on numerous websites and in various YouTube videos. In most models, the shark or the lion represents the competitor; the fox, the compromiser; the teddy bear, the accommodator; the turtle, the avoider; and the owl, the collaborator. If you are interested in identifying which animal you most resemble in coping style, go to www.elcamino.edu/faculty/bcarr/documents/ConflictManagementStyle.pdf.

Finding the Right Coping Style

Conflict resolution is an ongoing, dynamic process; and people can move from one coping style to another. This shift may occur from situation to situation or over time, especially as we age and mature. Consider the changes that occur in the coping styles of two sisters, Sora and Iris, who live in a busy suburb of Montreal. They both have cars, but they share a house with one parking space. Because Sora arrives home later in the afternoon than Iris, she is the one who has to look for alternative parking arrangements. Typically that means parking a distance from her house. For a long time, Sora does not complain. Eventually, however, she begins to feel unhappy with the arrangement. She decides to talk with her sister and to request a fairer arrangement. After discussing the problem, Sora and Iris arrive at a solution that is acceptable to both. If Sora has class before her sister in the morning, she will park in the driveway the previous evening. However, on the days that Iris has night classes, she will park in the driveway in order not to have to walk on her own after dark. This compromise satisfies both Sora and Iris.

In this example, we can see how Sora opts initially to use an accommodating style (giving in to her sister's behaviour) but later changes to a collaborating style (taking the interests of both girls into account). A typical compromise in this situation might have been the girls agreeing to park in the driveway on alternate weeks. That is, Iris would have the driveway parking space one week, and Sora would have the space the second week. This solution would not have met more than 50 per cent of the needs of either girl. Sora would have been rushed in the weeks she did not have the driveway space, and Iris would have had to walk home alone at night every other week. By identifying their interests through collaboration, they were able to arrive at a solution that worked for both of them. This example demonstrates how we often adopt different coping styles at different points in time, sometimes even to resolve the same conflict. See the "From Theory to Practice" box titled "What Kind of Animal Are You?" to find out which coping style(s) you use to respond to conflict.

OUTCOMES OF CONFLICT

Despite the negatives, conflicts do not have to be unproductive in their outcomes. Conflict can be dysfunctional or functional.[31] The difference between **dysfunctional conflict** and **functional conflict** relates to outcomes—that is, the extent to which the conflict has harmful versus beneficial consequences. Dysfunctional conflict has unproductive and often destructive outcomes. Functional conflict has at least some productive outcomes.

DYSFUNCTIONAL CONFLICT
Disagreements with unproductive or destructive outcomes.

FUNCTIONAL CONFLICT
Disagreements with productive or beneficial outcomes.

Dysfunctional Conflicts

Tension, stress, antagonism, hostility, and distrust signal the existence of a dysfunctional conflict.[32] You can recognize a dysfunctional conflict when the parties make accusatory and blaming statements or try to take advantage of each other. Other signs include controlling or distorting information, distracting people from completing their tasks, and getting in the way of decision making.[33] Couples in dysfunctional conflicts may express their feelings too strongly and fail to accept or respect the other's point of view. They may project their own unpleasant feelings onto the other person. When people fail to resolve their disagreements, the issues continue to plague the relationship; and eventually one or both of the individuals neglect or leave the relationship. While exiting a relationship may not be productive in the sense of maintaining the relationship, it is at least an active response. Neglect is a more passive response.[34] Both have negative consequences.

For an example of a dysfunctional conflict, consider the following scenario. Maureen is a young Irish Canadian raised in Deer Lake, Newfoundland. Imran is a young Pakistani Canadian, whose family emigrated from Rawalpindi, Pakistan. The two have been close friends since childhood. When it comes time to decide on university, Maureen chooses to pursue studies at the University of New Brunswick in Fredericton. Imran accepts an offer from Memorial University in St John's. They are both happy for each other but also disappointed they will be going to different schools. After leaving home in mid-August, they keep in touch for a few weeks. Once school starts, however, their emails and texts become less frequent. Maureen is particularly bad about writing. At Thanksgiving break, the two friends arrive home for the holiday, and Maureen's family invites Imran to their home for Thanksgiving dinner. The conversation unfolds in the following manner:

Maureen: Hi, Imran. Good to see you.
Imran: Yeah, sure.
Maureen: How is school?
Imran: It's all right. I guess they work you hard at UNB. No time to write, eh?
Maureen: Whoa!! Slow down! What's going on?
Imran: Nothing that would matter to you.
Maureen: That's pretty harsh.
Imran: Yeah, well, that's how I feel.
Maureen: Maybe you shouldn't have come if you feel this way. In fact, I think you should leave. It's Thanksgiving, and my mom worked hard on the meal.
Imran: You're probably right. See you around. Or not.
Imran turns around and leaves, slamming the door behind him.

In this situation, the conflict stems from Imran's resentment over infrequent contact with Maureen. As the situation escalates, Maureen becomes upset and defensive. The two friends become aggressive in their attacks on each other. The conflict is both overt and dysfunctional, which leads to a lose–lose ending.

Most conflicts can be resolved. However, all parties to a conflict must be motivated to resolve the dispute. That does not always happen. Sometimes one spouse wants a divorce; the other does not. In that situation, delaying and obstructing the settlement works to the benefit of the person who does not want a divorce. At other times, parties lack the information necessary to settle the conflict. One spouse may know the real reason for the divorce; the other may not. Parties to a conflict may have emotional reactions that have nothing to do with logic. They may be willing to face the most negative consequences rather than settle the conflict. Faced with a bitter divorce, a couple may choose to prolong the procedure and spend everything they have on lawyers in an effort to ensure that the other person gets nothing. In the end, however, both are losers; the only winners are the lawyers. Jeffrey Rubin made a colourful comment about the thinking processes behind these lose–lose dynamics: "We will both go down the rat hole but I am going to make sure that you go down first and a little bit further than I."[35]

"Never cut what you can untie."
JOSEPH JOUBERT

Functional Conflicts

Functional conflicts occur when people explore their differences and express their opinions in a respectful and productive way.[36] The result is increased trust and the establishment of authentic relationships. To see how the conflict between Maureen and Imran could have been more functional, consider the following dialogue.

Maureen: Hi Imran. Good to see you.
Imran: Hi Maureen. Nice to see you too. How's it going? Long time no news, partner.
Maureen: Yeah, sorry about that.
Imran: I guess they work you hard at UNB. I emailed and texted you a number of times, but you never got back to me. Anyway. . . .
Maureen: Honestly, Imran, things have been hectic. And when I thought of calling, it was too late for you in St John's or too early for me. You know me. I am not a big texter. I kept thinking it would be nicer to talk to you. I am sorry, but it wasn't like I didn't think about you.
Imran: It's okay, I get it. New classes, new profs, roommates. Yeah, roommates. We'll talk about that another time. St John's is way different from Deer Lake.
Maureen: Sounds like we have some things to talk about—but after dinner. I hear mom calling. Maybe when you get back to St John's, we can talk on weekends. Hey, what about Skyping?

In this alternative scenario, Maureen and Imran collaborate to create a supportive communication climate. They respond to each other in an empathic way, taking the perspective of the other person. They acknowledge each other's feelings, and their communication becomes descriptive rather than accusatory. In the end, their friendship moves in the direction of a win–win outcome. In short, the conflict is functional.

As the above example indicates, whether a conflict is functional or dysfunctional depends to a great extent on how both parties respond to the situation. See the "From Theory to Practice" box titled "Making Your Case in the Workplace" for an example of a workplace conflict that could end up as a functional or dysfunctional conflict, depending on the coping style and strategies of the middle manager.

from theory TO PRACTICE

Making Your Case in the Workplace

Imagine yourself in the following situation. You are a middle manager in a leading company that manufactures automobile parts. You have just come into work on a Monday morning after a relaxing weekend. You are in high spirits and looking forward to another week at work. Your secretary has arranged a manageable schedule, and everything seems to be under control. However, you are in for a rude shock. Upon checking your email, you find that upper management has reduced your department's budget; and they have assigned new and unrealistic goals to your team. You want to protest the cuts and the unachievable production goals, but you learn that the financial outlook statement you requested last week is not yet available. Without those figures, you will be unable to argue your case at the afternoon meeting of managers. What kinds of actions can you take to avoid a dysfunctional conflict with your boss? Should you voice your opinion or maintain a loyal silence? Which coping style could work best in this situation (competing, accommodating, avoiding, compromising, or collaborating)? What are the likely results of employing the different coping styles?

DEVELOPING A CIVIL WORKPLACE

The term *civility* implies a respectful awareness of others. In practice, civility means thinking about the impact of your words and actions before you employ them. It means being tolerant of differences and showing consideration for the needs of other people. Sometimes it means restraining yourself from being too blunt—looking for less hurtful words. In other words, civility implies courteous behaviour, politeness, and kindness in our interactions with others—treating people with dignity. In the following section, we will discuss behaviours associated with incivility in the workplace, the costs of an uncivil workplace, and ways to create a more civil work climate.

Behaviours Associated with Incivility

Uncivil behaviour is the opposite of civil behaviour. Uncivil behaviour includes acts of rudeness or insensitivity such as joking at the expense of others, showing intolerance for those who are different from us, sending emails that put down another person or group, gossiping, posting inappropriate pictures in the workplace, yelling or speaking in a loud voice, cursing or threatening another person, telling crude jokes, or making comments that belittle or humiliate others. Many of these behaviours fall into the category of bullying. To be considered as bullying, the behaviour must be "a repeated pattern of behaviour intended to intimidate, offend, degrade, or humiliate a particular person or group."[37] As we have learned earlier in this book, bullying behaviours can occur inside or outside the walls of an organization. Many bullies operate anonymously in cyberspace, posting information on Facebook or other social media sites.

> **"In dwelling, live close to the ground. In thinking, keep to the simple. In conflict, be fair and generous."**
>
> **LAO TZU**

At the violent end of the spectrum, uncivil behaviour can include an explosive and uncontrolled outburst of anger, destruction of property, or physical or sexual assault. Whereas bullying threatens our mental health, violence threatens our physical well-being. Nearly one-fifth of violence-related incidents occur in the workplace. The most common forms of workplace violence include physical assault (two-thirds of all cases), sexual assault, and robbery. Men are as likely as women to report being victims. Those most at risk are people working in social services, health, education, accommodation, and food services. Offices, factories, and stores are the most common locations where workplace violence occurs. In two-thirds of the cases, victims know the perpetrators of the violence, who are sometimes co-workers or former co-workers. In 93 per cent of the incidents, the accused are men acting alone; over half are under 35.[38]

Many believe that uncivil behaviours such as bullying and harassment precede workplace violence.[39] According to Jacqueline Power of the University of Windsor's Odette School of Business, 40 per cent of Canadians have experienced one or more acts of workplace bullying.[40] According to a US study, 71 per cent of workplace bullies hold a higher rank than those they bully; 17 per cent are coworkers, peers, or colleagues; and 12 per cent hold a lower rank than their targets. Both the bullies (58 per cent) and their targets (80 per cent) are often women.[41] In Canada, federal and provincial legislation addresses issues of violence and harassment in the workplace. See the "Professional Contexts" box for a discussion of the consequences one woman faced after she verbally threatened a co-worker.

*professional*CONTEXTS

Threatening Words Can Get You Fired

On 12 November 2005, anesthesiologist Marc Daniel stabbed former girlfriend and co-worker Lori Dupont to death in the recovery room at the Hôtel-Dieu Grace Hospital in Windsor, Ontario. Subsequently, in 2007, a coroner's jury recommended a review of the province's Occupational Health and Safety Act (OHSA). As a result of this review, Ontario Bill 168 came into force in June 2010. This bill amended the OHSA to require employers and employees to take steps to prevent and address issues of workplace violence.

One of the first employees to be dismissed under this legislation was Donna Hudson, a long-term employee of the City of Kingston. The City fired Hudson for making a death threat against a co-worker. Although Hudson acknowledged having anger management problems, she appealed the decision.

Hudson was not a model employee. She had a record of poor attendance. She had received warnings or disciplinary actions on several occasions for slamming doors, swearing, and engaging in angry confrontations with co-workers and supervisors. On one occasion, she received a three-day suspension for confrontational behaviour with the local union president (John Hale). After this event, Hudson took a three-month leave of absence with sick pay. Upon returning to the workplace, she verbally abused a co-worker and received a warning letter. The city then paid for Hudson to attend anger management classes; however, two days after completing the course, Hudson made a verbal threat to Hale. In response to a request not to talk about a deceased friend, Hudson replied to Hale, "Yes, and you will be too." Hale took the threat seriously, and the City of Kingston terminated Hudson's employment.

After hearing the case, arbitrator Elaine Newman broadened and helped to clarify the boundaries of Bill 168. She noted that Hudson's behaviour qualified as workplace violence under Bill 168, which includes the following as one possible definition of *workplace violence*: "a statement or behaviour that is reasonable for a worker to interpret as a threat to exercise physical force against the worker, in a workplace, that could cause physical injury to the worker." Thus, the act clearly includes threatening language under the heading of workplace violence. Newman also noted that, under Bill 168, employees have a responsibility to report such language and employers have a legal obligation to investigate and address the reports.

Newman also identified a number of factors that would be appropriate for an employer to consider when deciding how to respond to threats of violence in the workplace. Those factors included "the history of discipline, level of seniority, seriousness of the misconduct, impact of the misconduct, and likelihood of improvement of behaviour." She also observed that employers should ask questions such as the following: If returned to the workplace, will the employee conduct himself or herself in way that does not threaten the safety of others? Is it likely that the individual will repeat the problematic behaviour in the future?[42]

In Hudson's case, no physical act of violence occurred. However, the threat resulted in emotional harm to the distraught victim, who believed that his work colleague was capable of carrying out the death threat. Ultimately, Hudson's dismissal serves as a warning that workers, employers, and union leaders should look seriously at the implications of Bill 168.[43]

Costs of an Uncivil Workplace

What are the costs of incivility in the workplace? The costs of a disrespectful workforce include less motivated employees, increased absenteeism, frequent turnover, lower productivity, and a defensive and negative work climate.[44] The organization bears the burden in increased costs, reduced profits, and legal expenses associated with unhappy customers and employees.[45] The individual, on the other hand, bears the cost in terms of reduced job satisfaction and threats to self-concept and career. How much we feel respected and valued in the workplace can affect our overall sense of self. If our co-workers and bosses treat us as if we have little value, we may come to see ourselves in the same way.[46] We also feel a negative impact when the organization devalues our co-workers. When one member of a team receives unfair treatment, the performance of the entire team suffers.[47]

Our health also depends on our feelings of being respected and valued in the workplace. A disrespectful organizational climate causes employee burnout and other health issues.[48] In this environment, employees feel stressed, depressed, anxious, and sometimes even suicidal.[49] In 2008, the United States Veterans Health Administration launched a series of activities around the theme *civility, respect, and engagement in the workforce* (CREW). The CREW project tried to encourage more respect in interpersonal interactions, more cooperation in teamwork, more fair conflict resolution processes, and greater tolerance for individual differences.[50] All of these behaviours promote a civil environment and reduce the costs associated with an uncivil workplace.

Creating a Civil Work Climate

We learned in Chapter 8 that emotional intelligence (EQ) weighs more heavily than IQ in deciding whether someone gets ahead in an organization.[51] An important part of EQ involves knowing how to be respectful in our interactions with other people. The communication skills associated with civility—which include active listening, not interrupting, responding in a thoughtful way, and choosing our words carefully—have a positive impact on EQ. A civil workplace, inhabited by people with high EQs, nurtures not only people, but also productivity.

In the following section, we will consider the ideas of Jack Gibb, who offers instruction on how to create a more positive organizational **climate**. In creating a more positive climate, we are also creating a more civil workplace. The term *climate* refers to the emotional tone of relationships or the way people feel about each other. The verbal and nonverbal communication behaviours of the people in the environment create this tone.

CLIMATE The emotional tone of a relationship or interaction.

Gibb proposes that positive climates arise from supportive verbal behaviours, and negative climates arise from defensive verbal behaviours.[52] So he sets out to identify the kinds of **supportive communication** that create positive climates and the kinds of **defensive communication** that create negative climates. He identifies six types of defensive communication and six types of supportive communication. Table 9.1 depicts these twelve behaviours, paired as opposites.

SUPPORTIVE COMMUNICATION Behaviours that reduce defensiveness and demonstrate respect for the feelings of the other person.

DEFENSIVE COMMUNICATION Behaviours people use when they perceive a threat to their emotional well-being.

As in our personal lives, defensive communication in the workplace establishes barriers that limit the effectiveness of the work group and, ultimately, the organization. A good manager creates a supportive and positive climate in which everyone feels free to listen and to contribute ideas. To accomplish this task, managers need to look closely at their own communication patterns in the workplace and ask themselves the question: "Are my employees defensive because of their nature, or have I done something to contribute to that state?"[53]

Let us look at the six pairs of supportive and defensive communication in order to understand their impact on communication climate in organizations.

TABLE 9.1 The Gibb categories of defensive and supportive communication.

DEFENSIVE COMMUNICATION	SUPPORTIVE COMMUNICATION
1. Evaluation	1. Description
2. Control	2. Problem Orientation
3. Strategy	3. Spontaneity
4. Neutrality	4. Empathy
5. Superiority	5. Equality
6. Certainty	6. Provisionalism

SOURCE: J.R. Gibb, "Defensive Communication," *Journal of Communication* 11, no. 3 (1961): 141–8. Copyright © 2006, John Wiley and Sons.

Evaluation vs Description

EVALUATION Passing judgment on a person, idea, or object.

The first type of defensive communication involves the act of **evaluation**. An evaluative message judges the other person (either positively or negatively). This kind of message suggests that the evaluator is in a position (often of superiority) to pass judgment. A statement such as "You left all your dirty dishes everywhere! You're such a slob!" is clearly evaluative. The attack includes the accusatory *you*, and it labels the other person as a thoughtless slob. Even positive statements such as "That's a *beautiful* drawing," "You're so *pretty*," or "That's a *great* skateboard" involve judging an object, person, or possession. For that reason, they can lead to defensive behaviours.

DESCRIPTION Offering thoughts and feelings without judging.

In contrast, **description** provides a way to offer thoughts and feelings without judging. Using *I* language (e.g., "*I* get really upset when *I* walk into the apartment and see dirty dishes everywhere.") does not blame the other person. *I* language says how we feel about the situation. People tend to respond less defensively to descriptive statements of this nature.

Imagine that two colleagues, Aliya and Victoria, get together at one of their homes to work on a project for their consulting business. Partners in a graphics design firm, they are supposed to present their first sketches to a client the next morning. As they get started, Aliya realizes that she forgot to bring their last set of sketches to the meeting. The women consider their options.

Victoria has two choices in responding to Aliya's mistake. She can attack Aliya and say something like "I can't believe you're so irresponsible! How could you forget the reason for our meeting?" Perceiving this evaluative response as an attack, Aliya would probably become defensive and return the attack with words such as "You know I'm having a difficult time at home right now. I wish you had reminded me. Besides, you might remember that you lost our client list last year. It took weeks to replace the information."

In this scenario, both women would feel defensive, angry, and upset. As a result, their work plan could fall apart, along with their partnership. Note how the accusatory *you* has the potential to escalate a conflict.

In contrast to this defensive response, Victoria has a second option. To protect the partnership (and work session), she can choose a descriptive response, framed from the *I* perspective, such as the following: "Oh no! That is a problem because they are expecting the drawings tomorrow. I wish I had reminded you, but I've been so busy. Do you have any ideas about what we can do?"

Control vs Problem Orientation

CONTROL Ignoring the other person's input while forcing that person to accept your decisions.

The second type of defensive communication relates to assertions of **control**. When we attempt to control another person through our language, the other person will probably respond in a defensive way. In this sort of interaction, the defensive messages create a power dynamic whereby each person tries to gain the upper hand. Controlling statements like "Here, let me do it," or "We'll do it this way," or "I've made up my mind" also contribute to defensiveness because they ignore the rights of the other person to participate in decision making.

PROBLEM ORIENTATION Focussing on finding solutions.

In contrast to controlling, **problem orientation** focusses on finding solutions rather than being right. More collaborative in nature, problem orientation allows both parties to save face. *We* language characterizes problem orientation: "We need to figure out how we can both be satisfied," or "What do you think we should do?" or "Let's see if we can come up with a better way to handle this issue." Problem orientation produces results because it eliminates the power struggle and focusses on finding a solution. See the "From Theory to Practice" box for an example of how students can negatively perceive feedback from their professors if it does not convey a problem orientation.

Parents of toddlers often find themselves in power struggles with their children over issues related to eating, getting dressed, changing from one activity to another, and tidying up. Rather than using control (e.g., "Pick up your toys!"), many parents find it more effective to use problem orientation and collaborative language: "As soon as we have these toys picked up, we can have our snack. How about it?"

from theory TO PRACTICE

When Is Negative Too Negative?

Supervisors in any situation can learn from a study of how students feel about instructor feedback. Melanie Weaver identified four types of feedback disliked by students. Those four types were (1) feedback that does not identify anything positive in the student's work, (2) feedback that is too general or vague to indicate what needs to be improved, (3) feedback that does not provide information on *how* to improve in the future, and (4) feedback that is unrelated to the criteria for doing the assignment.[54] Think about the feedback that you have received from employers or instructors. Which kinds of comments were most useful? Which ones were not helpful at all? What kinds of feedback would you have liked to receive?

Strategy vs Spontaneity

The third kind of defensive communication involves **strategy**, a communication approach in which the communicator hides his motives. Such behaviour can be both dishonest and manipulative. Let us say that you are buying a bicycle. While you are examining the bicycle, the seller tells you that another buyer will be arriving in a few minutes to look at the same bike. In fact, there is no second buyer; the seller lied to you to make you feel pressure to purchase the bike. Real estate agents sometimes use the same strategy, misrepresenting the number of offers or exaggerating the size of the bids in order to close the deal at a higher price. While these sorts of pressuring strategies may lead to a sale, they can backfire. If the buyer finds out about the manipulation, he will feel negatively about the transaction and the seller. As a result, he will probably become defensive and walk away from the sale.

STRATEGY Hiding one's motives and manipulating someone into doing what you want them to do.

SPONTANEITY Being open and honest in interactions.

NEUTRALITY Showing lack of interest in the other person or that person's ideas.

By way of contrast, **spontaneity** requires being honest with others instead of manipulating them. If a seller gives you time to make your purchasing decision and answers your questions honestly, these behaviours build a relationship based on trust. Perhaps you end up not buying the bicycle or the house. But the trust you have developed for the salesperson may mean that you will purchase another bicycle or another piece of real estate from him in the future, or you will tell others about the good service that he provides.

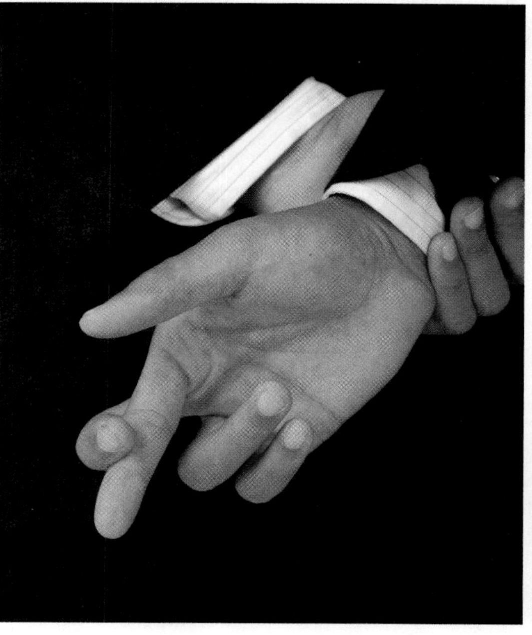
© VII-photo/iStockphoto

Neutrality vs Empathy

Neutrality is the fourth type of defensiveness. When we behave in a way that suggests neutrality, we convey a lack of interest in the ideas of others, their activities, or their decisions. For example, responses such as "I don't care" or "You decide" when a friend says "What do you want to do tonight?" suggest disinterest or (worse) disengagement. Let us say that a friend tells you about getting negative feedback from her boss. You respond "Oh, really?" while checking messages on your cellphone. Your friend may interpret your response as showing a lack of concern for her well-being. Looking away while someone is talking to you suggests the same indifference. In brief, if you use neutrality in your communication, you might send a message that you do not value or respect the other person.

Empathy is the opposite of neutrality. Recall from Chapter 8 that the practice of empathy requires that you put yourself in the shoes of the other person. When you empathize, you try to understand and accept the other person's feelings. You listen closely to what she has to say. Empathy implies an ability to see things from the perspective of the other person. A response such as "Wow, you must be really upset after all the work you did on that assignment" says that you are listening and you care about the other person.

Superiority vs Equality

SUPERIORITY
Behaving as though you are better than others.

The fifth type of defensiveness is **superiority**. Superiority surfaces when speakers imply they are better than those with whom they communicate. Of course, some people are more skilled, knowledgeable, or experienced than others in specific areas. But if they emphasize their superiority through their words and actions, defensiveness usually results. As an example, senior managers usually possess more experience than their junior subordinates. This higher level of experience does not mean they know everything; but when they act as if they are all-knowing, lower-level employees are less likely to speak out at meetings, offer suggestions, or engage in problem solving. **Equality**, in contrast, is a supportive form of communication. It becomes visible when people treat others as equals.

EQUALITY
Behaving as though you are equal to others.

Certainty vs Provisionalism

CERTAINTY
Conveying the message "I am always right."

The sixth and final type of defensive communication is **certainty**. Speakers create defensiveness when they convey the message "I am always right." This message usually has a negative impact on communication climate. For example, teenagers tend to respond negatively when parents make statements such as "I know what is going to happen next" or "Take it from me, that brand is no good" because this language implies that the parents think they know everything.

PROVISIONALISM
Acknowledging different points of view or different interpretations of events.

In contrast to certainty is **provisionalism**, characterized by communication that accepts the possibility for different points of view or different interpretations of events. Provisionalism conveys a spirit of openness to the input of other people. If parents say to a teenager, for example, "You might want to think about . . . " or "Have you considered . . . " or "Here's a thought . . . ," they send the message that they value the decision-making ability of the teen. Parents will meet less resistance when they use provisional language.

USING THE AWARENESS WHEEL TO MANAGE OUR CONFLICTS

Created by Sherod Miller, the awareness wheel can help us to understand, clarify, and communicate our feelings and thoughts on some topic (see Figure 9.2).[55] These actions can help us to avoid rushing to judgment, making perceptual errors, and communicating inaccurate perceptions to others.

Imagine, for example, that we want to communicate the experience of not receiving a promotion. To use the wheel, we place the issue in the hub. Next we begin at any one of five places (or spokes) on the wheel. Our options include *I sense*, *I think*, *I feel*, *I want*, and *I do*.

If we begin with *I sense*, we might explain how we received a letter that said we were not chosen for the promotion. We processed this information through our visual sense. Perhaps our boss tried to soften the rejection by leaving a complimentary voicemail message. When we listen to the message, we receive the information through an auditory channel. Using first-person language to describe what we have sensed, we could say, "I received the letter of rejection that you sent to me" or "I heard your voice mail."

Moving next to *I think*, we offer some insight into what we are thinking on the topic. For example, we might say, "Based on my past evaluations, I thought I would receive the promotion." Expressing our *feelings*, we might say, "I felt very disappointed. I had been counting on the promotion." Moving to *I want*, we try to express our intentions. In this case, we might say, "I want to understand why I did not receive the promotion and what I need to improve in order to do better the next time." Finally, in terms of *doing*, we could conceivably say, "I will do my best to incorporate your suggestions into my personal action plan for the coming year."

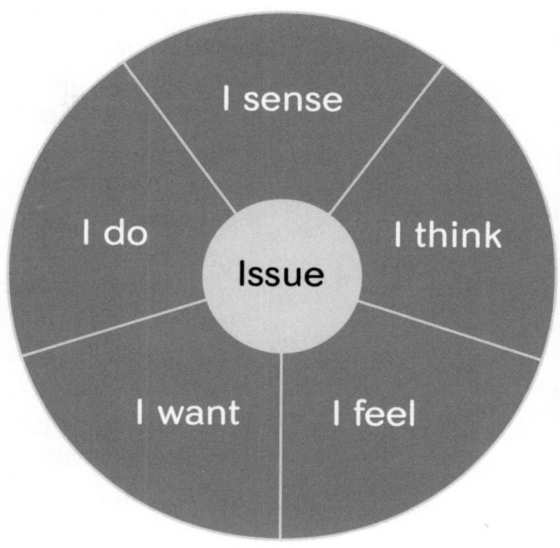

FIGURE 9.2 The awareness wheel.

SOURCE: Based on http://www.primarygoals.org/models/awareness-wheel/

The awareness wheel can be very helpful for resolving conflict. Councillors such as Sue Bronson use the awareness wheel in workplace and family mediations. Keeping the wheel in mind, Bronson asks questions aimed at getting her clients to understand the complex nature of their thoughts, feelings, and wants on a troubling issue. She believes that once people understand that they have more than one feeling and more than one want to be satisfied, they will become more flexible. Identifying these alternative feelings and wants allows the parties in conflict to shift positions without losing face. Bronson also helps her clients to understand that multiple possibilities exist for resolving any conflict. Ultimately, she believes that even if the parties in conflict do not resolve their differences at her sessions, they will develop a greater understanding of themselves. This greater clarity might lead, at a later date, to a resolution to the conflict. Bronson developed five questions that correspond to the spokes on the awareness wheel: "What do you see and hear? What meaning does it hold for you? How do you feel? What do you want? What are you willing to do?"[56]

TIPS FOR MANAGING CONFLICT

As we have seen in this chapter, the ways by which we manage and deal with conflict can have an impact on the outcome of the process. If managed effectively, conflict affords us an opportunity to work through our concerns as friends, a couple, co-workers, and family members. To conclude this chapter, let us look at some tips for effectively managing conflict and negotiating differences.

Get more information. Make sure you are not missing important details. Also make sure that you and the person with whom you are in conflict have the same information.

Ask questions if you think you have misunderstood something the other person has said or done. Flawed communication causes and aggravates many conflicts.

Get your emotions under control. Take a deep breath and approach interactions with a positive outlook. Keep in mind the saying "like attracts like"; if you are positive, perhaps the other person will respond in kind.

Make sure you understand what you are sensing, thinking, and feeling. Once you understand your own perceptions, thoughts, and feelings, you can better communicate your needs to someone else.

Know what you want—your bottom line. Too often we complain about what is wrong, but we never identify the criteria for an acceptable solution. How can we expect others to identify acceptable solutions if we do not know what we want?

Deal with conflict. If you avoid conflict, people may at first perceive you as a peaceable or agreeable person, bringing harmony into your interpersonal environment. However, if you consistently avoid conflict, others may come to see you as someone who is weak and unable to handle conflict. Expressing your feelings and thoughts is a healthy way to deal with conflict.

Avoid overly aggressive behaviours. Remember the scenario where Maureen and Imran criticized each other and made personal attacks. Their aggressive responses to each other created an unproductive, defensive communication climate.

Listen to others with an open mind. Give the other person a chance to express himself or herself. When that person has finished, stop to consider his or her perspective. When people believe you have heard them, they are likely to respond more favourably. For more tips on effective listening, refer to Chapter 5.

Bring hidden conflicts into the open. Words and actions spoken or done in secret to sabotage another person only accelerate the negative effects of conflict.

Use language that creates a supportive communication climate. Language that defuses tensions can help to create a positive environment.

Work towards building trust. Developing trust is critical to managing conflict effectively. Building trust now may also help you to navigate difficulties in the future.

Be mindful of cultural differences. If you are in conflict with someone whose cultural background differs from your own, take the time to learn more about their culture. This knowledge may help you to understand their rituals, beliefs, and actions.

Be aware of gender dynamics. Keep in mind that there are differences in how men and women communicate. These differences have the potential to generate or aggravate conflict.

Be aware of power dynamics. Approach each conflict with a clear understanding of how power differences can ease or worsen the situation.

Avoid bullying others and report all instances of bullying in the workplace. Psychological damage can be as serious as physical damage, and organizations have an obligation to protect employees. If you believe that someone poses a physical danger to you or others, report the matter to someone in authority.

number of features and
nflict, as well as ways of
ining sources of conflict,
, and values; personality
conflicting goals or roles;
t or different information;
e and non-distributable
les; and stressful situations. We also looked at the differences between overt (open) and covert (hidden) conflicts and discussed the importance of more open communication.

In our discussion of the stages of conflict, we examined the three acts through which people typically move when they experience conflicts. Sometimes parties in conflict never progress beyond Act I, characterized by negative words and actions. At other times, they reach a stalemate in Act II, which has the potential to be a period of transition. The parties must be willing to change their strategies if they are to reach Act III. If they manage to reach Act III, they have a chance of resolving their conflicts in a productive way.

We also discussed the five coping styles of managing conflict: competing, accommodating, avoiding, compromising, and collaborating. We looked at possible outcomes, which can be either functional (productive) or dysfunctional (unproductive) in nature. In relation to organizational settings, we examined how to develop a civil workplace. The use of supportive communication strategies, as illustrated in the Gibb model and the awareness wheel, can help to improve organizational climates.

REVIEW QUESTIONS

1. According to this chapter, what are some major factors that give rise to conflict? Can you think of additional factors that give rise to conflict?
2. What are the characteristics of passive-aggressive behaviour? Have you ever displayed this kind of behaviour? Do you know others who use passive-aggressive behaviour to achieve their purposes? When someone uses this sort of behaviour, how do you feel?
3. What are the benefits and/or drawbacks of each of the five coping styles discussed in this chapter? Which coping style do you most commonly use when faced with conflict? Do you think it is an effective style? If not, what steps could you take to start using a more effective style?
4. Have you ever been the victim of bullying in the workplace? How did it make you feel? Did you experience any health problems as a result of the bullying? Do you think that your work suffered? Did you report the events to anyone? What action, if any, was taken to address the situation?
5. Which of the communication behaviours outlined in Gibb's model do you tend to use in communicating with friends, family, and colleagues? What is the impact of your choices? What might you do to create a more supportive relational climate in the future?

SUGGESTED ACTIVITIES

1. Think of an issue that has created conflict for you in the past. Use the awareness wheel to generate some statements that would help you to move through your feelings on this topic.
2. Form a group of at least four people and create role plays that illustrate the various sources of conflict: differences in beliefs, attitudes, and values; personality differences; incompatible and conflicting goals or roles; interdependencies; insufficient or different information; poor communication; scarce and non-distributable resources and power struggles; and stressful situations. Act out your role plays and ask your classmates to identify as many sources of conflict as possible.
3. Using a large piece of poster board and paints or markers, create a design that illustrates the climate in some organization where you have worked. Discuss why you made the choices you made with this poster.
4. Create an individual or group mandala that reflects the kind of organization in which you would like to work. (A mandala is a multi-coloured circular pattern with many smaller parts such as triangles, squares, stars, and internal circles.) For examples and ideas on how to create a mandala, go to www.wikihow.com/Draw-a-Mandala. After creating the mandala, explain what each part represents.
5. Imagine your ideal organization. Then take the class on a guided visualization of how this ideal organization could look. For more information on guided imagery, go to http://creatingminds.org/tools/guided_imagery.htm. You can also refer to the example of a guided fantasy that appears in the appendix; see page 325.

CHAPTER 10

Group Decision-Making: Leadership and Process

CHAPTER OUTLINE

learning OBJECTIVES

- To understand the value of primary work groups and project-specific groups in organizations
- To understand the role of leaders in guiding group processes
- To gain insights into how to define and analyze problems—both causes and effects
- To learn about creative and rational problem-solving techniques
- To become acquainted with problems associated with groupthink
- To learn about the importance of commitment in implementing group decisions
- To understand the importance of evaluating what worked and did not work

forSTARTERS

Deadly Decisions

Some group decisions have deadly consequences. In March 1997, 39 members of a doomsday cult called Heaven's Gate, based in San Diego, California, decided to take their own lives. They used vodka to wash down a deadly amount of phenobarbital mixed with applesauce or pudding. Police believed that plastic bags, placed over the heads of cult members, ensured the deaths of any who did not die from the drugs. The ages of the participating members ranged from 20 to 72. One suicide victim was Canadian.

The victims of the mass suicide lay on tidy bunk beds, with $5.00 bills and quarters in their pockets and neatly packed suitcases at the foot of their beds. Women and men alike wore the same black outfits—long-sleeved shirts, pants, and Nike shoes—making identification difficult. Purple shrouds covered their upper bodies.

The members of the cult believed their deaths would transport them to an unidentified flying object (UFO). They thought the UFO would arrive on the tail of the Hale–Bopp comet. A videotape, left behind, explained that they would be shedding their human shells in order to reach heaven via the UFO. According to Dr Brian Blackbourne, the San Diego County medical examiner, the mass suicide seemed to be a well-planned and well-executed group decision. Evidence suggested that Marshall Applewhite, a man who compared himself to Jesus Christ, led the cult. Applewhite apparently played a major role in the collective decision to commit suicide.[1]

In different but also deadly scenarios, the National Parole Board of Canada (later renamed the Parole Board of Canada) made group decisions that came under heavy scrutiny and criticism. In 1995, for example, the Board decided to release Robert Bruce Moyes on parole, despite 36 convictions for crimes that included attempted murder. After Moyes participated in the murder of seven people less than a year later, many questioned how the Board had arrived at this decision. Again in 2002, the public questioned the Board's decision to grant parole to a convicted criminal. This time the man in question was convicted murderer

© Purestock/Alamy

INTRODUCTION

Earlier chapters have described the kinds of interpersonal relationships that come into play in our home, social, and work environments. This chapter will focus on work environments, with an emphasis on leadership, problem solving, and decision making in groups. Group work in organizations can take place in **primary work groups** or **project-specific work groups**. As you may imagine group work is important in many organizational settings. Primary work groups are those groups in which employees interact every day, based on their positions within the organization. Project-specific groups, on the other hand, bring together teams for more specialized purposes—to accomplish specific tasks or achieve shared goals.

PRIMARY WORK GROUPS Groups in which employees interact every day, based on their positions within the organization

PROJECT-SPECIFIC WORK GROUPS Groups of employees brought together for specialized purposes.

Traditionally, primary work groups in organizations remained relatively stable over time. That is, the groups were long-standing in nature. In today's environment, however, the term *long-standing* carries meanings different from 50 years ago when employees stayed in the same organization for most of their careers. Modern organizations experience frequent turnovers related to reorganization, mergers, and employee desires to seek

Conrad Brossard. While out on parole, Brossard raped and murdered a woman named Cecile Clement.

These two group decisions had fatal consequences despite the best intentions of group members. Parole boards operate in a high-stress climate, with members torn between the need to protect society and the need to show compassion for those who genuinely regret their crimes. Parole board members also face constant public scrutiny; and whenever the worst-case scenarios occur, they must answer for their decisions.

One final example of deadly group decision-making involves child-welfare officials in Calgary, Alberta. The officials became a target for criticism in 2011 when an independent review determined that 14-month-old Elizabeth Velasquez had died from unnatural causes—the result of physical abuse. Before the girl's death, her grandparents had repeatedly reported suspicions of abuse to social services as well as the police. Yet neither organization took actions to remove the girl from her parents' home. In a press interview, Bruce Anderson (Elizabeth's grandfather) stated: "Whatever way you look at it, someone at social services made some bad, bad decisions."[2]

As with parole board decisions, the choices that confront social service teams often entail high-risk decision-making. If members act too quickly, they can destroy a family that still has some chance of mending itself. On the other hand, if they delay for too long or fail to act, they face the possibility that children will suffer—sometimes even die. Their choices are not easy ones, which leads many social workers to argue for strong "evidence-based practice and decision making"—a shift from authority-based decisions.[3]

Unlike members of more collectivist societies such as China and Japan, North Americans often fear the power of group decisions. We fear giving up individual control. We feel that group decisions may not be as good as individual ones. We suspect that the personal biases or motivations of group members may negatively influence the outcomes. We may assume, for example, that parole board members have some inappropriately liberal biases or hidden agendas.[4] Or we may fear the influence of a persuasive group leader, as in the case of the Heaven's Gate cult. We may fear the outcomes of a flawed group process, based on inadequate information, as happens in some child custody and child welfare cases. We may question the motives of insurance company panels that review claims for patients. Or we may think that group members will want so badly to be accepted by peers that they will follow the herd and support bad decisions. When joining groups ourselves, we may fear unequal sharing of responsibilities. All of these hesitations about group process come into play when we make choices about when and how to use groups.

As you read this chapter, ponder the following questions. How do the decisions outlined above reflect some of the broader concerns that we have about group process? What kind of role, if any, could groupthink have played in the decision of the Heaven's Gate members to commit mass suicide? Do you think that Applewhite reflected functional, situational, emergent, or transformational leadership? Which of the approaches to leadership might have characterized the parole board and social services panels?

new challenges and opportunities. At other times, the turnovers come from employee dissatisfaction with their current jobs or the organization at large. In training workshops, Canadian government communicators often say that their project teams change constantly, with no team being the same at the end as at the beginning of the project.

We can trace some of these changes to the 1970s, a time of great transformation in Canadian organizations. Many youth saw their parents and other older adults laid off by companies in which these adults had planned to retire. At the same time, organizations were merging and changing hands. No positions were safe, including those of executives. Films such as *After the Axe* (see the "From Theory to Practice" box) detail the plight of senior executives who faced unexpected and painful career changes when their organizations disappeared, retooled, or hired younger employees at lower salaries. Change management became a popular career for many communicators.

Trends toward globalization and new technologies also played a role in changing the face of organizations in Canada. The workplace became increasingly diverse, posing challenges for group work. More women joined the workforce, and a growing number of people from various racial, ethnic, and religious backgrounds gained representation. New technologies demanded new skills and proficiencies, drawing many organizations to hire an increasing number of young people (sometimes displacing older workers who did not have the same computer skills). Older workers sometimes retired or looked for jobs that did not require competency in the new technologies. See the "Professional Contexts" box for a discussion of the impact of social media in the workplace.

Despite the above trends, organizations continue to rely on primary work groups to fulfill the major work of the organization. They also rely increasingly on project-specific groups, in which employees come together to solve problems, develop proposals, and carry out specialized tasks. Members of these task-specific teams often represent more than one primary work group in the organization. They may even involve participation from outside the organization. As organizations expand their operations into other regions and countries, a growing number of these interactions occur in virtual space.

from theory TO PRACTICE

After the Axe

The National Film Board of Canada holds a classic film called *After the Axe*. This film depicts the issues faced by top-level executives when they were laid off in the 1970s—a time of economic crisis for many firms. The film looks at the challenges faced by the men who had to forge new identities in a challenging economic environment. Even with the help of "head hunters" (firms that specialize in placing high-level executives), few were able to secure comparable employment. Many months later, some (like the composite character in this film) still had no jobs. Go to www.nfb.ca/film/after_axe to view the film. As you watch the film, keep in mind the ideas on self-concept we discussed in Chapter 2. Many of these ideas apply equally well to this case study.

Project-specific groups work on solving a specific problem or exploring a specific issue. They might be responsible for identifying and developing a new strategy, mission statement, venture, or practice. The output of the group effort could be a design, a plan, or a proposal. A proposal might argue for upper management to invest more money in research and development, to involve more partners in a business venture, or to adopt a new organizational approach. Within government, proposals often take the form of argumentation briefs, where team members ask for additional funding for projects, advocate the extension of programs, or explain the implications of proposed policy changes.

> **"No one can whistle a symphony. It takes a whole orchestra to play it."**
>
> H.E. LUCCOCK

Outside the organization, people come together in chat rooms and group meet ups that allow them to pursue a wide variety of personal interests. This chapter will focus, however, on professional and business contexts. More specifically, we will look at the role of leadership in—and requirements for—productive problem-solving and effective decision-making in group process. The chapter will conclude with tips on how to improve group decision-making. In the appendix that follows this chapter, we will discuss how to put together and present an effective team presentation.

GUIDING THE GROUP THROUGH THE PROCESS: A LEADERSHIP PERSPECTIVE

The question of leadership arises early in any group process. Some leaders are elected; others are appointed; still others are emergent. Emergent leaders assume a position of influence during one of the early meetings of a group. A variety of approaches characterize the study of leadership. In earlier periods, people attached a lot of credibility to the

*professional*CONTEXTS

Impact of Social Media on the Workplace

According to a 2012 survey commissioned by Deloitte, 45 per cent of executives believe that social media have an important role to play in establishing positive organizational cultures. Social media accomplish this end, they say, by connecting employees to the company, its leaders, and other employees. Only 27 per cent of non-executive employees, on the other hand, agree that social media make a positive contribution to workplace culture. They place more importance on regular and candid communication, employee recognition, and access to managers and leaders.[5] The Core Beliefs and Culture survey results reflected the views of 303 executives and 1005 US residents. The residents were 18 years or older and full-time employees of companies with at least 100 employees.

A 2012 survey by Kelly Services identified similar views regarding the use of social media in the workplace. Out of 170,000 people in 30 countries, only 15 per cent approved of personal use of social media at work. More than half of those participating in the Kelly Global Workforce Index (KGWI) survey said that failure to separate personal and professional connections can create problems. They expressed the view that, rather than improving organizational climate, social media contribute to a less harmonious work culture.[6]

Social media have also raised other issues of concern for employees such as background checks on applicants, monitoring and control of employees' online activities, and disciplining or firing employees for discussing work-related issues on social sites. Some employees complain that they are asked to promote the company's business on their personal web pages. Others say that their employers are claiming ownership of pages used to promote work, even when the employee leaves the business. When companies provide employees with cell phones, they expect those employees to be available 24 hours a day.

Not every employer is as enthusiastic about social media as the executives surveyed by Deloitte. Nucleus Research Inc. of Boston, Massachusetts, blames a 1.5 per cent loss of company productivity on employee activity on Facebook. Morse (a consulting firm specializing in IT services and technology) claims that British companies lose 2.2 billion a year as a result of employee activity on social media sites. Other reports suggest that employees may be spending more time on Facebook and Twitter at work than they are spending at home. Their profiles show less activity on Facebook and Twitter in the evenings and on weekends.[7]

Many employers believe they have lost control of the situation. Increased use of mobile devices makes it difficult to control or block access to social media at work. And when employees post comments on Facebook or tweet (at home or at work), they represent the company even if they do not intend to do so. When their comments call the integrity of the company into question or depict the employees in an unfavourable light, the company reputation suffers. In addition, employers find it difficult to track and respond in a timely fashion to rumours and misinformation. Statements may appear out of context, and employees may deliberately or accidentally release confidential information. A single highly publicized mistake can cause severe damage to the employee or company. Some organizations also worry that excessive time spent on social media encourages poor writing skills in employees. Despite these concerns, a 2010 survey by Cisco Systems Inc. revealed that only one in five companies has a social media policy.[8]

Whether supporters or detractors of social media, most people agree that social media will remain part of organizational landscapes. It is also clear that social media have an important role to play in the branding and marketing of businesses and governments. When used responsibly, they increase the visibility of the organization, allow marketing and communication personnel to reach larger numbers of people than would otherwise be possible, and improve customer and client service. Moreover, some academic studies point to the opportunities in social media for improving organizational climate and culture, reducing the felt isolation of teleworkers, and increasing job satisfaction.[9] These views support the opinions of executives sampled in the Deloitte study.

idea that leaders are born, not made.[10] Few hold this belief now, however; and newer theories have taken its place.

The **functional approach** sees leadership as a series of functions or duties performed by the leader.[11] These functions might include motivating, assigning tasks, coordinating meetings, maintaining a positive group climate, or others. In general, a functional approach to leadership sees the necessity for leaders to perform tasks, satisfy the needs of individual group members, and maintain the group.

FUNCTIONAL APPROACH An approach that sees leadership as a series of functions.

© redsnapper/Alamy

The **situational approach** involves studying leadership from the perspective of situations in which leaders find themselves. According to situational theory, leaders have a dominant style. Some are authoritarian (highly controlling). Others are democratic (taking the opinions of others into account in decision making) or laissez-faire (leaving decisions to group members). Situational theory argues that different situations call for different kinds of leadership.[12] Groups may prefer an authoritarian leader in stressful and uncertain conditions. In times of economic crisis and war, for example, people look to their leaders to exercise strong and decisive leadership. When the situation changes, however, preferences may also change. People will often rebel against authoritarian leadership in times of economic prosperity and peace. In these situations, they may prefer a more democratic style of leadership. Laissez-faire leadership tends to be the least productive in most situations. Situational views of leadership also take cultural factors into account since some countries and cultures vary in their preferences and tolerance for different kinds of leadership.[13]

SITUATIONAL APPROACH An approach that sees leadership as dependent on situation, with no one best approach.

EMERGENT APPROACH An approach that sees leadership as emerging from a leaderless group via a process of elimination.

The **emergent approach** originated with Ernest Bormann and colleagues at the University of Minnesota.[14] Bormann's research indicated that leaders emerge from leaderless groups by a process of elimination. That is, the leader is the one who remains standing after the group has rejected all other contenders. The first to be eliminated are the silent members of the group, then the overly talkative and the overly aggressive. In a second round of eliminations, the group rejects those who lack clarity or direction or who appear too meek and unwilling to accept credit for ideas or actions. Most groups choose leaders who show a high level of commitment to playing a role in the group process.[15] Emergent leaders also demonstrate a blend of male and female strengths, focussing on both tasks and people.[16] Nonetheless, men tend to fare better when it comes to being chosen. Although women perform slightly higher than men on the socio-emotional dimension and equally well on the task dimension, men get more credit than women for their performance.[17] Groups with two or more males typically reject female contenders for emergent leadership.[18]

TRANSFORMATIONAL APPROACH An approach that sees leaders as visionaries who challenge and mentor.

A final approach is the **transformational approach**, which sees true leaders as visionaries and mentors, who challenge existing ways of thinking.[19] In the context of group work, transformational leaders place a heavy value on new and creative approaches to problem solving. They also assume that groups have the motivation and capacity to move in these new directions. Transformational leaders believe the average employee can make a valuable contribution to the organization.[20] In addition, they encourage the group to adopt a new shared vision of where the organization should be going.

SIX STEPS IN PROBLEM SOLVING

In an effort to reach a decision, small groups must proceed through a series of steps (Figure 10.1). They must define and analyze the problem, establish criteria for solutions,

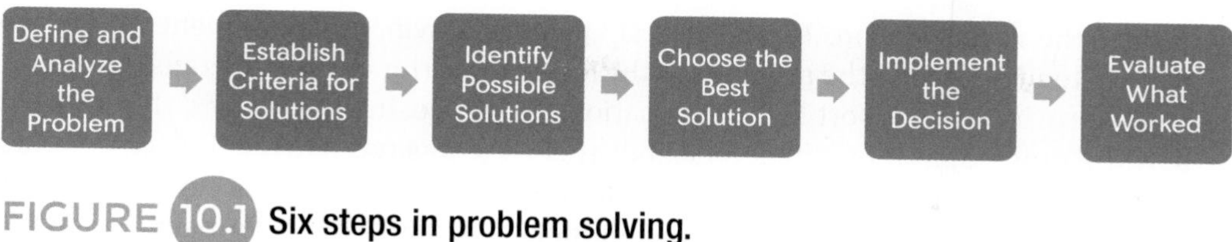

FIGURE 10.1 Six steps in problem solving.

identify possible solutions, choose the best solution, implement the decision, and evaluate what worked. The following discussion identifies and describes what happens at each of these six stages.

Step 1: Defining and Analyzing the Problem

Before we can find solutions to a problem, we must understand the problem—its nature and complexities. So the first step in group problem-solving involves defining and analyzing the problem. Let us explore this step using the issue of obesity in teenagers.

We may realize that obesity in teenagers has become a serious societal concern. In looking for information on the topic, we can learn about the origins of the problem from Statistics Canada databases and other sources. We can identify the ideal weight for teens in terms of the body mass index (BMI). We can compare trends over time and predict whether the problem will worsen in the future. Researching the problem enables us to gain a better understanding of its origins and characteristics. Thus it helps us to *define* the problem.

To provide a focus for discussion of teen obesity, we may want to frame the problem in the form of an **open-ended question** such as the following: How can we solve the problem of obesity in teenagers? Open-ended questions encourage exploration and discussion. We should avoid **closed-ended questions**, which request only a *yes* or a *no* answer. The following are examples of closed-ended questions: Does diet affect obesity in teenagers? Should we have more exercise programs in schools in order to help teens to stay fit?

OPEN-ENDED QUESTIONS Questions that encourage a full and detailed response.

CLOSED-ENDED QUESTIONS Questions that request a *yes* or a *no*.

When we *analyze*, we look at both causes and effects. The root cause of obesity in teenagers, for example, may be poor diet and lack of exercise. Poor diet may come, in turn, from limited family income, lack of time available to parents to prepare healthy meals, and easy access to fast food options in high schools and restaurants. Lack of exercise may stem from reliance on cars and buses (instead of walking) for transportation, scarcity of exercise programs in schools, and excessive time spent sitting in front of computers and televisions. So solving the problem of obesity in teens requires an understanding of all of the factors that contribute to obesity.

> "Problems are only opportunities in work clothes."
> HENRI J. KAISER

To gain support for proposed solutions, we must also understand the possible effects of unsolved problems. Obesity in teenagers, for example, can lead to poor self-image, increased risk of illness, more absences from school, more trips to the doctor, unnecessary stress on the health care system, and weaker performance by students in classrooms.

Sometimes we misdiagnose a problem. Misdiagnoses often result from too little information, and they can lead groups to misdirect their efforts. In 2012, Quebec students blamed the provincial government for high tuition rates in universities. As a result, many took to the streets in a protest directed at Quebec's provincial government. In fact, the issue extended beyond the province to the federal government, which transfers money to the province to support higher education in Quebec. In other words, the students saw the problem as a provincial one; but this view was too narrow. This case shows that before we can arrive at a workable solution, we must be able to accurately identify and fully understand the problem. For a humorous example of this principle, go to the "Professional Contexts" box titled "The Value of Understanding the Problem."

In setting up group sessions dedicated to definition and analysis of a problem, leaders may wish to establish an online meeting space (e.g., through Google Groups) to allow members to share their research in advance of face-to-face meetings.[21]

Step 2: Establishing Criteria for Solutions

Serious analysis of a problem—its history, root causes, and effects—leads us logically to the second step in the problem-solving process: establishing criteria for solutions. Obviously, any solution must be capable of solving the problem. However, solutions must meet multiple criteria before we can consider them to be feasible. In the case of obesity in teenagers, we can speculate that the solutions should be ones that the community and parents will accept and support. The solutions should be cost effective. They should be ethical. They should not cause physical or psychological harm to the youth, and they should not create new problems. The solutions should be practical, capable of being implemented in a reasonable length of time. They should take the food habits and culture of the community into account. Good criteria allow us to choose the best solutions; they also give us a tool to use in evaluating whether our solution has worked after we implement it.

Step 3: Identifying Possible Solutions

Step 3 of problem solving involves idea generation. Many recent studies have questioned whether groups or individuals can produce a larger range of high-quality ideas.[23] In fact, the answer to this question is complicated. The effectiveness of group problem-solving depends on a number of different factors. For example, a study involving

*professional*CONTEXTS

The Value of Understanding the Problem[22]

The printing presses of a major newspaper began to malfunction on the Saturday before Christmas. None of the technicians could track down the problem. As time ticked on, the manager of the newspaper grew increasingly anxious. If they could not fix the problem in time to print the Sunday paper, they would lose a considerable amount of advertising revenue. Finally, the manager made a frantic call to a retired technician who had worked with these presses for decades: "We'll pay anything—just come in and fix the problem!"

When the technician arrived, he walked around for a few minutes, surveying the presses. Then he approached one of the control panels and opened it. He removed a key from his pocket and turned a screw one-half of a turn. Satisfied, he turned to the manager and said, "The presses will now work correctly." After the manager thanked the technician profusely, he told him to submit a bill for his work.

The bill arrived a few days later—for $10,000! Thinking the amount was too much, the manager asked the technician to itemize his charges. He hoped the technician would reduce the amount once he had to identify how little he had done. The revised bill arrived: $1 for turning the screw; $9,999 for knowing which screw to turn.

computer simulations showed that groups can generate more ideas than individuals if they exchange ideas in writing, alternate between group and individual activities, and include people from different backgrounds with diverse experiences.[24]

A second computer-mediated study found that personality factors make a difference in numbers and diversity of ideas produced in group situations. **Extroverts** generate more unique and diverse ideas than do **introverts** when they also get a moderate to large number of ideas from outside. (In this context, *moderate to large* implies 20 to 40 ideas.) In other words, extroverts perform better than introverts when they receive stimulation from the ideas of others.[25] Extroverts are also more inclined than introverts to actively seek ideas from outside.[26]

EXTROVERTS
People who enjoy the company of others.

INTROVERTS
People who enjoy more alone time.

In the quest to find effective problem-solving techniques, groups may use either more creative or more rational strategies. The following discussion will explore techniques associated with each of these strategies.

Creative Problem-Solving Techniques

The best solutions come from a process that includes a creative stage.[27] A supportive attitude on the part of leaders also makes a difference when it comes to creative thinking. Motivational speaker and author Zig Ziglar speaks of "stinking thinking," which discounts novel ideas and discourages creative input from group members. He says that leaders must encourage group members to consider many different alternatives and discourage them from putting down the contributions of others.[28] Sometimes group leaders use children's toys in an effort to change the group dynamics from rational and serious to playful and creative. Allowing sufficient time for idea generation can also lead to more creative solutions.

In the following section, we will examine some of the most common techniques used to draw creative input from group members. These techniques include brainstorming, brainwriting, working in nominal groups, brainsketching, mind mapping, synectics, fantasy chaining, and crowdsourcing.

Brainstorming

Creativity theorist Alex Osborn fathered the most familiar and widely used idea-generation technique: **brainstorming**.[29] In brainstorming, a facilitator introduces the problem, and group members take turns generating ideas. The goal is to produce as many solutions as possible. The focus is on quantity over quality, unusual ideas, piggybacking (adding to the ideas of others), and withholding of criticism until the evaluation phase. A related technique is **reverse brainstorming**, in which the facilitator asks the group to identify what could make the problem worse. Once group members have generated ideas about what *not* to do, they consider the benefits of doing the opposite.[30]

BRAINSTORMING
An idea-generation technique that involves group discussion aimed at generating as many ideas and solutions as possible.

REVERSE BRAINSTORMING
An idea-generation technique that involves identifying what could make the problem worse before looking at what could make it better.

As suggested above, group members must observe several rules during a brainstorming session. First, no member should evaluate or criticize the ideas of another person until the group has exhausted all possibilities for solutions. (When we think we are being judged, we feel less free to suggest unconventional ideas.) Second, the group leader should encourage wild ideas because farfetched ideas can lead to breakthroughs in thinking about a problem. Third, members should try to build on the ideas of others and to combine ideas. Finally, they should value quantity over quality of ideas. The greater the number of ideas, the more likely good ideas will emerge. Brainstorming groups can generate hundreds of ideas in a single session, although some will be repetitious.[31]

Christopher Robbins/Thinkstock

Like other creative problem-solving techniques, brainstorming has received its share of criticism in recent years. A number of studies have found, for example, that group brainstorming sessions generate fewer ideas than comparable numbers of individuals working alone on the same problem.[32] Several findings explain this loss of productivity in group brainstorming. Group sessions can produce "free riders" and "social loafers." Free riders think others can solve the problem equally well without their participation; so they do not bother to contribute.[33] In a similar way, social loafers invest less effort if they believe the group will claim credit for the final product.[34] Like free riders, social loafers feel little motivation or accountability. In response, others in the group may decrease their efforts in order to avoid being "suckers"—taking the load of the work while others sit back and listen.[35] Most commonly, group members fail to contribute because they fear being negatively judged.[36] Finally, the necessity to wait one's turn can cause losses in idea generation.[37] Despite these demonstrated liabilities, the use of trained facilitators improves results in brainstorming sessions.[38]

> **"It is better to have enough ideas for some of them to be wrong, than to be always right by having no ideas at all."**
> EDWARD DE BONO

Brainwriting

BRAINWRITING An idea-generation technique involving exchange of ideas on paper in a group setting.

The technnique known as ***brainwriting*** is similar to brainstorming, but it tends to have better results. Brainwriting involves individuals writing their ideas on a sheet of paper and then passing the sheet to another person in the group. Group members can choose to build on the ideas of others or to generate entirely new ideas. Brainwriting stimulates thought processes but does not reduce productivity. With brainwriting, group members do not have to wait for their turn to offer suggestions. They can respond immediately in writing once they see the ideas of others. These ideas may cause them to move in new and unplanned directions.[39]

> **"There are two kinds of people, those who do the work and those who take the credit. Try to be in the first group; there is less competition there."**
> INDIRA GANDHI

The question of whether computer-mediated communication (CMC) increases the quantity and quality of ideas in a brainwriting (and brainstorming) sessions has not been clearly answered. Some studies have found that computer-mediated sessions can increase the number of novel ideas,[40] as well as improve the quality and richness of ideas.[41] Others have arrived at less positive or less conclusive results.[42]

Nominal Group Technique

NOMINAL GROUP TECHNIQUE An idea-generation technique in which group members work independently at first and then share their initial ideas.

Most people agree that, on the whole, nominal groups tend to outperform brainstormers.[43] Participants do not interact with each other during the first stages of the **nominal group technique**. That is, they are a group in name only. The process begins with group members responding in writing to a question posed by a moderator. In an organizational setting, a nominal group may address questions related to structures, issues, resources, costs, or personal feelings and concerns.

> "Creative problem-solving is looking at the same thing as everyone else and thinking something different."
> ALBERT SZENT-GYORGI

After recording ideas independently, group members proceed to the second stage of the nominal group process. Each member reads her or his first idea aloud in a round-robin fashion—one at a time. After each group member has shared one idea, the facilitator asks participants to share subsequent ideas in the same way. The group continues in a series of rounds until they have exhausted all ideas. Once an individual member has shared her or his complete list, that person falls silent until all remaining ideas are on the table.

Once the process of sharing has ended, participants have the option of engaging in group brainstorming, building on the ideas of others, and evaluating the contributions. If these latter stages occur, the group obtains the advantages of collective (as well as individual) idea generation.

The nominal group technique has some advantages over group brainstorming. No one can be a free rider with the nominal group technique; all members participate. Members do not have to wait to record their ideas. The generation of ideas occurs on an individual basis prior to group sharing. Nominal groups do not tend to focus on a single aspect of the problem or follow a single chain of thought. Finally, evaluation does not occur during the sharing of ideas.[44]

Brainsketching and Mind Mapping

Still another alternative to brainstorming, **brainsketching** involves the representation of ideas in graphic (rather than written or spoken) formats. This form of idea generation builds on approaches used by design artists, who often produce fast and messy sketches of ideas for logos, structures, or other projects. The nature of sketching encourages creativity because everyone attaches different meanings to drawings. As illustrated in the famed Rorschach inkblot test, different people can look at the same drawings and arrive at vastly different interpretations. One person may see a butterfly; another may see an airplane. Ambiguity—that is, lack of specificity—works in favour of creativity.

BRAINSKETCHING An idea-generation technique that involves sketching ideas on paper, followed by sharing with others.

Whereas facilitators in brainstorming and nominal group sessions generally record the group's ideas, participants in brainsketching sessions most commonly perform the work themselves. In what has been called a "reflective conversation"[45] with themselves, designers sketch out ideas on giant notepads, electronic blackboards, or flipcharts. Others add to the drawings, often superimposing their ideas over the original contribution and sometimes adding written comments. In this way, the group generates a "collective graphic memory,"[46] capable of being preserved and accessed at a later time.

In brainsketching sessions at the Delft School of Industrial Design Engineering, group members complete their first sketches on sheets of paper, which they then pass to colleagues. In turn, they

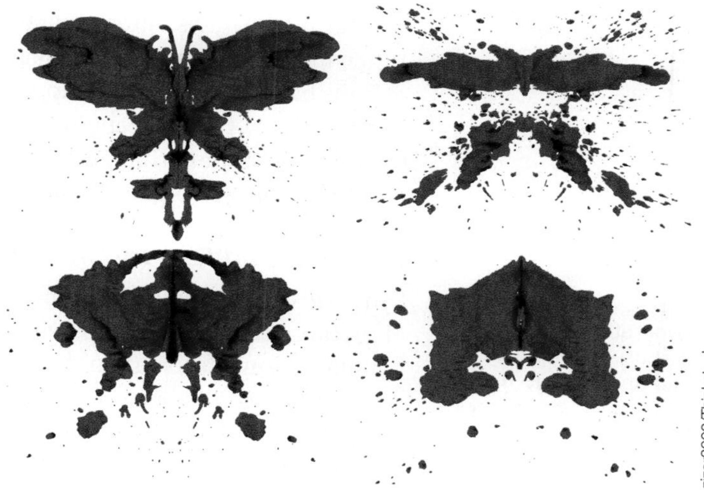
zizar2002/Thinkstock

receive the work of their peers. After exchanging sketches, group members continue to sketch; but this time they use the sketches of others as a source of inspiration for new concepts. Sometimes they modify or add to the sketches of others. Between rounds, a facilitator sometimes encourages members to build on the ideas of others. After five rounds, the idea-generation process stops.[47]

Variations in the brainsketching process sometimes take place. For example, group members may move from one station to the next to work with charts that have been taped to walls. Although typical brainsketching sessions require members to be silent throughout the sketching process, some designers like to talk about their ideas as they sketch. Studies by Remko van der Lugt asked group members to explain their ideas to the group after each round of sketching. By adding a verbal dimension to the brainsketching activity, van der Lugt hoped to combine the benefits of brainstorming and brainsketching.[48] And in fact, some benefits did result. For example, when asked to explain and discuss their ideas, group members made more connections and did a better job of building on the ideas of others. Subsequent studies, however, have not obtained the same positive results.

Brainsketching has several clear advantages. First, as suggested above, it promotes highly creative and varied solutions. If each member of a group processes the information in a different way, the ideas and solutions (generated by the group) will be more diverse. In addition, sketches allow more possibilities for building on the ideas of others. For example, one person may build on one part of a drawing; another may build on a different part.

Brainsketching also has its disadvantages. Participants without design experience tend to build on the ideas of others rather than contribute new ideas or offer alternatives. With proper instruction, non-designers can create sketches that convey their ideas; however, they often hesitate to attempt drawing. As a consequence, non-designers tend to accept and work within the frames set by designers; and many probably hesitate to contribute in sessions with people who have design experience.[49]

MIND MAPPING An idea-generation technique that uses a single word or idea placed at the centre of a piece of paper to stimulate more ideas.

Similar to brainsketching in its visual nature, **mind mapping** begins with placing a single word or topic at the centre of a sheet of paper. That word or topic stimulates connections with other ideas, which the mind mappers place on spokes radiating from the central term. The creative process radiates outward as those ideas continue to generate additional ideas. Mind mappers use colours, lines, images, arrows, and other symbols in creating the maps. After generating the initial ideas, they look for additional linkages. When mind mappers identify linkages, they visually connect related concepts. A number of firms have created mind-mapping software to assist in the idea-generation process.[50]

Advocates of mind mapping claim that the process works in conjunction with how the brain functions. That is, it uses right brain creativity to produce the ideas and left brain reasoning to organize the concepts.[51]

Synectics and Fantasy Chaining

SYNECTICS An idea-generation technique that uses metaphors and analogies to make the strange familiar and the familiar strange.

Synectics has its roots in brainstorming. However, synectics relies heavily on the use of metaphors and analogies, whose purpose is to "make the strange familiar and the familiar strange."[52] Its originator, William J. Gordon, claimed that "to make the familiar strange is to distort, or transpose the everyday ways of looking and responding . . . it is the conscious attempt to achieve a new look at the same old world, people, ideas, feelings, and things."[53]

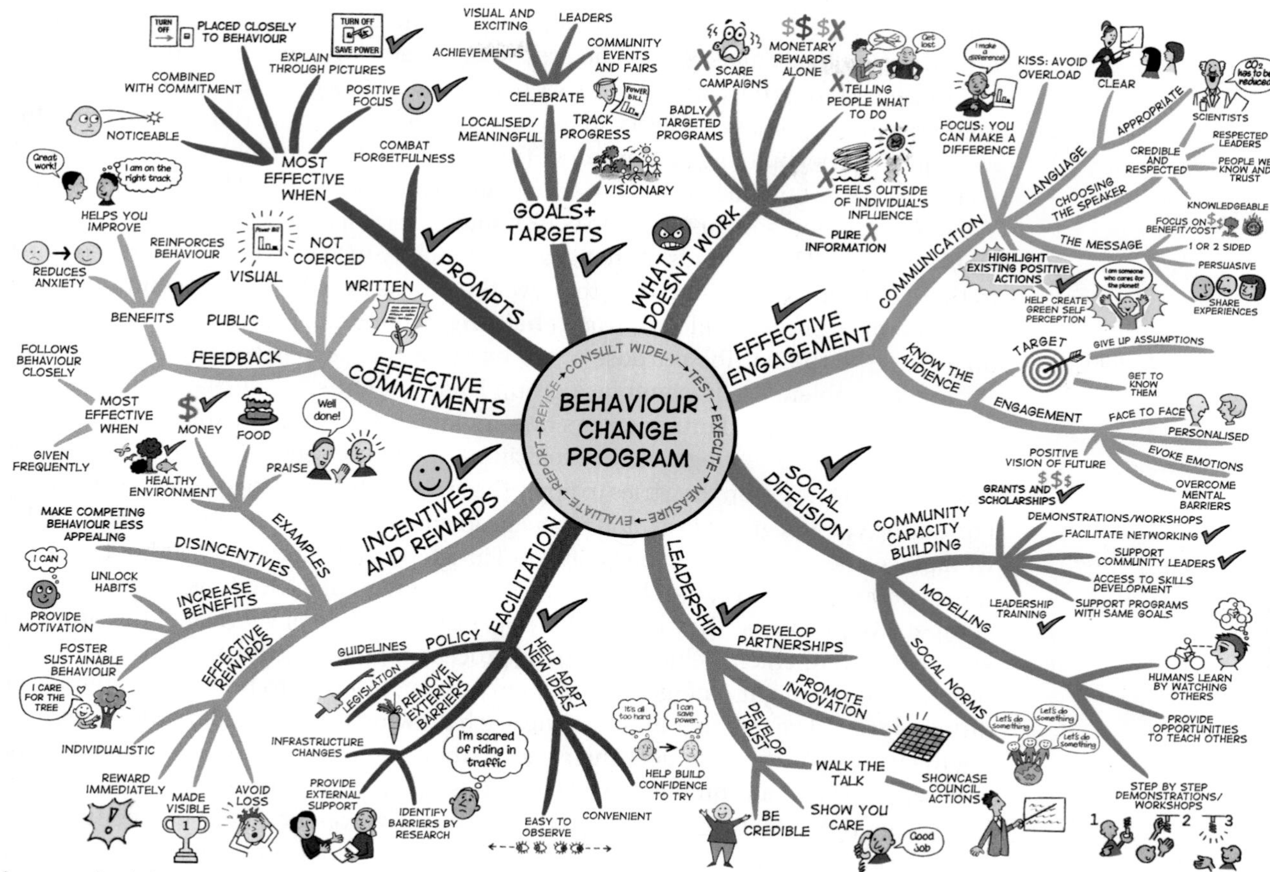

Source: www.learningfundamentals.com.au

Synectics usually involves a group of six to eight participants, plus a leader. After the leader briefly introduces the problem, the group paraphrases it. For example, a group of structural engineers might need to decide upon changes to building codes to make the structures more earthquake proof. If engaged in a synectics exercise, the group might reword the question as a "how to" statement: "how to make buildings more earthquake proof." After paraphrasing the problem, the group members proceed to generate an analogy or fantasy story that will allow them to explore the problem in a creative way.

> "Imagination is more important than knowledge."
> ALBERT EINSTEIN

An **analogy** uses a known concept to explain an unknown or less familiar one. So if a group is trying to brainstorm solutions for the stalled economy, for example, they might compare the situation to an army of ants that encounter an obstacle when trying to secure food for their queen. The ants have options such as relocating, looking for a new food source, finding new pathways to their food source, regrouping and assisting each other in reaching the goal, or resting for a time in hopes that the situation will change. After exploring the ant analogy, the group attempts to transfer the solutions to their real problem—the stagnant economy.

ANALOGY A figure of speech that uses something familiar to explain something less familiar.

In another problem-solving situation, a group leader might ask, "How can we in our wildest fantasy solve the problem of overcrowding in classrooms?" Group members might propose analogies that involve overselling seats on airplanes, overpopulation of some animal species, or long lineups at a movie theatre. Then they transfer the insights from these fantastic analogies to the problem of overcrowding in classrooms.

Another strategy (also in the category of analogies) asks group members to imagine themselves as buildings or objects. In the case of engineers considering requirements for earthquake-proof buildings, for example, the discussion leader might say: "Imagine that you are an office building in Vancouver, and an earthquake occurs. How would you feel? What would others see happening to you? If someone is measuring your vital signs, what would they find? What kinds of changes might make you feel better?" After responding to these questions, the group tries to move their ideas into the form of solutions.

FANTASY CHAINING
An idea-generation technique that involves group creation of a story based on a fantastic theme.

In a similar process called **fantasy chaining**, group members create a story based on a fantastic theme. The purpose of the exercise is to help the group to respond to some real problem.[54] For example, a group leader might suggest that members take "time out" and go on a fantasy excursion—an imagined trip to the top of a mountain, to the seaside, or to a jungle. After exploring some of the scenery and qualities of the places visited, the group then tries to apply these characteristics to the problem at hand. For example, if the group is exploring the problem of excessive competitiveness in the workplace, they might apply the qualities of jungle environments such as hot temperatures and an uncomfortable climate to the kind of workplace that results from highly competitive practices. They might also apply the principle of survival of the fittest to employees' competitive behaviours. In the process of exploring the problem in this way, some solutions might emerge. Group members might point to how many animals of diverse species live together in the jungle, each drawing what it needs without disrupting the ability of others to meet their needs. They might also note that the survival of some species depends on the survival of others; all are interdependent.

At other times, fantasy chaining starts with a single word or phrase that comes from the description of a problem. For example, the statement of a problem related to global warming could include the words *tsunami* or *starving polar bears*. Someone in the group then uses one of these concepts in a wild story about the problem. Each group member adds to the story. After everyone has contributed and the story appears to have reached a conclusion, the leader asks the group to consider absurd and impractical solutions to the problem. Finally, the group considers whether any of the absurd solutions could be made more practical and workable in order to apply the ideas to the issue of global warming.

In closing, we should note that different authors and practitioners use different fantasy processes. The above reflect a few basic approaches; however, they are not comprehensive. Many variations exist.[55]

Crowdsourcing

CROWDSOURCING
A practice where organizations invite large groups of Internet users to generate and share ideas on their products and services.

OPEN SOURCE
Approaches that allow and encourage a free flow of information into an organization.

Crowdsourcing refers to a practice where organizations invite large groups of Internet users to generate and share ideas on their products and services. Crowdsourcing falls under the heading of an **open-source** approach because it allows a free flow of information into the organization from customers, clients, employees, and the public at large.[56] Open-source practices such as crowdsourcing assume that knowledge and expertise no longer rest exclusively within the boundaries of the organization. Rather the survival and prosperity of large companies depend on their ability and willingness to capture intelligence inside as well as outside their walls.

Examples of open-source projects include Wikipedia; Galaxy Zoo, where web users help astronomers in exploring the universe; and OpenStreetMap, where users contribute geographic information to create detailed maps. British Petroleum issued a call to the masses for assistance in solving the 2010 *Deepwater Horizon* oil spill, which occurred in the Gulf of Mexico; the proposed solutions appeared on YouTube and TV programs. Police departments have long reached out to the public to help identify and provide information on the whereabouts of persons of interest in criminal investigations. Municipal governments have made a practice of holding town halls to ask citizens to contribute their solutions to pressing government problems.

Tom De Spiegelaere/Thinkstock

Within the world of business, the most frequent discussions of open-source approaches to knowledge creation concern innovation.[57] Open innovation requires going outside the organization in a quest for new ideas—then pooling this knowledge with the ideas generated by internal research and development (R&D) units. Closed innovation, on the other hand, supports a culture that relies solely on the efforts of R&D and other internal groups. Increasing numbers of business leaders think that open-source approaches such as crowdsourcing can lead to more creative solutions. The underlying belief is that "2 heads—or 2000 or 20,000—are better than one."[58]

Since crowdsourcing occurs via the Internet, the community of contributors is largely anonymous; and they may or may not receive compensation for their efforts. When given, compensation most often involves recognition. For example, the organization might generate a list of top contributors, which it posts on its website.[59]

Summary

In summary, we can see how groups have access to many different creative problem-solving techniques. We have discussed some of the most popular, including brainstorming, brainwriting, the nominal group technique, brainsketching, mind mapping, synectics, fantasy chaining, and crowdsourcing. Each has its strengths and weaknesses; and the choice of techniques depends largely on the nature of the problem, the resources available, and group preferences. To obtain practice using the creative problem-solving techniques we have discussed, go to the "From Theory to Practice" box on titled "Let's Get Creative: The Problem of Too Few Doctors in Canada."

> **"Never tell people how to do things. Tell them what to do and they will surprise you with their ingenuity."**
>
> GEORGE S. PATTON

Rational Problem-Solving Techniques

Organizations can also approach the task of problem solving through more rational and logical (as opposed to creative) techniques. These sorts of techniques rely heavily on the results of research and data. Some of the most common forms of rational problem-solving groups are Delphi panels, quality circles, and focus groups.

Delphi Panels

The problem-solving technique known as the ***Delphi method*** engages panels of experts in multiple rounds of problem solving or forecasting of future events or scenarios.[66] The

DELPHI METHOD
A structured method of decision making that engages panels of experts in multiple rounds of problem solving or forecasting.

from theory TO PRACTICE

Let's Get Creative: The Problem of Too Few Doctors in Canada

According to a 2011 report by the Fraser Institute, a think tank based in British Columbia, the shortage of doctors in Canada continues to worsen. Canada now ranks twenty-sixth out of 28 countries with publicly funded health care. The ratio of doctors to patients is 2.3 to 1000, compared to an average of 3 to 1000 in other developed countries.[60]

Problems related to the shortage of physicians include people without family doctors, long waiting lists for surgeries, unacceptable waiting times for cancer patients who require immediate treatment, difficulty getting appointments with specialists, long waiting times in emergency rooms, and outdated or inadequate numbers of medical equipment for diagnosing and treating patients. Almost 7 per cent of Canadians were unable to locate a family doctor in 2010. Those with enough money sometimes go to other countries for treatment that is either unavailable or inaccessible in Canada.[61]

We have been training more doctors in recent years, but not enough to maintain the current ratios, let alone improve them. The Fraser report projects that, over the coming decade, the situation will continue to deteriorate. In 2010, statistics showed that about 38 per cent of Canadian doctors were aged 55 or older.[62] As these doctors retire, they will need to be replaced by younger doctors. Unfortunately, surveys and other studies suggest that younger doctors work fewer hours and provide fewer services per week than do older doctors. In other words, as more young doctors replace the aging physicians, they will be caring for fewer patients.[63]

Should we be concerned about these statistics? Yes. The Organization for Economic Co-operation and Development (OECD) found a relationship between higher physician-to-population ratios and greater life expectancy in developed countries.[64] The Fraser report also notes that a higher physician-to-population ratio is associated with longer lives and lower mortality rates.[65]

What are your suggestions for solving the problem? Working in groups, use one of the creative problem-solving techniques to arrive at solutions. Your choices include brainstorming, brainwriting, the nominal group technique, brainsketching, mind mapping, synectics, fantasy chaining, and crowdsourcing.

Rand Corporation developed this well-respected technique for gathering ideas from experts within the organization. It works particularly well in conflict situations, where face-to-face communication is difficult.[67] Depending on the nature of the problem, the experts on the panel may come from similar or diverse backgrounds. Technical expertise plays a big role, for example, when the problem relates to some technical area. Interdisciplinary perspectives are more important, however, when the problem has a less specific focus. Some problems call for a mix of specialists and generalists.[68]

Basic steps in the Delphi method include defining the problem, identifying the type of expertise required to solve the problem, selecting a sample of experts to act as participants, preparing and distributing a questionnaire to the participants, and analyzing responses for level of agreement. Ten to fifteen participants can be sufficient when the group shares a common background. Studies requiring a more diverse group of experts demand a larger number of participants. Some Delphi studies engage as many as several hundred persons. Participants should have a good knowledge of the subject matter, a credible performance record in related areas, enough time to participate, and an appreciation of rational approaches to problem solving.

After selecting an appropriate number of participants, the researchers explain the purpose and importance of the study, the roles of the participants, and the questions to be answered. The questionnaire itself contains a clear statement of the problem. It also asks participants to provide opinions and reasoning on the topic, facts that played a role in their thinking, and any additional information that could help in decision making.

Once each participant has completed the questionnaire, the researchers review the responses. After identifying areas of agreement and disagreement (as well as points requiring clarification), they prepare and distribute a second questionnaire. This second questionnaire includes summaries of group responses to the first questionnaire. The researchers also provide any additional information or explanations requested by participants. After reviewing the summaries and the new information, participants can revise their positions if they wish. Where responses vary greatly from the norm, the researchers ask participants to explain their positions.

The researchers then circulate a second round of responses to participants for their reaction. This procedure continues until **consensus** emerges, usually after at least three rounds. By *consensus*, in this situation, we mean a condition whereby all participants accept a solution or decision even if they do not agree with it. The final report summarizes the goals, process, and results of the exercise.[69]

CONSENSUS General acceptance of (if not agreement with) a decision among all members of a group.

Weaknesses in the Delphi technique include the possibility for inclusion of participants with insufficient knowledge or motivation and the possibility that the organization will delay or never implement some recommendations. Nonetheless, Delphi compares favourably to other problem-solving techniques in terms of cost and the number of working hours required for participation and processing of results.[70]

The focus on expertise, prior experience with a problem, facts, logic, and reasoning differentiates this process from the more creative problem-solving strategies. With creative problem-solving, outside insights and novel perspectives weigh more heavily. Even the forecasting aspects of the Delphi method rely on statistical and mathematical formulas.

Like the Delphi method, medical panels rely on people with a high level of expertise. To learn more about how these panels function, see the "Professional Contexts" box.

Quality Circles

The **quality circle** is a type of problem-solving group traditionally employed in factory settings. The employees who make up a quality circle attempt to solve problems related to their day-to-day jobs. In other words, they do not attempt to solve problems that originate either below or above them or in some other part of the organization. Once employees have identified problems and possible solutions, they make recommendations to management. They also implement and monitor the results of any solutions approved by management.

QUALITY CIRCLE A group of employees who meet regularly to identify, discuss, and try to solve work-related issues.

Originally a Japanese concept, quality circles rely on—and encourage—teamwork. Leaders and members receive training in problem-solving and group-process techniques. The supervisors of employees normally function as quality-circle leaders. However, they must remove their supervisory hats when they assume the role of group facilitator. Like other facilitators, they must be non-directive, non-judgmental, and supportive. Facilitators link quality-circle members with others in the organization who hold information on specific topics, and they attempt to resolve issues that arise between group members.

To achieve results from quality circles, management must be willing to invest time and resources in the process. They must also attach value to the output of the quality circles. When management acts on the circles' recommendations, they show confidence in the employees. They also demonstrate confidence when they give the members significant issues on which to work.

*professional*CONTEXTS

A Case Study in Group Process with a Medical Team

When patients and their families face serious health conditions, medical teams come together to advise and offer counsel to the families. Medical specialists, family doctors, nurses, physical and occupational therapists, psychiatrists, dieticians, and others make up these teams. The specific makeup of the team depends on the medical condition of the patient and the anticipated outcome of treatments. Prior to meeting with the patient, team members must consult with one another and reach a preliminary consensus on how to proceed. Their decisions may involve a series of alternatives to present to the patient and family members. Whatever their preliminary decisions, they must stay open to modifying their views at the time of discussions with the patient and his or her family. The following fictitious case demonstrates a medical situation where a team might come together to decide what to recommend to the patient and his family.

At 88 years of age, Jerry Haiman developed bone cancer in one of his legs. His family doctor passed his case to an oncologist at the local hospital. After examining the X-rays, the oncologist shared the X-rays and his recommendation with a surgeon. The oncologist did not believe that chemotherapy alone could halt the spread of the cancer. However, he thought that surgery might be a workable option. The surgeon agreed. She said that Jerry might survive if they amputated his leg and followed the surgery with chemotherapy. They relayed this information to Jerry's family doctor.

Given Jerry's advanced age and history of heart problems, his family doctor did not believe that he could withstand the surgery and chemotherapy. He also believed that Jerry might have a difficult time adjusting to the loss of a leg. Jerry had lost his wife two years earlier, and he did not have anyone at home to care for him. He would be forced to enter a nursing home, an option that he had refused to consider after his wife died.

Since the doctors could not agree on the best way to proceed, they decided to convene a meeting. They invited all parties involved in Jerry's case—the surgeon, two oncologists (specialists in chemotherapy and radiation), Jerry's family doctor, a physiotherapist, and a psychiatrist. At the recommendation of the family doctor, the group also invited a specialist in pain management.

The oncologist who had met with the surgeon took the lead at the meeting. He introduced the purpose for their meeting and gave some background facts. He asked the family doctor to fill in details about the patient. He also directed the attention of the group to certain facts in the patient file. Following those introductory comments, he opened the discussion. It did not take the group long to diagnose the problem, and they moved quickly

Focus Groups

FOCUS GROUP
A group interview with a central purpose that guides the discussion.

Defined as a "discussion group with a purpose,"[71] a **focus group** is a special kind of group interview.[72] Originally corporations used focus groups almost exclusively for market research—to find out whether members of these groups liked new products or services. However, various organizations now apply the techniques in many other situations. Businesses employ focus groups to learn how employees feel about policies, to get ideas on planned innovations, and to involve employees in decision making. Governments use focus groups to learn more about the opinions of outside publics—what people believe and why they hold these beliefs. Politicians use focus groups to track shifts in public opinion, to make choices on how to deal with issues, and to discover weaknesses in the positions of the opposition. Some say that focus groups may be the only good method for getting information on highly sensitive issues (e.g., insurance fraud or tax evasion).[73]

Focus-group participants meet at a preset time and place to discuss a single topic, which may have multiple parts. Their discussions typically involve six stages: building positive group relations and clarifying the task, exploring broad questions, exploring questions of particular interest to the researcher, filling out a questionnaire or completing some other activity, evaluating the extent to which participants have met the goals of the discussion, and concluding with final comments from the participants *into considering criteria for solutions. Taking the age of the patient and the likely recovery time into account, they decided that any solution should (1) offer the hope of extending Jerry's life by at least two years, (2) enable him to function with the help of home care since he did not want to go into a nursing home, (3) not result in an unmanageable level of pain, and (4) be acceptable to the patient.*

All agreed that possible solutions included surgery, chemotherapy, radiation, and cryosurgery—or a combination of any two of the above. The less frequently used option was cryosurgery, which induces a condition of extreme cold that kills cancer cells. In addition, the team acknowledged that hospice care should be on their list of possible recommendations, should the treatment(s) fail.

The group did not encounter conflict until they reached the stage of deciding upon the best solution. At that time, the oncologist introduced a number of studies that supported the superiority of surgery when combined with other treatments such as chemotherapy and radiation. He explained that chemotherapy and radiation are almost never effective on their own. The surgeon discussed some advances in the area of cryosurgery. The psychiatrist and social worker agreed with the family doctor that amputation would be too hard on a person of Jerry's age.

At this point, the specialist in pain management suggested that they should revisit the criteria they had set earlier. After examining each proposed solution against the criteria, the group reached consensus on a treatment option—cryosurgery. Each member of the group drew on his or her expertise in arriving at the decision.

The surgeon pointed out that cryosurgery is less invasive than surgery. The family doctor supported the option because it would not necessitate amputation of the limb. The pain management specialist said that the option would meet the third criterion, as the pain should subside once the tissue healed. The physiotherapist believed that, along with a period of rehabilitation, cryosurgery could result in renewed mobility for Jerry. The psychiatrist believed cryosurgery offered the best alternative from a mental health perspective. The two oncologists raised questions about the long-term effectiveness of cryosurgery, which is still largely unknown, and about whether Jerry's insurance company would cover the cryosurgery. In the end, however, they said they could live with the recommendation of cryosurgery.

With the decision in place, the family doctor agreed to speak with Jerry and his representatives to discuss the team recommendation, and the meeting adjourned.

and the posing of unanswered questions by the moderator.[74] Not all stages occur in every focus group.

A focus-group discussion could centre on corporate image, a product or program, a candidate for political office, or another concern or issue. The following illustrate the kinds of questions to which a focus group might respond: What do you like or dislike about the company website? What, if anything, could be improved? How do you feel about the recent hikes in tuition? Which logo do you prefer? Why? As these questions suggest, focus groups bring people together to discuss their feelings and knowledge on a chosen topic, to acquire new insights, or to refine existing insights. Questions work better than statements in getting participants to share their perceptions, feelings, and opinions on topics.

Government- and university-based researchers often rely on focus groups to learn about social issues. In 2008, Health Canada conducted a series of eight focus groups with youth who had experienced substance abuse problems. The discussions centred on better ways to help youth with substance abuse problems.[75] In 2009, researchers at Brock University conducted focus groups with black youth from the Greater Toronto Area to find out their views on a proposal to build a new black-focussed high school.[76] In 2000, the Canadian Council on Social Development (CCSD) conducted six focus groups with immigrant youth living in Toronto, Montreal, and Vancouver. The CCSD wanted to learn more about the lifestyle patterns, challenges, and service needs of new immigrant youth.[77]

Deciding upon Number of Participants and Criteria for Inclusion

Not everyone agrees on the ideal number of participants for focus groups, but most groups have a moderator and eight to twelve participants. Ideally, focus groups should be large enough to include everyone who can make a contribution but not so large as to discourage participation.[78] Those who argue for smaller numbers say it is easier to fill groups and establish a close, friendly atmosphere with four or five participants.[79] In support of smaller groups, one study showed that increasing group size from four to eight did not double the quantity of ideas or significantly increase the quality of ideas.[80] Others claim, however, that larger groups result in more participation and better ideas.

In establishing focus groups, organizers take demographics into account. Factors like age, sex, language, ethnicity, region of residence, and income can influence results. Focus groups work best when participants share similarities with others in the group. When people feel inferior to other group members, they are uncomfortable expressing their opinions. They are more likely to go along with those who appear to be better educated, wealthier, or more experienced. In a similar way, bringing together individuals of widely varying ages can result in "parent–child" interactions and more argumentative discussions.[81] Ethnicity can also influence patterns of participation, with some groups exerting influence over others.[82] Placing more than one to two experts in a larger group of relatively uninformed individuals poses similar challenges. Experts can dominate a discussion and lower levels of participation by others who know less about the topic.[83]

Placing managers and their employees in the same focus groups can also be problematic. Differences in status can inhibit employees from expressing their open and honest opinions. Managers may feel the need to hide their true feelings and opinions from those beneath them in the organizational structure. Placing people from different organizational units in the same focus group can also sabotage results. When members of different business units interact in one focus group, they may feel the need to defend their special organizational interests.

As noted in other chapters, men and women communicate differently. In mixed-gender focus groups, men typically exercise more influence than women. Wives usually follow the lead of their husbands in focus groups; and even if they disagree with their spouses, they may remain silent. Therefore, a focus group with four married couples may reflect the views of only four individuals (not eight).[84]

Some researchers also warn against having friends in the same focus group.[85] Friends mean loss of anonymity, which can lead participants to feel less free to state their true thoughts. In addition, people often endorse their friends' points of view, even when they do not agree with those views.[86] Further, when friends "pair off," their private conversations can disrupt the group process and lessen the chances that others will participate.[87]

In conclusion, putting together highly diverse groups in terms of status, income, ethnicity, expertise, or other factors can sabotage the process. The presence of spouses or partners and friends can also affect the results.[88] To avoid these problems, the researcher must be very careful when selecting participants for a focus-group session.

Recruiting Participants

Organizations use various means to identify likely participants for focus groups. Sometimes they get the names from membership lists, organizational records, or directories (offline or online). At other times they recruit in person at a specific location. They might even ask current participants to suggest the names of friends who might be interested in participating in future groups. Experts say that if you pull names from a directory, you need to be sure the participants fit the profile. Many also advise that you should over-recruit by 20 per cent when pulling names from broad directories such as telephone listings.[89]

In our age of Internet access, new kinds of recruiting procedures and communication channels have become available. Many firms now reach potential focus-group participants by email or through recruiting notices posted on web pages. Many large companies rely on tech-savvy recruiting firms, which have large specialized databases. Challenges come, however, from the growing numbers of youth who rely solely on cell phones rather than land lines. Their names generally do not appear in telephone or other directories, making them more difficult to find and recruit.

Newsletter announcements, group invitations, and announcements at meetings usually get few responses.[90] Personal invitations, which explain the basis for selection, generate more interest. Recruiters' chances of filling their focus-group quotas will improve if they recruit in the right places. For example, if a video game company wants to find out what people think about their online games, they might install banners asking for volunteers on their websites. People will be most interested in participating in groups that address topics of interest to them. In general, explaining the value of the study furthers the chance that people will agree to participate.

A cash incentive (even if it is small) tends to encourage higher rates of participation. The amount of money offered usually depends on the anticipated difficulty of obtaining participants in a particular category. Recognized experts, business executives, physicians, lawyers, doctors, and engineers typically expect larger than average incentives.[91] Offers for free (or even discounted) products or services—as well as refreshments—also entice some individuals to participate in a focus group.

Rudyanto Wijaya/Thinkstock

Choosing a Setting

Organizations conduct focus groups in many different kinds of settings. Some use conference or meeting rooms, sometimes equipped with two-way mirrors. Others rent hotel or motel rooms. Whatever the choice, participants should feel at ease in the setting. A pleasant and easily accessible physical environment helps to create this sense of well-being. Holding the focus group at a highly desirable location may increase the chance that people will agree to participate and will arrive at the designated place on time. Ideally, one table should accommodate all participants in a focus group. Holding sessions at the workplace sometimes creates a threatening environment for employees.[92]

Moderating a Focus Group

Focus groups function best when participants see the moderator as one of them. To encourage that end, moderators can dress and behave in ways that conform to group norms. A moderator might wear a suit, for example, when facilitating a session with corporate executives. A sweater and pants might be more appropriate with a group of graphic artists.

In general, moderators should have good background knowledge of the topic being discussed, the ability to recognize good reasoning and relationships between ideas, and good facilitation skills. Ideally, they should share some background similarities with the participants, which will help participants see them as part of the group. A sense of humour and a friendly demeanour are also important.[93]

Taking a few preliminary steps can help a focus-group session to get off to a good start. First, the moderator should appoint an assistant who will attend to details such as taping the session, taking notes, looking after the physical needs of participants, and welcoming late arrivals. Appointing an assistant frees the moderator to concentrate on the group discussion. Second, the moderator must decide on how to document the session. This involves setting up any necessary recording equipment and ensuring that paper and pens are available for note taking. Even if the moderator makes an audio or video recording of the session, either the moderator or her assistant should still plan to take notes. Sometimes recorders fail to function or background noise interferes with the quality of the recording. In addition, notes can be useful in post-session analysis because they capture the note taker's personal thoughts and feelings about the events.[94] Although an assistant can observe and take notes from behind a two-way mirror, this practice takes away from the confidentiality of the process and threatens the comfort of some participants.[95]

The moderator can also prepare and distribute name tags. Name tags encourage participants to get to know each other and make it easier for moderators to call people by name. However, when the subject matter is sensitive (e.g., sexual harassment, family violence, or supervisor–subordinate relationships), participants may not want to use their last names.

The moderator begins the session by greeting participants, explaining the reasons for their selection, introducing the topic, and previewing the agenda for the session. She announces the length of the session; break times; the availability of refreshments (if any); and policies on smoking, use of cell phones, and other issues. She invites participation from all members and sets rules on turn taking. In an effort to establish a climate of openness and sharing, she welcomes different points of view and encourages negative as well as positive comments.

The moderator also indicates whether confidentiality will be protected. If representatives of the sponsoring company are observing the session, she informs the group. If the sessions are to be recorded, she explains the reasons and requests permission. Moderators attempt to anticipate concerns in order to reduce anxiety and stress.[96]

After making initial comments, the moderator asks members to introduce themselves. Then she "warms up" the group by asking an interesting question or suggesting that the group share stories or anecdotes on the topic under discussion.[97] Getting the group to react to an object, photograph, drawing, or video or audio recording can also stimulate early participation in the focus group.[98]

Most focus-group discussions move from the general to the specific. That is, moderators begin with open-ended questions and end with closed-ended questions. **Non-directive interviewing** allows control to shift from the interviewer to the interviewee and back again. The interviewer offers the topics for discussion, but an interactive conversation ensues. This conversation allows the researcher to obtain deeper insights into the thoughts and feelings of participants. For example, the interviewee may bring up important

NON-DIRECTIVE INTERVIEW An interview that relies on open-ended questions.

issues that the interviewer had not planned to discuss (e.g., because the interviewer was not aware of the issues or did not realize their importance). As a result, non-directive interviews can lead to unexpected findings.

Through its reliance on *yes–no* or closed-ended questions (e.g., Do you like the new parking policy?), **directive interviewing** enables a focus group to cover a larger number of topics. However, this style of interviewing closes some avenues of discussion before they can yield interesting results. Closed-ended questions lead to **single-loop learning**. With single-loop learning, we get only the information that we know how to request.[99] In some cases, we do not know enough about the topic to ask the right questions.

© OrangeDukeProductions/iStockphoto

DIRECTIVE INTERVIEW An interview that relies on *yes–no* or closed-ended questions.

SINGLE-LOOP LEARNING Learning that provides answers to questions we know how to ask.

Some of the most productive groups go in unexpected directions. For example, a discussion that begins with reactions to a new product might end with a critique of the manufacturer's hiring policies, a subject of equal importance to the company. Yet many organizations also want simple, specific answers to predetermined questions of interest. Do customers like a new product? Are employees interested in learning more about history of the business? Will a new company logo alienate existing clients? As a result, the best approach to moderating focus groups generally falls somewhere between the extremes of directive and non-directive. In other words, the best approach is to begin with open-ended questions and conclude with closed-ended ones, as suggested in the preceding discussion.

For a two-hour focus group, the moderator generally asks five to ten questions[100] Even though the discussion format can be flexible, moderators should prepare some questions in advance in case the discussion dies prematurely or fails to move in the desired direction. For organizational purposes, the moderator can divide the session so that the participants concentrate on only one question or issue at a time.[101]

Throughout the discussion, the moderator tracks the extent to which the focus group is meeting its objectives. The experienced moderator never loses sight of where the group should be at the end of the discussion. At some point, moderators may encourage a narrowing of focus to address main areas of interest. Occasional summaries and gentle prompting can help to refocus a group that has strayed from the topic. The moderator monitors the mood of the group; and when interest flags, she must be ready to move the group to the next issue. In cases involving sensitive issues, the moderator can invite individuals to share private thoughts or experiences on paper. The moderator then shares the ideas and experiences with the group but maintains the anonymity of the contributors.

> *"Would you tell me, please, which way I ought to go from here?"*
> *"That depends a good deal on where you want to get to."*
> *"I don't much care where . . . "*
> *"Then it doesn't matter which way you go."*
> LEWIS CARROLL, *ALICE IN WONDERLAND*

The best moderators take care not to signal acceptance or non-acceptance of an idea through verbal or nonverbal behaviours (e.g., nodding the head or saying "that's a great idea"). They treat participants as equals, taking care not to champion some points of view over others. Good moderators are good listeners, and they avoid over-directing. Friendly, consistent behaviours throughout the session can make all participants feel their views are valued.

To encourage balanced group participation, moderators can look in the direction of a less vocal participant when asking a question. If the person closes the communication channel by looking away, however, the moderator should look elsewhere for a response. Avoiding the gaze of a participant who tends to dominate the discussion can also encourage balanced participation.[102] If one participant has a much higher level of expertise than the rest of the group, the moderator can appoint this individual as a resource person—to offer facts or explanations on points of confusion. The moderator can suggest that such an expert should avoid expressing an opinion that could unduly influence the discussion.

Moderators typically avoid asking *why* people feel as they do.[103] They also avoid calling directly on individuals or going around the table to ask for positions on an issue. Participants may avoid taking a position because they do not have an opinion on the topic or because they are ill-informed. But once they have stated a position on an issue, they may feel the need to defend the position. At other times, they may be embarrassed to state an opinion on a particular topic. Progressing systematically around a group can also be boring for participants, especially if some people take a long time to state their opinions. Others may give brief responses that cut off the possibility for further questioning.

The average focus-group session lasts for one to two hours. Part of maintaining a friendly interpersonal environment is beginning and ending a focus-group session on time. Group members can become openly hostile if held beyond the time they have been asked to meet. Therefore, the moderator must manage time well. That is, she must keep the group on track and ensure participating members cover all necessary points, while not stifling or shutting off discussion too soon in important areas.

Step 4: Choosing the Best Solution

As the previous discussions suggest, groups may explore many different options when trying to solve a problem. In creative problem-solving, they may engage in brainstorming, brainwriting, the nominal group technique, brainsketching, mind mapping, synectics, fantasy chaining, or crowdsourcing to arrive at these options. In rational problem-solving, they use other formats such as the Delphi method, quality circles, and focus groups. No matter the means used to explore alternatives, however, the decision makers must eventually choose the best solution.

Thus, the fourth stage in the problem-solving process involves deciding which solutions can provide the best results for the group. At this point, conflict may occur as not everyone will agree on the best solution. Contrary to popular thought, this period of conflict is not necessarily a bad development. Classic studies suggest that the best solutions come from groups that go through a conflict phase prior to reaching consensus.[104]

Avoidance of conflict can lead to the "illusion of agreement," which masks the true feelings of group members and results in poor group decisions. Irving Janis labelled this desire to conform to dominant group opinion as **groupthink**. He said that groupthink occurs most often in highly cohesive groups with a long history or that value harmony. Characteristics of groupthink include an obvious dislike for conflict, a strong desire to reach consensus without debate, the appearance of unanimous agreement, a sense that nothing can hurt the group, the presence of pressures to conform, tendencies toward

GROUPTHINK The tendency for group members to conform to majority opinion in order to avoid conflict.

self-censorship, rationalization of the group's position, and a tendency to support the group leader.[105]

Referencing *The Righteous Mind* by Jonathan Haidt, a contributor to *The Washington Post* wrote in March 2013 that the leadership of the Roman Catholic Church meets all the criteria for groupthink. The organization is powerful. It has been around for a very long time. The leaders draw on moral arguments to justify their actions and decisions and manage their institutional reputation. They have low tolerance for members who advocate a different point of view, and they discourage debate and free expression of ideas.[106] We can also see groupthink at work in some courtroom trials. See the "Professional Contexts" box for an example of group pressures in jury deliberations.

Ideally, groups move out of the conflict phase and come to consensus on the basis of the best available information and insights. In practice, however, groups often have a tendency to go with the majority opinion and to support the leader even when they

*professional*CONTEXTS

Deadlocked Juries

Pressures to conform to group decisions can be enormous in charged atmospheres such as murder trials. The movie *Twelve Angry Men*, often studied in group dynamics, depicts one such situation. In this classic film, a lone holdout eventually convinces his fellow jurors to acquit the defendant in a murder trial. Despite being fictionalized, the level of conflict depicted in this film is not uncommon in murder trials. The scene replays itself time and again in jury deliberations. The National Center for State Courts in the United States reports that hung juries (juries unable to reach a verdict due to disagreement) result in about 6 per cent of cases under their jurisdiction.

In May 2012 a jury in Sarnia, Ontario, failed to reach agreement on the murder trial of Craig Short, accused of killing his 48-year-old wife Barbara Short. The jury indicated they had reached an impasse, which they would not be able to overcome. Similarly, in November 2010, a Nova Scotia jury informed Supreme Court Justice Glenn MacDougall that they were hopelessly deadlocked in the trial of Bernard Frederick Hartling, accused of murdering Kenneth McNamara. In both cases, the judge accepted the jury's statement and ordered a new trial.

Some judges, however, are less willing to take the pressure off dissenting jurors. The cost of trials—especially high-profile ones—makes hung juries an expensive proposition for all involved. As a consequence, the United States Supreme Court approved what has come to be known as a "dynamite charge." A dynamite charge allows a judge to tell deadlocked jurors to continue deliberating until they reach a verdict. For example, in May 2012, the judge in the murder trial of William Balfour, ex-brother-in-law to the Oscar-winning actress and singer Jennifer Hudson, told the jurors to return to deliberations. He did not accept their inability to reach a verdict. Ultimately, the jury found Balfour guilty; he got three life sentences for murdering Hudson's mother, brother, and seven-year-old nephew.

An earlier example occurred in December 2007 in New York. Three days before Christmas, a jury informed Judge Barbara Kahn that they were unable to agree on a verdict in the murder trial of John White. White was standing trial for the shooting death of a Long Island youth, Daniel Cicciaro. The trial was racially charged since John White was black, and his teenage victim was white. Rejecting the statement of deadlock on Friday afternoon, Kahn ordered the jury to resume deliberations. Faced with the likelihood of being closeted for the holiday weekend, the jurors returned a unanimous guilty verdict the next day.[107]

Following the trial, two jurors filed an official complaint. They claimed the other jurors and the judge had placed them under psychological pressure to renounce their position, which would have acquitted the defendant. They alleged that they had changed their votes from innocent to guilty after a 12-hour session in which hostile fellow jurors demanded a change of vote. They said that the upcoming holiday weekend had also created pressures for them.

In the latter two cases, jurors holding the minority view felt the necessity to give way to majority opinion. Ultimately their decisions resulted from normative influence (group pressures to conform), not informational influence (fact-based persuasion).[108]

do not agree with the decision. Two examples of such a tendency occur in a 2012 episode of the horror television series *The Walking Dead*.[109] The first instance arises after Randall Culver (Michael Zegen) reveals that his former group raped and murdered two teenage girls and their father. Arguing that Randall poses a threat to the group, Rick Grimes (Andrew Lincoln) engineers group consensus on the matter of executing Randall. Although Dale Horvath (Jeffrey DeMunn) tries hard to convince the others that Randall should not die, he is unable to break the consensus. A second example of group consensus occurs after a "walker" (a zombie) attacks Dale. Even though not all feel confident in their decision, the group quickly reaches consensus that they should shoot Dale in order to end his suffering.

Pressured group decisions can lead to disastrous consequences.[110] Consider the case of the Challenger space shuttle. Prior to the shuttle's launch on 28 January 1986, space engineers from Morton Thiokol, Inc. (a subcontractor to NASA) warned against launch. Thiokol engineers were concerned that the abnormally cold Florida temperatures might cause a structural failure in their product (the O-rings). They recommended waiting until the temperature reached 53 degrees Fahrenheit (11.7 degrees Celsius). One Thiokol engineer warned that it was "against goodness" to launch. Under pressure from NASA, however, Thiokol management pressured the engineers to agree to the launch. In the end, an O-ring failed during launch; the shuttle broke apart just over a minute after it left the ground, killing all seven astronauts on board.[111]

An example from Canada involved the collapse of a mall roof in Elliott Lake, Ontario, in June 2012. The collapse resulted in two deaths and over twenty injuries. The mall had been beset by structural problems for about 15 years. Despite repeated complaints from patrons and mall personnel and warnings from experts, administrators continued to ignore the serious leaks, rusting beams, and falling tiles. In the absence of research into the group meetings of mall administrators, we cannot say definitively that groupthink occurred in this situation; however, it is highly likely that at least some mall administrators argued the need for repairs. Yet no actions were taken, suggesting that the group reached consensus on their lack of action.

Cloaked in anonymity, group members can hide behind the decisions of others. They may be more willing to fire someone, for example, if they do not have to attach their names as individuals to the decision. At the same time, they may be more willing to make unpopular but necessary decisions if they do not have to take individual responsibility for the decision. When some people indicate a willingness to take risks, others sometimes follow their lead.[112]

Although the above examples suggest the possibility for negative outcomes to be associated with groupthink, many experts believe that true (not pressured) consensus generates high-quality—as well as more creative—decisions.[113] As noted earlier in this chapter, the term *consensus* does not imply total agreement. It does not mean that the decision was the first choice of every group member or that no one expressed disagreement. Rather *consensus* implies that all participating members have reached the point in the discussion that they believe they can live with the group decision. This end point in collective agreement generally means that the group has listened to everyone and considered what all members had to say with attention and respect. As a result, at the implementation phase, members are more likely to support the decisions.[114]

The Japanese rely heavily on consensus in their decision-making processes. When faced with a problem in their day-to-day work, lower-level employees have the option of drafting and circulating a document known as a *ringisho*. The *ringisho* states the problem, suggests a solution, and outlines the reasons for accepting the solution. The originators of the document circulate the *ringisho* to all concerned parties, who review and stamp the document to indicate they have read and approved it. If anyone disapproves or requests changes, he returns the *ringisho* to the responsible employees. When decisions are major in nature, the employees may consult with others prior to writing the *ringisho* in order to minimize conflict and disagreement.

The top executive rarely disapproves the document—both because it has been heavily vetted, but also because the lower-level employees typically take management perspectives into account in writing the document. In criticism, some say that the *ringi* mode of decision making is too slow for today's environment; and some Japanese organizations have reduced the number of individuals who must review a document. Nonetheless, this consensual system fits well with the Japanese world view, which places a heavy emphasis on the collective as opposed to the individual. Even in meetings of managers, the normal mode of operation in Japan is to seek consensus.[115]

Step 5: Implementing the Decision

After the group has decided on the best solution, either the organization or responsible individuals have to implement the decision. A major factor governing whether someone follows through with implementation relates to the concept of **commitment**.[116] Commitment implies a sense of connection with a decision—the feeling that you had a role in arriving at that decision and that you have verbally or nonverbally pledged to bring the decision to life. Jay Hall defines commitment as a feeling of "attraction, belonging, and ownership . . . the unifying force which holds the group together."[117] In many regards, commitment equals motivation—in this case, motivation to stay involved in the group process from its beginnings to its implementation.

COMMITMENT
Acceptance of and motivation to support an idea or concept.

What helps to create commitment in group settings? Commitment comes from active participation in the group process, feeling that your comments are valued, and feeling that you had some input into the decision. When others start to dominate discussions, some participants lose this commitment and drop out of the group process. Participants with little or no commitment may say, "Yes, that's a good decision"; yet they may feel no obligation to do anything to implement the decision. They are saying, in essence, "It's your decision. So make it work."[118]

Commitment also comes when the organization shares the results of discussions and implements group recommendations.[119] When recommendations drop into a black hole, never to be seen again, people lose commitment and stop participating. Groups need to know that the organization values the hard work they put into arriving at their decision.

Step 6: Evaluating What Worked

Following the implementation of a decision, organizations need to understand what worked and what did not work. An idea can be good but not workable. A group of architects may design a beautiful building that is impossible to construct. Understanding why the design does not work will help the group create more realistic designs in the future. Organizations and individuals do not want to keep making

"The measure of success is not whether you have a tough problem to deal with, but whether it is the same problem you had last year."
JOHN FOSTER DULLES

the same mistake. If you are manufacturing a new type of bicycle, you do not want to continue production if the bicycles are falling apart; you want to figure out *why* the bicycles are falling apart. Enduring organizations learn from their failures. Evaluation of solutions enables this kind of learning.

TIPS FOR IMPROVING GROUP DECISION-MAKING

Ideas for improving group decision-making have appeared throughout this chapter. A summary of some of the most important points appears below.

Decide on a leader whose leadership style best suits the needs of the group. If the group is under a very tight deadline, you may want to choose an authoritarian leader. If your task is to come up with creative solutions that will benefit everyone, a more democratic leader will be a better option. In business situations, a transformational leader—someone with a vision who can mentor others and move the group forward—is often the best choice.

If you are acting in a leadership role, focus on achieving task results as well as meeting the needs of the group members. The leader's job is to keep everyone productive and on task. As a result, leadership duties often include motivating people and maintaining a positive group climate, as well as performing functional duties such as assigning tasks and coordinating meetings.

Be open to the ideas of others. Encourage everyone to express his or her views and show respect for all group members, even when you disagree.

Come prepared. Do background research before coming to a group meeting so that you have a solid understanding of the facts concerning the problem the group is trying to solve.

Use both creative and rational problem-solving techniques to generate solutions. Creative problem-solving techniques are useful because they can lead to innovative ideas. Rational problem-solving techniques are useful because they tend to produce reliable solutions based on specialized knowledge, research, and data.

In arriving at the best solution, aim for consensus rather than unanimity. While complete agreement may be out of reach, the process of reaching true consensus can generate high-quality decisions.

Help to implement the group decision. Show your commitment to the project by actively working to make the decision a reality. If you are a leader, encourage group members to take ownership of the decision to keep them motivated.

Identify and learn from your successes and failures. Even if the chosen action did not solve the problem, understanding why the action failed can help you to make better decisions in the future.

SUMMARY

This chapter has examined the topic of group decision-making and dynamics, especially in the context of organizations. First, we looked at different approaches to understanding leadership exercised in group settings. Then we looked at the six stages of problem solving. The first stage involves defining and analyzing the problem. In exploring this topic, we saw how both causes and effects come into play when analyzing problems. Establishing criteria for solutions constituted the second stage in the problem-solving sequence, laying the groundwork for the third stage: identifying possible solutions. The search for possible solutions can involve creative problem-solving (brainstorming, brainwriting, nominal group technique, brainsketching, mind mapping, synectics, fantasy chaining, and crowdsourcing) and/or rational problem-solving techniques (Delphi panels, quality circles, and focus groups). The fourth stage in the problem-solving sequence involves choosing a best solution. This stage can be highly contentious, and some groups fall prey to groupthink in their efforts to avoid conflict. The fifth stage in problem solving involves implementing the selected decision. Successful implementation depends on commitment, and commitment depends on members' feeling as if they have played a role in arriving at the decision. The sixth stage in problem solving entails evaluating the extent to which the group achieved their objectives. Finally, we looked at tips for improving group interactions.

REVIEW QUESTIONS

1. Why do many North Americans fear the power of group decisions? Can you think of any situations (other than those mentioned in this chapter) in which group decisions could prove dangerous or even deadly?
2. In what ways can new communications technologies facilitate group interaction? Are there any drawbacks to using these technologies in organizational group contexts?
3. What are the different approaches to studying leadership, as outlined in this chapter? Which approach(es) do you find most helpful?
4. How can group leaders contribute to a good socio-emotional climate within the group as a whole?
5. Why are creative problem-solving techniques useful in identifying possible solutions? What are the benefits of using rational problem-solving techniques?
6. What is the purpose of a focus group? What kinds of factors should you take into account when choosing participants for a focus group? What is the role of the moderator in a focus group?
7. What are the six steps in problem solving? At which stage is conflict most likely to arise? Why? Why is the criteria-setting step important in arriving at a good solution?

SUGGESTED ACTIVITIES

1. Attend a meeting of your local student federation, a club, or some other organization. Observe how group members interact with one another to solve problems and make decisions. After the meeting, record your thoughts in response to the following questions. What role did each member of the group play? Did any members threaten to derail the meeting? Did any members go out of their way to promote group cohesion? Did the group have a leader? If so, was she or he appointed, elected, or emergent? In what ways did the leader facilitate group discussion? Did conflict play a role in the meeting? If so, did the conflict enable the group to arrive at creative solutions? Did groupthink prevail at any point? Did group members arrive at consensus in the end?
2. Form a group with three or more members of your class. Imagine that you and your classmates are members of an engineering design team at General Motors (GM). You want to design a car with some new features that will allow GM to increase its market share. Engage in a brain-sketching exercise to arrive at creative solutions to this problem. When you have finished, share your group's results with the rest of your class.
3. Form a group with three or more members of your class. Use fantasy chaining techniques to brainstorm solutions to the following problem. Your school has insufficient parking to meet the needs of staff, students, and visitors. The campus does not have room for expansion, but it wants to improve the situation for drivers.
4. Form a group with four other members of your class. Pretend you are members of a quality circle at your workplace. You are faced with the following problem. You have not been producing enough bottle caps. You need to figure out the reason for the slowdown in production with your group. Arrive at some solutions that you can recommend to management.

APPENDIX

Making a Team Presentation[1]

Imagine the following scenario. The course instructor has assigned a group presentation on environmental problems to Fiona, Han, Sosê, and Réjean. The four students meet to discuss their strategy for the presentation. Fiona volunteers to deliver a talk on disappearing wildlife. Han offers to research and present a discussion on toxic dumps. Sosê offers to put together a presentation on sick building syndrome. Réjean says that he will discuss the problem of plastics being dumped into the ocean. Having allocated tasks successfully, the four leave the meeting with a sense of confidence that they have achieved a credible plan.

The day arrives for the group presentation. Each member rises and makes a 15-minute PowerPoint presentation. The quality varies from one presentation to the next, depending upon the skills of the presenter. At the end of the four lectures, the members sit down, satisfied they have fulfilled the requirements of the assignment. Certainly, they have achieved the most basic goal of delivering an oral presentation. But did they achieve the teaching and learning objectives for the assignment? Did they choose the right strategies to reach their audience? Did they use their time wisely? Did the audience learn anything from the presentation? Would classmates be able to answer content-based questions at the end of the presentation if requested?

The response to these questions is "no" when novice presenters fail to develop presentations that reflect broadly accepted design, learning, teaching, and oral presentation strategies. Too often they rely on the most common teaching technique, the lecture; and they equate hearing with remembering and learning. The transmission of information is one-way, offering little opportunity for feedback. This scenario repeats itself again and again in classrooms around the country, in a range of subjects from business to engineering to health care to policing.

As the numbers of students in classrooms increase, time demands rarely permit individual presentations; and so instructors call on their students more and more frequently to give small-group presentations. In a similar way, most large organizations stress project work; and presentations become a team effort. Team presentations create new challenges, different from the requirements for individual presentations or speeches. At the same time, group presentations offer new teaching and learning opportunities for students. The classroom becomes an exciting forum for learning when students exercise creativity and strategy in their oral presentations, engaging their audiences through active learning techniques.

This appendix introduces the basic principles of how to design and deliver an effective team presentation. More specifically, we look at steps in planning the presentation; ideas for making the presentation as effective as possible; suggestions for activities; best practices for managing group dynamics; and effective delivery techniques. This discussion will focus on team—as opposed to individual—elements in preparing the presentation.

When discussing the management of group dynamics, we will refer to speakers or presenters as *facilitators* in order to de-emphasize the lecture component. A facilitator frames and guides the process of learning; the role is dynamic, interactive, and two-way.

ESTABLISHING A THEME AND OBJECTIVES

You know the topic on which you will be presenting. Now your team members must work together to prepare the presentation. The first steps involve deciding upon a theme for the presentation and identifying teaching and learning objectives.

Choosing a Theme

First, the group meets to decide upon a theme for the presentation. A presentation on communication planning could focus, for example, on the relationship among different kinds of planning—strategic, operational, and work planning—to show how everything fits together. When designing a presentation on cultural differences in communication, you could have a theme such as "different but equal." Your theme for a talk about email communication could be "email etiquette." Deciding on a title for your presentation can help you identify your theme.

Themes are important because they help you stay focussed. If ideas are too scattered, your presentation will seem confused and disorganized. So choosing a theme, early in your planning, prevents a disoriented approach to the subject matter.

Setting Teaching and Learning Objectives

The next step in the process is establishing teaching and learning objectives or goals.[2] These objectives define what a group wants to achieve in the presentation. For example, in a presentation on risk management in businesses, group members might decide upon the following *teaching objective*: "to convey the importance of risk management in the current business environment and to identify strategies for dealing with high-risk situations." Teaching goals are written from the perspective of the presenters, who are *teaching* the audience about their chosen theme.

The team should also write *learning objectives*, which they frame from the perspective of the audience. Learning objectives tell audience members what they will get from the presentation in the way of information and/or skills. In framing learning objectives for a presentation on risk management in businesses, you could write that (at the end of the group presentation) the audience should be able to

- discuss at least three reasons that organizations should identify risk-management strategies,
- identify four major threats to small businesses that would justify these strategies,
- reflect in writing upon several contemporary theories of risk management,
- pinpoint six common elements that appear in the strategies of corporations noted for successful risk-management practices, and
- generate at least two statements that could appear in a risk-management plan and explain how these statements reflect current theories and best practices.

In addition to being audience-centred, the learning objectives should be specific, unambiguous, measurable, positive, and realistic.[3] If you wanted to add a behavioural learning objective, you could write the following: "You should be able to demonstrate familiarity with several theories of risk management in a role-play exercise." Ways to test for understanding should be immediately obvious and clear. In this example, the presenting team members could test for knowledge by giving a quiz that covers key points from the presentation. Or they could test for ability to apply the theories by asking the audience to write a short risk-management plan.

Consider a second example. The *teaching goal* for a presentation on assertiveness training could be "to provide skills in assertiveness." The *learning objectives*, written with the needs of the audience in mind, could be the following:

At the end of the session, audience members should be able to

- analyze their own communication styles to identify assertive and nonassertive behaviours,
- diagnose situations that call for more assertive behaviours,
- identify the techniques for communicating assertively, and
- apply assertiveness techniques in interactions with aggressive personalities.

As you can see, the learning objectives for assertiveness training are audience-centred. They are specific and clear in wording. They are measurable in the sense that the presenters could test the ability of the audience to meet their goals. They are positive in wording, and they are realistic and achievable.

You should state the teaching and learning objectives in the beginning of your presentation and repeat them at the end. Doing so contributes to the reduction of anxiety (in presenters as well as audience members),[4] focusses audience attention on relevant concepts,[5] and increases learning.[6] If you put the teaching and learning objectives on PowerPoint slides, they will be clear to the audience.

TAKING AUDIENCE MAKEUP INTO ACCOUNT

A consideration of the audience should be the starting point for designing any presentation. Presenters need to be sensitive to differences related to such factors as age; occupation; gender; personality; levels of knowledge; cultural background; and beliefs, attitudes, and values.

Student presenters cannot assume that all members of their audience will be young adults with little to no career experience. With the trend toward lifetime learning, more seniors are returning to the classroom. In addition, the focus on "just-in-time" learning sends many professionals back to school to retool and learn new skills. These older adults and professionals have more experiences and different kinds of experiences from their younger cohorts. Moreover, they may have organized the experiences differently.[7] Seasoned adults almost always prefer an interactive classroom that allows them to share their life and work experiences and to learn from one another. They want to know how they can apply what they learn inside the classroom to their lives outside the classroom.

Gender and personality also influence learning preferences. Women in general prefer a wider variety of activities than do men, and they have stronger needs for collaborative sharing of ideas. Men in general (especially younger men) prefer a more analytical and active experimenter style of learning. That is, they prefer a learning style that involves watching and doing. But . . . it's not that simple. More apprehensive women also like the analytical and active experimenter style of learning; less apprehensive women prefer innovative approaches to learning.[8] Less flexible personalities favour a more direct and formal teaching style (e.g., lectures), and more optimistic personalities appreciate a wider variety of learning activities.[9] In short, people have many different preferences as to how they want to learn, which creates the need for flexible and varied approaches to classroom presentations.

In terms of levels of knowledge, different audience members may be more familiar with some topics than others. Older individuals may know more about the activism of Jane Fonda, but younger individuals may know more about the charitable work of Lady Gaga. Women may know more about current styles in women's clothing, but men may connect more with references to contact sports such as wrestling or boxing. Even so, we need to take care not to stereotype audiences. Wrestling has a number of female fans, and many top fashion stylists are men.

Beliefs, attitudes, and values also influence how audiences receive a presentation. To the extent that presenters can identify the beliefs, opinions, and values of the audience on any given topic, they will be in a better position to achieve their teaching goals. When people do not agree with positions presented by speakers, they tend to tune out or forget the information. Nonetheless, arriving at an accurate assessment of audience values is not so easy. Appearances can be deceiving. Someone who looks very conservative in the classroom—with a tidy haircut and neatly ironed clothes—may spend her evenings playing in a punk band. Most of us have multiple identities; and we make choices, depending upon our mood and circumstances, to wear one or the other on any given day. The best approach for group presenters is generally to adopt a "something-for-everyone" approach in the design of their presentation.

The meaning of symbols can change from one cultural context to the next. Upon planning a trip to his home country in the late 1960s, a young man from India confided in one of the authors of this text, "I am worried because I have cut my hair, and my father will be angry." What an interesting comment, she thought—that this man's father would be upset with him for cutting his hair. At that moment, across the country, young hippie males were engaged in daily confrontations with their parents because they *refused* to cut their hair! What is politically correct also changes as groups redefine themselves in cultural and political terms. In recent history, gay and lesbian individuals have added positive content to words such as *queer*, a highly charged and politically incorrect term in earlier years.

TAKING LEARNING PRINCIPLES INTO ACCOUNT

Learners retain approximately 10 per cent of what they read, 20 per cent of what they hear, 30 per cent of what they see, 50 per cent of what they see *and* hear, 70 per cent of what they say, and 90 per cent of what they say *and* do.[10] In classroom situations, a retention rate of 10 per cent is common,[11] probably because of heavy reliance on lectures as a way to transmit information. Further, learners tend to lose focus—and retain less information—when they have to sit through overly long lectures that do not meet their priorities. What do these findings imply for the design of group presentations?

First, oral presenters should actively engage their audiences in the learning process.[12] Lectures offer a fast, efficient way of transmitting large quantities of information, but the results in terms of learning are often questionable. Some say that, instead of trying to "cover" the content, instructors should aim to "uncover" the material by using a number of interactive demonstrations and problem-solving activities that engage learners.[13]

Second, presenters should be careful to avoid bombarding the audience with too much information at one time. Educators have learned that lectures should be broken into learning "chunks," no more than fifteen minutes in length.[14] In a one-hour presentation, groups should limit lecture components to five-minute chunks for maximum effectiveness. In a three-hour presentation, presenters should adhere to ten-minute "mini-lectures."

Third, presenters should do more than just lecture. People vary greatly in how they prefer to learn. Some prefer to learn new material by listening (auditory), by reading or viewing (visual), by touching (tactile), or by doing (kinesthetic).[15] Auditory learners might get the most out of hearing an audio recording of a speech or listening to music while they work. Visual learners might want to examine photographs, see graphical depictions of the material, or watch a film or television show. Those with a preference for the tactile might like to work on the computer, use their hands to construct a model, or take notes. The kinesthetic learner likes to practise the skill.

Finally, as suggested in the previous section, team members should design their presentations with the needs and priorities of their audience in mind. Professionals in training courses want to acquire information, learn how to apply it, and move to the next point.[16] They enjoy the stimulation of discussing ideas; but at the end of the day, they want to know how they can use the ideas. Since time is important to professionals, they will lose interest quickly if they think a presenter is wasting their time. Because they are less interested than younger learners in being entertained, older learners place less importance on liking the instructor.[17]

TAKING MULTIPLE INTELLIGENCES INTO ACCOUNT

In 1983, Howard Gardner, professor of education at Harvard University, developed a comprehensive theory of multiple intelligences that explains and amplifies many of the above ideas.[18] This popular theory advocates the existence of nine potential pathways to learning:

- linguistic intelligence (ability to understand, use, and appreciate words),
- logical-mathematical intelligence (ability to think in logical terms, to reason abstractly, and to see numerical patterns),
- visual-spatial intelligence (ability to think in images and pictures and to see visual and spatial patterns),
- bodily-kinesthetic intelligence (ability to exercise control over body movements and to handle objects with ease),
- musical intelligence (ability to produce and appreciate melody and rhythm),
- interpersonal intelligence (ability to interact easily with others, to understand their socio-emotional needs, and to respond in a way that furthers the relationship),

- intrapersonal intelligence (ability to connect with one's inner feelings, motivations, and values),
- naturalist intelligence (ability to appreciate and relate to the world of nature), and
- existentialist intelligence (ability to enjoy thinking about deep questions such as the meaning of life and human existence).

According to Gardner, all human beings possess all nine intelligences; however, people vary in the extent to which they possess any single intelligence. Therefore, one person may be very good at calculating the distance of stars from earth (logical-mathematical intelligence) but limited in the ability to play soccer (bodily-kinesthetic intelligence) or to feel comfortable in a social setting (interpersonal intelligence). Another person might win applause for being able to play the violin beautifully (musical intelligence) but have a difficult time creating images on paper (visual-spatial intelligence). A third person might have the ability to survive in an arctic environment under harsh winter conditions (naturalist ability) but be unable to express his feelings to himself or others (intrapersonal and linguistic intelligences).

When oral presentations by groups depend strictly on words, some audience members may be unable to relate to—or learn from—the presentation. The bodily-kinesthetic learner may grow restless and anxious to find a way to express herself in a more dynamic way. The visual-spatial learner may want to see pictures and photographs that illustrate the ideas being discussed. The interpersonal learner may become bored with presentations that do not allow interaction with others. In order to satisfy her need for interaction, she may write notes to the person sitting next to her. The musical learner may lose interest and quietly slip an earphone into one ear. The logical-mathematical learner may drift into his own dream state, wondering how to convert the ideas to a chart with statistics. The naturalist learner may pay more attention to the squirrels on the lawn outside the room than to the speakers. In such as a situation, the linguistic learner may be the only person whose needs are recognized and met.

APPLYING WHAT WE HAVE LEARNED

The following discussion will examine how we can apply our knowledge of audiences, learning principles, and activities based on multiple intelligences to an agenda for the team presentation. In determining the agenda, the presenting group needs to arrive at an appropriate mix of lecture and other activities. The activities should recognize different needs of the audience (e.g., whether they like to work alone or in groups). They should also engage audience members in active and experiential learning based on principles of learning and the nine intelligences.[19]

Adapting to Your Audience

Learners vary in whether they like to work alone, in dyads (two people), or in small groups.[20] Some people prefer to learn from their peers, while others like to draw their knowledge from authority figures. Introverts (people who enjoy alone time) and extroverts (people who enjoy time with others) also differ in preferences.[21] Introverted learners like activities such as questionnaires, handouts, work sheets, gallery exercises, and computer exercises that they can do at home or in a quiet setting. Extroverted learners like activities that bring them into contact with other people. Examples include icebreakers, brainstorming, games and simulations, read-arounds, role plays, and discussions. Extroverts are not shy about expressing their points of view, and these activities enable a dynamic exchange with other people.

If you are presenting to an audience with strong similarities, you may have some idea of which learning styles would appeal to the group. For example, computer analysts probably like activities that employ logic and reasoning. Musicians probably enjoy activities with aural content more than logical exercises. A video-recorded interview with a top researcher would appeal to visual learners and those who like to get their information from experts. With a diverse audience, however, the best approach may be "something-for-everyone."[22]

Appealing to the Nine Intelligences

The "something-for-everyone" approach also makes sense when we apply the theory of multiple intelligences to classroom contexts. The diversity in student populations creates the need for flexibility. Presentations with the broadest appeal generally include auditory (lecture, discussion, music, read-arounds, storytelling), visual (handouts, overheads, gallery exercises, maps, timelines), tactile (worksheets, card sorting, artwork), and kinesthetic (movement, role plays, icebreakers).[23]

As you plan your activities, ask yourself whether you have achieved a balance in your planned activities? If the activities place too much emphasis on language, restructure them to get more variety. For example, if you plan to make a presentation on television reality shows, consider using the following mix of activities:

- lecturing on the popularity of current reality shows (appeal to linguistic intelligence);
- asking the audience to guess the ratings for five of the top shows (appeal to logical-mathematical intelligence);
- presenting a graph showing the increasing popularity of reality shows over time (appeal to visual-spatial intelligence);
- showing a video clip from an episode of *The Amazing Race* (appeal to naturalist, bodily-kinesthetic, and visual-spatial intelligences);
- asking the audience to reflect on whether they would consider trying out for a show such as *The Bachelor* or *The Bachelorette*, where they would have little privacy (appeal to intrapersonal intelligence);
- asking the audience to think about what the popularity of reality shows reveals about modern society and what it might mean for the future of our society (appeal to existentialist intelligence);
- requesting that members of the audience act out a boardroom scene from *Celebrity Apprentice*, involving high levels of conflict with other people (appeal to interpersonal intelligence); and
- asking the audience to create a plot line for a new reality show (linguistic intelligence), to design a logo for the new show (visual-spatial intelligence), and to choose the music for the show (musical intelligence).

PLANNING ACTIVITIES FOR THE AGENDA

In preparing a presentation, group members must establish the order of lecture components and other activities. They should also set limits on the time to be spent on any single part of the presentation. In a one-hour presentation, facilitators should adhere to five-to-ten minute lecture segments in order to allow time for a variety of other activities. A sample agenda for a one-hour presentation on Aboriginal sentencing circles might look something like the following. Note that each item on the agenda relates to a different kind of learner.

10:00 to 10:05	Welcome, with Aboriginal music in background (musical)
10:05 to 10:10	Icebreaker with physical element (kinesthetic)
10:10 to 10:20	Lecture on Aboriginal sentencing circles—history and applications (linguistic)
10:20 to 10:30	Sketch of a medicine wheel to show relationship to restorative justice (visual)
10:30 to 10:50	Simulation of sentencing circle (interpersonal)
10:50 to 11:00	Debriefing and analysis of what happened (logical)

The following section describes some popular activities that can help facilitators break up their presentation. Although most often used in adult training situations, these activities appeal to students of all ages. The following activities are explored: icebreakers, energizers, guided fantasies, storytelling, gallery exercises, read-arounds, timelines, card sorting, case studies and scenarios, fishbowl exercises, role plays, creating artwork, and using slides and video clips.

Icebreakers

The first item on any presentation agenda should be an icebreaker, an activity designed to make people comfortable with one another and with the facilitators. The icebreaker may be tied directly to the theme of the presentation, or it may be unlinked. In either case, the purpose of the activity is to "break the ice" and establish a strong group dynamic.

Examples of icebreakers abound. One icebreaker asks members of the audience to remove their shoes and to place one shoe on the floor in the middle of the room. Then everyone takes a shoe from the pile and attempts to locate its owner. After identifying the owner, the person collects enough information to introduce the other person to the larger group. Another icebreaker involves asking people to pull pieces of toilet paper from a roll passed around the group. They are not told how much paper to pull. Afterwards they must answer as many questions about themselves as the numbers of sections of paper that they hold. A third icebreaker requires individuals to describe a favourite childhood game.

Some icebreakers have a largely physical component. For example, the game "human knot" requires group members to hold hands while trying to disentangle themselves. The floor game Twister requires that participants assume difficult body positions that bring them into close physical contact with others. This kind of physical contact allows group members to become familiar with one another.

One caution is in order. People from more reserved or traditional cultures, which place strict limits on male–female interactions, may resist participating in high-contact icebreakers. Older individuals may also feel uncomfortable participating in some of the more physical exercises. People who feel sensitive about their weight may be uncomfortable with an icebreaker that requires them to sit on a balloon and then answer the question that is inside the balloon. Before selecting an icebreaker, group presenters should assess the appropriateness of the activity and the probable level of acceptance by participants.

Depending on their nature, icebreakers hold appeal for many different kinds of learners. The more physical icebreakers appeal to bodily-kinesthetic learners and those who enjoy tactile experiences. Icebreakers that require listing of personal qualities appeal to learners with intrapersonal and linguistic intelligences. People with interpersonal intelligence enjoy icebreakers that require interacting with other people; and people with musical intelligence respond to icebreakers that require singing, dancing, or chanting.

Energizers

During a presentation of three or more hours, facilitators should make use of energizers. Energizers engage a group in some kind of physical activity that allows a break from a demanding mental task. A popular energizer is shoot the rabbit. To play this game, audience members divide into small groups. Each person then decides upon which of three objects she will represent: a wall, a rabbit, or an arrow. On cue, each person takes a position to represent the chosen object. The following criteria determine the winner:

- An arrow beats a rabbit, since it can kill a rabbit.
- A wall beats an arrow, since it can stop an arrow.
- A rabbit beats a wall, since it can jump over a wall.

If a tie occurs—that is, if two or more people choose the same object—the players repeat the game until there is a winner.

Other energizers require participants to move about the room, talk to other people, sing, or dance. Songs accompanied by actions, such as clapping or stomping, are especially dynamic. Applauding latecomers at the beginning of the session or after a break also activates a sleepy group and adds a touch of laughter to the setting. Some energizers require that people keep balls or balloons in the air, much as they would do in a volleyball game. To make the exercise more difficult, facilitators can ask participants to sort the balloons into colour clusters as they work to keep them in the air.

Professional facilitators and trainers rely heavily on energizers in longer presentations. They understand that audiences lose focus if they do not have the opportunity to move about from time to time. Energizers have particular appeal to learners with bodily-kinesthetic intelligence, as well as those with interpersonal intelligence. Learners who enjoy tactile experiences also enjoy many types of energizers.

Guided Fantasies

Guided fantasies ask participants to relax, close their eyes, and visualize scenes and experiences. The facilitator talks the group through a visualization experience such as the following:

Imagine a day in your life as a medical doctor in 2040. You get up at your usual time—7:30 a.m. You take a cup of strong black coffee into your office to begin your work day—at home, of course. Your office is bright and cheerful. Large windows overlook a lake, and the sun arches higher in the morning sky as you look out over the glistening water. A few geese light in a nearby pond. You feel comfortable, sitting with a pair of slippers and light robe in a comfortable easy chair. A breeze wafts through the room and rustles a few papers on your large mahogany desk. Checking the calendar, you notice that the date is 15 January. But you don't feel the cold because you are in a "cocooned" office. Last night, before you went to bed, you programmed your office for mid-April. The computer program set the temperature, the images that you see outside the windows, and the general ambiance for a beautiful spring day. You can hear the flapping of the wings of the geese from time to time. To alert your staff to the fact that you are now on duty, you press a button, embedded in your wrist. Promptly, you receive a mental image of your schedule for the day, set to run until 5:30 p.m., with an hour for lunch. Before switching to an interactive screen, you program your internal computer for a business day. That means that you will not appear in a robe and slippers to your patients. You will appear in a light grey business suit with a red tie. No need for uniforms in this virtual world! Finally you switch to an interactive screen on your computer, which shows a hologram of your first patient. She sits at a table with her child. Her dress has a pleasant floral pattern. (She was able to discern the fact that your office was set for spring, and she "dressed" for the occasion as well.) You switch the audio to interactive mode. "Hello there. I see that (oops, need a name, another button to push) Jimmy is having some problems with his (ah, another button, virtual scan of body) throat. I'll order the prescription (push another button). Have a good day."

Guided fantasies need not be futuristic. You could, for example, conduct a guided fantasy that leads people through a desired response to an assault or a guided fantasy that asks people to imagine the life of someone who lived in the eighteenth century. Alternatively, you could lead a group through a visualization exercise that would help them to enter a meditative state. Learners with linguistic intelligence, as well as those with visual-spatial intelligence, enjoy guided fantasies. Depending on the nature of the visualization, other intelligences such as the naturalist may also come into play. Those who like auditory and imaginative experiences are receptive to guided fantasies.

Storytelling

The facilitator can use a story (real or imaginary) to generate reflection on a given topic. The following legend of the dream catcher, for example, could lead into a discussion of dreams, mythology, Aboriginal culture, or any one of a number of other topics:

A long time ago, the Ojibwa people lived in a place known as Turtle Island. To ensure that the babies of the tribe enjoyed peaceful sleep, Spider Woman wove little dream catchers on the tops of their cradle boards. Bad dreams stuck in the spider-like webs, while the good dreams slipped through the openings. Each morning, with the first rays of dawn, the bad dreams died. In later years, Spider Woman found it hard to make her way to all the cradle boards. So others in the tribe—the grandmothers, mothers, and sisters—began to help to weave the magical webs. They used hoops from willow trees, sinew from animals, and cords from plants to make the dream catchers. In honour of ancient traditions, they connected the web to the hoop at seven or eight points. The number seven represents the Seven Prophecies and the number eight represents Spider Woman's eight legs.[24]

Storytelling as a teaching strategy offers a way of reaching out to imaginative learners and to those with visual-spatial and linguistic intelligence. People who enjoy auditory experiences also like storytelling.

Gallery Exercises

Gallery exercises use pictures and video clips to stimulate thought and discussion on a topic relevant to the theme of the presentation. Assume, for example, that you want to sensitize managers to behaviours that could be interpreted as sexual harassment. You could include in your presentation a series of PowerPoint slides that depict inappropriate behaviours. One slide could show a manager with a hand on the shoulder of a female subordinate. Another slide could show a manager who has invaded the personal space of an employee by leaning over his shoulder as he sits at his desk. A short video clip could depict employee reaction to an off-colour joke told by an employer or an invitation to go for drinks at a local bar. Gallery exercises appeal, in particular, to learners with visual-spatial intelligence.

Read-Arounds

Read-arounds are similar to tryouts in theatre. Participants take turns reading aloud from material provided by the group facilitators. This material could come from a poem, a play, a story, a report, a book, or some other source. Imagine that you are making a presentation on superstitious behaviours. In turn, each person from the group might read one point from a study on the most common superstitions in North America. Read-arounds appeal to the auditory learner and to the learner with linguistic intelligence.

Timelines

Timeline activities call upon participants to develop a calendar of events. If you were making a presentation on crisis communication planning, for example, you might ask participants to construct a timeline of when things could go wrong in a given situation. Afterwards you could compare and discuss their examples. Timeline activities appeal to learners with logical-mathematical intelligence.

Card Sorting

With card-sorting activities, facilitators ask volunteers to sort and order cards in terms of priorities, time sequence, or some other organizational scheme. The cards may pertain to duties that have to be performed, the different parts of some task, or the distinguishing features of some situation. If you were making a presentation on change management, the card-sorting exercise could involve establishing the order for undertaking various change management activities. The facilitators use this information as a takeoff point for discussion. Card-sorting appeals to tactile learners, as well as logical-mathematical and linguistic learners.

Case Studies and Scenarios

Case studies describe some incident that has occurred in the past. If you are making a presentation on airport security, for example, you could present (either orally or in writing) a case study that points to inadequacies in the system. Then you could ask participants to divide into small groups to review the case and to arrive at solutions to the problems. Afterwards you could facilitate a discussion of the findings. Organizations often develop case studies of best practices and worst practices, from which their members can draw lessons.

Whereas case studies concern the past, scenarios offer a glimpse into a possible future. Typically, scenarios depict a situation that could occur at some future date such as a natural disaster or a terrorist event. They ask participants to answer the question "What if?" What if an earthquake struck British Columbia? What if terrorists attacked the Montreal subway system? What if insufficient rain caused power shortages in Manitoba, an ice storm wreaked havoc in Quebec City, or a computer virus shut down air traffic control at the Lester B. Pearson International Airport in Toronto?

Both case studies and scenarios are attractive learning tools for people with logical-mathematical, linguistic, and interpersonal intelligences. If you include visuals (maps and photographs) with the exercises, you can also appeal to those with visual-spatial intelligence. Tactile learners like handling objects, papers, and other tangible items. Case studies and scenarios consume too much time for short presentations; however, a three-hour presentation may be able to employ limited versions of such narratives.

Fishbowl Exercises

A fishbowl is a structured discussion that allows participants to rotate between speaking and listening roles. A few participants (the fish) take seats in the middle of the larger group. They discuss their views on some assigned topic, while the others listen quietly. Whenever observers are ready to join the fishbowl discussion, they signal their interest by standing at their seats. Once a speaker has finished her turn making a statement and interacting with other members of the fishbowl, she surrenders her seat to a standing member of the listening audience. So the rotational process continues as various members join and leave the fishbowl discussion. Speaking is restricted to the four or five people in the fishbowl at any given time.

Facilitators prepare the group for the exercise by defining any relevant terms, identifying key concepts, and asking for questions about how to undertake the exercise. They might also distribute handouts or discussion guidelines. Handouts with terms, background information, and questions are helpful in stimulating an organized discussion. During the fishbowl discussions, the facilitators take notes. When the activity is over, they lead all participants in a group discussion. The facilitators prepare comments in advance on possible learning points for this discussion.

Sometimes facilitators divide groups along gender, occupational, ideological, or other lines in order to allow for the expression of minority or less popular views. The females in the group, for example, could be asked to conduct a fishbowl discussion on a topic such as division of responsibilities in the home. In that situation, the males are asked to listen without interrupting. Once the females have finished their discussion, the males replace them to present their views on the topic. Then the females listen, without responding, to the perspectives of the males.

With a topic such as discrimination in workplace environments, the facilitator may choose to create multiple groups. One group could represent the interests of women; another might reflect the interests of a linguistic minority; still another might represent the views of ethnic or cultural minorities. One by one, the members of the various groups take their places in the fishbowl and express their points of view on the topic of discrimination in the workplace.

Fishbowl activities hold strong appeal for learners with linguistic, bodily-kinesthetic, and interpersonal intelligences. The activity is also compatible with a preference for auditory learning. Because the activity requires thoughtful consideration, learners with logical-mathematical and intrapersonal intelligences would respond favourably, as well. Because fishbowl activities usually take about 15 minutes to complete, they are most appropriate in presentations that last several hours.

Role Plays

Role plays allow us to display and observe human interactions such as doctor–patient, male–female, and manager–employee. In a presentation on management theories, facilitators could ask participants to assume the role of employees in an organization with a scientific management philosophy or a human relations philosophy. In a presentation on intercultural variables in negotiation, facilitators could ask participants to assume the roles of business executives from two different cultures who are trying to negotiate an agreement. With some role plays, facilitators ask participants to model an effective behaviour, such as assertiveness, or to demonstrate an ineffective response such as aggressiveness or passivity. Role plays are attractive to learners with linguistic, bodily-kinesthetic, and interpersonal intelligences.

Artwork

Facilitators might give finger paints or other art supplies to members of the audience and ask them to create individual or group artworks that illustrate their perceptions of some topic, group, philosophy, or institution. Afterwards they lead the group in a discussion of the meanings and feelings behind the works of art. Tactile learners and those with visual-spatial, bodily-kinesthetic, and interpersonal intelligences enjoy this activity.

Slides and Video Clips

Most groups like presentations that include the use of slides and video clips. When using video clips in presentations, facilitators must limit the time given to the clips. No group should use more than one five-minute video clip or three two-minute clips in a one-hour presentation. Three-hour presentations can include more video clips; however, the clips should remain brief.

MANAGING GROUP DYNAMICS

An understanding of group dynamics improves the chances of an effective team presentation. The following discussion considers how groups can establish ground rules for interaction, use online technologies to share information, and take abilities and personality into account when assigning tasks and roles.

Establishing Ground Rules

Early in the project, the group needs to establish ground rules. Ground rules for meetings typically require that members arrive on time, come prepared, make constructive suggestions, treat team members with respect, and inform others if they cannot attend a meeting. More general ground rules could involve each member agreeing to do a fair share of the work, to use only reliable sources in researching the topic, and to complete tasks on time. Ground rules can also set out procedures for dealing with conflict. Some groups write a contract, in which they agree to assume certain responsibilities and to meet deadlines. They may even take a group picture to accompany the signed contract, as a sign of their commitment to the team.

Using Online Technologies to Share Information

To facilitate group sharing, students can connect and share materials online. Web-based software systems such as WebCT and Blackboard Learn allow students to upload and share files and create group presentations. Once an instructor has set up and granted students access to the system, group members can log in from their personal computers and interact at their convenience. All group members are able to access folders that contain the work of their group, but they cannot access the work of other groups. Groups can also use discussion forums to exchange ideas, either in real time or with a delay between posts. The major benefit of these systems is that they allow students to review comments as time allows. This means that group members are not bound by the time schedules of the other members.

Taking Abilities into Account in Assigning Tasks

When volunteering for tasks, group members should take the roles for which they are best suited. Every group needs a leader, who can take responsibility for guiding the group, assigning tasks where necessary, and ensuring that the group meets its deadlines. Other tasks include researching, writing and editing, interviewing, preparing PowerPoint slides and other visuals, assuming administrative and technical responsibilities, and facilitating the different parts of the presentation. Usually all group members share in the research phase of the project, but not all research the same parts of the topic. A person with good writing and editing skills should assume the role of editor for the entire project so that the final product has stylistic integrity. Another group member who is good at interacting with people could take charge of tasks such as interviewing or making telephone calls. Someone with artistic skills could prepare illustrations or take photos for the presentation, and an individual with technological skills could prepare the PowerPoint slides and video clips. Someone should be in charge of equipment necessary for the presentation. This person should also ensure that the group has a backup copy of all digital material on a flash drive. The person with the best organizational skills could take care of miscellaneous tasks such as purchasing the supplies required for the presentation, making name tags, and providing refreshments. Someone with musical interests could locate appropriate music to accompany the presentation or to play during break periods in long presentations.

Taking Personality into Account in Assigning Group Roles

In the fundamental interpersonal relations orientation (FIRO) model referenced in Chapter 8, William Schutz argues that the need for inclusion, control, and affection characterizes every group. In an effort to satisfy these needs, members assume different roles, which reflect their basic personality types.[25] Schutz identifies three personality types: autocrats, democrats, and abdicrats.

People who fit the personality profile of the *democrat* feel most comfortable in a sharing role, which encourages equal levels of contribution by all group members. No one individual dominates or submits to domination all the time. Rather each group member gets to enjoy being more influential some of the time, while allowing other group members to be more influential at other times. The *autocrat*, on the other hand, has a strong need for control; and he may work extra hard to take over and dominate groups. Despite wanting to control others, an *abdicrat* is reluctant to dominate. She may withdraw and let others take charge, behaving submissively in groups.

These basic personality tendencies influence the way that people behave in group settings. During group interactions and discussions, group members act out one or more of the following roles: task roles, relationship-building and maintenance roles, or self-centred and dysfunctional roles.[26] In connecting personality types with group roles, we can imagine that a democratic person is more likely to take a relationship-building and maintenance role, and an autocratic person is more likely to take a task role. Nonetheless, awareness of personality characteristics can help people to behave in functional rather than dysfunctional ways as they interact in group situations.

When members assume *task-oriented roles*, they act as initiators, information givers, information seekers, opinion givers, opinion seekers, elaborators, integrators, orienters, and/or energizers. *Initiators* propose new ideas, directions, and solutions. *Information givers* support their opinions with evidence, whereas *opinion givers* contribute only their personal views on a topic. *Information seekers* look for information and explanations, and *opinion seekers* ask others to provide and explain their ideas. By offering examples, stories, and explanations, *elaborators* clarify and build on ideas presented by others. *Integrators* act as synthesizers of ideas contributed by others. *Orienters* keep groups focussed on goals by summarizing and clarifying group contributions at different stages in the process. *Energizers* encourage members to participate more fully in the group process.

Those acting in *maintenance roles* nurture the interpersonal relationships in groups and try to increase group cohesiveness. They act as encouragers, harmonizers, tension relievers, gatekeepers, and/or followers. The *encourager* compliments the contributions of others. The *harmonizer* mediates conflicts by proposing compromises to the group, and the *tension reliever* uses humour to achieve a more informal and relaxed atmosphere. The *gatekeeper* uses body language and eye contact to encourage balanced participation from group members. The *follower* goes along with whatever others decide.

Unlike men, women tend to adopt supportive and inclusive behaviours when interacting with members of the opposite sex.[27] As a result, women are more likely than men to fall into follower and encourager roles. As encouragers, women tend to respond to interruptions, overlapping comments, and delayed feedback with "stroking" behaviours such as nodding or saying *yes* or *mmm hmm*. Women are also more likely to use tag questions (e.g., "I like that idea, *don't you*?") to avoid open disagreements. As discussed in Chapter 6, these kinds of questions convey uncertainty; however, they also serve a relational or maintenance function. They show respect for the other person through avoidance of blunt language. Women also use procedural suggestions—for example, "May I suggest . . . ," "I would like to propose that perhaps . . . ," or "Maybe we should . . ."—for similar purposes,

Dysfunctional roles prevent the achievement of group goals and threaten interpersonal relationships. Members who assume the roles of blockers, aggressors, dominators, recognition seekers, "anecdoters," distracters, confessors, and special-interest pleaders can derail a discussion or cause friction and disruption. The *blocker* complains and offers negative feedback when others try to move the discussion forward. The *aggressor* insults, criticizes, and points to the mistakes of group members. *Dominators* monopolize proceedings by interrupting or flattering others, whereas *recognition seekers* focus group attention on their own achievements. The *anecdoter* takes the group on side trips with irrelevant stories (often about personal experiences); and the *distracter* uses antics, jokes, and irrelevant comments to divert the group from task-oriented goals. The *confessor* talks about personal problems, revealing fears and perceived inadequacies. The *special-interest pleader* seeks favours for someone who is not present.

If a group has at least some members operating in maintenance roles, it will have an easier time negotiating conflict situations. Early in the life of the group, members may want to consciously adopt certain maintenance roles. Not only in group meetings, but also on the day of presentation, the group will need to function as a team.

To understand how these group roles operate in practice, consider the following fictitious transcript of a group meeting involving university students. In this dialogue, the students are discussing what to do about the problem of rising tuition fees. They cannot decide whether to collect a petition, stage a protest on Parliament Hill, or organize a walkout at the university. As you read through the transcript, try to identify some of the functional (task-oriented and maintenance) and dysfunctional roles taken by participants in this group meeting.

Ella: Okay, I think we should get started. We need to decide what to do if the government votes to raise our tuition. We all know the problem, right? And we've spent several meetings talking about how we can't afford to stay in school if tuition keeps rising. So today we should talk about our options. I see you've got an idea, Jamal. What do you think?

Jamal: I think we need to stay cool about this. The students in Quebec lost a lot of time when they went on strike, and they didn't end up with much. I can't afford to lose that kind of time.

Nada: Yeah, I agree. My parents said they won't keep helping me if I don't stay in school. And I'm so stressed at the moment. I just got dumped by my boyfriend, and I can't deal with anything else.

Erica: I know what you mean. I just lost my job. And my dog died.

Morgan: Sorry, Erica. That's heavy.

Emilie: Wow, you've had a lot of problems. It must be hard on you. I've already missed a lot of classes. I don't know if I can afford to miss more.

Solan: My friend emailed me some jokes the other day about students who miss school. I had to laugh. One bro said he missed class because he thought he would be sick, but he wasn't after all!

Harper: I think we need to stay on track. We've all had a lot of issues. But what should we do about the problem? I saw a CBC report. It said tuition rose almost 300 per cent in Alberta between 1990 and 2007. Where's it all going?

Morgan: That's ugly. Yeah, let's focus. What do you think, Erica? Should we organize a walkout?

Jamal: I think we should go to the media first—see what we can get in the way of public support. It's going to hurt a lot of students if we walk out.

Harper: I think we need to pull together on whatever we decide. We should air our views; then we need to find a way to get everyone to co-operate.

William: I'm ready to walk out. I say we vote now and not waste any more time talking.

Sasha: I organized a protest one time when I was in high school. The cafeteria food sucked, and nobody was doing anything about it. So everybody got together at my place, and we made signs and marched outside the lunch room.

Morgan: Rad.

Sasha: Everybody was really happy with me. You know, because I was the one who led the protest.

William: Yeah, Sasha! We all know how great you are.

Sasha: There's no need to chirp at me.

Ella: Hey, I agree with Harper. We need to work together. If we have differences, let's talk about them and stop attacking each other. Nada, you look as if you'd like to say something. What—

William: I'm not attacking. I'm just laying it out there for you. I think we should stop talking and start acting.

Nada: I know Jacob wanted to come to the meeting today, but he wasn't able. So I'd like to present his ideas. He said that he's in favour of a petition and a protest on Parliament Hill. After all, it's the federal government that's cut subsidies to the provinces.

Jamal: That's right. They have. Good point, Nada.

Nada: It was really Jacob's idea. I've been so upset by being dumped that I can't think straight any more.

Solan: Well, you know what they say. Better to lose a lover than love a loser.

Erica: Hah.

Emilie: Tell me about it. My ex started dating my best friend after I left for university. Well, he wasn't my "ex" then; you know what I mean.

Solan: Yeah, that reminds me of a joke I heard last week.

William: Give it a rest, Solan.

Morgan: I heard a funny one too. What do you call a porcupine with a carrot in each ear?

Solan: Anything you want 'cause he can't hear you anyway!

Ella: I'd like to summarize what we've covered so far.

William: Well, we've covered the death of Erica's dog, the boyfriend problems of Nada and Emilie, and . . . .

Erica: Cut it out, William. I heard you got dumped by your girlfriend last week. Yeah, I know about that. No need to act so superior.

Ella: There seems to be some disagreement on what we should do. I'd like to check out how many of you are supporting each position. I'll start with you, Shania. What is your position?
Shania: I'm good with whatever the rest of you think. Tell me what you want me to do.
Ella: Are you sure you don't have a position? I'd like to hear from everyone.
Harper: Yes, it's important that we all feel good about our decision.
Shania: No. I mean it. I'm good with whatever you guys decide.
Jamal: I'd like to add to what Harper said earlier. Maybe we need to focus on facts. I've been doing some reading too. We know the tuition rates are rising more in some provinces than others. So maybe we should compare what's happening in Alberta with what's happening elsewhere. Our increases are much higher in Alberta than in some other provinces like PEI. Like I said earlier, I'm for moving in stages—not jumping immediately to a walkout.
William: You already know my opinion.
And the discussion continues. . . .

PRACTISING AND DELIVERING THE PRESENTATION

Every group needs to conduct a dry run prior to the day of presentation, preferably in the same physical setting. Those who are responsible for technical matters such as setting up the PowerPoint presentation or operating lights and sound will need to coordinate their efforts with the presenters. Video recording the practice presentations allows the opportunity for the group members to review their performance before the final presentation.

This section of the discussion will consider the requirements for setting up the room, making an impression through dress, sharing responsibilities for the presentation, interacting with other team members and the audience, reaching the entire audience, managing the feedback process, and distributing supplementary materials.

Setting Up the Room

Presenting group members should arrive early enough to adjust for unexpected problems—microphones or digital players that do not function, missing lecture podiums or computer cables, blocked access to a wireless network, or a room in disarray. Presenters may also want to adjust the temperature settings of the room, if temperature controls are accessible. In addition, groups offering refreshments will want to set out their offerings before the audience arrives. Although not usually required, refreshments such as home-baked muffins or freshly brewed coffee help to make audiences feel more comfortable. Some presenters choose refreshments that fit with their presentation (e.g., fresh fruit for a presentation about tourism in the Caribbean or a vegetable tray and bottled water for a presentation on yoga).

Arriving early will also give you a chance to assess and adjust the seating arrangement (unless the chairs are bolted in place). Ideally, the arrangement of seating should be appropriate for the presentation to be delivered. You may want to position chairs or tables in a U-shaped or more friendly arrangement that encourages interaction. You may also want to position the chairs so they face away from potentially distracting elements such as windows, doors, or artwork.

Intimate spaces that allow for maximum eye contact and a sense of closeness work best for short presentations. If you are making a half-day or longer presentation to a group, however, you should try to arrange for a room with ample space for milling and talking, stretching, and moving about the room. As a facilitator, you need sufficient space to conduct icebreakers and energizers; and the group needs adequate space to perform activities. Sometimes instructors are able to relocate groups to settings that are more conducive to learning and conducting interactive exercises. If you do relocate to a different room, you need to announce the change and post signs to the new location for those who are not present for the announcement or who arrive late.

Making an Impression through Dress

The manner of dress will vary from one group presentation to the next. Team members often choose to dress in a more formal manner than they would normally dress. Sometimes they colour co-ordinate their dress in order to appear more professional, wearing the same colours of shirts, skirts, and/or slacks as their teammates. The most frequent choices are colours that the students already have in their closets, such as black and white. Occasionally, students choose to wear costumes that reflect the theme of their presentation. If they are speaking on the topic of dealing with difficult customers in a restaurant, they might dress like servers. If they are talking about cross-cultural communication in a tropical setting like Hawaii, they might wear floral shirts or dresses.

Sharing Responsibilities

Group members should plan in advance who will perform all necessary tasks on the day of the presentation. One person could greet audience members as they enter the room and distribute name tags (if appropriate), a copy of the agenda, and materials for group exercises. Another person could run background music to establish a mood. A third person could wander through the room encouraging audience members to sit near the front.

The presentation itself should be a co-operative effort, with tasks distributed evenly among team members. The mantra should be "different but equal." One of the better speakers should introduce the team and the topics to be covered by each presenter. The same person should summarize and conclude the discussion at the end.

Members who are comfortable with managing group interactions should facilitate various parts of the presentation, as well as question-and-answer sessions and follow-ups to exercises. Sometimes two group members co-facilitate a part of the presentation, with one fielding questions and the other recording comments on a flip chart or a white board. During small group activities, team members with good interpersonal skills can move around the room, checking on group progress and answering questions. Meanwhile, other team members can use the time to ready for the next part of the presentation. When one person makes a PowerPoint presentation, an assistant can manage the console, relieving the presenter of technical responsibilities—operating lights, sound, and PowerPoint or performing other tasks. The focus should always be on the presenter.

Interacting during the Presentation

Interaction among team members during the presentation conveys a sense of co-operation and team spirit. While group members should avoid interrupting one another during lectures, interjections from different team members during discussions or question-and-answer sessions add dynamism to the presentation. They also make the team look knowledgeable, interested, and comfortable with one another. Uninvolved members should sit (as a group) in locations that do not draw attention from the presenters. Their listening postures should convey interest in the presentation. They should not be scanning the room or slumping in a bored posture. Speakers should also refer to presenters who came before them and note how their contribution will relate to other topics in the team presentation, including those that will come later in the agenda.

The presenters should also help to facilitate interaction among audience members. When audience members are engaged in small group activities, one or more team members should circulate among the groups to be sure they understand the exercise. In group exercises, leaders will generally emerge from every small group; however, if a group seems to be struggling with an exercise, team members should move to their aid, respond to questions, and assist in organizing the group.

Reaching the Entire Audience

When giving the presentation, group members should be careful to communicate "outside the kite." Speakers tend to communicate in a kite-shaped pattern, ignoring audience members seated in front and rear corners. In a theatre-style or straight-row seating arrangement, speakers must take care to maintain eye contact with all members of the audience, not just those who are sitting in the "action zone." If the audience is large, speakers can create the perception that they are communicating with everyone by catching the eye of some individuals in all parts of the room.

Presenters should also try to sound spontaneous when speaking. While preparing for the presentation generally involves many practice runs, the presentation itself should sound unrehearsed. Presenters should use PowerPoint slides and note cards only as a guide, not as a script. The group should *not* put detailed information on the slides—only brief bullets and visuals. Otherwise the slides will compete with the words of the speaker. Speakers should also avoid distributing materials during the presentation.

Speakers can close some of the psychological distance that separates them from the audience by moving away from the podium or computer console as they speak. They can rely on a team member or use a remote control to change slides. Other factors that create positive feelings toward speakers include use of humour, an expressive voice, smiling, a relaxed body posture, a sense of warmth, good eye contact, and an energetic delivery with gestures and movement. Speakers should seem approachable. A wealth of research, including a review of 81 different studies, has identified a relationship between these speaker characteristics and student learning.[28] These findings apply to classrooms in North America;[29] but they may not apply equally well to regions of the world, where people expect and prefer a more formal and restrained approach to speaking (e.g., Japan or Thailand).

Managing the Feedback Process

Managing the feedback process involves knowing how to ask questions, acknowledge and respond to questions and comments, and reframe and redirect questions.

Asking Questions

When asking questions, facilitators should observe certain rules. Questions should be prepared before the presentation takes place. They should be open-ended, answerable, clearly worded, important, and thought-provoking. Some questions do not require a response, only consideration by the audience. Facilitators should also be aware of gender and power dynamics, and they should allow audience members enough time to think about and answer the questions.

Questions should be *planned in advance*, and they should be *open-ended*. Recall from Chapter 10 the benefits of asking open-ended questions. These sorts of questions encourage in-depth responses. They give people the freedom to generate their own answers and discuss those answers in whatever terms they choose. As a result, they draw out much more information than do closed-ended questions. If you choose nonetheless to ask a close-ended question in a presentation, you should be prepared to follow with an open-ended probe. An example follows: "Do you prefer less directive or more directive styles of leadership? Why did you choose that style?"

Facilitators should ask *questions that the audience can answer*. If you ask questions that are too controversial, too complicated, or too technical, you may get little or no response. People do not like to give politically incorrect answers, even if their belief structures vary from the social norms of the day. If you want answers to multiple questions, ask the additional questions as follow-up after audience members respond to the first question. Do not ask all the questions at once. Alternatively, you can put several questions on a PowerPoint slide and ask the audience to consider one point at a time. Finally, questions should not require expertise that is lacking in the audience. If you ask lower-level employees, for example, to respond to a question that requires management experience, they will have no idea of the appropriate answer. In a similar way, questions that call for highly technical expertise are inappropriate if audience members do not have the required knowledge and skills.

Questions should be *clearly framed and important*. Facilitators should plan different ways to ask the same questions in the event that the audience does not understand the original question. The questions should be important enough to demand the consideration and time of the members of the audience. When an answer is too obvious or a concern too trivial, people will be reluctant to answer the question.

Questions should also be *thought-provoking*. They should encourage audience members to think about matters in greater depth. Some questions are intended only to provoke thought, not to get actual responses. Facilitators might ask the following question, for instance: "Consider for a moment. What do you think could happen next if we don't change direction—if we don't stop the gradual takeover of our civil liberties? Civil liberties, once lost, can become fugitives from justice."

Facilitators can direct questions to the entire audience or to specific individuals or sub-groups. Or they can go from one to another audience member in the manner of a relay. If a small task group has generated a response to some problem, for example, the facilitator can ask a question of the following sort: "John, I know that your group has arrived at a pretty creative answer to this problem. Could you share your ideas with the group?"

Group presenters must take care not to embarrass people by calling upon individuals who may not have an opinion or information on a topic. Usually, when people do not know the answer to a question, they avoid the eye gaze of the interrogator. When participants close the line of communication in this way, facilitators should look elsewhere for a respondent.

When asking questions, facilitators should be aware of gender dynamics. The communication patterns of men and women vary in group situations. In mixed-gender groups, men tend to interrupt women; answer questions not addressed to them; start new conversation threads; and generally dominate the discussion. They also tend to "perform" for women,[30] and they are less likely to accept influence in mixed-gender groups. Women have a more difficult time getting and holding attention in mixed-gender groups.[31] Women are also less comfortable than men when discussing controversial subjects.[32] A good facilitator takes these kinds of gender dynamics into account.

Facilitators should also take status differences into account. High status individuals feel more comfortable than low status individuals in expressing their points of view. They are more likely to raise controversial topics and to exert influence over others.[33] At the same time, they are less likely to allow others to influence them or to change their opinions.[34]

Finally, facilitators should give ample time for people to think about and respond to their questions. At the same time, they should not allow silence to make audience members uncomfortable. If the facilitators think the audience has not understood a question, they should rephrase rather than repeat it. If no one volunteers an answer, facilitators should be prepared to answer the question themselves or move on to the next question.

Acknowledging and Responding to Comments and Questions

When acknowledging comments and questions, facilitators should find a way to involve a maximum number of audience members in the discussion. If some people answer every question, it does not allow time for others to voice an opinion or idea. One way to exercise control as a facilitator is to direct your eye gaze away from those who respond quickly and to look in the direction of more silent audience members. You might need to say, "I've received some really interesting responses from some of you, but I would like to know the opinions of others as well." Then you could look in the direction of someone who has not responded. If that person closes the communication channel by looking away, however, you must locate another respondent.

In another case, you could say: "Jennifer has offered one perspective to us, but I would like to get at least three or four other views. I'll give you a couple of minutes to think about the question." Some people are slower to respond to questions, because they like to give thoughtful, measured responses. If you go consistently to the first person who raises a hand to answer, you miss input from people who like to think through problems before answering. Different people have different personalities. Giving that extra time for thought can result in wider involvement among group members.

You should always acknowledge the responses of those who answer a question and, whenever possible, integrate the ideas into summaries and conclusions. You should rephrase the thoughts to show you are listening and understanding. Rephrasing can also help to clarify the responses for the larger group. You should try to position the idea within the framework of their discussion. If you do not understand a response, you should ask for clarification.

If a response reveals lack of understanding, you should not put down the contributor. If you undermine the contribution of even one person in a group, others will be reluctant to offer their ideas. Audience members are often as nervous as presenters. They fear looking unintelligent or uninformed in front of their peers. In work situations, they fear they might be overlooked for a promotion if they seem incompetent in training sessions. For that reason, responses from some audience members will be timid and tentative. Facilitators must offer encouragement and (when warranted) compliments to those who put themselves at risk. If responses are not on target, you can still acknowledge points of interest in the remark and thank the person for contributing to the discussion. Even if a comment is off the mark, you can say something like "That is a very thought-provoking comment. I'd like to have more time to think about it before responding."

Often a person will raise an idea or ask a question about something that you plan to discuss later in the presentation. In that case, you might want to say: "You've raised a very important point, and we will be discussing it later in the presentation. Perhaps you can hold comments on this point for now. You're just a bit ahead of the rest of us." When you reach the point where you planned to discuss the topic, refer back to the question and acknowledge the individual who raised the point. If you decide to respond to a question that takes the discussion off track, take the time after answering to return to the departure point.

If you do not know the answer to a question, you should tell the group that you will check and get back to them with the answer. If you need more time to think about the question, you can ask the person to repeat it or say that you will come back to the point later in the presentation. A sample response follows: "To be honest, I haven't given much thought to that question. But it is an interesting one, and I will get back to you before the end of the period." You might want to write the question on a flip chart or white board to allow more time to consider it before responding to the person.

Notice the kind of language that you use in facilitation. Effective facilitation is courteous, sensitive to the feelings of participants, and encouraging in tone. When you employ *we* language as a facilitator, you assume more of the responsibility for what does not work in the presentation. Mistakes and problems become *our mistakes and problems*—not *your mistakes* and *your confused understanding*. Your body language should also be supportive and encouraging. The use of qualifiers such as *a bit*, *a little*, and *somewhat* can soften the impact of less positive responses. If you say "There appears to be *some* misunderstanding on this point," you have avoided saying "You have misunderstood this point." The first statement is less *bare*. Adding some flesh softens the impact of the statement. As noted in earlier chapters, women tend to use this kind of language more frequently than men do.

Using the example of a misunderstanding, we can also observe some other points about appropriate language to use in group facilitation. When you use *indirect language*, you soften the impact. If you say, for example, "*There* appears to be some confusion on this point," you have avoided saying "*You* are confused." This kind of language serves the function of allowing those who are among the confused to save face. In addition, this example illustrates a third point. If you say "There *appears to be* some misunderstanding," you sound less dogmatic than when you say "There *is* some misunderstanding." While you should avoid this kind of indirect and powerless language in many settings (e.g., the workplace), the language is appropriate in group facilitation. In facilitated sessions, you want to encourage audience participation and to offer feedback that others will accept without defensiveness.

Redirecting Questions

Sometimes facilitators redirect questions to the larger group. In a session on retirement planning, someone might ask about the best savings plans. As a facilitator, you could redirect the question to the larger group: "What are your experiences with some of the savings plans? Which ones would you recommend?" In a presentation on the increasing costs of automobile insurance, an audience member might ask for more information about specific insurance plans. Again you could say: "Most of you are in the same age and risk group as the person who asked the question. Would some of you be willing to share what you pay for insurance?" At other times, you might want to redirect a question to the person who asked it: "That is a good question. Do you have any ideas on the topic?"

Providing Handouts and Other Supplementary Materials

Materials provided to participants should be professional in appearance. Handouts should be neatly packaged or bound, preferably with cerlox (comb) or spiral binding. These handouts typically include the agenda, materials for group exercises, copies of the PowerPoint presentation, and references. Instead of binding the materials, some teams provide folders to each audience member. If the team does not distribute name tags as people enter the room, they may include the name tags in folders that also contain handouts, blank paper, pens, and small favours.

Facilitators can also set up various supplementary materials at the front of the presentation space. Flip charts and white boards can help facilitators, as well as audience members, to collect and record ideas during discussions. They can also be useful during group activities. If facilitators make reference to a book, they should have the book with them. Visual aids—such as PowerPoint slides, photos, illustrations, posters, video clips—are highly desirable in long presentations.

GLOSSARY

accommodating (coping style) Resolving a conflict by giving in to what the other party or individual wants.

active perceivers Individuals who choose the amount and type of information they receive.

adaptors Body movements that relieve tension or satisfy self or bodily needs.

affect displays Body movements that tell others about our emotional state.

agreeableness The perceived warmth and friendliness of a person.

analogy A figure of speech that uses something familiar to explain something less familiar.

androgynous A mix of both feminine and masculine traits.

archetypal metaphor A metaphor that refers to basic elements of the earth and human experience.

assimilation The process of being absorbed into a larger group.

assimilation effect Heightened self-esteem following a favourable social comparison.

asynchronous communication Communicators exchange messages with a time delay between messages.

avatar An online visual representation of an individual.

avoiding (coping style) Withdrawing from a conflict.

bafflegab The use of unnecessarily long or complicated words that other people do not understand.

bald language Blunt or direct language.

beneficial impression management Efforts to create positive impressions of close others.

body-image disturbance Reduced levels of satisfaction with our bodies and a downward spiral in how we see our physical selves.

bonding social capital Benefits that result from close relationships with parents, children, and other family members.

brainsketching An idea-generation technique that involves sketching ideas on paper, followed by sharing with others.

brainstorming An idea-generation technique that involves group discussion aimed at generating as many ideas and solutions as possible.

brainwriting An idea-generation technique involving exchange of ideas on paper in a group setting.

breadth of perceptual field The amount of information we take into our visual or other perceptual systems.

bridging social capital Benefits that result from connections with friends and close associates.

bullying A form of aggressive behaviour that includes punching, name calling, or spreading rumors.

certainty Conveying the message "I am always right."

channel The medium used to transmit a message.

chronemics The study of how people perceive, structure, value, and react to time.

climate The emotional tone of a relationship or interaction.

closed-ended questions Questions that request a *yes* or a *no*.

cocktail party effect A phenomenon where we hear one voice out of a medley of conversations and background noises.

coercive power Power that comes from making threats or intimidating people.

cognitive complexity The capacity to use a number of viewpoints to make sense of complex information.

collaborating (coping style) Resolving conflict in a way that allows both sides to satisfy their wants.

collective identity The characteristics of our personal identity that we share with members of a larger group.

collectivism Focus on group needs and goals.

coming-apart phase Five stages that contribute to a movement away from intimacy.

coming-together phase Five stages through which couples move as they build intimacy.

commitment Acceptance of and motivation to support an idea or concept.

communication predicament of aging (CPA) model A model that predicts the relationship among aging cues, stereotyping, and communication behaviour.

competency One's expertise in a given area.

competing (coping style) Forcing a resolution by pushing for one's own needs or solution.

compromising (coping style) Resolving a conflict by meeting in the middle.

computer-mediated communication (CMC) The process of using a computer to communicate messages.

concealable stigmatized identity An identity that carries a stigma and that can be hidden from others.

confirmation bias The tendency to attend to information that confirms our beliefs and to ignore information that contradicts our beliefs.

conflict Disagreement between two or more parties who see themselves as having opposing goals or values.

connotative meaning Meaning that takes context and relationships into account.

consensus General acceptance of (if not agreement with) a decision among all members of a group.

content meaning See **denotative meaning**.

context Circumstances surrounding a situation.

contrast effect Feelings of inadequacy and lowered self-esteem following an unfavourable social comparison.

control Ignoring the other person's input while forcing that person to accept your decisions.

convergence Uniting or bringing together, as in speech that emphasizes similarities.

conversation style The way we present and express ourselves when conversing with others.

conversational self-focus Focus on oneself to the exclusion of others in a conversation.

counter-stereotyping Effort to eliminate stereotypes by focussing on similarities.

covert conflict Hidden conflict, not always known to the other party.

credibility The extent to which you are believable to others.

crowdsourcing A practice where organizations invite large groups of Internet users to generate and share ideas on their products and services.

cultural identity Characteristics we share with others from the same or similar cultural backgrounds.

culture The shared ideas, traditions, norms, symbols, and values that define a community.

culture bound Restricted by cultural influences.

cyberbullying Malicious communications in the form of text messages, emails, or postings on social and personal websites.

defensive communication Behaviours people use when they perceive a threat to their emotional well-being.

deferential language Language characterized by courteous respectfulness and submissiveness.

deliberative listening Listening to learn, often from a critical perspective.

Delphi method A structured method of decision making that engages panels of experts in multiple rounds of problem solving or forecasting.

denotative meaning The literal or dictionary meaning of a word.

description Offering thoughts and feelings without judging.

destination Where the message ends up.

directive interview An interview that relies on *yes–no* or closed-ended questions.

disclaimers Phrases that devalue statements by drawing attention to potential faults.

divergence Separating, as in speech that emphasizes differences.

doublespeak Language that deliberately disguises the true meaning of a potentially unpleasant idea.

dynamism One's boldness, energy, and assertiveness.

dysfunctional conflict Disagreements with unproductive or destructive outcomes.

effects The intended or unintended impact(s) of a message.

emblems Body movements that stand on their own as a replacement for words.

emergent approach An approach that sees leadership as emerging from a leaderless group via a process of elimination.

emoticons Graphic representations of facial expressions that convey mood.

emotional appeals Appeals based on the expected emotional responses of an audience.

empathic listening Listening from the perspective of the other person.

empathy An active and mindful effort to understand the experience of another person and share that person's feelings.

equality Behaving as though you are equal to others.

equivocality Possibility for words and actions to have multiple interpretations.

ethnic identity Characteristics we share with others with a common ancestry.

euphemism An expression meant to be less offensive or disturbing than the word or phrase it replaces.

evaluation Passing judgment on a person, idea, or object.

expectancy violation theory Theory that explains how violation of expectations can alter first impressions.

expert or information power Power that comes from knowledge or expertise.

external noise Interference from an environmental source.

extroverts People who enjoy the company of others.

face work Politeness strategies aimed at making other people feel better about themselves.

fantasy chaining An idea-generation technique that involves group creation of a story based on a fantastic theme.

feedback Response to a message or activity.

field of experience The totality of all we are at the moment of communication.

focus group A group interview with a central purpose that guides the discussion.

friendships Relationships involving people with shared activities and interests, ranging from the personal to the intimate.

functional approach An approach that sees leadership as a series of functions.

functional conflict Disagreements with productive or beneficial outcomes.

fundamental interpersonal relations orientation (FIRO) Theory that holds that we form interpersonal relationships in order to meet our need for inclusion, control, and affection.

gender identity Characteristics we share with others of a particular gender.

global self-esteem Self-esteem that shows in many aspects of our lives.

groupthink The tendency for group members to conform to majority opinion in order to avoid conflict.

hard architecture Buildings and other structures designed to stand strong and to resist human imprint.

hearing A physical process that occurs when the eardrum absorbs sound vibrations and sends the sensations to the brain.

hedges Phrases or words such as *sort of* and *somewhat* that protect against the risk of making a direct statement.

hedging Using words that show uncertainty or reduce the negative impact of what we are saying.

hesitations Words such as *um* or *well* that act as fillers and convey uncertainty.

high self-monitors People who are very aware of the opinions of others.

high-context cultures Cultures that place great importance on context and rely to a lesser degree on words.

historical self An outdated self, someone we used to be.

hyperpersonal theory Theory that suggests that we use limited online cues to construct idealized images of another person.

ideal personal type An individual who wants to be liked but feels comfortable in situations that may result in dislike.

ideal self The person we would like to be.

ideal social person An individual who meets her inclusion needs in a balanced way.

identity The characteristics that allow others to recognize us.

illustrators Body movements that accent or work in unison with what is said verbally.

immediacy A sense of likeability and approachability established through communication behaviours that draw people closer together.

immediacy behaviours Verbal and nonverbal behaviours that suggest a teacher's willingness to approach and to be approached by students.

impression formation theory Theory related to how we put together different pieces of information to form an impression of a person.

impression management The way we create impressions of ourselves in the eyes of others.

individualism Focus on individual needs and goals.

inference An educated guess when we do not have all the necessary information.

information source Where the message is conceived.

in-group A group of which one is a member.

instrumental Aimed at achieving a specific goal or purpose.

interdependent Reliant on other people for safety, survival, and support.

internal noise Interference from an internal source.

internal working model A mental picture that helps us understand some aspect of our world.

intimacy The state of having a close, authentic connection with another person.

intonation The way the voice rises and falls as we speak.

introverts People who enjoy more alone time.

jargon Words or expressions that have meaning for members of a specific profession or other group but that have little or no meaning to outsiders.

Johari window A self-awareness model that helps us to identify and understand the open, hidden, shared, and unknown parts of the self.

kinesics Communication through body movements, posture, stance, and hand gestures.

language misuse Use of words in the wrong context, improper grammar, or incorrect pronunciation.

legitimate power Power that comes from holding an office, title, or other legitimate position.

life scripts Storylines that we create to guide us through life.

linguistic determinism The idea that language determines our thinking.

linguistic identity Characteristics we share with others who speak a common language.

linguistic relativity The idea that people who speak different languages perceive and think about the world differently.

linking social capital Benefits that result from relationships with people in positions of power who are outside of our usual network.

listening A mental process that involves interpreting messages that others have transmitted.

load-induced blindness Inability to see as a result of information overload in the visual field.

logical appeals Appeals based on logic and reasoning.

looking-glass self How we think others see us.

low self-monitors People who do not worry about the opinions of others.

low-context cultures Cultures that rely heavily on words rather than context.

malapropism Switching of an intended word with another word of similar sound or spelling that has a different meaning.

metalanguage Language that describes or comments on language.

metaphor A figure of speech that reveals something about one thing by implicitly comparing it to something else.

mind mapping An idea-generation technique that uses a single word or idea placed at the centre of a piece of paper to stimulate more ideas.

monochronic cultures Cultures that view time as rigidly linear and rely heavily on clocks and schedules to regulate events.

mood contagion The idea that we can "catch" the mood of someone else much like we catch a cold.

myth of perfection The false notion that a state of perfection exists and is attainable.

national identity Characteristics we share with others from a particular country.

need for affection The need to feel liked by others.

need for control The need to influence our relationships, decisions, and activities and to let others influence us.

need for inclusion The need to be connected to other people.

neutrality Showing lack of interest in the other person or that person's ideas.

noise Interference that occurs in the transmitting or receiving of signals.

nominal group technique An idea-generation technique in which group members work independently at first and then share their initial ideas.

non-directive interview An interview that relies on open-ended questions.

nonverbal communication Communication that does not involve language.

nonverbal leakage The nonverbal behaviours that unintentionally reveal true inner states.

one-up, one-down situations Two-person interactions in which one person clearly holds more power than the other.

onomatopoeia Words that sound like what they describe.

open access Unrestricted and uncontrolled sharing of information on open platforms, accessible to everyone.

open source Approaches that allow and encourage a free flow of information into an organization.

open-ended questions Questions that encourage a full and detailed response.

optical communities A social group that shares a similar view of the world.

other-orientation Thinking about the other person's interests, needs, knowledge, and situation when you speak.

out-group A group of which one is not a member.

overpersonal Characteristic of an individual who seeks to establish close relationships with everyone, regardless of whether others show interest.

oversocial The tendency to work extra hard to seek interaction and attention from others.

overt conflict Conflict involving open disagreement.

own-race bias The idea that accuracy increases when we identify specific members of our own race.

paralanguage Elements of speech that are not recognized as language.

paraphrasing Using our own words to help us understand and/or reflect back our understanding of what another person has said.

paraphrasing content Summarizing the main verbal message.

paraphrasing emotions Summarizing how the speaker feels about what he or she is telling you.

passive receivers Individuals who rely on others to select information for them.

perception The process of sensing, interpreting, and reacting to the physical world.

perception-checking A process for confirming what we think we have seen, heard, or experienced.

perspective-taking Looking at a situation from the other person's point of view.

phonological rules Rules governing the sounds that appear in a language.

physiological noise Interference from a biological condition or function.

pitch The degree of highness or lowness with which we speak.

polychronic cultures Cultures that view time as elastic and believe events will happen when they are meant to happen.

powerful language Language that conveys authority.

powerless language Language that does not convey authority.

pragmatic rules Rules that take context into account when arriving at meaning.

primary work groups Groups in which employees interact every day, based on their positions within the organization.

problem orientation A focus on finding solutions.

project-specific work groups Groups of employees brought together for specialized purposes.

provisionalism Acknowledging different points of view or different interpretations of events.

proxemics The study of how people perceive and use space.

psychological noise Interference from a mental state.

quality circle A group of employees who meet regularly to identify, discuss, and try to solve work-related issues.

question statements Statements spoken as questions, expressing doubt through rising intonation.

quotatives Words used to introduce quotes in conversation.

racial identity Characteristics we share with others with respect to racial heritage.

rapport A positive relationship characterized by mutual liking and effective communication.

real self The person we actually are.

receiver Mechanism for decoding the message.

reference group A group whose opinions we value and in which we hold or aspire to membership.

referent The object or idea to which a symbol refers.

referent power Power that comes from personal attractiveness.

reflected appraisal See **looking-glass self**.

regional identity Characteristics we share with others from a particular region of a country.

regulators Body movements that control the flow of conversation.

relational meaning See **connotative meaning**.

relationship boundaries The limits to which we are willing to go to establish or maintain a relationship.

relationships of choice Relationships we actively seek out and choose to develop.

relationships of circumstance Relationships that develop because of situations or circumstances in which we find ourselves.

religious identity Characteristics that relate to a belief system and/or a sense of belonging to a particular religion.

remembering The process of recalling information.

report talk Talk that focusses on content rather than relationships.

responding The process of providing feedback to show that understanding has occurred.

restricted code Language and gestures with special meanings that only the members of a certain group understand.

reverse brainstorming An idea-generation technique that involves identifying what could make the problem worse before looking at what could make it better.

reward power Power that comes from offering benefits or gifts.

selecting The process of focussing on certain stimuli and ignoring others.

selective perception The process by which we see and retain certain kinds of information while ignoring or discarding other kinds of information.

self-categorization theory The idea that we see ourselves as both individuals and group members, whereas we see others as either individuals or group members based on other factors.

self-concept Relatively constant thoughts and feelings about who we are and how we differ from other people.

self-criticism The tendency to pay more attention to information that supports a negative view of the self.

self-disclosure Sharing of personal information about oneself in conversations.

self-efficacy Our perceived ability to accomplish something or to make a difference.

self-enhancement The tendency to pay more attention to information that supports a positive view of the self.

self-esteem Our perception of our overall value.

self-fulfilling prophecy A prediction or belief that leads to its own fulfillment.

self-grooming Cleaning and tidying behaviours, which often characterize courtship behaviours.

self-image Our views of ourselves.

self-monitoring The extent to which we regulate our behaviours in order to look good to others.

self-serving A focus on what serves our own purposes and makes us look best.

self-serving bias The tendency to credit our successes to internal or personal factors and our failures to external or situational factors.

self-verification theory Theory that says that we want others to see us as we see ourselves.

semantic rules Rules that relate to the agreed-upon meanings of words.

sexual harassment Unwanted sexual attention or the inappropriate promise of rewards for sexual favours.

signal The message.

significant others People whose opinions matter to us and influence how we perceive ourselves.

simultaneous access Unrestricted access to information flowing from mass media and reaching everyone at the same time.

single-loop learning Learning that provides answers to questions we know how to ask.

situational approach An approach that sees leadership as dependent on situation, with no one best approach.

sociability One's likeability.

social capital A resource based on interpersonal connections that can be converted into economic and other benefits.

social comparison theory Theory that holds that we look to others for a standard of comparison.

social exchange theory Theory that explains how people weigh the perceived costs and rewards of relationships in deciding to maintain or end them.

social friendships Friendships that go beyond the boundaries of the workplace.

social information processing theory Theory that investigates how we process various types of information in collaborative settings such as social media.

social penetration theory Theory that suggests the importance of self-disclosure in moving from less intimate to more intimate relationships.

social presence theory Theory that explores the effects of sensing another's presence in a social interaction.

social reality A generally agreed upon understanding of the world around us, created through interactions with other people.

sociofugal setting A physical setting that pushes people apart.

sociopetal setting A physical setting that brings people together.

soft architecture Buildings and other structures that allow personalization of spaces.

source credibility appeals Appeals based on the personal attractiveness of a communicator to the audience.

speech–thought differential The difference between the rate at which a speaker conveys a spoken message and the speed at which a listener processes the information.

spontaneity Being open and honest in interactions.

standpoint theory Theory that holds that our background and experiences determine our perspective.

static evaluation Use of language that does not take change into account.

status One's standing in relationship to others.

stereotypes Popularly held beliefs about a type of person or group of persons that do not take individual differences into account.

strategic ambiguity Use of unclear and vague language to accomplish goals.

strategy Hiding one's motives and manipulating someone into doing what you want them to do.

superiority Behaving as though you are better than others.

supportive communication Behaviours that reduce defensiveness and demonstrate respect for the feelings of the other person.

symbol Something that stands for or suggests something else.

synchronous communication Communicators exchange messages in real time.

synectics An idea-generation technique that uses metaphors and analogies to make the strange familiar and the familiar strange.

syntactic rules Rules governing the arrangement of words and punctuation in a sentence.

tag questions Phrases that, when tagged onto the end of sentences, change statements into questions (e.g., "don't you think?").

TAR effect A tendency to dislike the person who criticizes someone else rather than disliking the person who is criticized. (*TAR* stands for *transfer of attitudes recursively*.)

territoriality Our desire and efforts to mark our territory and defend it against invasion.

thought The mental image that we associate with a symbol and its referent.

tone The vocal quality that conveys emotion.

transactional theory Theory that sees communication as a dynamic process, involving continuous changes in communicators and environments.

transformational approach An approach that sees leaders as visionaries who challenge and mentor.

transmitter Mechanism for encoding the message.

triangle of meaning A model that explains the relationship among words, things, and their meanings.

triangular theory of love Theory proposing that passion, commitment, and intimacy characterize romantic relationships.

trickle-down access Controlled and restricted access to information, flowing mostly downward.

trustworthiness One's character or integrity.

turn taking The process of deciding who will speak at any given time during a conversation.

turning points Events or interactions that signal changes in the relationship.

underpersonal Characteristic of an individual who feels undervalued and seeks to avoid close relationships.

undersocial The tendency to avoid interaction with others.

understanding The process of assigning meaning to the stimuli we have selected.

undifferentiated Low scores on both feminine and masculine traits.

up talking A speech pattern in which the voice rises in pitch at the end of a statement.

validation Confirmation of our sense of worth and value.

Valleyspeak A variety of English characterized by up talking and excessive use of the word *like*.

verbal communication Communication that involves spoken, written, or signed language.

vocal fry A low vocal register that often sounds creaky or rattling.

warranting theory Theory that says we are more likely to believe information that someone cannot manipulate.

working friendships Friendships that are restricted to the workplace and limited in emotional investment.

NOTES

CHAPTER 1

1. Aristotle, *Rhetoric*, vol. 11, trans. W.R. Roberts (Oxford: Clarendon Press, 1924; New York: Modern Library, 1954), 90–1.
2. E.M. Rogers and D.K. Bhowmik, "Homophily-Heterophily: Relational Concepts for Communication Research," *Public Opinion Quarterly* 34 (1970): 523–38; E.M. Rogers and F.F. Shoemaker, *Communication of Innovations* (New York: Free Press, 1971); J.C. McCroskey, V.P. Richmond, and J.A. Daly, "Toward the Measurement of Perceived Homophily in Interpersonal Communication" (paper presented to the International Communication Association Convention, New Orleans, April 1974); V.P. Richmond, J.C. McCroskey, and J.A. Daly, "The Generalizability of a Measure of Perceived Homophily in Interpersonal Communication" (paper presented to the International Communication Association Convention, Chicago, April 1975); R.L. Atkinson, R.C. Atkinson, E.E. Smith, and D.J. Bem, *Introduction to Psychology*, 10th ed. (San Diego, CA: Harcourt Brace Jovanovich, 1990), 713.
3. E. Haley, "Organization as Source: Consumers' Understandings of Organizational Sponsorship of Advocacy Advertising," *Journal of Advertising* 25 (1996): 19–36.
4. F.S. Haiman, "The Effects of Ethos in Public Speaking," *Speech Monographs* 16 (1949): 192; C.I. Hovland and W. Weiss, "The Influence of Source Credibility on Communication Effectiveness," *Public Opinion Quarterly* 16 (1961): 635–50.
5. See discussions by B.W. Eakins and R.G. Eakins, *Sex Differences in Human Communication* (Boston: Houghton Mifflin, 1978), 38–49; P.H. Bradley, "The Folk-Linguistics of Women's Speech: An Empirical Examination," *Communication Monographs* 48, no. 1 (1981): 73–90.
6. See, for example, M.L. Houser, "Are We Violating Their Expectations? Instructor Communication Expectations of Traditional and Nontraditional Students," *Communication Quarterly* 53 (2005): 213–28; W.J. Potter and R. Emanuel, "Students' Preferences for Communication Styles and Their Relationship to Achievement," *Communication Education* 39 (1990): 234–9; G. Sorensen, "The Relationships among Teachers' Self-Disclosive Statements, Students' Perceptions, and Affective Learning," *Communication Education* 38 (1989): 259–76; J. Gorham, "The Relationship between Verbal Teacher Immediacy Behaviors and Student Learning," *Communication Education* 37 (1988): 40–53; V. Downs, M. Javidi, and J. Nussbaum, "An Analysis of Teachers' Verbal Communication within the College Classroom: Use of Humor, Self-Disclosure, and Narratives," *Communication Education* 37 (1988): 127–41; L.R. Wheeless, "Self-Disclosure and Interpersonal Solidarity: Measurement, Validation, and Relationships," *Human Communication Research* 3 (1976): 47–61.
7. L.K. Guerrero and T.A. Miller, "Associations between Nonverbal Behaviors and Initial Impressions of Instructor Competence and Course Content in Videotaped Distance Education Courses," *Communication Education* 47 (1998): 30–42.
8. W.C. Minnick, *The Art of Persuasion* (Boston: Houghton Mifflin, 1957).
9. See, for example, B. Reeves, J. Newhagen, E. Maibach, M. Basil, and K. Kurz, "Negative and Positive Television Messages: Effects of Message Type and Context on Attention and Memory," *American Behavioral Scientist* 34 (1991): 679–94. See also Minnick, *The Art of Persuasion.*
10. W.L. Schramm, "How Communication Works," in *The Process and Effects of Mass Communication*, ed. W. Schramm (Urbana, IL: University of Illinois Press, 1954), (pp. 3-26).
11. S.H. Kaminski, "Communication Models," accessed 16 July 2013, www.shkaminski.com/Classes/Handouts/Communication%20Models.htm#DancesHelicalSpiral1967.
12. D.C. Barnlund, "Transactional Model of Communication," in *Foundations of Communication Theory*, ed. K.K. Sereno and C.D. Mortensen (New York: Harper and Row, 1970), 99.
13. S. Ferguson, *Public Speaking in Canada: Building Competency in Stages* (Toronto: Oxford University Press, 2006).
14. N. Nunn, "Communication Breakdown," editorial, *Morgan County Citizen*, 18 January 2013, www.morgancountycitizen.com/?q=node/22294.
15. C. Heller, "Chaz Bono Opens Up about Sex Change," *On the Red Carpet*, 5 September 2011, www.ontheredcarpet.com/Chaz-Bono-opens-up-about-sex-change-Video/8120359.
16. B. Hallman, "After Sandy, Communication Breakdown Hampered Efforts to Find Evacuated Seniors," *Huffington Post*, 16 November 2012, www.huffingtonpost.com/2012/11/16/sandy-communication-evacuated-seniors_n_2141699.html.
17. B. Holl (VP/Publisher of Learning A–Z), "Reading Challenge with an Unusual Reward," *Bob's Blog* (blog),

10 July 2012, http://blog.readinga-z.com/bobs_blog/2012/07/reading-challenge-with-an-unusual-reward.html.

[18] J.R.P. French and B. Raven, "The Bases of Social Power," in Group Dynamics, ed. D. Cartwright and A. Zander (New York: Harper and Row, 1959), 150–67.

[19] C. Arribas, "Honesty of the Long Distance Runner," *El País*, 12 December 2012, http://elpais.com/elpais/2012/12/19/inenglish/1355928581_856388.html; D. Trifunov, "Iván Fernández Anay's Kindness Reaffirms Faith in Athletes for Some," *Global Post*, 18 January 2013, www.globalpost.com/dispatches/globalpost-blogs/world-at-play/ivan-fernandez-anayas-kindness-reaffirms-faith-athletes-so.

[20] A. Picard, "Communication Breakdown: How Canadians Were Let Down on E. Coli Response," *Globe and Mail*, 7 October 2012, www.theglobeandmail.com/news/national/communication-breakdown-how-canadians-were-let-down-on-e-coli-response/article4595708.

[21] C. Strohm, "9/11 Communication Failures Still Baffle FAA, Defense Officials," *Government Executive*, 21 June 2004, www.govexec.com.

[22] Ibid.

[23] Ibid.

[24] Ibid.

[25] Ibid.

[26] "Doing the 'Right' Things to Correct Wrong-Site Surgery," *Patient Safety Authority* 4, no. 2 (June 2007): 29, 32–45, http://patientsafetyauthority.org/ADVISORIES/AdvisoryLibrary/2007/jun4(2)/Pages/29b.aspx.

[27] S. Rice, "Patients, Beware of Wrong-Side Surgeries," *CNN*, 28 April 2011, www.cnn.com/2011/HEALTH/04/28/ep.wrong.side.surgery/index.html.

[28] "Doctors Perform Surgery on the Wrong Body Part about 40 Times a Week," KSL News Radio, 25 September 2012, www.ksl.com/?nid=895&sid=22296561.

[29] Rice, "Patients, Beware."

[30] John Hopkins Medical Institutions, "RX for Wrong Site Surgery: Two Minutes of Conversation," *Science Daily*, 24 January 2007, www.sciencedaily.com/releases/2007/01/070123143242.htm.

[31] F.L. Cohen, D. Mendelsohn, and M. Bernstein, "Wrong-Site Craniotomy: Analysis of 35 Cases and Systems for Prevention," *Journal of Neurosurgery* 113, no. 3 (2010): 461–73.

[32] "Seventy Patients Had Surgery on Wrong Part of Body, NHS Data Reveals," *Guardian*, 29 October 2012, www.guardian.co.uk/society/2012/oct/29/nhs-mishaps-data-published.

[33] M. Rogers, R. Cook, R. Bower, M. Molloy, and M. Render, "Barriers to Implementing Wrong Site Surgery Guidelines: A Cognitive Work Analysis," *IEEE Transactions on Systems, Man, and Cybernetics—Part A: Systems and Humans* 34, no. 6 (November 2004): 757–63.

[34] M. Makary, A. Mukherjee, J.B. Sexton, D. Syin, E. Goodrich, E. Hartmann, L. Rowen, D.C. Behrens, M. Marohn, and P.J. Pronovost, "Operation Room Briefings and Wrong Site Surgery," *Journal of the American College of Surgeons* 204, no. 2 (February 2007): 236–43, www.surgicalpatientsafety.facs.org/research/makary.pdf.

[35] C.C. Greenberg, S.E. Regenbogen, D.M. Studdert, S.R. Lipsitz, S.O. Rogers, M.J. Zinner, and A.A. Gawande, "Patterns of Communication Breakdowns Resulting in Injury to Surgical Patients," *Journal of the American College of Surgeons* 204, no. 4 (April 2007): 533–40.

[36] "Mokusatsu: One Word, Two Lessons," accessed 14 July 2013, www.nsa.gov/public_info/_files/tech_journals/mokusatsu.pdf.

[37] A. Mehrabian, *Nonverbal Communication* (Chicago: Aldine-Atherton, 1972).

CHAPTER 2

[1] M. Prince, "Self-Concept, Money Beliefs and Values," *Journal of Economic Psychology* 14 (1993): 161–73.

[2] Ibid.

[3] J.F. Rosenblith, *In the Beginning: Development from Conception to Age Two* (Newbury Park, CA: Sage, 1992).

[4] G.H. Mead, *Mind, Self, and Society: From the Standpoint of a Social Behaviorist* (Chicago: University of Chicago Press, 1934); A. Allport, *Personality: A Psychological Interpretation* (New York: Holt, Rinehart, & Winston, 1937); E.H. Erikson, *Childhood and Society* (New York: Norton, 1950).

[5] S. Onkvisit and J. Shaw, "Self-Concept and Image Congruence: Some Research and Managerial Implications," *Journal of Consumer Marketing* 4 (1987): 17.

[6] S. Coopersmith, *The Antecedent of Self-Esteem* (San Francisco, CA: Freeman, 1967); A. Bandura, "Self-Efficacy Mechanism in Human Agency," *American Psychologist* 37 (1982): 102–47; L. Steinberg, *Adolescence* (New York: McGraw-Hill, 1998).

[7] D.G. Gardner and J.L. Pierce, "Self-Esteem and Self-Efficacy within the Organizational Context: An Empirical Examination," *Group and Organization Management* 23, no. 1 (1998): 48–70.

[8] For a meta-analysis of a large number of studies in this area, see T.A. Judge and J.E. Bono, "Relationship of Core Self-Evaluations Traits—Self-Esteem, Generalized Self-Efficacy, Locus of Control, and Emotional Stability—With Job Satisfaction and Job Performance: A Meta-Analysis," *Journal of Applied Psychology* 86 (2001): 80–92.

[9] M. Rokeach, *Beliefs, Attitudes and Values: A Theory of Organization and Change* (San Francisco, CA: Jossey-Bass, 1968).

[10] E. Berne, *Games People Play: The Basic Handbook of Transactional Analysis* (New York: Ballantine Books, 1964, 1996).

11 R.F. Baumeister and D.M. Tice, "Anxiety and Social Exclusion," *Journal of Social and Clinical Psychology* 9 (1990): 165–95; M.B. Setterlund and P.M. Neidenthal, 1993, "Who Am I? Why Am I Here?: Self-Esteem, Self-Clarity, and Prototype Matching," *Journal of Personality and Social Psychology* 65 (1993): 769–80.

12 The term *self-fulfilling prophecy* was coined by Robert Merton in 1948. See R.K. Merton, "The Self-Fulfilling Prophecy," *Antioch Review* 8 (1948): 193–210.

13 I. Brown, "The Idea of Canada, on Display," *CTV News*, 14 February 2010, www.ctvolympics.ca.

14 K.T. Kishida, D. Yang, K.H. Quartz, S.R. Quartz, and P.R. Montague, "Implicit Signals in Small Group Settings and Their Impact on the Expressions of Cognitive Capacity and Associated Brain Responses," *Philosophical Transactions of the Royal Society* 367 (2012): 704–16, http://rstb.royalsocietypublishing.org/content/367/1589/704.abstract?sid=5fc88e56-8a71-4a9b-be8d-ad3fa88c631e.

15 "Study Suggests Group Settings Can Sometimes Diminish Expressions of Intelligence," Virginia Tech press release via EurekAlert!, 23 January 2012, http://therapytoronto.ca/news/?p=896.

16 N. Shields, "Self-Concept Is a Concept Worth Considering," *Physical and Occupational Therapy in Pediatrics*, 29 (2009): 23–6.

17 Mead, *Mind, Self, and Society*; Allport, *Personality*; Erikson, *Childhood and Society*.

18 P. Lockwood and Z. Zunda, "Outstanding Role Models: Do They Inspire or Demoralize Us?' in *Psychological Perspectives on Self and Identity*, ed. A. Tesser, R. Felson, and J. Suls (Washington, DC: American Psychological Association, 2000), 147–71.

19 B.D. Olson and D.L. Evans, "The Role of the Big Five Personality Dimensions in the Direction and Affective Consequences of Everyday Social Comparisons," *Personality and Social Psychology Bulletin* 25 (1999): 1498–1508.

20 Ibid.

21 J.V. Wood and K.I. Van der Zee, "Social Comparisons among Cancer Patients: Under What Conditions Are Comparisons Upward and Downward?," in *Health, Coping, and Well-Being*, ed. B.P. Buunk and F.X. Gibbons (Mahwah, NJ: Lawrence Erlbaum, 1997), 299–328.

22 C.S. Johnson and D.A. Stapel, "When Different Is Better: Performance Following Upward Comparison," *European Journal of Social Psychology* 37 (2007): 258–75; C.S. Johnson and D.A. Stapel, "No Pain, No Gain: The Conditions under which Upward Comparisons Lead to Better Performance," *Journal of Personality and Social Psychology* 92 (2007): 1051–67.

23 C.S. Johnson, M.I. Norton, L.D. Nelson, D. Stapel, and T.L. Chartrand, "The Downside of Feeling Better: Self-Regard Repair Harms Performance," *Self and Identity* 7 (2008): 262–77.

24 W.B. Swann, "To Be Adored or to Be Known: The Interplay of Self-Enhancement and Self-Verification," in *Handbook of Motivation and Cognition: Foundations of Social Behaviour*, ed. R.M. Sorrentino and E.T. Higgins (New York: Guilford Press, 1990), 408–48; S.E. McNulty and W.B. Swann, "Identity Negotiation in Roommate Relationships: The Self as Architect and Consequence of Social Reality," *Journal of Personality and Social Psychology* 67 (1994): 1012–23; W.B. Swann, "The Self and Identity Negotiation," *Interaction Studies* 6 (2005): 69–83.

25 M. Plunkett, "Serendipity and Agency in Narratives of Transition: Young and Women," in *Turns in the Road: Narrative Studies of Lives in Transition*, ed. D.P. McAdams, R. Josselson, and A. Lieblich (Washington, DC: American Psychological Association, 2001), 151–75.

26 A.D. Cast, J.E. Stetts, and P.J. Burke, "Does the Self Conform to the Views of Others?," *Social Psychology Quarterly* 62 (1999): 68–82.

27 C.S. Ellis-Hill, "Change in Identity and Self-Concept: A New Theoretical Approach to Recovery Following a Stroke," *Clinical Rehabilitation* 14 (2000): 279–87.

28 E.T. Cotter and E.W. Gonzalez, "Self-Concept in Older Adults: An Integrative Review of Empirical Literature," *Holistic Nursing Practice* 23 (2009): 335–48.

29 G.A. Kelly, *The Psychology of Personal Constructs* (New York: Norton, 1955); A. Friedman, "Toward a Sociology of Perception: Sight, Sex, and Gender," *Cultural Sociology* 5, no. 2: 187–206.

30 C.H. Cooley, *Human Nature and the Social Order* (New York: Scribner's, 1902).

31 S. Krashinsky and H. Sung, "Do You Love or Hate Dove's New Viral Campaign?," *Globe and Mail*, 18 April 2013, www.theglobeandmail.com/report-on-business/video/video-do-you-love-or-hate-doves-new-viral-campaign/article11369812.

32 R.B. Felson and M.A. Zielinsky, "Children's Self-Esteem and Parental Support," *Journal of Marriage and the Family* 61 (1989): 727–35.

33 S.S. Luthar and S.J. Latendresse, "Children of the Affluent," *Current Directions in Psychological Science* 14 (2005): 49–53.

34 J.H. Fouts, "Birth Order, Age Spacing, IQ Differences, and Family Relations," *Journal of Marriage and the Family*, 42 (1980): 517–31.

35 Ibid.

36 A. Susman-Stillman, M. Kalkoske, and B. Egeland, "Infant Temperament and Maternal Sensitivity as Predictors of Attachment Security," *Infant Behavior and Development* 19 (1996): 33–47; G.W. Holden, J.D. Stein, K.L. Ritchie, S.D. Harris, and E.N. Jouriles, "Parenting Behaviors and

Beliefs of Battered Women," in *Children Exposed to Marital Violence: Theory, Research, and Applied Issues*, ed. G.W. Holden, R. Geffner, and E.N. Jouriles (Washington, DC: American Psychological Association, 1998), 298–334; J.D. Osofsky, "Children as Invisible Victims of Domestic and Community Violence," in *Children Exposed to Marital Violence: Theory, Research, and Applied Issues*, ed. G.W. Holden, R. Geffner, and E.N. Jouriles (Washington, DC: American Psychological Association, 1998), 95–117; A.A. Levendosky and S.A. Graham-Bermann, "Behavioral Observations of Parenting in Battered Women," *Journal of Family Psychology* 14 (2000): 80–94; B.B. Rossman and J.G. Rea, "The Relation of Parenting Styles and Inconsistencies to Adaptive Functioning for Children in Conflictual and Violent Families," *Journal of Family Violence* 20 (2005): 261–77.

37 J. Borrego Jr, M.R. Gutow, S. Reicher, and C.H. Barker, "Parent–Child Interaction Therapy with Domestic Violence Populations," *Journal of Family Violence* 23 (2008): 495–505.

38 Sapphire, *Precious* movie commentary, presentation to the International Society for the Study of Trauma and Dissociation (ISSTD), Atlanta Hilton Hotel, 16 October 2010. See www.isst-d.org/education/precious-commentary.htm.

39 S.L. Murray, J.G. Holmes, and D.W. Griffin, "The Benefits of Positive Illusions: Idealization and the Construction of Close Relationships," *Journal of Personality and Social Psychology* 70 (1996): 79–98; S.L. Murray, J.G. Holmes, and D.W. Griffin, "The Self-Fulfilling Nature of Positive Illusions in Romantic Relationships: Love Is Not Blind but Prescient," *Journal of Personality and Social Psychology* 71 (1996): 1155–80.

40 S.L. Murray and J.G. Holmes, "Seeing the Self through a Partner's Eyes: Why Self-Doubts Turn into Relationship Insecurities," in *Psychological Perspectives on Self and Identity*, ed. A. Tesser, R. Felson, and J. Suls (Washington, DC: American Psychological Association, 2000), 173–97.

41 Ibid.

42 Ibid.

43 Swann, "The Self."

44 N.L. Collins, "Working Models of Attachment: Implications for Explanation, Emotion, and Behavior," *Journal of Personality and Social Psychology* 71 (1996): 810–32; B.R. Karney, T.N. Bradbury, F.D. Fincham, and K.T. Sullivan, "The Role of Negative Affectivity in the Association between Attributions and Marital Satisfaction," *Journal of Personality and Social Psychology* 66 (1994): 413–24; Murray and Holmes, "Seeing the Self."

45 J.W. Santrock, *Children* (New York: McGraw-Hill, 2008).

46 S. Boesveld, "Anti-Bullying Programs: Ignored and Insufficient," *Globe and Mail*, 22 February 2010, www.globeandmail.com.

47 M. Shah, "Facebook Launches Anti-bullying Campaign," *Sun News*, 15 November 15 2012, www.sunnewsnetwork.ca/sunnews/sciencetech/archives/2012/11/20121115-094350.html.

48 M. Mandel, "Fatal Bullying Case Goes to Court," *Toronto Sun*, 21 November 2011, www.torontosun.com/2011/11/21/fatal-bullying-case-goes-to-court.

49 "8 Ontario Girls Arrested in High School Bullying Case," *CBC News*, 19 October 2012, www.cbc.ca/news/canada/toronto/story/2012/10/19/london-bullying-arrests-girls-cyber.html.

50 J. O'Hara and M. Podgorny, "Supreme Court Rules Privacy Interest of Minors Trumps Freedom of the Press in Cyber-bullying Case," *McMillan*, October 2012, www.mcmillan.ca/Supreme-Court-rules-privacy-interest-of-minors-trumps-freedom-of-the-press-in-cyberbullying-case.

51 R. Rosenthal and L. Jacobson, *Pygmalion in the Classroom: Teacher Expectation and Pupils' Intellectual Development*, (New York: Holt, Rinehart, and Winston, 1968).

52 See, for example, J.B. Hinnant, M. O'Brien, and S.R. Ghazarian, "The Longitudinal Relations of Teacher Expectations to Achievement in the Early School Years," *Journal of Educational Psychology* 101 (2009): 662–70.

53 R. Rosenthal and D.B. Rubin, "Interpersonal Expectancy Effects: The First 345 Studies," *Behavioural and Brain Sciences* 1 (1978): 377–415.

54 L. Jussim and K.D. Harber, "Teacher Expectations and Self-fulfilling Prophecies: Knowns and Unknowns, Resolved and Unresolved Controversies," *Personality and Social Psychology Review* 9 (2005): 131–55.

55 M.R. Hebl and E.B. King, "You Are What You Wear: An Interactive Demonstration of the Self-Fulfilling Prophecy," *Teaching of Psychology* 31 (2004): 260–2.

56 T.L. Good and S.L. Nichols, "Expectancy Effects in the Classroom: A Special Focus on Improving the Reading Performance of Minority Students in First-Grade Classrooms," *Educational Psychologist* 36 (2001): 113–26.

57 R.H. Barnsley and P.E. Barnsley, "Hockey Success and Birthdate: The Relative Age Effect," *Canadian Association for Health, Physical Education, and Recreation Journal* 51 (1985): 23–8.

58 T.E. Daniel and C.T.L. Janssen, "More on the Relative Age Effect," *Canadian Association for Health, Physical Education, and Recreation Journal* 53 (1987): 21–4.

59 A.H. Thompson, R.H. Barnsley, and G. Stebelsky, "Born to Play Ball: The Relative Age Effect and Major League Baseball," *Sociology of Sport Journal* 8 (1991): 146–51.

60 J. Hansford, "I Am Aboriginal Campaign Builds Self-Esteem," *Windspeaker* 7, no. 4 (2009), http://imap.ammsa.com/publications/windspeaker/i-am-aboriginal-campaign-builds-self-esteem.

61 Ibid.

62 Ibid.

63 B. Wadenstein and G. Ahlström, "Ethical Values in Personal Assistance: Narratives of People with Disabilities," *Nursing Ethics* 16 (2009): 759–74.

64 Shields, "Self-Concept."

65 J.S. Livingston, "Pygmalion in Management," *Harvard Business Review* (September–October 1988), reprinted as an *HBR* classic with a retrospective comment in 2003.

66 Ibid.

67 Ibid.

68 L. Eichler, "How to Flex Your Confidence Muscle," *Globe and Mail*, 17 February 2012, www.theglobeandmail.com/report-on-business/careers/career-advice/leah-eichler/how-to-flex-your-confidence-muscle/article2342361.

69 J.M. Cohoon and W. Aspray, eds, *Women and Information Technology: Research on Under-Representation* (Boston: MIT Press, 2006); L. Knight, "Wanted: Less Excuses and More Competitive Women," *Forbes*, 1 October 2012, www.forbes.com/sites/forbeswomanfiles/2012/01/10/wanted-less-excuses-and-more-competitive-women.

70 Eichler, "How to Flex."

71 D.J. Kelley, C.G. Brush, P.G. Greene, and Y. Litovsky, "The 2010 Women's Report," *Global Entrepreneurship Monitor*, 6 January 2012, www.gemconsortium.org/news/757/gem-2010-womens-report.

72 S. Garner, "A Closer Look at Female Entrepreneurship and Success," GoForth Institute, 4 February 2012, http://canadianentrepreneurtraining.com/a-closer-look-at-female-entrepreneurship-and-success.

73 V. Milazzo, *Wicked Success Is Inside Every Woman* (Hoboken, NJ: Wiley, 2011).

74 V. von Pfetten, "Prostitution: A User's Manual," *Huffington Post*, 11 March 2008, www.huffingtonpost.com/2008/03/11/prostitution-a-users-ma_n_90788.html.

75 F. Xue, S. Zhou, and P. Zhou, "Effects of Ideal Body Images—Translatable across Gender and Culture?" (paper presented at the annual meeting of the International Communication Association, San Diego, CA, 27 May 2003).

76 D.G. McDonald and H. Kim, "When I Die, I Feel Small: Electronic Game Characters and the Social Self," *Journal of Broadcasting and Electronic Media* 45 (2001): 241–58.

77 S. Boden, "Dedicated Followers of Fashion? The Influence of Popular Culture on Children's Social Identities," *Media, Culture, and Society* 28 (2006): 289–98.

78 M.C. Martin and P.F. Kennedy, "Advertising and Social Comparison: Consequences for Female Preadolescents and Adolescents," *Psychology and Marketing* 10 (1993): 513–30.

79 A. Garner, H.M. Sterk, and S. Adams, "Narrative: Analysis of Sexual Etiquette in Teenage Magazines," *Journal of Communication* 48 (1998): 59–78.

80 J. Wood, "Want to Get Rid of Negative Thoughts? Throw Them Away," *Psych Central*, 2012, http://psychcentral.com/news/2012/11/27/want-to-get-rid-of-negative-thoughts-throw-them-away/48160.html.

81 Ibid.

82 A. Ellis, *Overcoming Destructive Beliefs, Feelings, and Behaviors: New Directions for Rational Emotive Behavior Therapy* (New York: Prometheus Books, 2001).

83 A.C. Downs and S.K. Harrison, "Embarrassing Age Spots or Just Plain Ugly? Physical Attractiveness Stereotyping as an Instrument of Sexism on American Television Commercials," *Sex Roles* 13 (1985): 9–19.

84 B. Silverstein, L. Perdue, B. Peterson, and E. Kelly, "The Role of the Mass Media in Promoting a Thin Standard of Bodily Attractiveness for Women," *Sex Roles* 14 (1986): 519–32; B. Silverstein, B. Peterson, and L. Perdue, "Some Correlates of the Thin Standards of Bodily Attractiveness for Women," *International Journal of Eating Disorders* 5 (1986): 895–905. See filmmaker Jean Kilbourne's *Killing Us Softly 4: Advertising's Image of Women* (Northhampton, MA: Media Education Foundation, 2010) for a more recent analysis of the effects of idealized depictions of women in advertisements.

85 D.M. Garner, P.E. Garfinkel, D. Schwartz, and M. Thompson, "Cultural Expectations of Thinness in Women," *Psychological Reports* 47 (1980): 483–91.

86 L. Percy and M.R. Lautman, "Advertising, Weight Loss, and Eating Disorders," in *Attention and Affect in Response to Advertising*, ed. E.M. Clark and T.C. Brock (Hilldale, NJ: Lawrence Erlbaum Associates, 1994), 301–11.

87 A.E. Andersen and L. DiDomenico, "Diet vs Shape Content of Popular Male and Female Magazines: A Dose-Response Relationship to the Incidence of Eating Disorders?," *International Journal of Eating Disorders* 11 (1992): 283–7.

88 P.R. Owen and E. Laurel-Seller, "Weight and Shape Ideals: Thin Is Dangerously In," *Journal of Applied Social Psychology* 30 (2000): 979–90.

89 A. Proud, "How Does She Do It! Megan Fox Shows Off Her Incredible Post-baby Figure in Unforgiving Leggings," *Mail Online*, 22 November 2012, www.dailymail.co.uk/tvshowbiz/article-2236676/Megan-Fox-shows-incredible-post-baby-figure-unforgiving-leggings.html.

90 J. Coupland, "Time, the Body, and the Reversibility of Ageing: Commodifying the Decade," *Ageing and Society* 29 (2009): 953–76.

91 V. Low, "What Is a Cougar Exactly?," Plenty of Fish forum, 6 November 2007, http://forums.plentyoffish.com/datingPosts7531027.aspx.

92 T.F. Cash and P.E. Henry, "Women's Body Images: The Results of a National Survey in the USA," *Sex Roles* 33 (1995): 19–28; C.R. Kalodner, "Media Influences on Male

and Female Non-eating Disordered College Students: A Significant Issue," *Eating Disorders* 5 (1997): 47–57; E. Stice and H.E. Shaw, "Adverse Effects of the Media Portrayed Thin-Ideal on Women and Linkages to Bulimic Symptomatology," *Journal of Social and Clinical Psychology* 13 (1994): 288–308.

93 J. Rabak-Wagener, J. Eickhoff-Shemeck, and L. Kelly-Vance, "The Effect of Media Analysis on Attitudes and Behaviors Regarding Body Image among College Students," *Journal of American College Health* 47 (1998): 29–35.

94 C.M. Peat, N.L. Peyerl, and J.J. Muehlenkamp, "Body Image and Eating Disorders in Older Adults: A Review," *The Journal of General Psychology* 135 (2008): 343–58.

95 M.A. Graham, C. Eich, B. Kephart, and D. Peterson, "Relationship among Body Image, Sex, and Popularity of High School Students," *Perceptual Motor Skills* 90 (2000): 1187–93.

96 M. Tiggemann, "Media Influences on Body Image Development," in *Body Image: A Handbook of Theory, Research, and Clinical Practice*, ed. T.F. Cash and T. Pruzinsky (New York: Guilford Press, 2002), 91–98; M. Tiggemann, "Media Exposure, Body Dissatisfaction, and Disordered Eating: Television and Magazines Are Not the Same!" *European Eating Disorders Review* 11 (2003): 418–30; M. Tiggemann, "Television and Adolescent Body Image: The Role of Program Content and Viewing Motivation," *Journal of Social and Clinical Psychology* 24 (2005): 361–81. Also, for a meta-analytic review, see L.M. Groesz, M.P. Levine, and S.K. Murnen, "The Effect of Experimental Presentation of Thin Media Images on Body Satisfaction: A Meta-analytic Review," *International Journal of Eating Disorders* 31 (2002): 1–16; or see A. Hendriks, *Examining the Impact of Repeated Exposure to Ideal Mediated Body Images on Body Satisfaction, Self-Esteem, and Disordered Eating in Females* (PhD dissertation, University of Arizona, 2002), Dissertation Abstracts International 63 (2002): 1173.

97 D. Garner, "Survey Says: Body Image Poll Results," *Psychology Today*, 1 February 1997, www.psychologytoday.com.

98 R. Galler, *Pleasure and Danger: Exploring Female Sexuality* (Boston: Routledge & Kegan Paul Books, 1984); S.D. Stone, "The Myth of Bodily Perfection," *Disability and Society* 10 (1995): 413–24.

99 D.K. Eaton et al., *Youth Risk Behavior Surveillance—United States, 2005.* (Atlanta, GA: National Center for Chronic Disease Prevention and Health Promotion, Centers for Disease Control and Prevention, 9 June 2006).

100 L. Nguyen, "Celebrity Pregnancies Blamed for Eating Disorders among Pregnant Canadians," Canadian Press, 23 July 2012, www.canada.com/health/story.html?id=6975166.

101 K. Harrison, "The Body Electric: Thin-Ideal Media and Eating Disorders in Adolescents," *Journal of Communication* 50 (2000): 119–44; Hendriks, *Examining the Impact.*

102 H.D. Posavac, S.S. Posovac, and E. Posovac, "Exposure to Media Images of Female Attractiveness and Concern with Body Weight among Young Women," *Sex Roles* 38 (1998): 187–201; L.J. Heinberg and J.K. Thompson, "Body Image and Televised Images of Thinness and Attractiveness: A Controlled Laboratory Investigation," *Journal of Social and Clinical Psychology* 14 (1995): 325–38; T.C.J. Nio, *Cultivation and Social Comparison of the Thin-Ideal Syndrome: The Effects of Media Exposure on Body Image Disturbance and the State Self-Esteem of College Women* (PhD dissertation, Southern Illinois University Carbondale, 2003), Dissertation Abstracts International 64 (2003): 2688; J. Blechert, T. Nickert, D. Caffier, and B. Tuschen-Caffier, "Social Comparison and Its Relation to Body Dissatisfaction in Bulimia Nervosa: Evidence from Eye Movements," *Psychosomatic Medicine* 71 (2009): 907–12; D.A. Hargreaves and M. Tiggemann, "Muscular Ideal Media Images and Men's Body Image: Social Comparison Processing and Individual Vulnerability," *Psychology of Men and Masculinity* 10 (2009): 109–19.

103 E. Goffman, *The Presentation of Self in Everyday Life* (New York: The Overlook Press, 1959); W.B. Swann, "Identity Negotiation: Where Two Roads Meet," *Journal of Personality and Social Psychology* 53 (1987): 1038–51; McNulty and Swann, "Identity Negotiation in Roommate Relationships."

104 C.S. Lamb, L.A. Jackson, P.B. Cassiday, and D.J. Priest, "Body Figure Preferences of Men and Women: A Comparison of Two Generations," *Sex Roles* 28 (1993): 345–58.

105 J.K. Thompson, "Body Shape Preferences: Effects of Instructional Protocol and Level of Eating Disturbances," *International Journal of Eating Disorders* 10 (1991): 193–8.

106 Nguyen, "Celebrity Pregnancies."

107 Ibid.

108 S. Grogan and H. Richards, "Body Image: Focus Group with Boys and Men," *Men and Masculinities* 4 (2002): 219–23; G. Cohane and H.G. Pope Jr, "Body Image in Boys: A Review of the Literature," *The International Journal of Eating Disorders* 29 (2001): 373–9; D.R. McCreary and D.K. Sasse, "An Exploration of the Drive for Muscularity in Adolescent Boys and Girls," *Journal of American College Health* 48 (2000): 297–304.

109 Rabak-Wagener et al., "The Effect of Media Analysis."

110 M. Tiggemann, Y. Martins, and A. Kirkbride, "Oh to Be Lean and Muscular: Body Image Ideals in Gay and Heterosexual Men," *Psychology of Men and Masculinity* 8

(2007): 15–24; M.P. McCabe and L.A. Ricciardelli, "Body Image Dissatisfaction among Males across the Lifespan: A Review of Past Literature," *Journal of Psychosomatic Research* 56 (2004): 675–85.

[111] M.P. McCabe and L.A. Ricciardelli, "A Longitudinal Study of Body Change Strategies among Adolescent Males," *Journal of Youth and Adolescence* 32 (2003): 105–13; McCabe and Ricciardelli, "Body Image Dissatisfaction."

[112] D. Schooler and M.L. Ward, "Average Joes: Men's Relationships with Media, Real Bodies, and Sexuality," *Psychology of Men and Masculinity* 7 (2006): 27–41; S.J. Duggan and D.R. McCreary, "Body Image, Eating Disorders, and the Drive for Muscularity in Gay and Heterosexual Men: The Influence of Media Images," *Journal of Homosexuality* 47 (2004): 45–58.

[113] R. Olivardia, H.G. Pope Jr, J.J. Borowiecki, and G. Cochane, "Biceps and Body Image: The Relationship Between Muscularity and Self-Esteem, Depression, and Eating Disorder Symptoms," *Psychology of Men and Masculinity* 5 (2004): 112–20; G. Cafri, J. Strauss, and J. K. Thompson, "Male Body Image: Satisfaction and Its Relationship to Well-Being Using the Somatomorphic Matrix," *International Journal of Men's Health* 1 (2002): 215–31; R. Olivardia, "Body Image and Muscularity," in *Body Image: A Handbook of Theory, Research, and Clinical Practice*, ed. T.F. Cash and T. Pruzinsky (New York: Guilford Press, 2002).

[114] R.D. Schope, "Who's Afraid of Growing Old? Gay and Lesbian Perceptions of Aging," *Journal of Gerontological Social Work* 45 (2005): 23–38.

[115] I. Tossell, "Naked Guy. Click. Naked Guy." *Globe and Mail*, 14 February 2010, www.the globeandmail.com.

[116] J. Raskauskas and A.D. Stoltz, "Involvement in Traditional and Electronic Bullying among Adolescents," *Developmental Psychology* 43 (2007): 564–75.

[117] R. Bjerke and P. Polegato, "How Well Do Advertising Images of Health and Beauty Travel across Cultures? A Self-Concept Perspective," *Psychology and Marketing* 23 (2006): 865–84.

[118] Xue, Zhou, and Zhou, "Effects of Ideal Body Images."

[119] J.M. Taylor, C. Gilligan, and A.M. Sullivan, *Between Voice and Silence: Women and Girls, Race and Relationship* (Cambridge, MA: Harvard University Press, 1995).

[120] K. Parnell, R. Sargent, S.H. Thompson, S.F. Duhe, R.F. Valois, and R.C. Kemper, "Black and White Adolescent Females' Perceptions of Ideal Body Size," *Journal of School Health* 66 (1996): 112–8.

[121] M. Milkie, "Social Comparisons, Reflected Appraisals, and Mass Media: The Impact of Pervasive Beauty Images on Black and White Girls' Self Concepts," *Social Psychology Quarterly* 62 (1999): 190–210.

[122] P.H. Collins, *Black Feminist Thought: Knowledge, Consciousness, and the Politics of Empowerment* (New York: Routledge, 1990); B. Greene, "Africa American Women," in *Woman of Color: Integrating Ethnic and Gender Identities in Psychotherapy*, ed. L. Comas-Diaz and B. Greene (New York: Guilford), 10–29.

[123] V.L. De Francisco and A. Chatham-Carpenter, "Self in Community: African American Women's Views of Self-Esteem," *The Howard Journal of Communications* 11 (2000): 73–92.

[124] G.R. Henriques, L.G. Calhoun, and A. Cann, "Ethnic Differences in Women's Body Satisfaction: An Experimental Investigation," *Journal of Social Psychology* 136 (1996): 689–97.

[125] S. Vazire, "Who Knows What about A Person? The Self–Other Knowledge Asymmetry (SOKA) Model," *Journal of Personality and Social Psychology* 98 (2010): 281–300.

[126] D.L. Stewart, "Perceptions of Multiple Identities among Black College Students," *Journal of College Student Development* 50 (2009): 253–70.

[127] D.E. Hamachek, *Encounters with Others: Interpersonal Relationships and You* (New York: Holt, Rinehart and Winston, 1982, cited in R. B. Adler, L.B. Rosenfeld, R.F. Proctor II, & C. Winder, *Interplay: The Process of Interpersonal Communication*, 3rd Canadian edition (Toronto: Oxford University Press, 2012): 49

[128] J.S. Jackson, W.R. McCullough, and G. Gurin, "Family, Socialization, Environment, and Identity Development in Black Americans," in *Black Families*, ed. H.P. McAdoo (Thousand Oaks, CA: Sage, 1997), 252–66.

[129] De Francisco and Chatham-Carpenter, "Self in Community."

[130] Ibid.

[131] A.C.H. Szeto, R.M. Sorrentino, S. Yasunaga, Y. Otsubo, S. Kouhara, and I. Sasayama, "Using the Implicit Association Test across Cultures: A Case of Implicit Self-Esteem in Japan and Canada," *Asian Journal of Social Psychology* 12 (2009): 211–20.

[132] De Francisco and Chatham-Carpenter, "Self in Community."

[133] M.S. Kim, *Non-Western Perspectives on Human Communication: Implications for Theory and Practice* (Thousand Oaks, CA: Sage Publications, 2002).

[134] See, for example, S.E. Taylor and J.D. Brown, "Illusion and Well-Being: A Social Psychological Perspective on Mental Health," *Psychological Bulletin* 103 (1988): 193–210.

[135] See, for example, S. Kitayama and M. Karasama, "Implicit Self-Esteem in Japan: Name Letters and Birthday Numbers," *Personality and Social Psychology Bulletin* 23 (1997): 736–42.

[136] S. Kitayama, H. Takagi, and H. Matsumoto, "Seiko to Shippai No Kiin: Nihonteki Jiko No Bunka-Shinrigaku" ["Causal Attribution of Success and Failure: Cultural Psychology of Japanese Selves"], *Japanese Psychological Review* 38 (1995): 247–80.

[137] E.C. Chang and K. Asakawa, "Cultural Variations on Optimistic and Pessimistic Bias for Self versus a Sibling: Is There Evidence for Self-Enhancement in the West and for Self-Criticism in the East When the Referent Group Is Specified?," *Journal of Personality and Social Psychology* 83 (2003): 569–81.

[138] J.J. Bauer and H.A. Wayment, "The Psychology of the Quiet Ego," in *Transcending Self-Interest: Psychological Explorations of the Quiet Ego*, ed. H.A. Wayment and J.J. Bauer (Washington, DC: American Psychological Association, 2000), 9.

[139] D. Harris, F. Biberica, and S. Wright, "Happiness, Inc.: Wayne Dyer Lives His Positive Thinking Philosophy," ABC News, 29 November 2009, http://abcnews.go.com/Health/positive-thinking-treat-lecturer-authors-chronic-lymphocytic-leukemia/story?id=9201959.

[140] W.W. Dyer, *Wishes Fulfilled: Mastering the Art of Manifesting* (Carlsbad, CA: Hay House, 2012).

CHAPTER 3

[1] This box is based on A. Janca and C. Bullen, "The Aboriginal Concept of Time and Its Mental Health Implications," *Australasian Psychiatry* 11 (2003): S40–4.

[2] A. Friedman, "Toward a Sociology of Perception: Sight, Sex, and Gender," *Cultural Sociology* 5, no. 2 (2011): 187–206.

[3] See, for example, S. Soto-Faraco, "Multisensory Contributions to the Perception of Vibrotactile Events," *Behavioural Brain Research* 196, no. 2 (2009): 145–54; L. Shams and R. Kim, "Crossmodal Influences on Visual Perception," *Physics of Life Reviews* 7, no. 3 (2010): 269–84.

[4] M. Auvray and C. Spence, "The Multisensory Nature of Flavor," *Consciousness and Cognition* 17, no. 3 (2008): 1016–31.

[5] B. Stuckey, "The Taste of Sound," *Salon*, 11 March 2012, www.salon.com/2012/03/11/the_taste_of_sound. Also see B. Stuckey, *Taste What You're Missing: The Passionate Eater's Guide to Getting More from Every Bite* (New York: Free Press, 2012).

[6] Stuckey, "The Taste of Sound."

[7] P.J. Kellman and P. Garrigan, "Perceptual Learning and Human Expertise," *Physics of Life Reviews* 6, no. 2 (2009): 53–84.

[8] Moody Institute of Science, *Sense Perception* (Whittier, CA: Science Institute, 1968), VHS.

[9] S. Ferguson and S.D. Ferguson, "High Resolution Vision Prosthesis Systems: Research after 15 Years," *Journal of Visual Impairment and Blindness* 80 (1986): 523–7.

[10] B.A. Wright and M.B. Fitzgerald, "Sound-Discrimination Learning and Auditory Displays." *Proceedings of the 2003 International Conference on Auditory Display*, Boston, MA, 6–9 July 2003.

[11] E.E. Jones, *Interpersonal Perception* (New York: Freeman, 1990); S.E. Taylor, A.P. Letitia, and D.O. Sears, *Social Psychology*, 10th ed. (Upper Saddle River, NJ: Prentice Hall, 2000).

[12] J. Bruner and L. Postman, "On the Perception of Incongruity: A Paradigm," *Journal of Personality* 18 (1949): 206–23.

[13] E.F. Loftus, *Eyewitness Testimony*, rev. ed. (Cambridge, MA: Harvard University Press, 1996).

[14] A. Koestler, *The Act of Creation* (New York: MacMillan, 1964).

[15] S. Penrod, E.F. Loftus, and J. Winkler, "The Reliability of Eyewitness Testimony: A Psychological Perspective," in *The Psychology of the Courtroom*, ed. N. Kerr and R. Bray (New York: Academic Press, 1982), 119–68.

[16] B. Malinowski, *Argonauts of the Western Pacific: An Account of Native Enterprise and Adventure in the Archipelagoes of Melanesian New Guinea* (London: Routledge and Kegan Paul, 1922).

[17] Friedman, "Toward a Sociology of Perception."

[18] Janca and Bullen, "The Aboriginal Concept of Time."

[19] M. Henneberger, "Out, Damned Spot: The 'Mindbugs' of Bias that Sneak into Our Brains," *Washington Post*, 7 February 2013, www.washingtonpost.com/blogs/she-the-people/wp/2013/02/07/out-damned-spot-the-mindbugs-of-bias-that-sneak-into-our-brains/?wpisrc=nl_headlines.

[20] T. Masuda and R.E. Nisbett, "Culture and Change Blindness," *Cognitive Science* 30 (2006): 381–99.

[21] E. Zerubavel, *Social Mindscapes: An Invitation to Cognitive Sociology* (Cambridge, MA: Harvard University Press, 1997); T. Laqueur, *Making Sex: Body and Gender from the Greeks to Freud* (Cambridge, MA: Harvard University Press, 1990).

[22] T. Kuhn, *The Structure of Scientific Revolutions* (Chicago: University of Chicago Press, 1996 [1962]).

[23] A.-M. Leach, B.J. Cutler, and L. Van Wallendael, "Lineups and Eyewitness Identification," *Annual Review of Law and Social Science* 5 (2009): 157–78; H.F. Fradella, "Why Judges Should Admit Expert Testimony on the Unreliability of Eyewitness Testimony," *Federal Courts Law Review* 3 (2006): 1–29.

[24] See www.innocenceproject.org.

[25] L.O. Shermer, K.C. Rose, and A. Hoffman, "Perceptions and Credibility: Understanding the Nuances of Eyewitness Testimony," *Journal of Contemporary Criminal Justice* 27, no. 2 (2011): 183–203; G.L. Wells and D.S. Quinlivan, "Suggestive Eyewitness Identification Procedures and the Supreme Court's Reliability Test in Light of Eyewitness Science: 30 Years Later," *Law and Human Behavior* 33 (2009): 1–24; H.F. Fradella, "Editor's Introduction: Forensic Science and Criminal Justice," *Journal of Contemporary Criminal Justice* 27, no. 2 (2011): 128–32.

26 N. Brewer and A. Burke, "Effects of Testimonial Inconsistencies and Eyewitness Confidence on Mock-Juror Judgments," *Law and Human Behavior* 26 (2002): 353–64; N.D. Brewer and G. Wells, "Eyewitness Identification," *Current Directions in Psychological Science* 20, no. 1 (2011): 24–7; Leach et al., "Lineups and Eyewitness Identification."

27 G.B. Moskowitz and P. Li, "Egalitarian Goals Trigger Stereotype Inhibition: A Proactive Form of Stereotype Control," *Journal of Experimental Social Psychology* 47, no. 1 (2011): 103–16.

28 B. Stewart and B. Payne, "Bringing Automatic Stereotyping under Control: Implementation Intentions as Efficient Means of Thought Control," *Personality and Social Psychology Bulletin* 34, no. 10 (2008): 1332–45.

29 P.S. Jaya and M. Porter, "Asking for Apples from a Lemon Tree: Some Experiences of Immigrant Women in Newfoundland and Labrador," in *Immigrant Women in Atlantic Canada: Challenges, Negotiations, and Re-Constructions*, ed. E. Tastsoglou and P.S. Jaya (Toronto: Canadian Scholars Press, Women's Press, 2011), 87–118.

30 M. Carrasco, "Visual Attention: The Past 25 Years," *Vision Research* 51 (2011): 1484–1525.

31 For reviews, see D.M. Beck and S. Kastner, "Top-Down and Bottom-Up Mechanisms in Biasing Competition in the Human Brain," *Vision Research* 49 (2009): 1154–65; also J.H. Reynolds and L. Chelazzi, "Attentional Modulation of Visual Processing," *Annual Review of Neuroscience* 27 (2004): 611–47.

32 M. Csikszentmihalyi, *Flow: The Psychology of Optimal Experience* (NY: Harper, 2008).

33 K.F. Muenzinger, *The Psychology of Behavior* (New York: Harper, 1942).

34 J.S.P. Macdonald and N. Lavie, "Load Induced Blindness," *Journal of Experimental Psychology* 34, no. 5 (2008): 1078–91.

35 For more on gender and selective perception, see D.J. Herrmann, M. Crawford, and M. Holdsworth, "Gender Linked Differences in Everyday Memory Performance," *British Journal of Psychology* 83, no. 2 (1992): 221–31; E.F. Loftus, M.R. Banaji, J.W. Schooler, and R. Foster, "Who Remembers What? Gender Differences in Memory," *Michigan Quarterly Review* 26 (1987): 64–85.

36 P. Powers, J. Andriks, and E. Loftus, "The Eyewitness Accounts of Males and Females," *Journal of Applied Psychology* 64, no. 3 (1979): 339–47.

37 Friedman, "Toward a Sociology of Perception"; G. Kleege, *Sight Unseen* (New Haven, CT: Yale University Press, 1999); M. Jay, "Sartre, Merleau-Ponty, and the Search for a New Ontology of Sight," in *Modernity and the Hegemony of Vision*, ed. D. Levin (Berkeley, CA: University of California Press, 1993), 143–85; G. Lakoff and M. Johnson, *Metaphors We Live By* (Chicago: University of Chicago Press, 1980).

38 Friedman, "Toward a Sociology of Perception."

39 E.M. Rogers and R. Agarwala-Rogers, *Communication in Organizations* (New York: Free Press, 1976), 91.

40 J.E. Newhagen and B. Reeves, "Emotion and Memory Responses for Negative Political Advertising: A Study of Television Commercials Used in the 1988 Presidential Election," in *Television and Political Advertising: Psychological Processes*, vol. 1 (Hillsdale, NJ: Lawrence Erlbaum, 1991), 197–220; J.L. Monahan, "Thinking Positively: Using Positive Affect when Designing Health Messages," in *Designing Health Messages: Approaches from Communication Theory and Public Health Practice*, ed. R.L. Parrott and E. Maibach (Thousand Oaks, CA: Sage, 1995), 81–98; N.H. Frijda, "The Laws of Emotion," *American Psychologist* 43 (1988): 349–58; G.M. Garramone, C.K. Atkin, B.E. Pinkleton, and R.T. Cole, "Effects of Negative Political Advertising on the Political Process," *Journal of Broadcasting and Electronic Media* 34 (1990): 299–311.

41 Leach et al., "Lineups and Eyewitness Identification."

42 W.J. Livesley and D.B. Bromley, *Person Perception in Childhood and Adolescence* (New York: J. Wiley, 1973).

43 T.A. Ito and G.R. Urland, "Race and Gender on the Brain: Electrocortical Measures of Attention to Race and Gender of Multiply Categorizable Individuals," *Journal of Personality and Social Psychology* 85 (2003): 616–26, cited in J. Ruscher and E. Hammer, "The Development of Shared Stereotypic Impressions in Conversation: An Emerging Model, Methods, and Extensions in Cross-Group Settings," *Journal of Language and Social Psychology* 25, no. 3 (2006): 221–43.

44 D.Y. Tsao and M.S. Livingstone, "Mechanisms of Face Perception," *Annual Review of Neuroscience* 31 (2008): 411.

45 L.J. Postman, J.S. Bruner, and E. McGinnies, "Personal Values as Selective Factors in Perception," *Journal of Abnormal and Social Psychology* 43 (1948): 142–54.

46 J. Senger, "Seeing Eye to Eye: Practical Problems of Perception," in *Intercom: Readings in Organizational Communication*, ed. S. Ferguson and S.D. Ferguson (Rochelle Park, NJ: Hayden Book, 1980): 144–5.

47 D.M. Buck and E.A. Plant, "Interorientation Interactions and Impressions: Does the Timing of Disclosure of Sexual Orientation Matter?," *Journal of Experimental Social Psychology* 47 (2011): 333–42

48 D.R. Ames, L.K. Kammrah, A. Suppes, and N. Bolger, "Not So Fast: The (Not-Quite-Complete) Dissociation between Accuracy and Confidence in Thin-Slice Impressions," *Personality and Social Psychology Bulletin* 36, no. 2 (2010): 264–77.

49 D.T. Gilbert, "How Mental Systems Believe," *American Psychologist* 46 (1991): 107–19; C. Hendrick and

A.F. Costantini, "Effects of Varying Trait Inconsistency and Response Requirements on the Primacy Effect in Impression Formation," *Journal of Personality and Social Psychology* 15 (1970): 158–64; Jones, *Interpersonal Perception.*

[50] H.M. Buckley and M.E. Roach, "Attraction as a Function of Attitudes and Dress," *Home Economics Research Journal* 10 (1981): 88–97.

[51] A.C. Brandt, R. Vonk, and A. van Knippenberg, "The Source Effect: Person Descriptions by Self versus Others Have Differential Effects on Impression Formation," *Personality and Social Psychology Bulletin* 35 (2009): 965–77.

[52] J.B. Walther, B. Van Der Heide, L. Hamel, and H. Shulman, "Self-Generated versus Other-Generated Statements and Impressions in Computer-Mediated Communication: A Test of Warranting Theory Using Facebook," *Communication Research* 36 (2009): 229–53; J.B. Walther and M.R. Parks, "Cues Filtered Out, Cues Filtered In: Computer-Mediated Communication and Relationships," in *Handbook of Interpersonal Communication*, 3rd ed., ed. M.L. Knapp and J.A. Daly (Thousand Oaks, CA: Sage, 2002), 529–63.

[53] A. El-Alayli, C.J. Myers, T.L. Petersen, and A.L. Lystad, "'I Don't Mean to Sound Arrogant, but . . .': The Effects of Using Disclaimers on Person Perception," *Personality and Social Psychology Bulletin* 34, no. 1 (2008): 130–43.

[54] The content of this box is adapted from pp. 47–50 of S. Ferguson, *Public Speaking in Canada: Building Competency in Stages* (Toronto: Oxford University Press, 2006). It references the documentary film *The Good Times Are Killing Me* (California and New York: TVTV, 1975), available online at http://mediaburn.org/video/the-good-times-are-killing-me-3. See also G.A. Miller, "The Magical Number Seven, Plus or Minus Two: Some Limits on Our Capacity for Processing Information," in *Readings in the Psychology of Cognition*, ed. R.C. Anderson and D.P. Ausubel (New York: Holt, Rinehart, and Winston, 1965), 241–67.

[55] B. Gawronski and E. Walther, "The TAR Effect: When the Ones Who Dislike Become the Ones Who Are Disliked," *Personality and Social Psychology Bulletin* 34, no. 9 (2008): 1276–89.

[56] N.C. Hartsock, "The Feminist Standpoint: Developing the Ground for a Specifically Feminist Historical Materialism," in *Discovering Reality: Feminist Perspectives on Epistemology, Metaphysics, Methodology, and Philosophy of Science*, ed. S. Harding and M.B. Hintikka (Dordrecht: Reidel, 1983), 283–310; J.T. Warren and D.L. Fassett, *Communication: A Critical/Cultural Introduction* (Thousand Oaks, CA: Sage, 2011).

[57] Based on Adam Green, "A Pickpocket's Tale: The Spectacular Thefts of Apollo Robbins," *New Yorker*, 7 January 2013, www.newyorker.com/reporting/2013/01/07/130107fa_fact_green#ixzz2JruqEIHP.

[58] See "Kirk Bloodsworth," *Innocence Project*, accessed 27 June 2013, www.innocenceproject.org/Content/Kirk_Bloodsworth.php. See also J. Wagner, "As Maryland Votes on Death Penalty Repeal, Exonerated Man Becomes a Living Reminder," *Washington Post*, 14 March 2013, www.washingtonpost.com/local/md-politics/as-maryland-votes-on-death-penalty-repeal-exonerated-man-becomes-a-living-reminder/2013/03/14/8fb87e84-8ca8-11e2-9838-d62f083ba93f_story.html?wpisrc=nl_headlines.

[59] N.C. Schaeffer, "Hardly Ever or Constantly: Group Comparisons Using Vague Qualifiers," *Public Opinion Quarterly* 55 (1991): 395.

[60] S. Schnall, K.D. Harber, J.K. Stefanucci, and D.R. Proffitt, "Social Support and the Perception of Geographical Slant," *Journal of Experimental Social Psychology* 44 (2008): 1246–55.

[61] M. Moore, *Fahrenheit 9/11* (Santa Monica, CA: Lions Gate, 2004), DVD.

[62] J. Terhaar, M.K. Boettger, C. Schwier, G. Wagner, A.K. Israel, and K.-J. Bär, "Increased Sensitivity to Heat Pain after Sad Mood Induction in Female Patients with Major Depression," *European Journal of Pain* 14 (2010): 559–63; M.K. Boettger, C. Schwier, and K.-J. Bär, "Sad Mood Increases Pain Sensitivity upon Thermal Grill Illusion Stimulation: Implications for Central Pain Processing," *Pain* 152 (2011): 123–30.

[63] S. Bambauer-Sachse and H. Gierl, "Can a Positive Mood Counterbalance Weak Arguments in Personal Sales Conversations," *Journal of Retailing and Consumer Services* 16 (2009): 190–6.

[64] S.K. Johnson, "Do You Feel What I Feel: Mood Contagion and Leadership Outcomes," *Leadership Quarterly* 20, no. 5 (2009): 814–27.

[65] J.P. Forgas, S.M. Laham, and P.T. Vargas, "Mood Effects on Eyewitness Memory: Affective Influences on Susceptibility to Misinformation," *Journal of Experimental Social Psychology* 41 (2005): 574–88; J.P. Forgas, "The Upside of Feeling Down: The Benefits of Negative Mood for Social Cognition and Social Behaviour," (paper presented at the Sydney Symposium of Social Psychology: Social Thinking and Interpersonal Behaviour, Sydney, Australia, 2011); J.P. Forgas, "Can Negative Affect Eliminate the Power of First Impressions? Affective Influences on Primacy and Recency Effects in Impression Formation," *Journal of Experimental Social Psychology* 47 (2011): 425–9.

[66] J.P. Forgas, "When Sad Is Better than Happy: Negative Affect Can Improve the Quality and Effectiveness of Persuasive Messages and Social Influence Strategies," *Journal of Experimental Social Psychology* 43 (2007): 513–28.

67 Forgas et al., "Mood Effects on Eyewitness Memory."

68 Forgas, "Can Negative Affect"; H. Bless and K. Fiedler, "Mood Regulation of Information Processing and Behavior," in *Affect in Social Thinking and Behavior*, ed. J.P. Forgas (New York: Psychology Press, 2006), 65–84; G.H. Bower, "Mood Congruity of Social Judgments," in *Emotion and Social Judgments*, ed. J.P. Forgas (Oxford: Pergamon Press, 1991), 31–55.

69 J.R. Huntsinger, J. Lun, S. Sinclair, and G.L. Clore, "Contagion without Contact: Anticipatory Mood Matching in Response to Affiliative Motivation," *Personality and Social Psychology Bulletin* 35, no. 7 (2009): 909–22.

70 E. Hatfield, J.T. Cacioppo, & and R.L. Rapson, *Emotional Contagion* (Cambridge, UK: Cambridge University Press, 1994); R. Neumann and F. Strack, "'Mood Contagion': The Automatic Transfer of Mood between Persons," *Journal of Personality and Social Psychology* 79 (2000): 211–223; Huntsinger et al., "Contagion without Contact."

71 A.P. Brief and H.M. Weiss, "Organizational Behavior: Affect in the Workplace," *Annual Review of Psychology* 53 (2002): 279–307.

72 R. Neumann and F. Strack, "'Mood Contagion.'"

73 P.M. Niedenthal, L.W. Barsalou, P. Winkielman, S. Krauth-Gruber, and F. Ric, "Embodiment in Attitudes, Social Perception, and Emotion," *Personality and Social Psychology Bulletin* 9, no. 3 (2005): 184–211; Huntsinger et al., "Contagion without Contact."

74 J.C. Biesanz, L.J. Human, A.-C. Paquin, M. Chan, K.L. Parisotto, J. Sarracino, and R.L. Gillis, "Do We Know When Our Impressions of Others Are Valid? Evidence for Realistic Accuracy Awareness in First Impressions of Personality," *Social Psychological and Personality Science* 2, no. 5 (2011): 452–9.

75 Ibid.

76 Huntsinger et al., "Contagion without Contact"; C. Anderson, D. Keltner, and O.P. John, "Emotional Convergence in Close Relationships," *Journal of Personality and Social Psychology* 84 (2003): 1054–68; Neumann and Strack, "'Mood Contagion'"; S. Oishi and H.W. Sullivan, "The Predictive Value of Daily vs Retrospective Well-Being Judgments in Relationship Stability," *Journal of Experimental Social Psychology* 42 (2006): 460–70.

77 Huntsinger et al., "Contagion without Contact."

78 R.S. Weill and G. Rees, "A New Taxonomy for Perceptual Filling-In," *Brain Research Reviews* 67 (2011): 40–55.

79 R. Rasmussen, A. Esgate, and D. Turner, "On Your Marks, Get Stereotyped, Go! Novice Coaches and Black Stereotypes in Sprinting," *Journal of Sport and Social Issues* 29, no. 4 (2005): 426–36.

80 N.O. Rule, N. Ambady, R.B. Adams, and C.N. Macrae, "Accuracy and Awareness in the Perception and Categorization of Male Sexual Orientation," *Journal of Personality and Social Psychology* 95 (2008): 1019–28; Buck and Plant, "Interorientation Interactions and Impressions"; V. Purdie-Vaughns, and R.P. Eibach, "Intersectional Invisibility: The Distinctive Advantages and Disadvantages of Multiple Subordinate-Group Identities, *Sex Roles* 59 (2008), 377–91.

81 S.J. Ko, C. Judd, and I. Blair, "What the Voice Reveals: Within- and Between-Category Stereotyping on the Basis of Voice," *Personality and Social Psychology Bulletin* 32, no. 6 (2006): 806–19.

82 S.J. Ko, C. Judd, and D. Stapel, "Stereotyping Based on Voice in the Presence of Individuating Information: Vocal Femininity Affects Perceived Competence but Not Warmth," *Personality and Social Psychology Bulletin* 35, no. 2 (2009): 198–211.

83 Ibid.

84 L. Jackson, V. Esses, and C. Burris, "Contemporary Sexism and Discrimination: The Importance of Respect for Men and Women," *Personality and Social Psychology Bulletin* 27, no. 1 (2001): 48–61.

85 T. Conley and B. Collins, "Gender, Relationship Status, and Stereotyping about Sexual Risk," *Personality and Social Psychology Bulletin* 28, no. 11 (2002): 1483–94.

86 A. Watson, V. Ottati, and P. Corrigan, "From Whence Comes Mental Illness Stigma?," *International Journal of Social Psychiatry* 49, no. 2 (2003): 142–57.

87 P. Veazie, "Projection, Stereotyping, and the Perception of Chronic Medical Conditions," *Chronic Illness* 2, no. 4 (2006): 303–10.

88 C. Ryan, D. Robinson, and L. Hausmann, "Stereotyping among Providers and Consumers of Public Mental Health Services," *Behavior Modification* 25, no. 3 (2001): 406–42.

89 "*Harry's Law* Canceled: NBC Pulls Plug on Kathy Bates Legal Drama," *Huffington Post*, 11 May 2012, www.huffingtonpost.com/2012/05/11/harrys-law-canceled-kathy-bates_n_1510785.html.

90 J.C. Turner, "Self-Categorization and the Self-Concept: A Social Cognitive Theory of Group Behavior," in *Advances in Group Processes; Theory and Research*, vol. 2, ed. E.J. Lawler (Greenwich, CT: JAI, 1985), 77–122; J.C. Turner and K.J. Reynolds, "Self-Categorization Theory," in *Handbook of Theories of Social Psychology*, vol. 2, ed. P.A.M. Van Lange, A.W. Kruglanski, and E.T. Higgins (Thousand Oaks, CA: Sage Publications, 2012): 399–17; D.R. Ames and E.C. Bianchi, "The Agreeableness Asymmetry in First Impressions: Perceivers' Impulse to (Mis)judge Agreeableness and How It Is Moderated by Power," *Personality and Social Psychology Bulletin* 34, no. 12 (2008): 1719–1736; A.J.C. Cuddy, S.T. Fiske, and P. Glick, "The BIAS Map: Behaviors from Intergroup Affect and Stereotypes,"

Journal of Personality and Social Psychology 92 (2007): 631–48.

[91] Buck and Plant, "Interorientation Interactions and Impressions."

[92] Buck and Plant, "Interorientation Interactions and Impressions"; E.A. Plant and P.G. Devine, "The Antecedents and Implications of Interracial Anxiety," *Personality and Social Psychology Bulletin* 29, no. 6 (2003): 790–801; E.A. Plant and D.A. Butz, "The Causes and Consequences of an Avoidance-Focus for Interracial Interactions," *Personality and Social Psychology Bulletin* 32 (2006): 833–46; R.K. Mallett, T.D. Wilson, and D.T. Gilbert, "Expect the Unexpected: Failure to Anticipate Similarities When Predicting the Quality of an Intergroup Interaction," *Journal of Personality and Social Psychology* 94 (2008): 265–77; J.N. Shelton, "Interpersonal Concerns in Social Encounters between Majority and Minority Group Members," *Group Processes and Intergroup Relations* 6 (2003): 171–85.

[93] J.A. Cameron and Y. Trope, "Stereotype-Biased Search and Processing of Information about Group Members," *Social Cognition* 22, no. 6 (2004): 650–72.

[94] S. Quadflieg, N. Flannigan, G.D. Waiter, B. Rossion, G.S. Wig, D.J. Turk, and C.N. Macrae, "Stereotype-Based Modulation of Person Perception," *NeuroImage* 57 (2011): 549–57. For additional information on stereotyping of gender and racial groups, see K. Kawakami and J. Dovidio, "The Reliability of Implicit Stereotyping," *Personality and Social Psychology Bulletin* 27, no. 2 (2001): 212–25.

[95] K. Kahn and P. Davies, "Differentially Dangerous? Phenotypic Racial Stereotypicality Increases Implicit Bias among Ingroup and Outgroup Members," *Group Processes and Intergroup Relations* 14, no. 4 (2011): 569–80.

[96] R.C. Hutter, R.J. Crisp, G.W. Humphreys, G.M. Waters, and G. Moffitt, "The Dynamics of Category Conjunctions," *Group Processes and Intergroup Relations* 12 (2009): 673–86.

[97] G. Ku, C. Wang, and A.D. Galinsky, "Perception through a Perspective-Taking Lens: Differential Effects on Judgment and Behavior," *Journal of Experimental Social Psychology* 46, no. 5 (2010): 792–8.

[98] T.F. Pettigrew and L. Tropp, "A Meta-analytic Test of Intergroup Contact Theory," *Journal of Personality and Social Psychology* 90 (2006): 751–83; R.K. Mallett and T. Wilson, "Increasing Positive Intergroup Contact," *Journal of Experimental Social Psychology* 46 (2010): 382–7; Plant and Butz, "Causes and Consequences."

[99] Ruscher and Hammer, "Development of Shared Stereotypic Impressions."

[100] C. Stangor, G. Sechrist, and J. Jost, "Changing Racial Beliefs by Providing Consensus Information," *Personality and Social Psychology Bulletin* 27, no. 4 (2001): 486–96.

[101] A.S. Waggoner, E.R. Smith, and E.C. Collins, "Person Perception by Active Versus Passive Perceivers," *Journal of Experimental Social Psychology* 45 (2009): 1028–31.

[102] I. Blair, "The Malleability of Automatic Stereotypes and Prejudice," *Personality and Social Psychology Review* 6, no. 3 (2002): 242–61; M. Monahan, "The Education of Racial Perception," *Philosophy and Social Criticism* 36, no. 2 (2010): 209–29; N. Wyer, "The Roles of Motivation and Ability in Controlling the Consequences of Stereotype Impression," *Personality and Social Psychology Bulletin* 26, no. 1 (2000): 13–25.

[103] A. Furnham, *The Psychology of Behaviour at Work* (Sussex, UK: Taylor & Francis, 1997); E. Goldstein, *Sensation and Perception* (San Francisco, CA: Brooks Cole, 1998).

[104] For a discussion of the importance of promoting intergroup harmony, as opposed to just focussing on differences, see B. Park and C. Judd, "Rethinking the Link between Categorization and Prejudice within the Social Cognition Perspective," *Personality and Social Psychology Review* 9, no. 2 (2005): 108–30.

[105] R.B. Adler, L.B. Rosenfeld, R.F. Proctor II, & C. Winder, *Interplay: The Process of Interpersonal Communication*, 3rd Canadian edition (Toronto: Oxford University Press, 2012).

[106] E.T. Hall, *Beyond Culture* (New York: Random House, 1976).

[107] E.B. Ryan, H. Giles, G. Bartolucci, and K. Henwood, "Psycholinguistic and Social Psychological Components of Communication by and with the Elderly," *Language and Communication* 6 (1986): 1–24.

[108] J. Lennox Terrion and M. Lagacé, "Communication as Precursor and Consequence of Subjective Social Capital in Older People: A New Perspective on the Communication Predicament Model," *Social Theory and Health* 6 (2008): 239–49.

CHAPTER 4

[1] B. Brumfield, "Who's Who on the Internet, Who Knows," *CNN Tech*, 17 January 2013, www.cnn.com/2013/01/17/tech/teo-online-identity/index.html?iid=article_sidebar.

[2] CNN Staff, "TV Show *Catfish* Focuses on Fake Internet Relationships," *CNN*, 17 January 2013, www.cnn.com/2013/01/16/sport/manti-teo-controversy-catfish/index.html.

[3] S. Stryker, "Identity Theory: Developments and Extensions," in *Self and Identity: Psychosocial Perspectives*, ed. K. Yardley and T. Honess (Chichester, UK: Wiley, 1987).

[4] R.J. Shavelson, J.J. Hubner, and G.C. Stanton, "Self-Concept: Validation of Construct Interpretations," *Review of Educational Research* 46 (1976): 407–41.

[5] J. Luft, *Group Processes: An Introduction to Group Dynamics* (Palo Alto, CA: National Press Books, 1970).

[6] J.M. Cheek and S.R. Briggs, "Self-Consciousness, Self-Monitoring, and Aspects of Identity" (paper presented at

the meeting of the American Psychological Association, Los Angeles, CA, 1981). Also see J.M. Cheek and S.R. Briggs, "Self-Consciousness and Aspects of Identity," *Journal of Research in Personality* 16 (1982): 401–8; E.E. Sampson, "Personality and the Location of Identity," *Journal of Personality* 46, (1978): 552–68; R. Hogan and J.M. Cheek, "Identity, Authenticity, and Maturity," in *Studies in Social Identity*, ed. T.R. Sarbin and K.E. Scheibe (New York: Praeger, 1983), 339–57; J.M. Cheek, "Identity Orientations and Self-Interpretation," in *Personality Psychology: Recent Trends and Emerging Directions*, ed. D.M. Buss and N. Cantor (New York: Springer-Verlag, 1989), 275–85; J.M. Cheek, L.R. Tropp, L.C. Chen, and M.K. Underwood, "Identity Orientations: Personal, Social, and Collective Aspects of Identity" (paper presented at the meeting of the American Psychological Association, Los Angeles, CA, 1994); J.M. Cheek, S.M. Smith, and L.R. Tropp, "Relational Identity Orientation: A Fourth Scale for the AIQ" (paper presented at the meeting of the Society for Personality and Social Psychology, Savannah, GA, 2002); K J. Gergen, *The Saturated Self: Dilemmas of Identity in Contemporary Life* (New York: Basic Books, 1991).

7 W. James, *The Principles of Psychology* (Cambridge, MA: Harvard University Press, 1890).

8 R.A. Neimeyer, "Narrative Disruptions in the Construction of the Self," in *Constructions of Disorder: Meaning-Making Frameworks for Psychotherapy*, ed. R.A. Neimeyer and J.D. Raskin (Washington, DC: American Psychological Association, 2000), 207–42; J. Conway, *When Memory Speaks: Exploring the Art of Autobiography* (New York: Vintage Books, 1998).

9 A. Shah, "Alice in Wonderland," (winning essay submitted for the Office for International Students and Scholars Essay Contest at Michigan State University), 2005, oiss.isp.msu.edu/documents/essay_winners/05/AartiShah.pdf.

10 For other examples, see S. Kim, "Creating Campus Communities: Second-Generation Korean-American Ministries at UCLA," in *GenX Religion*, ed. R.W. Flory and D.E. Miller (New York: Routledge, 2000), 92–112; S. Park, "'Korean American Evangelical': A Resolution of Sociological Ambivalence among Korean American College Students," in *Asian American Religions: The Making and Remaking of Borders and Boundaries*, ed. T. Carnes and F. Yang (New York: University Press, 2004), 182–204.

11 S. Bem, "On the Utility of Alternative Procedures for Assessing Psychological Androgyny," *Journal of Consulting and Clinical Psychology* 45 (1977): 196–205.

12 R.M. Hoffman and L.D. Borders, "Twenty-Five Years after the Bem Sex-Role Inventory: A Reassessment and New Issues regarding Classification Variability," *Measurement and Evaluation in Counseling and Development* 34 (2001): 39–55.

13 H. Tajfel, *Human Groups and Social Categories* (Cambridge, UK: Cambridge University Press, 1981); M.J. Rotheram and J.S. Phinney, "Introduction: Definitions and Perspectives in the Study of Children's Ethnic Socialization," in *Children's Ethnic Socialization: Pluralism and Development*, ed. J.S. Phinney and M.J. Rotheram (CA: Sage Publications, 1987).

14 M. Eisenbruch, "Cross-Cultural Aspects of Bereavement II: Ethnic and Cultural Variations in the Development of Bereavement Practices," *Culture, Medicine, and Psychiatry* 8 (1984): 315–47; J.S. Phinney, "Ethnic Identity in Adolescents and Adults: Review of Research," *Psychological Bulletin* 108 (1990): 499–514; D.W. Sue and D. Sue, *Counselling the Culturally Different: Theory and Practice* (New York: John Wiley and Sons, 1990); S. Sue and D.W. Sue, "Chinese American Personality and Mental Health," *Amerasia Journal* 1 (1971): 36–49; P. Saran, *The Asian Indian Experience in the United States* (Cambridge, MA: Schenkman Publishing, 1985); N. Kibria, *Family Tightrope: The Changing Lives of Vietnamese Americans* (Princeton, NJ: Princeton University Press, 1993); N. Hutnik, "Patterns of Ethnic Minority Identification and Modes of Social Adaptation," *Ethnic and Racial Studies* 9 (1986): 150–67; L. Uba, *Asian Americans: Personality Patterns, Identity, and Mental Health* (New York: Guilford Press, 1994).

15 J.E. Helms, "Introduction: Review of Racial Identity Terminology," in *Black and White Racial Identity: Theory, Research, and Practice*, ed. J.E. Helms (New York: Greenwood Press,1990).

16 D.T. Sanchez, M. Shih, and J.A. Garcia, "Juggling Multiple Racial Identities: Malleable Racial Identification and Psychological Well-Being," *Cultural Diversity and Ethnic Minority Psychology* 15 (2009): 243–54.

17 K. Jurva and P.S. Jaya, "Ethnic Identity among Second-Generation Finnish Immigrant Youth in Canada: Some Voices and Perspectives," *Canadian Ethnic Studies* 40, no. 2 (2008): 109–28.

18 L.J. Francis, "Attitude and Longitude: A Study in Measurement," *Character Potential*, 8 (1978): 119–130; L.J. Francis, "Attitudes towards Christianity during Childhood and Adolescence: Assembling the Jigsaw," *Journal of Beliefs and Values* 14 (1993): 4–6; J.E. Greer and L.J. Francis, "Measuring Rejection of Christianity among 14- to 16-year-old Adolescents in Catholic and Protestant Schools in Northern Ireland," *Personality and Individual Differences* 13 (1992): 1345–8.

19 K.J. Ajrouch and A.M. Kusow, "Racial and Religious Contexts: Situational Identities among Lebanese and Somali Muslim Immigrants," *Ethnic and Racial Studies* 30, no. 1 (2007): 72–94.

20 G. Marshall, s.v. "Sapir–Whorf hypothesis," in *A Dictionary*

of Sociology (1998), *Encyclopedia.com*, www.encyclopedia.com/doc/1O88-SapirWhorfhypothesis.html.

21 I. Peritz, "Non-Natives Evicted from Mohawk Reserve," *Globe and Mail*, 15 February 2010, www.theglobeandmail.com/news/national/non-natives-evicted-from-mohawk-reserve/article4308902.

22 "Saving a Tribal Language," *Futurist* 44, no. 1 (2010), 9.

23 Government of Canada, "Aboriginal Languages Initiative—Aboriginal Peoples' Program," 6 October 2011, www.pch.gc.ca/eng/1267285112203.

24 S. Hall, "Cultural Identity and Diaspora," in *Theorizing about Diaspora*, ed. J E Braziel and A. Mannur (Hoboken, NJ: Blackwell Publishing, 2003), 233–45.

25 O. Sensoy, R. Sanghera, G. Parmar, N. Parhar, L. Nosyk, and M. Anderson, "Moving beyond Dance, Dress, and Dining in Multicultural Canada," *International Journal of Multicultural Education* 12, no. 1 (2010): 1–15; P. Jackson, "The Politics of the Streets: A Geography of Caribana," *Political Geography* 11, no. 2 (1992): 130–51.

26 K.H. Karim, "Mapping Diasporic Mediascapes," in *The Media of Diaspora*, ed. K.H. Karim (London: Routledge, 2003); W. Li, "Ethnic Broadcasting and Ethnic Relations: A Comparative Study between Canada and China" (master's thesis, University of Ottawa, 2010); C. Murray, "Media Infrastructure for Multicultural Diversity," *Policy Options* 29, no. 4 (Montreal, QC: Institute of Research on Public Policy, 2008): 63–7.

27 A.D. Smith, *National Identity* (Reno, NV: University of Nevada Press,1991).

28 G. Hofstede, *Culture's Consequences: Comparing Values, Behaviors, Institutions, and Organizations across Nations*, 2nd ed. (Thousand Oaks, CA: Sage, 2001).

29 G. Hofstede and M. H. Bond, "The Confucius Connection: From Cultural Roots to Economic Growth," *Organizational Dynamics* 16, no. 4 (1988): 4–21; G. Hofstede and G.J. Hofstede, *Cultures and Organizations: Software of the Mind*, 2nd ed. (New York: McGraw Hill, 2005); G. Hofstede and R.R. McCrae, "Personality and Culture Revisited: Linking Traits and Dimensions of Culture," *Cross-Cultural Research* 38, no. 1 (2004): 52–88; G. Hofstede, G.J. Hofstede, M. Minkov, and H. Vinken, *Values Survey Module 2008 Manual* (January 2008), www.geerthofstede.nl/media/229/manualvsm08.doc.

30 J. Jedwab, "Canadian Society: More American than European" (results of a poll conducted for the Association for Canadian Studies), 2004, referenced at www.acs-saec.ca/polls/collective.

31 S.D. Ferguson, H. Horan, and A. Ferguson, "How Others See the US: A View from Canada," in *Images of the US around the World: A Multicultural Perspective*, ed. Y. Kamalipour (Albany, NY: State University of New York Press, 1999), 157–78.

32 M. Adams, "Fire and Ice: The US, Canada, and the Myth of Converging Values," Environics Research Group, accessed 16 July 2013, http://old.ppforum.ca/common/assets/speeches/en/micheal_adams_presentation.pdf.

33 Ferguson et al., "How Others See the US."

34 P.M. Valkenburg, A.P. Schouten, and J. Peter, "Adolescents' Identity Experiments on the Internet," *New Media and Society* 7, no. 3 (2005): 383–402.

35 S.L. Calvert, "Identity Construction on the Internet," in *Children in the Digital Age: Influences of Electronic Media on Development*, ed. S.L. Calvert, A.B. Jordan, and R.R. Cocking (Westport, CT: Praeger, 2002), 57–70; E.F. Gross, "Adolescent Internet Use: What We Expect, What Teens Report," *Journal of Applied Developmental Psychology* 25 (2004): 633–49; A. Lenhart and M. Madden, *Teens, Privacy and Online Social Networks* (Washington, DC: Pew Internet and American Life Project, 2007); P.M. Valkenburg and J. Peter, "Adolescents' Identity Experiments on the Internet: Consequences for Social Competence and Self-Concept Unity," *Communication Research* 35 (2008): 208–31.

36 Valkenburg, Schouten, and Peter, "Adolescents' Identity Experiments."

37 K.S. Newman, C. Fox, and D. Harding, *Rampage: The Social Roots of School Shootings* (New York: Basic Books, 2005).

38 B. Plummer, "Social Roots of School Shootings," *WONKBLOG* (blog), *Washington Post*, 18 December 2012, www.washingtonpost.com/blogs/wonkblog/wp/2012/12/18/the-small-town-roots-of-school-shootings.

39 K. Newman, "In School Shootings, Patterns and Warning Signs," *CNN Opinion*, 17 December 2012, www.cnn.com/2012/12/17/opinion/newman-school-shooters/index.html.

40 Ibid.

41 Ibid.

42 Ibid.

43 C.L. Toma, J.T. Hancock, and N.B. Ellison, "Separating Fact from Fiction: An Examination of Deceptive Self-Presentation in Online Dating Profiles," *Personality and Social Psychology Bulletin* 34 (2008): 1023–36; C.L. Toma and J.T. Hancock, "Looks and Lies: The Role of Physical Attractiveness in Online Dating Self-Presentation and Deception," *Communication Research* 37 (2010): 335–51.

44 Toma, et al., "Separating Fact from Fiction."

45 J.T. Hancock and C.L. Toma, "Putting Your Best Face Forward: The Accuracy of Online Dating Photographs," *Journal of Communication* 59 (2009): 367–86.

46 A.L. Gonzales and J.T. Hancock, "Identity Shift in Computer-Mediated Environments," *Media Psychology* 11 (2008): 167–85.

47 D.M. Quinn and S.R. Chaudoir, "Living with a Concealable Stigmatized Identity: The Impact of Anticipated Stigma, Centrality, Salience, and Cultural

Stigma on Psychological Distress and Health," *Journal of Personality and Social Psychology* 97 (2009): 635.

48 Quinn and Chaudoir, "Living with a Concealable Stigmatized Identity." Based on work of J. Crocker and B. Major, "Social Stigma and Self-Esteem: The Self-Protective Properties of Stigma," *Psychological Review* 96 (1989): 608–30.

49 E. Goffman, *Stigma: Notes on the Management of Spoiled Identity* (Englewood Cliffs, NJ: Prentice-Hall, 1963).

50 Quinn and Chaudoir, "Living with a Concealable Stigmatized Identity." See also J.E. Pachankis, "The Psychological Implications of Concealing a Stigma: A Cognitive-Affective-Behavioral Model," *Psychological Bulletin* 133 (2007): 328–45.

51 W.B. Swann, "The Self and Identity Negotiation," *Interaction Studies* 6 (2005): 69–83; E. Berne, *Games People Play: The Basic Handbook of Transactional Analysis* (New York: Ballantine Books, 1964, 1996); C. Steiner, *Scripts People Live: Transactional Analysis of Life Scripts* (New York: Grove/Atlantic, 1994); T.A. Harris, *I'm OK—You're OK* (New York: Harper Paperbacks, 2004).

52 K. Leslie, "Gerard Kennedy Reaches Out to Protestors at Liberal Leadership Convention," *Toronto Star*, 26 January 2013, www.globalnews.ca/canada/gerard+kennedy+reaches+out+to+protesters+at+liberal+leadership+convention/6442796325/story.html.

53 M. Rokeach, *The Three Christs of Ypsilanti* (New York: A.A. Knopf, 1964).

54 W.B. Swann Jr, "Self-Verification: Bringing Social Reality into Harmony with the Self," in *Psychological Perspectives on the Self*, vol. 2, ed. J. Suls and A. G. Greenwald (Hillsdale, NJ: Erlbaum, 1983), 33–66.

55 B. Givens, written testimony for US Senate Judiciary Subcommittee on Technology, Terrorism, and Government Information, chaired by Senator Jon Kyl, Privacy Rights Clearinghouse, posted 12 July 2000, www.privacyrights.org/ar/id_theft.htm.

56 W.B. Swann Jr and S.J. Read, "Self-Verification Processes: How We Sustain Our Self-Conceptions," *Journal of Experimental Social Psychology* 17 (1981): 351–72.

57 W.B. Swann Jr and C.A. Hill, "When Our Identities Are Mistaken: Reaffirming Self-Conceptions through Social Interaction," *Journal of Personality and Social Psychology* 43 (1982): 59–66.

58 Ibid.

59 M. Snyder, "Self-Monitoring of Expressive Behaviour," *Journal of Personality and Social Psychology* 30 (1974): 526–37.

60 J. Potter, "Self-Monitoring: Do You Censor What You Say?," accessed 16 July 2013, www.outofservice.com/self-monitor-censor-test/results/?raw=53.

61 E. Goffman, *The Presentation of Self in Everyday Life* (New York: Overlook Press, 1959).

62 C.H. Cooley, *Human Nature and the Social Order* (New York: Charles Scribner's Sons, 1902); Goffman, *The Presentation of Self*; E. Goffman, *Frame Analysis* (New York: Doubleday, 1974); G.H. Mead, *Mind, Self and Society* (Chicago: University of Chicago Press, 1934); G.H. Mead, *The Philosophy of the Act* (Chicago: University of Chicago Press, 1938); James, *The Principles of Psychology*.

63 B.R. Schlenker and T.W. Britt, "Beneficial Impression Management: Strategically Controlling Information to Help Friends," *Journal of Personality and Psychology* 76, no. 4 (1999): 559–73; A.J. DuBrin, *Impression Management in the Workplace: Research Theory and Practice* (New York: Routledge, 2010).

64 Sanchez et al., "Juggling Multiple Racial Identities."

65 Goffman, *The Presentation of Self*.

66 B.R. Schlenker and B.A. Pontari, "The Strategic Control of Information Management: Impression Management and Self-Presentation in Daily Life," in *Psychological Perspectives on Self and Identity*, ed. A. Tesser, R. Felson, and J. Suls (Washington, DC: American Psychological Association, 2000), 199–232.

67 B.R. Schlenker, "Self-Presentation," in *Handbook of Self and Identity*, ed. M.R. Leary and J.P. Tangney (New York: Guilford, 2003), 492–518.

68 J.P. Caughlin and S. Petronio, "Privacy in Families," in *Handbook of Family Communication*, ed. A.L. Vangelisti (Mahwah, NJ: Lawrence Erlbaum, 2004), 379–412.

69 J.F. Nussbaum, S. Ragan, and B. Whaley, "Children, Older Adults, and Women: Impact on Provider–Patient Interaction," in *Handbook of Health Communication*, ed. T.L. Thompson, A.M. Dorsey, K.I. Miller, and R. Parrott (London, UK: Lawrence Erlbaum, 2003), 183–204.

70 Caughlin and Petronio, "Privacy in Families"; M.P. Pagano, *Interactive Case Studies in Health Communication* (Sudbury, MA: Jones and Bartlett, 2010).

71 Caughlin and Petronio, "Privacy in Families."

72 Ibid.

73 G.A. Fine, "Friends, Impression Management, and Preadolescent Behavior," in *The Development of Children's Friendships*, ed. S.R. Asher and J.M. Gottman (New York: Cambridge University Press, 1981), 29–52.

74 D.M. Newman, *Sociology: Exploring the Architecture of Everyday Life* (Thousand Oaks, CA: Pine Forge Press, 2009).

75 K. Alpizar, R. Islas-Alvarado, C.R. Warren, and M.S. Fiebert, "Gender, Sexuality, and Impression Management on Facebook," *International Review of Social Sciences and Humanities* 4, no. 1 (2012): 121–5.

76 Ibid.

77 Schlenker and Britt, "Beneficial Impression Management."

78 A.K. Przybylski and N. Weinstein, "Can You Connect with Me Now? How the Presence of Mobile

Communication Technology Influences Face-to-Face Conversation Quality," *Journal of Social and Personal Relationships* 30, no. 3 (2012): 237–46.

79 J.R. Roney, "Effects of Visual Exposure to the Opposite Sex: Cognitive Aspects of Mate Attraction in Human Males," *Personality and Social Psychology Bulletin* 29, no. 3 (2003): 393–404.

80 V. Griskevicius, J.M. Tybur, J.M. Sundie, R.B. Cialdini, G.F. Miller, and D.T. Kenrick, "Blatant Benevolence and Conspicuous Consumption: When Romantic Motives Elicit Strategic Costly Signals," *Journal of Personality and Social Psychology* 93, no. 1 (2007): 85–102.

81 D. Dosmukhambetova and A. Manstead, "Strategic Reactions to Unfaithfulness: Female Self-Presentation in the Context of Mate Attraction Is Linked to Uncertainty of Paternity," *Evolution and Human Behavior* 32, no. 2 (2011): 106–17.

82 R.R. Vallacher, D.M. Wegner, and J. Frederick, "The Presentation of Self through Action Identification," *Social Cognition* 5 (1987): 301–22.

83 L.L. Carli, "Gender, Language, and Influence," *Journal of Personality and Social Psychology* 59 (1990): 941–51; B.M. DePaulo, "Nonverbal Behavior and Self-presentation," *Psychological Bulletin* 2 (1992): 203–43; D. Tannen, *Talking from 9 to 5: Women and Men in the Workplace: Language, Sex, and Power* (New York: Avon Books, 1994); S. Lee, B.M. Quigley, M.S. Nesler, A.B. Corbett, and J.T. Tedeschi, "Development of a Self-Presentation Tactics Scale," *Personality and Individual Differences* 26 (1999): 701–22.

84 DuBrin, *Impression Management in the Workplace*.

85 Ibid.

86 F. Norris, "RadioShack Chief Resigns after Lying," *New York Times*, 21 February 2006, www.nytimes.com/2006/02/21/business/21radio.html?_r=0.

87 "Yahoo Ousts CEO over Resumé," *Globe and Mail*, 14 May 2012, www.theglobeandmail.com/report-on-business/video/video-yahoo-ousts-ceo-over-rsum/article2431672.

88 DuBrin, *Impression Management in the Workplace*.

89 B. Safani, "Lying to Get a Job: Nine Famous Fibbers," *AOL Jobs*, 26 January 2011, http://jobs.aol.com/articles/2011/01/26/lying-to-get-a-job.

90 K.D. Tomassi, "Most Common Resumé Lies," *Forbes*, 23 May 2006, www.forbes.com/2006/05/20/resume-lies-work_cx_kdt_06work_0523lies.html.

91 E.E. Jones and T.S. Pittman, "Toward a General Theory of Strategic Self-Presentation," in *Psychological Perspective on the Self*, ed. J. Suls (Hillsdale, NJ: Lawrence Erlbaum, 1982), 231–61.

92 R.E. Guadagno and R.B. Cialdini, "Gender Differences in Impression Management in Organizations: A Qualitative Review," *Sex Roles* 56 (2007): 483–94.

93 O.P. John and R.W. Robins, "Accuracy and Bias in Self-Perception: Individual Differences in Self-Enhancement and the Role of Narcissism," *Journal of Personality and Social Psychology* 66, no. 1 (1994): 206–19; W.K. Campbell and G.D. Reeder, "Narcissism and Comparative Self-Enhancement Strategies," *Journal of Research in Personality* 34 (2000): 329–47.

94 T.E. Becker and S.L. Martin, "Trying to Look Bad at Work: Methods and Motives for Managing Poor Impressions in Organizations," *Academy of Management Journal* 38 (1995): 174–99.

95 Jones and Pittman, "Toward a General Theory."

96 "Bullying Prevention: Nature and Extent of Bullying in Canada," Public Safety Canada, 18 July 2011, www.publicsafety.gc.ca/res/cp/res/2008-bp-01-eng.aspx; P. O'Connell, D. Pepler, and W. Craig, "Peer Involvement in Bullying: Insights and Challenges for Intervention," *Journal of Adolescence* 22 (1999): 437–52; G. Colvin, T. Tobin, K. Beard, S. Hagan, and J. Sprague, "The School Bully: Assessing the Problem, Developing Interventions, and Future Research Directions," *Journal of Behavioural Education* 8, no. 3 (1998): 293–319.

97 See *Eyes on Bullying*, www.eyesonbullying.org/index.html.

98 D.T. Gilbert and E.E. Jones, "Perceiver-Induced Constraint: Interpretations of Self-Generated Reality," *Journal of Personality and Social Psychology* 50 (1986): 269–80.

99 W.H. Turnley and M.C. Bolino, "Achieving Desired Images while Avoiding Undesired Images: Exploring the Role of Self-Monitoring in Impression Management," *Journal of Applied Psychology* 86 (2001): 351–60.

100 Becker and Martin, "Trying to Look Bad."

101 W.R. Gove, M. Hughes, and M.R. Geerkin, "Playing Dumb: A Form of Impression Management with Undesirable Side Effects," *Social Psychology Quarterly* 4 (1980): 89–102.

102 For examples, see J. Rosenberg and N. Egbert, "Online Impression Management: Personality Traits and Concerns for Secondary Goals as Predictors of Self-Presentation Tactics on Facebook," *Journal of Computer-Mediated Communication* 17, no. 1 (2011): 1–18; N.B. Ellison, C. Steinfield, and C. Lampe, "The Benefits of Facebook 'Friends': Social Capital and College Students' Use of Online Social Network Sites," *Journal of Computer-Mediated Communication* 12 (2007): 1143–68; C. Ross, E.S. Orr, M. Sisic, J.M. Arseneault, M.G. Simmering, and R.R. Orr, "Personality and Motivations Associated with Facebook Use," *Computers in Human Behaviour* 25 (2009): 578–86; S.T. Tong, B. Van Der Heide, L. Langwell, and J.B. Walther, "Too Much of a Good Thing: The Relationship between Number of Friends and Interpersonal Impressions on Facebook," *Journal of*

Computer-Mediated Communication 13 (2008): 531–49; J.B. Walther, B. Van Der Heide, S. Kim, D. Westerman, and S.T. Tong, "The Role of Friends' Appearance and Behaviour on Evaluations of Individuals on Facebook: Are We Known by the Company We Keep?" *Human Communication Research* 34 (2008): 28–49; S. Zhao, S. Grasmuck, and J. Martin, "Identity Construction on Facebook: Digital Empowerment in Anchored Relationships," *Computers in Human Behaviour* 24 (2008): 1816–36; J. Zywica and J. Danowski, "The Faces of Facebookers: Investigating Social Enhancement and Social Compensation Hypotheses; Predicting Facebook and Offline Popularity from Sociability and Self-Esteem, and Mapping the Meanings of Popularity with Semantic Networks," *Journal of Computer-Mediated Communication* 14 (2008): 1–34; E.S. Orr, M. Sisic, C. Ross, M.G. Simmering, J.M. Arseneault, and R.R. Orr, "The Influence of Shyness on the Use of Facebook in an Undergraduate Sample," *Cyber Psychology and Behaviour* 12, no. 3 (2009): 337–40.

103 A. Lenhart, P. Hitlin, and M. Madden, *Teens and Technology* (Washington, DC: Pew Internet and American Life Project, 2005).

104 D.G. Oblinger and J.L. Oblinger, "Is It Age or IT: First Steps toward Understanding the Net Generation," in *Educating the Net Generation*, ed. D.G. Oblinger and J.L. Oblinger (Washington, DC: EDUCAUSE), www.kwantlen.ca/academicgrowth/resources/EduCausepub7101.pdf.

105 J. Short, E. Williams, and B. Christie, *The Social Psychology of Telecommunications* (New York: John Wiley and Sons, 1976).

106 J.B. Walther, "Interpersonal Effects in Computer-Mediated Interaction: A Relational Perspective," *Communication Research* 19 (1992): 52–90; B.A. Olaniran, "Social Information Processing Theory (SIPT): A Cultural Perspective for International Online Communication Environments," *IGI Global*, 25 November 2011, 45–6, www.igi-global.com/viewtitlesample.aspx?id=55560.

107 E. Griffin, "Social Information Processing Theory of Joseph Walther," *A First Look at Communication Theory*, 8th ed. (New York: McGraw Hill, 2012).

108 J.B. Walther and M. Parks, "Cues Filtered Out, Cues Filtered In: Computer-Mediated Communication and Relationships," in *Handbook of Interpersonal Communication*, 3rd ed., ed. M.L. Knapp and J.A. Daly (Thousand Oaks, CA: Sage Publications, 2002), 529–63.

109 Walther, "Interpersonal Effects."

110 J.B. Walther and K.P. D'Addario, "The Impacts of Emoticons on Message Interpretation in Computer-Mediated Communication," *Social Science Computer Review* 19, no 3 (2001): 324–47.

111 D. Derks, A.E.R. Bos, and J.V. Grumbkow, "Emoticons and Online Message Interpretation," *Social Science Computer Review* 26, no. 3 (2008): 379–88; Y. Liu and D. Ginther, "Managing Impression Formation in Computer-Mediated Communication," *Educause Quarterly* 50, no. 1 (2001): 50–54; Zhao et al., "Identity Construction on Facebook."

112 N. Kennedy and M. Macko, "Social Networking Privacy and Its Effects on Employment Opportunities," in *Convenient or Invasive—The Information Age*, ed. K.R. Larson and Z.A. Voronovich (Boulder, CO: Ethica, 2007).

113 J.G. Noll, C.E. Shenk, J.E. Barnes, and F.W. Putnam, "Childhood Abuse, Avatar Choices, and Other Risk Factors Associated with Internet-Initiated Victimization of Adolescent Girls," *Pediatrics* 123 (2009): e1078–83, http://pediatrics.aappublications.org/content/123/6/e1078.full.pdf.

114 Ellison et al., "The Benefits of Facebook 'Friends.'"

115 Tong et al., "Too Much of a Good Thing?"

116 Ibid.

117 C.A. Kleck, C.A. Reese, D.Z. Behnken, and S.S. Sundar, "The Company You Keep and the Image You Project: Putting Your Best Face Forward in Online Social Networks" (paper presented at the Annual Meeting of the International Communication Association, San Francisco, CA, May 2007).

118 Ellison et al., "The Benefits of Facebook 'Friends.'"

CHAPTER 5

1 R.I. Sutton, *Good Boss, Bad Boss: How to Be the Best . . . and Learn from the Worst* (New York: Business Plus, 2010).

2 K.E. See, E.W. Morrison, N.B. Rothman, and J.B. Soll, "The Detrimental Effects of Power on Confidence, Advice Taking, and Accuracy," *Organizational Behavior and Human Decision Processes* 16, no. 2 (2011): 272–85.

3 P.G. Hepper and S. Shahidullah, "The Development of Fetal Hearing," *Fetal and Maternal Medicine Review* 6 (1994): 167–79.

4 J.-P. Lecanuet, C. Granier-Deferre, A.Y. Jacquet, I. Capponi, and L. Ledru. "Prenatal Discrimination of Male and Female Voice Uttering the Same Sentence," *Early Development and Parenting* 2 (1993): 217–28.

5 Hepper, "Unraveling Our Beginnings."

6 L.K. Steil, "Listening Training: The Key to Success in Today's Organizations," in *Listening in Everyday Life: A Personal and Professional Approach*, ed. M. Purdy and D. Borisoff (Lanham, MD: University Press of America, 1997), 213–37.

7 R.F. Verderber, *The Challenge of Effective Speaking*, 11th ed. (Belmont, CA: Wadsworth Thomson Learning, 2000), 36.

8 *The Power of Listening* (Scarborough, ON: McGraw-Hill Films, 1978), filmstrip.

9 L. Barker, K. Gladney, R. Edwards, F. Holley, and C. Gaines, "An Investigation of Proportional Time

Spent in Various Communication Activities by College Students," *Journal of Applied Communication Research* 8, no. 2 (1980): 101–10.

10 D. Bird, "Teaching Listening Comprehension," *Journal of Communication* 3 (1953): 127–30; D. Bird, "Have You Tried Listening?," *Journal of the American Dietetic Association* 30 (1954): 225–30.

11 R. Emanuel, J. Adams, K. Baker, E.K. Daufin, C. Ellington, E. Fitts, J. Himsel, L. Holladay, and D. Okeowo, "How College Students Spend Their Time Communicating," *International Journal of Listening* 22, no. 1 (2008): 13–28.

12 B.R. Burleson, "A Constructivist Approach to Listening," *International Journal of Listening* 25, no. 1 (2011): 27–46, p. 29.

13 A.W. Bronkhorst, "The Cocktail Party Phenomenon: A Review on Speech Intelligibility in Multiple-Talker Conditions," *Acta Acustica United with Acustica* 86 (2000): 117–28.

14 R. Edwards, "Listening and Message Interpretation," *International Journal of Listening* 25, no. 1/2 (2011): 47–65.

15 Ibid.

16 G.D. Bodie, D.L. Worthington, M. Imhof, and L. Cooper, "What Would a Unified Field of Listening Look Like? A Proposal Linking Past Perspectives and Future Endeavors," *International Journal of Listening* 22 (2008): 103–22; G. Brown, "Investigating Listening Comprehension in Context," *Applied Linguistics* 7, no. 3 (1986): 284–302.

17 Edwards, "Listening and Message Interpretation."

18 R. Oxford and D. Crookall, "Research on Language Learning Strategies: Methods, Findings, and Instructional Issues," *Modern Language Journal* 73, no. 4 (1989): 404–19.

19 Burleson, "A Constructivist Approach to Listening."

20 M.J. Beatty and S.K. Payne, "Listening Comprehension as a Function of Cognitive Complexity: A Research Note," *Communication Monographs* 51, no. 1 (1984): 85–9; J.W. Neuliep and V. Hazelton Jr, "Enhanced Conversational Recall and Reduced Conversational Interference as a Function of Cognitive Complexity," *Human Communication Research* 13 (1986): 211–24; G.D. Bodie and M. Fitch-Hauser, "Quantitative Research in Listening: Explication and Overview," in *Listening and Human Communication in the Twenty-First Century*, ed. A.D. Wolvin (Oxford, UK: Blackwell, 2010), 46–93.

21 B.R. Burleson, L.K. Hanasono, G.D. Bodie, A.J. Holmstrom, J.J. Rack, J.G. Rosier, and J.D. McCullough, "Explaining Gender Differences in Responses to Supportive Messages: Two Tests of a Dual-Process Approach," *Sex Roles* 61 (2009): 265–80; B.R. Burleson, J.D. McCullough, G.D. Bodie, J.J. Rack, A.J. Holmstrom, L.K. Hanasono, and J. Gill-Rosier, "It's How You Think about It: Effects of Ability and Motivation on Recipient Processing of and Responses to Comforting Messages" (paper presented at the annual meeting of the International Communication Association, Montreal, QC, 2008); B.R. Burleson, G.D. Bodie, J.J. Rack, A.J. Holmstrom, L. Hanasono, and J.N. Gill, "Good Grief: Testing a Dual-Process Model of Responses to Grief-Management Messages" (paper presented at the annual meeting of the National Communication Association, Chicago, IL, 2007).

22 Burleson, "A Constructivist Approach to Listening."

23 B.R. Burleson, "Constructivism: A General Theory of Communication Skill," in *Explaining Communication: Contemporary Theories and Exemplars*, ed. B.B. Whaley and W. Samter (Mahwah, NJ: Lawrence Erlbaum, 2006), 105–28, p. 122.

24 J.M. Brendel, J.B. Kolbert, and V.A. Foster, "Promoting Student Cognitive Development," *Journal of Adult Development* 9, no. 3 (2002): 217–22.

25 Burleson, "Constructivism: A General Theory."

26 J. Andrade, "What Does Doodling Do?," *Applied Cognitive Psychology* 24, no. 1 (2010): 100–6.

27 C.B. Fried, "In-Class Laptop Use and Its Effects on Student Learning," *Computers and Education* 50 (2008): 906–14.

28 C. Croo and D. Barrowcliff, "Ubiquitous Computing on Campus: Patterns of Engagement by University Students," *International Journal of Human–Computer Interaction* 13, no. 2 (2001): 245–56; M. Grace-Martin and G. Gay, "Web Browsing, Mobile Computing, and Academic Performance," *Educational Technology and Society* 4, no. 3 (2001): 95–107; H. Hembrooke and G. Gay, "The Laptop and the Lecture: The Effects of Multitasking in Learning Environments," *Journal of Computing in Higher Education* 15, no. 1 (2003): 46–64.

29 Grace-Martin and Gay, "Web Browsing."

30 C.A. Sanderson, K.B. Rahm, and S.A. Beigbeder, "The Pursuit of Intimacy Goals in Close Friendships," *Journal of Social and Personal Relationships* 22 (2005): 75–98.

31 L.B. Rosenfeld and G.L. Bowen, "Marital Disclosure and Marital Satisfaction: Direct-Effect versus Interaction-Effect Models," *Western Journal of Speech Communication* 55 (1991): 69–84; E.M. Waring and G. J. Chelune, "Marital Intimacy and Self-Disclosure," *Journal of Clinical Psychology* 39 (1983): 183–9.

32 H.T. Reis and P. Shaver, "Intimacy as an Interpersonal Process," in *Handbook of Personal Relationships*, ed. S. Duck (Chichester, UK: Wiley, 1988), 367–89.

33 F. Warren, "Frank Warren: Half a Million Secrets," TED Talks video, filmed February 2012, posted 9 April 2012, www.ted.com/talks/frank_warren_half_a_million_secrets.html.

34 Ibid.

35 F. Wolff, *Perspective Listening* (New York: Holt, Rinehart, and Winston, 1983).

36 Aboriginal Human Resource Council, "Tips on Working with Aboriginal Colleagues: Listening," 19 September

2001, www.aboriginalhr.ca/en/resources/getstarted/Listening.

37 C.D. Shepherd, S.B. Castleberry, and R.E. Ridnour, "Linking Effective Listening with Salesperson Performance: An Exploratory Investigation," *Journal of Business and Industrial Marketing* 12, no. 5 (1997): 315–22.

38 R.P. Ramsey and R.S. Sohi, "Listening to Your Customers: The Impact of Perceived Salesperson Listening Behavior on Relationship Outcomes," *Journal of the Academy of Marketing Science* 25, no. 2 (1997): 127–37.

39 S. Saha, S.H. Taggart, M. Komaromyand, and A.B. Bindman, "Do Patients Choose Physicians of Their Own Race?," *Health Affairs* 19, no. 4 (2000): 76–83.

40 Q. Ngo-Metzger, A.T.R. Legedza, and R.S. Phillips, "Asian Americans' Reports of Their Health Care Experiences: Results of a National Survey," *Journal of General Internal Medicine* 19, no. 2 (2004): 111–19.

41 S. Meryn, "Improving Doctor–Patient Communication: Not an Option but a Necessity," *British Medical Journal* 316, no. 7149 (1998): 1922–30.

42 M.K. Marvel, R.M. Epstein, K. Flowers, and H.B. Beckman, "Soliciting the Patient's Agenda: Have we Improved?," *Journal of the American Medical Association* 281 (1999): 283–7.

43 W. Levinson, D.L. Roter, J.P. Mullooly, V.T. Dull, and R.M. Frankel, "Physician–Patient Communication: The Relationship with Malpractice Claims among Primary Care Physicians and Surgeons," *Journal of American Medical Association* 277, no. 7 (1997): 553–9.

44 M. Lynn and K. Mynier, "Effect of Server Posture on Restaurant Tipping," *Journal of Applied Social Psychology* 23, no. 8 (1993): 678–85.

45 M.P. Nichols, *The Lost Art of Listening: How Learning to Listen Can Improve Relationships* (New York: Guilford Press, 2009).

46 J. Brownell, "Perceptions of Effective Listeners: A Management Study," *Journal of Business Communication* 27, no. 4 (1990): 401–15.

47 Ibid.

48 Ibid.

49 Ibid.

50 Ibid.

51 T. Klingberg, *The Overflowing Brain: Information Overload and the Limits of Working Memory*, trans. N. Betteridge (New York: Oxford University Press, 2009).

52 T. Särkämö, M. Tervaniemi, S. Laitinen, A. Forsblom, S. Soinila, M. Mikkonen, T. Autti et al., "Music Listening Enhances Cognitive Recovery and Mood after Middle Cerebral Artery Stroke," *Brain* 131 (2008): 866–76

53 N.R. Simmons-Stern, A.E. Budson, and B.A. Ally, "Music as a Memory Enhancer in Patients with Alzheimer's Disease," *Neuropsychologia* 48 (2010): 3164–7.

54 C.M. Tomaino, "Music Therapy to Benefit Individuals with Parkinson's Disease," *Movement Disorders* 21, no. 13 (2006): S29.

55 P. Camille, "Talking with Concetta Tomaino: The Power of Music," 24 December 2012, www.caring.com/interviews/concetta-tomaino-about-music-therapy-for-alzheimer-s-patients.

56 Särkämö et al., "Music Listening Enhances Cognitive Recovery."

57 M.A. Just, P.A. Carpenter, T.A. Keller, L. Emery, H. Zajac, and K.R. Thulborn, "Interdependence of Non-Overlapping Cortical Systems in Dual Cognitive Tasks," *NeuroImage* 14 (2001): 417–26.

58 R.G. Nichols, "What Can Be Done about Listening?," *The Supervisor's Notebook* 22, no. 1 (1960).

59 S.R. Covey, *The Seven Habits of Highly Effective People* (New York: Simon and Schuster, 1989).

60 C.R. Rogers and F.J. Roethlisberger, "Barriers and Gateways to Communication," *Harvard Business Review* (July/August 1952): 28–34.

61 B.R. Burleson, "Comforting Messages: Features, Functions, and Outcomes," in *Strategic Interpersonal Communication*, ed. J. Daly and J. Wiemann (Hillsdale, NJ: Lawrence Erlbaum, 1994), 135–61; B.R. Burleson, T.L. Albrecht, and I.G. Sarason, *Communication of Social Support: Messages, Interactions, Relationships, and Community* (Thousand Oaks, CA: Sage, 1994).

62 Covey, *The Seven Habits*.

63 R.E. Crable, *One to Another: A Guidebook for Interpersonal Communication* (New York: Harper and Row, 1981).

64 Grace-Martin and Gay, "Web Browsing."

65 eCompliance Safety, "Safety Update," 25 January 2012, www.ecompliance.ca/club-zero/archive/20090422-Cell-Phone-Use-While-Driving.

66 M.A. Just, T.A. Keller, and J.A. Cynkar, "A Decrease in Brain Activation Associated with Driving when Listening to Someone Speak," *Brain Research* 1205 (2008): 70–80.

67 Nichols, "What Can Be Done about Listening?"

68 A. Strage, Y. Baba, S. Milner, M. Scharberg, E. Walker, R. Williamson, and M. Yoder, "What Every Student Affairs Professional Should Know: Student Study Activities and Beliefs Associated with Academic Success," *Journal of College Student Development* 43 (2002): 246–66.

69 R.F. Verderber, *The Challenge of Effective Speaking*, 11th ed. (Belmont, CA: Wadsworth Thomson Learning, 2000), 36.

70 University of Waterloo Counselling Services, "Curve of Forgetting," accessed 9 August 2013, http://uwaterloo.ca/counselling-services/curve-forgetting.

71 Ibid.

72 S. Mackie, "Quick Tip: Speed Listen to Podcasts on Your iPhone/iPod," 14 May 2010, http://gigaom.com/2010/05/14/quick-tip-speed-listen-to-podcasts-on-

your-iphoneipod; S. Pavlina, "Overclock Your Learning," 6 August 2007, www.stevepavlina.com/blog/2007/08/overclock-your-audio-learning.

[73] See C. Harrington, *Student Success in College: Doing What Works!* (Boston, MA: Wadsworth Publishing, 2012).

[74] Covey, *The Seven Habits*, 122.

[75] C. Rogers and R.E. Farson, "Active Listening," in *Organizational Communication*, ed. S.D. Ferguson and S. Ferguson (New Brunswick, NJ: Transaction Publishers): 319–34.

[76] Carl Rogers, *A Way of Being* (Boston: Houghton Mifflin, 1980), 10. Copyright © 1980 by Houghton Mifflin Harcourt Publishing Company. Copyright © renewed 2008 by David E. Rogers and Natalie Rogers. Extract reprinted by permission of Houghton Mifflin Harcourt Publishing Company. All rights reserved.

[77] M.L. Mclaughlin and M.J. Cody, "Awkward Silences: Behavioral Antecedents and Consequences of the Conversational Lapse," *Human Communication Research* 8 (1982): 299–316.

[78] Ibid.

[79] A. Mehrabian, *Silent Messages* (Belmont, CA: Wadsworth, 1971).

[80] J.H. Wirth, D.F. Sacco, K. Hugenberg, and K.D. Williams, "Eye Gaze as Relational Evaluation: Averted Eye Gaze Leads to Feelings of Ostracism and Relational Devaluation," *Personality and Social Psychology Bulletin* 36 (2010): 869–82.

[81] M.F. Mason, E.P. Tatkow, and C.N. Macrae, "The Look of Love: Gaze Shifts and Person Perception," *Psychological Science* 16 (2005): 236–9.

[82] J.F. Dovidio and S.L. Ellyson, "Decoding Visual Dominance: Attributions of Power Based on Relative Percentages of Looking while Speaking and Looking while Listening," *Social Psychology Quarterly* 45, no. 2 (1982): 106–13.

[83] See J.H. Ellerby, *Working with Aboriginal Elders* (Winnipeg: University of Manitoba Native Studies Press, 2001). See also P. Chin, "Chinese Americans," in *Culture and Nursing Care: A Pocket Guide*, ed. J.G. Lipson, S.L. Dibble, and P.A. Minarik (San Francisco: University of California-San Francisco Nursing Press, 1996), 74–81.

[84] A. Rashidi and S.S. Rajaram, "Culture Care Conflicts among Asian-Islamic Immigrant Women in Us Hospitals," *Holistic Nursing Practice* 16, no. 1 (2001): 55–64.

[85] R.G. Nichols and L.A. Stevens, "Six Bad Listening Habits," in *Are You Listening*?, ed. R.G. Nichols and L.A. Stevens (New York: McGraw-Hill, 1957).

[86] M. Sonnby-Borgström, P. Jönsson, and O. Svensson, "Emotional Empathy as Related to Mimicry Reactions at Different Levels of Information Processing," *Journal of Nonverbal Behavior* 27, no. 1 (2003): 3–23.

[87] G.D. Bodie and S.M. Jones, "The Nature of Supportive Listening: The Role of Verbal Person Centredness and Nonverbal Immediacy," *Western Journal of Communication* 76, no. 3 (2012): 250–69.

[88] T. Royce, "The Negotiator and the Bomber: Analyzing the Critical Role of Active Listening in Crisis Negotiations," *Negotiation Journal* 21, no. 1 (2005): 5–27.

[89] G. M. Vecchi, V. B. V. Hasselt, and S. J. Romano, "Crisis (Hostage) Negotiation: Current Strategies and Issues in High-Risk Conflict Resolution," *Aggression and Violent Behavior* 10 (2005): 533–51.

[90] T. Royce, "The Negotiator and the Bomber."

[91] A. Coyle, "Qualitative Research in Counselling Psychology: Using the Counselling Interview as a Research Instrument," in *Counselling Psychology: Integrating Theory, Research and Supervised Practice*, ed. P. Clarkson (London, UK: Routledge, 1998), 56–73.

[92] S. Myers, "Empathic Listening: Reports on the Experience of Being Heard," *Journal of Humanistic Psychology* 40, no. 2 (2000): 148–73.

[93] I. Grayling and K. Stevenson, "A Trainer's Perspective," in *Workplace Bullying in the NHS*, ed. J. Randle (Abingdon, UK: Radcliffe Publishing, 2006), 77–96.

[94] C. Rogers, *Client-Centred Therapy: Its Current Practice, Implications and Theory* (Boston: Houghton Mifflin, 1951).

[95] Nichols, *The Lost Art of Listening*.

CHAPTER 6

[1] P. McMahon, "Top Five Reasons Planes Crash," *Discovery*, accessed 28 May 2012, www.discoverychannel.ca/Article.aspx?aid=14378.

[2] M. Gladwell, *Outliers: The Story of Success* (London, UK: Penguin Books, 2010).

[3] Ibid.

[4] Ibid.

[5] Ibid.

[6] Ibid.

[7] Ibid.

[8] Ibid.

[9] Ibid.

[10] C.K. Ogden and I.A. Richards, *The Meaning of Meaning: A Study of the Influence of Language upon Thought and of the Science of Symbolism* (London, UK: Routledge and Kegan Paul, 1923).

[11] B. Geery, "Thirty-nine Words for Snow," *YoBeat*, 22 January 2009, www.yobeat.com/2009/01/22/38-words-for-snow.

[12] C.B. Mayhorn, M.S. Wogalter, and V.C. Conzola, "Perceptions of Sport-Utility Vehicle (SUV) Safety by SUV Drivers and Non-drivers," in *Advances in Human Factors, Ergonomics, and Safety in Manufacturing and Service Industries*, ed. G. Salvendy (Boca Raton, FL: CRC Press, 2010), 986–97.

13 J.M. Ackerman, V. Griskevicius, and N.P. Li, "Let's Get Serious: Communicating Commitment in Romantic Relationships," *Journal of Personality and Social Psychology* 100, no. 6 (2011): 1079–94.
14 Ibid.
15 Ibid.
16 A. Russell and T. Falconer, *Drop the Worry Ball: How to Parent in the Age of Entitlement* (Mississauga, ON: John Wiley and Sons, 2012).
17 Ibid.
18 Language Samples Project, "Phonology," 2001, http://ic-migration.webhost.uits.arizona.edu/icfiles/ic/lsp/site/Phonology.html.
19 "The Hawaiian Language," *Vacation Rental in Princeville Kauai and Kauai Travel Guide*, accessed 29 July 2013, www.vacationrentalkauaihawaii.com/language-hawaii-rentals.html.
20 B. Hayes, *Introductory Phonology* (Malden, MA: Blackwell, 2008).
21 L. Truss, *Eats, Shoots and Leaves: The Zero Tolerance Approach to Punctuation* (London, UK: Profile Books, 2003).
22 N. Chomsky, *Syntactic Structures* (The Hague/Paris: Mouton, 1957).
23 C. Eble, *Slang and Sociability: In-Group Language among College Students* (Chapel Hill: The University of North Carolina Press, 1996); C. Eble, "Slang," In *Language in the USA: Themes for the Twenty-First Century*, ed. Edward Finegan and John R. Rickford (Cambridge, UK: Cambridge University Press, 2004), 375–86.
24 A. Reyes, "Appropriation of African American Slang by Asian American Youth," *Journal of Sociolinguistics* 9, no. 4 (2005): 509–32.
25 L. Cherry Wilkinson, A. Cherry Wilkinson, F. Spinelli, and C.P. Chiang, "Metalinguistic Knowledge of Pragmatic Rules in School-Age Children," *Child Development* 55, no. 6 (1984): 2130–40.
26 S. Ting-Toomey, *Communicating across Cultures* (New York: Guilford Press, 1999), 10.
27 L. Von Schneidemesser, "Soda or Pop?," *Journal of English Linguistics* 24, no. 4 (1996): 270–87.
28 A. Jacot de Boinod, *The Meaning of Tingo and Other Extraordinary Words from around the World* (London, UK: Penguin Books, 2006).
29 K. Pidduck. "What Did Y'all Say?," in S.D. Ferguson, *Public Speaking in Canada: Building Competency in Stages* (New York: Oxford University Press, 2007), 136–7.
30 R.J. Lingwood, P. Boyle, A. Milburn, T. Ngoma, J. Arbuthnott, R. McCaffrey, S.H. Kerr, and D.J. Kerr, "The Challenge of Cancer Control in Africa," *Nature Reviews Cancer* 8, no. 5 (2008): 398–403.
31 E. Sapir, *Language* (New York: Harcourt Brace, 1921); E. Sapir, "The Status of Linguistics as a Science," in *Selected Writings*, ed. D. Mandelbaum (Berkeley: University of California Press, [1929] 1951); B. Whorf, "Science and Linguistics," in *Language, Thought and Reality*, ed. J.B. Carroll (Cambridge, AM: MIT, [1940] 1956); B.L. Whorf, "The Relation of Habitual Thought and Behavior to Language," in *Language, Thought and Reality*, ed. J.B. Carroll Cambridge, MA: MIT, [1941] 1956).
32 R. Boswell, "Ottawa Fears Suit over Native Languages," *National Post*, 16 February 2012, http://news.nationalpost.com/2012/02/16/ottawa-fears-suit-over-native-languages.
33 J. Penhale, "More Indigenous Language and Culture Needed on Canada's Airwaves," *Rabble.ca*, 14 May 2012, http://rabble.ca/news/2012/05/canada-needs-more-indigenous-culture-radio.
34 Ministry of Aboriginal Relations and Reconciliation, "Pre-school Language Nest Program," Government of British Columbia, accessed 28 May 2012, www.gov.bc.ca/arr/cultural/fcf/pslnp.html.
35 Ministry of Aboriginal Relations and Reconciliation, "Language and Culture Immersion Camps," Government of British Columbia, 28 May 2012, www.gov.bc.ca/arr/cultural/fcf/lcic.html.
36 M. Cardwell, "The Fight to Revitalize Canada's Indigenous Languages," *University Affairs*, 8 November 2010, www.universityaffairs.ca/fight-to-revitalize-canadas-indigenous-languages.aspx.
37 D. Hruschka, M. Christiansen, R. Blythe, W. Croft, P. Heggarty, S. Mufwene, J. Pierrehumbert, and S. Poplack, "Building Social Cognitive Models of Language Change," *Trends in Cognitive Science* 13, no. 11 (2009): 464–9.
38 S.A. Tagliamonte, *Variationist Sociolinguistics: Change, Observation, Interpretation* (Malden, MA: Wiley-Blackwell, 2012).
39 Ibid.
40 E. Banville and A. Gradstein, "Drippin' Episode," *Zoey 101*, season 3, episode 17, directed by D. Kendall, aired 21 October 2007 on Nickelodeon.
41 S. Tagliamonte and D. Denis, "Linguistic Ruin? Lol! Instant Messaging and Teen Language," *American Speech* 83, no. 1 (2008): 3–33.
42 K. Axtman, "'R U Online?': The Evolving Lexicon of Wired Teens," *Christian Science Monitor*, 12 December 2002, www.csmonitor.com/2002/1212/p01s01-ussc.html.
43 Tagliamonte and Denis, "Linguistic Ruin? Lol!," 26.
44 P. Eckert, "Language and Gender in Adolescence," in *Handbook of Language and Gender*, ed. J. Holmes and M. Meyerhoff (Oxford, UK: Blackwell, 2003); P. Eckert, "Adolescent Language," in *Language in the USA: Themes for the Twenty-First Century*, ed. E. Finegan and J. Rickford (New York: Cambridge University Press, 2004), 361–74.

45 L. Wolk, N.B. Abdelli-Beruh, and D. Slavin, "Habitual Use of Vocal Fry in Young Adult Female Speakers," *Journal of Voice* 26, no. 3 (2012): 111–16.

46 S.A. Tagliamonte, "So Different and Pretty Cool: Recycling Intensifiers in Toronto, Canada," *English Language and Linguistics* 12, no. 2 (2008): 361–94; S.A. Tagliamonte and A. D'Arcy, "Peaks beyond Phonology: Adolescence, Incrementation, and Language Change," *Language Variation and Change* 85, no. 1 (2009): 58–108; S. Tagliamonte and A. Darcy. "Frequency and Variation in the Community Grammar: Tracking a New Change through the Generations," *Language Variation and Change* 19, no. 2 (2007): 199–217.

47 S.A. Tagliamonte, "Be Like: The New Quotative of English," in *The New Sociolinguistics Reader*, ed. N. Coupland and A. Jaworski (New York: Palgrave/Macmillan, 2009), 75–91.

48 Tagliamonte and Denis, "Linguistic Ruin? Lol!," 25.

49 M. Heidegger, *An Introduction to Metaphysics*, trans. R. Manheim (New Haven, CT: Yale University Press, 1959), 13.

50 P. Berger and T. Luckmann, *The Social Construction of Reality: A Treatise in the Sociology of Knowledge* (Garden City, NY: Doubleday, 1966), 52.

51 Y. Shibata, *Governing Employees: A Foucauldian Analysis of Deaths from Overwork in Japan*, Social and Cultural Research Occasional Paper series (North Point, Hong Kong: Centre for Qualitative Social Research, 2012).

52 J. Kelly, "Baby Talk," *How I Met Your Mother*, season 6, episode 6, directed by P. Fryman, aired 25 October 2010 on CBS.

53 C. Hax, "Agreeing on a Child's Name," *Washington Post*, 26 April 2013, www.washingtonpost.com/lifestyle/style/carolyn-hax-agreeing-on-a-babys-name-family-trips-loaded-with-guilt/2013/04/26/7ab9b1c2-a1f9-11e2-be47-b44febada3a8_story.html?wpisrc=nl_headlines.

54 A. Mehrabian, *The Name Game: The Decision that Lasts a Lifetime* (New York: Penguin Group, 1992); A. Mehrabian, "Characteristics Aattributed to Individuals on the Basis of Their First Names," *Genetic, Social, and General Psychology Monographs* 127 (2001): 59–88.

55 L. Rosenkrantz and P.R. Satran, *Beyond Jennifer & Jason, Madison & Montana* (New York: St Martin's Press, 2000).

56 Ibid.

57 G. Stupnitsky and L. Eisenberg, "The Convention," *The Office*, season 3, episode 2, directed by K. Whittingham, aired 28 September 2006 on NBC.

58 D. Tannen, *Conversational Style: Analyzing Talk among Friends* (New York: Oxford University Press, 2005); D. Tannen, *You Just Don't Understand: Women and Men in Conversation* (New York: Ballantyne, 1990); D. Tannen, *Gender and Discourse* (New York: Oxford University Press, 1996).

59 C.I. Hovland, I.L. Janis, and H.H. Kelley, *Communication and Persuasion* (New Haven, CT: Yale University Press, 1953).

60 L.L. Haleta, "Student Perceptions of Teachers' Use of Language: The Effects of Powerful and Powerless Language on Impression Formation and Uncertainty," *Communication Education* 45, no. 1 (1996): 16–28.

61 D. Tannen, "Conversational Style," in *Psycholinguistic Models of Production*, ed. H.W. Dechert and M. Raupach (Norwood, NJ: Ablex, 1987), 251–67.

62 Tannen, "Conversational Style."

63 Tannen, *You Just Don't Understand*.

64 N.A. Mendoza, H.M. Hosch, B.J. Ponder, and V. Carrillo, "Well . . . Ah . . . : Hesitations and Hedges as an Influence on Jurors' Decisions," *Journal of Applied Social Psychology* 30, no. 12 (2000): 2610–21.

65 L. Hosman and S. Siltanen, "Hedges, Tag Questions, Information Processing, and Persuasion," *Journal of Language and Social Psychology* 30, no. 3 (2011): 341–9; Leaper and Robnett, "Women Are More Likely"; L. Carli, "Gender and Social Issues," *Journal of Social Issues* 57, no. 4 (2001): 725–41.

66 A.H. Rosenstein, H. Russell, and R. Lauve, "Disruptive Physician Behavior Contributes to Nursing Shortage," *Physician Executive* 28 (2002): 8–11.

67 E. Gjerberg and L. Kjolsrod, "The Doctor–Nurse Relationship: How Easy Is It to Be a Female Doctor Co-operating with a Female Nurse?," *Social Science and Medicine* 52 (2001): 189–202.

68 L.I. Stein, "The Doctor–Nurse Game," *Archives of General Psychiatry* 16 (1967): 699–703.

69 L. MacKey, *Conflicts in Care Medicine and Nursing* (London, UK: Chapman and Hall, 1993).

70 M.B. Wanzer, M. Booth-Butterfield, and K. Gruber, "Perceptions of Health Care Providers: Communication Relationships between Patient-Centered Communication and Satisfaction," *Health Communication* 16 (2004): 363–84.

71 M.B. Wanzer, M. Wojtaszczyk, and J. Kelly, "Nurses' Perceptions of Physicians' Communication: The Relationship among Communication Practices, Satisfaction, and Collaboration," *Health Communication* 24 (2009): 683–91.

72 C. Leaper and R.D. Robnett, "Women Are More Likely than Men to Use Tentative Language, Aren't They?," *Psychology of Women Quarterly* 35, no. 1 (2011): 129–42.

73 C. Glaser, *Gendertalk Works: 7 Steps for Cracking the Gender Code at Work* (New York: Jedco Press, 2007).

74 A. Nooritajer, A. Mahfozpour, and A. Nouruzi-Nejad, "The Head Nurses Participatory Decision Making at the Educational Hospitals of IUMSHS (Iran University of Medical Sciences and Health Services)," *Journal of Health Administration* 10, no. 28 (2007): 7–14.

75 M.J. Beatty and R.R. Behnke, "Teacher Credibility as a Function of Verbal Content and Paralinguistic

Cues," *Communication Quarterly* 28, no. 1 (1980): 55–9; Ferguson, *Public Speaking*; J.L. Terrion, "Making More Powerful Presentations," *Canadian Government Executive* 3 (2000): 30–1.

76 J. Mulholland, *The Language of Negotiation: A Handbook of Practical Strategies for Improving Communication* (London, UK: Routledge, 1991).

77 Ibid.

78 E.K. Alexander and J.H. Lord, "Impact Statements: A Victim's Right to Speak, a Nation's Responsibility to Listen," National Victim Center and Mothers against Drunk Driving, 15 July 1994, www.ncjrs.gov/ovc_archives/reports/impact/welcome.html.

79 Ibid.

80 D. Adams, "The Pirate Planet," *Doctor Who*, serial 99, episode 2, directed by P. Roberts, aired 7 October 1978 on BBC.

81 Ferguson, *Public Speaking*, 107.

82 E.M. Eisenberg, "Ambiguity as Strategy in Organizational Communication," *Communication Monographs* 51 (1984): 227–42; J.L. Terrion and B. Ashforth, "From I to We: Humor, Metaphor, and Equivocality in the Development of a Temporary Group," *Human Relations* 55 (2002): 55–88.

83 C. Hignite, "Craigslist Secrets Exposed: Prostitution in the Dating Ads," *Examiner.com*, 1 October 2010, www.examiner.com/article/craigslist-secrets-exposed-prostitution-the-dating-ads.

84 Ibid.

85 A. Hess, "The Secret Prostitution Code and What It Says about Johns," *Washington City Paper*, 27 October 2009, www.washingtoncitypaper.com/blogs/sexist/2009/10/27/the-secret-prostitution-code-of-johns.

86 E. Eisenberg, *Strategic Ambiguities: Essays on Communication, Organization, and Identity* (Thousand Oaks, CA: Sage Publications, 2007); K.E. Weick, *The Social Psychology of Organizing*, 2nd ed. (Reading, MA: Addison-Wesley, 1979).

87 Eisenberg, *Strategic Ambiguities*, 5.

88 Eisenberg, *Strategic Ambiguities*, 11.

89 Based on Ferguson, *Public Speaking in Canada*, 107.

90 Ibid.

91 M.M. Osborne and D. Ehninger, "The Metaphor in Public Address," *Speech Monographs* 29 (1962): 223–34.

92 M. Miller, "Canceled? Nah: The TV Industry Uses Less Objectionable Words to Kill Off a Show," *Los Angeles Times*, 2 July 2007, http://articles.latimes.com/2007/jul/02/entertainment/et-canceled2.

93 W. Lutz, *Doublespeak: From Revenue Enhancement to Terminal Living: How Government, Business, Advertisers, and Others Use the Language to Deceive* (New York: Harper Collins, 1990). Also W.D. Lutz, *Doublespeak Defined: Cut through the Bull**** and Get to the Point* (New York: Harper Resource, 1999).

94 Lutz, *Doublespeak: From Revenue Enhancement to Terminal Living*. Also Lutz, *Doublespeak Defined*.

95 A. Curtis, *The Century of the Self*, documentary miniseries, aired 17 March–7 April 2002 on BBC Four.

96 "Cigarette Use among Teens Inches Downward: Rate Is Higher in Rural Areas," *CA: A Cancer Journal for Clinicians* 52 (2002): 3–4.

97 P. Lin, "The One where Chandler Doesn't Like Dogs," *Friends*, season 7, episode 8, directed by K.S. Bright, aired 23 November 2000 on NBC.

98 Estabon, "What Does the Word "Dating" Mean to You?," Yahoo forum, 2009, http://answers.yahoo.com/question/index?qid=20090528122041AAaWS7Y.

99 J. McCann, "Dating or Seeing Someone . . . What Is the Difference?," Plenty of Fish forum, 20 December 2005, http://forums.plentyoffish.com/datingPosts2772626.aspx.

100 J. Pimlott, "*Fag Hags*: Women Who Love Men," *Passionate Eye*, aired 29 September 2005 on CBC.

101 H. Duff, "Think before You Speak ('That's So Gay')," YouTube video, 8 October 2008, www.youtube.com/watch?v=TVicCD8FmMs.

102 The discussion of politically correct language comes from Ferguson, *Public Speaking*, pp. 143–5.

103 Haleta, "Student Perceptions."

104 R.A. Schwartz-Mette and A.J. Rose, "Conversational Self-Focus in Adolescent Friendships: Observational Assessment of an Interpersonal Process and Relations with Internalizing Symptoms and Friendship Quality," *Journal of Social and Clinical Psychology* 1, no. 28 (2009): 1263–97.

105 J.C. McCroskey, "Communication Competence and Performance: A Research and Pedagogical Perspective," *Communication Education* 31, no. 1 (1982): 1–7; B.H. Spitzberg, "Communication Competence as Knowledge, Skill, and Impression," *Communication Education* 32, no. 3 (1983): 323–9.

106 Ferguson, *Public Speaking*.

107 A.N. Shelby and N.L. Reinsch Jr, "Positive Emphasis and You-Attitude: An Empirical Study," *Journal of Business Communication* 32, no. 4 (1995): 303–26.

108 D.J. O'Keefe and J.D. Jensen, "Do Loss-Framed Persuasive Messages Engender Greater Message Processing than Do Gain-Framed Messages? A Meta-Analytic Review," *Communication Studies* 59, no. 1 (2008): 51–67.

109 K.O. Locker, *Business and Administrative Communication*, 4th ed. (New York: Irwin/McGraw-Hill, 1997).

110 B. Meglino and M. Korsgaard, "The Role of Other Orientation in Reactions to Job Characteristics," *Journal of Management* 33 (2007): 57–83, 59.

CHAPTER 7

1 Paul Ekman Group, "Paul Ekman," 2013, www.paulekman.com/content/paul-ekman.

2 J. Foreman, "A Conversation with Paul Ekman: The 43 Facial Muscles that Reveal Even the Most Fleeting Emotions," *New York Times*, 5 August 2003, www.nytimes.com/2003/08/05/health/conversation-with-paul-ekman-43-facial-muscles-that-reveal-even-most-fleeting.html.
3 Paul Ekman Group, "Paul Ekman."
4 S. Weinberger, "Airport Security: Intent to Deceive?," *Nature* 465 (2010): 412–15, www.nature.com/news/2010/100526/full/465412a.html.
5 "Oprah's Lance Armstrong Interview Viewed by 28 Million Worldwide," *Huffington Post*, 22 January 2013, www.huffingtonpost.com/2013/01/22/oprahs-lance-armstrong-interview-28-million-worldwide_n_2530338.html.
6 C.K. Goman, "Why Lance Armstrong Looks Like a Liar," *Forbes*, 18 January 2013, www.forbes.com/sites/carolkinseygoman/2013/01/18/why-lance-armstrong-looks-like-a-liar.
7 S.A. Beebe and J.T. Masterson, *Communicating in Small Groups: Principles and Practices*, 9th ed. (Boston, MA: Pearson, 2009); also see R.B. Adler, L.B. Rosenfeld, R.F. Proctor II, and C. Winder, *Interplay: The Process of Interpersonal Communication*, 3rd Canadian ed. (Toronto, ON: Oxford University Press, 2012).
8 M. McLuhan, *Understanding Media: the Extensions of Man* (Cambridge, MA: MIT Press, 1964).
9 Canadian Association of the Deaf, "Terminology," accessed 3 May 2013 www.cad.ca/terminology_links.php.
10 A. Kondolojy, "ABC Family Announces All ASL Episode of *Switched at Birth*," *TV by the Numbers*, 11 January 2013, http://tvbythenumbers.zap2it.com/2013/01/11/abc-family-announces-all-asl-episode-of-switched-at-birth-to-air-monday-march-4/165052.
11 See P. Ekman and W.V. Friesen, "The Repertoire of Nonverbal Behaviour: Categories, Origins, Usages, and Coding," *Semiotica* 1 (1969): 49–98; P. Ekman and W.V. Friesen, *Unmasking the Face* (Englewood Cliffs, NJ: Prentice Hall, 1975); V.P. Richmond and J.C. McCroskey, *Nonverbal Behaviour in Interpersonal Relations* (Boston, MA: Allyn and Bacon, 2004).
12 P. Ekman and W.V. Friesen, "Hand Movements," *Journal of Communication* 22 (1972): 353–74.
13 R.E. Axtell, *Gestures: The Do's and Taboos of Body Language around the World* (New York: Wiley, 1998).
14 Ekman and Friesen, "Hand Movements."
15 See H. Sacks, E.A. Schegloff, and G. Jefferson, "A Simplest Systematics for the Organization of Turn-Taking for Conversation," *Language* 50 (1974):696–735.
16 See S. Duncan, "Some Signals and Rules for Taking Speaking Turns in Conversations," *Journal of Personality and Social Psychology* 23 (1972): 283–92.
17 See M.L. Knapp and J.A. Hall, *Nonverbal Communication in Human Interaction* (New York: Holt, Rinehart, and Winston, 2010).
18 Ekman and Friesen, "The Repertoire of Nonverbal Behaviour."
19 D.L. Roter, R.M. Frankel, J.A. Hall, and D. Sluyter, "The Expression of Emotion through Nonverbal Behaviour in Medical Visits: Mechanisms and Outcomes," *Journal of General Internal Medicine* 21, no. S1 (2006): S28–S34.
20 Ibid.
21 Ekman and Friesen, "Hand Movements."
22 A. Mehrabian, *Silent Messages* (Belmont, CA: Wadsworth, 1971).
23 M. Argyle, F. Alkema, and R. Gilmour, "The Communication of Friendly and Hostile Attitudes by Verbal and Nonverbal Signals," *European Journal of Social Psychology* 1 (1971): 385–402.
24 H. Aviezer, Y. Trope, and A. Todorov, "Body Cues, Not Facial Expressions, Discriminate between Intense Positive and Negative Emotions," *Science* 338, no. 6111 (2012): 1225–9.
25 Ibid.
26 R. Chillot, "The Power of Touch," *Psychology Today*, 11 March 2013, www.psychologytoday.com/articles/201302/the-power-touch.
27 D.T. Gilbert, "How Mental Systems Believe," *American Psychologist* 46 (1991): 107–19; C. Hendrick and A.F. Costantini, "Effects of Varying Trait Inconsistency and Response Requirements on the Primacy Effect in Impression Formation," *Journal of Personality and Social Psychology* 15 (1970): 158–64; E.E. Jones, *Interpersonal Perception* (New York: Freeman, 1990).
28 Gilbert, "How Mental Systems Believe"; Hendrick and Costantini, "Effects of Varying Trait Inconsistency"; Jones, *Interpersonal Perception*; S.E. Asch, "Forming Impressions of Personality," *Journal of Abnormal and Social Psychology* 41(1946): 258–90; H.H. Kelley, "The Warm–Cold Variable in First Impressions of Persons," *Journal of Personality* 18 (1950): 431–9; W.D. Crano, "Primacy versus Recency in Retention of Information," *Journal of Social Psychology* 101 (1977): 87–96.
29 N.P. Li, J.M. Bailey, D.T. Kenrick, and J. A. Linsenmeier "The Necessities and Luxuries of Mate Preference: Testing the Trade-Offs," *Journal of Personality and Social Psychology 82* (2002): 947–85.
30 A.H. Eagly, R.D. Ashmore, M.G. Makhijani, and L.C. Longo, "What Is Beautiful Is Good, but . . . : A Meta-analytic Review of Research on the Physical Attractiveness Stereotype," *Psychological Bulletin* 110 (1991): 109–28.
31 D.R. Ames and E.C. Bianchi, "The Agreeableness Asymmetry in First Impressions: Perceivers' Impulse to (Mis)judge Agreeableness and How It Is Moderated by Power," *Personality and Social Psychology Bulletin* 34, no. 12 (2008): 1719–36.

32 Ames and Bianchi, "The Agreeableness Asymmetry"; D.R. Ames, L.K. Kammrath, A. Suppes, and N. Bolger, "Not So Fast: The (Not-Quite-Complete) Dissociation between Accuracy and Confidence in Thin-Slice Impressions," *Personality and Social Psychology Bulletin* 36, no. 2 (2010): 264–77; J.C. Biesanz, L.J. Human, A.-C. Paquin, M. Chan, K.L. Parisotto, J. Sarracino, and R.L. Gillis, "Do We Know When Our Impressions of Others Are Valid? Evidence for Realistic Accuracy Awareness in First Impressions of Personality," *Social Psychological and Personality Science* 2, no. 5 (2011): 452–9.

33 J. Denrell, "Why Most People Disapprove of Me: Experience Sampling in Impression Formation," *Psychological Review* 112, no. 4 (2005): 951–78.

34 Ames et al., "Not So Fast," 273.

35 See B. Grayson and M.I. Stein, "Attracting Assault: Victims' Nonverbal Cues," *Journal of Communication* 31, no. 1 (1981): 68–75.

36 R. LaHaie, "Why Is Everybody Always Picking on Me? Short Circuiting the Victim Selection Process," accessed 11 June 2013, http://empowernet.ca/wp-content/uploads/2013/05/Why-Is-Everybody-Always-Picking-On-Me.pdf.

37 C.N. Macrae and S. Quadflieg, "Perceiving People," in *The Handbook of Social Psychology*, 5th ed., ed. S. Fiske, D.T. Gilbert, and G. Lindzey (New York: McGraw-Hill, 428–63).

38 M. Weisbuch, N. Ambady, A.L. Clarke, S. Achor, and J.V.V. Weele, "On Being Consistent: The Role of Verbal–Nonverbal Consistency in First Impressions," *Basic and Applied Social Psychology* 32 (2010): 261–8.

39 J.K. Burgoon, "A Communication Model of Personal Space Violation: Explication and an Initial Test," *Human Communication Research* 4 (1978): 129–42.

40 L.J. Sanna and K.J. Turley, "Antecedents to Spontaneous Counterfactual Thinking: Effects of Expectancy Violation and Outcome Valence," *Personality and Social Psychology Bulletin* 22 (1996): 906–19.

41 M. Casserly, "Ten Body Language Tics that Could Cost You the Interview—and the Job," *Forbes*, 26 September 2012, www.forbes.com/sites/meghancasserly/2012/09/26/10-body-language-tics-that-could-cost-you-the-interview-and-the-job.

42 P. Andersen, *Nonverbal Communication: Forms and Functions (Mountain View, CA: Mayfield, 1999).*

43 Casserly, "Ten Body Language Tics."

44 M. Casserly, "'You Look Like a Convict' and the Most Common Pitfalls of Interviewing over Skype," *Forbes*, 3 September 2012, www.forbes.com/sites/meghancasserly/2012/10/03/you-look-like-a-convict-common-pitfalls-of-skype-video-interviews.

45 Mehrabian, *Silent Messages*, 1.

46 A. Mehrabian, "Some Referents and Measures of Nonverbal Behaviour," *Behaviour Research Methods and Instrumentation* 1 (1969): 203–07, 203.

47 V.P. Richmond and J.C. McCroskey, "The Impact of Supervisor and Subordinate Immediacy on Relational and Organizational Outcomes," *Communication Monographs* 67, no. 1 (2000): 85–95; V.P. Richmond, J.C. McCroskey, and A.D. Johnson, "Development of the Nonverbal Immediacy Scale (NIS): Measures of Self- and Other-Perceived Nonverbal Immediacy," *Communication Quarterly* 51 (2003): 502–15; L.L. Hinkle, "Nonverbal Immediacy Communication Behaviours and Liking in Marriage," *Communication Research Reports* 16 (1999): 81–90.

48 J.K. Burgoon, T. Birk, and M. Pfau, "Nonverbal Behaviours, Persuasion, and Credibility," *Human Communication Research* 17 (1990): 140–69.

49 J.J. Teven and J.L. Winters, "Pharmaceutical Representatives' Social Influence Behaviours and Communication Orientations: Relationships with Adaptive Selling and Sales Performance," *Human Communication* 10, no. 4 (2007): 465–86.

50 P.D. Cherulnik, K.A. Donley, T.S.R. Wiewel, and S.R. Miller, "Charisma is Contagious: The Effect of Leaders' Charisma on Observers' Affect," *Journal of Applied Social Psychology* 31 (2001): 2149–59.

51 R. Greene, *The Five Communication Secrets that Swept Obama to the Presidency* (New York: Films Media Group, 2008), DVD.

52 C.K. Goman, "Body Language Will Make or Break Future Leaders," *Forbes*, 8 February 2012, www.forbes.com/sites/carolkinseygoman/2012/08/02/body-language-will-make-or-break-future-leaders.

53 S.C. Johnson and A.N. Miller, "A Cross-cultural Study of Immediacy, Credibility, and Learning in the US and Kenya," *Communication Education* 51 (2002): 280–92.

54 J.F. Andersen, "Teacher Immediacy as a Predictor of Teaching Effectiveness," in *Communication Yearbook*, vol. 3, ed. D. Nimmo (New Brunswick, NJ: Transaction Books, 1979), 543–59.

55 Ibid.

56 Andersen, "Teacher Immediacy"; L. Pogue and K. AhYun, "The Effect of Teacher Nonverbal Immediacy and Credibility on Student Motivation and Affective Learning," *Communication Education* 55 (2006): 331–44; L.J. Christensen and K.E. Menzel, "The Linear Relationship between Student Reports of Teacher Immediacy Behaviours and Perceptions of State Motivation, and of Cognitive, Affective, and Behavioural Learning," *Communication Education* 47 (1998): 82–90; D.M. Christophel, "The Relationship among Teacher Immediacy Behaviours, Student Motivation, and Learning," *Communication Education* 39 (1990): 323–40.

57 D.H. Kelley and J. Gorham, "Effects of Immediacy on Recall of Information," *Communication Education* 37 (1988): 198–207.

[58] J.L. Chesebro and J.C. McCroskey, "The Relationship of Teacher Clarity and Immediacy with Student State Receiver Apprehension, Affect, and Cognitive Learning," *Communication Education* 50 (2001): 59–68; V.P. Richmond, J.S. Gorham, and J.C. McCroskey, "The Relationship between Selected Immediacy Behaviours and Cognitive Learning," in *Communication Yearbook 10,* ed. M.L. McLaughlin (Newbury Park, CA: Sage, 1987), 574–90.

[59] K.A. Rocca, "College Student Attendance: Impact of Instructor Immediacy and Verbal Aggression," *Communication Education* 53 (2004): 185–95.

[60] M.A. Jaasma and R.J. Koper, "The Relationship between Student-Faculty Out-of-Class Communication to Instructor Immediacy and Trust, and to Student Motivation," *Communication Education* 48 (1999): 41–7.

[61] A. Moore, J.T. Masterson, D.M. Christophel, and K.A. Shea, "College Teacher Immediacy and Student Ratings of Instruction," *Communication Education* 45 (1996): 29–39.

[62] A. Kerr, *Teaching and Learning in Large Classes at Ontario Universities: An Exploratory Study* (Toronto: Higher Education Quality Council of Ontario, 2011).

[63] P.L. Witt and P. Schrodt, "The Influence of Instructional Technology Use and Teacher Immediacy on Student Affect for Teacher and Course," *Communication Reports* 19 (2006): 1–15.

[64] J.L. Cooper and P. Robinson, "The Argument for Making Large Classes Seem Small," in *New Directions for Teaching and Learning: Energizing the Large Classroom,* J.L. Cooper and P. Robinson (San Francisco, CA, Jossey-Bass, 2000), 5–16.

[65] L.K. Guerrero and K. Floyd, *Nonverbal Communication in Close Relationships* (Mahwah, NJ: Lawrence Erlbaum, 2006); J.T. Wood, *Interpersonal Communication—Everyday Encounters*, 7th ed. (Belmont, CA: Wadsworth, 2013).

[66] M. Knapp, *Interpersonal Communication and Human Relationships* (Boston: Allyn and Bacon, 1984).

[67] M.R. Cunningham and A.P. Barbee, "Communication Dynamics in the Initiation of Romantic Relationships," in *Handbook of Relationship Initiation*, ed. S. Sprecher, A. Wenzel, and J. Harvey (New York: Taylor and Francis, 2008), 97–120.

[68] M.M. Moore, "Human Nonverbal Courtship Behaviour—A Brief Historical Review," *Journal of Sex Research* 47 (2010): 171–80, 178.

[69] Ibid.

[70] M.L. Knapp and A.L. Vangelisti, *Interpersonal Communication and Human Relationships*, 4th ed. (Boston: Allyn and Bacon, 2000), 323.

[71] M.A. Fitzpatrick, *Between Husbands and Wives: Communication in Marriage* (Sage: Newbury Park, 1988).

[72] Guerrero and Floyd, *Nonverbal Communication*; Wood, *Interpersonal Communication.*

[73] S.R. Covey, *The Seven Habits of Highly Effective People* (New York: Simon and Schuster, 1989), 79–80.

[74] P. Ekman and W.V. Friesen, "Constants across Cultures in the Face and Emotion," *Journal of Personality and Social Psychology* 11 (1971): 124–9.

[75] C.L. Kleinke, "Gaze and Eye Contact: A Research Review," *Psychological Bulletin* 100 (1986): 78–100.

[76] C. Perilloux, J.A. Easton, and D.M. Buss, "The Misperception of Sexual Interest," *Psychological Science* 23, no. 2 (2012): 146–51.

[77] L.A., Samovar, R.E. Porter, and E.R. McDaniel, *Communication between Cultures* (Belmont, CA: Thomson Higher Education, 2007).

[78] Duncan, "Some Signals and Rules."

[79] M. Argyle and J. Dean, "Eye Contact, Distance, and Affiliation," *Sociometry* 28, no. 3 (1965): 289–304.

[80] Burgoon et al., "Nonverbal Behaviours, Persuasion, and Credibility."

[81] Argyle and Dean, "Eye Contact, Distance, and Affiliation."

[82] M. Argyle and M. Cook, *Gaze and Mutual Gaze* (Oxford, UK: Cambridge University Press, 1976).

[83] P.J. Hills and M.B. Lewis, "Sad People Avoid the Eyes or Happy People Focus on the Eyes? Mood Induction Affects Facial Feature Discrimination," *British Journal of Psychology* 102 (2011): 260–74.

[84] C.C. Tigue, D.J. Borak, M. O'Connor, C. Schandl, and D.R. Feinberg, "Voice Pitch Influences Voting Behaviour," *Evolution and Human Behaviour* 33 (2012): 210–16.

[85] C.A. Klofstad, R.C. Anderson, and S. Peters, "Sounds Like a Winner: Voice Pitch Influences Perception of Leadership Capacity in Both Men and Women." *Proceedings of the Royal Society B* 279, no. 1738 (7 July 2012): 2698–704.

[86] N. Miller, G. Maruyama, R.J. Beaber, and K. Valone, "Speed of Speech and Persuasion," *Journal of Personality and Social Psychology* 34, no. 4 (1976): 615–24.

[87] C.J. Carpenter, "A Meta-analysis and an Experiment Investigating the Effects of Speaker Disfluency on Persuasion," *Western Journal of Communication* 76, no. 5 (2012): 552–69; N.A. Mendoza, H.M. Hosch, B.J. Ponder, and V. Carrillo, "Well . . . Ah . . . : Hesitations and Hedges as an Influence on Jurors' Decisions," *Journal of Applied Social Psychology* 30, no. 12 (2000): 2610–21.

[88] R.J. Duffy, M.F. Hunt Jr, and T.G. Giolas, "Effects of Four Types of Disfluency on Listener Reactions," *Folia Phoniat* 27 (1975): 106–15.

[89] A. Belford, "Left out in the Cold by Revival of Old Rules," *New York Times*, 12 October 2010, www.nytimes.com/2010/10/13/world/asia/13iht-bali.html?_r=1&.

[90] R. Birdwhistell, *Introduction to Kinesics: An Annotation System for Analysis of Body Motion and Gesture* (Louisville, KY: University of Louisville, 1952).

[91] Ekman and Friesen, "The Repertoire of Nonverbal Behaviour."

[92] R. Laneri, "Body Language Decoded," *Forbes*, 23 June 2009, www.forbes.com/2009/06/23/body-language-first-impression-forbes-woman-leadership-communication_print.html.
[93] Ibid.
[94] Greene, *The Five Communication Secrets.*
[95] D.R. Carney, A.J. Cuddy, and A.J. Yap, "Power Posing: Brief Nonverbal Displays Affect Neuroendocrine Levels and Risk Tolerance," *Psychological Science* 21, no. 10 (2010): 1363–8.
[96] Andersen, *Nonverbal Communication.*
[97] T. Field, *Touch* (Cambridge, MA: MIT Press, 2003).
[98] Field, *Touch.*
[99] Ibid.
[100] R. Everett-Green, "New Gizmos Add a Physical Component to Online Relationships," *Globe and Mail*, 18 October 2012, www.theglobeandmail.com/life/fashion-and-beauty/fashion/new-gizmos-add-a-physical-component-to-online-relationships/article4621846/?cmpid=rss1.
[101] Ibid.
[102] T. Grandin, "Calming Effects of Deep Touch Pressure in Patients with Autistic Disorder, College Students, and Animals," *Journal of Child and Adolescent Psychopharmacology* 2, no. 1 (1992): 63–72.
[103] L. Guerrero, P.A. Andersen, and W.A. Afifi, *Close Encounters: Communication in Relationships*, 4th ed. (Thousand Oaks, CA: Sage Publications, 2012).
[104] Field, *Touch.*
[105] Andersen, *Nonverbal Communication.*
[106] Chillot, "The Power of Touch."
[107] Guerrero et al., *Close Encounters.*
[108] S. Johnson, *Hold Me Tight: Seven Conversations for a Lifetime of Love* (New York: Little, Brown, 2008).
[109] Chillot, "The Power of Touch."
[110] D. Gibson, *Stories about Storytellers* (Toronto: ECW Press, 2011).
[111] Field, *Touch.*
[112] G. Stone, "Appearance and the Self," in *Human Behaviour and Social Processes: An Interactionist Approach*, ed. A. Rose (Boston: Houghton Mifflin, 1962), 86–116.
[113] J.G. Noll, C.E. Shenk, J.E. Barnes, and F.W. Putnam, "Childhood Abuse, Avatar Choices, and Other Risk Factors Associated with Internet-Initiated Victimization of Adolescent Girls," *Pediatrics* 123 (2009): e1078–83, http://pediatrics.aappublications.org/content/123/6/e1078.full.pdf.
[114] S. Au, F. Khandwala, and H. Stelfox, "Physician Attire in the Intensive Care Unit and Patient Family Perceptions of Physician Professional Characteristics," *JAMA: Internal Medicine* 173, no. 6 (2013): 465–7.
[115] S. Milgram, "Behavioral Study of Obedience," *Journal of Abnormal and Social Psychology* 67 (1963): 371–8.
[116] S. Ghumman and A.M. Ryan, "Not Welcome Here: Discrimination towards Women Who Wear the Muslim Headscarf," *Human Relations* 66 (2013): 671–98.
[117] Ibid.
[118] Ibid.
[119] P. Waldie, "Two Canadian Links to Discovery of Richard III," *Globe and Mail*, 4 February 2013, www.theglobeandmail.com/news/world/two-canadian-links-to-discovery-of-richard-iii/article8158525.
[120] Ibid.
[121] M. Lüscher, *The Lüscher Colour Test* (New York: Pan Books, 1972).
[122] F.M. Adams and C.E. Osgood, "A Cross-cultural Study of the Affective Meanings of Color," *Journal of Cross-cultural Psychology* 4, no. 2 (1973): 135–56.
[123] C. Gill, "Cross-cultural Meanings of Colour in Brand Design," 28 April 2010, www.trulydeeply.com.au/madly/2010/04/28/cross-cultural-meanings-of-colour-in-brand-design.
[124] L. Jacobs, C. Keown, R. Worthley, and K. Ghymn, "Cross-cultural Colour Comparisons: Global Marketers Beware!," *International Marketing Review* 8, no. 3 (1991): 21–30.
[125] M. Mitchell, "Savvy International Manufacturers Need to Know Their Colours," University of Illinois News Bureau, 6 February 1997, http://news.illinois.edu/ii/97/970206/colors.html.
[126] Gill, "Cross-cultural Meanings of Colour."
[127] Ibid.
[128] E.T. Hall, *The Hidden Dimension* (New York: Doubleday, 1966).
[129] M. Sobociński, "On Proxemics and Territoriality in Communicative Behaviour of Man: A Communiqué," in *Consultant Assembly III: In Search of Innovatory Subjects for Language and Culture Courses*, ed. Z. Wasik (Wroclaw, Poland: Philological School of Higher Education, 2010), 127–37, www.wsf.edu.pl/upload_module/wysiwyg/Wydawnictwo%20WSF/Consultant%20Assembly%20III.pdf#page=129.
[130] E.T. Hall, *The Silent Language* (Garden City, NY: Doubleday, 1959).
[131] Ibid.
[132] F. Steele, *Physical Settings and Organization Development* (Reading, MA: Addison-Wesley, 1973). Also see A. Mehrabian, *Public Places and Private Spaces* (New York: Basic Books, 1976).
[133] M. Korda, "Office Power—You Are Where You Sit," in *With Words Unspoken: The Nonverbal Experience*, ed. L.B. Rosenfeld and J.M. Civikly (New York: Holt, Rinehart, and Winston, 1976).
[134] Ibid.
[135] Ibid.
[136] G.M. Goldhaber, *Organizational Communication*, 4th ed. (Dubuque, IA: Wm. C. Brown, 1986).
[137] Korda, "Office Power."
[138] Goldhaber, *Organizational Communication.*
[139] F.D. Becker, *Workspace: Creating Environments in Organizations* (New York: Praeger, 1981).

[140] Korda, "Office Power."

[141] See R. Sommer, *Tight Spaces: Hard Architecture and How to Humanize It* (Englewood Cliffs, NJ: Prentice Hall, 1974).

[142] H. Osmond, "Function as Basis of Psychiatric Ward Design," *Mental Hospitals* 8 (1957): 23–9.

[143] T. Levine, K. Serota, and H. Shulman, "The Impact of *Lie to Me* on Viewers' Actual Ability to Detect Deception," *Communication Research* 37, no. 6 (2010): 847–56.

[144] Weinberger, "Airport Security."

[145] P. Castillo and D. Mallard, "Preventing Cross-cultural Bias in Deception Judgments: The Role Expectancies about Nonverbal Judgments," *Journal of Cross-cultural Psychology* 43, no. 6 (2012): 967–78.

[146] M. Mead, review of *Darwin and facial expression*, by Paul Ekman, *Journal of Communication* 25 (1975): 212.

[147] Ibid.

[148] A. Mehrabian, "Silent Messages," www.kaaj.com/psych/smorder.html.

CHAPTER 8

[1] Andrea is a fictitious name.

[2] D. Goleman, "The Emotionally Intelligent Salesman," accessed 8 February 2013, http://danielgoleman.info/the-emotionally-intelligent-salesman.

[3] P. Bourdieu, "The Forms of Capital," in *Handbook of Theory and Research for the Theory of Sociology of Education*, ed. J.G. Richardson (New York: Greenwood Press, 1986), 241–58.

[4] R.D. Putnam, *Bowling Alone: The Collapse and Revival of American Community* (New York: Simon and Schuster, 2000); M. Woolcock, "The Place of Social Capital in Understanding Social and Economic Outcomes," *Isuma* 2 (2001): 11–17.

[5] Woolcock, "The Place of Social Capital."

[6] J. Bowlby, *Attachment and Loss, Vol. 1: Attachment* (New York: Basic Books, 1969/1982).

[7] Woolcock, "The Place of Social Capital."

[8] Putnam, *Bowling Alone*, 312; E.T. Pascarella and P. Terenzini, "Predicting Voluntary Freshman Year Persistence/Withdrawal Behavior in a Residential University: A Path Analytic Validation of the Tinto Model," *Journal of Educational Psychology* 52 (1983): 60–75; A.W. Astin, *What Matters Most in College: Four Critical Years Revisited* (San Francisco, CA: Jossey-Bass, 1983).

[9] Woolcock, "The Place of Social Capital."

[10] Bourdieu, "The Forms of Capital."

[11] Putnam, *Bowling Alone*; R.D. Putnam. "Social Capital: Measurement and Consequences," *Isuma* 2 (2001): 41–51.

[12] M.D. Resnick, L.J. Harris, and R.W. Blum, "The Impact of Caring and Connectedness on Adolescent Health and Well-being," *Journal of Paediatrics and Child Health* 29 (1993): S3–9.

[13] L.B. Hendry and M. Reid, "Social Relationships and Health: The Meaning of Social 'Connectedness' and How It Relates to Health Concerns for Rural Scottish Adolescents," *Journal of Adolescence* 23 (2000): 705–19.

[14] J. Lennox Terrion, "Building Social Capital in Vulnerable Families: Success Markers of a School-Based Intervention Program," *Youth and Society* 38 (2006): 155–76.

[15] J.D. Teachman, K. Paasch, and K. Carver, "Social Capital and Dropping Out of School Early," *Journal of Marriage and the Family* 58 (1996): 773–83.

[16] N. Keating, J. Swindle, and D. Foster, "The Role of Social Capital in Aging Well," in *Social Capital in Action: Thematic Policy Studies*, ed. Government of Canada (Ottawa: Policy Research Initiative, 2005), 24–48, www.policyresearch.gc.ca/doclib/SC_Thematic_E.pdf.

[17] C. Bjørnskov, "Social Capital and Happiness in the United States," *Applied Research in Quality of Life* 3 (2008): 43–62.

[18] K.A. Lochner, I. Kawachi, R.T. Brennan, and S.L. Buka, "Social Capital and Neighborhood Mortality Rates in Chicago," *Social Science and Medicine* 56 (2003): 1797–805.

[19] W. Schutz, *FIRO: A Three Dimensional Theory of Interpersonal Behavior* (New York: Holt, Rinehart, and Winston, 1958).

[20] R.F. Baumeister and M.R. Leary, "The Need to Belong: Desire for Interpersonal Attachments as a Fundamental Human Motivation," *Psychological Bulletin* 117 (1995): 497–529.

[21] "Workplace," Canadian Centre on Substance Abuse, 25 May 2011, www.ccsa.ca/Eng/Topics/Populations/Workplace/Pages/default.aspx.

[22] R. Granfield and W. Cloud, *Coming Clean: Overcoming Addiction without Treatment* (New York: New York University Press, 1999); J. Coleman, "Social Capital in the Creation of Human Capital," *American Journal of Sociology* 94, suppl. 95 (1988): S94–120.

[23] W. White and W. Cloud, "Recovery Capital: A Primer for Addiction Professionals," *Counselor: The Magazine for Addiction Professionals* 9 (2008): 22–7.

[24] D.A. Wolfe, P.G. Jaffe, and C.V. Crooks, *Adolescent Risk Behaviors: Why Teens Experiment and Strategies to Keep Them Safe* (New Haven, CT: Yale University Press, 2006).

[25] B.M. Booth, D.W. Russell, W.R. Yates, P.R. Laughlin, K. Brown, and D. Reed, "Social Support and Depression in Men During Alcoholism Treatment," *Journal of Substance Abuse* 4 (1992): 57–67.

[26] J. Lennox Terrion, "The Experience of Post-secondary Education for Students in Recovery from Addiction to Drugs or Alcohol: Relationships and Recovery Capital," *Journal of Social and Personal Relationships* 30, no. 1 (2013), 3–23.

[27] J. MacCormack, S.M. Hudson, and T. Ward, "Sexual Offenders' Perceptions of Their Early Interpersonal Relationships: An Attachment Perspective," *The Journal of Sex Research* 39, no. 2 (2002): 85–93.

[28] P. Klaus, "Thank You for Sharing: But Why at the Office?," *New York Times*, 18 August 2012, www.nytimes.com/2012/08/19/jobs/sharing-too-much-information-in-the-workplace.html?_r=0. For recommendations on what to share, see also B. Schlacter, "Eight Dos and Don'ts of Talking about Your Personal Life on the Job," 2 January 2013, http://comerecommended.com/2013/01/8-dos-and-donts-of-talking-about-your-personal-life-on-the-job.

[29] P. Jenkins, *Monster* (United States: Media 8 Entertainment, 2003), DVD.

[30] N. Thibaut and H. Kelley, *The Social Psychology of Groups* (New York: Wiley, 1959).

[31] S.D. Bacharach and E.J. Lawler, "Power Dependencies and Power Paradoxes in Bargaining," *Negotiation Journal* 2, no. 2 (1986): 167–74.

[32] "The History of the Human Library," Human Library Organisation, 2012, http://humanlibrary.org/the-history.html.

[33] J. Whitehouse, "Borrowed Time," 7 November 2011, www.thegridto.com/city/local-news/borrowed-time/2010.

[34] Bowlby, *Attachment and Loss.*

[35] See L.A. Sroufe and J. Fleeson, "Attachment and the Construction of Relationships," in *Relationships and Development*, ed. W. Hartup and Z. Rubin (Hillsdale, NJ: Lawrence Erlbaum, 1986), 51–71.

[36] Bowlby, *Attachment and Loss.*

[37] L.M. Youngblade and J. Belsky, "Parent–Child Antecedents of Five-Year-Olds' Close Friendships: A Longitudinal Analysis," *Developmental Psychology* 28 (1992): 700–13.

[38] K.A. Kerns, "Individual Differences in Friendship Quality and Their Links to Child–Mother Attachment," in *The Company They Keep: Friendship in Childhood and Adolescence*, ed. W.M. Bukowski, A.F. Newcomb, and W.W. Hartup (New York: Cambridge University Press, 1996), 137–57.

[39] N.L. McElwain, C. Booth-LaForce, J. Lansford, X. Wu, and W.J. Dyer, "A Process Model of Attachment-Friend Linkages: Hostile Attribution Biases, Language Ability, and Mother–Child Affective Mutuality as Intervening Mechanisms," *Child Development* 79 (2008): 1891–906.

[40] N.L. McElwain, C. Booth-LaForce, and X. Wu, "Infant–Mother Attachment and Children's Friendship Quality: Maternal Mental-State Talk as an Intervening Mechanism," *Developmental Psychology* 47 (2011): 1295–311.

[41] Truth and Reconciliation Commission of Canada, *Truth and Reconciliation Commission of Canada: Interim Report* (Winnipeg, MB: Author, 2012), www.attendancemarketing.com/~attmk/TRC_jd/Interim%20report%20English%20electronic%20copy.pdf.

[42] N.F. Davin, "Report on Industrial Schools for Indians and Half-Breeds," 14 March 1897.

[43] Aboriginal Healing Foundation, *Aboriginal People, Resilience, and the Residential School Legacy* (Ottawa: Author, 2003), www.ahf.ca/downloads/resilience.pdf.

[44] Ibid.

[45] See W.W. Hartup, "Adolescents and Their Friends," *New Directions for Child and Adolescent Development* 60 (1993): 3–22.

[46] Aboriginal Healing Foundation, *Aboriginal People.*

[47] Ibid.

[48] CBC News, "FAQs on Residential Schools and Compensation," *Residential Schools: A History of Residential Schools in Canada*, 16 May 2008, www.cbc.ca/news/canada/story/2008/05/16/f-faqs-residential-schools.html.

[49] Aboriginal Healing Foundation, www.ahf.ca.

[50] C.L. Bagwell, M.E. Schmidt, A.F. Newcomb, and W.M. Bukowski, "Friendship and Peer Rejection as Predictors of Adult Adjustment," *New Directions for Child and Adolescent Development* 91 (2001): 25–49.

[51] F.E. Aboud and M.J. Mendelson, "Determinants of Friendship Selection and Quality: Developmental Processes," in *The Company They Keep: Friendship in Childhood and Adolescence*, ed. W.M. Bukowski, A.F. Newcomb, and W.W. Hartup (New York: Cambridge University Press, 1996), 87–112; F.E. Aboud and J. Sankar, "Friendship and Identity in a Language-Integrated School," *International Journal of Behavioral Development* 31 (2007): 445–53.

[52] Hartup, "Adolescents and Their Friends."

[53] D. Buhrmester, "Need Fulfillment, Interpersonal Competence, and the Developmental Contexts of Early Adolescent Friendship," in *The Company They Keep: Friendship in Childhood and Adolescence*, ed. W.M. Bukowski, A.F. Newcomb, and W. Hartup (New York: Cambridge University Press, 1996), 158–85.

[54] Buhrmester, "Need Fulfillment"; W.M. Bukowski, M. Brendgen, and F. Vitaro, "Peers and Socialization: Effects on Externalizing and Internalizing Problems," in *Handbook of Socialization: Theory and Research*, ed. J.E. Grusec and P.D. Hastings (New York: Guilford Press, 2007), 355–81; J. Youniss, *Parents and Peers in Social Development: A Sullivan-Piaget Perspective* (Chicago: University of Chicago Press, 1980).

[55] Bowlby, *Attachment and Loss.*

[56] W.M. Bukowski, B. Laursen, and B. Hoza, "The Snowball Effect: Friendship Moderates Escalations in Depressed Affect among Avoidant and Excluded Children," *Development and Psychopathology* 22 (2010): 749–57.

[57] E. Gooren, P. van Lier, H. Stegge, M. Terwogt, and H. Koot, "The Development of Conduct Problems and Depressive Symptoms in Early Elementary School Children: The Role of Peer Rejection," *Journal of Clinical Child and Adolescent Psychology* 40 (2011): 245–53.

[58] W.K. Rawlins, *Friendship Matters: Communication, Dialectics, and the Life Course* (New Brunswick, NJ: Transaction Publishers, 2008).

[59] W. Furman and D. Buhrmester, "Age and Sex Differences in Perceptions of Networks of Personal Relationships," *Child Development* 63 (1992): 103–15; B. Laursen and V.A. Williams, "Perceptions of Interdependence and Closeness in Family and Peer Relationships among Adolescents with and without Romantic Partners," *New Directions for Child Development* 78 (1997): 3–20.

[60] Buhrmester, "Need Fulfillment."

[61] Ibid.

[62] S. Harter, "Self and Identity Development," in *At the Threshold: The Developing Adolescent*, ed. S.S. Feldman and G.R. Elliott, 352–87 (Cambridge, MA: Harvard University Press, 1990).

[63] H.T. Reis and P. Shaver, "Intimacy as an Interpersonal Process," *Handbook of Personal Relationships*, ed. S. Duck (Chichester, UK: Wiley, 1988), 367–89.

[64] E.H. Erikson, *Identity: Youth and Crisis* (New York: Norton, 1968).

[65] R. Pea, C. Nass, L. Meheula, M. Rance, A. Kumar, H. Bamford, M. Nass et al. "Media Use, Face-to-Face Communication, Media Multi-tasking, and Social Well-being among 8- to 12-Year-Old Girls," *Developmental Psychology* 48, no. 2 (2012): 327–36.

[66] Bukowski et al., "The Snowball Effect"; J.B. Kupersmidt, J.D. Coie, and K.A. Dodge, "The Role of Peer Relationships in the Development of Disorder," in *Peer Rejection in Childhood*, ed. S.R. Asher and J.D. Coie (New York: Cambridge University Press, 1990), 274–308; J.G. Parker and S.R. Asher, "Peer Relations and Later Social Adjustment," *Psychological Bulletin* 102, no. 3 (1987): 357–89.

[67] R. Lev-Wiesel, O. Nuttman-Shwartz, and R. Sternberg, "Peer Rejection During Adolescence: Psychological Long-Term Effects—a Brief Report," *Journal of Loss and Trauma* 11 (2006): 131–42.

[68] Erikson, *Identity*.

[69] Buhrmester, "Need Fulfillment"; B. Laursen, "Closeness and Conflict in Adolescent Peer Relationships: Interdependence with Friends and Romantic Partners," in *The Company They Keep: Friendships in Childhood and Adolescence*, ed. W.M. Bukowski, A.F. Newcomb, and W.W. Hartup (New York: Cambridge University Press, 1996), 186–210.

[70] K. Radmacher and M. Azmitia, "Are There Gendered Pathways to Intimacy in Early Adolescents' and Emerging Adults' Friendships?," *Journal of Adolescent Research* 21 (2006): 415–48.

[71] Ibid.

[72] See W.K. Rawlins, "Being There and Growing Apart: Sustaining Friendships During Adulthood," in *Communication and Relational Maintenance*, ed. D.J. Canary and L. Stafford (New York: Academic Press, 1994), 275–94.

[73] M. Monsour, *Women and Men as Friends: Relationships across the Life Span in the Twenty-First Century* (Mahwah, NJ: Lawrence Erlbaum, 2002).

[74] D. Knox and C. Schacht, *Choices in Relationships: An Introduction to Marriage and the Family* (Belmont, CA: Wadsworth, 2010).

[75] R.G. Adams, "Friendship During the Later Years," in *Blackwell Encyclopedia of Sociology*, ed. George Ritzer (2007), *Blackwell Reference Online*, www.sociology encyclopedia.com/subscriber/tocnode?id= g9781405124331_chunk_g978140512433112_ss1-69.

[76] Keating, Swindle, and Foster, "The Role of Social Capital."

[77] C. Cannuscio, J. Block, and I. Kawachi, "Social Capital and Successful Aging: The Role of Senior Housing," *Annals of Internal Medicine* 139 (2003): 395–9.

[78] P. Eng, E. Rimm, G. Fitzmaurice, and I. Kawachi, "Social Ties and Change in Social Ties in Relation to Subsequent Total and Cause-Specific Mortality and Coronary Heart Disease Incidence in Men," *American Journal of Epidemiology* 155 (2002): 700–9.

[79] D. Doran and J. Almost, "Exploring Worklife Issues in Provincial Correctional Settings," (Toronto: Lawrence S. Bloomberg Faculty of Nursing, University of Toronto, 2010).

[80] M. Shields, *Findings from the 2005 National Survey of the Work and Health of Nurses* (Ottawa: Industry Canada and Canadian Institute for Health Information, 2006).

[81] Doran and Almost, "Exploring Worklife Issues."

[82] Rawlins, *Friendship Matters.*

[83] Ibid.

[84] A.N. Salvaggio, M. Streich, J.E. Hopper, and C.A. Pierce, "Why Do Fools Fall in Love (at Work)? Factors Associated with the Incidence of Workplace Romance," *Journal of Applied Social Psychology* 41, no. 1 (2011): 906–37.

[85] Canadian Human Rights Commission, *Anti-Harassment Policies for the Workplace: An Employer's Guide* (Ottawa: Government of Canada, 2006).

[86] Statistics Canada, *Marriages, by Type of Marriage and Month, Canada, Provinces and Territories, Annual*, CANSIM Table 101-1001 (Ottawa: Statistics Canada, 2011).

[87] S. Page, *If I'm So Wonderful Why Am I Still Single?*, rev. ed. (New York: Three Rivers Press, 2002).

[88] K. Engelhart, "Online Dating and the Search for True Love—or Loves," *Maclean's*, 30 January 2013, www2. macleans.ca/2013/01/30/true-loves.

[89] A. Shimo, "Reeling in a Date: Plenty of Fish Has Become the Dating Site for the Masses," *Maclean's* 121, no. 29 (2008): 37–8.

[90] J. Hall, N. Park, H. Song, and M. Cody, "Strategic Misrepresentation in Online Dating: The Effects of

Gender, Self-Monitoring, and Personality," *Journal of Social and Personal Relationships* 27, no. 1 (2010): 117–35.

[91] J.L. Gibbs, N.B. Ellison, and C.-H. Lai, "First Comes Love, Then Comes Google: An Investigation of Uncertainty Reduction Strategies and Self-Disclosure in Online Dating," *Communication Research* 38 (2011): 70–100.

[92] D. Couch and P. Liamputtong, "Online Dating and Mating: Perceptions of Risk and Health among Online Users," *Health, Risk and Society* 9, no. 3 (2007): 275–94.

[93] S. Turkle, *Alone Together: Why We Expect More from Technology and Less from Each Other* (New York: Basic Books, 2011).

[94] R.J. Sternberg, *The Triangle of Love: Intimacy, Passion, Commitment* (New York: Basic Books, 1988).

[95] M. Knapp, *Interpersonal Communication and Human Relationships* (Boston: Allyn and Bacon, 1984).

[96] "Description of *Notes for a Film about Donna and Gail*," *Canadian Film Encyclopedia*, accessed on 29 August 2013, http://tiff.net/CANADIANFILMENCYCLOPEDIA/content/films/notes-for-a-film-about-donna-and-gail.

[97] V.J. Derlega and J.H. Berg, *Self-Disclosure: Theory, Research, and Therapy* (New York: Springer, 1987).

[98] C. Bruess and J. Pearson, "Interpersonal Rituals in Marriage and Adult Friendship," *Communication Monographs* 64 (1997): 25–46.

[99] C. Bruess and J. Pearson, "'Sweet Pea' and 'Pussy Cat': An Examination of Idiom Use and Marital Satisfaction over the Life Cycle," *Journal of Social and Personal Relationships* 10 (1993): 609–15.

[100] Knapp, *Interpersonal Communication.*

[101] Ibid.

[102] J. Gottman, J. Markman, and C. Notarius, "The Topography of Marital Conflict: A Sequential Analysis of Verbal and Nonverbal Behaviour," *Journal of Marriage and the Family* 39 (1977): 461–77; J. Gottman and N. Silver, *The Seven Principles for Making Marriage Work: A Practical Guide from the Country's Foremost Relationship Expert* (New York: Three Rivers Press, 2000); J.M. Gottman, "Predicting the Longitudinal Course of Marriages," *Journal of Marital and Family Therapy* 17, no. 1 (1991): 3–7; J.M. Gottman and L.J. Krokoff, "The Relationship between Marital Interaction and Marital Satisfaction: A Longitudinal View," *Journal of Consulting and Clinical Psychology* 57 (1989): 47–52; J.M. Gottman and A.L. Porterfield, "Communicative Competence in the Nonverbal Behaviour of Married Couples," *Journal of Marriage and the Family* 43 (1981): 817–24.

[103] Gottman and Silver, *Seven Principles.*

[104] S.S. Spielmann, S. Joel, G. MacDonald, and A. Kogan, "Ex Appeal: Current Relationship Quality and Emotional Attachment to Ex-partners," *Social Psychological and Personality Science* 4, no. 2 (2013): 175–180.

[105] N. Kalish, *Lost and Found Lovers* (New York: William Morrow, 1997).

[106] Ibid.

[107] Statistics Canada, Health Statistics Division, "Canadian Vital Statistics, Divorce Database and Marriage Database," 2011, cited in Human Resources and Skills Development Canada, "Indicators of Well-Being in Canada, accessed 12 September 2013, www4.hrsdc.gc.ca/.3ndic.1t.4r@-eng.jsp?iid=76; American Psychological Association, "Marriage and Divorce," 2013, www.apa.org/topics/divorce/index.aspx.

[108] Derlega and Berg, *Self-disclosure.*

[109] I. Altman and D. Taylor, *Social Penetration: The Development of Interpersonal Relationships* (New York: Holt, Rinehart, and Winston, 1973).

[110] J. Luft, *Group Processes: An Introduction to Group Dynamics* (Palo Alto, CA: National Press Books, 1970).

[111] D.I. Tamir and J.P. Mitchell, "Disclosing Information about the Self Is Intrinsically Rewarding," *Proceedings of the National Academy of Sciences* 109, no. 21 (2012): 8038–43.

[112] J. Pennebaker, *Opening Up: The Healing Power of Confiding in Others* (New York: Guilford, 1997).

[113] J.W. Pennebaker and S.K. Beall, "Confronting a Traumatic Event: Toward an Understanding of Inhibition and Disease," *Journal of Abnormal Psychology* 95 (1986): 274–81.

[114] R.I.M. Dunbar, A. Marriott, and N.D.C. Duncan, "Human Conversational Behaviour," *Human Nature* 8 (1997): 231–46; N. Emler, "A Social Psychology of Reputation," *European Review of Social Psychology* 1 (1990):171–93; N. Emler, "Gossip, Reputation, and Social Adaptation," in *Good Gossip*, ed. R. Goodman and A. Ben Ze'ev (Lawrence: Kansas University Press, 1994), 117–33.

[115] C.R. Miller and D. Shepherd, "Blogging as Social Action: A Genre Analysis of the Weblog," *NTO: The Blogosphere*, accessed 20 August 2013 http://blog.lib.umn.edu/blogosphere/blogging_as_social_action_a_genre_analysis_of_the_weblog.html.

[116] Ibid.

[117] H. Qian and C.R. Scott, "Anonymity and Self-Disclosure on Weblogs," *Journal of Computer-Mediated Communication* 12 (2007): 1428–51.

[118] Ibid.

[119] Ibid, p. 1431.

[120] Ibid, p. 1441.

[121] Putnam, *Bowling Alone.*

[122] C. Derber, *The Pursuit of Attention: Power and Ego in Everyday Life* (New York: Oxford University Press, 2000).

[123] Gottman and Silver, *Seven Principles.*

[124] Ibid.

[125] Gerdes and Segal, "A Social Work Model."

[126] J.H. Larson, *The Great Marriage Tune-Up Book: A Proven*

Program for Evaluating and Renewing Your Relationship (San Francisco: Jossey Bass, 2002).

[127] Gottman and Silver, *Seven Principles*.

[128] A.W. Gouldner, "The Norm of Reciprocity: A Preliminary Statement," *American Sociological Review* 25 (1960): 161–78.

CHAPTER 9

[1] This case is fictitious; however, we have based the subsequent discussion on concepts that appear in R.J. Wilson, B. Huculak, and A. McWhinnie, "Restorative Justice Innovations," *Behavioral Sciences and the Law* 20 (2002): 363–80.

[2] R. Reed, *The American Indian in the White Man's Prisons: A Story of Genocide* (San Francisco, CA: Uncompromising Books, 1993).

[3] The facts presented in this discussion appeared in "Let Muslims Use Sharia in Family Disputes: Report," *Globe and Mail*, 20 December 2004, www.theglobeandmail.com/servlet/story/RTGAM.20041220.wsharia1220; "Shariah Law: FAQs," CBC News, 26 May 2005, www.cbc.ca/news/background/islam/shariah-law.html; A. Korteweg, "Lessons from the 2003–2006 'Sharia Debate,'" 12 December 2012, http://korteweg.wordpress.com/tag/arbitration-act-1991; and "Ontario Premier Rejects Use of Shariah Law," CBC News, 9 September 2005, www.cbc.ca/news/canada/ontario-premier-rejects-use-of-shariah-law-1.523122.

[4] J. Gatlin, A. Wysocki, and K. Kepner, "Understanding Conflict in the Workplace," University of Florida IFAS Extension, June 2002, http://edis.ifas.ufl.edu/hr024.

[5] S. Reynolds and E. Kalish, "Managing Collaborative Conflict Resolution," 2002, cited in Gatlin et al., *Understanding Conflict*.

[6] D. Weeks, *The Eight Essential Steps to Conflict Resolution* (New York: Penguin Putnam, 1994), p. 4.

[7] G. Hofstede, *Culture's Consequences: Comparing Values, Behaviours, Institutions, and Organizations across Nations*, 2nd ed. (Thousand Oaks, CA: Sage, 2001).

[8] M.L. Egan and M. Bendick Jr, "Combining Multicultural Management and Diversity into One Course on Cultural Competence," *Academy of Management Learning and Education* 7, no. 3 (2008): 387–93.

[9] L. Bayer, *The Power of Civility: Top Experts Reveal the Secret of Social Capital* (San Francisco, CA: Thrive Publishing, 2011); also see L. Bayer, "Welcome to the Center for Organizational Cultural Competence," 2013, www.culturalcompetence.ca.

[10] D. Berry, *Health Communication: Theory and Practice* (New York: Open University Press, 2007).

[11] L.M. Vanderford, T. Stein, R. Sheeler, and S. Skochelak, "Communication Challenges for Experienced Clinicians: Topics for an Advanced Communication Curriculum," *Health Communication* 13, no. 3 (2001): 261–84; E. Vegni, S. Visioli, and A.E. Moja, "When Talking to the Patient Is Difficult: A Physician's Perspective," *Communication and Medicine* 2, no. 1 (2005): 69–76; S.M. Wolf, V.M. Willimas, M.R. Parker, S.N. Parikh, W.A. Nowlan, and W.D. Baker, "Patient's Shame and Attitudes Toward Discussing the Results of Literacy Screening," *Journal of Health Communication* 12 (2007): 721–32.

[12] B. Cottrell, P.S. Jaya, and E. Tastsoglou, "Navigating Anti-violence Work in Atlantic Canada in a Culturally Sensitive Way" (report submitted to Status of Women Canada, 2006).

[13] A.C. Filley, *Interpersonal Conflict Resolution* (Glenview, IL: Scott, Foresman, 1975), p. 4.

[14] M. Deutsch, "Conflicts: Productive and Destructive," in *Conflict Resolution through Communication*, ed. F.E. Jandt (New York: Harper and Row, 1973).

[15] K.A. Jehn, "A Multimethod Examination of the Benefits and Detriments of Intragroup Conflict," *Administrative Science Quarterly* 40, no. 2 (1995): 265–82; Deutsch, "Conflicts."

[16] A.O. Hirschman, *Exit, Voice, and Loyalty: Responses to Decline in Firms, Organizations, and States* (Cambridge, MA: Harvard University Press, 1970); A.O. Hirschman, "Exit, Voice, and Loyalty: Further Reflections and a Survey of Recent Contributions," *Social Science Information* 13 (1974): 7–26.

[17] E. Yong, "Justice Is Served, but More So after Lunch: How Food Breaks Sway the Decisions of Judges," *Discover: The Magazine of Science, Technology, and the Future*, 13 April 2011, http://blogs.discovermagazine.com/notrocketscience/2011/04/11/justice-is-served-but-more-so-after-lunch-how-food-breaks-sway-the-decisions-of-judges.

[18] Deutsch, "Conflicts."

[19] C. Buehler and B.B. Trotter, "Nonresidential and Residential Parent's Perceptions of the Former Spouse Relationship and Children's Social Competence Following Marital Separation: Theory and Programmed Intervention," *Family-Relations* 39 (1990): 395–404.

[20] L.R. Pondy, "Organizational Conflict: Concepts and Models," *Administrative Science Quarterly* 12, no. 2 (1967): 296–320.

[21] The information in this section is based on J.Z. Rubin, "Conflict from a Psychological Perspective," in *Negotiation: Strategies for Mutual Gain*, ed. L. Hall (Newbury Park, CA: Sage Publications, 1993), 123–37.

[22] J.R.P. French and B. Raven, "The Bases of Social Power," in *Group Dynamics*, ed. D. Cartwright and A. Zander (New York: Harper and Row, 1959).

[23] A. Hawks, "Janelle Evans and Leah Messer Threaten to Quit *TeenMom2* over Money," *Starcasm.net*, 14 March 2012, http://starcasm.net/archives/148179.

[24] S. Hess, "Contestants Angry over *Biggest Loser* Twitter Reaction," *WebProNews*, 22 February 2012, www.webpronews.com/contestants-angry-over-biggest-loser-2012-02.

[25] AP, "Teresa Guidice Wants *Jersey Shore*–Type Pay," *Hollywood Reporter*, 9 January 2012, www.hollywoodreporter.com/news/teresa-giudice-wants-jersey-shore-27305.

[26] P.S. Jaya, "The Discourse of Power in Organizations: Set in 'Caste'?" (poster session at the Critical Management Studies Workshop at the Annual Meeting of the Academy of Management, Chicago, IL, 1999).

[27] S.D. Ferguson, *Researching the Public Opinion Environment* (Thousand Oaks, CA: Sage, 2000).

[28] R.H. Kilmann and K.W. Thomas, "Interpersonal Conflict-Handling Behaviour as Reflections of Jungian Personality Dimensions," *Psychological Reports* 37 (1975): 971–80.

[29] R. Fisher and W.L. Ury, *Getting to Yes: Negotiating Agreement without Giving In* (New York: Penguin Books, 1983).

[30] The Mennonite Conciliation Service of Akron, Pennsylvania, references the contribution of Norman Sawchuck. See http://peace.mennolink.org/cgi-bin/conflictstyle/inventory.cgi?printable=1, accessed on May 16, 2013.

[31] A.C. Amason, "Distinguishing the Effects of Functional and Dysfunctional Conflict on Strategic Decision Making: Resolving a Paradox for Top Management Teams," *Academy of Management Journal* 39, no. 1 (1996):123–48.

[32] K. Thomas, "Conflict and Negotiation Processes in Organizations," in *Handbook of Industrial and Organizational Psychology*, vol. 3, 2nd ed., ed. M.D. Dunnette and L.M. Hough (Palo Alto, CA: Consulting Psychological Press, 1990), 651–717; D. Zillman, "Cognition-Excitation Interdependencies and Aggressive Behavior," *Aggressive Behavior* 14 (1988): 51–64; C. De Dreu and L.R. Weingart, "Task versus Relationship Conflict, Team Performance, and Team Member Satisfaction: A Meta Analysis," *Journal of Applied Psychology* 88, no. 4 (2003): 741–9.

[33] See D.W. Barclay, "Interdepartmental Conflict in Organizational Buying: The Impact of Organizational Context," *Journal of Marketing Research* 22, no. 2 (1991): 145–59; B.J. Jaworski and A.K. Kohli, "Market Orientation: Antecedents and Consequences," *Journal of Marketing* 57, no. 2 (1993): 53–70; De Dreu and Weingart, "Task versus Relationship Conflict"; R.W. Ruekert and O.C. Walker, "Interactions between Marketing and R&D Departments in Implementing Different Business Strategies," *Strategic Management Journal* 8, no. 3 (1987): 233–48.

[34] C.E. Rusbult, I.M. Zimrod, and L.K. Gunn, "Exit, Voice, Loyalty, and Neglect: Responses to Dissatisfaction in Romantic Involvements," *Journal of Personality and Social Psychology* 43, no. 6 (1982): 1230–42.

[35] Rubin, "Conflict from a Psychological Perspective," 127.

[36] R. Baron, "Positive Effects of Conflict: A Cognitive Perspective," *Employee Responsibilities and Rights Journal* 4, no. 1 (1991): 25–36; R.A. Cosier, "The Effects of Three Potential Aids for Making Strategic Decisions on Predictions Accuracy," *Organizational Behavior and Human Performance* 22 (1978): 295–306; D. Tjosold, "Implications of Controversy Research in Management," *Journal of Management* 11, no. 3 (1985): 21–37.

[37] Alberta Learning Information Service, "Bullies at Work: What to Know, What You Can Do," accessed 18 May 2013, http://alis.alberta.ca/ep/eps/tips/tips.html?EK=11608.

[38] S. de Léséleuc, "Criminal Victimization in the Workplace," Canadian Centre for Justice Statistics, 2004, http://safetysoftware.ca/downloads/Stats%20Canada%20-%20Criminal%20Victimization%20in%20the%20Workplace%202004.pdf.

[39] Canada Safety Council, "Workplace Violence Takes a Toll on Employers," *Safety Canada* 55, no. 1 (2013), https://canadasafetycouncil.org/safety-canada-online/article/workplace-violence-takes-toll-employers.

[40] "40% of Canadians Bullied at Work, Expert Says," CBC News, 6 December 2011, www.cbc.ca/news/canada/windsor/story/2011/12/06/wdr-cbsa-bullying-johnston.html.

[41] Alberta Learning Information Service, "Bullies at Work."

[42] N. Keith, "Bill 168 in Action at Union Arbitration," *Occupational Safety*, 12 January 2012, www.cos-mag.com/Legal/Legal-Columns/bill-168-in-action-at-union-arbitration.html.

[43] For a discussion of this case, see J. Tetreault, "Verbal Threats as Workplace Violence: The Effects of Bill 168 Are Beginning to Show," *Canadian Lawyer Magazine*, 12 December 2011, www.canadianlawyermag.com/3962/verbal-threats-as-workplace-violence.html; C. Cosh, "Keep a Close Eye out for the Signs," *McLean's*, 16 December 2010, www2.macleans.ca/2010/12/16/a-close-eye-out; Keith, "Bill 168 in Action at Union Arbitration."

[44] For relevant discussions, see E. Pinel and N. Paulin, "Stigma Consciousness at Work," *Basic and Applied Social Psychology* 27, no. 4 (2005): 345–352; S. Lim, L.M. Cortina, and V.J. Magley, "Personal and Workgroup Incivility: Impact on Work and Health Outcomes," *Journal of Applied Psychology* 93 (2008): 95–107; K. Osatuke, S.C. Moore, C. Ward, S.R. Dyrenforth, and L. Belton, "Civility, Respect, Engagement in the Workforce," *Journal of Applied Behavioral Science* 45, no. 3 (2009): 384–410.

[45] Osatuke et al., "Civility, Respect, Engagement in the Workforce."

46 D. De Cremer and T.R. Tyler, "Am I Respected or Not? Inclusion and Reputation as Issues in Group Membership," *Social Justice Research* 18, no. 2 (2005): 121–53; R. Hodson, *Dignity at Work* (Cambridge, UK: Cambridge University Press, 2001); D.T. Miller, "Disrespect and the Experience of Injustice," *Annual Review of Psychology* 52 (2001): 527–53.

47 J.A. Colquitt, "Does the Justice of the One Interact with the Justice of the Many? Reactions to Procedural Justice in Teams," *Journal of Applied Psychology* 89, no. 4 (2004): 633–46.

48 L. Ramarajan and S.G. Barsade, "What Makes the Job Tough? The Influence of Organizational Respect on Burnout in the Human Services," November 2006, http://knowledge.wharton.upenn.edu/papers/1327.pdf.

49 C.M. Pearson and C.L. Porath, "On Incivility, Its Impact and Directions for Future Research," in *The Dark Side of Organizational Behavior*, ed. R.W. Griffin and A.M. O'Leary-Kelly (San Francisco, CA: Jossey-Bass, 2004), 403–25; C.M. Pearson and C.L. Porath, "On the Nature of Consequences, and Remedies of Workplace Incivility: No Time for 'Nice'? Think Again," *Academy of Management Executive* 19 (2005): 7–25.

50 Osatuke et al., "Civility, Respect, Engagement in the Workforce."

51 D. Goleman, *Leadership: The Power of Emotional Intelligence* (North Hampton, MA: More than Sound, 2011).

52 J.R. Gibb, "Defensive Communication," *Journal of Communication* 11, no. 3 (1961): 141–8.

53 D.C. Smith, "Teaching Managers to Relate: Using Feedback to Bolster Commitment and Morale," *Journal Of Diversity Management* 3, no. 3 (2008): 7–12.

54 M.R. Weaver, "Do Students Value Feedback? Student Perceptions of Tutors' Written Responses," *Assessment and Evaluation in Higher Education* 31, no. 3 (2006): 379–94.

55 S. Miller and P.A. Miller, *Core Communication: Skills and Processes* (Evergreen, CO: Interpersonal Communication Programs 1997).

56 W. Morris, "Interpersonal Communication Skills in Community Art: An Introduction to the Awareness Wheel," accessed 4 September 2013, www.wendymorris.org/resources/communicationcommunityart.pdf.

CHAPTER 10

1 S. Lindlaw, "Astral Cult, Expecting UFO Rendezvous, Leaves 39 Lifeless 'Containers,'" Associated Press, 28 March 1997, http://old.chronicle.augusta.com/stories/1997/03/28/tec_206008.shtml.

2 N. Moharib, "'Not a Complex Case': Grand-dad Says a Child with Broken Legs Was Reported to Cops . . . and That Should Have Been Enough," *Calgary Sun*, 26 August 2011, www.calgarysun.com/2011/08/26/not-a-complex-case.

3 A. Shlonsky and L. Gibbs, "Will the Real Evidence-Based Practice Please Stand Up? Teaching the Process of Evidence-Based Practice to the Helping Professions," *Brief Treatment and Crisis Intervention* 4, no.2 (2004): 137–53; E. Gambrill, "Evidence-Based Practice: An Alternative to Authority-Based Practice," *Families in Society: The Journal of Contemporary Human Services* 80, no. 4 (1999): 341–50; E. Gambrill, "Evidence-Based Practice: Sea of Change or the Emperor's New Clothes?," *Journal of Social Work Education* 39, no. 1 (2003): 2–23; Children's Aid Society of Brant, "Evidence-Based Practice and Decision Making in Child Welfare Services," accessed 11 September 2012, www.casbrant.ca.

4 See I.N. Engleberg and D.B. Wynn, *Working in Groups* (Boston: Houghton Mifflin, 2007), 43–4, for a discussion of how hidden agendas can influence group interactions.

5 Deloitte, "Core Beliefs and Culture Survey" (survey conducted by Harris Interactive), 14 June 2012, www.deloitte.com/view/en_US/us/press/Press-Releases/917ed0b3d26e7310VgnVCM2000001b56f00aRCRD.htm.

6 Kelly Services, "Kelly Services Workforce Global Index Survey," June 2012, www.kellyservices.ca/CA/About-Us/Kelly-Global-Workforce-Index/Social-Media-in-the-Workplace---June-2012.

7 M. Brooks, "Does the Use of Social Media Have an Adverse Effect on Workplace Productivity and the Reputations of Employers?," *Mel Brooks—Thoughts on Business, Management, and Leadership* (blog), 19 January 2013, http://melbrookssa.wordpress.com/2013/01/19/does-the-use-of-social-media-have-an-adverse-effect-on-workplace-productivity-and-the-reputations-of-employers.

8 C. Lovering, "Negative Effects of Social Media on Business," *Chron*, accessed 5 May 2013, http://smallbusiness.chron.com/negative-effects-social-media-business-25682.html.

9 F. Awolusi, "The Impacts of Social Networking Sites on Workplace Productivity," *Journal of Technology, Management, and Applied Engineering* 28, no. 1 (2012): 2–5, www.atmae.org/jit/Articles/Awolusi-Social-Networking-Work-Productivity-2012-01-30.pdf.

10 See the critique of trait theory in Fiedler, "Style or Circumstance."

11 See S.A. Beebe and J.T. Masterson, *Communicating in Small Groups: Principles and Practices*, 20th ed. (Boston: Pearson, 2012), 286–8.

12 F.E. Fiedler, "Style or Circumstance: The Leadership Enigma," in *INTERCOM: Readings in Organizational Communication*, ed. S. Ferguson and S.D. Ferguson (Rochelle Park, NJ: Hayden Book Company, 1988), 184–91. Also see discussion of Fiedler's theories in S.D. Ferguson and S. Ferguson, *Organizational*

Communication, 2nd ed. (New Brunswick, NJ: Transaction Publishers, 1990).

13 Beebe and Masterson, *Communicating in Small Groups*. Also see Ferguson and Ferguson, *Organizational Communication*.

14 E. Bormann, *Discussion and Group Methods*, 2nd ed. (New York: Harper and Row, 1975).

15 Ibid.

16 V.P. Hans and N. Eisenberg, "The Effects of Sex Role Attitudes and Group Composition on Men and Women in Groups," *Sex Roles* 12 (1985): 477–90.

17 Beebe and Masterson, *Communicating in Small Groups*.

18 Bormann, *Discussion and Group Methods*.

19 P.M. Senge, "Rethinking Leadership," *Executive Excellence* 15, no. 5 (1998): 16–17.

20 See D. McGregor, *The Human Side of Enterprise* (New York: McGraw-Hill, 1960).

21 *The Ultimate WebCT Handbook: A Practical and Pedagogical Guide to WebCT*, accessed 2 October 2004, www.ultimatehandbooks.net/excerpts/presentations.html.

22 This often-told story has appeared in various forms online and in print. It is not clear whether the story is based in fact, but it provides a clear illustration of the importance of being able to accurately define a problem in order to solve it.

23 See M.K. Perttula, C.M. Krause, and P. Sipilä, "Does Idea Exchange Promote Productivity in Design Idea Generation?," *CoDesign* 2, no. 3 (2006): 125–38.

24 V.R. Brown and P.B. Paulus, "Making Group Brainstorming More Effective: Recommendations from an Associative Memory Perspective," *Current Directions in Psychological Science* 11, no. 6 (2002): 208–12.

25 J.H. Jung, Y. Lee, and R. Karsten, "The Moderating Effect of Extraversion–Introversion Differences on Group Idea Generation Performance," *Small Group Research* 43, no. 1 (2012): 30–49.

26 M.W. Eysenck, *Attention and Arousal* (New York: Springer, 1982).

27 B. Johnson, "Characteristics of Effective Decision Building," in *INTERCOM: Readings in Organizational Communication*, ed. S. Ferguson and S.D. Ferguson (Rochelle Park, NJ: Hayden Book Company, 1988), 325–31.

28 Beebe and Masterson, *Communicating in Small Groups*.

29 A.F. Osborn, *Applied Imagination* (New York: Scribner's, 1953).

30 J.E. Eitington, *The Winning Trainer* (Houston, TX: Gulf Publishing, 1989).

31 Osborn, *Applied Imagination*.

32 M. Diehl and W. Stroebe, "Productivity Loss in Brainstorming Groups: Toward the Solution of a Riddle," *Journal of Personality and Social Psychology* 53, no. 3 (1987): 497–509; M. Diehl and W. Stroebe, "Productivity Loss in Idea-Generating Groups: Tracking Down the Blocking Effect," *Journal of Personality and Social Psychology* 61, no. 3 (1991): 392–403; B. Mullen, C. Johnson, and E. Salas, "Productivity Loss in Brainstorming Groups: A Meta-analytic Integration," *Basic and Applied Social Psychology* 12 (1991): 3–24.

33 N.L. Ken and S.E. Bruun, "Dispensability of Member Effort and Group Motivation Losses: Free Rider Effects," *Journal of Personality and Social Psychology* 44, no. 1 (1983): 78–94; D.D. Henningsen, M.G. Cruz, and M.L. Miller, "Role of Social Loafing in Predeliberation Decision Making," *Group Dynamics: Theory, Research, and Practice* 4, no. 2 (2000): 168–175.

34 S.J. Karau and K.D. Williams, "Social Loafing: A Meta-Analytic Review and Theoretical Integration," *Journal of Personality and Social Psychology* 65, no. 4 (1993): 681–706; J.A. Shepperd, "Productivity Loss in Performance Groups: A Motivation Analysis," *Psychological Bulletin* 113, no. 1 (1993): 67–81.

35 J. Orbell and R. Dawes, "Social Dilemmas, in *Progress in Applied Social Psychology*, vol. 1, ed. G. Stephenson and H. H. Davis (New York: Wiley, 1981), 37–65; P.W. Mulvey, L. Bowes-Sperry, and H.J. Klein, "The Effects of Perceived Loafing and Defensive Management on Group Effectiveness," *Small Group Research* 29 (1998): 394–415; P.W. Mulvey and H.J. Klein, "The Impact of Perceived Loafing and Collective Efficacy on Group Goal Processes and Group Performance," *Organizational Behavior and Human Decision Processes* 74 (1998): 62–87; P.B. Paulus, V. Brown, and A.H. Ortega, "Group Creativity," in *Social Creativity in Organizations*, vol. 2, ed. R.E. Purser and A. Montuori (Cresskill, NJ: Hampton Press, 1999), 151–76; J.J. Seta, C.E. Seta, and S. Donaldson, "The Impact of Comparison Processes on Co-actors' Frustration and Willingness to Expend Effort," *Personality and Social Psychology Bulletin* 17 (1991): 560–68.

36 L.M. Camacho and P.B. Paulus, "The Role of Social Anxiousness in Group Brainstorming," *Journal of Personality and Social Psychology* 68 (1995): 1071–80.

37 T.S. Larey and P.B. Paulus, "Group Preference and Convergent Tendencies in Small Groups: A Content Analysis of Group Brainstorming Performance," *Creativity Research Journal* 12, no. 3 (1999): 175–84.

38 S.K. Isaksen and J.P. Gaulin, "A Re-examination of Brainstorming Research: Implications for Research and Practice," *Gifted Child Quarterly* 49, no. 4 (2005): 315–29; T.J. Kramer, G.P. Fleming, and S.M. Mannis, "Improving Face-to-Face Brainstorming through Modeling and Facilitation," *Small Group Research* 32, no. 5 (2001): 533–57.

39 Isaksen and Gaulin, "A Re-examination of Brainstorming Research."

[40] A.B. VanGundy, *Idea Power: Techniques and Resources to Unleash the Creativity in Your Organization* (New York: AMACOM, 1992); also A.B. VanGundy, *Techniques of Structured Problem Solving*, 2nd ed. (New York: Van Nostrand Reinhold, 1988). Also Beebe and Masterson, *Communicating in Small Groups.*

[41] P. Lowry, T. Roberts, N. Romano, P. Cheney, and R. Hightower, "The Impact of Group Size and Social Presence on Small-Group Communication: Does Computer-Mediated Communication Make a Difference?" *Small Group Research* 37, no. 6 (2006): 631–61.

[42] Ibid.

[43] Larey and Paulus, "Group Preference and Convergent Tendencies."

[44] A.L. Delbecq and A. Van de Ven, "A Group Process Model for Problem Identification and Program Planning," *Journal of Applied Behavioral Science* 7, no. 4 (1971): 466–92.

[45] D.A. Schön and G. Wiggins, "Kinds of Seeing and Their Functions in Designing," *Design Studies* 13, no. 2 (1992): 135–52.

[46] R. van der Lugt, *Sketching in Design Idea Generation Groups* (PhD dissertation, Delft University of Technology, 2001).

[47] Ibid.

[48] R. Van der Lugt, "Developing a Graphic Tool for Creative Problem Solving in Design Groups," *Design Studies* 21, no. 5 (2000): 505–22. Also Van der Lugt, *Sketching in Design Idea Generation Groups.*

[49] R. Van der Lugt, "Brainsketching and How It Differs from Brainstorming," *Creative Innovation Management* 11, no. 1 (2002): 43–54.

[50] T. Buzan, "Power of Mind Mapping," accessed 15 September 2012, www.thinkbuzan.com/intl.

[51] "Mind Mapping," accessed 15 September 2012, www.mindmapping.com.

[52] W.J. Gordon, *Synectics: The Development of Creative Capacity* (New York: Harper and Row, 1961).

[53] Ibid.

[54] E.G. Bormann, "Fantasy and Rhetorical Vision: The Rhetorical Criticism of Social Reality," *Quarterly Journal of Speech* 58 (1972): 396–407; E. Bormann, "Fantasy Theme Analysis and Rhetorical Theory," in *The Rhetoric of Western Thought*, 5th ed., ed. J. Golden, G. Berquist, and W. Coleman (Dubuque, IA: Kendall/Hunt, 1992), 365–84.

[55] T. Proctor, *Creative Problem Solving for Managers: Developing Skills for Decision Making and Innovation*, 3rd ed. (New York: Routledge, 2009).

[56] B. Still, "A Dozen Years after Open Source's 1998 Birth, It's Time for OpenTechCom," *Journal of Technical Writing and Communication* 40 (2010): 219–28.

[57] H. Chesbrough, *Open Innovation: The New Imperative for Creating and Profiting from Technology* (Boston: Harvard Business School Press, 2003).

[58] E.A. Sullivan, "A Group Effort: More Companies Are Turning to the Wisdom of the Crowd to Find Ways to Innovate," *Marketing News* 44 (2010): 23–30.

[59] M.J. Antikainen and H.J. Väätäjä, "Rewarding in Open Innovation Communities—How to Motivate Members?," *International Journal of Entrepreneurship and Innovation Management* 11 (2010): 440–56; B.A. Huberman, D.M. Romero, and F. Wu, "Crowdsourcing, Attention, and Productivity," *Journal of Information Science* 35 (2009): 758–65.

[60] N. Esmail, "Canada's Physician Supply," *Fraser Forum*, March/April 2011, http://www.fraserinstitute.org/uploadedFiles/fraser-ca/Content/research-news/research/articles/canadas-physician-supply.pdf. Also see summary of report in CTV News release, "Canada's MD Shortage to Worsen: Fraser Report," 17 March 2011, www.ctvnews.ca/canada-s-md-shortage-to-worsen-fraser-report-1.620173.

[61] Ibid.

[62] Ibid.

[63] N. Esmail, "Demographics and Canada's Physician Supply," *Fraser Forum*, December 2007/January 2008, at http://www.fraserinstitute.org/uploadedFiles/fraser-ca/Content/research-news/research/articles/demographics-and-canadas-physician-supply.pdf.

[64] Z. Or, "Exploring the Effects of Health Care on Mortality across OECD Countries", *OECD Labour Market and Social Policy Occasional Papers* 46 (2001), http://dx.doi.org/10.1787/716472585704.

[65] Esmail, "Canada's Physician Supply."

[66] A more complete discussion of the Delphi method appears in S. Ferguson, *Researching the Public Opinion Environment: Theories and Methods* (Thousand Oaks, CA: Sage Publications, 2000).

[67] A.L. Delbecq, A.H. Van de Ven, and D.H. Gustafson, *Group Techniques for Program Planning: A Guide to Nominal Group and Delphi Processes* (Glenview, IL: Scott, Foresman, 1975), 7–16.

[68] R.J. Tersine and W.E. Riggs, "The Delphi Technique: A Long-Range Planning Tool," in *Organizational Communication*, 2nd ed., ed. S.D. Ferguson and S. Ferguson (New Brunswick, NJ: Transaction Books, 1988), 500–9.

[69] Ibid.

[70] Ibid.

[71] BT Organizational Development, *Focus Groups: Involving Employees Creatively to Influence Decisions* (London, UK: Industrial House, 1997).

[72] E. Babbie, *Survey Research Methods* (Belmont, CA: Wadsworth, 1990).

[73] A. Reid, "Public Affairs Research," in *The Canadian Public Affairs Handbook: Maximizing Markets, Protecting Bottom Lines*, ed. W.J. Wright and C.J. DuVernet (Toronto: Carswell, 1988), 117–46.

74 H. Mariampolski, "The Resurgence of Qualitative Research," *Public Relations Journal* 40, no. 7 (1984): 21–3.

75 Health Canada, "Best Practices—Early Intervention, Outreach and Community Linkages for Youth with Substance Abuse Problems," accessed 10 July 2012, www.hc-sc.gc.ca/hc-ps/pubs/adp-apd/bp-mp-intervention/summary-sommaire-eng.php.

76 M.K. Gordon and D.M. Zinga, "'Fear of Stigmatization': Black Canadian Youths' Reactions to the Implementation of a Black-Focussed School in Toronto," *Canadian Journal of Educational Administration and Policy*, 131 (26 March 2012), ww.umanitoba.ca/publications/cjeap/pdf_files/gordon_zinga.pdf.

77 Canadian Council on Social Development, "Cultural Diversity: Immigrant Youth in Canada," accessed 4 November 2012, www.ccsd.ca/subsites/cd/docs/iy/hl.htm.

78 M.G. Cruz, F.J. Boster, and J.I. Rodriguez, "The Impact of Group Size and Proportion of Shared Information on the Exchange and Integration of Information in Groups," *Communication Research* 24 (1997): 291–313.

79 J.H. Watt and S.A. Van Den Berg, *Research Methods for Communication Science* (Boston: Allyn and Bacon, 1995).

80 E.F. Fern, "The Use of Focus Groups for Idea Generation: The Effects of Group Size, Acquaintanceship, and Moderator on Response Quantity and Quality," *Journal of Marketing Research* 19, no. 1 (1982): 1–13.

81 D.E. Morrison, *The Search for a Method: Focus Groups and the Development of Mass Communication Research* (Luton, UK: University of Lutton Press, 1998). See also E. Noelle-Neumann, *The Spiral of Silence: Public Opinion—Our Social Skin*, 2nd ed. (Chicago: University of Chicago Press, 1993).

82 E.H. Witte and J.H. Davis, *Understanding Group Behavior: Small Group Processes and Interpersonal Relations*, vol. 2 (Mahwah, NJ: Lawrence Erlbaum, 1996).

83 BT Organizational Development, *Focus Groups*.

84 R.A. Krueger, *Focus Groups: A Practical Guide for Applied Research*, 2nd ed. (Thousand Oaks, CA: Sage, 1994).

85 W.L. Neuman, *Social Research Methods: Qualitative and Quantitative Approaches*, 3rd ed. (Boston: Allyn and Bacon, 1997).

86 D.W. Stewart and P.M. Shamdasani, *Focus Groups: Theory and Practice* (Newbury Park, CA: Sage, 1990).

87 BT Organizational Development, *Focus Groups*.

88 D.L. Morgan, *Focus Groups as Qualitative Research* (Newbury Park, CA: Sage, 1988).

89 Morgan, *Focus Groups as Qualitative Research*.

90 Krueger, *Focus Groups*.

91 Krueger, *Focus Groups*.

92 R.A Krueger, "Quality Control in Focus Group Research," in *Successful Focus Groups*, ed. D.L. Morgan (Newbury Park, CA: Sage, 1993), 65–88.

93 Stewart and Shamdasani, *Focus Groups*.

94 W. Jackson, *Methods: Doing Social Research* (Scarborough, ON: Prentice Hall, 1999).

95 Krueger, "Quality Control in Focus Group Research."

96 A.P. Hare and M.F. Davies, "Social Interaction," in *Small Group Research: A Handbook*, ed. A.P. Hare, H.H. Blumberg, M.F. Davies, and M.V. Kent (Norwood, NJ: Ablex, 1994), 169–93.

97 R.D. Wimmer and J.R. Dominick, *Mass Media Research: An Introduction*, 3rd ed. (Belmont, CA: Wadsworth, 1997).

98 D.M. Dozier and F.C. Repper, "Research Firms and Public Relations Practices," in *Excellence in Public Relations and Communication Management*, ed. J.E. Grunig (Hillsdale, NJ: Lawrence Erlbaum, 1992).

99 C. Argyris, "Single-Loop and Double-Loop Models in Research on Decision Making," *Administrative Science Quarterly* 21, no. 3 (1976): 363–75.

100 Krueger, *Focus Groups*.

101 M.S. Hanna and G.L. Wilson, *Community in Business and Professional Settings*, 3rd ed. (New York: McGraw-Hill, 1991).

102 Ibid.

103 Krueger, *Focus Groups*; Reid, "Public Affairs Research."

104 See, for example, A.B. Fisher, *Small Group Decision Making: Communication and the Group Process* (New York: McGraw-Hill, 1974). More recent studies include R. Holtz and N. Miller, "Intergroup Competition, Attitudinal Projection, and Opinion Certainty: Capitalizing on Conflict," *Group Processes and Intergroup Relations* 4 (2001): 61–73.

105 CRM Learning, *Groupthink*, 2nd edition (Carlsbad, CA: CRM Learning, 2010), DVD; also I. Janis, *Victims of Groupthink* (Boston: Houghton Mifflin, 1972).

106 L. Miller, "Roman Catholic Leaders Need to Get Rid of Their Groupthink," *Washington Post*, 8 March 2013, http://articles.washingtonpost.com/2013-03-08/national/37561393_1_american-cardinals-transparency-curia.

107 M.K. Miller and B.H. Bornstein, "Do Juror Pressures Lead to Unfair Verdicts?," *Judicial Notebook, Monitor on Psychology* 39, no. 3 (March 2008): 18, www.apa.org/monitor/2008/03/jn.aspx.

108 Ibid.

109 A. Kang, "Judge, Jury, Executioner," *Walking Dead*, season 2, episode 11, directed by G. Nicotero, aired 4 March 2012 on AMC.

110 D.D. Henningsen, M.L.M. Henningsen, J. Eden, and M.G. Cruz, "Examining the Symptoms of Groupthink and Retrospective Sensemaking," *Small Group Research* 37 (2006): 36–64; W. Safire, "On Language: Groupthink—A Collaborative Search for Coinage," *New York Times Magazine* (6 August 2004), section 6, p. 16, cited in Beebe and Masterson, *Communicating in Small*

Groups; Johnson, "Characteristics of Effective Decision Building."

[111] CRM Learning, *Groupthink*.

[112] N.E. Friedkin and E.C. Johnsen, "Social Influence Networks and Opinion Change," *Advances in Group Processes* 16 (1999): 1–29; also N.E. Friedkin, "Choice Shift and Group Polarization," *American Sociological Review* 64 (1999): 856–75.

[113] M.A. Renz, "The Meaning of Consensus and Blocking for Cohousing Groups," *Small Group Research 37, no. 4 (2006)*: 351–76; R.Y. Hirokawa, "Consensus Group Decision-Making, Quality of Decision and Group Satisfaction: An Attempt to Sort 'Fact' from 'Fiction,'" *Central States Speech Journal 33 (1982)*: 407–15; J. Hall, *Toward Group Effectiveness* (Conroe, TX: Teleometrics, 1971); Johnson, "Characteristics of Effective Decision Building."

[114] Johnson, "Characteristics of Effective Decision Building."

[115] S.D. Ferguson and S. Ferguson, "The Japanese Management Model: An Example for the US," in *Organizational Communication*, ed. S.D. Ferguson and S. Ferguson (New Brunswick, NJ: Transaction Publishers, 1990), 124–39.

[116] N.R.F. Maier, "Assets and Liabilities in Group Problem Solving: The Need for an Integrative Function," in *Organizational Communication*, ed. S.D. Ferguson and S. Ferguson (New Brunswick, NJ: Transaction Publishers, 1990), 417–30.

[117] Hall, *Toward Group Effectiveness*, 2.

[118] Ibid.

[119] Beebe and Masterson, *Communicating in Small Groups*.

APPENDIX

[1] Most of the content of this appendix first appeared in S.D. Ferguson, *Public Speaking in Canada: Building Competency in Stages* (Toronto: Oxford University Press, 2006).

[2] Little agreement exists in the management literature on the differentiation between *goals* and *objectives*. Some use *goals* to suggest a broader focus and *objectives* to suggest a more narrow focus; others use the terms in the opposite way. See P.G. Bergeron, *Modern Management in Canada: Concepts and Practices* (Scarborough, ON: Nelson Canada, 1989), 254.

[3] J.E. Brooks-Harris and S.R. Stock-Ward, *Workshops: Designing and Facilitating Experiential Learning* (Thousand Oaks, CA: Sage Publications, 1999), 55–6. See also P.N. Blanchard and J.W. Thacker, *Effective Training* (Toronto: Prentice Hall, 2005), 122–4; L. Stoneall, "The Case for More Flexible Objectives," *Training and Development* (August 1992): 67–9.

[4] See sources such as the following: J. Colquitt and J. Lepine, "Toward an Integrative Theory of Training Motivation: A Meta-analytic Path Analysis of 20 Years of Research," *Journal of Applied Psychology* 85 (2000): 678–707; Blanchard and Thacker, *Effective Training*, 126; J. Lewis, "Answers to Twenty Questions on Behavioral Objectives," *Educational Technology* (March 1981): 27–31.

[5] P.N. Blanchard and J.W. Thacker, *Effective Training: Systems, Strategies, and Practices*, 2nd ed. (Upper Saddle River, NJ: Pearson Education, 2007), 193.

[6] Lewis, "Answers to Twenty Questions."

[7] J.R. Kidd, *How Adults Learn* (New York: Association Press, 1955), 44.

[8] K.K. Dwyer, "Communication Apprehension and Learning Style Preference: Correlations and Implications for Teaching," *Communication Education* 47 (1998): 137–50.

[9] J.A. Daly and C.A. Diesel, "Measures of Communication-Related Personality Variables," *Communication Education* 41 (1992): 405–14.

[10] A study completed by the US Department of Health, Education, and Welfare is referenced in W.E. Arnold and L. McClure, *Communication, Training, and Development*, 2nd ed. (Prospect Heights, IL: Waveland Press, 1996), 38.

[11] CRM Productions, *The Power of Listening* (Scarborough, ON: McGraw-Hill Films, 1978), VHS.

[12] D.A. Brunson and J.F. Vogt, "Empowering Our Students and Ourselves: A Liberal Democratic Approach to the Communication Classroom," *Communication Education* 45 (1996): 73–83.

[13] S.S. Wulff and D.H. Wulff, "Of Course I'm Communicating; I Lecture Every Day: Enhancing Teaching and Learning in Introductory Statistics," *Communication Education* 53 (2004): 92–102; also P. Smagorinsky and P.K. Fly, "The Social Environment of the Classroom: A Vygotskian Perspective on Small Group Process," *Communication Education* 42 (1993): 157–71.

[14] J. Middendorf and A. Kalish, "The Change-up in Lectures" (unpublished manuscript, Indiana University, 1995), cited in P.H. Andrews, J.R. Andrews, and G. Williams, *Public Speaking: Connecting You and Your Audience*, 2nd ed. (Boston: Houghton Mifflin Company, 2002), 54.

[15] R. Dunn and K. Dunn, *Teaching Secondary Students through Their Individual Learning Styles: Practical Approaches for Grades 7–12* (Boston: Allyn and Bacon, 1993).

[16] M.L. Houser, "Are We Violating Their Expectations? Instructor Communication Expectations of Traditional and Nontraditional Students," *Communication Quarterly* 53 (2005): 213–28; also M.D. Richardson and K.E. Lane, "Andragogical Concepts for Teachers of Adults," *Catalyst for Change* 22 (1993): 16–18.

[17] Ibid.

[18] H. Gardner, *Frames of Mind: The Theory of Multiple Intelligences* (New York: Basic Books, 1983).

[19] See, for example, D.A. Kolb, *Experiential Learning: Experience as the Source of Learning and Development* (Englewood Cliffs, NJ: Prentice Hall, 1984).
[20] Dunn and Dunn, *Teaching Secondary Students.*
[21] Brooks-Harris and Stock-Ward, *Workshops*, 30–1.
[22] Arnold and McClure, *Communication, Training, and Development*, 21.
[23] Brooks-Harris and Stock-Ward, *Workshops*, 29.
[24] This passage is a paraphrased version of "The Legend of the Dream Catcher." Online at www.y-indianguides.com/pfm_st_dreamcatacher.html. Accessed July 26, 2004.
[25] W. Schutz, *FIRO: A Three Dimensional Theory of Interpersonal Behavior* (New York: Holt, Rinehart, and Winston, 1958).
[26] M. Burgoon, J.K. Heston, and J. McCroskey, "Communication Roles in Small Group Interaction," in *Organizational Communication*, 2nd ed., ed. S.D. Ferguson (New Brunswick, NJ: Transaction Publishers, 1990), 386–90; K. Benne and P. Sheats, "Functional Roles of Group Members," *Journal of Social Issues* 4 (1948): 41–9.
[27] D. Tannen, *Framing in Discourse* (London, UK: Oxford University Press, 1993).
[28] See, for example, J.L. Chesebro and J.C. McCroskey, "The Relationship of Teacher Clarity and Immediacy with Student State Receiver Apprehension, Affect, and Cognitive Learning," *Communication Education* 50 (2001): 59–68; also P.L. Witt, L.R. Wheeless, and M. Allen, "A Meta-analytical Review of the Relationship between Teacher Immediacy and Student Learning," *Communication Monographs* 71 (2004): 184–207.
[29] See, for example, Q. Zhang, "Immediacy, Humor, Power Distance, and Classroom Communication Apprehension in Chinese College Classrooms," *Communication Quarterly* 53 (2005): 87–108; J.C. McCroskey, A. Sallinen, J.M. Fayer, and R.A. Barraclough, "Nonverbal Immediacy and Cognitive Learning: A Cross-cultural Investigation," *Communication Education* 45 (1996): 200–11; and J.C. McCroskey, A. Sallinen, J.M. Fayer, and R.A. Barraclough, "A Cross-cultural and Multi-behavioral Analysis of the Relationship between Nonverbal Immediacy and Teacher Evaluation," *Communication Education* 44 (1995): 281–91.
[30] R.A. Krueger, *A Practical Guide for Applied Research*, 2nd ed. (Thousand Oaks, CA: Sage, 1994).
[31] E.H. Witte and J.H. Davis, *Understanding Group Behavior: Small Group Processes and Interpersonal Relations*, Vol. 2 (Mahwah, NJ: Lawrence Erlbaum, 1996).
[32] E. Noelle-Neumann, *The Spiral of Silence: Public Opinion—Our Social Skin*, 2nd ed. (Chicago: University of Chicago, 1993).
[33] Ibid.
[34] Witte and Davis, *Understanding Group Behavior.*

INDEX